ANDREW MARVELL

ANDREW MARVELL
The Chameleon

❋

NIGEL SMITH

YALE UNIVERSITY PRESS
NEW HAVEN AND LONDON

For information about this and other Yale University Press publications, please contact:
U.S. Office: sales.press@yale.edu   www.yalebooks.com
Europe Office: sales @yaleup.co.uk   www.yaleup.co.uk

Set in Arno Pro by IDSUK (DataConnection) Ltd
Printed in Great Britain by TJ International Ltd, Padstow, Cornwall

Library of Congress Cataloging-in-Publication Data
Smith, Nigel, 1958–
Andrew Marvell: the chameleon / Nigel Smith.
     p. cm.
  Includes bibliographical references.
  ISBN 978–0–300–11221–4 (alk. paper)
  1. Marvell, Andrew, 1621–1678. 2. Poets, English–Early modern, 1500–1700–Biography.
3. Legislators–Great Britain–Biography. 4. Marvell, Andrew, 1621–1678–Political and
social views. 5. Politics and literature–Great Britain–History–17th century. 6. Great
Britain–Politics and government–1660–1688. I. Title.
  PR3546.S65 2010
  821'.4–dc22   2010009130

A catalogue record for this book is available from the British Library.

10 9 8 7 6 5 4 3 2 1

CONTENTS

✳

ILLUSTRATIONS

✳

Maps

PREFACE AND
ACKNOWLEDGEMENTS

✳

This biography was researched and written in the years following the publication in 2003 of my edition of Andrew Marvell's poems in the Longman Annotated English Poets series. The initial research, which grew out of the work for the poetry edition, but which had far more detailed recourse to the kinds of archive in which life records are contained, took place from 2004 to 2006, followed by a sustained period of further research, reflection and writing. During the last three decades, and especially during the last fifteen years, Marvell has ceased to be regarded merely as an interesting literary figure who straddled the worlds of poetry and politics, and who wrote a handful of important poems, but has become the focus of such attention as befits an author of high literary quality: one whose peculiar greatness brings him into the first division of seventeenth-century authors, second only to Milton, and in the company of Jonson, Donne and Dryden. In addition to recent scholarly editions of the poetry, there is now also a full and properly annotated edition of Marvell's prose (edited by Annabel Patterson, Martin Dzelzainis and N.H. Keeble 2 vols, 2003), the first time Marvell's prose has been published in complete form for more than a hundred years. In the years after the appearance of these editions academic interest in Marvell blossomed to the extent that there is now an international society dedicated to the study of Marvell in addition to a noticeable increase in scholarly gatherings and publications on him and his writings.

Modern biography of Marvell is understandably scarce. Augustine Birrell's study of 1905 was succeeded by Pierre Legouis's remarkable *thèse* of 1928, the first extensively documented work that brought together the double career of politician and poet. Legouis's findings were published in English, compressed and revised, in 1965, and a new life, taking account of scholarly discovery from the 1960s to the 1990s, was published in 1999 by Nicholas Murray. The purpose of my own biography is to make Marvell known to the widest possible readership, in the light of the most recent editions and scholarly work, much of which was unknown to Murray. I offer my own interpretation of events, circumstances and writings, but I am deeply indebted to Birrell, Legouis and Murray and to all of Marvell's biographers, from Thomas Cooke to Hilton Kelliher, the author of Marvell's life in the recent *Oxford Dictionary of National Biography*, for helping to represent the life of a man who preferred to be secretive, and for thinking it was a life worth shaping as biography.

My greatest debt in these pages is to Nicholas von Maltzahn, whose monumental chronology of Marvell's life records (2005) establishes the new standard to which all Marvell study must rise and whose authority on Marvell's life records is now unsurpassed. I am deeply grateful for all of his help, his willingness to share information, his patience and the astute judgement displayed when reading my manuscript. As a result the exposition is sharper, and he has saved me from many errors. I must also thank two other leading Marvell scholars whose knowledge, insight and close friendship have been just as valuable in the construction of this life: Annabel Patterson (our greatest critical advocate of seventeenth-century political literature) and Martin Dzelzainis. These three are my touchstones of judgement. Other Marvellians who have directly helped me in research and writing include Warren Chernaik, Alastair Fowler, Vitaly Eyber, Estelle Haan, Paul Hammond, Derek Hirst, Edward Holberton, Art Kavanagh, N.H. Keeble, George Klawitter, Sean McDowell, Paul Mathole, Ian Parker, Timothy Raylor, Gilles Sambras and Steven Zwicker. A longer list of Renaissance and seventeenth-century experts who have helped with discussions sometimes dating back many years includes Sharon Achinstein, John Barnard, Maureen Bell, Tom Corns, John Creaser, Ariel Hessayon, Ann Hughes, John Kerrigan, Timothy Kircher, Charles-Edouard Levillain, Rhodri Lewis, David Loewenstein, Sarah Mortimer, David Norbrook, William Poole, Steve Pincus, Diane Purkiss, John Rogers, Peter Rudnytsky, George Southcombe, Phil Withington, Blair Worden and the two anonymous readers for the publisher.

But in fact my debts of gratitude in encountering Marvell are even older. Like Marvell's father, I am a southerner who went to live in the north. I bought my first (of many) copies of Elizabeth Story Donno's Penguin edition of Marvell's poems on a weekend trip to Cambridge in the summer of 1977; but it was as an undergraduate that I first encountered a discussion of Marvell in his home town of Hull in 1978, the year of the tercentenary of Marvell's death, celebrated by an important series of lectures in the university there (none of which I attended). I am deeply grateful to the inspiration and guiding hands of F. John Hoyles and Arthur Pollard, my two tutors in English, deeply opposed in many of their views, but united by a critical evangelism that still drives me. H.A. Lloyd in the Hull History Department made me begin to understand the work of the historian, and made me think hard about tying together literature and history, which has turned out to be my life's furrow. I sat at the feet of J.P. Kenyon and I spent many hours reading in Philip Larkin's outstanding library.

It was in Hull too that I experienced the landscape into which Marvell was born, and grew to know how it shapes the mind: for showing me the civilization of Holderness I am beholden to Patsy and Colin Stoneman. Somewhat like Marvell, I have revisited Hull over the years and found that the distinctiveness of the place and its people, its zest for liberty and righteous causes (from Andrew Marvell and William Wilberforce to Amy Johnson and Mick Ronson) is always manifest. Three years later I returned to London, and Stephen Brook introduced me to the literary world of the capital: the beginning of a journey into cosmopolitanism.

I am indebted to the librarians of the following libraries for their hospitality and help: the Special Collections Department of the Firestone Library, Princeton University; the Bodleian Library, Oxford University; Corpus Christi College Library, Oxford; the British Library; Cambridge University Library; Hull Central Library; Hull University Library; Inner Temple Library, London; Nottingham University Library; and to the archivists of the following archives: Hertfordshire Record Office, Hertford; Hull City Archives; the Public Record Office, London; London Guildhall; London Metropolitan Archives; The Royal Society, London; Westminster Record Office, London. I am deeply grateful for research and research leave support from the Dean of the Faculty and the University Committee for Research in the Social Sciences and Humanities, Princeton University, the John Simon Guggenheim Foundation and the National Humanities Center.

I must acknowledge the continuing friendship in scholarship and beyond of, in the UK, Averil Cameron, John Carey, Ralph Hanna and Nick McDowell, in the US Leonard Barkan, Nick Barberio, Paul Muldoon and the members of Rackett, Michael Wood, Susan Stewart, Oliver Arnold, Jeff Dolven, Anthony Grafton, Peter Lake, David Aers, Jerry Passannante, Russ Leo, Stephen Fallon and Gordon Teskey, and in both places Alastair and Florence Minnis. They have all been involved in discussions about this work, and some have read drafts. My graduate students at Princeton have been most helpful in offering opinions during the final stages of preparation, in particular Elizabeth Melly, Joe Moshenska, Julianne Werlin, Matthew Harrison and James Rutherford. I thank my agent Peter Robinson. To these names I must add my deep gratitude once again to my longstanding editors at Yale University Press, Robert Baldock (now Director at the London office) and Candida Brazil, who have as usual given enormous, generous support in addition to their editorial acumen. Carolyn Guile has offered unending, delightful and caring companionship not least during the final stages of composition. I much appreciate her patience. As ever the buck stops with me.

NS
Princeton, NJ
9 May 2010

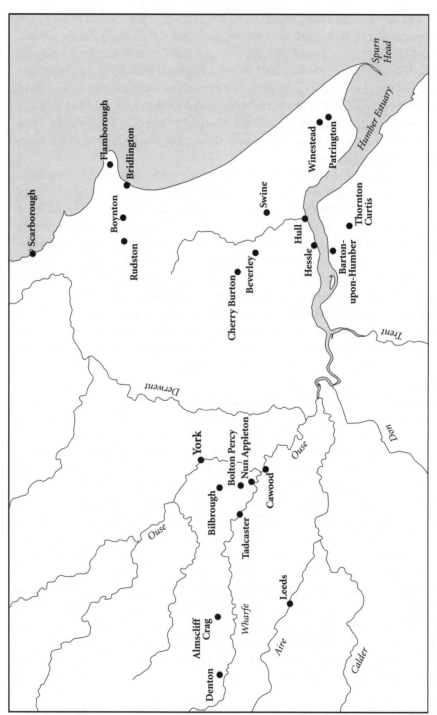

Marvell's Yorkshire

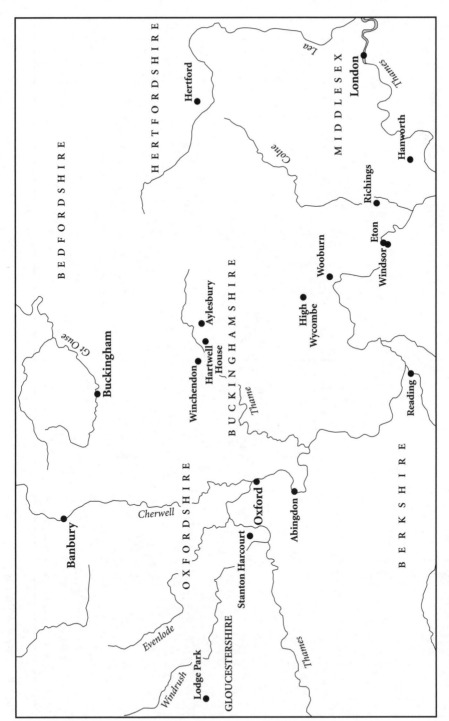

Marvell's London and surrounds

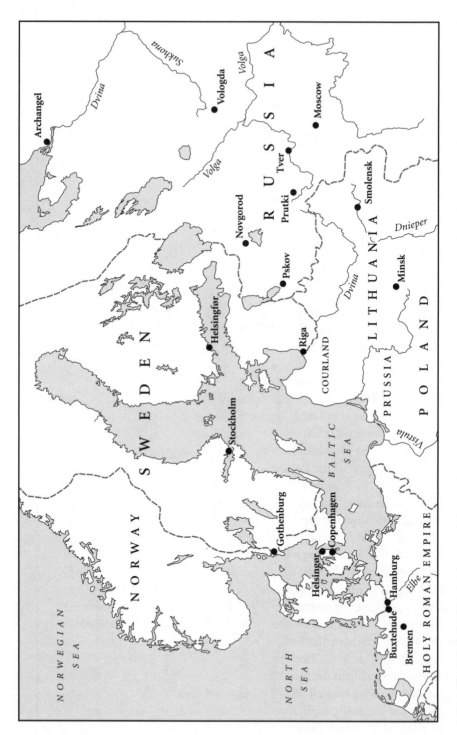

Marvell's travels in Russia

✳

CHAPTER 1

INTRODUCTION:
THE PROBLEM OF ANDREW MARVELL

Whig Hero and the Use of the Anecdote

WHAT THE WORLD HAS thought about Andrew Marvell and why it has thought so has much to do with the political situation in London during the days, weeks and months after Marvell's death in August 1678. These would establish him posthumously as a hero of the emergent Whig party during the Exclusion Crisis of 1678 to 1681, and from this political conflagration Marvell's early biographies would grow. They would tell us much about some aspects of Marvell (a lot less about others), and would involve a fair degree of fabrication, but would also leave much else in the dark.

The unfolding of political events in the months after Marvell's death reads like the prophecy of the Popish conspiracy in church and state that Marvell had made in *An Account of the Growth of Popery and Arbitrary Government* (1677) come true. Marvell had managed to stir up the kingdom with his *Account*, published the previous January, and probably mostly written during the previous May.[1] 'Stir up' is an understatement, since Marvell had done much more than this. By offering a close analysis of Parliamentary procedure in 1677 and political history during the previous ten years, *An Account* had shown the steady undermining of English liberties.[2] The pamphlet laid the blame at the door of pro-Catholic courtiers led by the King's brother, James, Duke of York (the future James II), and more immediately claimed it was a conspiracy of the King's chief minister, the Earl of Danby, with the bishops of the Church of England, who sat in the House of Lords.[3] The further and more serious implication, discernible to the reader through the layers of typical Marvellian irony, was that the King himself was guilty of misleading Parliament, the representative of the English people, by demanding funds without actually acting on the purpose for which those funds had been procured (war with France). The previous ten years, if not longer, looked in Marvell's view like those of a monarch not ruling as he was supposed to in Parliament, but arbitrarily, seeking to move around Parliament and govern without it, yet with an ideally limitless supply of money sanctioned by it. This was the final meaning Marvell drew from the very many intervals (called 'prorogations') imposed by the King on Parliamentary sessions in a single Parliament that had been elected in 1661 and that would not be dissolved until 1679.[4] The *Account* pointed a finger of accusation at Charles II and said 'enough': it left no doubt in the reader's mind that Charles had governed in a constitutionally unEnglish way, making England more like its neighbour France, Roman Catholic in religion, and governed arbitrarily by Louis XIV. The French king had earlier secretly underwritten Charles's military funding needs in return for a promise (again made secretly) that Charles would make England once again Catholic. Marvell's charge was scandalous but ultimately true. By August 1678, he had a reputation as a skilled and amusing satirist on the important issue of religious toleration. Written according to Sir Robert Southwell by a 'good smart pen', the *Account* made Marvell a major political commentator and operator even though he had not owned up to his authorship: the tract and he were an utter sensation.[5]

Keeping his identity as author secret was vital to the success of the enterprise. The evidence of a widespread conspiracy of Roman Catholics, indigenous and foreign, designed to ensure a Catholic succession of the monarchy and future for England was widely believed and caused a massive crisis in church and state. Titus Oates made his allegations of a 'Popish plot' in late September, and on 12 October Sir Edmond Berry Godfrey went missing. His body was discovered one week later, his murder widely suspected to be the work of Catholic agents.[6] The immediate outcome was the fall of the Earl of Danby, the King's chief minister, and, at long last, the summoning of a new parliament: the dissolution of the old, which had been elected in 1661, came on 24 January 1679. In the medium term, the huge political battle known as the Exclusion Crisis took its three-year course. In it the Whig and Tory parties formed as the issue of the Protestant succession of the monarchy was debated.[7]

Perhaps early in 1679, the republican and Whig poet and conspirator John Ayloffe, who would be executed for treason in 1685, wrote the powerful verse satire 'Marvell's Ghost'.[8] No longer was Marvell a composer of surreptitiously circulated poetry on affairs of state and mostly unsigned tracts: he was now a subject of the poetry itself and a hero to boot, denouncing Stuart oppression ever more strongly. Four more separate poems of this kind are known to exist, one from 1687, one from 1690, another from 1691 also entitled 'Marvell's Ghost', and yet one more from 1697 perhaps deliberately designed to be published with a collection of Marvell's state poems.[9] Marvell's political verse, of which a great deal will be said in the following pages, began to have a greater impact too. The attributions of much opposition poetry to Marvell grew although many of these would prove to be incorrect: his reputation and association with a certain kind of poem (for instance, the Advice-to-a-Painter poem) was the cause. Dryden made decidedly negative allusions to Marvell at this time, comparing him to the scurrilous Elizabethan Puritan pamphleteer Martin Marprelate in the preface to *Religio Laici* (1682), and Tory poetry further railed at Marvell's associations with Whig grandees such as Buckingham and Shaftesbury. This added to the names that Marvell would be called by his enemies, as well as by some more even-handed judges: 'sneering', 'untowardly'. Those who read Marvell's pamphlet were regarded by Tories as credulous Whigs, and Marvell's *An Account of the Growth of Popery and Arbitrary Government* (1677) was regarded as fuel, among other writings, for the Rye House Plot of 1683 against the lives of the King and his brother and heir the Duke of York. Roger L'Estrange now regarded *An Account* as part of a larger plot to exclude James from the succession. He even claimed that Marvell 'dreamed' the idea of the Popish plot and complained that the controversialist had been canonized 'if not for Saint, yet for a Prophet, in shewing how pat the Popish Plot falls out to his conjecture'.[10] Furthermore Marvell's tract was evidence of a republican conspiracy, he claimed, that had its roots in a culture of lewd tavern dwellers, led by the Earl of Shaftesbury, in his view the supreme aristocratic turncoat. This was all part of a hero's afterlife: Marvell's biography began with this posthumous reputation as Whig patriot, hero of political liberty and religious toleration, a reputation that would be carried through the eighteenth century on the wings of the Glorious Revolution of 1688 to 1689 and the Whig ascendancy that followed.

LIVES OF THE POET

Yet Marvell is not merely a subject for those interested in politics and history. He is also of great interest to us for his poetry, and for the last hundred years of greater interest as the poet rather than the politician. Because his poetry is notoriously both brilliant and difficult, he is regarded as an author of high literary quality: certainly in the first division of seventeenth-century poets, second only to Milton and in the company of Jonson, Donne and Dryden. But much of that quality has to do with indecipherability, with irresolvable ambiguities, with seeing things all ways at once and yet never really revealing what the hidden author thinks. He deliberately hides himself in his verse, and clearly it was a form of escape, just as he apparently liked to retreat into gardens or secluded studies.

Just as it was once conventional to claim that Marvell did not write serious poetry after 1660, so it has been usual to claim that he had no reputation as a poet until the nineteenth century. In fact amidst the most fervent parading of Marvell's patriotism, he was never entirely forgotten as a poet during the eighteenth century. In addition to the limited appearance of some of the lyrics in anthologies, his first two editors and biographers, Thomas Cooke and Edward Thompson, readily recognized him as a poet (Cooke only presents the poetry, a small selection of letters and no controversial prose, and judges Marvell's poetry to have 'the Effect of a lively Genius, and manly Sense, but at the same Time seem[s] to want that Correctness he was capable of making'). This played a crucial role in the development of Marvell's poetic reputation.[11] Thompson considered Marvell original, and a significant force of innovation in English poetry. Nonetheless, Cooke and Thompson thought of Marvell primarily as the patriot MP ('a Man, who always thought for the Good of his Country and the Glory of Religion')[12] and devoted such materials as they had to an essentially political life. It is not hard to see why. Cooke's entire career as man of letters was associated with Whig causes. Thompson was from Hull, and decidedly a Whig; his seminal three-volume edition of Marvell's works, with Life, was published in 1776, the year of the outbreak of the American Revolutionary War. In this particular book, Marvell appeared as a hero of liberty in pro-American propaganda.[13]

A third life appeared in the same year as Cooke's edition, 1726, in Latin, and then in English translation in 1727 and 1728. This was of an entirely different order: fourteen pages and some further references, all of a hostile nature, in Samuel Parker's *De Rebus sui Temporis Commentariorum Libri Quatuor* (*Bishop Parker's History of his Own Time* as it appeared in English). Parker had in fact written this in 1686 and was intent on settling scores with Marvell after the *Rehearsal Transpros'd* controversy of 1672–3, in which literary fracas he had generally been considered Marvell's inferior. Marvell is judged by Parker to be a slanderer and malign rebel, like Milton, and also a member of the radical Whig Green Ribbon Club; before that, claimed Parker, he had joined the conspiratorial sixty MPs in the Cavalier Parliament who had attempted to maintain Commonwealth and/or Protectorate principles. When Marvell was, in Parker's view, silenced by vocal opposition to his voice in the Commons, he had resorted to malign, clandestine activity outside Parliament. Here then was the Tory and High Church opposite to the Whig myth.

Parker joined the tradition, to which Samuel Butler had already contributed, of regarding Marvell as innately wicked, impudent and sour (as opposed to witty). Abandoned by his father, and cast out of college, claimed Parker, Marvell scraped a living as a penniless poetaster until at Milton's pleadings he was employed as a Cromwellian undersecretary, and published 'The First Anniversary of the Government under His Highness the Lord Protector'. Marvell was also a hypocrite because he had defended Charles II's Declaration of Indulgence in 1672 but argued against it in 1677.

Speculative, foundationless stories continued to abound in the brief lives of Marvell attached to editions of his poetry through the nineteenth century. The Boston edition of 1857, with a prefatory notice based on the *Edinburgh Review* notice of Henry Rogers, assumed that Milton and Marvell probably met for the first time in 1640s Rome (in this he follows Thompson), and went to the Vatican to discuss the shortcomings of the Roman church.[14] But Rogers also makes much of running mere rumour to ground: and it is humbling for any biographer to see someone so exposed to posterity's greater hindsight even as they seek to be scrupulous with the truth, and to root out 'those fictions which have gained extensive circulation only because they have been felt to be not intrinsically improbable'.[15] Thus, even in Augustine Birrell's life of 1905 the Skinner family's funding of Marvell's education is regarded as 'quite possible', but is in fact a groundless speculation. The other strategy in these biographies, like the earlier Whig hagiography, is to devote considerable space to identifying Marvell's impeccable moral qualities and to praising them. Dating should also be mentioned: there is a tendency in the early biographies to date poems to the earliest possible moment. Thompson assumed that the poem on Maniban was written during Marvell's first visit to France in the 1640s, whereas correspondence now suggests a more probable and much later date of 1676.[16] Finally there is plagiarism. With sparse available details, earlier biographers were left to repeat each other in a very absolute way. Rogers thus noticed that John Dove, the author of the first biography of the poet that was not part of an edition, had taken without acknowledgement parts of Isaac D'Israeli's 1814 account of the quarrel between Marvell and Parker and an unsigned essay of 1824/5 in the *Retrospective Review*.[17]

MODERN LIVES OF THE MODERN POET

The sense of Marvell as author if not poet was very important both to Marvell lovers and haters. For Thompson, Marvell's writings were seamlessly connected to the life of a new kind of public figure, one of the 'first patriots that this, or any other country hath produced': 'he hath given us so pure and perfect an image of his own mind in the immortal monuments of his wit and writings, and in the incorruptibility of his life and actions'.[18] The anonymous author of the account of Marvell published in the *Retrospective Review* in 1824/5 thought that the writings, with their 'poetical genius' and sense of 'irreproachable' character, were quite enough as a life record: biographical material in family history was simply 'dull'.[19] At this time, however, Marvell's reputation as a poet took considerable steps forward. Hartley Coleridge thought in 1832 that Marvell would have been more famous as a poet had he not been important as a politician, but surely the principles of assessment had changed when John Ormsby, writing in the *Cornhill Magazine* in 1869, opined that with five editions of his poetry extant since his death Marvell had a poetic popularity exceeded only by Milton, Dryden and Samuel Butler.[20]

The modern era of Marvell biography – the era that begins with the assumption that at the least Marvell was a major poet as well as a politician and therefore should have a poet's life, and that that life should be as detailed and impartial as possible – starts with Pierre Legouis's *thèse* of 1928: a painstaking gathering together of very many different materials. It used a variety of documentary materials, and is a very impressive achievement for someone writing abroad and outside English language culture (although Legouis did visit English libraries and archives, and met and corresponded with several experts, including the great historian of the Civil War, C.H. Firth). It was fashioned considerably before modern literary biography had attained the standards of competence to which we are now used, although it looked to the example of Masson's monumental study of Milton.[21] Its impact has to be seen in the light of T.S. Eliot's widely influential essay of 1921, commemorating Marvell's birthday but also sealing his reputation as a major poet in the English and European traditions.[22] Even so, much of the life was still hard to write: in 1965 the elderly Legouis published a condensed, updated version of his study in English. That Marvell's father's death happens on page 7 of this version (p. 17 in the original) underlines Legouis's own claim that his book was more poetry commentary than biography. By page 20, Marvell has arrived at Nun Appleton, but his life was more than half over. Of the original 449 pages of French text, just 144 were devoted to the life.

No one attempted a full-scale biography until the last eleven years. Nicholas Murray is a professional biographer who numbers Matthew Arnold, Aldous Huxley, Bruce Chatwin and Franz Kafka among his subjects. His 1999 Life of Marvell aimed to bring together the poet and the politician and to show his 'dedicated avocation, . . . energy, imagination, moral commitment and literary skill' all at work at once inside one personality.[23] No early modern scholar, Murray constructed his life from readily available sources, and treats Marvell very much as if he were a modern man of letters, comparable to Matthew Arnold or to T.S. Eliot (Arnold actually appears in these pages to help define Marvell as a moral reformer).[24]

In truth, and as Murray is the first to admit, new life records concerning Marvell require much extremely careful and laborious searching in national and local record offices and other archives. An up-to-date edition of the letters (in addition to the new edition of the prose, unavailable to Murray), including those addressed to as well as those written by Marvell, is now needed: several remain uncollected.[25] A true biography, and one that finally escapes from the myths that have been present in Marvell's biography, cannot be written until a new foundation of the documentary knowledge of Marvell's life has been laid. After Legouis, the most valuable work in making the conditions possible for a comprehensive life of Marvell has been conducted on this level; in respect of genealogy by Pauline Burdon and more generally by Hilton Kelliher. Kelliher's most impressive earlier achievement was an exhibition at the British Library of documents that went to make up Marvell's life, accompanied by a catalogue.[26] The intention was not to provide a complete biography but to give a detailed representation of the documents that did exist; and to allow each one enough space for considered interpretation. Biographical evidence is replaced by a 'map' of evidence, with microscopic attention paid to the 'dots' themselves, rather than to the narrative that joins them up, and this tendency has been brought to a magnificent fullness with Nicholas von Maltzahn's 2005 *Chronology* of Marvell's life records, a detailed descriptive and evaluative list of the different types of evidence. It seems a more honest way to proceed: for the time being and until we have better tools to work with, the 'map' provides us with a series of departure points in which Marvell's views and attitudes might be addressed in forensic detail. It will be evident that the following pages are deeply indebted to this work. There's no doubt too that the recent annotated editions of Marvell's poetry and prose have added more detail to this picture through their findings with regard to the composition, circulation and publication details of many of the works. In this respect Kelliher's recent extensive discussion of the manuscript circulation of the 'Last Instructions to a Painter' explains Marvell's connections with the Harley family in more detail, and overcomes the inevitable effects of compression in a shorter life.[27] What follows could not have been written without the painstaking researches of a number of Marvell scholars.[28]

Literary criticism has played its role in improving Marvell's biography too. One important area that has contributed greatly to the possibility of writing an informed life of Marvell is the scholarly attention paid to the public poetry. It is from the contextual understanding of the Cromwell poems and the Restoration verse satires in the publications of John M. Wallace, Annabel Patterson, Warren Chernaik, Blair Worden, Derek Hirst, Steven N. Zwicker and David Norbrook that a picture of Marvell as political creature and political thinker was able to emerge.[29] The poetry was shown to be the work of an arch-political observer, enforced by an informed knowledge of advanced contemporary political theory, and to be part of the historical process itself. It is here that we see emerging Marvell the follower of Machiavelli, user of Hobbes, inheritor of interest theory. Marvell suddenly had a serious political life before as well as after 1660. The same might be said in respect of Marvell's knowledge of visual art in John Dixon Hunt's 1978 study, which is particularly valuable in evoking the Europe through which Marvell travelled and the England in which he spent the early 1650s.[30]

SO TO PROCEED

Yet there are some concrete facts concerning Marvell's life, and reasonably solid extrapolations that we can make from them. It is a start. He was born in East Yorkshire to a clergyman father who was making his way from humbler origins: his grandfather was a yeoman farmer from Cambridgeshire. He was educated in classic fashion at Hull Grammar School, and within a Protestant household whose head, his father, was open to the full range of difference fomenting in the English church, having himself come from the Puritan environment of Emmanuel College, Cambridge. He continued to be educated in humanist Protestant fashion at Trinity College, Cambridge, and by all accounts he proved the worth of his meagre scholarship by performing as a good scholar. Elected to a scholarship, he had every expectation that he would pursue a profitable career in the church and possibly the university.

Everything changed with the loss of his father and the deprivation of his scholarship. His lifeline was cut off and he had to find a new means of subsistence. This meant, perhaps disagreeably to him for much of the time, seeking the preferment of greater men for a living. A short period trying to find a way in early 1640s London, perhaps in the London households of important northern families, perhaps in search of a teaching appointment, gave way to a resolve to mortgage his property inheritance and to spend the sum he realized travelling in Europe in order to gain a thorough knowledge of other languages and cultures. He was aiming at being a secretary, and perhaps beyond it there might be a career in a higher diplomatic appointment.

But it took a long time for this to happen, and there were many, including Philip Meadows and Joseph Williamson, who would sweep past him on the secretarial route to considerable wealth and influence.[31] He had to settle for life as a far more humble kind of educated servant: a tutor in a noble household, and a tutor in a clergyman's household to the heir of another very rich gentleman. He spent some time probably in London at the end of the 1640s, probably at first in Royalist company, and certainly writing in a poetry circle some of his very best poetry. Perhaps in pursuit of patronage, perhaps genuinely as an address on the cusp of a new age, he wrote his first poem about Oliver Cromwell. Some further poems in praise of the republican ethos betoken yet more gestures towards employment by writing the right sort of poem for England's new leaders, and perhaps already Marvell was functioning as an intelligence agent in this period; that is, a spy. But then came four to five years spent in Eton and associated environs as tutor to William Dutton, the ward of Oliver Cromwell.

From this point onwards, Marvell's life as civil servant and MP can be written with a confidence based on relatively full records of correspondence and rich Parliamentary and other political sources for the time. That life, with its subject paying assiduous detail to the committee work of the House of Commons, was marked by a reluctance and very probably an inhibition to speak in the Commons: only a very few speeches are recorded. These are in places tortuous: oral eloquence was not Marvell's forte, and he may well have found public speaking difficult. But he did not avoid controversy: physical collisions or exchange of blows with other MPs threatened to ruin his career as a representative on at least two occasions. Nonetheless his work as a political operator is evident and was impressive for its serious application. In addition to keeping the Mayor and Aldermen of Hull abreast of affairs in Westminster, we know that he operated in favour of religious toleration, and against the threat of an absolutist monarchy.

Then there is the life of the poet, and first of all some hard realities. It was known to the earlier biographers that Marvell, like other poets, for example Jonson and Cowley, died poor, even though they were all 'incomparable' poets:

Marvell was considered alongside Milton, Cowley and Spenser as a flower of Cambridge.[32] Two significant perspectives are opened up immediately. The first is that Marvell was compelled to be a servant for his entire adult life, and that anxieties about his personal and social status and identity were no doubt a consequence of this indubitable fact. He was sharply aware of his non-elite status, howsoever he was also sometimes called a gentleman (and sometimes mockingly so). He wrote to Sir Henry Thompson of 'that duty of those in our station to doe right to any gentleman'.[33] He lived modestly, an adult lifetime of living largely in small rooms in inns and other people's houses. Sir Henry Thompson for one was keen to help him by identifying a rich Puritan widow who would have given him substance. The other perspective is offered by the straightforward evidence that Marvell was acknowledged at an early stage, within five years of his death, two years after the publication of the *Miscellaneous Poems*, as one of the great ('incomparable') poets. From this point of view, the assumption that he had no reputation as a significant poet until much later is one more myth.

It will also become apparent in the pages that follow that Marvell was supremely aware of himself as a literary artist. For someone who was so self-consciously aware of the way in which others around him and just before him had sounded their own trumpets, proclaiming themselves latter-day Virgils, Ovids or Lucans, Marvell is remarkable for the degree to which he is able in his verse and his prose to speculate on his own career as a poet even while refusing the terms of aggrandizement claimed by his contemporaries. This even helps us tie his poetry to his political career. Among all the kinds of imitation and echoing of ancient and modern poets that he offered in his writing, he prized above all others Ovid and considered himself in some senses a version of the great Roman poet. But this aspect of literary and biographical self-consciousness was not all straightforward and involved negation. Jonson, Milton, Herrick, Cowley, D'Avenant and Katherine Philips all took pains to make their voices major, distinctive and above or beyond the tradition that had formed them. Marvell is a poet who denied this sense of poetic egotism by a form of studied imitation (echoing all of the people named above and many more) but who nonetheless made a virtue and indeed a highly creative resource of being other men's (and women's) mirrors. Interestingly Thompson saw this, although he chose to relate it to Marvell's ethical excellence: 'as men are more or less mirrours to each other, such was Mr Marvel to the world, that all men might so clearly discern perfection in him, as to dress, and even ornament themselves, by so compleat a pattern'.[34]

And personality? We have evidence of a very hot temper, of someone who did not suffer fools gladly and who seems to have reacted with excessive violence or agitation when frustrated. Contemporaries, albeit hostile critics, saw a man with a sneer. He enjoyed snide laughter at those who deserved to be treated with contempt. This may well have been part of his psychological make-up, although there are plenty of things that would have given him cause for jealousy and frustration. He spoke of the closeness in expression between a smile and a frown, saying that there is so little difference between them, and he appeared to know the complicated and unpleasant psychology behind that closeness. One hostile contemporary portrayed him as an androgynous personality, perhaps a literal physical one too.[35] If he had a sneer it was a very civilized one, and the energy of its probing intelligence and judgement runs through *The Rehearsal Transpros'd* even as Marvell depicts his enemies as crazed animals. His ability to see himself in others and them in him is startling, and that is as true for Samuel Parker as it was for his far less deadly enemy Richard Flecknoe. If all men were mirrors of each other, this was a device for revealing darkness as much as light.

Underneath his defence of toleration and his discussion of the relationship between liberty and necessity, Marvell names the savage within us all. Many of his friends as well as his adversaries made substantial fortunes; Marvell made very little money and remained in debt in the closing years of his life. He had plenty of cause to be resentful, and resentment may well have built up in his personality however much he tried to dispel it. A good deal of adversity that prevented him from 'getting on in life' culminated in a perpetual frustration. He was bitterly aware of those less talented people who had surpassed him, and whose principles he found repellent. Or was his taciturn nature and caution, read by most people as a lack of charm, a further compounding reason for his neglect and slow progress? He was obstinate and stubborn, in certain circumstances sly. This is evident in the accounts of his tactless behaviour as a diplomat. His hopes for a diplomatic career were high, but we cannot be too surprised that he was not rewarded in this way. All in all, his temperament was far better suited to being a spy, which he evidently was for several periods in his life.

The teachings of poetry and politics, of faith and of men's manners, left him with an overriding sense of sympathy. It is both an aesthetic principle and an ethical foundation of his idea of toleration. He sees things from the viewpoint of the other, even if that other is his purported enemy. The other is always in some sense the same, and those who lacked this quality or understanding of sympathy were to be held at arm's length or even detested: men like the Anglican divine Samuel Parker, Marvell's first big controversial opponent, or the graphologist Joseph de Maniban. For a man who could also manifest tactlessness and considerable anger, such perceptions of sympathy seem like a big contradiction. Marvell had an acute sense of his own contribution to poetic tradition within the broader field of literary history, but he kept this achievement and understanding almost entirely within himself. Unlike major talents such as Milton and Dryden, and unlike lesser contemporary poetic talents like Waller and Cowley, he kept his literary views and achievement almost entirely silent: we only know about it from the works that were published after his death. To make a public showing in the literary world was to exert one's ego, and this he determinedly refused to do. Thus, his notion of sympathy arose from the position of someone who denied himself as a public literary ego in the first age of criticism and critical reputation, and it gains purchase for being so articulated.

The speculation based on the poetry, that Marvell was open to many configurations of sexual relationship that evaded most of his contemporaries, or that evaded their ability to write about them, demands our attention. In this field of strongly heterosexual poetry, Marvell stands out for his ability to express male-male, female-female and young-old relationships: any permutation you like, but not what we normally expect. Was he then so disposed that he himself stood outside the heterosexual norm? And is this an aspect of himself that is part of his silence and his secrecy? For answers to these questions, you will certainly have to read on.

There are psychological and social dimensions to his character that also merit further consideration. Was the quality of his torment, the source of his anger, the peculiar way in which the benefits of patriarchy were lost to him: first through the death of his father, then his own failure to progenerate? Was he a Tristram Shandy of the seventeenth century, even (to believe one of the sources) an emasculated man, an effective eunuch, unable to participate in the relationships between men and women and the making of families, and so forced either to console himself in conversation with his talented nephew, or to confront his own uselessness in the species, living a life to no purpose?

This book is an uncovering of the covering up of Marvell's life that has taken place. It is an assembly of the documentary materials and acts of interpretation that constitute Marvell's biography, and an explanation of how an East Yorkshire vicar's son became the most effective political and religious satirist of his day, one of the greatest lyrical and political poets in the English language, and in his time one of the most advanced thinkers in respect of toleration and free thinking. In both poetry and the theory of toleration Marvell was a mould-breaker, remaking categories on the eve of modernity in poetry, religion and politics. For this reason, his life and his writing are worthy of anyone's attention today: they address serious matters in today's world of shifting values and encroachments on personal and civil liberty. The world is suffering the consequences of a financial crisis that has its origins, it is alleged, in the greed of those who operate the financial system; today, improperly equipped soldiers fall in battle on distant plains while politicians corruptly reap financial benefits from the taxpayer. Marvell would have understood all of these matters with innate wisdom, and his writings still address them. But it is the way he found revelation of the personal and connected it with the public that is so unusual and so instructive.

❊

CHAPTER 2

ROOTS

HOLDERNESS AND WINESTEAD

ANDREW MARVELL WAS BORN in the vicarage at Winestead, East Yorkshire, on 31 March 1621. Winestead is situated in the Holderness region of the county, a flat expanse of land spreading east from the city of Kingston upon Hull towards the North Sea. Due east and on the coast is Withernsea, in the seventeenth century little more than a few meagre dwellings. Extending south to make a barrier between the sea and the Humber estuary is Spurn Head, periodically broken by the sea, its shape thereby constantly changed by the strident waters. It is one of England's ends, a place of dunes seldom rising more than three yards, with seawater all around. On the end was an isolated lighthouse, in the Middle Ages just a beacon kept ablaze by a hermit. To the north the Yorkshire Wolds curve, beginning west of Hull and arching north and east, above Beverley, to meet the sea at Flamborough, where flocks of crying seagulls populate the cliffs, and where, further back in time, the Danes invaded. To the west of Flamborough, along the path of the old Roman road from York to Bridlington, lies the village of Rudston, and before the village, on a hilltop on which the church was eventually built, is the Rudston Monolith, the tallest standing stone in Britain, a needle projecting abruptly from the ground like a spear hurled at the earth by an angry god or indeed the devil. This gigantic monolith is almost eight metres in height; it has been traced to a depth of sixteen feet below the surface without reaching the bottom. It is of fine-grained oolitic grit, dragged sixteen miles from its parent rock in the north-eastern moorlands near Whitby. The deep past of the pagans is never far from sight in East Yorkshire.

Holdernesss was wild country even in the 1600s. Much of the land, especially near the river, was practically at sea level. Inland travel might well be by boat, not down rivers so much as across marshes. That's how the Norman church at the village of Swine just to the north-east of Hull was reached. Hull was a good Reformation town, and the church was present to all in Holderness: out of the flat plain rises the magnificent spire of the parish church in Patrington – the so-called 'Queen of Holderness'. But the Reformation did not reach this far so easily. When the Quaker George Fox passed through in the 1650s, dodging thuggish constables as he went, up on the Wolds, and where the Wolds become the North Yorkshire moors, he found churches still with their medieval paintings visible, not whitewashed.[1]

Less marshy than Swine was Winestead, about thirteen miles south-east of Hull and one and a half miles north-west of Patrington. In Marvell's time it was on the Humber. At its heart was the church, begun in 1170: nothing more than an oblong chancel and nave, dedicated to St Germanus, Bishop of Auxerre, one of whose fingers had been brought to Selby Abbey in 1150. This dedication at Winestead suggests an early Christian settlement there. The church was a low Gothic structure, surrounded by lofty trees that give it an air of deep solemnity (plate 1). In the interior was a stone monument, representing the late Sir Robert Hildyard lying in armour. This stood in an unusual part of the church, being placed immediately before the pulpit. Here in 1347 Sir Robert Hilton, Lord of Swine, founded a chantry at the altar of Our Lady for prayers to be said for his own soul, and for the souls of Dame Margaret, his consort, his father and mother. It became the burial place of the Hildyards.

Early in the seventeenth century the decayed south aisle was demolished by the third Sir Christopher Hildyard, when he erected the Hildyard chapel. This chapel, built of stone, occupies the easternmost bay of the aisle. The Hildyards had acquired the patronage of the church through a marriage in 1417 between Sir Robert and Isobell, co-heiress of Sir Robert Hilton. The story resembles the history of Marvell's future Yorkshire patrons, the Fairfaxes. Apart from the strengthening of the roof, little else was done to the church during the seventeenth century.

The most prominent monument is the altar tomb of Sir Christopher Hildyard, bearing a recumbent effigy of the knight in plate armour. He died in 1602. Another is the effigy of a priest in a similar posture, somewhat mutilated, and apparently belonging to the fifteenth century. Two Sir Christophers, uncle and nephew, were High Sheriffs of Yorkshire in the reign of Elizabeth. Sir Robert, the son of the latter, was a gentleman of the privy chamber to King Charles I, and a colonel in the royal army during the Civil War. He was a doughty warrior, and slew in single combat the Scottish champion who challenged any gentleman in the royal army to meet him. For this he was made, on the field, a knight banneret. Is he then the knight banneret referred to at the end of Marvell's poem 'The Unfortunate Lover'? All these figures were reminders of the leaders of the world into which Marvell was born: the caste of people to whom he should show deference, or, in the case of the priest, a reminder of the role in life to which he might be expected to aspire.

But these people were also passing from the world, as bloodlines were disrupted and the social and political change that Marvell would witness. The ancient residence of the Hildyards, a little west of the church, was surrounded by a moat, in which William, only son of Sir Christopher Hildyard, Knt, was drowned. In consequence of this melancholy event, it is supposed, Sir Christopher pulled down the old mansion and built a new one, in 1579, at the northern extremity of the lordship. The moated site is now a garden. Little happened after 1620. Even Andrew Marvell senior, the father of the poet, was accused of negligence in letting repairs in the chancel go unmade, and for this was summoned before the Archbishop of York in 1619.

NEW-MADE CLERGYMAN

Andrew Marvell senior was born in approximately 1585 at Meldreth in south-west Cambridgeshire, one of the two sons of Andrew Marvell (d. 1628), yeoman, and his wife, Johanne (d. 1615). The family, which had long been settled in the area, farmed some fifty acres of land in the village. But young Andrew was on the rise and would never be a farmer. He was admitted in 1601 to Emmanuel College, Cambridge, and elected a scholar in 1604, graduating BA in 1605 and proceeding MA in 1608. After entering the diaconate at York in March 1607 he was in November of the following year licensed by the Bishop of Ely to serve as curate and schoolmaster at Melbourne, adjacent to his birthplace. But any plans he had to stay in the south were quickly altered. By January 1609 his signature as curate appears in the register of burials at Flamborough in the East Riding of Yorkshire, and he was ordained a priest in York Minster on 30 May (Trinity Sunday). He had finally found his vocation in a part of the country far distant from his home.[2]

At Cherry Burton near Beverley, on 22 October 1612, Marvell married Anne Pease, daughter of George and Ann, who had been baptized in Flamborough on 1 March 1584.[3] On 23 April 1614 he was formally inducted as Rector of Winestead by Marmaduke Brooke, the Dean and Parson of Seaton Ross.[4] Here in Winestead all Marvell's five children would be baptized: two sons (Andrew, the poet, born 31 March 1621; John, born 7 September 1623) and three daughters (Anne, born 14 March 1615; Mary, born 20 October 1616; Elizabeth, born 28 September 1618). Of his sons only Andrew would reach manhood; John was buried at Winestead on 20 September 1624.

Ten days after John's death, Marvell senior was elected Master of the Charterhouse Hospital in the important port of Hull, a quarter of a mile beyond the town's north walls in Sculcoates (see plate 3). It was also known as 'God's House'. The family moved to Hull and took up residence in the master's house, which stood apart from the Charterhouse. For the young Andrew, Winestead would become a remote memory. At the same time, Marvell senior became a preacher at Hull's Holy Trinity Church, the predominant church in the town and the closest building it had to a cathedral (plate 2).[5]

Holy Trinity is a proud church: the third church building on the site, it was and remains the largest by area of all English parish churches. If the churches at Flamborough and Winestead did not remind Marvell and his family of the pre-Reformation past of the church, here it was absolutely unavoidable. To be so dominated by not one or two but four ecclesiastical buildings helps to explain why religion was always a priority and the marker of the horizon in Marvell's world. The church was originally only a chapel of ease to Hessle, from which it was separated by Act of Parliament, and made a vicarage, only in 1661, under the patronage of the Corporation. In this later act of separation the adult Marvell would play a significant role.

In the Charterhouse Andrew senior was joined in 1626 by his father (also Andrew) and his brother Edward and family (including Edward's baby son Andrew, born in November of this year), perhaps fleeing the plague or in grandfather Andrew's case, Charles I's forced loan. In due course his daughters became the wives of Hull townsmen, Anne (b. 1615) marrying James Blaydes in 1633, Mary (b. 1617) marrying Edmond Popple in 1636, and Elizabeth (b. 1618) marrying Robert More by 1642. The Alureds, to whom the Marvells would also become related by marriage, also lived in the Charterhouse at this time. Their lives intertwined: in April 1628, the Reverend Marvell signed the will of Henry Alured, and his wife Ann determined, along with the widow of the former Master of the Charterhouse, what Alured's daughter would need by way of household goods. Little Andrew, Edward's son, less than two years old, died and was buried in Holy Trinity on 4 June 1628.[6]

The Charterhouse, situated just north of the old city, was founded in 1384 by Michael de la Pole, first Earl of Suffolk, a Hull boy made good. It was conceived by his father, William, and founded after his death by Michael as a house for poor people, the elderly and those who had fallen on hard times. Originally, it was a monastery for thirteen monks of the Carthusian order, one of whom was to be Prior. Now there were to be thirteen poor men and thirteen poor women, one of the former of whom was to be master; the Prior and monks and the Master and the poor folk might live together, or separately. The Lord Mayor of Hull and the Corporation selected the residents and the Master, the right being granted in 1552 by King Edward VI as a thank-you for services to the Crown. When the Marvells moved in there were twelve residents in the almshouses. The Charterhouse had gardens surrounded by a brick wall.

Hull's experience of the Reformation itself was distinctive and significant. Unlike the situation in many other provincial towns, former monks and friars did not find new roles in the reformed church, or remain resident in the town: there were no such places to be had. The reborn Charterhouse was stocked from outside, and Marvell senior was part of that new order. In Holy Trinity

Church there had been a large number of chantry priests and with the abolition of the chantries they all disappeared. Andrew Marvell junior's early world contained far, far fewer clergymen than his forebears would have known. Into this vacuum came in the reign of Edward VI vigorous evangelical preaching, Hull's first Protestant preacher being John Rough, a Scot and sometime associate of John Knox, who had been invited in 1547 to preach in northern England by Lord Protector Somerset. From this point Protestantism took hold among the clergy, Hull having a disproportionate number of clergymen who resisted the return to Catholicism in Mary's reign, while there was little obvious revival of pre-Reformed practice among the laity. The return of Protestantism with Elizabeth's accession was warmly greeted, the Corporation seizing the initiative to endow preaching appointments. Protestants brought from the south into the city, such as Melchior Smith, who came in 1561 from Boston in Lincolnshire to be Vicar of Holy Trinity, tended to be of the more godly sort. Smith disapproved of the vestment regulations and what he regarded as the idolatrous communion practices that remained in the Elizabethan settlement. Allegedly, he defamed bishops in his sermons and introduced Anabaptist notions of the equality of all men; preaching was for him the central part of his ministry. The establishment of the lectureship eventually held by Marvell senior was a further enhancement of Protestantism in Hull, made in 1573 by an agreement between Edmund Grindal, then the Archbishop of York, Smith the Vicar, and the Corporation. It was a final victory over some lingering instances of anti-Protestant 'filibuster', such as having the organ played for so long that the sermon was edged out, and continuing the practice of extensive bell ringing on funeral days and All Saints' Day. The first lecturer, Griffith Briskin, a man of similar persuasions to Smith, was very successful in raising a loyal following among the congregation during the last two decades of the century, this while emphasizing severe moral reformation.[7] The gathering of poor relief by Hull townspeople under the aegis of Protestantism – and where church met corporation – was in this period impressive and exceptional.[8] It is therefore not entirely surprising that Richard Perrot, the Laudian or High Church divine, who arrived as Vicar of Hessle and Hull in 1616, and who would in 1627 controvert the great legal scholar John Selden on the history of tithes, had little impact on the religious complexion of the town.[9] Perrot and Marvell senior disagreed on the nature and extent of preaching, an issue that was settled finally by the Corporation on 15 November 1626. Early in the new year, Marvell senior was officially licensed as lecturer in Holy Trinity.

During Marvell's stewardship of the Charterhouse the number of almspeople was increased, the fabric and chapel were extensively repaired, and annual accounts faithfully rendered.[10] These original buildings came to be levelled during the Civil War. Marvell senior dispersed the not insubstantial income of £55 for the poor.In fact the total income of the rents to the Charterhouse was £118, but £63 disappeared in annual running costs, and the cost of building and repairs ran to £118 15s. 6d. Six rooms for poor women were added. He managed to pay each resident 14d. a week, slightly more than twice the amount originally intended in the foundation, although the six new residents would have to endure a mere 8d. a week until some further capital charges had been covered, since the total income was limited. In any case, there was good reason, as Marvell senior stated, to fear that the income of the Charterhouse might drop, through a general recession, or through the decline of the tenant farmers who paid the rents. Indeed, the plague years of the mid-1630s meant that income was restricted; Marvell senior did most of the repairs in the last eighteen months of his life, from August 1639 onwards. It was not an easy situation: Marvell feared a potential decline of annual income of up to 23 per cent, and indicated that the foundation did not have the contingency sum that the founders had recommended, while the Charterhouse had the responsibility for the upkeep of several buildings in the town, as well as the Charterhouse buildings themselves. In addition, the Charterhouse walls were in 1640 reported to be ruinous in many places. With the money that was left over in these circumstances (some £8 a year), Marvell senior wanted to build a ceiling in the hall and above it a new room that would function as a library, no doubt warmed by the large fireplace below in the hall. The library would be open to any in Hull who could make use of it. Otherwise, according to his son, he 'lived with some measure of reputation, both for Piety and Learning: and he was moreover a Conformist to the established Rites of the Church of *England*, though I confess none of the most over-running or eager in them'.[11]

It is true, as we know, that early on he fell out with the Vicar of Hull about preaching, and as late as 1639 was ordered by the diocese to read, in hood and surplice, more of the Prayer Book liturgy before his weekly lecture. Yet some autograph complaints against local separatists and notes on the necessity of observing church ritual suggest that his was a moderate Puritanism, just as his son later claimed. Puritanism it was nonetheless, and we can surely expect nothing less from a graduate of Emmanuel College, the new home of Puritan churchmanship in Cambridge. Yet, as will become plain, the character of Marvell senior's 'Puritanism' was not at all as we might expect and its distinctiveness would have a lasting influence on his son.

Hull may have been laid out by monks, but its standing as a port meant that it had enormous military significance.[12] It was a staging post for any campaign a monarch might wish to wage in Scotland, and although it seems far to the south it was always refortified in time of conflict with the Scots for fear that it might be a target for attack from the north, or from an invasion sailing from Europe. In addition to the medieval walls around the town on the west bank of the River Hull, there was a fierce defensive rampart bound by two block-houses and with a castle halfway along protecting the port from the east. This was built during Henry VIII's reign after Hull had fallen temporarily to Pilgrimage of Grace rebels in 1536. The south blockhouse at least could rake the entrance to the Hull with ordnance fire if so desired, and the King certainly supplied the defences with some powerful artillery pieces. From the 1540s onwards a considerable garrison was billeted in the defences and the town. These soldiers, plus the militia officially funded, drilled and led by the Mayor (the 'Trained Bands'), would have made the town feel very military indeed. As a child, Marvell would witness the fortifying of the extant defences in readiness for projected English involvement in the Thirty Years War (1,350 soldiers had sailed from Hull in 1626 to support the King of Denmark), and the danger of attack from Spain and the Spanish Netherlands.[13] New earthworks were thrown up and some doubtful gates closed: all traffic was directed through three heavily guarded gates. Moving around was not as easy as it once had been, and at these times travellers were scrutinized at the town entrances.

Marvell commended the delight of seeing the militia drill: 'I can not but remember, though then a child, those blessed days when the youth of your own town were trained for your militia, and did methought become their arms much better then any soldiers that I haue seen there since.'[14]

Reading was clearly of great importance to Marvell senior: it was his great pleasure and his source of edification. He worried that his proposal for a library in the Charterhouse might be seen as self-seeking but pointed up the benefits to an establishment of having a book-reading master. These were habits that were inherited by his son. The Rev. Marvell saw himself as a 'scholar' and that all of his duties in Hull, and those of his successors, would be dependent upon the frequent use of the scholar's tools: books. And after all, the annual stipend of the master was not so great; the additional attraction of a scholarly library would bring clergymen of quality more readily into Hull. As he put it, the library would be a 'common well' for scholars. The Corporation needed well-informed divines who would engage in controversy with those in error, if necessary, and especially those who might drift in (he talks of 'an irresolute staggerer') from a ship at the port. The purity of English Reformation doctrine had to be maintained.[15] In the back of his mind was a growing sense that from this work of charity could be fashioned eventually a college and even a university. Book accumulation was to be pursued by a call for public donation and by modest and ongoing purchases from the foundation. Marvell left his own library, or a very large part of it, as part of this founding collection. He said he was prepared to wait for the foundation to buy it from him. What then would happen to these books when he died? Would they pass to his son; would they be lost in the Civil War destruction of the Charterhouse?

The historian Thomas Fuller's anecdotal account of Marvell senior was taken in part from the testimony of a son-in-law, either James Blaydes, Edmond Popple or Robert More. It portrays him as 'most *facetious* in his *discourse*, yet *grave* in his *carriage*; a most excellent preacher, who, like a good husband, never *broached* what he had new *brewed*, but preached what he had pre-studied some competent time before'.[16]

Marvell senior corresponded on theological matters with brother ministers,[17] sometimes acrimoniously, while Fuller mentions that his 'excellent
comment upon Saint *Peter* is daily desired and expected'. During his ministry,
Marvell senior attracted just over £60 in funeral bequests, the most conferred
on any one clergyman in Yorkshire in this period. Several of his sermons
survive in manuscript. Besides those still preserved in Hull, 'Israel and
England parallel'd. or Some of their sinnes ballanced' was dedicated on
28 April 1627 to Anne Sadleir of Standon, Hertfordshire, sister of his
benefactor Bridget Skinner of Thornton Curtis, Lincolnshire, and another
patroness.[18] This is a handsome pocketbook-sized presentation copy, written
in an extremely fine hand. A copy of the address that, although recently under
quarantine from the plague, he delivered at the funeral of John Ramsden,
Mayor of Hull, on 8 December 1637 also survives.[19] In the latter,the analogy
between physical and political bodies is the starting point: although the wound
in a body politic (from the death of a mayor) might heal quickly after three
days, Marvell has come to rub the sore, as would be the case with a natural
wound. The imagery of Ramsden as a sun is notable, magisterial in its effect,
and should be associated with the reference to God as axeman, cutting off
useless branches. Such terms are therefore those of the regicide that will come
in the following decade but here applied to a civic context. There is no guarantee at all that a good magistrate will succeed a previously good one (even like
Nero's good first five years of government); therefore there is every reason to
fear a political eclipse. Those residents of Hull who heard the sermon would
be under no illusion that their sin was not a part of the cause of Ramsden's
death in the plague season.

The sermon dedicated to Mrs Sadleir begins with 1 Cor. 10: 7, 'Be ye not
Idolators as were some of them.'[20] The anxious preface, in which he apologizes
for writing later than he should have done and acknowledges that perhaps it
would have been better for him to have left it unsaid, is similar to his son's nice-
ness in respect of patronage. The sermon is described as a 'payment' as if it
were rent, and even the scribe is mentioned as being keenly involved in its
production and fearful of Mrs Sadleir's censure. But Marvell instructs in
patience as he apologizes and the work and wit of his sermon are buried inside
his preface. Appropriately, his study is described as 'poore'.

The Rev. Marvell proceeds with Judges 5: 8, 'They have chose new gods.'
Marvell describes himself as wishing he were like the musicians described in
the ancient Greek musician and poet Timotheus of Miletus, who could change
people's moods by changing the tone of his playing.[21] It is the time of a public
fast and people must be sombre. Apart from the appeal of music there is also
the wit that makes music and its variety of moods come together with the
seeming seriousness of the fast. It is a startling effect and quite unexpected;
certainly more so than the simile of the Bible as a looking glass, 'God's sacred
mirrour', that follows (sig. 3ʳ), in which may be discerned our own times (and

later God's bounties are compared to a pair of spectacles or a perspective glass).
The Bible is brought alive in the most animated way, with references to it being
full of examples of offenders (pp.16–17). There are analogies woven throughout
the text, each continually extending the imaginative scope of the discourse. As
striking as the music analogy is a comparison of men with grasshoppers (p. 15),
anticipating his son's poetry.[22] The resolution of the text begins with Marvell
senior's characteristic Ramist diagram. National characteristics turn out to be
sins, including the English obsession with newfangledness. Another theme that
surfaces is that of apparent free will: the Israelites chose to seek new gods (p.30).
One wonders how far Marvell senior was prepared to go in illustrating God's
response to the Israelites when he describes Him as being passionately discontented, just as Julius Caesar was when stabbed, more by the ingratitude than the
wound itself (referring to Suetonius). The false gods are exemplified wittily but
most daringly in a quotation from Horace on Priapus: 'By descent I am a block
no better than my neighbours I was fayre to have been hewed into a bench or
settle but being an unshapely piece for any such service at ye last he resolved to
make a Saint or a God of me (p.63)'.[23] The English have become obsessed with
worldly wealth and are covetous, enjoying pleasure and luxury and the claims
of Bacchus (drinking) and Venus (idolizing proud mistresses), and they have
succumbed to vainglory. They have so many idols that they are condoning the
pagan Saxons who named the days of the week after their deities. Instead,
Marvell senior exhorts his listeners to heed Origen in his homily on Jude: for
whatever weighs heaviest in the balance of affections is to be made a god: and
this will reconcile us with God's purposes. Elsewhere, Marvell senior shows
deep respect for the Church of England, 'ye paradise of the world' (p.21),
and the Archbishop (of Canterbury or York?), the 'Pope of ye other world'
(p.52). His son's later sense of pre-Civil War England as a lost paradise must
draw on such views.

   Most of Marvell senior's sermons are gathered in the manuscript book that
survives in Hull Central Library.[24] Scriptural exegesis in its examples comes
with a great deal of learning. A sermon opens with an invocation not of the
Bible but of Aristotle: 'The Councell of Aristotle to Callisthenes for discretion
in Court Conference is not an unfit remembrance for him wch is a spokesman
at a festivall solemnity. . . . Either speak very little or things very pleasing[.] I
purpose to make use of both for the present.'[25] Marvell senior's sermons are
neither particularly Laudian nor Puritan, in their fusion of biblical and classical learning, and in their pointed use of rhetorical devices such as repetition.
We can certainly see the early formation of Marvell junior's own humour,
eclecticism and wise caution:

   Is not thyr bonus δαίμων [daemon] recta ratio? Do not the Stoicks desire a
   blessed man to be one that lives according unto reason? . . . Paul tells us of
   unreasonable men. Peter tells us of unreasonable beasts. These p[er]haps are

Pauls beasts after the maner of men. Our doctrine letts us see the world peopled w[th] beasts. The furious is a beare robbed of her whelps. Ye lecher a goat or a horsleach not leaving till she be full, nor full till she burst. The drunkard a swine or a poisoned rat, that drinks as long as it can stand. The subtile a fox. The malicious a mad dog. The envious a dog in a manger. The idle a dormouse. The swaggrer a Colt unbridled. The ignora[n]t a nasse. The impatient a resty jade that seekes to cast his burden. So that the world is a wildernesse full of beasts; Circes island where all are turned into beasts wch have not Moly that is reason for a Counter Charme. Hence Pythagoras his transmigration of mens soules into beasts when men for want of reason are turnd bestiall. The whole world is a Bedlem or Fooliana.[26]

There's much imagery here accessible and familiar to someone not learned; the use of the animal comparisons in that respect is interesting. Here in Marvell senior's preaching we have the reference to the herb Moly in precisely the same way that it is referred to in Milton's *Comus* (ll. 635–40; written at the same time as this sermon); that is, as a preservative against transformation into a beast. Elsewhere, metaphor and simile develop easily from engagement with the Bible, suggesting a habit of deep familiarity and use that would have rubbed off on the young poet. St Luke was a physician, and so a sermon for a new mayor in a time of plague is to be taken from a scripture that must be regarded as a cure for a disease.[27]

Marvell senior objects to mortification in a Roman Catholic sense, and indeed seems to recommend strongly that the body be not denied in any act of mortification. Along the way he objects to 'Pythagorean' vegetarianism as well as to 'friarlike mortification'. Being a hermit is like being a boar or a werewolf, the anchoret like a rabbit in its burrow. Similarly, but on the level of theological concepts, he accused another clergyman, Richard Harrington, of maintaining superstition by defending the idea of Christ's descent into Hell, strictly speaking unscriptural, despite the several texts in the Bible that have been associated with it. Behind his reasoning lay his suspicion of the Athanasian Creed, which was its direct source, together with the Apostles' Creed.[28]

Yet in the sermon book there are a number of spiritual treatises that look more properly like the interests of a Laudian or even a Roman Catholic: 'Historia de vita et gestis Jesu Christus in sum Maria Collecta cum Epistolis Agbari ad Jesu et Jesu ad Agbari cum Epistolaq Lentuli ad Tiberum.'[29] It may well be that, despite the clash between Marvell and Perrot, there were also some points of contact and influence. At some point in these years he gave to Anne Sadleir, his patroness, a copy of a fifteenth-century commentary on the Ten Commandments, together with directions for visiting the sick.[30] In many ways the manuscript is a companion piece to the sermon book, an earlier version of it. Once in circulation with a laywoman, it represents both a sustaining of that earlier tradition of medieval feminine piety, and a development of post-Reformation lay piety, which often used medieval spiritual sources; and it was of a theological kind that often gave the orthodox or bishops some offence. Perhaps Marvell senior and Mrs Sadleir understood that these books were for private devotion alone. In a more public context, they become something quite different and more challenging. Thomas Fuller noted that Marvell senior's excellent commentary on St Peter would do more good were it in print, but that this was prevented by the envy and covetousness of whoever he knew possessed the manuscript volume: someone who acknowledged Marvell's powers as a pious author and exegete but could not bear to see him have the praise.[31]

The one chief remaining text in the sermon book is one of the most controversial books of the time, being reviled across Christendom and burned in many places, including England. Marvell senior had a copy of the Racovian Catechism in his collection: the most concise statement of the Polish Socinian church, which was anti-Trinitarian, refused the belief that Christ's atonement automatically brought at least some of mankind grace, and expounded further views on toleration that most Protestants as well as Catholics found utterly abhorrent.[32] The force of Faustus Socinus's (1539–1604) teachings lay in his denial that Christianity was a sacrificial religion, that Adam's Fall applied to all men, and that Christ's atonement was necessary to anyone's redemption.[33] Socinus argued that Christ's life and death were to be taken only as an inspiring example. It may even be that the text was Marvell senior's translation, although connections have been drawn with one of the earliest English Socinians, Paul Best, who came from Elmswell near Driffield; his family had property in Beverley and he returned there during his lifetime.[34] While the link with Best cannot at present be definitively confirmed, the question remains as to why Marvell had this inflammatory document at all. Perhaps, like Best, he was drawn by anti-Trinitarianism itself, a confident development of Protestant thought and a line that would mark him as moving towards some extreme of the Puritan diaspora, along with Best, John Biddle and the many others who came after them. But then again, the Racovian Catechism was attractive to Laudians, even to some Catholics, because of its elevation of Christ's priesthood, even if Jesus was denied a place as part of the Godhead. Others, often but not only associated with the High Church, admired the Socinians on account of their elevation of reason. Some of the other patristic and late-medieval writings associated with Marvell senior suggest that this was the more likely set of connections. After all, he was ready to disagree with the more extreme Puritans in Hull, and he strongly objected to their treatment of him. Either way, we still have to decide whether this text was, as has been suggested, intended for private consumption by Marvell or for circulation. Even the most privately kept document was evidence of one of the most subversive theological works published in this period. Marvell senior's ownership of it attests to a growing awareness of the insufficiency of scripturally based proofs of the Trinity, and the associated views that came with it. Key Puritans like John Owen railed against anti-Trinitarianism's dangers, but by the end of the century a new form of Christianity had become important in England. It might be called Enlightenment religion, but never confessing in public its true nature, in fact it harboured powerful critiques on the idea of the Trinity from men as eminent as Locke and Newton.[35] This modulated version of Socinianism certainly had an impact on the influential Puritan divine Richard Baxter and his followers, as Owen feared (and even though Baxter repudiated the Socinians on the status of Christ's atonement).[36]

So, in the light of this evidence, does Andrew Marvell senior look like a religious radical? That does not seem very likely from the sermons that have survived. The first sermon in the sermon book volume was preached on the occasion of the installation of a new mayor at Hull on St Luke's Day, 18 October 1636. It is decidedly conformist, socially as well as theologically, in its stance, reminding the listener over and over again of the way in which we are all parts of hierarchies; everyone is subject to someone else:

> so that thou suffer not to let slip or to be shaken out the commandement mouth word, countenance, or pleasure of y[e] King of Kings God or rather of his viceregent the king on earth, and that in regard (there is reason for what I require) in regard of the word (which I find in the originall) that you should not slight or falsify, & the rather because it is back'd wth an Oath wch you should not violate: W[th] the oath of God; of god in regard of attestation by whom you have sworne, or observation who is privy to your oath & behaviour afterward or obligation, by which you are tyed to him who is a God by title, & by resemblance of authority likewise.[37]

Elsewhere there is a strong and explicit disagreement with the Arminians on their purported position that denying free will removes the efficacy of the grace bought by Christ. Also against the Arminians, he objected in a private dispute against the right to the sacrament of all who present themselves, as opposed to those 'to [w]home he (Jesus) gave himself'.[38] Surely those who were 'scandalous impenitents' should be debarred. There are tables in another sermon setting out the nature and advantageousness of sacrifices.[39]

In the dispute, Marvell senior displays all of the qualities of an age when belief in original sin was almost universal: there are children who will indelibly be hypocrites and will dissemble affection, even though a charitable person will want to believe the best. He noted the degree of punishment of all kinds of enormity for the purpose of reformation and thought that this was worthy of further enquiry. Regular sacrifices in the ceremonies of worship due to God have resulted, Marvell senior argues, in the wonder that while the town itself was plague-ridden, no other surrounding communities had been affected. It is then the sinners among those of Hull who must be sacrificed for the sake of the sound; otherwise they will all be lost. In November 1638, the Archbishop of York, Richard Neile, and his court did not think that Reverend Marvell would be above helping them to execute their order that prayers be read daily in Hull Trinity Church, in the face of expected intransigence from Richard Perrot and his curate John Gouge.[40] Yet they had to insist on 14 August 1639, when he was summoned to appear before the Chancellor or Vicar General of the Archbishop's court, that he read the later part of the prayers or service from the Book of Common Prayer, in his hood and surplice, on Wednesdays and Sundays, and at other times when he preached at Holy Trinity. On 12 October, he had to appear again before the Chancellor to be ordered to read the entire 'Second Service'. Yet again, the order was insisted upon on 14 December, and on 31 January 1640: Neile was on to his case.[41]

Perhaps the book list that immediately precedes the Racovian Catechism tells all, with its huge variety of opinions and approaches: Andrewes, Kellet, the Greek Bible, the famous commentary on biblical apocalypse *Clavis Apocalyptica* by Joseph Mede, Lambert Danaeu, the Calvinist scriptural commentator and anti-witch authority, Zanchius, Sarpi's *History of the Council of Trent*, Cyril, Peter Martyr on Samuel, Damascen.[42] It is an intriguingly broad synthesis typical of the early seventeenth-century Protestant consensus, in which the High Church, the Anabaptists and the Socinians came close to shaking hands, but never quite close enough.

The final piece in the sermon book is a list of disagreements with the Puritans in Hull who rejected Marvell senior's ministry, having first promised to be guided by him.[43] They said they wanted to debate the status of Christ's merit but never did. Instead, they concealed their opinions from him, while letting them be known to others. He said they could not lawfully meet in household assemblies to worship, and challenged their denial of infant baptism, only to be accused himself of being a secret believer in adult baptism. In the light of Marvell senior's possession of something as heterodox as the Racovian Catechism, one might wonder whether this might not be a reasonable accusation. But at the same time, they had attacked his use of godfathers as erroneous and superstitious. They had, it would seem, approached members of the Marvell family and made insinuations, while suggesting to others that Marvell senior was a hypocrite. They had singled him out for wearing the surplice for preaching, while leaving others who also adopted this practice alone. All of this criticism circulated as rumour, a whispering campaign that Marvell senior felt to be particularly undermining. They would not meet him and instead sent him letters that were unsigned and undated; he had no means of replying, although it might be remembered that these apparent Baptist separatists needed to keep their identities secret since most of their worship was illegal and subject to suppression. Clearly, Marvell senior was caught between the Archbishop of York on the one hand and the emergent Baptists of Hull on the other, and felt exposed to the latter while the former was closely scrutinizing him. Was the document written in his defence at an investigation? We might imagine another divine being rather more dismissive of these separatists. Here, the attitude of openness and toleration, despite holding his own line, is notable.

SCHOOLDAYS

Funds that would before 1539 have gone to chantries, and other means by which people hoped to enhance their status in the afterlife with money left to the church, were diverted after the Reformation to poor relief and to education. Hull already had its grammar school, founded in 1479, along with a chantry to support it by Bishop Alcock, successively Bishop of Rochester, Worcester, and Ely, and afterwards Lord Chancellor of England.[44] It stood on South Church Side facing Holy Trinity Church. It had flourished until the reign of Edward VI, when all free schools and chantries were suppressed and their revenues seized. The people of Hull objected to this proceeding, and ultimately the school was re-established. In 1548 the Chantry Commissioners allowed the salary of the schoolmaster (who had been a priest) to remain in place; it simply passed to the oversight of the Corporation. About 1578, the building having fallen into decay, Alderman William Gee, who was thrice Mayor of Hull, opened a subscription for the purpose of repairing it. This resulted in the erection of a new school in 1583–85, a rectangular brick building, in the financing of which Alderman Gee was joined by the Corporation of Hull; the Corporation added a second storey, which was used as an exchange and assembly room. It remains there today, a schoolroom of twenty by seventy feet, with large windows facing both north and south. Alderman Gee not only contributed £80 and 20,000 bricks, but also left two houses in the 'Butchery' (now Queen Street) for the benefit of the school. The cost of rebuilding was £600. In 1586 the school was declared, by inquisition, the property of the Crown. In the following year the Queen gave the schoolhouse, the garden, and other tenements, 'formerly given to superstitious uses', to Luke Thurcross, the then Mayor, and others. The appointment of masters passed to the Corporation in 1604. In 1629, when Marvell would have attended school, Hull Grammar School was waiting for him.

Before the Reformation, grammar schools were an aspect of the church: places where Latin, the language of the church, was taught. Lateran Councils of 1179 and 1215 legislated that all cathedrals and substantial churches should have grammar schools. The growth of urban centres gave rise to a greater need for education; hence Hull Grammar School emerged shortly after the creation of the town as a chartered borough. The grammar schools were the engine of social transformation in the early modern period, much as they have been at times since then, the growth in their numbers a reflection of rising gentry and merchant prosperity. They enabled the socially humble but talented to join the ranks of the educated elite; in some cases they made powerful clerics out of poor boys. The schools were the means by which the Reformation was transmitted with relative unity, through uniform primers and catechisms, and in many instances the episcopal licensing of schoolmasters. Mantuan's eclogues, especially the ninth in the series, strong on anti-papal sentiment, were one example of Renaissance Latin poetry assimilated into a curriculum containing a far greater number of ancient authors.

While the schools catered for the gentry, they were also open to those boys who would become apprentices in the superior trades and handicrafts. Marvell, the son of a successful divine and grandson of a yeoman farmer, studied in Hull Grammar School alongside the sons of poor journeymen. It was by and large a local school, the gentry and substantial families in the outlying regions preferring the schools at Beverley and Pocklington, perhaps on account of their greater number of university scholarships. This does not mean that some Hull boys were not sent elsewhere, as some were, but it does mean that some very close ties of urban confraternity were being solidified at the most formative period in most citizens' lives. It was something that would mark them for the rest of their lives. Of the relationships Marvell formed at school, that with William Lister, son of Sir John Lister, twice Mayor of Hull in his time, was of lasting significance. William was an MP himself in the 1650s and became Recorder to the Corporation, residing in London and often operating with Marvell when he was MP in the 1660s. The early shared experience lay behind their ability to work together later. The school was the only means of education in the tight-knit community within the city walls: socially and geographically it was at the centre of local life. The schoolmaster was therefore a figure of considerable standing in the town, his house lying between the school and the vicarage, directly opposite Holy Trinity Church.

The grammar school curriculum was daunting. The idea was to teach boys to write and speak highly competent Latin, to read and write decent Greek, learn some Hebrew, and engage in some Bible scholarship and theology. Literature was the medium by which Latin and Greek were taught, so grammar school boys were taught to read Cicero, Virgil, Ovid, Horace, Terence, Homer, Hesiod, Aesop, Aristophanes, Plutarch, Erasmus and so on. They moved as quickly as possible from simple dialogues to the more demanding challenges of Cicero and Terence. Greek and Hebrew were reserved for the upper school. The technique of quite literally 'bashing' Latin grammar into the boys, by the master's liberal use of his birch or his rod, is well attested. It has been described as a world of 'cruel and brutal violence'.[45] The mechanics of learning – the very process of memorizing vocabulary and grammar, as well as more advanced aspects like the quantitative scanning of Latin verse – mattered much more than any understanding on the part of the boys of what they were reading. To this should be added the fact that this was a very small world, with pupils being taught in one room by one or two persons only. For those being taught, it was an intense experience and there was nowhere to hide.

Every school day would begin at six, with a two-hour midday break at eleven, and afternoon school ending at five or six o'clock. One half-day might be devoted to play: usually on Butcroft just outside the town walls. In the winter, starting an hour later and finishing an hour earlier might economize on lighting costs. The school itself was divided into two. The Upper School sat in desks grouped around the master on a raised platform in the top third of the room, while the usher supervised the rest of the Lower School. The boys were organized in 'forms' corresponding to age, and sat opposite each other. The master taught from a huge wooden desk, symbolizing his power, that could only be entered by a door (its seat was therefore like a pew) and was surmounted by a huge canopy or sounding board. Robert Witty, the eventual creator of the spa at Scarborough, Marvell's friend and associate, to whom he wrote dedicatory poems, was usher at the Grammar School from 1633 until 1641. This was just at the time when Marvell was leaving for university, but it is not impossible that they first met here.

Because the pay was poor the ushers were young and there was a rapid turnover of staff. In 1630, Marvell's second year, no usher could be attracted, a parent complained and Anthony Stevenson, a Hull man, was appointed to the post. Most of the masters and the ushers were local, and the ushers were typically very recent university graduates. Marvell would have known two masters: James Burney, master from 1613 to 1632, and Anthony Stevenson, master from 1632 to 1646. The masters were certainly substantial figures on the local scene but they found their stipends insufficient to support a family. Burney retreated with his young family to be Vicar of Beverley Minster in May 1632. Stevenson supplemented his income by taking on the chaplaincy of Trinity House in 1642, and eventually found that he had to take a living to keep his family, with an income three times the size of his schoolmaster's income. As the incumbent of Roos, Stevenson was among the Nonconformist divines to be ejected in 1662 – one of the people whom Marvell spent much of his time defending in the 1670s. Both Burney and Stevenson had attended Trinity College, Cambridge, the former the son of a merchant, the latter the son of a tailor. Trinity would become Marvell's college. Stevenson took the enrolment of the school to about a hundred boys, several of whom would become Puritan ministers themselves.

While it cannot be proved, the likelihood is that Marvell's father paid no fees for his son; these were 4s. per quarter for the son of a burgess, and whatever the master charged for a 'stranger'. Smaller contributions, no more than pennies, were used to buy brooms for cleaning and the master's birches. At the time of Stevenson's appointment, the town bench tried to restrict the relatively onerous customary donation of candles. A feast was held by the master for the boys just before Shrovetide, and funded by voluntary donations from the parents. The other widely practised custom of Exclusion also took place: six weeks before Christmas, the master was shut out of the schoolroom until he had offered sufficient extra playdays. Customarily too, the boys would hang their daily exercises from the windows to show the excluded master they had completed their work. Contemporaries were aghast at the violent, foul-mouthed disorderliness that often accompanied this ritual in which the supposed authority of the master was temporarily suspended.

Marvell's allusions to his schooldays fit perfectly with this picture. Take, for instance, the throwaway reference in *The Rehearsal Transpros'd* that touches on a central paradox for the Grammar School: godly boys were taught ancient literature that was often profane in content. Hence 'whether it alluded to Io that we read of at School, the Daughter of Inachus; and that as Juno persecuted the Heifer, so this was an *He-Cow*.'[46] Io was raped by Jupiter and then turned into a heifer to hide the crime from Juno. The story comes from Ovid, *Metamorphoses*, I. 590–667. Clearly he thought the discipline of the Grammar School left mental as well as physical scars on boys. Marvell says his opponent of the 1670s, Samuel Parker, once 'emancipated' from the grammar school cannot but help defame it. The harshness of the Restoration bishops is a repetition of what they learned at school: 'they seem to have contracted no *Idea* of wisdom, but what they learnt at School, the Pedantry of Whipping'.[47] In Marvell's eyes then, the abuse of beating boys was transferred later into other areas of life.

Marvell did not miss an opportunity elsewhere to make capital of other people's school experiences. Parker, he noted in *Rehearsal Transpros'd*, went to St Paul's School, where Milton had studied earlier. And Parker's logic, alleges Marvell, is on the level of a schoolboy: 'except the manufacture and labour of your periods, you have done no more than any School boy could have done on the same terms.' In Mr Smirke, Marvell has a low opinion of scanning. When Francis Turner, Marvell's target, claimed he has 'scann'd' Herbert More, Turner's target, Marvell says this is a 'hacking and vain repetition', as when at grammar school pupils are made to scan unremarkable lines from Ovid's *Metamorphoses* before understanding what the words mean: 'as I remember, this *Scanning* was a liberal Art that we learn'd at Grammar-School; and to *Scan* verses as he does the Authors Prose, before we did, or were obliged to understand them'.[48] Within much of the satire is the suspicion that behind every arrogant divine lies 'the dullest School-boy, the rankest Idiot, no nor the veriest Animadverter'.[49]

In fact, the school, which was the only institution of education most of the pupils would ever attend, required no more than the ability to read as an entrance qualification. In practice, however, most of the boys would have been taught to write before they attended the school, perhaps being instructed by a scrivener: several were hired by the Corporation to teach writing to the children of burgesses.

Hull Grammar School did not begin to keep a register until 1635. There is thus no record of Marvell's attendance, but it is improbable that he did not attend it, and his later descriptions of grammar school experience are several and vivid. There was no other such school to attend in the vicinity. It is also likely that his father provided some extra tuition since the Reverend Marvell is known to have tutored other boys, including those of his son's godfather.[50]

The earliest poem we know by Marvell was written at university but it is quintessentially part of his grammar school experience, being a reworking of the second ode in the first book of Horace's odes to meet the occasion of the birth of a royal princess. 'Ad Regem Carolum Parodia' involves a very strict and ancient use of 'parody', a counter-song or reply using very nearly the same words and phrases as the original. Lines 45–9 involve the substitution of just one word; in all other respects these are Horace's lines. The modern sense of comic or ironic version of an original was certainly known in the sixteenth century, but Marvell clearly means 'imitation' as if in an academic exercise. Indeed, some of Marvell's lexical inventions in his Latin poem may have been suggested by marginal notes in the annotated editions of Horace. Marvell kept the shape of Horace's poem by choosing words with similar sounds or spellings to Horace's originals. This is done even to the extent of failing to match the seventeenth-century context. The beginningsof Marvell's poetry writing may be seen to flow directly from the grammar school classroom.[51]

During the Civil War and Commonwealth, the school no doubt suffered, and much effort was invested in renovation when John Catlyn became school-master in 1665. Marvell must have regarded this with some reserve: for all the extensive refurbishment that took place, Catlyn was an inveterate Royalist and had Royalist sentiments carved in Greek in the master's desk:

> Ευτειχουν τρια στεμματ εχεις βασιληιον αστν:
> Τοϋνεχα τον Δωτην τον βασληα φιλει.

> O well-built royal town, thou hast three crowns,
> Therefore love the king, thy benefactor.

TRINITY

Hardly anyone went from Hull to Oxford. Of the eighty boys who went to university between 1613 and 1716, all but three went to Cambridge. Marvell matriculated at Trinity College, Cambridge, on 14 December 1633. He was twelve years of age. He joined as a subsizar, the most meagre of the undergrad-uates who worked for their board and education fees. To put this in perspective, the future Leveller and General Baptist, Richard Overton, who would regularly present himself in the 1640s as the legal victim of a rigidly stratified society, was a sizar, a notch higher than Marvell, at Queens' College.[52] Subsizars received no allowance for food but paid only 4d. for their tuition. Marvell's annual livery money was 6s. 8d. Being one so young, even by contemporary standards, we might imagine he was considered a prodigy.

King Henry VIII founded Trinity College in 1546 as one of the very last acts of his life. His intention was to establish an institution that would produce the future leaders of the reformed church, and he formed Trinity through the amalgamation of two existing colleges – King's Hall and Michaelhouse. King's Hall had received its charter in 1337 and occupied buildings that are now the northern parts of Trinity's Great Court. Michaelhouse, founded in 1324 by Hervey de Standon, Chancellor of the Exchequer to Edward II, occupied buildings to the southern side of Great Court. From the outset Trinity was a much richer institution than King's Hall and Michaelhouse put together: their joint endowments amounted to less than a quarter of those of Trinity. Most of this endowment was derived from land and other property that had belonged to dissolved monasteries, but it also included small private estates purchased by the King.

Queen Elizabeth I appointed Thomas Nevile as Master of Trinity in 1593: from then until 1615, Nevile designed and presided over the architectural development of Trinity to form the basis of what it is today. During his mastership, Great Court was created using existing structures to form a single coherent space. He replaced the decaying Michaelhouse buildings with the Hall and privately funded the building of Nevile's Court.

The college grew rapidly in importance during the century after its foundation and by 1564 already accounted for about a quarter of the total number of resident members of the university. It was much patronized by the prominent families, with many leaders of the time receiving their education at Trinity. Sir Edward Coke, Lord Bacon and the Earl of Essex were undergraduates in the late sixteenth century; in the seventeenth century, the college supplied six of the translators of the Authorized Version of the Bible from among its resident Fellows, and counted among its members the poets George Herbert, John Suckling, Abraham Cowley and John Dryden, as well as Marvell.

Hull Grammar School was an intensive immersion in Latin and Greek learning but the university made more extensive demands. To us today these look like an extension of the capacity to read, write, speak and translate the ancient languages. Every day began at 5 a.m. with an assembly in the college chapel for an hour-long morning service. Then there was a break for breakfast, followed by college-based studies in Latin, Greek, logic, mathematics and philosophy. The students gathered from each college in the public schools to hear four hours of University Exercises, which were lectures by the university professors. All of this before lunch, after which an hour or two was spent listening to declamations and disputations of contending graduates: the exercises recorded by Milton as his 'prolusions' and in which the art of 'paradiastole' – the defending of one position, and then its redescription so as to attack it – was honed. There followed a time for private study or recreation until evening service in chapel and dinner in hall. College gates were closed at 9 p.m., and undergraduates were expected to remain within them.

During hours of instruction, speech was supposed to be in Latin, Greek or Hebrew. Drinking, gaming and visits to fairs were banned, although the taverns in the town were frequented, despite the fact that corporal punishment took place: at 7 p.m. every Thursday in Trinity College, for instance. If we are to believe his later reminiscences, Marvell was not averse to a game of cards.

For seven years, Marvell put up with this discipline, the first four-year quadrivium leading to a BA degree, and then three years for the MA. Many students left after the first part, perhaps to attend the Inns of Court in London, or to pursue another course. Marvell's serious intent to study strongly suggests that a clerical and indeed academic career was intended; as does his eventual acceptance of a scholarship on 13 April 1638. Marvell was then entitled to an annual stipend of 13s. 4d., with a further shilling a week for food. He had been admitted to the fellowship as a scholarship student. When he graduated in Lent Term of 1639, the food allowance was raised by 2d. a week. At about this time, on 27 February (Ash Wednesday), Marvell signed articles affirming his loyalty to the royal supremacy in church and state and his acceptance of the Book of Common Prayer and the Thirty-Nine Articles of the Church of England: and he had to do this before he could receive his degree, which he was taking a year later than he should have done.[53] Whether or not he had an inkling of this at the time, Marvell would eventually find himself pursuing not an academic or a clerical career but that towards which so many of the Trinity men pushed themselves: a career in the service of the state, exactly what Henry VIII had wanted. But from October 1640, he was one of the Lady Bromley scholars, receiving 3s. 4d. every quarter.[54]

Cambridge was the engine house of English Puritanism. Several of its colleges were famous for producing Puritan divines and it was in the later sixteenth century that a group of scholars began to codify a body of divinity commensurate with the broadly godly consensus. Foremost among these was William Perkins, who has a claim to be called the Puritan Aquinas, and whose compendious writings exercised an influence throughout the seventeenth century and beyond. The great Puritan preacher, Richard Sibbes, was Master of St Catharine's College, and we have already noticed that Andrew Marvell senior studied at Emmanuel College, a new foundation of 1584 with decidedly Puritan inclinations. Marvell himself would come to know well one of Oliver Cromwell's chaplains, Peter Sterry, a significant Puritan and Platonist thinker, and an Emmanuel graduate.

But the university contained other elements and was not simply Hull Grammar School writ large against a fen, as opposed to an estuarial river. The university was expanding rapidly in these years, Nevile's construction of the Great Court at Trinity being the foremost example of this. The breakdown of the Calvinist consensus of the later sixteenth century was reflected in Cambridge, where Arminianism and even pseudo-Catholicism were embodied in the new and highly ornate chapel at Peterhouse, and in the fellowship of this

old establishment. High Church ritual and the beauty of holiness were venerated in chapel services. In Trinity, the chapel was similarly 'beautified', which
included moving the altar to the east end and placing it behind rails. This was
not uncontroversial, and Marvell himself would later write critically on the
caustic consequences of Laud's time as English primate.

A third way was evident and nowhere more so than in Trinity College. This
was the most Protestant attempt to justify the existence of eternal verities
through Platonic philosophy.[55] Benjamin Whichcote and John Sherman were
two divines who held such views, the former associated with Trinity and the
latter a fellow of the college whose lectures Marvell may be supposed to
have heard. Whichcote's pupil Henry More of Christ's College would turn his
controversial skills against Descartes, and would become Cromwell's favoured
choice in unrealized plans for a national church in the 1650s. Whichcote was
a founder of the school that would become Restoration Latitudinarianism,
stressing the foundations of religion in reason. Sherman was an influential
teacher whose published exercises, originally given in Trinity chapel, convey
an idea of how the young Marvell was being equipped to think about and write
poetry in the most detailed manner. It was Sherman's view that poetry
perfectly reconciles with divinity: it is the best way to write about God, and
always was, even indirectly, as in the case of the ancients.[56]

Another distinguished and influential fellow, who had been in the College
since 1613 and was elected to a fellowship five years later, was Herbert
Thorndike, friend of George Herbert and able scriptural scholar.[57] He was an
expert in Syriac in particular and would provide these sections in Brian
Walton's 1657 Polyglot Bible. Thorndike was a defender of episcopacy but he
would eventually propose a universal Christianity based on the agreements of
the first six General Councils of the early church. It was his interest in the early
church that led to his defence of prayers for the dead, call for return to the discipline of penance and assertion of a mystical and objective presence in the
Eucharist. This of course looked very Roman Catholic. He would resurface in
Marvell's later life.

In a more mundane way than Whichcote's novel postulations, several of
Marvell's later poems show an engagement with the study of logic that
must stem back to these years. Using logic poetically was no new thing in
seventeenth-century verse, as a famous poem like John Donne's 'The Flea'
makes plain with its specious use of the syllogism. But Marvell's knowledge of
the history of reasoning is extremely precise, as exemplified in 'The Definition
of Love'. The poem is an exercise in different kinds of explanation, logic, and
logic's subversion by paradox and oxymoron. Geometry, through Euclidean
rules, is a structure for the poem: 'given: love itself; required: its definition;
construction, the images of space and line; proof, the argument from those
images that culminates in the QED of the last stanza'.[58] The poem also employs
an Aristotelian mode of definition to define love: definition by difference. Thus,

magnanimity is confronted by despair (l. 5), hope by fate (ll. 7–11). The poem involves a series of 'definitions', and is thus concerned with the very nature of definition itself, and the fear that definition may after all be a circular process. The poem actually deals with confusion rather than definition. At lines 9–10: 'And yet I quickly might arrive/Where my extended soul is fixed', 'extended' means (a) possessing dimensions in time and space, or (b) strained. That the soul as well as the body might have extension was a contentious philosophical debate, intensified in the mid-seventeenth century by the spread of Cartesian ideas. Henry More, the most prominent of the Cambridge Platonists, vigorously maintained that the soul did have extension: 'let us first consider [the soul] a while, what she is in her own Essence, without any reference to any *Body* at all, and we shall find her a *Substance extended and indiscernible* . . . she hath as ample, if not more ample, *Dimensions* of her own, then are visible in the Body she has left.'[59] Marvell's speaker suggests that, unconfined by his body, his soul reaches out to the object of its desire. These insights are undoubtedly the work of a poet at the height of his powers, but the training that made them possible began at Cambridge and in Trinity College in the 1630s.

Another example of a kind of poetic innovation that Marvell witnessed in his time at Trinity was the sung poetic dialogue. The dialogues that survive in his corpus are usually regarded as slight pieces, but they were meant to be sung, and the simple diction leaves ample and appropriate space for the music. Marvell would have been among the first to witness this form in English, and by all accounts it provided a most effective and poised way of expressing duality.[60]

There is much more drama in Marvell's poetry and prose than has usually been supposed. One of the starting points here in Marvell's theatrical experience would have been a performance of a Latin play by Abraham Cowley, *Naufragium Ioculare, Comoedia* on 2 April 1638. It has been suggested that the many Latin references to Marvell's name in the character of the sententious tutor Gnomicus mean that he might have played the part himself.[61] Cowley's name triggers a set of associations with the other literary figures and emergent poets who were studying at Trinity College or elsewhere in Cambridge in these years. Cowley was the most accomplished and already highly rated as a poet while an undergraduate. Milton paid attention to Cowley at this time, and thought him the most significant of the English poets. There was also Samuel Barrow, the physician and lawyer, who would later publish a Latin prefatory poem to Milton's *Paradise Lost*, alongside Marvell's now famous English poem on Milton's epic. Thomas Randolph had graduated with an MA in 1632, just before Marvell went up; he was elected to a fellowship but resided with his father in Northamptonshire until his untimely death in 1635. Randolph's prowess as playwright and poet are well attested; the performance of his *The Jealous Lovers* before the King and Queen in 1632, with students playing the parts, would have been fresh in college memories, while he was given a fitting monument in the 1638 posthumous publication of *Amyntas, or The Impossible Dowry*, together with English and Latin poems, a volume that Marvell undoubtedly read and by which he was impressed, to judge by his later borrowing from it. At the very end of his time in Cambridge, the Villiers brothers, George, second Duke of Buckingham, and Francis, would arrive, already fatherless and both important people in Marvell's future. In addition there were figures with whom Marvell would be associated in the future, such as Buckingham's protégé, Martin Clifford, later involved in the publication of Buckingham's play *The Rehearsal* and the author of the iconoclastic *Treatise on Humane Reason* (1675).[62] The point of these references to acquaintance is to show that while Marvell would certainly have met those from similar backgrounds, with similar limited means, he also had opportunity to rub shoulders with those of decidedly greater elevation and means. It was to be a route to greater preferment and advancement in future, although it would have served to remind Marvell of the very limitations defined by his social origins.

Less well known was Nathaniel Whiting (1611/12–82), who proceeded to MA at Queens' College in 1635, and may have been in the university after this date before being ordained as a priest in Peterborough in 1639. He was a Cambridge poet throughout the decade and contributed to the volume produced in 1633 to celebrate the birth of the future James II, before embarking on a career as a schoolmaster and Puritan divine in Northamptonshire. If Marvell did not know him personally, he certainly read his published verse. *Le hore di recreatione, or, The Pleasant Historie of Albino and Bellama* and *Il insonio insonado, or, A Sleeping-Waking Dreame* were published in one volume in 1637, and it seems that Marvell read this volume carefully and borrowed passages from it in poetry he wrote later in life.[63] We have the image of Marvell reclusively immersed in a book while lying on grass: this would have been ideal reading matter. Its fanciful nature, 'farcical, ribald, anti-Roman Catholic burlesque romance, employing a far-fetched, archaic, would-be "metaphysical", and obscure vocabulary . . . "graceless and slatternly" ', would in fact open the door for several Marvellian insights into the relationship between sexuality and religion.[64]

John Milton, a member of Christ's College, took his MA in 1632 and left Cambridge, retiring first to Hammersmith, and then in 1637 to Horton in Buckinghamshire. He was beginning to make his mark as a published poet when Marvell was an undergraduate. *Comus* appeared in print in 1637, having first been performed in 1634, but more importantly for Marvell, *Lycidas* appeared in the commemorative volume for Edward King in 1638. There is no single poem in English that Marvell mulled over and quoted as significantly as Milton's great and innovative elegy.[65] Marvell would come to understand it exactly as Milton had intended: as not merely an elegy for a lost acquaintance but a map of the risks involved and debts paid in being a poet. It may well be that Marvell did not come to understand the poem this well until some time later. Nonetheless, it was in these years that he must first have encountered it. Finally, another poet who would matter in Marvell's future was Richard Lovelace. Although an Oxford man, he visited Cambridge in 1637, the year that Marvell first appeared in print as a poet. A Cambridge poet who later strayed to Oxford was the wealthy Thomas Stanley of Pembroke Hall, who arrived in Cambridge in 1637. He was a relative of Lovelace, and a poet and patron who would also matter to Marvell in the future.

As the decade closed, Marvell was involved in something that has never been satisfactorily explained, and probably never will be. It is highly probable that an attempt was made to convert him to Roman Catholicism and to have him operate thereafter as an agent on behalf of the Roman Catholic cause in England. Marvell's earlier eighteenth-century editor, Thomas Cooke, reported that Marvell senior was alarmed by a rumour that his son was about to become a Jesuit. He found his son in a bookshop, either in some kind of employment, or just browsing, remonstrated with him and sent him back up to Cambridge. The story, which on the showing of this evidence alone is little more than myth, is in fact confirmed by the existence of a letter of about January 1640 to Marvell senior from John Norton, Vicar of Welton, ten miles west of Hull, concerning the recruitment by Catholics at Peterhouse, Cambridge, of Norton's son. Norton asks Marvell's advice in respect of what he had done with his son, and demands some punishment for the perpetrators.[66]

It would seem that Norton junior, a St Catharine's undergraduate, was invited to dinner at the house of a town 'gentlewoman' where was present Mr Nicols, a fellow of Peterhouse, and two other MAs who were probably not fellows of a college. Then proceeded an invitation to live in a house with these men and in return receive free board and lodging and eventually preferment at Somerset House, all for the sake of a conversion to Rome. The incident found its way to the ears of the Vice-Chancellor, John Cosin, who investigated and had Nicols officially deny Catholic principles.[67]

This is strong evidence. Nor is it implausible. The Catholic community enjoyed greater confidence in the 1630s than it had done for decades. In part, this was to do with a Catholic queen, Henrietta Maria, and greater influence for certain Catholics at court, such as Walter Montague, the author of some important court entertainments.[68] This presence extended to the universities, especially Cambridge, despite its reputation as the Puritan university. The Laudians no longer regarded the Church of Rome as Antichrist but as false brethren, and in a more general sense English Protestantism had borrowed unapologetically from Catholic, especially Counter-Reformation, literature as it sought to build its own devotional literature.[69] In the area of devotional poetry in particular, the gap between Protestant and Catholic was very narrow or did not exist, as in the case of the Laudian and eventual Roman Catholic Peterhouse divine and poet Richard Crashaw, or the poetry of the future New Model Army radical John Saltmarsh.[70] There were several allegations of undergraduate abduction by Catholics in 1630s Cambridge. Young Andrew's skills as a linguist were probably already known in Cambridge, and in this respect his services could be very useful, even vital. The presence in his own poetry of some important translated recusant works suggests earlier familiarity with them, perhaps gained in this period; for example, the emblem book by the Jesuit Henry Hawkins, *Partheneia Sacra* (1633) (plate 4).

Cambridge completed Andrew Marvell's literary education and brought him into contact with skilled and elevated people who would define the course of his life. It also exposed him to tensions that would remain with him for the rest of his life.

CHAPTER 3

❋

A DECADE OF CRISES

DEATH IN THE HUMBER

DURING MARVELL'S SEVEN YEARS at Cambridge, the other members of the Marvell family still lived at the Charterhouse in Hull. Andrew Marvell senior continued to be a useful and esteemed man in his community. The archives of Hull contain evidence that he was called upon to verify and witness the authenticity of documents, and sign his name under them, and in January 1631 he was left £13 6s. 6d. in the will of Thomas Ferries, an alderman of Hull.[1] In October 1630, George Pease, possibly his father-in-law, left him 40s. in his will; in December 1635 he was left £5 in the will of Alexander Swan of St Mary's. Finally, he was left £3 by Sir John Lister and made a trustee of the hospital that Lister left money to build. He was doing well. Andrew junior would have been expected to return every summer during the vacation to witness the changes that the years had brought.

But the scene began to darken in the later 1630s. Marvell might prudently have kept away; perhaps his menial service at Trinity was extended during the summer recess. From July 1635, Hull was stricken with a serious plague epidemic, which in turn greatly damaged trade. Evidence suggests that commerce virtually ceased: there were in addition challenges from privateers and pirates, and Dutch disputes to fishing rights. Many activities in the city ceased; it was in every sense a disaster:

In the month of July, anno 1635, the plague, which, for some time past, has raged in several of the sea-port towns abroad, made its appearance in this town, notwithstanding all the wise precautions taken to prevent it, and spread with great rapidity. Many of the inhabitants left their houses, and spread into the country: strict watch was kept both night and day; and the gates were kept continually shut, except when provisions were brought in: all assemblies and meetings were forbidden; the schools were discontinued, and the churches entirely unfrequented. The whole town soon exhibited a scene of horror, silence, and distraction: the streets were unfrequented, and the country people fearing to attend the markets, made provisions excessively dear.[2]

It was recorded that there were in this period some 2,730 plague deaths in the city, not counting those who left the city and died of it elsewhere, and deaths from other causes. This is astonishing for a city of about six thousand people: 45 per cent of the population died during the course of the 1630s.[3] Plague came again in mid-August 1637; enormous unemployment and destitution followed: relief could not be found from local taxes, or by an appeal to the rest of Yorkshire, so that the magistrates were forced to appeal nationally to the charity of the wealthy. Even if all members of the Marvell family escaped the infection, protected by the distance of the Charterhouse from the city, they knew very many of the dead. One such was John Ramsden, the Mayor of Hull, who died on 7 December 1637, and left £5 in his will to the Reverend Marvell. At his funeral, Marvell senior, who breached regulations in attending it and risked his life, preached a 'most excellent Sermon to the mournfull Auditors which was after printed'.[4] And in recognition of his services at this time, Reverend Marvell – along with two other preachers – was voted, on 3 January 1638, 20s. by Hull Trinity House. As Master of the Charterhouse, Marvell was given a further £56 3d. to give to the poor in general at this harsh time. The Marvell household may have been affected too: their servant Jane Pease, a relation of Mrs Marvell, was buried in Holy Trinity Church on 29 October 1637.

Five days after Marvell matriculated in Cambridge, on 19 December 1633, his eldest sister Anne married James Blaydes, the son of a Yorkshire MP, in the chapel of the Charterhouse. In August 1636 Marvell was probably present at the wedding of his second-oldest sister Mary, again in Charterhouse Chapel, to Edmond Popple. He is described as a 'nautam', that is, a sailor, but this was a synonym for a merchant, a man who would soon become an influential figure in Hull's commercial, corporate and administrative life, and a man with the key to his brother-in-law's political future. The Marvells were embedding themselves in the successful, prosperous middle class of Hull. Yet, as we saw in the last chapter, Reverend Marvell was also feeling the wind of contention blowing in the church. On the one hand, he would incur in 1639 the displeasure of the Laudian Archbishop of York, Richard Neile, and on the other, he was a stumbling block for the ambitions of the earliest Nonconformists in the city, and they let him know it.

Time was catching up with the older generations. Marvell's grandfather had died in 1628, and was buried in Holy Trinity on 13 April. On the same day ten years later, the very day that Marvell was admitted to a scholarship at Trinity College, his mother died in Hull. We do not know how she died, but we do know that she was buried at Holy Trinity Church on 28 April 1638. Although he later refers to his father, Marvell remains silent about his mother in his writings. But Marvell senior was not in the habit of wasting time. Seven months later, on 27 November, he married Lucy Harries at Norton in Derbyshire. This was where Lucy lived. She had been married twice already (to William Harries (d. October 1631) and before then to Francis Darley (d. 1616), but she was from Hull and was the daughter of John Alured, whose family lived next door to the Charterhouse in the Old Carthusian priory. The Alureds were important local people whose members would hold another key to Andrew junior's future. Whatever else was in this new marriage, Andrew Marvell senior was doing what he had arranged for his daughters: making an advantageous match with an important Hull family. The fruit of such matches was already evident. On 4 February 1638, William Popple had been born to Marvell's sister Mary and her husband Edmond. He would become the most important member of the Marvell family for the poet and politician, and later on a significant figure in national political and economic life.

Andrew senior and Lucy remained married for the next twenty months, and thanks to his scholarship, Andrew junior was able to reside and study in Cambridge, and to dabble with Catholicism. Then tragedy struck: his father was drowned while crossing the Humber on 23 January 1641. Earlier and in respect of library use in the Charterhouse he had complained of 'infirmityes seasing upon me daily', but there is no other evidence to suggest that he was not going to live a long and healthy life. No one should underestimate the impact this had on Andrew junior. It took him many years to recover, for he had lost his guiding light and support in the world.

The two major surviving accounts both report that Marvell senior was in the company of Mrs Skinner, the daughter of Sir Edward Coke, the famous common law authority. They also report that the boat was from Barrow upon Humber, on the Lincolnshire side, and that it became stranded on sand-banks through the carelessness or the drunkenness of the boatman. The more colourful account has the Reverend Marvell contemplating his end cheerfully as the water took him, shouting 'Ho for Heaven!'[5] Most probably it was not like this.

Whatever these accounts tell us, in losing his father Marvell had lost the means to a certain career. His father was the one man who could have held him to what was probably his goal – to be an academic or a career clergyman. There is no doubt that Marvell's talent had been spotted, but there had been distrac-tions, perhaps religious, certainly social. Marvell senior was a reliable source of income: he had prospered in the church and local people of substance honoured him by giving him money. He was probably able on these donations alone to keep his son well enough. But with his death this ongoing supplement to the stipend dried up. His affairs in Hull were wound down: on 8 May, Marvell's stepmother Lucy presented accounts for the Charterhouse and paid the balance of £75 2s. to the new master, William Stiles. There was little in reserve to fall back upon since Marvell senior would have had to produce the dowries for the marriages of his daughters to substantial people. It is true that his aunt (Jane Grey, the remarried widow of his father's brother Edward) enabled him to have some property in Meldreth, the original Marvell family home, forty-seven and a half acres of copyhold, which he mortgaged to his brothers-in-law for £260, repayable in two instalments on the eve of his majority. At the same time, he paid a fine of £3 in order to retain the house and two and a half acres in Meldreth known as 'the Marvells' or 'Meldreth Court'.[6]

But the broader context is that he was generally poor, and, as it would happen, any hope of a lifeline in the university and the church was to be denied within months. In short, he was very talented but away from Hull, in trouble, and with no certain future.

The death of his father meant that Marvell was orphaned, and while this literally meant that he was dependent to some extent on his sisters and their husbands, his stepmother and his aunt, in a more extended sense it may well have given rise to a long-term reflection upon the nature of being an orphan. This is certainly the dominant theme of 'The Unfortunate Lover', one of the most accomplished yet mysterious of Marvell's lyrics. It is usually associated with the later 1640s and the execution of Charles I. But if it was written before, or written with a strong memory of what came before, its revelations are remarkable.

II

'Twas in a shipwrack, when the seas
Ruled, and the winds did what they please,
That my poor lover floating lay,
And, ere brought forth, was cast away:
Till at the last the master-wave
Upon the rock his mother drave;
And there she split against the stone,
In a Caesarean sectiòn.

III

The sea him lent those bitter tears
Which at his eyes he always wears:
And from the winds the sighs he bore,
Which through his surging breast do roar.
No day he saw but that which breaks
Through frighted clouds in forkèd streaks;
While round the rattling thunder hurled,
As at the fun'ral of the world.

IV

While Nature to his birth presents
This masque of quarr'lling elements;
A num'rous fleet of corm'rants black,

> That sailed insulting o'er the wrack,
> Received into their cruel care
> Th'unfortunate and abject heir:
> Guardians most fit to entertain
> The orphan of the hurricane.

(ll. 9–32)

It is a picture of abject misery, presenting an heir to nothing much but pain and the whim of Fortune; although the force of poetic inventiveness has been seen to remove the emotional claim of experience so far that most have felt the poem is in some sense an allegory. So the storm and the rough sea become a metaphor for life and its cruelties or unfathomable turns. Marvell carries it especially well with his sharp sense of the visual emblem and what it could do for poetry. Yet what is equally striking is the extended comparison of the ship on a stormy sea with the term of a pregnancy, and childbirth as shipwreck. The mother and motherhood are represented as a scene of violence with no direct emotional reference, except that childbirth breaks mothers. There are those who have argued that this is evidence of traumatic childhood experience, perhaps abuse.[7] I would not go this far, but the poem does touch upon a long-standing sense of denial of happiness and well-being, and directs unhappiness and lack of reconciliation at the figure of the mother. What then about the father?

As the new term approached in September 1641, the authorities at Trinity College – the Master and eight senior fellows – acted decisively after a period in which they had clearly gathered evidence concerning five scholars. It is recorded that having been for some time suspected of being married or of not 'keeping their days' (residing in college for a required period of time), the students were to lose their scholarships and to leave the college within three months.[8] Since the full term of residence for an MA had been abolished in 1608 and attendance requirements had probably diminished to a very low level (perhaps just a few public exercises), it may well be that Marvell had done something fairly outrageous, but we do not know the details. Living a gambling life in London might have been an escape for an unhappy young man, seriously out of sorts after his father's death. Perhaps the Master and fellows felt they needed to make examples of them. Whatever it was, the ejection was to pitch Marvell into the harsher world of London. Without the support of his father, this was a monstrous blow. It excluded Marvell from the most obvious secure career route in the church, from which he was now effectively severed in disgrace. Given his abilities, it could have been a remarkable career, perhaps leading to high preferment: surely he would have made an impressive bishop. In consequence, a sense of some distaste for aspects of the clergy never left him from then onwards, despite his keen interest in theology and ecclesiology. He would hardly ever keep the company of divines (there are some notable exceptions), and forthwith cut his coat from a different cloth. His father saved him from a Catholic future, perhaps from being whisked away to Spain and a life of service in Spanish America.[9] Now when he needed his father even more, Andrew senior was not there to catch him when he fell.

COWCROSS

After Cambridge Marvell went to London. There is a local tradition in Hull that he became a clerk there, perhaps for his brother-in-law Edmond Popple, but this seems very unlikely.[10] He had until Christmas 1641 to be out of his rooms in Trinity College. We next have evidence of him in London on 8 February 1642. One to a maximum of four months is insufficient time for a clerkship. He simply went to London.

Marvell's residence in Cowcross in 1642 is usually explained as a matter of the proximity of Clerkenwell to the Inns of Court (see plate 5). It is true that the Inns are a walk of some ten to fifteen minutes away, but this was a fair distance in the seventeenth century. More compelling is the fact that Cowcross was very close to the Charterhouse, which had been founded in 1371, the fourth Carthusian monastery in England. Marvell's father had been master of the Hull Charterhouse, and it seems equally if not more likely that the poet had gone in search of patronage here. After the spectacularly bloody way in which the Reformation came to the Charterhouse in Clerkenwell (the Prior was hanged, drawn and quartered in 1534, sixteen more monks and lay brothers were executed), the Carthusian monastery was refounded as a hospital (i.e. an almshouse) and a school, just like its counterpart in Hull. The poet might well have sought, with the help of a family connection, some teaching duties, and perhaps saw the chance of further preferment when the schoolmaster, Mr Brooke, was so evidently a diehard Royalist. He beat boys who expressed Parliamentary sympathy and was dismissed in 1643.[11] One of the other scholars dismissed from Trinity along with Marvell was Thomas Carter, who had been Master of Highgate School since 1639. Perhaps it was an opportunity for a worthy young man with proper connections and a history of association with another Charterhouse.

Clerkenwell was home before the Reformation to two more monastic houses: the convent of St Mary's, Clerkenwell, which stood on the site of the present St James's parish church, while the Order of the Knights Hospitallers of St John of Jerusalem had its English headquarters in the precinct (both were founded in the mid-twelfth century). Clerkenwell took its name from the Clerk's Well in Farringdon Lane. In the Middle Ages, the London parish clerks performed annual mystery plays there, some cycles taking three or even eight days to perform. It was a pleasant place at this time, with meadows, pastures, streams and mills interspersed with the religious houses. But violence in the name of religion was never far away in this period. One of the most important and sensational of the burnings of the proto-Protestant Lollards, that of Sir John Oldcastle, took place in Clerkenwell in 1417.

Perhaps Marvell was already there in the summer of 1641, having abandoned his Cambridge rooms. He was certainly present by 8 February 1642, when he witnessed a deed of property sale from Sir William Savile of Thornhill to Thomas, Viscount Savile, Baron of Pontefract and Castlebar. Savile seems to have lived in the Clerkenwell area. On 17 February, Marvell signed an oath of loyalty to the Protestant faith, the King, the Parliament and the rights and liberties of subjects, ordered by Parliament on 3 May 1641, but he did not make contributions for relief of the suffering Irish Protestants (there had been a revolt of Roman Catholics in Ireland in 1641) on 23 February and 11 March, which suggests that he was a resident in someone else's house: perhaps Savile's. Whatever Marvell was doing in these suburbs just to the north of the city, an area to which he would return to live in the 1660s, he remembered vividly the scene on the short, steep streets around the River Fleet, such as the singers on the seedy Saffron Hill. Cowcross cannot have been too savoury, however fashionable the rest of Clerkenwell might have been in the earlier seventeenth century. Through its narrow compass were driven animals on their way for purchase and slaughter at Smithfield. The demands of both the market and growing urbanization produced this kind of ballad: 'At Cowcross and at Smithfield/I have much pleasure found,/Where wenches like to fairies/Did often trace the ground.'[12] There were also two theatres in Clerkenwell, the Fortune, between Golden Lane and Whitecross Street, rebuilt after a fire in 1621, and the Red Bull, originally a pub, on Woodbridge Street, off the southern end of St John Street. Both played the older popular drama of Marlowe and Dekker, famous for its spectacles and sensationalism. Marvell would have had time to visit these before he left the country and before all the theatres were closed in July 1642.

A few days after signing the loyalty oath, on 21 February, he witnessed the signing of a deed of mortgage, probably in one of the Inns of Court, either Gray's Inn or Furnivall's. The deed recorded the transfer of land and other property from Sir William Savile to Thomas, Viscount Savile, the sale of which he had witnessed a week earlier. The Saviles were extremely wealthy northern nobility, and Marvell had been drawn into a distinctly Yorkshire transaction, as the property transferred was located in Darrington, Yorkshire. For Marvell, it was so much training for what would come. Perhaps at this stage he was in the service of, or hoped to be in the service of, one of the Saviles. They had an address in St John's or 'St Jones', not the street but the area of Clerkenwell around Cowcross comprising St John's Lane as well as St John's Street. Was Marvell a resident in one of their houses? Despite the stews, despite the presence in Clerkenwell of the Bridewell, a prison for vagabonds of both sexes, and of the presence of the stocks at the bottom of St John's Street, the company was encouraging: the Cavendishes, the Chaloners, the earls of Northampton all had residences, aristocratic mansions no less, in the neighbourhood. It is not insignificant that Sir William Savile was a strong Royalist: he would die fighting for his cause at York in 1644.[13]

Did Marvell write any poetry in this period? The indebtedness of the 'The Coronet' to Donne's sequence *La Corona*, and Herbert's 'The Wreath', and the echoes of sixteenth-century verse, suggest an early date of composition during this time, or perhaps in the last weeks at Cambridge:

The Coronet

> When for the thorns with which I long, too long,
>   With many a piercing wound,
>   My Saviour's head have crowned,
> I seek with garlands to redress that wrong:
>   Through every garden, every mead,
> I gather flow'rs (my fruits are only flow'rs)
>   Dismantling all the fragrant tow'rs
> That once adorned my shepherdess's head.
> And now when I have summed up all my store,
>   Thinking (so I myself deceive)
>   So rich a chaplet thence to weave
>   As never yet the King of Glory wore:
>   Alas, I find the serpent old
>   That, twining in his speckled breast,
>   About the flow'rs disguised does fold,
>   With wreaths of fame and interest.
> Ah, foolish man, that would'st debase with them,
> And mortal glory, Heaven's diadem!
> But Thou who only could'st the serpent tame,
> Either his slipp'ry knots at once untie,
> And disentangle all his winding snare:
> Or shatter too with him my curious frame:
> And let these wither, so that he may die,
> Though set with skill and chosen out with care.
> That they, while Thou on both their spoils dost tread,
> May crown thy feet, that could not crown thy head.

(ll. 1–26)

'The Coronet' belongs to a tradition of early seventeenth-century divine poetry concerned to make holy (and hence criticize, reject or 'convert') the literary ingenuity of the late sixteenth-century courtly lyric, exemplified by the verse of Sir Philip Sidney, whose work is also echoed in this poem. The poem is generally presumed to be a Protestant, Calvinist, and even Puritan, vehicle. Yet it has also been argued that – somewhat at odds with its sense of the frailty of all human art – the poem is most successfully achieved because Marvell is in fact implicitly criticizing the Puritan castigation of human invention. After all, the poem itself is a beautiful invention.[14]

All through this period the fabric of church and state was crumbling. On Monday, 22 August 1642 matters went past the point of no return when the King raised his standard at Nottingham. On 23 April, Sir John Hotham, the Parliamentary commander of Hull, had refused to open the gates of the town to the King and his soldiers. Trinity College signalled its loyalty to the Crown. Under the name of 'Francis Cole' Cowley published the prologue and epilogue of a college entertainment for the King as an anti-Roundhead satirical pamphlet. In addition to its exploitation of poetic and theatrical devices, this work contains clear indications of loyalty, such as a woodcut of the playwright presenting a copy of the entertainment to His Majesty.[15] While a new arrival in the Marvell family occurred with the birth on 23 October of Andrew's niece Elizabeth, daughter of his sister Elizabeth and her husband Robert More, at some point in these months the young ex-scholar, novice poet and would-be talented man of letters slipped out of the country with most of what he had in the world. Marvell would be attracted by Cowley's keen sense of the change that had come upon the world of letters with the growing division of the nation when he came to commend Lovelace's poetry in verse later in the decade. Herbert Thorndike managed to ride out much of the 1640s, but he would finally be ejected from his fellowship in 1646 when Parliament tightened its grip on the university. Considerable numbers of defeated Royalists would accept exile in continental Europe after the major defeats of the mid- and later 1640s. Others, like the philosopher Thomas Hobbes, chose to leave the country before the major fighting broke out – in Hobbes's case as early as 1640.[16]

ABROAD

Marvell left England in late 1642 or 1643, and he would stay away for four years. He would miss the major action of the Civil War and the defeat of the King's armies, in the north at Marston Moor and then decisively at Naseby. This was to be the lot of many exiles in this period, although Marvell clearly did not leave the country primarily to avoid the war. He took a gamble with his limited means, using the money he had gained from the mortgage arranged with his brothers-in-law or by selling another portion of the Cambridgeshire property in order to fund travel and gain the experience of foreign lands and languages that would make him indispensable as a secretary.[17] Perhaps he hoped to gain such contacts for future employment with well-connected English gentlemen he would meet along the way.

Milton listed the countries Marvell visited in this order: Holland, France, Italy and Spain.[18] This makes sense geographically, suggesting a series of arduous land journeys once a year on average to reach the next country, then a sea journey to reach Spain from Italy and one more to reach home again. But if Marvell was in Italy in early 1646, it would have made his Spanish stay somewhat short, and this scenario does not sit well with the description of the

fencing lessons in Madrid, where there is the impression of a lengthier residence. While Milton's list is indeed logical, it may be that Spain came before
Italy. It was not the most extensive tour but it was certainly broad-ranging and
credible as a strategy for gaining experience.

Uncertainty about the details of this period in Marvell's life leaves us to
resort to the many records of his exposure to continental culture throughout
his verse and prose: they provide us with a very rich resource for understanding the new sensations he encountered and how they shaped his
growing mind. If we put these responses in the historical context of those
places as they were in the seventeenth century, T.S. Eliot's description of
Marvell as a quintessentially European poet begins to take on substantial
new life: not merely a Latin poet as Eliot meant but one open to the variety
of European vernaculars.[19] Before we go to Holland, we should also pay
attention to Samuel Hartlib's observation of 1655 that Marvell had 'spent
all his time in travelling abroad with Noblemens Sones'.[20] It may not have
been such a bad engagement to remain a private tutor. Hartlib reported of
Edmund Page, sometime fellow of King's College, Cambridge, that he earned
an annuity from the Earl of Devonshire of £100 as tutor to his son – a not
inconsiderable sum.

The Dutch republic, or the United Provinces, as it called itself, was the most
remarkable state in early modern Europe. Much energy has been spent in the
last generation in making its exciting history come alive to us today.[21] The
Dutch Republic emerged as a separate state only in 1579, when it had rebelled
in the name of Protestantism against its Spanish overlord. The princes of
Orange, who had governed the Netherlands for the King of Spain, finally threw
in their lot with the local assemblies, especially the Estates of Amsterdam. A
long war ensued down to the end of the century and well into the next one, as
the borders of what would become modern Holland, and much later, Belgium
(then called the Spanish Netherlands), were established.

When Marvell reached the Netherlands the republic was about to reach the
zenith of its success. The war with Spain had been concluded, and in 1648
would come the Peace of Westphalia that ended the Thirty Years War in
Europe in which the Dutch were also caught up. The necessity of keeping
many men under arms had meant that the office of stadholder, which had
passed down through the male line of the House of Nassau, was strong. The
princes of Orange, whose job was to maintain and command the army, kept a
powerful and influential court in the Hague which had flourished under the
first three stadholders: William the Silent, Prince Maurice and Prince
Frederick Henry. They were aided by influential partners, especially the wife of
Frederick Henry, Amalia van Solms, and they were well connected by marriage
with appropriate European houses, not least the Stuarts.

In the mid-century, and at the time of Marvell's later visits, the office of
stadholder would be very seriously compromised by heirs who were too

young, and by anti-monarchical suspicion from the republican element in the state. This predicament points to two notable features of the United Provinces: it was a federal republic with several relatively decentred components, and two preponderant forces, namely the Stadholder and the Estates General in Amsterdam. It was also a more thoroughly modern middle-class society than most parts of Europe and especially England. The focus on the cities and their productive and trading power was the source of Dutch success and it was entirely necessary in the context of the war with Spain. Once that threat was more or less removed, Dutch trade expansion flourished, with highly profitable colonial activity beginning in Java around 1600 and spreading to the other islands in the Malay archipelago. To the outsider, the Dutch polity looked confusing, or even insane, and its efficiently gathered wealth either cloying or revealing of a gross materialism that showed the Dutch up for what they were. At the same time, their artistic and engineering skills were much admired: the English governing elite conducted a long-term entertainment of Netherlandish intellectuals, artists and inventors.[22] Marvell would write a verse satire against the Dutch ('The Character of Holland') in February 1653 during the First Dutch War, based as much on stereotypical English views as on his own experience of the country, and playfully acknowledging on a poetic level the interaction of English and Dutch culture despite their animosity at the time of his composition.[23]

The United Provinces, especially the Hague, was unusually full of English and Scottish people at this time. Royalists had moved into exile here. Marvell's arrival in Holland followed that of Queen Henrietta Maria in February 1642, on what would be a year's mission to raise funds, arms and troops for her husband Charles I's cause. She had hopes of persuading the Dutch to intervene on the King's behalf, and it was not an ill-founded policy: the court was already well used to the presence and influence of Elizabeth of Bohemia, Charles I's sister, in exile since shortly after the Battle of the White Mountain in 1618. Amalia van Solms had entered the Hague for the first time in 1618 in the train of the retreating Elizabeth, and her husband Frederick V, Elector of the Palatinate. Elizabeth's second eldest surviving son, Rupert, would later be a significant Royalist soldier and commander. Further in the future, according to some evidence, he would become a close friend of Marvell.[24] But while the poet stayed in Europe, Henrietta Maria returned to England in February 1643 with £2 million, several convoys of arms and a detachment of professional veteran soldiers, sailing into Bridlington, just to the south of Flamborough.

In Holland, Marvell encountered the well-ingrained and flourishing painting industry that created a body of fine art the achievements of which were unparalleled in its own time or since. This new world where courtly culture easily met the middle classes, and where the most tolerant society in western Europe had resulted in remarkable philosophical views, was rather different from the world

Marvell had left behind in London. Unlike in England, writers did not necessarily need patrons, and indeed it was expected that they would be self-supporting. The greatest Dutch poet of the seventeenth century, Joost van den Vondel, remained a silk-shop keeper for his entire career, using his profits to underwrite his publications. The popular Amsterdam playwright Jan Vos was a glazier. Poetry societies were notably cross-class experiences: the diplomat P.C. Hooft had a poetry society that met at his castle at Muiden, outside Amsterdam. In it were Vondel, Vos, Anna Roemer Visscher and her sister Maria Tesselschade Visscher, the great courtly poet and secretary to the Stadholder, Constantijn Huygens, and the poet Caspar Barlaeus. Anna Roemer Visscher developed the ability to engrave poems on the backs of glasses with a diamond point. There is nothing like this in the English tradition in its combination of the arts of poetry composition, calligraphy and glass engraving. And this is to say nothing of the fact that it was a woman poet who was at once the author and the artisan, a woman who was a prominent member of society and who was indubitably middle class if also well born. Several members of the group were accomplished musicians, including Anna Visscher and Huygens himself. The Muiden group met in private and was a very high-class example of the salon-style association that typified Dutch literary society.

The academies of Amsterdam were also where theatrical performances took place and a nascent national theatre had begun around 1610–20, rather later than their English counterpart, on account of the war with Spain. The leading playwrights were Vos, a glazier specializing in tragedy, and Bredero, a some-time painter who wrote comedies. Unlike the English tradition, Dutch acting was oratorical rather than mimetic, and it was hard to have a play performed and make a profit.[25] The Calvinist authorities insisted that plays be performed in almshouses, and that money from the ticket sales be given to the almshouse after the performance. Among Bredero's plays the outstanding example was *The Spanish Brabanter*, which has been consistently revived since its performance in 1618. Ironically for a play that celebrates Dutch nationhood, it is an adaptation of the Spanish romance *Lazarillo de Tormes*. But this is appropriate, given that the Brabanter Jerolimo is tainted with Spanish influence, being a Brussels minor gentleman who has come to live in Amsterdam. The pervasive sense of confusion – many exchanges in the play can be reduced to: 'I have no idea what you are saying to me' – is redolent of Dutch nation formation and the linguistic complications that this involved.

Vos's *Aran en Titus, of Wraak en Weerwraak* (1641) bears a relationship to Shakespeare's *Titus Andronicus* and may well be indebted to it. Vos was famous and popular for verbal bombast and scenic violence. Titus's sense of revenge is grim indeed:

My pain is constant and intense, and I do not wish anyone a world that is
better. I really want to torment others with my pain. I want no one to escape.

But even after acknowledging this – as after nearly every crime I have committed – and facing these facts, there is no catharsis. I do not acquire any deeper insights into myself. My story yields no new understanding. This confession is meaningless.

Probably the most significant figure for Marvell was Huygens, and it may be that in the company of the noblemen he was instructing he was able to secure an audience with this extremely important man. Huygens had a country house near Voorburg called Hofwyk (literally: 'court avoid' by means of a pun on 'wyck'), finished in 1642, and Marvell may well have been attracted to Huygens by his friendship with Donne, some of whose verse he had already translated into Dutch, and by Huygens's long association with English statesmen.[26]

In Huygens's book, *Hofwyck* (1651), his house is imagined as the head, the gardens as the body, of a person. Two passages in particular anticipate 'Upon Appleton House'.

> My birches abound as white as church tapers,
> Which drip their wax in graves, stand not so strong,
> White-barked this tree, white as the virgin wax
> New gathered from the hive; I see things but dimly,
> So shadowy the greenness, and so green the shade

> . . . I speak not now of nightingales, although they nest
> Within my grove, outsinging the other darling birds
> I speak of one more eminent.[27]

'Upon Appleton House' may be indebted to Huygens's *Hofwyk*, although Marvell cannot have seen a printed copy of the poem when he visited the Netherlands in the 1640s.

If the United Provinces was the most advanced place in western Europe in terms of toleration, trade, politics, culture and social structure, France was a frightening mixture of the advanced and the repressive. A shocking set of philosophical views looked to most people like atheism whilst on the other hand, rigorous attempts at state management required more and more authority to emanate from the centre of power at court, in particular from the king's chief administrator Cardinal Richelieu. The latter configuration of power is of course known as absolutism and it had a distinct impact upon poetry. The libertine poets, like Théophile de Viau (1590–1626), who were widely read in England, not least by Marvell and his future employer Thomas, Lord Fairfax, were followers of Montaigne and Charron, the sceptic philosophers. They were also known to be morally debauched: Viau himself was a homosexual, and homosexual passion is evident in some of his verse. Richelieu subjected the libertines to a purge and then privileged the neoclassical poets and the ethos that would characterize the Académie Française.[28] At the same time, many French intellectuals had fled to places where freedom of thought was tolerated. Among them was René Descartes, beneficiary of freedom in Amsterdam and at the court of Queen Kristina of Sweden.

Viau came from a Huguenot family and had served with the Protestants under the comte de Candale in 1615–16. He was then pardoned and allowed to come to court, where his powers as poet and dramatist were recognized. Under the influence of Lucilio Vanini (self-styled Giulio Cesare), Viau became an epicurean and one who challenged the idea of the immortality of the soul. After a prolonged trial in 1618, Vanini was condemned, as an atheist, to have his tongue cut out, and to be strangled at the stake and his body burned to ashes. The sentence was executed in Toulouse on 9 February 1619. In the same year Viau was banished from court, and travelled in England. In 1622 'Le Parnasse satyrique' was attributed to him (in fact he was one among several authors in the collection); he was denounced as a heretic by the Jesuits, particularly in the work of Father François Garasse (*La Doctrine curieuse des beaux esprits de ce temps, ou prétendus tels*, 1623–24), and was sentenced to appear barefoot at Notre Dame to be burned alive. Not surprisingly, he went into hiding and the sentence was carried out in effigy. Attempting to escape to England again, he was captured and held in Paris for two years. The trial that followed occasioned a serious debate for and against him, with the result that he was finally perpetually banished. With less than a year to live he spent the remaining months of his life in Chantilly under the protection of the duc de Montmorency. With his death went a poetry of intense emotion and extravagant baroque imagery.

Equally typical of French poetry is the light erotic verse where persuasions to love are at once courtly and dignified, and yet also implicitly erotic, confronting and expressing sexual encounters and sexual practice in an uncannily tangible way. Such is the case with Viau's 'Elegie', which starts with an acknowledgement of human transience in the ageing of the mistress. The lover confesses that in this circumstance he finds happiness in his own self-love, and ends with a celebration of artistic jouissance. The writing of the elegy has purged effortlessly the poet-lover's melancholy. He says he is now healed and no longer needs his mistress as his muse, but the energy in the verse is a sure sign of abundant sexual energy. As ever, Viau says what he really means indirectly. He produces a picture of a decidedly capricious lover who uses argument merely as a means to sexual gratification or just the love of performing endlessly as a seducer:

> Each loves self always a little more than lover;
> We rarely follow them into the tomb;
> The rights of love give way to the laws of nature.
> For myself, if I were to see, in the humour that I am in,
> Your soul fly away to the eternal nights,
> Whatever the power of your charms practiced on me,

> I would console myself with a few tears. . . .
> Heaven be praised! Cloris, I am healed.
>
> . . .
>
> I have changed my subject,
> Carried away by the pleasure of feeling my easy inspiration
> Confidently address my re-appeased passion
> And play as it pleases on the topic of love,
> With no goal today except to rhyme
> And without asking your beautiful eye to brighten
> These verses, where I took no care to please you.[29]

Marvell's 'Daphnis and Chloe', probably written shortly after the European tour, is just such a poem of apparently authentic, desperate, frustrated male desire met by feminine coyness, Daphnis's plight undercut by the final realization that he is 'executed' for love's sake every night of the week:

> XXV
> At these words away he broke;
> As who long has praying ly'n,
> To his headsman makes the sign,
> And receives the parting stroke.
>
> XXVI
> But hence virgins all beware.
> Last night he with Phlogis slept;
> This night for Dorinda kept;
> And but rid to take the air.
>
> (ll. 97–104)

The poem is remarkable among Marvell's lyrics for its length and commitment to an intricate narrative form. It belongs to a long tradition of literature exposing amorous capriciousness: Chaucer's *Troilus and Criseyde* is an early example. But the form of the poem aligns it with the libertine poetry that was so crucial a part of Parisian culture and which circulated in manuscript as well as in print: precisely the kind of material that Marvell would have encountered when he arrived in the French capital.[30] Just like a French libertine poem, in 'Daphnis and Chloe' we have no way of judging the sincerity of either lover; we never quite know what drives them, apart from the assumption that there should be desperate lovers in the world, and that true love is threatened by the attractions of the other boy or girl just seen.

Viau was at the height of his notoriety in the 1620s, but libertine verse left a distinct literary atmosphere for the following decades. One poet who was writing in the 1640s was Marc Antoine Gérard, sieur de Saint-Amant, who had obtained a patent of nobility and attached himself to different great noblemen, including the duc de Retz and the comte d'Harcourt. After a military career and periods in Italy, England and Poland, Saint-Amant's later years were spent in France; he died in Paris. Saint-Amant produced a considerable body of verse, much of which was available in editions published at Rouen and Lyons in 1642 and 1643, and would become most famous for bacchanalian writing. His poetry also circulated quite widely in manuscript.[31] His *Albion*, a violent poetical attack on England, and *Rome ridicule* established the burlesque poem in France. In his later years he devoted himself to serious subjects and produced an epic, *Moyse Sauvé* (1653). At Nun Appleton in the early 1650s, Saint-Amant's poetry would be an important resource for both Marvell and his employer Lord Fairfax.

Marvell appears to have had some close contact with 'French youths', whom he refers to in his satire on Richard Flecknoe. Perhaps this was the result of staying in an educational and even monastic house, but since the words come in a poem intimately concerned with Rome, Marvell might well be talking about the French community there, focused on the church of San Luigi dei Francesi completed in 1589. This kind of reference may have been part of a burlesque poetry that would be widespread during the revolt against French royal authority in the later 1640s, the Fronde, by which time Marvell was back in England.[32]

Louis XIV had become king in 1643 at the age of five. Richelieu had died the year before, but his influence continued in French government policy under his successor, Cardinal Jules Mazarin. The mid-1640s was an unsettled time in which pressures that had begun at least two decades before were building up. The persecution of Viau was an example of one kind of harsh treatment that contributed to discontent. Paris in the 1640s was an uneasy place.

The city was also the home of many English Royalist exiles. But although Charles I's estranged queen and the Duke of Newcastle (the chief Royalist commander in the north) and his family became resident in Paris, this was not until 1644–45. Newcastle himself did not arrive from Hamburg until April 1645, by which time Marvell may well have been on his way out of the country. The exiles in Paris were less high-profile players on the scene, such as Thomas Hobbes who was yet to become the notorious author of *Leviathan*. Hobbes had been in Paris since 1641 and would remain at the heart of an exile community, especially after the defeats in 1644 of the Royalists in England, until he alienated many or most of them by the publication of his great work in 1651. Since he had been involved with French intellectuals since the 1630s he was central to the debates on the nature of matter and the connection between matter and mind that had preoccupied French philosophers. In particular, he had published a critique of Descartes, but more significantly had built a strong relationship with Marin Mersenne, the monk who was at the hub of international intellectual exchange.[33]

ROME AND MADRID

After France, we presume, Marvell travelled to the Italian peninsula. It is quite possible that he visited several places – Genoa, Livorno, Pisa and Florence, for instance – if he travelled south through France and then sailed from a southern port. On the way he may have passed through Geneva: Marvell would mock Samuel Parker in 1672 for erroneous geography of the city.[34] But the only place he records in his writing, the only place that leaves a substantial presence in his poetry, is Rome, and it is here that we must suppose he spent time in 1645–46. His verse recalls many situations and actions in which a Roman literary gentleman might participate. And Rome was then the city par excellence for architecture, art and letters.

Italian verse and Latin verse by Italians were sources for his poetry. One example is 'On a Drop of Dew', and its debts to the Marian poetry of Ippolito Capilupi; or the Florentine Marc'antonio Flaminio's (1498–1550) goat-girl, the inspiration for Marvell's 'Nymph Complaining for the Death of her Fawn'. There is also the more extensive significance of Italian literature popular in English translation: Giovanni Battista Guarini's (1538–1612) *Il Pastor Fido*, translated by Sir Richard Fanshawe (1647), was widely read as a Royalist text. Like all other aspiring men of letters, Marvell probably knew the Italian version. Giambattista Marino's poetry was a model for 'The Fair Singer', just as the widely influential Marino (1569–1625) himself was a model for Marvell as secretary-cum-poet.[35]

Painting was important too: Marvell's 'The Gallery' alludes to several famous Italian paintings, such as Botticelli's *Birth of Venus* and *Primavera*. Marvell was keen to show how in his time the cosmopolitan fashion for paintings had replaced the tapestries or arras-hangings favoured in the comparatively inward-looking Tudor and Jacobean England. Yet these paintings are Florentine, and the one Italian art collection to which the poem refers is that of the Duke of Mantua, from which Charles I purchased several works.

In the seventeenth century there was, however, nothing like a visit to Rome itself as a way of transforming one's verse by exposing it to the plastic arts that made the eternal city unique. Marvell responded, in particular, to the new sculpture of Gian Lorenzo Bernini (1598–1680), which he saw on his arrival in the city in 1645/46 – for example Bernini's 'Apollo and Daphne' (1622–25) (plate 6), the pair who figure in 'The Garden':

> When we have run our passions' heat,
> Love hither makes his best retreat.
> The gods, that mortal beauty chase,
> Still in a tree did end their race:
> Apollo hunted Daphne so,
> Only that she might laurel grow . . .

> (ll. 25–30)

Bernini's sculptures render the nymphs, other mythical figures and shepherds, frequent in classical and Renaissance literature (especially Ovid), in intimately human, naturalistic terms – a whole new aesthetic presentation of the body. He was himself indebted to older sculptures, such as one of 100 BC found at Pompeii, Pan teaching Daphnis to play the pipes, a sculpture that exudes homoerotic energy.

Marvell's 'Daphnis and Chloe', the most significant English literary treatment of the ancient lovers, was written in the light of this intensely real kind of sculpture. The 'disordered locks', 'Looks distracted' and 'rolling eyes' (ll. 34–5, 39) of Daphnis's passion (quite unlike the tender idyll evoked by Ravel in his much later musical work of the same name) might suggest the inspiration of a sculpture, but the surprisingly fickle conversation that follows comes from somewhere else: we will shortly find out where that is.

Of all the places he visited, Rome was the furthest from dingy England and its civil conflict, especially for a northerner like Marvell. It was a city and state generally at peace at this time, and shored up by the careful and often politically astute patronage of generations of popes. It was therefore a great time of building and artistic patronage. Pope Urban VIII (1623–44) may have been bellicose in his broader territorial aims and diplomatically subtle, but he employed Bernini to build the Palazzo Barberini and, among other features, the Fontana del Tritone was created during his papacy.

Pope Alexander VII's (1655–67) favourite word was 'theatre'. The building of fountains in the city had a long history: in summer they were the lifeblood of this arid, intensely hot place. When Marvell arrived in Rome, the magnificent basilica of St Peter's and the Vatican Palace as we know them had just been finished after more than a century's labour.

Roman houses and highly ornate gardens – the substantial and grandiose residences that were also built in this period, now that the city was no longer subject to immediate military threat – are present in Marvell's verse. Some were in the city itself, such as the Villa Borghese and its grounds. Marvell's 'The Garden' contains much that is English but also reflects the complex gardens just outside Rome at Villa Aldobrandini (1598–1604), a few miles to the south-east. There were water sculptures and herbal dials – as instanced at the end of Marvell's poem:

> How well the skilful gard'ner drew
> Of flow'rs and herbs this dial new;
> Where from above the milder sun
> Does through a fragrant zodiac run;
> And, as it works, th'industrious bee
> Computes its time as well as we.
> How could such sweet and wholesome hours
> Be reckoned but with herbs and flow'rs!

(ll. 65–72)

The significance of gardens built within Roman ruins, and of ruinous remnants surviving as centrepieces of gardens (statues, columns, friezes, with reliefs or writing on them) is reflected in the statue of the Nymph in 'The Nymph Complaining':

> First my unhappy statue shall
> Be cut in marble; and withal,
> Let it be weeping too: but there
> Th'engraver sure his art may spare;
> For I so truly thee bemoan,
> That I shall weep though I be stone:
> Until my tears, still dropping, wear
> My breast, themselves engraving there.
> There at my feet shalt thou be laid,
> Of purest alabaster made:
> For I would have thine image be
> White as I can, though not as thee.
>
> (ll. 111–22)

The grotto at Villa Aldobrandini contained paintings of Apollo, and of Daphne turning into a laurel, by Domenico Zampieri, the theme we have already seen treated by Bernini. Marvell's 'The Mower against Gardens' was a complaint in very English peasant terms against Italianate landscaping as well as Dutch horticulture. Marvell, in a playful way, imagines a parochial English rejection of these innovations:

> Luxurious man, to bring his vice in use,
>   Did after him the world seduce:
> And from the fields the flowers and plants allure,
>   Where Nature was most plain and pure.
> He first enclosed within the gardens square
>   A dead and standing pool of air: . . .
>
> 'Tis all enforced, the fountain and the grot;
>   While the sweet fields do lie forgot:
> Where willing Nature does to all dispense
>   A wild and fragrant innocence:
> And fauns and fairies do the meadows till,
>   More by their presence than their skill.
> Their statues polished by some ancient hand,
>   May to adorn the gardens stand:
> But, howsoe'er the figures do excel,
>   The gods themselves with us do dwell.
>
> (ll. 1–6; 31–40)

'Flecknoe, an English Priest at Rome' records a dinner in the early months of 1646 attended by the poet speaker and the Roman Catholic poet Richard Flecknoe, then resident in Rome. Perhaps the third character in the satire is George Villiers, Duke of Buckingham, or his brother Lord Francis Villiers, whom Marvell is thought to have known at this time.[36] Flecknoe was an example of the kind of poet that Marvell might have been or could still become: the entertainer, adviser to rich Catholic people. Flecknoe was a skilled lutenist and singer as well as a poet, but to Marvell's speaker it all sounds terrible – and is rendered so through gently mocking anti-Catholic jokes. The churches of Rome are present in the poem here. The speaker imagines himself as St Lawrence tortured by Flecknoe's dreadful verse; St Lawrence's gridiron was (and is) kept in a side chapel at San Lorenzo in Lucina:

> Straight without further information,
> In hideous verse, he, and a dismal tone,
> Begins to exercise, as if I were
> Possessed; and sure the Devil brought me there.
> But I, who now imagined my self brought
> To my last trial, in a serious thought
> Calmed the disorders of my youthful breast,
> And to my martyrdom preparèd rest. . . .
> . . . I, silent, turned my burning ear
> Towards the verse; and when that could not hear,
> Held him the other; and unchangèd yet,
> Asked still for more, and prayed him to repeat:
> Till the tyrant, weary to persecute,
> Left off, and tried t'allure me with his lute.
>
> (ll. 19–26; 31–6)

Being a good Catholic Flecknoe fasts at Lent, but this means, according to the poet's wit, that he is so thin, he fails to be a recognizable body until he is dressed; he is a 'basso relievo' of a man (l. 63), a sculpture or carving which does not project from its surface in proportion to its length and breadth, popular in Italian churches at this time. The speakers meet at the 'Pelican Inn', which was probably owned by the English College at Rome, and there is wordplay on pellicano (pelican) and pellegrino (pilgrim). The events the poem describes are finally turned in the poet's imagination into an ex-voto painting:

> . . . I, finding myself free,
> As one 'scaped strangely from captivity,
> Have made the chance be painted; and go now
> To hang it in S Peter's for a vow.
>
> (ll. 167–70)

The little painting would hang in St Peter's Basilica, along with all the other offerings.

Richard Flecknoe (*c.* 1605–*c.* 1677) was born in the vicinity of Little Harrowden, Orlingby Hundred, Northamptonshire (not in Ireland, as was once supposed). He is thought to have been converted to Roman Catholicism by a Jesuit at Liège in about 1620 and was imprisoned in Newgate shortly thereafter before he returned to Saint-Omer to study philosophy and theology. However, his connections with English Catholic peers in Northamptonshire, notably Lord Vaux, may mean that his Catholicism was actually rooted in his home background. He was ordained a priest (probably by the Jesuits; he was almost certainly a lay priest) in 1636, returned to England, and offended non-Jesuit priests in London with his staging of a 'lascivious play' (either *Love's Kingdom* or another work now lost) in early 1638. In 1640 Flecknoe left England, spent some time in the Spanish Netherlands, but left for Italy in 1644 because of continued violence in the north, and was in Rome by January 1645. The young Duke of Buckingham elevated Flecknoe to his 'poeticall Academy' of exiles in Rome, and the poet-musician-priest's grand associates while in Rome (including the Duchess of Lorraine, Cardinal Caraffa and the Duchess Maidalchini) are at odds with the picture painted by Marvell, although Flecknoe's tiny quarters that Marvell portrays would not have been inconsistent with his way of life. In the later 1640s, Flecknoe left Rome for Spain, Portugal and Brazil, before eventually returning to England in the 1650s.[37]

Flecknoe thrived upon and indeed made much of his patronage by aristocrats in England and on the continent. As a priest, he could offer advice, but he was also a minstrel and a raconteur. Most of his works were written quickly and geared specifically to the sensibilities of his patrons, eschewing aesthetic innovation. In all of this Marvell saw a double for himself and a possible poetic future: the Catholic Marvell. He was, I believe, decidedly repelled by this, to the extent that he wrote this brilliant satire, which is at one and the same time the purging of a choice that had been laid before him earlier in his Cambridge days.

The resonances in content and in style of Marvell's poem with earlier satires are many and complex. Despite this eclecticism the satire is highly original, developing an extended conceit in which the function of the emaciated poetaster's manuscript copies as clothing becomes the site for a series of playful, sometimes lurid, but not overtly hostile, observations upon, and engagements with, Roman Catholic habits and worship.

There are earlier roots too: the poem is not just about Rome as Marvell knew it but contains a poetic memory of earlier dinners. Flecknoe himself is presented as a priestly version of one of the characters at Trimalchio's dinner in Petronius's *Satyricon*: Seleucus, for instance, is a bore, as is Flecknoe with his bad verse, while Ganymede complains of poverty. Yet the poem also points to English subjects and materials. The funeral imagery bears close affinities, almost to the point of echo, not with Donne's satires, but with his elegiac poetry, as Donne's conceits were lifted from a panegyrical context and placed in a diametrically opposite framework. In Donne's *Anniversaries*, the dead Elizabeth Drury is imagined as wrapped in the 'rags of paper' of the poet's verse ('A Funeral Elegy', ll. 11–12); in Marvell's poem, Flecknoe dresses in the rags of his poetry. Elizabeth Drury was so pure it was as if she was transparent ('Flecknoe', ll. 59–60); Flecknoe is transparent because he has eaten so little. In funerary elegies poets said goodbye to their subjects; in his satire Marvell bid farewell to Flecknoe and all that he stood for.

Much of Marvell's poem appears to be a riposte to Flecknoe's ideals, beliefs, behaviour and poetry. Flecknoe's idealistic poetic, not unlike Milton's, sees music and poetry as a harmonious combination that reflects divine truth: 'which ballads . . . was in manner the sole relict of this divine Science, until *Claudio Montanvendo* [*sic*] (in our Fathers days) principally revived by his admirable Skill (like another *Prometheus*) conjoyning in one body again the scattered limbs of *Orpheus* (Musick and Poetry)'.[38] Whilst Flecknoe would go on to develop his own version of simple bawdy drollery and satire in the later 1650s, he also had an explanation for the simple diction and syntax of his idealizing earlier verse: 'so have I endeavour'd short periods and frequent rithmes, with words smooth and facile, such as most easily might enter into the mind, and be digested by the understanding'.[39] If Flecknoe was interested in mock-heroic drollery at that time in early 1646, when Marvell met him, some of the poem's imagery could be seen as an appropriate mock-heroic response, as well as an attack upon Flecknoe's notorious snobbery.

Flecknoe's poverty and his ceaseless search for patronage is documented in his own poetry. For Marvell it was 'hideous verse . . . and a dismal tone' ('Flecknoe', l. 20) and by contrast, Marvell's poem is notable for its highly wrought conceits and puns. The poem's construction of complex metaphors out of puns, usually directed at the mockery of Catholicism, has been noted.[40] Lines 9–18 are developed around the conceit of Flecknoe's room as a coffin, the theme being death, the decorations presenting Catholicism as 'a religion of spiritual death'. The space-saving ingenuity with which the room is constructed invokes the priest-holes of English recusant houses, with its associations of secrecy and (in Protestant eyes) deceit, as well as duress.

Thus, within the governing genre of satire 'Flecknoe' moves through a series of religious situations. The first is martyrdom, with the humorous presentation of the Protestant speaker as a 'martyr' to the Catholic priest's vile poetry. Foxe's *Acts and Monuments* is a background presence here: the reference to Nero (l. 126) recalls Foxe's account of the primitive church; both Foxe and Marvell use Suetonius as a source. We have seen how Marvell's speaker identifies with St Lawrence, since he turns first one then another 'burning ear' to Flecknoe, just as the saint asked his torturers to turn him over on the gridiron. Then comes Flecknoe's fasting for Lent, itself succeeded by the parodic communion of the meal. Flecknoe's body is wittily presented as the host, enabling allusions to the Catholic theology of transubstantiation (ll. 58–62), the doctrine of the Trinity and the authority of the Church's teaching (ll. 75–8), and Protestant–Catholic disputes concerned with the reading of the Latin Bible and the understanding of Scripture, in addition to the ridicule of Flecknoe's poetic practice.

Marvell makes a series of obscure and abstruse references in the service of humour, but he does so in the tone of a speaker who is supremely confident. The requirement of the rhyming couplet is expertly met and effortlessly combined with lively speech rhythms and conversational manners, which offer suspension, balance and interruptive variety within the regular iambic pattern. In this early poem, Marvell offers what the reader is meant to take as a thoroughly virtuoso, precocious performance, over and against the awful grotesquery of Flecknoe's songs, and their tuneless performances by the youth. Marvell would later say that one should always carry something venomous with one in order to ward off malicious attacks.[41] Becoming like Flecknoe was such a threat, and the poem is Marvell's pouch of poison that sees him off.

Marvell calls Flecknoe the chameleon poet (l. 82) in that he is so thin that his environment is visible through his body: thus he looks like what surrounds him. Marvell's guilty conscience or fear of becoming Flecknoe's mirror is never truer than in respect of this aspect of Flecknoe's identity. Marvell would shortly become the chameleon himself, but he seems to have had a good premonition that it would happen.

Marvell's speaker describes himself as a martyr to Flecknoe's terrible verse. Elsewhere in his poetry suffering martyrs have undeniable attractiveness. 'The Unfortunate Lover' is a truly exceptional poem.[42] Its title is lexically indebted to the heretical philosopher Giordano Bruno's *Heroic Frenzies* (1585) and his notion of the love-stricken poet-lover, '*infortunato amante*'. In 1600 Bruno himself was martyred for his beliefs in Rome: today a statue stands in the Campo dei Fiori where he was burned, commemorating his life and his brilliant insights. Like many Englishmen with an interest in the 'new philosophy' as well as poetic theory, Marvell would have been drawn to this man who had visited England in the later sixteenth century and had been connected with Sir Philip Sidney. Marvell's superb satire 'Last Instructions to a Painter' (1667) may be read as his most Roman poem. It is as if a superior Italian poet/painter was composing/painting the English and Dutch scene. Thought by some to be the greatest longer verse satire of its time, it contains a portrayal of the one hero in the Royal Navy of the Dutch raid on the Medway during the Second Dutch War (1664–67), amidst great English incompetence, militarily and at court, and mixes Ovid, desire and the history of persecution: a fantastic coming together of the quintessentially Marvellian, with Captain Archibald Douglas, Marvell's neo-Roman martyr-hero refusing dalliance with the nymphs, to become the greatest 'unfortunate lover' – or perhaps the most fortunate. This pastoral and erotic moment is totally fitting in such an

Italianate poem – which begins with the public poetry of Roman graffiti, often lewd or pornographic verse left in public places, most famously on the Pasquino statue of central Rome, near the Piazza Navona (see plate 7). Bernini considered Pasquino the greatest antique in Rome.

Marvell used this kind of verse as his model to satirize the King and his courtiers. He also took care to make poetry, sculpture and painting interrelate, a matter that was crucial to Renaissance Romans:

> After two sittings, now our Lady State,
> To end her picture does the third time wait.
> But ere thou fall'st to work, first, painter see
> It ben't too slight grown, or too hard for thee.
> Canst thou paint without colours? Then 'tis right:
> For so we too without a fleet can fight.
> Or canst thou daub a signpost, and that ill?
> 'Twill suit our great debauch and little skill.
> Or hast thou marked how antique masters limn
> The alley-roof with snuff of candle dim,
> Sketching in shady smoke prodigious tools?
> 'Twill serve this race of drunkards, pimps, and fools.
>
> (ll. 1–12)

Salvator Rosa (1615–73) was a painter-poet whose long periods of residence in Rome would have drawn Marvell's attention. The phallic references in the passage just quoted are related to sections in Rosa's verse satires, and Marvell appears to have been attracted by some of Rosa's paintings and prints.[43] His satirical poetry and plays made him unpopular in Rome (and a decided enemy of Bernini), to the extent that he had to leave the city at certain times. If there was an example of a painter and poet who pitted his art against the corrupt of the world and publicly sympathized with those who rebelled against tyranny and injustice, having used his talent first to create works of acclaimed beauty, this was he. If Flecknoe was an anti-model, Bruno – and more so Rosa – showed Marvell the way.

Restoration satire returns to a martyr: Archibald Douglas, almost certainly a Roman Catholic as well as a Scot, who was sacrificed by an incompetent English and Protestant administration. Douglas is likened to the Sun's Statue, a bronze statue, massive (six times lifesize) but beautiful and lifelike, and regarded as the image of the sun or of Rome herself. Made of gilded bronze and dating from the fourth century, it was held to have shone in the dark and rotated to face the sun constantly. One of the early popes (Sylvester I or Gregory I) ordered it to be melted by a huge fire; only the head and one hand, originally holding a sphere, survived and were placed on marble pillars in front of the Lateran Palace, the earlier residence of the popes. The history of persecution, beauty, heroism and desire all lie intertwined in art in Roman history and in Marvell's English present:

Like a glad lover, the fierce flames he meets,
And tries his first embraces in their sheets.
His shape exact, which the bright flames enfold,
Like the sun's statue stands of burnished gold.
Round the transparent fire about him glows,
As the clear amber on the bee does close,
And, as on angels' heads their glories shine,
His burning locks adorn his face divine.
But when in his immortal mind he felt
His altering form and soldered limbs to melt,
Down on the deck he laid himself and died,
With his dear sword reposing by his side,
And on the flaming plank, so rests his head
As one that's warmed himself and gone to bed.

(ll. 677–90)

The Sun's Statue was literally a fragment by Marvell's day, just like the Pasquino statue. Marvell's Douglas is a poetic statue, completing the Sun's Statue in a modern revival, just as Bernini's statues revived the past, against a backdrop of the loquacious, gossipy energies that make a lively capital, whether Rome or London. And if there is a Bernini statue in the background, it is most likely to be the remarkable ecstasy of St Teresa, in the Cappella Cornaro, in the church of Santa Maria della Vittoria.[44]

Marvell's Flecknoe is described as dressed in his own poems. In this he is not unlike the statue of Pasquino on which poems were pinned (see above, p. 57). And in this Roman world in which satirical statues spoke with the voice of, well, just about anybody, it is not too much to imagine Daphnis and Chloe as elegant pastoral statues given voice by very worldly lovers, indeed wearily worldly lovers, their innuendoes scarcely suppressed. By contrast Marvell's picture of Douglas, like Bernini's Apollo and Daphne, and St Teresa, embodies redemption in verse and art more generally, while Douglas's self-sacrificing action constitutes love's redemptive powers in a selfless, ultimate act, recalling all those Romans who fell or were martyred to make their city great.

In less extensive ways, other parts of the city are present in the poetry. 'The Third Advice to a Painter', written between late 1666 and January 1667, is propelled by the image of St Eustachio – the vision of a stag with a crucifix between its antlers. Such a sculpture existed (and exists) on the roof of the church of San Eustachio. Later on too, in 1671–72, and from the Lateran Palace – before the Vatican City was built, the place of officialdom and history – Marvell lifted lapidary poems for entries in a Louvre epigram competition announced by Louis XIV: 'There is not in the world a more holy house' is turned into 'compact house' (presumably a wry joke – the Louvre is about as compact as a whale). The architecture of ancient Rome glimmers in the background of the verse – the Janus Gates elsewhere in the Louis distichs, and the tiny cell built by

Romulus, the founder of Rome. And in 'Upon Appleton House', at line 46 is a reference to the *quadratura* considered by architects to be the basic structure and balance of a building: Leonardo's drawing of a man in a circle.

The Flecknoe poem provides a seemingly startling insight into the meaning of the prospect of staying on in Rome, as many visitors did. It might well have meant the adoption of an unpalatable poetic, or the prostituting of one's muse for the sake of a livelihood, or a conversion to the Roman church, or all of these. Marvell pulled back from it and left. Perhaps he had no choice, being engaged to his charges, whoever they were. But there is no doubt that of all the foreign influences on his mind and his art, Rome was the greatest, the most intense. In context, it is not difficult to see why.

He arrived next in Spain, and here it was the architectural creations of the Habsburg monarchs that most impressed him. It seems that he was for some months resident in Madrid in 1646 and 1647; he would have sailed from the Italian mainland to the port of Valencia and then travelled overland westwards to the capital. In 'Upon Appleton House' Marvell compares the Fairfax estate favourably with two Spanish residences:

> For you Thessalian Tempé's seat
> Shall now be scorned as obsolete;
> Aranjuèz, as less, disdained;
> The Bel-Retiro as constrained . . .

(ll. 753–6)

Aranjuèz and Bel-Retiro were royal residences in or near Madrid, with huge, impressive gardens and frequent masque performances (see plate 8). 'Bel-retiro' is properly *Buen Retiro*, so Marvell in 1651 even makes a Protestant and anti-Catholic joke ('Bel' is from Bel and the Dragon in the Apocrypha). The *Palacio Real* at Aranjuèz was built in the reign of Philip II by Juan Bautista de Toledo and Juan de Herrera, the same architects who worked on El Escorial. The palace's garden setting resonates with Nun Appleton because it was bordered by the River Tagus, and an artificial channel called 'La Ria' that separated garden from house. Statuary in the garden was dense and very largely Italianate from the beginning. Aranjuèz is forty-eight kilometres from Madrid, whereas Buen Retiro is right in the heart of the capital city. It was originally the royal retreat for Christmas and Easter; Philip IV began to build extensive gardens in 1632. During Marvell's visit they would have been new, and many of the walks and plazas bear the names of Spanish-speaking countries of the new world. Here the poetry societies that characterize seventeenth-century Madrid met.[45] Perhaps it was here that he first encountered in poetry the plant that carried his name. The great and controversial lyricist Luis de Góngora refers to the South American 'Marvel of Peru' and its quickly fading flower.

> The flower of the marvel
> of Peru reveals this truth,
> because afternoon steals from it
> the bloom that morning gave.[46]

Marvell would later deploy the image in a very different way in the 'The Mower against Gardens'.[47] This reference suggests that Marvell had had access to the royal courts. Is it possible that he was in company that benefited from the patronage of the Spanish Crown? His one reference in a letter suggests an extended and embedded residence, and one replete with instruction fit for a gentleman, if not also a courtier: 'My Fencing-master in *Spain*, after he had instructed me all he could, told me, I remember, there was yet one Secret, against which there was no Defence, and that was, to give the first Blow.'[48]

✳

CHAPTER 4

POETRY AND REVOLUTION

REACTION

MARVELL RE-ENTERED ENGLAND SOME time in 1647, probably in the autumn. It was a propitious time to do so, although it can hardly have been planned. Between 11 and 14 November, King Charles escaped from Hampton Court to the Isle of Wight only to find himself imprisoned anew in Carisbrooke Castle. As negotiating positions between King and Parliament hardened and as the King lost the upper hand, London became the site of strong and vibrant anti-Parliamentarian ferment. Cavaliers and Levellers alike had reason to object to Parliamentary positions and the Presbyterian–Independent alliance that lay behind it. The Scots, increasingly unhappy at the treatment of the King in England, threatened to pull away from the alliance. By the summer of 1648 the discontent and instability resulted in the outbreak of the Second Civil War, preceded in May by the Kentish Rising. The Royalists would find the response of the New Model Army fiercer than they could have imagined. A new bitterness and desperation entered affairs as the New Model commanders felt that the uprisings were beyond the usual conventions of military behaviour: the First Civil War having been won fair and square, the supporters of the King had no right to take up arms again.

Marvell found himself in the thick of the much disturbed literary culture of London. Several former Parliamentarian journalists had swapped sides, notably Marchamont Nedham, erstwhile editor of the Parliamentarian *Mercurius Britanicus*, now editor of the Royalist *Mercurius Pragmaticus*. Other figures on the scene were the enormously talented John Hall, another side-swapper, and author of an impressive volume of poems of 1646 that would much appeal to Marvell. A number of firm Royalist poets were publishing their work, such as Abraham Cowley, Marvell's senior at Trinity College by three years, and Oxford's Richard Lovelace, in many ways the exemplary Cavalier soldier-gentleman-poet, who had wasted his fortune in the King's cause.[1] Marvell paid careful attention to the work of all these poets and later came to know some of them personally, if he did not already know them.

While Charles was making his way southward in the journey that Marvell would later famously describe in his greatest political poem, the poet himself was raising more income. On 12 November 1647 he sold the rest of his Meldreth property for £80 to John Stacey, who had already purchased the land on either side of the house in 1642. Marvell was in Meldreth again on 23 December to complete the sale of the property.[2]

But where did he specifically reside? He appears to have returned first to Hull and was noted in Meldreth as a gentleman of the northern port. It is not impossible that he took up arms, for the Royalists, but given his successful avoidance of service thus far, that seems unlikely. It is most probable that he returned to the north-west edge of London – St John's, Clerkenwell and the Inns of Court. Perhaps, as the literary evidence suggests, he had to do with Thomas Stanley, the wealthy man of letters who was supporting a society of decidedly Royalist poets with food and board from his chambers in the Middle Temple.[3] The Meldreth sale would give him means for some time. Wherever he was, Marvell kept a low profile; he read and he wrote.

He also began to think about his vocation as a poet in war-torn England. Being an aspirant gentleman, even a Cavalier, almost inevitably meant writing verse: it was a facet of one's public identity, and at the same time fuelled an inner sense of identity commensurate with how one saw oneself in society. Marvell began to look at what had been published recently as he began to write the poems that eventually – a long time after his death – would be revered. Abraham Cowley had been in exile in Paris since as early as 1644, and Marvell may have met him there and seen some of his verse.[4] But it is more consistent with Marvell's habits of writing to have noticed, to have acquired and read repeatedly with much reflection, Cowley's *The Mistress* when it appeared in the weeks after 4 March 1647. Particular phrases find their way into Marvell's poems, perhaps some years ahead at this stage, as in the echo of Cowley's 'Either soft, or sweet, or fair' ('Nature', l. 18) in Marvell's 'All this fair, and soft, and sweet' ('Dialogue, Between the Resolved Soul, and Created Pleasure', l. 51), or the send-up in 'The Match' of Cowley's 'The Given Heart':

> Wo to her stubborn *Heart*, if once mine come
> Into the self same room;
> 'Twill tear and blow up all within,
> Like a *Grenado* shot into a *Magazin*
>
> (ll. 9–12)
>
> Thus all his fuel did unite
>   To make one fire high:
> None ever burn'd so hot, so bright:
>   And Celia that am I.
>
> (ll. 33–6)

Yet it is the spirit of Cowley's achievement in *The Mistress* as a whole that must have been so challenging and inspiring to Marvell – the consummate definition of libertine verse, even in a time of civil war.

We might say that the respect for Cowley is evident in the fact that Marvell largely responded to lines in *The Mistress* that he found memorable by echoing them, whereas other recently published poems became more profoundly reworked, shells to be made into better poetry.[5] Hence another volume, less well remembered than *The Mistress*, that Marvell read at this time was Thomas Philipot's *Poems* (1646):

> Thou art Natures Magazine,
> Or her casket rather, in
> Whose narrow precincts she hath pent
> The treasure that both Indies sent.
>
> (ll. 9–12)

By making Love do the gathering as well as Nature, Marvell creates an intriguing fiction:

The Match

I

Nature had long a treasure made
  Of all her choicest store;
Fearing, when she should be decayed,
  To beg in vain for more.

II

Her orientest colours there,
  And essences most pure,
With sweetest perfumes hoarded were,
  All as she thought secure.
  . . .

V

Love wisely had of long foreseen
  That he must once grow old;
And therefore stored a magazine,
  To save him from the cold.

VI

He kept the sev'ral cells replete
  With nitre thrice refined;
The naphtha's and the sulphur's heat,
  And all that burns the mind.
  . . .

(ll. 1–8; 17–24)

The bringing together of the components of an explosion is an opposite to 'The Definition of Love', a riposte to the logical divisiveness in that poem and its account of impossible love. Philipot was another Cambridge poet, whom Marvell may have known since the 1630s; he may have known Philipot's poetry while at Cambridge, since the 1646 volume was a gathering together of material written earlier.

'On a Drop of Dew' probably also comes from these years. The poem is self-mirroring in its very structure, just like a real drop of dew: the second half, on the soul, matches, point for point, the first half, applying the description of the dewdrop to the matter of the soul. The two-part structure could have been suggested by Thomas Stanley's 'The Bud' (1646). Stanley was another poet in the Hall/Lovelace circle at this time; indeed, as we shall see, he may well have been its leader.[6] It has been argued that the first eighteen lines of the poem are governed by the command 'See' (l. 1), and the rest of the poem by the conjunction 'So' (l. 19), in imitation of the structure of an emblem poem.[7] The metre of the first part of the poem, concerned with the dewdrop, alternates almost line by line (only two lines (4–5) have the same number of syllables): 'For the clear region where "twas born/Round in itself incloses/And in its little globe's extent,/Frames as it can its native element' (ll. 5–8). The second half of the poem, concerned with the soul, is marked by groups of lines with similar syllable lengths. The couplets at the end of each section imply clarity, resolution and stasis, as opposed to the undulating movement in the first parts of those sections. The syntax of the first eighteen lines (two nine-line sentences) is extremely difficult, with ellipses that obscure any clear relationship between clauses. The intention may have been to suggest the integrity of the dewdrop: just as the spherical drop shape is suggested by variant line length, so the syntax appears to 'run round' the surface of the drop in an endless chain: 'Restless it rolls and unsecure,/ Trembling lest it grow impure' (ll. 5–16). A similar effect is achieved in the Latin companion poem 'Ros'.[8]

Each section of the poem presents elements of the other in a markedly different kind of poetry. Thus, description and interpretation interpenetrate, just as both dewdrop and tear contain within themselves the greater and higher environment from which they come. In the first half, description of a natural object moves from literal observation through anthropomorphic description to psychological connotations: 'it the purple flower does slight,/ Scarce touching where it lies,/ But gazing back upon the skies,/ Shines with a mournful light' (ll. 9–12). The interpenetration of categories may be seen as a meditation on the complexities of description and interpretation, and the proximity or even interpenetration of subject and object. Yet these senses of fusion are undermined by the consistently impersonal nature of the viewpoint of the speaker, who never uses the first person. But impersonality is itself undermined by the refined and fastidious feelings attributed to the dewdrop and the soul: 'Rememb'ring still its former height,/ Shuns the swart leaves and blossoms green;/ . . ./ In how coy a figure wound,/ Every way it turns away:/ . . ./ Dark beneath, but bright above:/Here disdaining, there in love' (ll. 22–3, 27–8, 31–2). Is this not then a description of a self such as Marvell's: enclosed, secretive, yet deeply complex and highly reflective of the environment in which it rests? Like several other Marvell poems, it is worth writing the poem's 'biography' itself, so notable is its achievement.

Other poems written probably in this period propose similar situations in which objects and the speaker himself are insulated from the world around them and the world of values from which they come. 'Eyes and Tears' is balanced, with six stanzas on each side of the pivotal stanzas 7 and 8. Thus, the figure of the Magdalen is at the centre of the poem. Each stanza deals with a different aspect of, or image connected with, the poem's central concern, but some stanzas are more conceptually relevant than others (e.g. ll. 1 and 2, 12 and 13). Different kinds of causes of tears are dealt with: complaint (st. I), sorrow (st. II), pity (st. VI), grief (st. VII). Different sections of the poem employ repetition in order to create an effect of rising intensity, which sits paradoxically alongside the sense of stifled activity that weeping brings about. The effect is to focus the reader's attention upon the suspended moment of weeping, as if the entire fifty-six lines were addressing the picture or emblem of a weeper. We are left meditating on two objects, suspended, pendant-like, for our attention: eyes and tears. At the same time, we are made very subtly aware of the different qualities attached to weeping and to seeing:

VII

Yet happy they whom grief doth bless,
That weep the more, and see the less:
And, to preserve their sight more true,
Bathe still their eyes in their own dew.

VIII

So Magdalen, in tears more wise
Dissolved those captivating eyes,
Whose liquid chains could flowing meet
To fetter her Redeemer's feet.

(ll. 25–32)

Stanza VIII has a Latin version that was added at the end of the poem when it was published in 1681, and this has been seen as a kind of origin for the poem, growing as it may have done from this very Latin, and offering a completeness with which it informs and unites the other stanzas. These Latin lines belong to the English tradition inaugurated by the Elizabethan Jesuit Robert Southwell. But if this is so, the poem removes itself from the religious context suggested by the Latin lines: 'Christus' is demoted slightly to 'Redeemer'. This is at once experiential in a very narrow theological sense and at the same time aesthetic in a secular sense. The poem's appearance in the anthology Poetical Recreations (1688) confirms the transformation from sacred convention to secular lyric, a 'deconversion', so to speak, that the poem's origins and method of composition embody. Even so, some have felt that the poem subtly retains its religious identity, at the very least riding on the edge of Christian profession.[9]

Along with the echoes of Shakespeare, the presence of John Donne's poems that mention tears has been sensed (especially 'A Valediction: of Weeping' and 'Twicknam Garden') in this poem, but with a turning away (perhaps critically so) from Donne's dramatic confrontations of tearful lovers. What remains of Donne in Marvell is an echo of the phrasing of interpenetration: not, as in Donne, of the lovers but of the means of perception and expression: eyes and tears.[10] In other words, Marvell's poem is remarkable and original in itself, but also a highly intelligent commentary on English religious verse since the late sixteenth century and the confessional battleground of which it was a part. Perhaps too, with its distanced placing of the figure of the Magdalen, it is an acknowledgement of the rise of secular perspectives in Marvell's lifetime.

While Marvell read and worked away, in May 1648, events began to mount for a new Royalist rising and the real possibility of a counter-revolution. A Welsh insurgency had been contained but there was discontent in several English counties. The possibility of an army in support of the King marching south from Scotland was accompanied by unrest in London, which had had to be occupied by the New Model Army the previous July. On 21 May the Kentish Rising began. The Earl of Holland also raised forces, the purpose of which was to relieve the Royalists besieged in Colchester by Fairfax. It was 'planned to be a major rising, but turned out to be a very damp squib'.[11]

As we saw in Chapter 2, the Villiers brothers, George, second Duke of Buckingham, and Lord Francis, were sent to Cambridge, either just before or just after Marvell had left the university in 1641, but they enlisted with Prince Rupert and Lord Gerard in 1642. After the sequestering of their estates in 1643, they were sent on an extensive tour of the continent (where, as we also saw, they probably encountered Marvell in Rome) and on their return, Francis joined his elder brother in the Earl of Holland's rising. The distinguished Puritan soldier and historian Edmund Ludlow commented that Villiers had a romance with Mary Kirke, daughter of the poet Aurelian Townshend. According to Ludlow's account, it was because Francis Villiers had sent his company before him, having entertained Mary Kirke the night before, that he was exposed to the enemy. He was surprised by Parliamentary soldiers, refused to give himself up, and was killed on 7 July.[12] Indeed, Villiers was described in detail defending himself valiantly, with his back against a tree, his horse having been shot from under him. The manner of his death was most unchivalric (in keeping with the desperation and bitterness that characterized the Second Civil War), a Parliamentary soldier dashing off his helmet, then running him through from behind:

and (after he was dead) cut off his Nose, and then run him thorow and thorow the neck and cut and mangled his body in a most barbarous and inhumane manner: But that gallant Spirit expired with more honour then ever the proudest of the Rebels, or any of their tainted race will do to the worlds end: He scorned to ask quarter of a Rebel, and fought with 8 or 9 of the stoutest Butchers of the Army. But he is dead.

> When they dishonour'd and defam'd shall die,
> Valour and Fame shall crown his memory.[13]

To many commentators, the death of the young Cavalier was indicative of the senseless waste of war and the growing acknowledgement of the futility of these late Royalist risings. It was more than that. Villiers had featured in court portraiture since he was a child: as much as anyone he was the epitome of Cavalier beauty in life and art. His barbaric dissection must have seemed sickeningly awful to all who knew his short history. Even the Parliamentarian journalist, soon to be a prominent republican apologist, John Hall lamented: 'the *Lord Francis Villiers*, a fine yo[u]ng Gentleman *expiated* part of the folly of his companions, and dyed by a many wounds, which had been brave enough, had they been received in another cause'.[14]

Shortly after this sad event, Marvell wrote quickly and therefore with some unevenness 'An Elegy Upon the Death of My Lord Francis Villiers'. The poem, 128 lines long, was printed in a quarto pamphlet of one sheet of which only two known copies survive. The poem was not printed in the 1681 *Miscellaneous Poems*: Marvell, his poetic executors, or his publishers, may not have wanted to foreground an association with the Villiers family in the late 1670s and early 1680s, or to have acknowledged that he had written such an obviously Royalist poem, or perhaps his papers no longer contained a copy of it. The poet begins his lament by complaining that 'Fame' (i.e. journalism) should not have brought the news: the poet speaker appears to put his newsbook aside and write.[15]

It is, despite its shortcomings, a successful poem, maintaining an appropriate tenor of reserved regret (with occasional emotional heights) within the structure of rhymed heroic couplets and deftly placed enjambments. There are a number of images that are quietly placed either for effect or perhaps, through inexperience, lacking the more confident texturing of the later public poetry. The poem is structurally poised between the cultural forms associated with the Villiers family and early life (romance, courtly portraiture, extravagant buildings) and that which painting cannot represent: the horror of war and the pressure it places upon love. Paradoxically, the actual death of Villiers is described not literally, but through a series of romance, epic and mythical images (ll. 93–114).

There has been some debate on the nature of Marvell's allegiances in the 'Elegy'. The poem is apparently the most openly Royalist of Marvell's works, but grief expressed in personal terms is not blatantly political. The poem is under the sway of the general brutalization of affairs after the outbreak of the Second Civil War, and Villiers's death is ultimately blamed on fate, not Parliament, as if to suggest that Parliament was destined by fate to victory. Some go even further to see the poem as being in tension with Royalist elegy, not bearing its typical poetic character or sentiments.[16] The poem is from this viewpoint concerned not with a loyal subject but with a lover; it is 'a poem attempting to mediate between modes of representing its dead'. In this way, Marvell's verse has more in common with mourning elegies from the pre-war decades, with their use of heroic, romance and mythic components. Villiers is presented more or less as an art object, like the paintings his elder brother had sold to fund the Royalist rising.[17] But it is hard to see how the invocation to poets to take up arms (l. 126) could not be read at the very least as an oblique statement of Civil War Royalist allegiance. And what of the concern with valiant, even erotic, male beauty, characterized by Villiers's own self-observing powers? 'There is a narcissistic, self-enclosing movement about the gaze which is directed at himself, and which finds other masculine objects – even the eyes of an enemy soldier – to reflect it back, rather than the eyes of his mistress. Marvell's conceit labours to preserve the all-male circuit of vision.'[18] The inclusion of the Venus and Adonis story makes Villiers not only (through comparison with Adonis) an 'icon of male beauty', but also 'an unattainable object of sexual desire'. This is the passage in question:

> Lovely and admirable as he was,
> Yet was his sword or armour all his glass.
> Nor in his mistress' eyes that joy he took,
> As in an enemy's himself to look.
> I know how well he did, with what delight
> Those serious imitations of fight.
> Still in the trials of strong exercise
> His was the first, and his the second prize.
>
> (ll. 51–8)

It is an intense realization of the Cavalier as the lover of Cowley's *The Mistress*, but interestingly the enemy is Marvell the poet, apparently imagining an encounter in which the two fenced to hone their skills, and recalling his fencing lessons in Spain. Flecknoe was an opposite from whom the poet fled; here is a heroic 'opposite' locked in a mirroring gaze during a sword fight with the poem's speaker. Perhaps here we have evidence that ties up with the later allegation that Marvell had been a captain of a night watch.[19]

Marvell's poem is unique and outstanding in its time: no contemporary printed elegy goes as far as Marvell does in placing his subject in a heroic romance narrative, endowed with a character and a distinctive mode of perception. The poem has very little to do with any of the three other printed elegies on Villiers, in the largely critical poetry on his demise, although there are some resemblances with a published Latin elegy.[20]

However, the 'Elegy' fits far more tellingly with the manuscript culture of the Royalists in these years. One University College, London, manuscript is a folio

miscellany of some 220 poems and songs, largely by Royalist writers.[21] That the
volume has a Royalist bias is clear not least because it contains elegies both for
Francis Villiers and for Charles I: the first poem in the volume is an elegy for
Charles, and it immediately precedes the first two Villiers poems. Marvell's
connection with the volume is not merely through the shared elegizing of
Francis Villiers: also included is a version of Marvell's 'Dialogue between
Thyrsis and Dorinda' (entitled 'Thirsis & Dorinda'), one of the very few Marvell
lyric poems for which there is evidence of wide manuscript circulation. There
is also an echo of 'An Horatian Ode' in an elegy for Charles.[22]

In this manuscript are three elegies on Villiers: C.R.'s 'To my worthy friend
A: J: invitinge him to write somethinge on the Lord Francis Villers slayne in
their uncivill Warrs at Kingston upon Thames', A.J.'s 'The Answere', and G.T.'s
'On the Death of the Lord Francis Villers'. These three poems and Marvell's
elegy share an acknowledgement of Villiers's physical beauty, as well as some
classical parallels. The opening of G.T.'s poem is apparently indebted to the
beginning of Marvell's:

> Fame th'art deceivd, Lord Francis is not dead
> But thou wert by him, when his pure soule fled
> From his sadd body, yet thou art deceivd
> Tis wee alone, wee only are bereavd.

The similarity of Marvell's elegy to these poems suggests that he was indeed
closely involved with Royalist literary circles at this point. To judge from the
emotional tone of the passage, it was an association that extended to an invest-
ment in the refined ideals of high Royalism, if not so far as willingness to
enlist.[23] Perhaps, then, Marvell presented a copy of the poem to Chlora,
Villiers's sister, the Duchess of Richmond, and her husband.[24] Did they have
the poem printed in a small run of frail quarto sheets? Its rareness and absence
from the major London tract collection of the period collected by the
publisher George Thomason suggest that it was printed away from the capital,
perhaps on a secret Royalist press, and in limited numbers.

But unlike the other elegies, Marvell's poem is an acknowledgement of the
love culture of the Cavalier courtiers, one that, on the evidence of lyric poetry,
flouted the boundaries of relationships provided by marriage and family
honour. As we have seen, Villiers was held to have endangered himself by
sending on his troops and delaying to spend a night with Mary Kirke. A lock
of her hair was found on his corpse, sewn up inside a ribbon, presumably by
Mary herself. Marvell does not condemn this seemingly imprudent act but lets
it stand as a fitting testimony to Villiers's tragically noble character: if we will,
an entirely Royalist dilemma.[25] Does this explain the distance that Marvell
introduces when he seems to mock Villiers with the imagined hordes of lady
admirers who ride with him in the saddle (ll. 93–4)? Was he discussing even at

this time with John Hall the foibles of the Royalists? And what is Marvell hinting at when his speaker identifies himself as fencing with Villiers: more enemy than fencing partner (ll. 53–6)?

The Royalist hope expressed at the end of the poem was in vain, with the outcome possibly sealed even before it was finished. On 17 August 1648, Cromwell defeated the Scots at Preston, ending the Second Civil War. Through the autumn, events moved rapidly and shockingly into a new phase. In early December, Presbyterian MPs were excluded from Parliament in Pride's Purge. This allowed the Independents to have the upper hand: the way was open for the trial and execution of the King. Marvell clearly viewed the regicide of 30 January 1649 with something approaching traumatic apprehension. The imagery of sacrifice, blood and blood-guilt is spread throughout the lyric poetry,[26] implying that the execution kept a hold on the poet for a very long time.

But in the weeks before the regicide, Marvell most probably had his hand in a poem whose occasion properly belongs to events earlier in the year. This was his verse letter addressed to Richard Lovelace. Lovelace's famous volume of Cavalier verse, *Lucasta*, was licensed as early as 7 February 1648, but did not appear until May 1649. Publication was delayed by the actions of press censors and these circumstances are alluded to in Marvell's poem. Along with some of the other prefatory verse, Marvell's poem was probably written not long before publication, but certainly before the execution of the King, of which there is no mention. The volume was also delayed by Lovelace's imprisonment from June 1648 to April 1649, during which time his estates were sequestered. Perhaps the publication of *Lucasta*, Marvell's poem along with it, was part of a campaign to have Lovelace's sequestration fine reduced.

Lovelace was a handsome Cavalier hero and a respected poet. His physical beauty and the fineness of his verse were seen as interconnected and Marvell presents him as part of a lost courtly age:

> Our times are much degenerate from those
> Which your sweet Muse with your fair fortune chose,
> And as complexions alter with the climes,
> Our wits have drawn th'infection of our times.
>
> (ll. 1–4)

The new age is not merely of the Civil War; it is also of journalism, and journalism's wrecking of literary virtue. Marvell broadly imitates Horace's verse epistles which mention poets; but where the enemy for the ancients is an ill-educated rabble, Marvell's addresses a new age of debased literary activity and Puritan censorship. The unspoken difficulty was that Marvell was very nearly part of it, and in this sense his poem is an abrupt departure from the verse epistles of Ben Jonson where a continuity of values with the ancient past is celebrated, and where the context of war is explicitly absent. The understanding of the predicament of the Cavalier poet is startlingly acute, suggesting a profound engagement with the *Lucasta* volume. The poem is at once panegyric and elegy for a lost and bountiful pre-war culture, as it looks back in its form at the verse epistle by which Jonson's 'tribe' of followers communicated with each other, even as it shoots into a dark future.

It may be that Marvell was taking a pattern from his acquaintance John Hall, who also wrote a commendatory poem for Lovelace, but who himself had been lambasted for turning from apparently Royalist lyric writing to Parliamentary journalism in 1648.[27] But the poem's energy proceeds to explore the corruption of literary ideals in a way that is consistent with Lovelace's idealism. The singularity of high Caroline idealism has been replaced by double standards, confusing paradoxes and absurd propositions. Of all the poems addressed to Lovelace, Marvell's is quite distinctive in catching this moment but, like John Hall, Marvell sees that Lovelace was offering a new kind of heroic poem for the times, and in doing so had become a new kind of hero as a poet. In Marvell's eyes, Lovelace even becomes a hero in a romance narrative. Marvell is not alone in presenting a hostile front to the Presbyterians, then at the height of their censorious power, and here he shares a perspective with Royalists, Independents and Levellers alike. In this sense the poem appears to share terms with Marchamont Nedham's journalism, even though it ostensibly inveighs against such views. After the passage concerned with the Presbyterian censors the poem ends with a curious passage in which Lovelace's female admirers mistake the poet-speaker for one of the persecutors. He identifies himself as a would-be Cavalier, ready to defend the ladies or die alongside Lovelace. In doing so, Marvell makes himself as poet an agent, realizing himself as a desiring subject just as he had done in the Villiers elegy, as Echo to the presence of Narcissus. There is a hint too of being like the ladies in desiring Lovelace, a confession of entering the circles of mutual homoerotic admiration that marked some Cavalier relationships (and French libertine ones too). Marvell had addressed Lovelace in academic terms as an equal, 'Mr' ('*magister*', since both men had MAs), thereby suggesting his continuing attachment to an academic identity that had been lost in 1641. Likewise, the poem lauds a Royalist poet hero, but Royalism in the sense of veneration of Stuart rule itself is not extolled. The poem says goodbye to all that.

ROYALISM AND REPUBLICANISM

Marvell watched events during the anxious early months of 1649 as the state turned itself into a republic: 'free state' was the adopted name. The hopes that he had apparently invested in the last-ditch attempt at Royalist revival were dashed, and all literary endeavour would have to be redefined. To be a Royalist now meant supporting Prince Charles, the future Charles II, proclaimed king in Scotland on 5 February. It would mean possible exile, or surreptitious living, until the risings of 1650, all of which would be unsuccessful. Marvell's probable associates, those involved in the counter-revolution, were mopped up. Nedham was imprisoned and would not be released until he had promised to be a journalist for the victors: something he would do with application and originality.

Wherever Marvell was, he must have learned that in mid-May his nephew and probable godson, Andrew More, died and was buried on the 23rd in Holy Trinity Church, Hull. One month later, on 24 June, Henry, Lord Hastings, son and heir apparent of Ferdinando, seventh Earl of Huntingdon and young Cavalier hero, died of smallpox the day before his wedding. He was nineteen. The poets set to work and soon a memorial volume appeared, a collection of elegies assembled by Richard Brome, entitled *Lachrymae Musarum*, published quite soon after Hastings's death, once again as the signs of hasty compilation imply (e.g. ll. 74, 77). Marvell's poem appeared as the first in a 'postscript' of eight further elegies, since the bulk of the volume 'was printed before these following Papers were written or sent in'. Hastings's untimely death also drew poems from his mother, Lucy, Countess of Huntingdon, and from the brilliant classicist Bathsua Makin, both of which appear to echo Marvell's. Perhaps Marvell's success as an elegist for Villiers led some to encourage him to commemorate Hastings.

Lachrymae Musarum was covertly mourning the regicide as much as commemorating Hastings, who, after all, had achieved little in his short life, despite coming from a famous literary family, and despite the remarkable timing of his death. The leaf after the title page contained a decoration of the four crowns of England, Wales, Scotland and France, with insignia, which appeared on other Royalist publications at this time. Some evidence suggests that Hastings was present at the siege of Colchester from 12 June until 28 August 1648 (with his uncle, Baron Loughborough, a prominent Royalist commander), an event notorious for its Cavalier recklessness during the Second Civil War. It may well be that *Lachrymae Musarum* was meant to be understood not merely as an act of mourning but as one of resistance to the new regime.

The Hastings elegy incorporates some of the circumstances of the Hastings family, and the marriage of Lord Hastings to Elizabeth, daughter of Sir Theodore Turquet de Mayerne (1573–1655), physician to James I, Charles I, Henrietta Maria and eventually Oliver Cromwell. Hastings's parents came from two famous literary families. The literary and cultural patronage of the earls of Huntingdon at their country seat of Ashby de la Zouche in Leicestershire was extensive. Hastings's mother, Lucy, was the daughter of the poet and statesman Sir John Davies. Her mother was the controversial and notorious prophet (she had managed to prophesy the assassination of the Duke of Buckingham in 1626, and was critical of Charles I), Lady Eleanor Davies (or Douglas), whose publications had increased in frequency at the end of the 1640s, but who, not surprisingly, goes unmentioned in Marvell's poem. She published two versions

of a prophecy on the occasion of the death of her grandson in which she found
a parallel story in 2 Esdras 9–10. She regarded Henry's death as a symbol of the
tragedy that was occurring in the world at large.[28]

Mayerne, the other parent named in the poem, had been excluded from
the medical faculty at the University of Paris for being a Paracelsian and a
Protestant.[29] His presence in England ensured that (al)chemically prepared
remedies were incorporated into the English pharmacopoeia. Marvell refers to
Mayerne by name, and builds alchemical and pharmacopoeic imagery into the
poem's structure. Marvell has been seen to represent the union of Hastings and
Mayerne as a 'chemical wedding', symbolizing, and even partaking of, the
alchemical process of purification. Hastings's death is thus also the loss of the
immortal elixir, or stone.[30] Mayerne had been involved in the unsuccessful
treatment of James I on his deathbed in 1625: this earlier event may be recalled
in lines 57–8, so that 'to lose one member of the royal family might be regarded
as misfortune – the death of another [since Hastings claimed royal descent
from Edward IV] began to look like carelessness'.[31] The final lines of the poem
appear to make the best of a hopeless situation in respect of Mayerne's inability
to save Hastings:

> But what could he, good man, although he bruised
> All herbs, and them a thousand ways infused?
> All he had tried, but all in vain, he saw,
> And wept, as we, without redress or law.
> For man (alas) is but the heavens' sport;
> And art indeed is long, but life is short.

(ll. 55–60)

In Paris, Mayerne had been accused of injuring several patients with his treatment, but his reputation for exactitude in diagnosis and prescription remained
and grew after he came to live in England. He also wrote long letters of counsel
to his patients. Mayerne introduced chemical and alchemical cures (he
thought that the philosopher's stone was a panacea), to the fury of traditional
herbalists. A reference to Mayerne's daughter as a balsam tree refers to the tree
yielding balsam resin, used as a soothing balm but also regarded as a preservative essence in alchemical writing, and thought by Paracelsus to exist in all
bodies; so, in the image, Mayerne's daughter becomes the essence of Hastings,
preservation and perfection. In alchemical theory, the Tree of Life (to which
Marvell refers in line 20) contained the balsam that kept Adam in a state of
prelapsarian purity. After the Fall, that balsam could be discovered within the
human body, thereby returning man to the paradisal state.

But for Hasting's this did not happen, and the poem surreptitiously seems to
ridicule alchemy, in keeping with the scepticism of Ben Jonson, whose writing
was so important to Marvell at this time:

And Aesculapius, who, ashamed and stern,
Himself at once condemneth, and Mayerne
Like some sad chemist, who, prepared to reap
The golden harvest, sees his glasses leap.

(ll. 47–50)

The image in line 49 could be seen to mock alchemists; Marvell may have been trying to warn of the more tenuous aspects of alchemy. Aesculapius restored the dead Hymenaeus to life; Marvell was suggesting that what Aesculapius could do for Hymen, he cannot do for Hastings; and no more can Mayerne.[32] Aesculapius was punished by Jove for bringing the dead Hippolytus to life, and in a Christian universe, he is not redeemed. Indeed in some traditions Aesculapius was regarded as a false Christ, because he sought to redeem bodies but not souls. Aesculapius used herbs to cure Hippolytus, and cure by herbs was a godlike action in ancient poetry, but Lady Eleanor Davies implies that Hastings, 'by letting blood was cast away', although 'committed to no simple Doctors'.[33] The poem steps into this unsettling world even as it appears to console. Although the Hastings family was in serious financial straits at the end of the 1640s, Hastings's funeral itself was lavish and marked by a public procession in London (his body was finally interred at Ashby de la Zouche in July 1649), another act of Royalist demonstration.

Marvell's poem hints at Hastings's Royalism, but the other elegies in the volume make much more of this. Despite its Royalist associations (e.g. ll. 25–6), the poem offers but then withdraws Royalist implications. Thus, the absence of reference to the Earl of Huntingdon, Hastings's father, who gave the King no assistance, has been seen as a covert Royalist statement, but the reference to the monarchy of heaven (ll. 27–32) paints princes in a more tyrannous light. Marvell's fatalistic 'Therefore the democratic stars did rise,/And all that worth from hence did ostracize' is one thing, but Nedham's 'It is decreed, we must be drain'd (I see)/Down to the dregs of a Democracie' quite another.[34] It is as if Marvell, unlike his fellow poet contributors, was reading the situation carefully and guarding his own position, perhaps already in anticipation of preferment with the new regime. He was also characteristically sensitive to the complications within the Hastings family.

It is, of course, unsurprising that a series of poems produced by writers in a relatively closed world, with a shared literary culture, should be of a similar nature when addressing a singular issue. Nonetheless, the interconnectedness of the poems in *Lachrymae Musarum* is striking. Since Marvell's lament, along with Nedham's and Dryden's, among others, was submitted at a late stage, it is probable that he saw some of the earlier compositions and some of those in the postscript either before or during the writing of his own poem. The fact that some of the poems in the collection provided him with sources for some of his other poems is further evidence that he was part of a school of poets.

A second edition of *Lachrymae Musarum* was published in January 1650, and was received by Thomason on the 30th, the first anniversary of the regicide, an even clearer sign of Royalist affiliation. The sense of timing, of things on earth being influenced by greater forces, runs through the poem, and so in a larger sense the regicide itself dominates the poem. Hastings's death is as precisely timed as that of Charles:

> Alas, his virtues did his death presage:
> Needs must he die, that doth out-run his age.
> The phlegmatic and slow prolongs his day,
> And on Time's wheel sticks like a remora.
> What man is he, that hath not heav'n beguiled,
> And is not thence mistaken for a child?
> While those of growth more sudden, and more bold,
> Are hurried hence, as if already old.
> For, there above, they number not as here,
> But weigh to man the geometric year.
>
> (ll. 9–18)

The 'geometric year' is a year calculated by geometry: it would pass more quickly than a normal year. In Platonic tradition, it expresses each unit of time as part of a unifying eternity, usually described in the figure of a circle. The emblematic representation of man's life as four quarters of a circle, corresponding to the four seasons of the year, is graphically geometrical, and visually very powerful.

The precision of this part of the poem, and its confident construction as a whole, no doubt drew the attention of *Lachrymae Musarum*'s editor, Richard Brome. In both editions, Marvell's poem appeared as the first in a 'postscript' of nine elegies, since the bulk of the volume 'was printed before these following papers were written or sent in'. In the first edition, Marvell's poem appears on pages 78–80, but in one surviving copy of the first edition, as well as in the second edition, on unpaginated, inserted leaves, between pages 42 and 43, with the instruction 'Place this after fol. 42' printed at the foot of the first page. By moving the poem forward from the postscript, Brome placed Marvell among the company of fellow poets: Herrick, Denham and John Hall (although Nedham and Dryden's elegies remained in the postscript). He had been recognized.

This promotion of Marvell suggests a shared consciousness of his worth in the context of an acknowledged sphere of poets in London and Westminster at the very end of the 1640s: the Tribe of Ben, the group of younger poets who gathered around the elderly Ben Jonson in 1620s and 1630s London, now relocated in a new republican age. What Marvell was doing remains to be seen, but the closeness of his writing to some of those already or soon to be hired pens for the free state is evident. In particular, and as we have seen, there are echoes of Hall and Marchamont Nedham. Of Hall's significance, there will be more later. But

Nedham's interest in Machiavelli, and his startling reflection of distinct Machiavellian terminology, as instanced in his editorials for *Mercurius Politicus* and elsewhere, is present in Marvell's writing.[35] There's some evidence of this already in the Hastings elegy:

> But 'tis a maxim of that state, that none,
> Lest he become like them, taste more than one.
> Therefore the democratic stars did rise,
> And all that worth from hence did ostracize.
>   Yet as some prince, that, for state-jealousy,
> Secures his nearest and most loved ally;
> His thought with richest triumphs entertains,
> And in the choicest pleasures charms his pains.
>
> (ll. 23–30)

As well as the echo of Nedham's verse that we have already noted, there is also the hint of political theory. The maxim was fashionable in the early seventeenth century. It was popular with some republicans in the 1650s, but more often derided as an instrument of tyranny by others, including Milton and Algernon Sidney. The use of the word 'ostracize' reflects Nedham's and others' growing interest in the lessons that might be gained from ancient political and literary theory. In ancient Athens, those who were too wealthy, virtuous, popular or politically able could be banished by a vote in the assembly, in order to prevent a monarchy.[36] Of this register in his poetry, a new register for a new age, Marvell would soon make much more.

Most probably Marvell wrote 'The Nymph Complaining for the Death of her Fawn' in the early months of 1649. Its veiled references to Parliamentary or Scottish soldiers who carry blood-guilt for the fawn's murder associate the poem with a strain of Royalist pastoral verse in which Charles I's martyrdom is painfully lamented. The large amount of commentary devoted to the poem should leave no one in any doubt that it is as innovative as any of Marvell's major poems, the most astonishing achievement being the distinctive voice of the nymph herself, with its simplistic, sometimes awkward, diction and syntax, and trite puns and rhymes. Her grief is pinpointed by an inability to name the fawn directly: the pronoun 'it' is repeated twenty-six times. Into the nymph's words disappear the poet's views: the process of the poem's creation seems to involve a hiding of the views of the all too evident regicidal context that surrounds the poem. Marvell does not want to give too much away, and in any case it might not suit his career prospects with a new kind of regime. But the poem triumphs by isolating the nymph's pained expression and her evident delight in the now lost pleasures of the fawn, especially its feasting on roses – whatever that may mean.

The next public poem we have by Marvell shows both how acute a public observer he had become and how classical. This was his masterpiece 'An

Horatian Ode upon Cromwell's Return from Ireland', considered by many to be the greatest political poem in the English language. He had, it would seem, changed sides, and that will take some explaining.

At the time of the execution of Charles I in January 1649, Oliver Cromwell was second in command of the New Model Army, and politically influential in the purged House of Commons, the Rump Parliament. In the summer of 1649, he led a military expedition to Ireland where he achieved a series of victories against the Royalist and Catholic alliance at the Battles of Drogheda and Wexford, and the siege of Clonmel. Shortly after the siege, in late May 1650, he returned to England, landing at Bristol on the 28th and reaching Windsor on the 31st. The Irish threat to the new republic of England had been contained, but the Scottish threat remained. On 12 June, Sir Thomas Fairfax was appointed commander-in-chief of the army for a Scottish campaign, with Cromwell still second in command. However, Fairfax refused to enter Scotland without provocation, by which he meant a Scottish invasion of England. On 26 June, sitting high in public esteem after the Irish success, Cromwell replaced Fairfax as commander-in-chief (see plate 9). On 22 July, the Parliamentary forces invaded Scotland with Robert Overton, Governor of Hull, among the officers. The poem looks back upon the regicide, the birth of the republic, and the Irish campaign, and forward to the Scottish venture. It must have been composed in this brief interlude between Cromwell's two Celtic forays. There was a notable rise of patriotic feeling at this time despite the regicide. Marvell is acutely aware throughout the poem of the juxtaposition of fighting and writing, two alternative but related spheres – a juxtaposition often noticed by contemporaries.[37]

The poem's construction is complex and from this comes the vexed issue of what it stands for, or where its sympathies lie. One of the two poems that represent Marvell's earliest published work, 'Ad Regem Carolum Parodia' (1637), is, as we saw, a close imitation of the second ode in the first book of Horace's odes, or *Carmina*.[38] Horace, who fought for the republicans at Philippi, eventually accepted the rule of Augustus Caesar, and celebrated in verse the peace that then prevailed. Perhaps Marvell was aware that switching sides, and seeking to praise your former enemy so that it might benefit you, was enshrined in the very idea of a Horatian ode.

The compilation and translation of Horatian odes was in part a reaction to the experience of civil war. Mildmay Fane, second Earl of Westmorland's 'Fugitive Poetry' contains nineteen of Horace's odes in Latin and English, and two epodes, all decidedly Royalist.[39] But Marvell deliberately reverses Fane's Royalist Horatianism with an apparently republican poetics favouring action.

Similarities between the Ode (ll. 1–24, 113–14) and passages in Lucan's pro-republican *De bello civili* or *Pharsalia* (I, II. 144–57, 225–32, 239–43) also exist. It is clear from these examples that Marvell is not simply echoing Lucan and Thomas May's influential translation of the poem. There is a pattern of transformation in Marvell's borrowings by which the ironic structure of the

Ode is partly achieved. The treatment is a reversal of May's attitude to the uses of Roman history. May made comparisons between Rome and England in his *History of Parliament* (1647) to show how the histories of the two nations did not agree. In Marvell's poem, recollections of Horace and Lucan serve to evoke Roman responses to the ambiguities of power and right, centring on the name of Caesar. Charles I is called Caesar in the Ode (l. 23), but the context can only be his downfall (in May's *History of the Parliament*, Charles is presented as Caesar the usurper). By line 101, Cromwell has become the Julius Caesar who triumphantly overruns France, the point at which *De bello civili* begins. From this position, following the parallel with Caesar, Marvell could be seen as hinting at Cromwell's ambition for the Crown of England, an accusation made by Royalist and radical pamphleteers, and a possibility that Cromwell actively rejected in the mid-1650s. In terms of poetic models, a point of wit is made by situating Lucanic (and for that matter Lucretian) enormity inside Horatian restraint.[40] This would also chime with Marvell's interest in a poetry of the sublime, signalled by his echoes of John Hall's translation of Longinus. Longinus thought that Pindar's odes were the best sublime poems. It has been suggested that Marvell's 'elliptical account of Cromwell's career, with its sublime imagery and its long digression about Charles', may be seen also as an attempt to place a Pindaric ode inside a Horatian ode, just as Milton had been trying to locate Pindaric form inside the sonnet.[41] Marvell (and indeed Milton) in their writings from this period and later on were in fact replying to Cowley's 1647 announcement of his intention to write a Royalist sublime.[42] The energy assoc-iated with Pindaric and Lucretian poetry chimed with another important aspect of Cromwell's success. He was widely seen as an instrument of apoc-alyptic justice punishing those who had displeased God, and boasted that he was a force who would take liberty across Europe to Holland (helping the States General against the Stadholder), France (inspiring the Fronde) and Italy. In later 1650, the New Model Army was mooted as a potential support force for the Province of Holland in its dispute with the Stadholder, Willem II. Even openly Royalist publications accepted this interpretation, while other forces acknowledged by the Ode to be at work were 'fate' and 'nature'. In this respect, the poem has rightly been called a 'prophecy'.[43]

But how could Marvell have switched sides so easily? Was he in fact switching sides at all? There have always been disagreements as to how sympathetic Marvell is to Charles I, and how critical of Cromwell, in a poem that is osten-sibly one of praise. Cromwell was the 'force of angry heaven' but the regicides perfidiously claim divine backing in order to vindicate their cause. The difficulty of the Ode in this respect has made it a major example in critical debates concerned with the relative merits of internal and 'aesthetic' interpretation, and contextual or 'historical' interpretation. That Marvell's Ode should be read as a panegyric, and so be subject to rhetorical conventions, has tended to limit the more extreme speculations of earlier readings. The poem is a deliberative oration, a moderate delivery on a difficult subject, looking for possible advantages in the future. Or might we prefer a demonstrative form of encomium which shows or indicates rather than evaluates or weighs? There is the unexpected presence of the execution of Charles I exactly halfway through a panegyric on Cromwell.[44] Such a placing serves equally to point up the regicide as Cromwell's greatest achievement. Elsewhere Marvell can take a Royalist reading and turn it into a Parliamentarian one: most famously his appropriation of the story that Cromwell had tricked the King into moving to Carisbrooke Castle where he was subsequently imprisoned. These ironies rebound: was Marvell belittling Parliament by praising Cromwell in the title and not it? After all, in Marvell's verse Cromwell might be read as threatening to overawe the Parliament despite his apparent obedience to it. And would this have appealed to a republican spirit and poetry lover like Colonel Robert Overton, whom Marvell might have known in Hull in the late 1640s (see plate 10)?

These refined generic choices are the measure of Marvell's subtle understanding of both his art and the political situation. Through this complicated poetic play he could think himself into a republican mindset, a republican way of seeing things. Again, this was not untypical at the time: the new free state had to be invented and classical parallels regularly came to mind for Marvell's contemporaries. The Spanish ambassador wrote to Philip IV stating that he believed the purged Parliament and the Council of State had recreated the Roman republic.[45] It is not that Marvell was writing a political pamphlet (and the 'Ode''s circulation appears to have been strictly limited in the first instance, which, given his career, was just as well) but that the choices he made in respect of genre and imitation defined his ability to comment effectively on Cromwell's rise to power. Those who made the switch from king to republic were certainly well aware of the complexity of the issue. Nedham and Hall had both written Royalist as well as Parliamentarian journalism and both were capable of acknowledging elements of doubleness or compromise in their own positions. So it was with Marvell, who may well have written the poem for possible inclusion by Nedham in *Mercurius Politicus*. Perhaps too it was written as a presentation poem to someone powerful in the government who could help advance his career: perhaps Oliver Cromwell himself.

No doubt 'An Horatian Ode' takes its guidance from Machiavelli's *The Prince* in its consummate account of Cromwell's ambition and its constitution, and how he overcomes with 'industrious valour' (l. 33); Machiavelli's *industria* and *virtù* are the qualities required to overcome the stumbling blocks that Fortune puts in our way. It is the true prince who has the ability to 'mould' that which he inherits, to 'cast the kingdoms old/Into another mould' (ll. 35–6). Only at the end of Marvell's ode do the arts of peace intrude (at ll. 119–20), regarded as the same as the arts of war by Machiavelli. The poet himself devotes his art entirely to the demonstration of this Machiavellian vision: his muse gives way to the sublime poetry of his substantial living warrior-poet, Oliver

Cromwell. 'An Horatian Ode' is the first truly Machiavellian poem in the language even as it praises and assesses the new non-monarchical state of England.

Finally, Marvell's use of form and metre has been enthusiastically acclaimed: his ode has been hailed as one of the best, if not the best, English Horatian odes, being faithful in measure, diction and spirit. In his translations of Horace, begun in 1648 though not published until 1652, Sir Richard Fanshawe had begun to use the metre which has been called a 'remarkable thinking metre', 'an unusual pattern of pairs of rhymed four-beat and then three-beat lines, the delicate monosyllables of the second pair, the short lines, in effect undercutting the first pair'.[46] The alternate couplet lengths are antiphonal in character, as if two distinct voices were speaking. The diction is notable for the high incidence of words with a wide semantic range, always significantly deployed by Marvell, while the syntax features Latinate inversions, the two effects combining to create the famous reserved and ironic tone of the poem. The confusion or ambiguity is enhanced by grammatical openness: blast (l. 24) may be transitive or intransitive, Caesar's head subject or object; does Victory crown Cromwell or sit on his helmet (l. 98)? It is so totally fitting to the enormity of the moment:

> So restless Cromwell could not cease
> In the inglorious arts of peace,
>> But through advent'rous war
>> Urgèd his active star:
>
> And like the three-forked lightning, first
> Breaking the clouds where it was nursed,
>> Did thorough his own side
>> His fiery way divide.
>   . . .
>
> That thence the royal actor born
> The tragic scaffold might adorn,
>> While round the armèd bands
>> Did clap their bloody hands.
>
> He nothing common did, or mean,
> Upon that memorable scene;
>> But with his keener eye
>> The axe's edge did try.

                                            (ll. 9–16, 53–60)

We do not know whether Marvell took the Engagement Oath, which pledged loyalty by the taker to the new free state, but no one would have been preferred for state employment unless they had done so. The Ode is written from the position of one who has accepted the necessity of the oath, whatever their personal regrets, and by someone who was stirred by the challenge to the imagination of converting a monarchy into a republic.

Tom May

Thomas May (1599–1650), historian, poet, playwright, pamphleteer and translator, died on 13 November 1650. Marvell addressed his death soon afterwards in poetry. It was an extremely important demise in the world of letters. May's decision to follow Parliament (he was appointed its official historiographer) was not lightly forgiven by his former friends who went with the King. In the 1620s and 1630s, May had been a successful poet, playwright and translator, enjoying a considerable reputation at court. Aside from several Parliamentary pamphlets, and his *History of the Parliament of England* (1647), May was granted a licence to publish *The King's Cabinet Opened* (1645), a collection of captured royal correspondence used by Parliament to maximum propaganda effect. In his *Brief Lives*, Aubrey commented that May's 'translation of Lucan's excellent poeme made him in love with the republic, which tang stuck by him'. Elsewhere, Aubrey reported from the witness of others that, as a young man, May was 'debaucht *ad omnia*'.[47] May's poverty, mocked by Marvell in 'Tom May's Death' (l. 81), was in fact the result of unfulfilled expectations. He had been in line to inherit considerable property, but was a disappointed heir.[48] This circumstance ended May's hopes of a career in court politics, and was the main reason for his recourse to a career in letters.

Even after the Ode, Marvell could write a poem like this, a satire of a republican sympathizer. The poem is a travesty of May's views, and of the way he engaged through his poetry and his prose in public affairs. Although May was certainly partly responsible for the development of republican thought in mid-seventeenth-century England, he did not discountenance the possibility of a settlement with the King. His association with pro-Protestant foreign policy aristocrats in the 1620s places him in a tradition of belligerent anti-Catholic foreign policy stretching back to Elizabeth's reign. He was also in line with the views of prominent Parliamentary nobility in the Civil War, such as the Earl of Essex (who is compared to Brutus in May's *History*, 3.2). Only in the Latin translation of May's *Continuation* of Lucan's *De bello civili*, *Supplementum Lucani* (1640), where passages recording imperial clemency were suppressed, is genuine hostility to the monarchy registered.

The charge against May in Marvell's poem – that he has treacherously swapped sides – is only secondary. His real failing, in the eyes of the poem's main speaker, the dead Ben Jonson, is that he has alienated the true role of the poet by expressing classical republican views in partisan pamphlets and histories. This imaginative exploration of how Jonson would have read civil war and revolution literature mattered greatly to Marvell, enabling him to take further his understanding of the poet's predicament. 'Tom May's Death' understands that May's 'decline' began with the translation of Lucan's *De bello civili* or *Pharsalia* (1627), which the poem presents not as the complicatedly ambiguous epic it was for readers in the 1620s and 1630s, but very much as the reading matter of republicans and of Commonwealth supporters. It is May's *The History of the Parliament*, however, that has most offended Jonson's ghost (see ll. 71–4).

Marvell's poem pays no attention to May's own account of his developing historiography but reflects the fact that May was assumed by contemporaries to have been involved in the writing and production of Parliamentary propaganda and newsbooks. In his prefatory poem to May's translation of Lucan, Jonson had called May 'Mercury' (l. 24), but now he was assumed to be a Mercury of an undesirable sort. It could in fact be that May played a larger role in the newsbooks than is usually thought to be the case. The development of Nedham's republican views grew partly from his acquaintance with May, and May either was, or was assumed to be, responsible for the recessed republican parallels between Roman and English Civil War history that appeared in issues of *Mercurius Britanicus* and, just before May died, the early issues of *Mercurius Politicus*. Moreover, Marvell's poem gives evidence (ll. 39–46) of the alehouse meetings of republicans in the late 1640s, well witnessed in contemporary printed and manuscript sources. These were notoriously drunken, as Nedham himself admitted, and, where May was concerned, they must have appeared to Royalists as a specific perversion of Tribe of Ben tavern culture.[49]

The voice of Jonson complains against the 'Roman-cast similitudes' discussed by 'novice Statesmen', the kind of discussion of reason of state, 'interest' theory and republicanism that prevailed among journalists like May and Nedham, and gentlemen like Henry Marten, from the later 1640s onwards, and which would lead to the full-blown classical republicanism of the 1650s.[50] The evidence is scanty, but suggests that the hired pens of the Council of State, and some of the gentlemen within it or close to it, discussed and decided to project in print an image of a republic in the months leading up to May's death. In effect, some of the 'Tribe of Ben', Jonson's younger companions and admirers who kept him company in taverns during his declining years in the 1620s and 1630s, had become (in Jonson's ghost's view) anti-monarchist journalists (and desecrators of poetry) in the 1640s.

But how could Marvell have written 'Tom May's Death' so shortly after 'An Horatian Ode'? Nedham, a possible associate of Marvell's in the late 1640s, infamously changed sides and wrote both for and against the same figures and causes at different stages in his career. To write from the opposite point of view to that which one is supposed to support, or is paid to support, is entirely possible, especially among journalists. There is no reason why Marvell cannot have written 'An Horatian Ode' and then 'Tom May's Death'. Some have gone so far as to suggest that the two poems are 'companion pieces'. Those poems might be seen as 'rival experiments', 'exploring the challenges of different poetic modes both for opening alternative worlds of political connection and for their own linguistic challenges'.[51] But there are no complicated contextual relationships between 'Tom May's Death' and contingent events as there are in the Cromwell poems, 'Upon Appleton House', and the verse satires of the Restoration years. The real concern of the poem is poetry itself, and the role of the poet as a commentator on public affairs.

The poem belongs to the group of classical satirical forms put to use in the paper wars of the 1640s so decried in the verse epistle to Lovelace. In their use of the 'journey to the underworld' motif, their use of fantasy, and their dialogue form, they belong to the Lucianic tradition, given wide circulation by the northern humanists of the early sixteenth century, and in particular Erasmus, More and Rabelais. In their mixture of prose and verse, and in their combination of dialectic and fantasy, resolving matters of church and state through ridicule, they also belong to the Menippean tradition.

In the underworld of Marvell's poem, be it Elysium or Hades, the true state of the world is apparent. However much Jonson had valued May in life, and however he praised the virtue and patriotism of Roman republican heroes in his plays, his ghost revises his opinions. Once again too we see how crucial Jonson and his work were for Marvell. Behind the idea of 'the poet's time' is the idea of the poet as virtuous custodian of a community's history and honour, as voiced by the Italian humanists and instanced in Matteo Palmieri's praise of Dante.[52]

The Menippean satire to which Marvell's poem directly refers is the anonymous *The Great Assises Holden in Parnassus by Apollo and his Assessors* (1645).[53] 'Tom May's Death' takes the anxious concern with the state of poetry during the civil crisis in *The Great Assises* and uses it as a vehicle for anti-republican sentiments. Perhaps Marvell was playing an even more allusive game with the current literary scene. It has been suggested that the virtuous poet of lines 65–6 is D'Avenant, who had recently completed *Gondibert*, and was in prison on the Isle of Wight, in some danger of his life for his Royalism.[54] D'Avenant, preferred by Charles I to May as Laureate, 'laughs' in Marvell's poem to see the heavy irony of May's death as a confirmation of his self-denying Roman austerity (ll. 87–9). D'Avenant's own position was as complicated as Marvell's: he was a diehard Royalist, but *Gondibert* itself is critical of courts, and D'Avenant accepted the authority of the Commonwealth, even though *Gondibert*'s preface, and Thomas Hobbes's published reply to it, launched a distinctly anti-populist neoclassical and rational aesthetic. Marvell elsewhere appears to deride D'Avenant.

It was unconventional to have Jonson (and not a classical figure) passing judgment in a Menippean satire, and to an extent Jonson's authority is almost mocked. At the same time, Jonson's political views are made decidedly monarchical. Unlike Marvell's portrayal, Jonson's own earlier portrayal of Brutus and Cassius in *Sejanus* was as protectors of liberty. The allusion to one of Jonson's masques at the end of the poem suggests that Marvell had Jonson the court poet and entertainer in mind, not Jonson the classicist. Marvell is furthermore suggesting that had he lived through the 1640s Jonson would have substantially modified his views of classical literature and republics. Here Marvell the satirist wears a specific mask: that of Royalist Menippean.

Marvell's satire involves an acute parody at lines 21–4 of the first three lines of May's influential translation of Lucan's *De bello civili*. Self-defeat by drinking replaces civil conflict, and the heroic field of Pharsalia becomes an inn:

> Warres more then civill on Aemathian plaines
> We sing: rage licens'd; where great Rome disdaines
> In her owne bowels her victorious swords.
> (Lucan's *Pharsalia* (1626), trans. Thomas May, I. 1–3)

May's drinking also parodies the Roman republican ritual of drinking sacrificial blood, represented in the engraving on the title page of May's *A Continuation of Lucan's Historicall Poem* (1650). The fictional Jonson's voicing of the role of the true poet (ll. 65–70) is also a reversal of the real Jonson's commendatory poem to May's translation of Lucan:

> When, Rome, I read thee in thy mighty pair,
> And see both climing up the slippery stair
> Of fortunes wheel, by Lucan driven about,
> And the world in it, I begin to doubt:
> At every line some pin thereof should slack
> At least, if not the general engine crack.
> (Ben Jonson, 'To my Chosen Friend, The learned translator
> of Lucan, Thomas May, Esquire' (1627), ll. 1–6)

Marvell's poem is also notable for its detailed version of May's London: May lived at St Stephen's Alley, mentioned in line 6, or Canon Row, near King Street and Tothill Street, once the property of the Dean and Canons of St Stephen's Chapel, but the home of various noblemen and gentlemen in the seventeenth century, and notorious for its taverns. Yet these are fused with fictitious inn names – The Pope's Head . . . The Mitre (l. 7) – with Catholic and prelatical associations, thereby pointing up May's sense of irreverence. Henry Ayres, a genuine member of the Vintners' Company in the 1640s, enters the poem as a tapster at line 10. It ends with a transposed sense of masque imagery with which May as well as Jonson had once been associated. At the performance of a masque before the King and Queen by gentlemen of the Inns of Court in February 1634, the Lord Chamberlain, Philip Herbert, fourth Earl of Pembroke, broke his staff over May's shoulders, not realizing who he was (May was at this time in favour with Charles). Pembroke apologized the next day and paid May £50 in compensation. Pembroke died in 1650, and a satirical commemoration tied this event to May's later affiliations: 'To *Tom May* (whose pate I broke heretofore at a *Masque*) I give Five Shillings; I intended him more, but all that have read his *History of the Parliament* thinke *Five* shillings to[o] muche.'[55] May finally disappears: 'straight he vanished in a cloud of pitch,/Such as unto the Sabbath bears the witch.' This derives from Jonson's *The Masque of Queenes* (1609), lines 326–8: 'A cloud of pitch, a spur, and a switch,/To hast him away, and a whirlwind play/Before, and after, w'th thunder for laughter.' May's descent identifies him with the antimasque, as opposed to the masque heroes, who usually ascend heavenwards on masque machinery.

Nun Appleton

Cromwell's rise to command the New Model Army was dependent on Thomas, Lord Fairfax's resignation as commander-in-chief on 25 June 1650 (see plate 11). Fairfax had in any case been marginal to the army's political mobilization since June 1647, although he did have some success as a moderate, on the one hand reinstating MPs forced out by a Presbyterian backlash, but on the other frustrating attempts to promote radicals within the ranks. The summer of 1650 was, as we have seen, the context for the writing of 'An Horatian Ode'. Fairfax retired to his estates in Yorkshire, and set about building the future of his family. There were repairs and restorations to perform after property damage during the Civil War (especially to the York houses). It is often said that Fairfax retired to pursue his scholarly pursuits and to cultivate his garden. This is but a partial account: Fairfax had risked his family properties in the Parliamentary cause. There was much reconstruction to do; there was a daughter to educate and her marriage to settle. After all, she was Fairfax's only heir: on her future match a great deal rested. In addition to the York properties, there were three country houses with sizeable estates to be minded: Denton, the traditional seat of Thomas Fairfax's branch, where he grew up; Nun Appleton, a recently acquired property, and the projected home and dowry for his daughter Mary (see plate 12); and Bilbrough, in addition to the sequestered property on the Isle of Man acquired from the Duke of Buckingham.[56]

Marvell enters the scene late in the year; we presume he left London and travelled north to take up an appointment as Mary Fairfax's tutor, possibly after he had written 'Tom May's Death'. In all probability, northern connections were working for Marvell: the pro-Parliamentary and Puritan associations of the Hull Corporation (Fairfax had also been commander of the garrison at Hull when it was besieged by Royalist troops in 1643), the Fairfax connections in the West Riding, and the New Model Army, at last coincided. But that does not explain everything. Fairfax was a Presbyterian, his wife an enthusiastic one. Like the Presbyterians, he disapproved of the trial and execution of the King. He later claimed that he had always understood his charge as soldier and commander in the Parliamentarian cause as a Royalist act: to rescue the King from evil counsel. He did not think of himself or his family in the long term as being separated from those who fought for the King, and he would eventually play a critical role in sanctioning the Restoration. Might he already have had an interest in marrying his daughter when the time was right to a suitable heir, perhaps a returning Royalist; and might such a Royalist have been the young Duke of Buckingham, many of whose estates had fallen into Fairfax's hands as rewards from Parliament for his military service? Might therefore his chosen tutor be someone who actually knew the Duke of Buckingham, his habits and his tastes? This would have made Marvell a singularly appropriate choice, and Fairfax could have known about Marvell from literary kinsmen of his, whom it is likely that Marvell knew, such as Thomas Stanley.

The first poems Marvell wrote during his stay at Nun Appleton were two dedicatory pieces, one in Latin, one in English, for Robert Witty's (or Wittie's) translation of the French Huguenot physician James Primerose's *Popular Errours. Or the Errours of the People in Physick*. Witty's dedication is dated 30 November 1650, and his preface to the reader is signed 'From my house at Hull, Decemb. 2, 1650', so Marvell wrote his poem either in late 1650 or early 1651, but the translation had been completed years earlier, its appearance delayed by the Civil War. Witty was a Hull physician, who had been an usher in the Grammar School there between 1634 and 1642, responsible for teaching the lower forms; born in Beverley and the son of a baker, he had attended Beverley Grammar School, and had graduated from King's College, Cambridge, in 1633.[57] At Hull Grammar School he was able to borrow some medical books from the school library that enabled him to re-train as a physician. Witty was friendly with members of the Fairfax family in the Restoration;[58] it is likely that he was acquainted with them before 1660; he was practising medicine in Hull when Fairfax commanded the garrison during the siege of 1643. After treating patients in the garrison at Scarborough in 1648, he had picked up that a revolt there in favour of the King was imminent, and he rode post-haste back to Hull with the news. In East Yorkshire he was thus a Parliamentary hero of sorts. Before the Primerose translation had been printed Witty and his family moved to York, where he would prosper principally as the discoverer of the beneficial properties of Scarborough's mineral water. York was a lot closer to Nun Appleton than Hull, and so we may suppose he was no stranger to the Fairfax household. In late March 1658 Witty was called to treat a family near Nun Appleton poisoned with hemlock roots, which they had thought to be parsnips.[59] Perhaps it was Witty who recommended Marvell to Fairfax as a tutor for his daughter.

Primerose was the son of Gilbert, a Scottish divine, who had been received into the French reformed church, and had taught at Saumur (which Marvell would later visit in 1656), before he became a minister in the French church at London in the 1620s. Although admitted to the College of Physicians by Harvey, James controversially attacked the theory of the circulation of blood in a work of 1630. He published *De Vulgi in Medicina Erroribus* in Latin in 1638. Witty had translated Primerose's *The Antimoniall Cup twice cast* (1640), which

was added to the end of *Popular Errours*. In 1650 he added extra material for
Witty's translation.[60] Primerose died in Hull in 1659, and had probably been
resident there since 1634. It is highly likely that Marvell would have known
Primerose as well as Witty. Although Witty was a Presbyterian, Primerose had
been noted as a Roman Catholic in the later 1630s and it is likely that he
remained so. The collaboration between the two men is therefore unusual,
and a consequence of their shared respect for the medical profession and its
learning. Witty became the guardian of Primerose's sons after their father's
death.

While Marvell's Latin dedicatory poem addresses the contemporary issue of
publication, his English poem relates more extensively to the contents of
Popular Errours, a Galenist defence of (male) physicians against superstition,
mountebanks, empiricks, Paracelsian medicine, and the practice of popular
diagnosis and treatment by women. Such errors included the belief that the
linen of the sick ought not to be changed; that remedies ought not to be
rejected for their unpleasantness; and that gold boiled in broth will cure
consumption. The concern is emphasized by a woodcut in which an angel
holds back a woman so that a sick man can be treated by a physician. Marvell
makes reference to this image (in ll. 29–30), although the concerns of *Popular
Errours* are much broader.

Witty dedicates his translation to Frances Strickland, daughter of Thomas
Finch, Earl of Winchilsea, so that one kind of (gentle)woman is praised and
educated, while another, the female physician, is rebuked. Editors have usually
taken Marvell's reference to Celia in the poem to mean his tutee Mary Fairfax,
but there is also the possibility that he is obliquely addressing Frances
Strickland. And with good reason, because she too had married into a landed
East Yorkshire family, being the second wife of Sir William Strickland, whose
residence was at Boynton, just to the west of Bridlington.[61] Strickland was
strictly speaking an *arriviste* in the area: the family had originally come from
Lancashire in the north-west, and having been knighted in 1630, he was made
a baronet on 29 July 1641 by the King. This must have meant early support for
the King and his cause. Frances's father, the Earl of Winchilsea, was also a noted
supporter of the King. Nonetheless, Strickland was soon strongly associated
with the Parliamentary cause, and the family had had Puritan associations for
three generations; this is how he appeared as MP for Hedon in the Long
Parliament. He had also signed the Yorkshire petition presented to the King on
30 July 1640 and later took the Protestation Oath. Boynton was plundered by
Royalists in 1643 and incurred much destruction and loss of property, while
Strickland was compelled to take refuge in Hull when Scarborough declared for
the King in 1648. Strickland would represent York in both Protectorate parliaments, and was summoned by Cromwell to be part of his House of Lords. By
all accounts he was an influential, wealthy, magisterial Puritan who appeared in
markedly Puritan dress, part of the new establishment in East Yorkshire, and

someone to whom it would behove Witty (and by association Marvell) well to honour. Strickland was also very active as a committee man in Westminster, influencing legislation for the demolition of Popish monuments and the preparation of the Directory of Public Worship, and, although a Presbyterian, had not been excluded at Pride's Purge: his presence at the centre of power as a dedicatee had its uses too. Indeed in the autumn of 1650 he was most famous for having carried the news to London of Cromwell's victory at Dunbar on 3 September.

As prefatory verse to a translation, Marvell's poem is closely related to contemporary ideas and debates on translation. Although Primerose's text is medical in subject matter, Marvell treats it as if it were a poem. His paradoxical notion that the terser in English the more the Latin flourishes in translation is in opposition to the contemporary description of 'free translation' by the influential Royalist poet Sir John Denham who argued that the translator must add his own 'spirit' in order to avoid 'evaporation' in the original: 'I conceive it a vulgar error in translating Poets, to affect being *Fidus Interpres*; let that care be with them who deal in matters of Fact, or matter of Faith.'[62] But elsewhere, Marvell agrees with Denham that a translation into English should not permit the language to be corrupted or diluted by French and Italian elements or fashions.[63] He does this by mentioning 'Celia', who has been learning French and Italian, which, she says, she will treat only as adornments, remaining 'chaste' and authentically herself, howsoever she uses French or Italian wit. Here, Marvell's masterful poem, displaying far more intelligence than we might expect of a prefatory poem to a text of this kind, echoes the ending of the verse epistle to Lovelace, but instead of the horde of angry women rushing to Lovelace's defence, Marvell steps back from identifying with the women because they are criticized so much in Primerose's treatise. Primerose was as much against Paracelsian medicine as against women's remedies, so Marvell appropriately draws an analogy between translation and alchemy. In making the metal extremely shiny, polishing entirely obliterates it, just as (Paracelsian) alchemy damages base metal by vainly attempting to turn it into gold: 'To add such lustre, and so many rays,/That but to make the vessel shining, they/Much of the precious metal rub away' (ll. 10–12). This is consistent with the dispute Witty had with two 'chymists' concerning his promotion of Scarborough spa water in the 1660s.

During this time, Sir William Strickland continued organizing his estates and governing in East Yorkshire. We know that he excavated the ground under the Rudston Monolith, determining that the granite needle itself extended as far below the surface as it rose above ground and retrieving a very large number of human bones. This shows an antiquarian attitude and an interest in the material of local history that was characteristic of Fairfax; also that Strickland kept in close touch with Captain Adam Baynes, the Parliamentarian soldier and Commissioner of Leeds, who, like Sir William, profited greatly from the forfeited estates of Royalists. Meanwhile his younger brother Walter had been accruing valuable experience on the continent as Parliament's agent to the States General of the United Provinces. On 23 January 1651, Walter Strickland was chosen to accompany Oliver St John in his crucial embassy to Holland. The diplomatic aim was to construct a close alliance and negotiate political union between the two republics. The failure of the embassy was a major event in the build-up to the First Dutch War of 1652–4. A further example of Marvell's interest in exploiting these circles, whether in Yorkshire or in Westminster, is evident in his fine Latin poem, addressed to Strickland's partner in the mission, Oliver St John:

In Legationem Domini Oliveri St John ad Provincias Foederatas

> Ingeniosa viris contingunt nomina magnis,
>> Ut dubites casu vel ratione data.
> Nam sors, caeca licet, tamen est praesaga futuri;
>> Et sub fatidico nomine vera premit.
> Et tu, cui soli voluit respublica credi,
>> Foedera seu Belgis seu nova bella feras;
> Haud frustra cecidit tibi compellatio fallax,
>> Ast scriptum ancipiti nomine munus erat;
> Scilicet hoc Martis, sed pacis nuntius illo:
>> Clavibus his Jani ferrea claustra regis.
> Non opus arcanos chartis committere sensus,
>> Et varia licitos condere fraude dolos.
> Tu quoque si taceas tamen est legatio nomen
>> Et velut in scytale publica verba refert.
> Vultis Oliverum, Batavi, Sanctumve Johannem?
>> Antiochus gyro non breviore stetit.

(ll. 1–16)

On the Embassy of Lord Oliver St John
To the United Provinces

Apt names befall mighty men with the result that you would doubt whether they have been given by chance or by reason. For Fortune, although blind, nevertheless is a predictor of the future, and conceals the truth beneath a prophetic name. As for you, to whom alone the Republic wanted to be entrusted, whether you bring to the Dutch treaties or new wars, it was not in vain that this elusive encounter has befallen you; rather the duty was inscribed in your twofold name: in the latter, to be sure, messenger of war, but in the former, that of peace; by means of these keys do you rule over the iron bolts of Janus. There is no need to entrust hidden meanings to paper and to bury permitted deceptiveness in various forms of guile. Even if you too are

silent, yet your name is an embassy, and it relays official words just as in a
code. Is it Oliver or the sainted John that you want, Dutchmen? No tighter
was the circle in which Antiochus stood.

Oliver St John (?1598–1673) was Hampden's counsel during the Ship Money
crisis issue, and from 1648 Chief Justice of Common Pleas. By his first and
second marriages, he was connected with Cromwell, and by his third with
John Oxenbridge, the Puritan divine with whom Marvell would lodge in
Eton from 1653 to 1655. Of the two ambassadors, St John was regarded as the
senior partner, and was chosen not for his linguistic ability (his command of
European vernaculars was not strong), but because he was skilled in reconciling differences, especially for the sake of Protestant unity. St John's own
reluctance to accept the mission (he feared assassination; an earlier ambassador for the republic, Isaac Dorislaus, had been killed in 1649), and his
worries about the legitimacy of the republic, are of course absent from the
poem, as is the fact that Strickland was always more in favour of reconciliation
with the Dutch.

Like St John in his ambassadorial role, the poem is a committed extension of
the English republic's polity. The desired alliance was regarded by the English
government as the prelude to the union of the English and Dutch republics, the
two exemplary non-monarchical, godly, seafaring nations. The English delega-
tion arrived in the Hague on 17 March, but three months of negotiation ended
in failure. Dutch support for the alliance was partial and hindered by the power
of pro-Royalist Orange influence, despite the recent death of Willem II (the
struggle early in 1650 between Willem and the States General of Holland had
exerted an influence on English politics, with Orangists summoning Royalist
support, and the States General seeking military assistance from the New
Model Army). In late April, St John arranged for the ambassadors to be recalled.
By the summer of the following year, the two nations would be at war. Marvell's
comment, 'whether you bring to the Dutch treaties or new wars' (l. 6), is thus
remarkably prescient and quite at odds with available public information in
early 1651. We may reasonably infer that Marvell was party to information
limited to the circles of government; more than that, Marvell had a 'strong
awareness of the ideological stakes' of the mission.[64]

The poem has been thought to have been written in order for Marvell to win
employment with the new government; or perhaps he was already in its employ.
Its sentiments are undoubtedly republican and apocalyptic, reflecting Marvell's
connections just before he left London for Yorkshire. It has been suggested that
the poem also expresses (in its instances of images of peace and war) the poet's
anxieties concerning his commitment to the new regime and the dangers it might
hold for him.[65]

Can we speculate further? Is it possible that the poem was successful in its
probable attempt to win Marvell employment? Did he disappear to Westminster

in the early months of 1651 to help with the processing and translation of diplomatic correspondence? Or did he do this in Holland: was he active as a secretary there, or even as a spy? Thomas Scot was the spymaster in these years, and in his records there is no mention of Marvell as an employee: he derived his news about the United Provinces from 'Colonel Riley'.[66] But perhaps Marvell could have worked directly for St John and Strickland and would have sailed directly from Bridlington or Hull for Holland (see plates 13 and 14).

We should note that the poem connects Marvell with St John rather than Strickland, as might be expected. A further hypothesis is that Marvell wrote it later rather than earlier, after the initial optimistic negotiations with the Dutch had soured, and when war seemed likely.[67] This might suggest that Marvell had gone to Holland as part of the large diplomatic retinue, indeed perhaps as one of St John's party, and that he was working for the secretary of the embassy, John Thurloe, his future superior in the Protectorate government. This would make Marvell's arrival in Yorkshire later than has been supposed, so that he would have written several poems with Yorkshire connections from London or abroad.

Back at Nun Appleton, the daily routine of Marvell's life as tutor would have included hours to teach Mary, as well as unspecified but extensive time to talk with Fairfax himself, especially about matters of common interest, including poetry. The evidence in Marvell's Fairfax poetry is that patron and poet did talk to each other, and must have exchanged poems. How, then, did Marvell come to write his masterpiece 'Upon Appleton House'? For dates of composition, several allusions to recently published works provide the *terminus a quo*, in particular Robert Waring's dedicatory poem to William Cartwright's *Poems, Plays and Miscellanies*, dated by the bookseller Thomason 23 June. It has also been argued that a series of references to agricultural activity, Fairfax's movements, and public affairs (especially a series of threats to the fledgling 'free state'), associate the poem with the summer months of July and August 1651.[68]

Although the substantial house designed by John Webb and built by Lord Fairfax at Nun Appleton was once generally regarded as the house in Marvell's poem, it is now argued that Marvell was in fact referring to the much smaller dwelling built out of the nunnery and standing next to the ruined church.[69] This makes sense of the references in the poem itself (ll. 71–4, 87–8). Fairfax did not build the larger house until after 1650 (as opposed to the earlier dating of 1637–50), and he did so in order to enhance his daughter's dowry. The reference to the grand intentions of the 'foreign architect' in stanzas 1–3 suggests that Fairfax was planning the new house at this time, or perhaps even beginning work on the renovation, and that Marvell knew of this. Indeed, the poem may be read as responding to the architectural transformation of the house, with Fairfax making use of a stone quarry in 1652 at nearby Tadcaster; comparing the view on the estate to masque scenery fits with Webb's experience, since he had helped Inigo Jones design the Masquing House at Whitehall and masque scenery, notably for D'Avenant's *Salmacida Spolia* (1640).[70] Although the subject of the poem is the house at Nun Appleton, details of other Fairfax residences and estates, especially Denton, find their way into the poem.

The poem is, in the fullest sense, the product of a patronage relationship, and is quite unlike the published panegyrics that still praised Fairfax's martial heroism even after his retirement.[71] Marvell deals in depth with many aspects of Fairfax's antiquarian and literary interests, and the place of the Fairfax family in history. There are several allusions to and uses of texts that were in Lord Fairfax's library, from the poetic to the contemplative and occult. Marvell's poem is also related to the verse that was produced by other members of the Fairfax family in this period. The poet seems happy in this rural landscape. It might be part and parcel of epideixis to exude happiness, unlike the guardedness of most of his major public poems, but the speaker's joyful and reverential tone seems genuine.

The poem is regarded as advice to Fairfax not to indulge excessively in meditative, and possibly enthusiastic, interests that would go against the public standards of the Commonwealth (but others doubt whether a hired tutor would be in any position to give advice or criticism).[72] Although Fairfax was no supporter of extreme radicalism, he had succeeded in having appointed many hard-line Puritans as officers at the formation of the New Model Army in 1645, and his treatment of the Diggers in 1649 was moderate. Despite the easy retirement that the poem appears to offer, the north of England in 1651 experienced a most uneasy peace, with the enduring threat of a Royalist rising, and further Leveller insurgency against enclosure just to the east of the Fairfax estates. With the threatened invasion of a Scottish army at this time, the Council of State turned to Fairfax for his active participation, since the situation was now the one in which Fairfax had said he was ready to take up arms before he resigned. Fairfax's dilemma was whether he should take up arms for an uncertain cause, before the survival of the Commonwealth was guaranteed by its victory at Worcester on 3 September 1651. The choices facing Fairfax in the summer of 1651 are mapped on to the experiences and expressions of the various characters in the poem, but Marvell respects Fairfax's judgement by expressing no final viewpoint in the voice of the poem's narrator.

There is nonetheless no explicit reference to public events involving Fairfax in the period immediately preceding the poem's composition, and frankly no reason for them to be included. Marvell makes no reference to the fracas in which one of Fairfax's cousins was involved, in early April 1651, while representing the republic in Holland. These facts should have been known to Marvell through the extensive newsbook and pamphlet collection being assembled by Fairfax.

Just as the Fairfaxes were very interested in their family history, so that history is registered in the poem. Marvell settled into Nun Appleton life and it enclosed him. It has been suggested that the apparent invention of William Fairfax's rescue of Isabel Thwaites, with legal right on his side, may have functioned as an explanation designed to deter the fear that those who occupied former monasteries committed sacrilege.[73] Some country house poems explicitly praised those who avoided the re-use of monastic fabric (e.g. Robert Herrick in 'A Panegyrick to Sir Lewis Pemberton' (1648), l. 127). Fairfax employed the important antiquarian Roger Dodsworth (1585–1654) to copy and preserve manuscripts in York both before and after the siege there in 1644, and he was rewarded when a very large collection of Dodsworth's manuscripts came into his possession.[74] Fairfax's own interest in medieval learning (he possessed manuscripts that may have belonged to Isabel Thwaites) is reflected in the early part of Marvell's poem. Elsewhere, Marvell appears to take elements of local medievalism, and shows (as he does in other poems) how they have been positively transformed in the post-Reformation age.

The impeccably Protestant heritage presented in this history of the Fairfax family, and the anti-episcopal reference at lines 363–6 (there is a scarcely disguised reference to the 'ambitious' Archbishop of York John Williams who had fortified his residence, Cawood Castle), chimed with Fairfax's Presbyterianism and, more so, that of his wife. Noting the absence of Lady Fairfax by name – she is present only three times in the poem – it has been contended that Prioress Langton in the poem is a representation of the strong-willed wife of the Lord General.[75] She interrupted from the public gallery during the trial of the King, was in contact with Presbyterian Royalists, and seems to have successfully pressured her husband to resign his command in June 1650. A Roman Catholic allegory for intra-marital Protestant politics in the Reformation period of the sixteenth century was an appropriate way for Marvell to distance Fairfax from his wife's dangerous activities, while not drawing disapproval from Lady Fairfax herself. June 1651 saw the trial and execution of Christopher Love, a Presbyterian minister found guilty of conspiring with the Royalists. Perhaps too the poem contains a veiled reference to a pitiful chain of events involving a Catholic branch of the Fairfax family.[76]

The contact with Fairfax, and with his learned kinsmen in the district, such as Henry Fairfax, Rector of the parish of Bolton Percy, provided every opportunity to sharpen the literary endeavour that was now bearing fruit in such an ambitious way. After the city and its distractions, there would have been plenty of time to focus on literary gains of the last few years, and to assimilate them into his verse. There is no greater example of this than 'Upon Appleton House' itself and its construction. In it Marvell finally establishes his poetic identity and ruminates on his life's achievements thus far. Poems on country houses and estates stem from classical verse: on the one hand the praise of humble retreats in Horace and Martial, and on the other, the grand architecture acknowledged by Statius and Sidonius Apollinaris. The vogue, however, caught on in a serious way in the seventeenth century.[77] Marvell's poem is unusual and innovative in a number of ways: the indistinctness of the description of both house and estate, the presence of an observing persona, and its sheer length. His demonstration of his mastery of the genre's repertoire is signalled by the exhaustive range of possibilities, from park poem, to retirement and digressive observation.

'Upon Appleton House' is also a 'prospect' poem, another new and fashionable genre, popularized by Sir John Denham's *Cooper's Hill* (1641/2) and influenced by developments in landscape painting. Prospective poetry exploited the illusions presented to the viewer by landscapes, and derived social and political commentary from views. Although Marvell's poem deals with the history of the Fairfax family, as Denham's uses landscape as an opportunity to meditate upon English royal family history, Marvell is more concerned with illusion and the eye's survey of the Nun Appleton estate (e.g. sts XI, LVIII).

We may never know the precise nature and extent of their interaction, and whether Fairfax's verse influenced Marvell's, or vice versa, or both. What is clear is that 'Upon Appleton House' is full of echoes and reworking of some Fairfax poems, in particular his translation of Saint Amant's 'La Solitude' (1625; see l. 495), no doubt intended as a compliment. Fairfax's translation replicates Saint Amant's vivid interest in ruins and the quarries from which the rocks came, and their representation of an absolute retirement. For Marvell, ruins (ll. 87–9) are not the objects of contemplation but the occasion of the narrative of William Fairfax's rescue of Isabel Thwaites from the nuns – a small Gothic fiction. Other Fairfax poems reveal an interest in creation and perspective similar to that of 'Upon Appleton House'; for instance 'Wisdomes Antiquity': 'Whilst yet the earth unframed was,/ . . . I was, and when I wisely set/ The Hanging clouds I (th'Architect)/Gave to the sea itt circled shore'.[78] Marvell was also replying to Sir William D'Avenant's recently published heroic poem *Gondibert* (1651), with its pretentious claim to produce epic literature on subjects distanced from the present time, its grand claim for poetry as high architecture, its preference for books (as opposed to the book of nature), and the influence in its preface of Hobbes's psychological and political theories (see ll. 3, 20, 355–6).[79]

When it was a nunnery, Appleton House contained one of the most important scriptoria in England. Into Fairfax's library went some treasures of medieval manuscript literature, and a host of lesser but valuable handwritten books. There are some elements of medieval and pre-Reformation vocabulary and literature in the poem. Although *The Pricke of Conscience* is not among the surviving Fairfax manuscripts (unlike poetry by Chaucer, Gower and the *Cursor Mundi*), it was a popular text in Yorkshire monasteries and nunneries. The successive comparisons of the world as sea, wilderness, forest and battlefield in the second book of *The Pricke* (see ll. 1212–56) is comparable to Marvell's similes and metaphors in the poem; where *The Pricke* points to mortification, Marvell is concerned to demonstrate the potential for man's regeneration through contact with the natural world (see ll. 355, 568).

However, the text most fundamentally behind the poem, and the source of many individual episodes and phrases, is the Bible. The narrative is founded upon a series of carefully deployed allusions to and echoes of biblical language, from a variety of books, though largely Genesis and, secondarily, Revelation. Again, this was a compliment: Fairfax's own reverence for Scripture is attested by his nephew Brian Fairfax: 'He red diviner things then Druids knew,/ Such mistery's were then reveald to few,/ For his Chiefe study was Gods sacred Law,/ And all his Life did Comments on it draw'.[80]

So much for the context of this extraordinary, joy-giving poem. What of the poet and the character of the poet here? The closeness of the poet to the subject of his praise, despite his invisibility is evident, perhaps the most so in the witty rhymes. In his praise of Cromwell Marvell would later claim that he could only 'echo far behind' the Lord Protector, but with Fairfax in retirement, he 'echoes' in the sense of appearing as a retainer who understands how best to present his master to the world. That praise is then enhanced by the dimensions of the poet's mind, as he is able to see the startling transformation of perspectives that come across his mind's eye when he views different parts of the estate. The reader begins to sense how remarkable this is: 'The scene again withdrawing brings/A new and empty face of things' (ll. 441–2). A distinct 'I' of the poet emerges at line 521, a persona who takes delight in the pleasurable sadness of warbling pigeons, whose 'moaning' is 'mourning' (ll. 526–7), an apparent unhappiness despite the fact that the birds have evident mates. This perspective frees the speaker from worldly cares, 'I careless' deeply lost in Nun Appleton's nature. He becomes the Hermetic magus, 'I, easy philosopher,/ Among the birds and trees confer', and in such discourse can begin to fly, 'floating on the air' (ll. 561–2, 566). Not only does he enjoy union with nature, he also begins to resemble the symbols belonging to the wisdom of books on the natural world, and so, as in the commonplace that a mandrake plant looks like an upside-down man, he the speaker looks like 'an inverted tree' (l. 568).

Through the fantasy afforded by imagining himself as a magus Marvell can indulge himself in a version of that which he would never be: a senior clergyman, a bishop even, 'some great prelate of the grove', covered in oak leaves, ivy and caterpillars. The utter ease of finding rest by reclining on the velvet moss is most arresting, 'languishing with ease' as the wind blows his thoughts away. Finally, in retreat and repose there is a real self with a rich inner life. No passions can touch this figure – the arrows of love miss their mark or are deflected by the trees. It is here that the poet is enchained by plants, and, in the evening at the riverbanks, asked that he be staked out like a sacrifice left to drown with the rising tide. But in the poem's narrative he survives the drowning to make the comparison of the Wharfe with the Nile, and to offer his final identity in leisured retreat and pleasure as an angler, before the apparition of Mary Fairfax utterly dominates our attention in the poem. Before this moment, it is unclear whether anyone knows who is who in this primal world of entirely self-sufficient natural coexistence. Even the sun:

> ... its yet muddy back doth lick,
> Till as a crystal mirror slick;
> Where all things gaze themselves, and doubt
> If they be in it or without.

(ll. 635–8)

Such is Marvell's assessment of himself and his art, as he praises Mary Fairfax and her father. And these long sections where the mutual reflection of objects erases identity tells us much of Marvell's sense of himself as a poet. Not for him vatic or architectonic ego: just as his speaker disappears in the landscape, so he is unperceived as poet. He is but a servant and the poem is not circulating, either in manuscript or in print. For all its courage and originality it is an entirely private piece; its call to poetic virtue against the grandiose claims of D'Avenant goes almost entirely unnoticed.

Two other Fairfax locations became the subjects of a pair of poems, one in Latin, the other in English. The first is severely classical and addresses Almscliff Crag as well as Bilbrough. Marvell treats these markers of Fairfax country as the two pillars of Hercules (imagined as Fairfax himself) that were believed to straddle the straits of Gibraltar and mark the known extent of the world and of knowledge (the Rock of Gibraltar itself, and either Mount Acha or Jebel Musa, near Ceuta, Morocco). The poem echoes Lucretius' insistence in *De rerum natura* that one should understand as well as see. Almscliff Crag lies sixteen miles west of Bilbrough Hill across the floodplain of the River Wharfe. The major Fairfax residence of Denton lay a further nine miles upstream to the west. Bilbrough itself is five miles north of Nun Appleton. Where Almscliff is imposingly high, Bilbrough rises just 145 feet above sea level, albeit from a level plain. In Marvell's day the quarrying that would further flatten the hill had not taken place, and there were still trees on its summit. It is a symmetrical and smooth mound formed from glacial action: hence in every sense its gentleness.

Bilbrough itself was another Fairfax house, purchased by Sir William Fairfax in 1546 and the residence of Fairfax's great-grandfather, also called Sir Thomas (d. 1599). The poem might be regarded as a coda to 'Upon Appleton House' and where that larger poem ends with the praise of Lord Fairfax's daughter, this one includes the wooing of Lady Fairfax by her future husband. Did Marvell know the affection that Lady Fairfax held for the house at Bilbrough? In the church at Bilbrough she would be interred in 1665 and her husband would follow her in 1672. Marvell's poem is both mountain poem and grove poem, each examples of retirement poetry: a notable group in classical verse. The two trees named in the poem connote martial valour (ash) and sacredness (oak). The highest place guarantees the best-quality wood, and the most sacred kind of grove, the best place for retirement, meditation and contemplation. But Marvell eschews the strong association of groves with Royalism in the period made in a number of influential publications and later enforced by Charles II's escape after the Battle of Worcester by hiding in an oak tree.

Near the end of this poem in which the subject of praise, Lord Fairfax and his wooded hill, command undivided attention, the 'echoing' voice of the poet enters in a more personal way as the trees of the grove 'speak', whispering in the wind their knowledge of Fairfax's time among the forests of pikes and the mountains of dead soldiers. The phrases anticipate those that Marvell would use in 'The Garden', and it seems that the poet is making good a boast in 'Upon Appleton House' that he would, as it were, rather be a tree. The mountains of dead men in fact refers back to the elegy on Villiers, when Marvell's speaker vows to take revenge for Villiers's death in a poem where the speaker notices that the reader would like him to report the deaths of both Cromwell and Fairfax. 'But until then' he says; it did not happen and Fairfax would die peacefully in his bed at home although not on the same estate where Marvell had imagined himself one of the trees timelessly bearing witness to his hero patron.

Towards the end of his stay at Nun Appleton, Marvell wrote a poem on the daughter of an acquaintance living at Thornton Curtis, Lincolnshire, just south of the Humber. The poem was 'The Picture of Little T.C. in a Prospect of Flowers', the daughter Theophila Cornewell, aged between six and eight; her parents were Humphrey and Theophila, the latter a member of the Skinner family, known to both Marvell and Milton. The poem is a spectacular exercise in the suspension of sexual desire, even as the future sexual maturity of the girl is the unavoidable subject. Poems dealing with infant charm and future love embroilment go back to Greek lyrics; what is notable in Marvell's poem is the shock tactic of so many combined arresting poetic motifs – pastoral, *carpe florem*, *carpe diem*, triumph, prophecy, ekphrasis (including a fashion in portraiture where the subject is painted within a floral border), the Golden Age – coming together in a poetic space of suspended reflection. That might well have been entirely appropriate for a family who had already lost another daughter called Theophila as an infant, in 1643. A companion piece for 'To his Coy Mistress' or the praise of Mary Fairfax in 'Upon Appleton House', as well as a presentation piece for the Cornewell family, the poem brings into play the voyeurism of the poet-speaker, introducing a form of sexual desire that seems improper – that of older man for girl child – only to acknowledge that such desire is at a distance, at best in the realm of play, and in this case, the poet will die first; when Theophila reaches the height of her powers, he will most probably be dead. In all of this, what comes through as abundantly renewed is poetry itself.

We could say the same for the mower poems, at least three of the four being dated to these years: in these unusually dark pastorals the despair wrought on the mower by the cruel Juliana serves as a focal point to express the most uneasy sense of dislocation of this troubled period.[81] 'Damon the Mower''s keen visceral sense of living and working in the heat of a hot summer in communion with grasshoppers, frogs, snakes, dogs and chameleons, is vitiated by Juliana's wounding presence, and only death will cure it. There is the progressively darker 'The Mower to the Glow-worms', a single sentence that withholds its main verb until the final stanza, and where the vocabulary matches simplicity and sophistication:

> III
> Ye glow-worms, whose officious flame
> To wand'ring mowers shows the way,
> That in the night have lost their aim,
> And after foolish fires do stray;
>
> IV
> Your courteous lights in vain you waste,
> Since Juliana here is come,
> For she my mind hath so displaced
> That I shall never find my home.
>
> (ll. 9–16)

The vengeful alienation of 'The Mower's Song' is a fitting conclusion to one of Marvell's most accomplished imaginative projections:

> . . . ye meadows, which have been
> Companions of my thoughts more green,
> Shall now the heraldry become
> With which I shall adorn my tomb;
> For Juliana comes, and she
> What I do to the grass, does to my thoughts and me.
>
> (ll. 25–30)

And that's what Marvell had done by the end of 1652: he had renovated the grounds of English poetry. He had ridden the crest of post-regicidal lament, and certainly his verse had engaged in it, but more remarkably his poetry had remained apart, intact, following its own trajectory, because it had dared to face the future. The only problem was that hardly anyone, if anyone at all, could see this in his own time. We may doubt that any single person saw the collection of poems discussed here as one group. That laudatory assessment of his poetic achievements would have to begin in a distant future. No wonder there is a scarcely concealed grudge and even hostility towards the poets who did have fame: D'Avenant and Cowley in particular. Did he keep a book of poems at this time and try to publish it? And if not, why not? Is this how his great posthumous miscellaneous collection of 1681 began life?

CHAPTER 5

✳

THE TUTOR

IN PURSUIT OF EMPLOYMENT

MARVELL LEFT THE FAIRFAX household some time in 1652; perhaps in the spring or summer of the year. Once again, he was in pursuit of employment and probably to that end he kept company with influential people, such as the fashionable and popular George Colt and his wife Elizabeth, Adrian Scroop and John Spencer.[1] It was a world that was much changed from the turbulent and uncertain days following the execution of the King and the first year of the republic. There had been some settling of loyalties to the new state and several former Royalists had compounded. The literary and journalistic scene had proceeded apace, with Milton, Nedham and Hall driving at a coherent, educative and persuasive communication of the ideals and possibilities of republican culture, notably in the newsbook *Mercurius Politicus*.[2]

How Marvell maintained himself during this period is not known. Perhaps he had saved some funds from his stay with Fairfax. It would seem that he had some time for leisure in these days, since he wrote some of his greatest, best-remembered verse.[3] We are talking about nothing less than his most famous lyric 'To His Coy Mistress':

To His Coy Mistress

Had we but world enough, and time,
This coyness lady were no crime.
We would sit down, and think which way
To walk, and pass our long love's day.
Thou by the Indian Ganges' side
Shouldst rubies find: I by the tide
Of Humber would complain. I would
Love you ten years before the flood:
And you should, if you please, refuse

Till the conversion of the Jews.
My vegetable love should grow
Vaster than empires, and more slow.
An hundred years should go to praise
Thine eyes, and on thy forehead gaze.
Two hundred to adore each breast:
But thirty thousand to the rest.
An age at least to every part,
And the last age should show your heart.
For Lady you deserve this state;
Nor would I love at lower rate.
   But at my back I always hear
Time's wingèd chariot hurrying near:
And yonder all before us lie
Deserts of vast eternity.
Thy beauty shall no more be found;
Nor, in thy marble vault, shall sound
My echoing song: then worms shall try
That long preserved virginity:
And your quaint honour turn to dust;
And into ashes all my lust.
The grave's a fine and private place,
But none I think do there embrace.
   Now, therefore, while the youthful glew
Sits on thy skin like morning dew,
And while thy willing soul transpires
At every pore with instant fires,
Now let us sport us while we may;
And now, like am'rous birds of prey,
Rather at once our Time devour,
Than languish in his slow-chapped power.
Let us roll all our strength, and all
Our sweetness, up into one ball:
And tear our pleasures with rough strife,
Thorough the iron gates of life.
Thus, though we cannot make our sun
Stand still, yet we will make him run.

The poem has been seen as broadly in the tradition of Latin love elegy, pre- and post-Ovidian. More precisely, the poem is an example (almost to a self-parodic degree) of the *carpe diem* motif, most famously exemplified in Catullus's much-imitated fifth poem 'Vivamus, mea Lesbia, atque amemus' (Let us live, my Lesbia, and love). The coy mistress has been associated with the *castas puellas* ('decent girls') of another Latin elegist, Propertius (*Elegies*, I.i.5).[4] Within this structure come a series of allusions to the Greek and Latin erotic lyric tradition, the epigram, echoes of Lucretius's *De rerum natura*, and a more concrete set of local echoes to English poems (and, less frequently, plays) in or near this tradition, many of them circulated or published in the later 1640s and 1650s, in addition to echoes from the service for the Burial of the Dead in the Book of Common Prayer.

It has been argued that this 'parodic deconstruction of a cluster of inherited literary forms – the lover's complaint, the blazon, the *carpe diem* exercise' – transcends the limitations of these forms and their clichés to produce a 'radically new, outspoken, and vigorous evocation of sexual intimacy.'[5] Elsewhere, this effect has been described as 'literally, an expansion', pushing time, space and the abilities of praise poetry beyond its customary limits.[6] The poem thus refers to a tradition of coyness, in the sense of an exceeding of Protestant teaching on the marital sexual 'mean', the reconciliation of the two extremes in Herrick, and the case for a feminine exception in Philips.[7]

Then again, the poem relates to the *ars moriendi* tradition, with the sensuous depiction of death, the three-part formula encompassing past, present and future, and the speed of the moment of death as components therein. But a hint too of the Epicurean philosophy of living for the moment has been detected in the poem. The *carpe diem* motif was used by continental Epicureans, such as Montaigne, from the late sixteenth century onwards. The poem is, in that view, a very serious parody (from a Puritan point of view) of Epicurean beliefs, then prevalent at the exiled court in Paris and made public by Royalists, for example by Cowley in *The Mistress* (1647).[8] Thus 'vegetable' (l. 11) means 'plantlike' or 'treelike', characterized by slow, steady growth (in the Aristotelian scheme of vegetative, sensitive and rational souls, the first characterized only by growth) as in Lord Herbert of Cherbury's 'You well compacted groves': 'Pleasure of such a kind, as truly is/A self-renewing vegetable bliss'. But 'My vegetable love' carries another sense: if 'vegetable' is regarded (in witty terms) as a metaphorical noun, as well as an adjective, the phrase implies a long, slow erection of the penis. Epicureans thought that plants could love in the same way as humans.[9] Yet Epicurean beliefs are also undermined by being placed ironically alongside Providentialist references (e.g. ll. 29–30, 45–6). Images from Cowley are combined to rebut Epicureanism with exaggeratedly expressed Christian teachings concerning mortality (l. 24): Cowley is under attack. The reference to human desire as animalistic (l. 38) is also Epicurean: Marvell's representation is seen as ironically self-defeating at the speaker's expense, who is presented as an Epicurean with no knowledge of the realm of grace. A further important image of death is at line 24, 'Deserts of vast eternity', notable for its exclusion of any idea of romantic or theological afterlife. The classical source behind all the English, seventeenth-century versions may be Lucretius, *De rerum natura*, 1.1103: 'deffugiant subito magnum per inane soluta' (space without end or limit lies open to us in all directions).

Yet the poem alludes to the contemporary millenarian sense that the Second Coming of Christ was imminent. The 'conversion of the Jews' referred to the conjunction of the deluge and the conversion of the Jews (supposed to presage the millennium). As Zachary Crofton explained: 'There is an argument for it, it is analogical. It was in 1656 [BC], the flood came on the old world, and lasted fourty daies. Ergo in that year 1656 fire must come on this world and last fourty years.'[10] Millenarian ideas were popular among mid-seventeenth-century Puritans and negotiations were begun in the 1650s between the Commonwealth government and the Jews of Amsterdam in the hope that the return of the Jews to England would help bring on the millennium.

A significant identity issue is signalled when the male speaker of Marvell's poem is voicing Ovid's echo (hence the wordplay at line 27), and that the mistress corresponds to Narcissus (both are proud 'that neither youth nor Mayden' might them touch).[11] Paul Hammond notes the presence of vocabulary and thematic echoes from the Narcissus episode in Arthur Golding's earlier translation of Ovid's *Metamorphoses*. These comparisons are enhanced by further echoes of Ovid's Latin and of Renaissance commentaries on Ovid. Marvell may also have been attracted by finding his name in Latin three times in the Latin ('miratur . . . mirabilis . . . mirantia', *Metamorphoses*, 3.424, 503). Hammond argues that 'there are sufficient traces of the Narcissus story in Marvell's text to suggest that when he composed this poem about desire for a woman, Marvell's imagination was dwelling on other forms of desire'.[12]

Several commentators have seen the structure of the tripartite logical syllogism in the poem. Some have regarded the poem as one that out-Donnes Donne in its continuous argument, its rigidly syllogistic structure and its 'essentially dramatic tone'.[13] It has been argued that not the formal syllogism, but another kind of logical argument, the *reductio ad absurdum*, and a travesty of it, is present.[14] The conclusion that lust must be satisfied is fallacious, built on top of the opening proposition, 'Had we but world enough' and the acknowledgement of the foreshortening of time. Thus, the poem succeeds through a 'contrived collision between its emotional impulse and its purported form'. So, Marvell 'uses logic and illogic to disturb stereotypes, expose assumptions, and test the use of reason itself'.[15] In this way, the mistress is compelled not to think of her honour but to see that the only response to the claim of death is to seize life in a culminating moment of sexual fulfilment.

The tone of the speaker is crucial to the interpretation of the poem, but the images are deceptive in their apparently changing direction. The speaker reserves the indirectly named lower parts (including the genitalia) for the greatest praise, but then devotes better time (the 'last age', the millennium itself) to his mistress's heart. Elsewhere, conceptual opposites are used with pointed effect: not only is a very long lifetime (ll. 1–20) contrasted with the absence of time because of death, but vast space and distance (ll. 5–7) and absolute open space (l. 24) are contrasted with the confinement of the burial vault (l. 26).

All of the these meanings are finally brought together in the poem's climax, 'And tear our pleasures with rough strife,/ Thorough the iron gates of life' (ll. 43–4). The sense of the gates as the threshold between this world and the next is enforced by Horace, *Carmina*, 3.27.41, when Europa wonders whether she is awake or visited in a dream by a phantom that has flown through the *porta eburna* (ivory gate). The 'gates of life' are an inversion of the gates of death (Ps. 9: 13: 'thou that liftest me up from the gates of death'), which were iron: this is taken to be an image of the Harrowing of Hell; as well as 'For he hath broken the gates of brass, and cut the bars of iron in sunder'; Lucretius, *De rerum natura*, 1.415: 'vitai claustra resolvat' (open the gates of life [i.e. 'die']). And there is also the presence of the Book of Common Prayer's Collect for Easter Day: 'Almighty God, Who through Thine only begotten Son Jesus Christ has overcome death, and opened unto us the gate of everlasting life'. Marvell's echo of the Prayer Book is a parody of the Christian doctrine of resurrection: death is overcome not by resurrection in the afterlife but by life.[16] This was probably meant in an ironic way: the speaker thinks that lust will be rewarded with more pleasure in life; the Christian knows that the wages of sin (i.e. lust) are death.[17]

Perhaps such a richly allusive achievement gave him confidence when he finally met Milton for the first time in early 1653. The testimony of Marvell senior's patroness, Anne Sadleir, that Marvell had met Milton by 1649, and had helped him complete *Eikonoklastes* on account of the elder poet's blindness, is groundless, a post-regicide slur and possibly a confusion of Marvell and Milton's collaboration in 1653 or 1654.[18] Milton was not completely blind in 1649–50, and Marvell was otherwise occupied, perhaps completely differently disposed in opinion. It may be that Milton had already read Marvell, since it seems that his sonnet 'To the Lord General Cromwell', written in May 1652, contains a strong echo of 'An Horatian Ode'.[19] Now on 21 February 1653, Milton wrote to John Bradshaw, President of the Council of State, suggesting that Marvell become his assistant, in place of the German poet, Georg Weckherlin, who had died the previous week.[20] Milton hoped that Marvell, with his skills in modern languages and also his knowledge of the ancients, might become as useful to the state as Anthony Ascham, the remarkable political theorist who had been assassinated during his stay in Spain as Resident at Madrid. Was Milton trying to dispel any worries about Marvell's previous connections by saying that he was of an 'approved conversation'? To say that this was because he had lately come from Fairfax's household must stress religion rather than politics: Fairfax's difficulty with the regicide and the foreign policy of the republic must have been well known to Bradshaw. Milton also noted that it would be natural out of jealousy and 'aemulation' of Marvell's talents not to recommend him, and this is of course an echo of line 18 in Marvell's Ode, further proof that Milton was already tuned into Marvell's poetic powers.

It may be that Marvell wrote his impressive verse satire 'The Character of Holland' in order to impress Milton, or Bradshaw (possibly at Milton's suggestion). The former is more likely, since the poem is so full of Miltonic echoes. It would seem that the two men had recently met and the avenue to Milton could well have been opened by Marvell's erstwhile associates, Nedham and Hall. Milton's sense of Marvell's worth, and awareness that he was suited to be more than a secretary, are strongly affirmed: 'of singular desert for y^e: state to make use of . . . it would be hard for them to find a Man soe fit in every for y^t purpose as this Gentleman'. Although blind, Milton must have discerned the worth of Marvell's mind in his conversation and, in all probability, in hearing his verse. No doubt Marvell put on a good show, but it is hard to believe that Milton failed to understand someone of a different mind, someone not so ideologically committed as himself.

Marvell's poem celebrates English success in the First Dutch War (1652–54) which came during the winter of 1653, after eight months of indecision and occasional Dutch supremacy. On 26 November 1652, Robert Blake, George Monck and Richard Deane were appointed to command a reformed English fleet after complaints of inefficiency and cowardice. The Three Days Battle of 18–20 February 1653 was a notable success for the Commonwealth and Marvell's poem marks this event. There was a further series of victories for the British in this war, though none was quite so decisive.

As we know, Marvell had travelled in Holland during the 1640s, but whilst some of the details in the poem no doubt have their roots in personal observation derived from this tour, others were derived from publications concerned with the Dutch.

Rivalry between the English and the Dutch, largely of an economic nature, was no new matter in the 1650s. As early as 1608 James I challenged the right of the Dutch to fish freely for herring in what he claimed were English waters. Despite the genuine similarities and mutual sympathy between Dutch religion and politics and the practices of those who were gaining the upper hand in England in the 1640s, godly zeal also enhanced aggressive mercantilism in England.[21] Many merchants had Puritan leanings, and the 1640s saw a campaign in press and Parliament by a broad spectrum of interests to find a means of breaking Dutch trading pre-eminence, by force of arms if necessary. In 1649, the new republic, Cromwell in particular, sought security in a proposed 'alliance and union' with the Dutch, which would also help to silence Royalist refugees in exile. The Dutch, bewildered at first, were not prepared to compromise their own independence, in politics and trade, and the negotiations failed. As we have seen, the two British ambassadors sent to the Hague, St John and Strickland, were reputedly abused, especially by English Royalists and their sympathizers in Holland. They returned, insulted and angry, while the mercantile polemics in England grew.

The legal consequence of the failure of the alliance plan was the 1651 Navigation Act, which prohibited the import of goods to England in any vessel other than that of the country of origin of the goods, or of England. The

valuable trade in carrying was denied to the Dutch. In addition, the Act
insisted that the Dutch offer a deferential salute to English vessels when
encountering them in waters where English sovereignty was claimed.

Economic motives should not, however, be over-stressed. Thought to be
fellow travellers in the cause of Reformation and in trade, the Dutch were
revealed as false brethren when they eventually refused the alliance. Some
Dutch statesmen regarded English enmity as caused by the very existence
of their republic, and its prosperity. Lacking in ingenuity, the English, they
thought, were forced to resort to legal intimidation and naval thuggery to
plunder the fruits of Dutch success.

None of this information quite prepares us for 'The Character of Holland',
with its remarkable sense of instability – the sense that the Dutch land is really
water:

> Holland, that scarce deserves the name of land,
> As but th'off-scouring of the British sand;
> And so much earth as was contributed
> By English pilots when they heaved the lead;
> Or what by th'oceans slow alluvion fell,
> Of shipwracked cockle and the mussel-shell;
> This indigested vomit of the sea
> Fell to the Dutch by just propriety.
>
> . . .
>
> How did they rivet, with gigantic piles,
> Thorough the centre their new-catched miles;
> And to the stake a struggling country bound,
> Where barking waves still bait the forced ground;
> Building their wat'ry Babel far more high
> To reach the sea, than those to scale the sky.
>
> (ll. 1–8; 17–22)

The language tumbles away with negative inventiveness as the Dutch are vilified:
'off-scouring' comes from to 'offscour', to cleanse from defilement. Off-scouring
then is that which is removed during cleansing: filth; rubbish. Mere landscape is
soon left behind for a more critical look at the republican institutions of the
United Provinces. Marvell's interest here was in showing that he understood
politics, and how the Dutch stood in relation to the English:

> Who best could know to pump an earth so leak,
> Him they their Lord and country's Father speak.
> To make a bank was a great plot of state;
> Invent a shovel and be magistrate.
> Hence some small dyke-grave unperceived invades
> The power, and grows as 'twere a King of Spades.
> But for less envy some joint States endures,

Who look like a Commission of the Sewers.
For these *Half-anders*, half wet, and half dry,
Nor bear strict service, nor pure liberty.

(ll. 45–54)

Line 51 is an allusion to the republican government of the United Provinces, and the mixture of authority, between communal assemblies in the cities and the States General, and the protective role of the Stadholder, whose support was mainly in the provinces. Line 60's 're-baptize' refers to adult baptism, the mark of conversion and acceptance into a Baptist church. Before 1640, Holland was a place of refuge for many English Baptists, and the English General Baptists (who rejected the doctrine of predestination to damnation) had their origins in the Dutch Waterlander church, whose name is of course significant for Marvell's imagery throughout the poem. It is here that the mocking hostility of the poem appears to break down, for not only is Commonwealth England also tolerant of Baptists, but line 53's 'Half-anders' is a play on Hollanders, pointing up confusion but also echoing *andershalf*, Dutch for 'one and a half', implying that liberty means being more than one; having sympathy with the opposite side.

If there is a poet through whom Marvell speaks in this poem, as he spoke through Ben Jonson in 'Tom May's Death', then it is John Cleveland, the Royalist satirist. Echoes of Cleveland's acerbic and strikingly original manner are present, although already the generosity of spirit that we have just seen, and that was developed in 'Upon Appleton House', is undoing the satirical attack.[22] A presentation poem in these circumstances is, however, no place to assess poetic identity. Marvell would reserve his judgement of Cleveland for later.[23]

However accomplished the poem, its demonstration that Marvell was fit in ability and in sympathy 'for the state to make use of' was not successful. The position went to Philip Meadows, a fellow of The Queen's College, Oxford, since 1649. He was Thurloe's choice, and an indication of that remarkable figure's growing influence. Meadows would enjoy a rapid rise: he soon became full Latin Secretary, leaving Milton free for 'extraordinary' business; in 1656 he successfully completed a difficult and controversial embassy to Portugal and was rewarded with the means to buy a substantial estate in Suffolk (while also surviving an assassination attempt); in 1657 as ambassador to Denmark he was able to nego-tiate a difficult peace between Denmark and Sweden, if a temporary one; he was knighted in 1658, published important books on diplomacy, and continued into a great old age to have lucrative appointments in trade and excise commissions (he died in 1718, but was only five years younger than Marvell, outliving him by forty years).[24] Meadows made a dynasty from his success in 1653. Milton had felt that Marvell had the potential to become as important a diplomat as Ascham, the Commonwealth apologist, but it is very hard to imagine Marvell compassing quite so much as Meadows, with such decisiveness.[25] Thurloe was probably right:

this was not the job for the Yorkshireman. The aspirant secretary would have to settle for a less prestigious position.

On 20 April, a momentous political event took place that would have far-reaching consequences for everyone, Marvell included. The Rump Parliament, the representative of the republic, had sat for four years and nearly four months, but it had done so with decreasing momentum. Lassitude was its characteristic as conservatives and radicals produced a balance of inaction. In a move designed to forestall the return by election of a similarly indecisive body, Cromwell as head of the army discharged the Rump. New elections were to be held for a new kind of parliament in the summer. No one could have foreseen quite what would happen, but what happened was the end of the republic.

ISLAND FARM

Milton's attempt to have Marvell employed by the state had failed, but if 'The Character of Holland' and the other state poems had been shown to the powerful in the regime, there was a positive result. Marvell had come to the closer attention of Oliver Cromwell, who was rapidly asserting himself as the most eminent man in the country. In the summer of 1653, Marvell was appointed governor or tutor to William Dutton, a ward and prospective son-in-law of Cromwell. They were to lodge with John Oxenbridge, one of the new Puritan fellows of Eton College, and brother-in-law of Oliver St John, the ambassador addressee of Marvell's Latin verses of 1651. Marvell wrote on 28 July to thank Cromwell and to give an account of Dutton's behaviour and the order of Oxenbridge's household. From the letter, it sounds very much as if Dutton and his tutor had but recently arrived. By the summer of 1653, Cromwell had forced the Rump Parliament to dissolve and had set in train elections to the new Nominated or 'Barebones' Assembly, the most radical legislative body the Commonwealth would see. But by the end of the year Barebones would be abandoned while Oliver Cromwell would become the greatest figure in the nation with the establishment of the Protectorate, and the most feared soldier in Europe.

Eton College had been established by Henry VI in 1440 as a foundation for the education of twenty-five boys, and with the further aim of becoming a centre for the dispensing of charity. While the latter aim was never achieved, by Marvell's time it had acquired the reputation of the highest intellectual distinction. From its inception, the college elected annually several scholars to take places at King's College, Cambridge, and smaller numbers were sent on similar terms to some of the Oxford colleges. Its foundation was left intact by the Henrician Reformation. Its Provost, Head Master and Fellows constituted a long list of impressive intellectuals, equal to and often exceeding that of any single Oxford or Cambridge college, and it enjoyed a frequent exchange of personnel with the two universities. Marvell was not a fellow, and was never admitted to Eton privileges. He remained a private servant. Nonetheless, he moved among the community – the decidedly divided community – of Eton and its environs in this period, and it had a significant impact on him.

At the end of the sixteenth century, Queen Elizabeth had appointed Sir Henry Savile, already Warden of Merton College, Oxford, as thirteenth Provost. Savile had enormous academic prestige, being Elizabeth's private tutor in Greek and mathematics, and the translator of a famous edition of Tacitus. Later came Sir Henry Wotton, the diplomat and speculative thinker, and sometime patron of the younger Milton. With their presence Eton was the centre for some of the most advanced theological and philosophical thinking in the country. The resistance to the Calvinist synthesis that had spread in the English church from 1559 to the 1620s was conducted in part in conversations at Eton. Be it Arminianism, Socinianism or 'rational religion', these ideas were known in the fellowship of the college, and the most distinguished proponent of some of them was John Hales, revered in his own time for his willingness to converse, his civility and his generosity. Hales lived on into the 1650s, and it was Marvell's privilege, as he was well aware, to have made Hales's acquaintance.[26]

With its body of liberal, or better still 'anti-Calvinist', divines, it is no surprise to find Eton's fellowship siding with the King at the outbreak of the Civil War. This was certainly the conviction of Wotton's successor as Provost, Richard Steward, Dean of Chichester and Clerk of the King's Closet. Indeed, on the outbreak of the fighting, Steward left the college for the King, taking the college seal with him, and probably much of the plate. Parliament moved to control the college, restricting ceremonial clothes and practices and removing Steward from the provostship. In his place was put Francis Rous, a West Country gentleman, an MP and an influential and learned lay Puritan. As a young man, he had shown promise as a poet, had a strong reputation as a devotional writer with an uncommon knowledge of the mystical tradition, and was rewarded in 1653 by being made Speaker of the Barebones Parliament. When Parliament imposed the Engagement after the regicide, Hales among others refused to sign, and promptly lost his fellowship. He was compelled to reside near Eton in what had become an enclave for disgraced Anglicans, Richings Lodge, near Colnbrook, some two to three miles away, at the home of Lady Salter, the niece of Brian Duppa, Bishop of Salisbury. The Bishop of Chichester and poet, Henry King, also lived here in internal exile; Hales functioned as tutor to Mrs Salter's son, and as household chaplain, using the Anglican liturgy. It was this community and institution in transition, with expelled fellows and other divines in the countryside nearby, and a new generation of Commonwealth or Cromwellian fellows forging a Puritan ethos – and indeed a Cromwellian church – in the college, that Marvell entered in the summer of 1653.

Eton was and is a bucolic place. The college sits in the Thames Valley, on a flat grassy plain forming part of the north bank of the river, at a southerly bend in its course. Its name derives from Old English *eg-tun*: 'island farm'. It was indeed a pastoral landscape and here Marvell readily saw the connection with pastoral poetry, and the encounters he had with eminent Etonians were apt to be captured in pastoral form. From Virgil onwards, pastoral was concerned with the forming of poets' minds and convictions. Here, in his early thirties, and with some substantial achievements already behind him, this was so for Marvell.

Opposite Eton, and rising sharply above it, was Windsor, symbol of royal authority with its huge and complicated castle. It was in the Chapel of Windsor Castle that Charles I had been rapidly interred, in an unmarked casket. Was this known to the Cromwellian Etonians? If it was, it would surely have cast its shadow on them.

William Dutton was the son of a Royalist who had died in 1646. After his father's death he had been taken into the care of his exceedingly rich but retiring uncle, John, of Sherborne Court, Gloucestershire. Uncle John (see plate 16), whom Marvell met at this time during a trip to Sherborne, had prudently arranged for Cromwell to assume guardianship of his nephew after his death, and to be responsible for his education forthwith; he also named his nephew heir to his estate. Hence the job for Marvell. For Cromwell, the arrangement with Dutton, a prominent Cavalier, was typical of his policies of rapprochement and reconciliation, as well as being advantageous for his own family. The regime would benefit from the support of an influential person of extreme wealth and Cromwell had found a handsomely fitting husband for his youngest daughter, Frances. It must have been hard for Frances to contemplate William Dutton with enthusiasm: he was, according to his tutor, of a 'gentle and waxen disposition', which on the one hand meant that he was impressionable and apt to be educated, and on the other that he was already 'grown up' and formed to a large degree in virtue. While of course Marvell is giving a good account to Cromwell in terms he would want to hear, the third sense of 'waxen' might well be 'pallid', as the portrait of Dutton now at Sherborne suggests. And Marvell goes on to comment that Mrs (Jane) Oxenbridge's care of Dutton had already resulted in an improvement in his complexion. The portrait suggests a wholly un-Puritanical young man with an exaggeratedly pasty complexion: it sits uneasily both with contemporary portraiture and all contemporary ideals of manly appearance, as if Dutton himself were an insurmountable challenge to portraiture. By contrast, Frances's real object of devotion was Robert Rich, grandson to the Earl of Warwick, and another exceedingly wealthy young man, while public rumour had it that the exiled Charles II (as he had been proclaimed in Scotland) was also an interested suitor.

However, Marvell was teaching Dutton, and we may suppose the instruction involved lots of exercise in Latin, Greek and modern languages, much as Marvell had taught Mary Fairfax. Even if some of the historical writers were added to the poetry, nothing is so evident as that Marvell was going through the motions, and was uninterested in Dutton himself. The letter to Cromwell is as concerned with the writer as it is with its subject, and a letter nearly a year later to Milton makes no mention of Dutton whatsoever. Of more interest to Marvell, and by way of giving assurance to Cromwell, were the figures of John Oxenbridge and his wife.

Oxenbridge was the kind of previously wronged Puritan whom Cromwell liked to favour, and he was the brother-in-law of Cromwell's political associate Oliver St John, the addressee of one of Marvell's Latin poems.[27] He had been a Fellow of Magdalen Hall, Oxford, one of the few centres of Puritanism in the university. He had been dismissed by Archbishop Laud in May 1634 for imposing a demanding disciplinary system on his pupils, in addition to the normal academic requirements. He fled to the New World, and spent time in the Bermudas (twice: in 1635 and 1641), and eventually during the Restoration Surinam, Barbados and New England. In each place, he revealed his Independent (Congregationalist) church principles by becoming involved in experiments in church government.

Oxenbridge returned to England in the 1640s, and by the end of the decade was chaplain to the Governor of Hull, Robert Overton, who was a republican, millenarian, sympathetic to Fifth Monarchists, poet and friend of both Milton and Marvell. Marvell might have encountered him in the north in the early 1650s. Oxenbridge was then appointed Vicar of New Windsor, and in 1652 was made a Fellow of Eton College. Just as Marvell arrived in Eton, Oxenbridge's knowledge of the transatlantic world was both rewarded and exploited when he was made one of the commissioners for the government of the Bermudas; he would succeed as Governor of the Somers Island Company in 1655.

Marvell's poem 'Bermudas' was most probably a compliment to Oxenbridge and his wife, in conscious imitation of psalm poetry, and possibly also connected with his role as tutor of Dutton:

Bermudas

Where the remote Bermudas ride
In th'ocean's bosom unespied,
From a small boat, that rowed along,
The list'ning winds received this song.
    'What should we do but sing his praise
That led us through the wat'ry maze,
Unto an isle so long unknown,
And yet far kinder than our own?
Where He the huge sea-monsters wracks,
That lift the deep upon their backs.
He lands us on a grassy stage;
Safe from the storms, and prelates' rage.
He gave us this eternal spring,

Which here enamels ev'rything;
And sends the fowls to us in care,
On daily visits through the air.
He hangs in shades the orange bright,
Like golden lamps in a green night.
And does in the pom'granates close,
Jewels more rich than Ormus shows.
. . .
Oh let our voice His praise exalt,
Till it arrive at heaven's vault:
Which thence (perhaps) rebounding, may
Echo beyond the Mexique Bay.'
    Thus sung they, in the English boat,
An holy and a cheerful note,
And all the way, to guide their chime,
With falling oars they kept the time.

(ll. 1–20; 33–40)

English colonists came to the Bermudas nearly a hundred years after the European arrival there (the islands were named after the Spanish explorer Juan Bermudez). The poem is indebted to published accounts of the settlement of the Bermudas, but Marvell's idealizing ignores the disputes among the colonists, the punishment of some of them, conspiracies against the governors, the furore and squabbling caused by the pressure to ship ambergris back to England, instances of sodomy, and the unpopularity of Puritan activities, including Oxenbridge's, in the 1620s and 1630s. Marvell follows the writings on the Bermudas that were published for propaganda purposes, such as Lewis Hughes's *A Letter Sent into England from the Summer Islands* (1615), which claims the islands had a special destiny. Where Marvell used other accounts, the negative in the sources is rendered positive in the poem, whose imagined occasion may be the psalm sung by the first English visitors on their arrival.

'Bermudas' 'sounds rather like a metrical Psalm'.[28] Sandys's psalm translations were popular at court, and especially with the King. By 1651 they were widely recognized as part of the Royalist literature of lament of which *Eikon Basilike* was the most well known, and that Thomas Stanley had rendered in psalmic form as *Psalterium Carolinium*. Marvell could have witnessed their sung performance at Stanley's Hertfordshire estate.[29] To transfer this kind of verse into an obviously Puritanical context was to perform the kind of generic relocation characteristic of Marvell's political poems. Among the religious reforms debated by Puritans in the 1640s and 1650s was a new (and better) translation of the Book of Psalms. Marvell's highly wrought psalmic poem introduces refined courtly verse into the space of a godly household. The metrical variations and the nautical context suggest additionally the singing of a sea shanty. It may be that the poem was sung to the tune of, not a shanty, but a well-known ballad. But, whereas music usually lightens the burden of labour, this relationship is reversed in a poem that makes the praise of God pre-eminent: the work of rowing keeps time to the music, rather than vice versa. Did Dutton sing the music to Oxenbridge in a household entertainment, or was the poem intended to accompany the elevation of Oxenbridge to the Somers Island council?

Perhaps this was a covert way of paying a compliment, since Marvell was immediately impressed, so his letter to Cromwell testifies, with the Oxenbridges' godly household. Shortly after his expulsion from Oxford, Oxenbridge had married Jane Butler, the daughter of a Newcastle merchant. She accompanied John to the Americas and shared in his adverse circumstances. Marvell presents their household as a model: 'so godly a family as that of Mr Oxenbridge whose Doctrine and Example are like a Book and a Map, not onely instructing the Eare but demonstrating to the Ey which way we ought to trauell.' Oxenbridge had helped Marvell instruct Dutton, and Jane Oxenbridge had fed him and had organized his room 'that he may delight to be in it as often as his Studyes require'. Quite the mother, but more than that; for Jane had a reputation as a preacher to women and a scriptural interpreter of repute, who reportedly had a substantial influence on her husband's own sermon writing.[30]

Hales was the opposite of Oxenbridge, and while we cannot easily suppose that the two men met, Marvell knew and approved them both. By all accounts, Hales was astonishing, a prodigy in youth, who had worked with Savile on his edition of St John Chrysostom, and had been elected to fellowships at Merton College, Oxford, in 1605, and Eton in 1613. He was admitted to court circles when at Windsor, and in an annual trip to London visited theatres and kept the company of Jonson, D'Avenant and Falkland.[31] When in *The Rehearsal Transpros'd* (p. 130), Marvell looked back to the privilege while in Eton of knowing 'the living *remains* [his italics] of one of the clearest heads and best prepared brests in Christendom', he was alluding to the posthumously published *Golden Remains of the ever memorable Mr John Hales* (1659). Hales was close to being an Arminian (he had been present at the Synod of Dort and had been persuaded there to 'bid John Calvin good-night' – an unhelpful simplification), but although he had become Laud's chaplain in 1639, he disliked Laudian clericalism. In *The Rehearsal Transpros'd* Marvell would rely heavily upon Hales's account of schism and the extent to which it was caused by clerical ambition. Despite the charges of Socinianism, Hales struck Marvell as the epitome of conscionable virtue, as later bishops would not. Hales was more than a theologian, and took a keen interest in all branches of literature, including history, on which he wrote a short treatise, and poetry. Whilst having no reputation as a poet, he had edited poetry collections and is frequently, respectfully and affectionately mentioned in Cavalier verse. He knew Milton when the poet was living in retreat at Horton, not far from Eton. He was famous in his time and later for defending Shakespeare as at least the equal if not the better of all the ancient and living poets, and he had argued this in conversation with Ben Jonson, Sir John Suckling and other prominent figures on the Caroline literary scene.

Hales's *Tract concerning schisme and schismaticks*, written and circulated in manuscript, and published in print perhaps without the author's permission in 1642, is a remarkable document. It is famous for asserting that schism is caused by those with ecclesiastical authority, rather than those who have sincerely argued the case for separating from a church. Laud was certainly worried by the short treatise and subjected Hales to an interrogation. In fact, Hales does not quite argue this position in a singular way: he also admits that the cause of schism can in some cases be the fault of both parties. His immense knowledge of church history allowed him to express his distaste for the many times that controversy and schism among Christians had broken out over matters indifferent – more often than not inconsequential items of dates and incidentals of ceremonies. There is an unmistakable sense of his objection to episcopal ambition as well as superstition, especially when used to frighten people into obedience when their reason might teach them otherwise. There can be no doubt that Marvell learned greatly from, and incorporated, Hales's subtle logic and syntax into his writing. The same might be said for his humorous digressions. No one comes closer to Marvell among those he met in being able to think across Protestant and Catholic divisions, applying what Hales would have called a sceptical logic, and a generous one at that. No wonder that a very considerable section of the *Tract concerning schisme and schismaticks* was written out by Marvell in *The Rehearsal Transpros'd*, with Marvell introducing capitalization to emphasize the context in 1672: 'All pious Assemblies, in times of Persecution and Corruption, howsoever practised, are indeed, or rather alone, the Lawful Congregations: and Publick Assemblies, though according to form of Law, are, indeed, nothing else but RIOTS and CONVENTICLES, if they be stained with Corruption and Superstition.'[32] Hales also thought that the power of the keys could be exercised by anyone and that Holy Communion could be celebrated anywhere.

For Marvell, this was an example of 'Majesty and Beauty which sits upon the Forehead of masculine Truth and generous Honesty', an emptying out of 'Sloth . . . Fear . . . Ambition', as opposed to those churchmen, like Samuel Parker (whom we will meet properly later on), who 'must incite Princes to Persecution and Tyranny, degrade Grace to Morality, debauch Conscience against its own Principles, distort and mis-interpret the Scripture, fill the World with Blood, Execution, and Massacre'. Hales was entirely undone by the Civil War, having been ejected from his canonry at Windsor in 1644 and his Eton fellowship in 1649. When Marvell first met him in 1653, at least he had found a place of refuge. But he had been forced to sell his important library to maintain himself, even as he selflessly shared the proceeds with other redundant Anglicans. Just before or about the time that Marvell left Eton, towards the end of 1655 or in January 1656, Hales was compelled to leave Richings, since new laws forbade the harbouring of malignants, and to hide with the widow of a former servant in Eton, where he died on 19 May 1656. Aubrey's portrait is so remarkably arresting that it is still worth quoting at length. In this widow's 'handsome darke old-fashioned howse', with psalm sentences painted on cloth above the wainscot, a fashion that was by the 1650s well out of date, Hales appeared:

> a prettie little man, sanguine, of a cheerful countenance, very gentile, and courteous; I was received by him with much humanity: he was in a kind of violet-coloured cloath Gowne, with buttons and loopes (he wore not a black gowne) and was reading Thomas à Kempis; it was within a yeare before he deceased. He loved Canarie; but moderately to refresh his spirits.[33]

Marvell's other significant acquaintance at Eton was Nathaniel Ingelo (1620/1–83), another Independent divine who had been made a fellow of the college in 1650. He was the same age as Marvell, had a degree from Edinburgh, and was inserted by the Earl of Manchester as a fellow of Queens' College, Cambridge, in 1644.[34] With ecclesiology his similarities with Oxenbridge ended. A native of Bristol, and connected by kin to the mercantile elite of the city, Ingelo was a musical Puritan, and was known to have offended the congregation of Bristol Nonconformists to whom he ministered in the later 1640s with his attention to dress and his love of music: 'Take away my music, take away my life.' Oxenbridge was indefatigable and unstinting in his beliefs: for him the Restoration meant another transatlantic crossing, this time to be a minister and to end his life in Boston. Ingelo was a great survivor: he became Vice-Provost of Eton and was one of only two fellows to avoid deprivation in the early 1660s, remaining in this post until his death in 1683. Hales might have induced admiration with his character and career. Ingelo, from a mercantile city background and with strong artistic interests, was nearly a double for Marvell, but as a divine and fellow of the college, considerably more advanced.

Barebones Parliament had gathered in July 1653, when it discussed and proposed some hard-hitting reforms in, for instance, the areas of law and education. It was quite the opposite of the endlessly demurring Rump Parliament. The debates in Barebones bore the unmistakable tones of millenarian language, and it was soon evident to the army commanders that, just as they had once had to quell the populism of the Levellers, so they now had to deal with radical Puritans intent on reforming the property relations of the country. This time they faced a popular movement and a legislative assembly, itself internally incoherent, the combined weight of which was threatening to destabilize the nation.

So a council of senior officers met and wrote a new constitution investing far more power than before in a single executive officer: the Lord Protector. A coup of 12 December overthrew Barebones. If there were parliaments in this constitution, they were not clearly defined, and many would think this constitution looked like a return to monarchy by another name. Perhaps it gave the Protector even more power than the English monarch. Either way, Oliver Cromwell was proclaimed Lord Protector on 16 December 1653, to rule in conjunction with a Council of State, and with the only written constitution that has ever existed in the British Isles. Earlier he had rejected the offer of the Crown from some army officers.

Most of those gathered at Eton under the republic's patronage were in fact there as godly placemen. They were well favoured by Cromwell, and, like Marvell, were there at his wish. Under the Protectorate they would now find themselves more directly involved with Oliver's matters of state.

Angelo suo Marvellius

The early months of 1654 were taken up with participation, albeit for Marvell at a great distance, in one of the most spectacular as well as important events in the history of the Protectorate. The eminent lawyer Bulstrode Whitelocke, Keeper of the Great Seal and President of the Council, was chosen as ambassador to Sweden. The point of the mission was to win Swedish support to counterbalance the Dutch treaty with the Danes. Peace with the United Provinces was achieved in 1654, but it was not on the horizon when Whitelocke was appointed in September 1653. It would also be the first time that the Commonwealth, and by 1654 the Protectorate, had staged a large-scale embassy abroad: it had a lot to prove in the eyes of Europe. Quite apart from the hostile international reception of the regicide, the republic's diplomacy had already garnered a reputation for amateurism and lack of protocol. In every sense imaginable, this would prove to be an extraordinary mission.

The September appointment of Whitelocke was important for Marvell for he had already become involved in the beginnings of the embassy as an extended member of Cromwell's household. The Swedes had been trying to win support in the English Council of State for the release of some ships captured by the Commonwealth navy, and they had done this by a direct approach from Queen Kristina to Oliver Cromwell as chief military commander. She wanted trade and fishing agreements, an alliance against the powerful Dutch–Danish axis, and the right to employ Scottish mercenaries. She had even sent him a portrait in May 1653, as if he were a foreign prince. While Cromwell was not empowered to negotiate with her, and legally could not be approached by any diplomats, he nonetheless saw advantages in an Anglo-Swedish alliance (proposed by the Swedish ambassador in July), and, as his own frustration with Barebones Parliament grew, signalled his favour by having a remarkable portrait painted by Robert Walker as reciprocation for the one sent by Kristina (plate 15). Marvell was asked to produce a Latin verse epigram to accompany it. The sending of the picture was part of a manoeuvre that allowed Cromwell to keep the idea of Anglo-Swedish concord alive in the autumn of 1653 and in the period just preceding the establishment of the Protectorate, when he would have a much freer hand. The picture is notable for its portrayal of Cromwell as a Roman military commander, declaring the extent and limitations of his authority: in the military realm and without political and diplomatic remits, he is depicted wearing cuirass armour and a white mantle like the Roman *paludamentum*, the military counterpart to the civilian toga. In this respect the picture and epigram answer the Swedish queen's hint that Cromwell might be the founder of a new heroic dynasty of warrior kings like her own line, the Vasas.[35] To this extent too it is a key (and until very recently) overlooked piece of English republican iconography. Marvell's verse was painted into the bottom right-hand corner, squeezed on to the canvas by the miniaturist Jeremiah Meyer, with the Latin epigram explaining precisely how the picture should be read:

> Bellipotens virgo, septem regina trionum.
>   Christina, arctoi lucida stella poli;
> Cernis quas merui dura sub casside rugas;
>   Sicque senex armis impiger ora fero;
> Invia Fatorum dum per vestigia nitor,
>   Exequor et populi fortia jussa manu.
> At tibi submittit frontem reverentior umbra,
>   Nec sunt hi vultus regibus usque truces.

Powerful Virgin, Queen of the Seven Oxen. Christina, clear star of the northern pole. You see what wrinkles I have acquired under a hard helmet. Thus an old man, yet vigorous, I face my enemies while I press through the pathless tracks of the Fates and execute the strong commands of the people with force. But this image submits its brow more respectfully to you, nor are these features always hostile to kings. (trans. Holberton)

The sense of the lines remains very pro-Commonwealth (in imagery that harks back to 'An Horatian Ode') but is tactful towards monarchs, or at least this Swedish one and to Cromwell's age (he was old enough to be Kristina's father). It avoids any hint of a relationship beyond mutual respect.

Marvell's Eton companion Nathaniel Ingelo had known Whitelocke in Bristol when the latter was Recorder of that city; he accepted the invitation to join the embassy as one of Whitelocke's chaplains. Indeed, he had already accepted the post under the original leader of the embassy, Philip Sidney, Viscount Lisle, who had been approached in December 1652, when planning for the mission began, but who later withdrew on grounds of ill health. It was through Ingelo that Marvell would come to play a fuller role in the business of diplomacy. Whitelocke and his entourage departed in November; negotiations were concluded in April, and the embassy left Sweden in June, arriving back in London in early July.

At the heart of the planning for the mission was the astonishing figure of Queen Kristina. Born in 1626, she was the daughter of Gustavus Adolphus, the Vasa king who had taken Sweden firmly on to the European stage and made her a great power with his military successes in the Thirty Years War. His death at the Battle of Lützen in 1632 meant that Kristina came to the throne at the age of six. By then she was already a prodigy, and had delighted her father with early signs of scholarly promise. While she was a minor, Sweden was ruled by a regency, in which Count Axel Oxenstierna was the most influential figure: he remained Chancellor during the English embassy. In her minority years, Kristina kept long and rigorous hours of study, and the best available tutors were found for her, including Oxenstierna and the theologian Johannes Matthiae. While still a teenager, she had become a very plausible European intellectual, and proceeded to gather about her major intellectual figures of the time, the most famous of whom was René Descartes. She assembled what might be justly called a European super-salon, with a retinue of dazzling minds. The presence of advanced thinking was notable. Kristina herself has been described as a philosophical libertine and she produced a substantial body of her own writing. She had attended council meetings since 1640, when she was aged fourteen, and came into her majority and reigned as queen from 1644. She played a major role in concluding the Thirty Years War with the Peace of Westphalia in 1648. The English saw her as a model Protestant queen, a fitting counterpart in the far north to Cromwell, and these were the terms in which the embassy was launched. But the English were in for a great surprise.

Whatever her achievements, Kristina's position at home was neither as stable nor as straightforward as Whitelocke or Cromwell might have wished. In the eyes of many advisers, including Oxenstierna, who was dismissed and then recalled to office, the cost of the peace was too high, and insufficient attention had been paid to the terms of reparation that Sweden might have demanded. Kristina was accused of favouring the nobility; although she managed to avoid a civil conflict, and despite the advances she encouraged in industry, education and trade, the country as a whole had neither the ability nor the desire to maintain the extravagant court that came with her group of philosophers. She utterly refused marriage (one of her suitors was the future Charles II), which was dynastically a very serious issue. At least as grievous was the fact that she had secretly become a Roman Catholic, which was forbidden in Sweden. These last two circumstances led her in 1651 to contemplate abdication in favour of her younger cousin, the future Charles X. This was the uneasy situation that greeted the English embassy when it arrived in late 1653.

Whitelocke's voyage had been eventful enough: he had been delayed by adverse weather, and diverted by the pursuit of potential Dutch prizes. He set about impressing the Swedes, always appearing with at least forty armed men, as he organized his overland convoy of coaches to Uppsala. The envoy's first meeting with the Queen must have been a startling experience:

> In the next room beyond that (which was fayre & richly hanged) was the Q[ueen] herselfe, in the midst of it were great Candlestickes full of waxe lights Besides many torches.
>
> Wh[itelocke] perceived the Q[ueen]sitting att the upper end of the room in her chayre of State, of Crimson velvet & a Canopy over it, some Ladyes stood behind her, & many Lords, officers and gent[lemen] filled the roome . . .
>
> . . . rising from her Seate caused Wh[itelocke] to know her to be the Q[ueen] her habit being upwards like that of a man, she wore the Jewell of the Order of Amar[a]nta, her countenance was pale butt/sprightly, her demeanor full of Majesty & sweetnes.[36]

The amaranth was regarded as a flower from the Garden of Eden that never faded, and to this chivalric order that Kristina had recently created were admitted the King of Poland and several north German electors, in addition to Whitelocke himself. The knights in the order wore their 'jewels' signifying membership (in fact two As of gold and precious stones entwined in a green enamelled laurel wreath with the legend *Dolce nella memoria*) on a crimson scarf or gold chain. Whitelocke would have a series of equally unusual encounters, including concerts from her choir of Italian eunuchs and a meeting with the countess de la Gardie, who was probably Kristina's lover; he noted the strangeness of Laplanders visiting the court, and the frequency with which Kristina was whisked around the city and its environs in her sled.

At the centre of Marvell's involvement in the embassy was his fine Latin poem 'A Letter to Doctor Ingelo', or 'Angelo suo Marvellius' as it was known in manuscript, and the two smaller epigrams. We know that Marvell wrote the poem in Eton on 23 February. Probably he was invited to do so by Ingelo or perhaps even by Whitelocke through Ingelo. In Whitelocke's papers at Longleat House is a copy of the poem, a complete text of one of its versions.[37] It is dated 22 February 1653 (old style), which is when it was written; after the post arrived on 23 March it was transcribed for Whitelocke along with another poem, an ode by Sir Charles Wolseley, another Commonwealth stalwart.[38] On 30 March Whitelocke showed both poems to the Queen and he mentions specifically that 'je lui ai donné beaucoup de contentement par le lecture de certains vers Latins, envoyes d'Angleterre (a Monsieur Ingelo) qui es[t]oyent excellemment composes, et ausi d'une Ode qu'on m'a envoyé d'Angleterre'. After a tough session of diplomacy, Kristina had fallen 'into discourse of poetry', or of England. According to Whitelocke's original, 'a Copy of verses he had then about him, made by an English gent[leman] and sent hither to Wh[itelocke]. . . . the Q[ueen] was much delighted with them, and read them over severall times, and highly commended them, as she did those that Dr Whistler made, and she desired copyes of them, which were sent to her.' The embassy's physician Daniel Whistler, who was admitted to personal audiences with the Queen, had indeed written a Latin poem to her earlier in the visit. Marvell's poem is entitled 'Angelo suo Marvellius', signed 'Tuus Marvellius', and was copied by Whitelocke into the first version of his journal when he was shown the poem in Sweden by Ingelo ('miss[i] etiam fuerunt ab Amico quodam Etoniensi ad Dominum Ingelo versus sequentes elegantissimi' [the following very elegant lines were sent to Dr Ingelo from a friend in Eton). The significance of Kristina's praise cannot be over-stressed. She was frequently the subject of panegyrical praise, and many, many poems addressed to her survive.[39] Of all these, she clearly regarded Marvell's as one of the best, and it occupied her serious attention. It is so acute in its engage-ment with the mission that it is hard not to form the conclusion that Whitelocke provided precise advice as to his needs.

Poems were an effective and necessary part of the diplomatic process: they formed part of the exchange of gifts that accompanied embassies, and since they often contained narrative content they could be used to influence the direction of negotiations. They were also a good deal cheaper than the many gifts of coins that Whitelocke was expected to make as an ambassador. Perhaps it would be considered an uncouth breach in protocol for a private man to address the Queen directly, so the fiction of a poetic letter addressed to a friend worked well. One of the aims of the mission was to show Europe that England was not being run by a bunch of low-born zealots. Marvell's poem's sharp edge is in the implicit threat that if Kristina begins to act like or treat with the Dutch, or further delays signing what was supposed to be a very straightfor-ward treaty with the English, Ingelo will return and give critical accounts of her to men like Marvell. But Marvell's elegant, humanistic Latin verse letter to Ingelo is its own gentle threat, because it proves to Kristina that English insti-tutions are as capable of producing literary correspondents as any of the European scholars whom she had cultivated in the past; she should see her reputation – particularly with reference to Marvell's forceful interpretation of her favourite images and topics – as suggesting that Kristina and Cromwell share similar ideals and cultural heritage. Marvell can have known nothing of the abdication question when he wrote the poem, or finished writing it, on 23 February, but the other two poems that survive by Englishmen on the embassy make it the central issue. Marvell's poem had a very direct and different political end, and by the time Kristina heard the poem the treaty was well on the way to completion; Whitelocke signed it with Oxenstierna on 11 April. Perhaps because of its very avoidance of the sensitive issue of abdication, because it presented an idealized view of Kristina as she would have liked to be remembered, and no doubt because it was a successful poetic construction, it delighted her, and it helped Whitelocke negotiate. Nothing we know about its early reception suggests that Kristina took offence at the diplomatic under-tones. If she noticed them, she was already interested in seeing what she could make from the English, and enjoyed the poem's invitation to the game of praise and barter that was international diplomacy at this time.[40] At the very least she took care to see that it was copied into her own records.

Meanwhile, back in Eton, just before Kristina abdicated, but presumably before the English ambassador and his party sailed from Sweden, Marvell wrote to Milton on 2 June. He addressed Milton as 'my honoured Friend': clearly a significant friendship had developed, although not one based on daily association, or even frequent meetings. Yet there is strong evidence here of mutual respect and shared ideals and viewpoints between the gifted men of letters. The letter is so full of both humanist convention and sentiment, it is surprising not to find it written in Latin. It shows that they were in regular contact by correspondence, and this letter is but a footnote to a previous one, which had to be speedily concluded in order to go back to Westminster with the messenger, who had arrived only a few hours earlier that day. Milton had asked Marvell to present a letter and a copy of his *Defensio Secunda* to John Bradshaw, until recently President of the Council of State, and Marvell wrote the second letter in order to provide a fuller account of the presentation, and of his own pleasure in opening and reading Milton's letter to him. Through correspondence Marvell had probably been helping Milton to assemble the *Defensio Secunda*; perhaps too Milton had helped Marvell write his Swedish poetry. Bradshaw was apparently living near Eton, probably on his recently acquired estate at Hanworth. 'My Lord read not the letter while I was with him, which I attributed to our Despatch, and some other Businesse tending thereto.' Marvell suspected also that Bradshaw did not open his letter because he thought it might contain a request to employ Marvell, just like an earlier letter Milton had written in February 1653. Bradshaw praised Milton for his work as Foreign Secretary in Marvell's presence. Milton had also sent copies of the *Defensio Secunda* to Oxenbridge and to Marvell, and the younger poet expressed gratitude and was touched that he had been so honoured. In the letter to Milton he promised to learn the *Defensio* by heart and claimed that its quality was of the 'Height of the Roman eloquence',[41] by which he means that it is truly lofty, sublime discourse. He harks back to the republican moment of 1650 to 1652, and the raising by John Hall, himself an admirer of Milton, of Longinus's ideal of the sublime as that which occurs most readily in free states. As Milton's tract contains a defence of both his own career and that of the Commonwealth, Marvell imagines it as a monument, but one that seems so alive with successful rhetoric that it is musical architecture: 'When I consider how equally it turnes and rises with so many figures, it seems to me a Trajans columne in whose winding ascent we see imboss'd the severall Monuments of your learned victoryes.' Marvell would have seen the column in Rome in 1645.[42]

Marvell's reference was properly literary, since the rising frieze on the column suggested the opening of a scroll. Marvell refers to Milton having, in his view, the better of his two controverters, Claude de Saumaise and Alexander More, in defending the regicide and the honour of the English in removing their king. It has been suggested that Marvell's 'When I consider' echoes the beginning of Milton's famous sonnet on his blindness ('When I consider how my light is spent'), possibly written in 1652, so that some sympathetic insight into the relationship between the cost and the reward of service, both in the public and the private senses, is manifested. If that is the case, it suggests that a relationship of deep literary intimacy between the two men probably began before they met, when Marvell first read Milton's poetry. For the second time Marvell resorted to an image of a powerful figure writing his own place in history and being aware of doing so.[43] He would also have been aware of Milton's imitation in his *Pro populo anglicano defensio* (1650) of Pliny's praise of Trajan because he had stayed within the laws, recovering and restoring ancient Roman liberties. Pliny himself had insisted on justly violent tyrannicide in vengeance for leaders who strayed from the law.

In his letter, Marvell also asks after Colonel Robert Overton, Governor of Hull, Independent and Fifth Monarchist, who had been recalled to London from Scotland on suspicion of fomenting republican and Fifth Monarchist revolt in the northern army against the Protectorate. It may have been more than Hull that drew the two men together: Oxenbridge had himself been chaplain to Overton in Hull, and the Governor had been reluctant to lose him. Overton had clearly visited Milton, who had mentioned him in his letter to Marvell. Marvell's tone suggests fondness ('affectionate Curiosity') which may be construed as concern for the danger that Overton might be in, and the acquaintance hinted at with Overton connected to poetry, since Overton was much interested in contemporary verse and would leave behind him an important collection of manuscript verse.[44] Overton had a frank discussion with Cromwell, in which he was able to express his fear that Cromwell as Protector would become a tyrant, and Cromwell managed to convince him that that was not the case, that he, Oliver, would expect Overton to resign or rebel if ever he succumbed to such self-aggrandizement. As we shall see, it was a temporary reconciliation, and Overton would spend much of the rest of the decade in prison as a conspirator.

The mention of Overton's precarious position points up the change in politics that was sweeping in and that would eventually distinguish Marvell quite clearly from Milton. The dissolution of the Rump in April had signalled the beginning of Bradshaw's decline in influence. However much he stood on ceremony and held on to positions and privileges (even though it was originally stated that the Council of State should have no head), he was a believer in the republic and its ethos. He challenged Cromwell's right to dissolve the Rump, did not sit in Barebones Parliament, and did not take up his seat in the Parliament of 4 September 1654. Although the Rump's Council of State no longer existed, and therefore could have no President, Bradshaw remained Chancellor of the Duchy of Lancaster, and continued as head of the Court of Relief on articles of war. Soon he would refuse a lower legal position from Cromwell and, finding himself unelected to the Protectorate Parliament, rapidly became an opponent of Cromwell. Milton maintained his admiration for Bradshaw, but Marvell's livelihood increasingly depended upon Cromwell's patronage.

Marvell approves the fact that another friend of Milton, Cyriack Skinner, has seen the blind poet. Milton's letter had referred either to a visit from Skinner or to the fact that Skinner was now dwelling close to Milton. Skinner was another republican – at least he would be a member of Harrington's Rota Club in 1659–60 – and was a member of the northern Skinner family known to the Marvells, and with whom Marvell would have to do in future.

If Marvell was reading Milton, it would seem that Milton had also been reading Marvell, since the *Defensio Secunda* contains a reference to the story of the Judgment of Paris, a linchpin of Marvell's poem on Queen Kristina. The sense of growing intimacy and collaboration between the two poets is supported by the observation that if indeed Milton had seen Marvell's poem (and as he was Secretary for Foreign Tongues, material for dispatch might well have been reported to him) there may be a hint of friendly irony on Milton's part in the association of such conceits, with the older poet gently jibing at a man who, being still in his thirties, would have qualified as an adolescent in Roman usage.

Marvell seems to have stayed in the Oxenbridge household in the late summer of 1654, since on 3 August he witnessed leases on college houses in Eton, one of which was let to Oxenbridge.[45] He remained in Eton through the autumn, as the Lord Protector enhanced his powers. As every day went by, the poet-schoolmaster must have hoped for better things from his employer.

He certainly rendered him signal service by writing his greatest panegyric of Cromwell, *The First Anniversary of the Government under His Highness the Lord Protector*. It was probably composed between December 1654 and early January 1655 and thus not for the anniversary, but after it, to be circulated in print as a propaganda poem. An unsigned quarto edition appeared in the first month of 1655: Thomason dated his copy 17 January, and the pamphlet was advertised in *Mercurius Politicus*, 240 (1–18 January 1655) as 'newly printed and published'. As noted earlier, the Protectorate of Oliver Cromwell was established on 16 December 1653.

The poem presents as Cromwell's success his rule by the Instrument of Government, a written constitution drawn up by Colonel John Lambert and his associates. The Instrument represented a rejection of absolute parliamentary sovereignty and republican government, and a return to the deeply rooted national tradition of a mixed constitution. By the Instrument, power was in the hands of the Protector and his Council of State. The latter was meant to exercise a check on the executive. There was also to be an elected Parliament (which met first in September 1654), and successive election to the Council of

State achieved by a complicated voting system involving Protector, Parliament and Council.

The Protectorate was a godly government, and its first nine months (before the Parliament met) could boast impressive, zealous reformation, together with the settling of the war with Holland, and treaties with France and Denmark. Marvell's poem addresses the particular context of the first Protectorate Parliament of September 1654, which attempted to revise the Instrument, taking back some authority for Parliament from the Protector. Marvell is sensitive to the millenarian expectations generated by its meeting. The Instrument remained substantially unaltered, and was still the subject of debate when Cromwell dissolved the Parliament five days after 'The First Anniversary' appeared. Then began a process of further constitutional experiment which resulted in the 'rule' of the Major-Generals, later in 1655. Marvell says nothing of these matters because they had not yet appeared on the political agenda: he did not need to apologize for them. But he was apologizing for Cromwell's continuing singular power, which was frustrating to many, republican and Royalist alike.

The first year of the Protectorate was notable for a number of crises, many of which were indicative of the continuing instability of the state. On the domestic scene, republican hostility to the Protectorate was vigorous in the presses, and there were assassination attempts by Royalists and some disaffected republicans on Cromwell's life. The Quakers began to emerge as a significant force in the religious life of the nation: their message and their behaviour was often frightening and produced hostility, especially in provincial places. Many Puritans, the backbone of support for the Commonwealth, were disappointed by the government's failure to remove tithes. There were further complaints of legal abuses, and fears that a Protectoral court would lead to tyranny. Symbolic gestures against the Protector were frequent.

Yet none of these issues and movements feature explicitly in the poem. The single public force of opposition to the Protectorate that Marvell mentions is the Fifth Monarchist movement (the 'Chammish crew' of line 293), an association of radical Puritans, mostly Independents and Baptists, who expected the imminent Second Coming of Christ, who would rule over his saints for a thousand years before the Last Judgment. Fifth Monarchists applied the prophecies in the Books of Daniel and Revelation to their own time, and they believed that it was necessary (even by force of arms) to reform society in order to help bring on the millennium. They regarded the Protectorate as illegal, and protested against it from its inception.

Many Fifth Monarchists had previously looked to Cromwell as the hope of their godly vision. Cromwell himself shared a degree of millenarian sentiment but was bold in his opposition to the Fifth Monarchists because he thought they disturbed property relations, and because they were spiritually fractious. Marvell echoes the Protector's use of millenarian language in his speeches and, like

Cromwell, presents this as the true form of waiting upon the Lord, as opposed to more militant forms of millenarianism. Marvell's poem deftly responds to key Fifth Monarchist images and uses of the Bible: the poem avoids the passages from Daniel and Revelation popular with the Fifth Monarchists, and constructs an alternative image of the millennial state. To this extent, his portrait of Cromwell has been seen as that of the millenarian, Machiavellian state-builder, akin to the character of Olphaus Megalator (a thinly disguised and idealized Cromwell) in James Harrington's *Oceana* (1656).[46]

There were continued attempts to offer the crown to Cromwell and settle the succession on his heirs, in order to provide stability in the state. This was in opposition to the argument for an elective Protectorate, based upon the notion of an advantageous constitutional balance: 'If war be, here is the Unitive virtue (but nothing else) of *Monarchy* to encounter it; and here is the admirable Counsel of *Aristocracie* to manage it: if Peace be, here is the industry and courage of *Democracie* to improve it.'[47] The poem is not urging Cromwell to be King, but is a celebration of the Protector pure and simple: it closely mirrors the Protectorate understanding of statehood (Cromwell is a prince to the world, but a citizen at home).[48] This was common Commonwealth propaganda, as was the picture of Cromwell as providential ruler. The attachment of prophetic language to the figure of the Protector relates to Cromwell's own religious interests and behaviour. Marvell's theme of anti-monarchical and yet imperial sobriety (as in lines 387–90) was often echoed as a way of appreciating the godly government of the Protector.

Yet if the poem offers apparent support to the Protector, the opinions of its author may not be so readily identified with this stance. Six months before composing 'The First Anniversary' Marvell had expressed republican sentiments in a letter to Milton. Although Marvell does not so obviously qualify his praise of the Protector as Milton did in his *Defensio Secunda*, it may be that, like Nedham and Milton, he voiced outward support for the Protectorate while remaining privately worried by its threat to liberty. There are, significantly, no references to the republican opposition to the Protectorate, while the imagery of Parliament as a building (ll. 87–98) constitutes a modification of republican imagery from the early years of the Commonwealth (the *Defensio Secunda* is also echoed). As we have seen, Marvell was friendly with the republican army officer, Robert Overton, who was placed under arrest in late December. It is hard not to see some personal satisfaction in the balanced nature of the constitution:

> The common-wealth does through their centres all
> Draw the circumf'rence of the public wall;
> The crossest spirits here do take their part,
> Fast'ning the contignation which they thwart;
> And they, whose nature leads them to divide,

Uphold, this one, and that the other side;
But the most equal still sustain the height,
And they as pillars keep the work upright;
While the resistance of opposèd minds,
The fabric as with arches stronger binds,
Which on the basis of a senate free,
Knit by the roof's protecting weight agree.

(ll. 87–98)

Curiously, 'The First Anniversary' was entered in the Stationers' Register by its printer Thomas Newcomb (also the government's printer) only on 29 May. There is no apparent explanation for this delay, although the entry confirms Marvell as the author. The register did show Waller's panegyric at the same time, so it may be that Newcomb wanted to signal his ownership of an edition that had become profitable. The appearance of Waller's poem also signals how seriously Marvell's poem was taken to be, since we are now sure that it was a response to Marvell's, with Waller using Machiavelli to restructure Marvell's millenarian, Nedham- and Harrington-influenced vision of the Protectorate.[49]

SAUMUR

It was probably in the autumn of 1655, to coincide with the beginning of the academic and legal year, that Andrew Marvell, now thirty-four and a half years of age, accompanied his pupil William Dutton to France. This does not seem to have been part of a larger grand tour so much as a specific visit to Saumur, in the Loire, home to a Protestant academy of high repute, widely regarded as one of the chief centres of learning in the international Protestant world of the time. It makes sense to suppose that Dutton attended lectures by the eminent faculty of the academy while Marvell continued to function as his tutor and governor.

Saumur is an imposing and beautiful place: a town built around a castle, Château Saumur, that itself sits on top of an elevation rising above the south bank of the Loire at its junction with the Thouet River. The town extends to a long island that sits in the middle of the river, which is crossed by a many-arched bridge. It was a place of strategic military advantage (although its famous cavalry school was not founded until the eighteenth century) and administrative importance, and during the later Middle Ages experienced considerable development as a prosperous mercantile centre. It was also one of the homes of the French Reformation. During the French Wars of Religion in the 1560s, Calvinist discipline was installed and acts of iconoclasm committed against Catholic images. There was in these years a harking back to the town's earlier history: since the twelfth century, peasants had dug cave villages into the hillsides of the soft tuffeau stone along the Loire between Saumur and Montsoreau. During their persecution, the Huguenots used these troglodyte caves to hide in. In 1598 the Edict of Nantes protected French Protestantism, effectively creating a kind of double state, or at least a double society. The University of Saumur, founded in 1591 by its Huguenot Governor Philippe Duplessis-Mornay, the philosopher and friend of Sir Philip Sidney, opened in 1604 and became the university of French Protestantism before the revocation of the Edict of Nantes in 1685, whereupon the academy was closed. The late sixteenth and early seventeenth centuries, and in particular the reign of Henri IV (1594–1610), marked the high tide of French Protestant power and influence, while the fifty years before Dutton and Marvell's arrival had seen growing attrition between the French state, and especially the monarchy, and the Protestants. Louis XIII regarded Protestantism as a detestable heresy that, despite the protection afforded by the Edict, should be obliterated. And yet, since the Edict, Saumur and its region had managed to cultivate the practice of mutual toleration in this city of Protestants and Catholics. Saumur in this period does not conform to the picture of 'confessionalization', with different religious communities in the same place cultivating mutually exclusive worlds of education and employment.[50] Marvell and Dutton were entering a safe and civilized place, and yet also a war zone: a country divided by recent and recurring religious civil war, where the only conclusion in the 1685 revocation was the abolition of French Protestantism as a tolerated religion, and mass emigration of Huguenots to many countries. The young English heir and his tutor were subjected to French culture at its most tolerant, rich and multifarious; libertine and speculative in its habits, and no more so than at Saumur. Later on, from across the Channel in England during the 1660s and 1670s, Marvell must have looked with dismay at the growing intolerance and religious embitterment, as well as at what we know he abhorred: the absolutism of Louis XIV.

For a ward of Cromwell, Dutton's exposure to Saumur might seem surprising. The academy's high reputation was also a controversial one, and this was largely due to the long-standing presence of Moïse Amyraut (1596–1664), who had challenged in his teaching and publications the doctrine most closely associated with Calvin: predestination to damnation. The ensuing controversy, which echoed throughout the world of international Protestantism, was joined in the mid-1630s: Amyraut was widely interpreted as teaching universal salvation, something even more shocking than the free will of the Arminians. In 1641, Amyraut became principal of the Saumur academy and remained so until his death: his influence was enormous. By the 1650s, moderate Puritan divines like Richard Baxter understood Amyraut and the Saumur school to be pushing for a middle way between Calvin and Arminius – limiting free will with the proviso that God may predestine some to salvation. This is in fact the position that Milton offers in *Paradise Lost*, but Amyraut's views cannot have been acceptable to other divines close to Cromwell, like John Owen, whom Marvell would later defend. When we also learn that Amyraut, in common with nearly all Huguenots, had lectured on the evil of the English regicide, and after 1649 eliminated any element of non-monarchical thought from his political theory lectures, the choice seems perhaps even more surprising. But was John Dutton making the decisions for his nephew here?

Later on, in the last year of his life, Marvell would defend John Howe, another of Cromwell's chaplains, who, as a leading London Nonconformist minister, would attempt to reconcile Calvinists and Arminians by specific resort to Amyraut's theology.[51] Amyraut's influence was profound and extensive; for instance the later Quaker William Penn studied with him at one point. Howe's position was closely related to that of Richard Baxter, another Cromwell chaplain, who found Amyraut very useful. Baxter was Owen's chief opponent in the competition for designing a Commonwealth church. What Marvell saw and heard in Saumur was to be of extreme importance to him. Did the moderation of the Saumur theologians remind Marvell more of his father's position or of his more recent encounter with John Hales?

In Saumur, Marvell was not merely immersed in a theological culture. He was surrounded by important French men of letters, and the evidence of allusions in his own writings suggests that he knew several interesting and diverse local figures. The sojourn gives us the best insight into Marvell's exposure to French literary culture. Near to Saumur, in the Château des Réaux, lived Gédéon Tallemant des Réaux, a Protestant by birth but a colourful *libertin* and *bon vivant* by nature. Marvell's first modern biographer and editor, Pierre Legouis, noted that a phrase in *The Rehearsall Transpros'd: The Second Part*, referring to Rabelais's giant Pantagruel, had its source in Tallemant's *Historiettes*, a series of satirical portraits of courtiers.[52] Since the latter work was not published in print until 1834, it has been supposed either that Marvell saw a Tallemant manuscript or that both men heard the Rabelais anecdote in the locality. The former seems more likely: Tallemant had several manucripts in circulation, some of which have only very recently been discovered. Marvell seems to have admired Tallemant's wit, and used the opportunity of his rich work to extract further ludic moments for *The Rehearsall Transpros'd*. Tallemant compiled Manuscrit 673 (in the collection at La Rochelle) between 1649 and 1690, an astonishing collection of largely topical satirical poems and prose passages, by Tallemant himself, and a host of other famous writers. Tallemant added a considerable amount of glossing. If we ever doubt where the specific form of Marvell's 'Last Instructions to a Painter' came from, here is an answer.

Just outside Saumur, at Notre-Dame des Ardilliers, was another college established in 1619 by L'Oratoire de France, a society of secular priests, and called the Collège royal des Catholiques. On the same site was an Oratorian house for advanced studies in theology and philosophy. Although Roman Catholics, the Oratorians enjoyed friendly relations with the Protestant academy, even to the extent of participating in each other's academic exercises. In 1654 or 1655 Abel-Louis St-Marthe was appointed Father Superior of the house. Although he moved on to another appointment in Paris at the end of

March 1656, it is conceivable that he met Marvell in the early months of that year. This conjecture too was important to Legouis because he could not otherwise find a source for another reference in *The Rehearsal Transpros'd* to 'the two learned brothers of St. Marthe', one who wore a plain band and one who wore a ruff.[53] These were the twins Gaucher III and Louis St-Marthe, sons of Gaucher (Scévole) St-Marthe, a famous humanist. The twins were born in 1571, and Marvell recounts how similarly their minds worked. Louis eventually took orders, hence the plain band, while Gaucher, the *seigneur* of Mèrè-sur-Indre in Touraine, wore the *fraise* or ruff that was still common among the gentry in the reign of Louis XIII. Abel-Louis was the second son of Gaucher III, and Legouis conjectures that it was from him that Marvell learned of both his father and uncle. No surviving printed or manuscript source would have given him the information before *The Rehearsal Transpros'd* was published in 1672. Abel-Louis was also a poet, and had a strong interest in architecture, but his primary occupation in the mid-1650s was the completion of a revision of his father and uncle's jointly authored *Histoire généalogique de la maison de France*, originally published in 1619. Abel-Louis saw the book into print just after Marvell and Dutton had left Saumur in September, his uncle Louis having died on 29 April, and his father some six years prior to that. The other major French publication during 1656 was Pascal's *Provinciales*, the notorious manifesto of the Jansenist movement. The Oratorians openly accepted the Pope's condemnation of Jansenism, but Abel-Louis was suspected of complicity in the movement, resulting in his eventual exile from Paris and his resignation of the generalship of his society. Abel-Louis displayed notable moral austerity and was certainly associated with the home of Jansenism, the Port-Royal community.

A third notable literary presence was Louis La Forge (1632–66), the disciple of Descartes. He had established a medical practice at Saumur in 1653. As an active participant in the intellectual life of both Protestant and Catholic institutions, La Forge was responsible for the dissemination of Cartesian ideas in both the Oratorians' house, and in the Protestant Academy, where it was officially adopted a few years later. When Marvell alludes to Descartes in *The Rehearsall Transpros'd: The Second Part*, was he in fact referring to an earlier version of La Forge's writings, texts that would not appear in print until the 1660s?[54]

We can associate only one very short three-line poem by Marvell with the stay in Saumur. This is the translation into Latin of four French lines from Georges de Brebeuf's translation of Lucan's epic *De bello civili*, which Marvell had used prominently in the construction of 'An Horatian Ode'. De Brebeuf's translation had appeared in 1655, and it seems most likely that Marvell saw it the following year and in Saumur. The French translation is relatively free, and Marvell was drawn to de Brebeuf's elaboration not on military valour but on the ability of words to capture images and sounds – a sophisticated version of the *ut pictura poesis* topos: 'The former [the Phoenician] afforded with eloquent characters, with a quill as his medium, the art of suggesting sounds to the eyes and of painting speech, and he transferred thought to paper, hearing to the eyes.' Was this written as an example for Dutton to follow, or as a compliment for someone in Saumur, or indeed, after Marvell's return to England, perhaps as a further demonstration of his skill with languages, and in connection with his entry into the civil service? Whatever the circumstance of composition, the translation is a further instance of Marvell's growing interest in the relationship between the verbal and the visual.

Marvell did not go unnoticed in Saumur. Scots divines played a highly significant role in the academy: John Cameron (*c.* 1579–1623) was another principal who ranked second only to Amyraut as an expounder of Saumur theology. His countryman Alexander Calander, who taught pupils in a house owned by his sister in the town, revealed that he was an intimate of Dutton and Marvell when, away from the city, he asked a friend, Joseph Williamson (the future master of intelligence for Charles II), to convey his 'humble salutations' to the couple in a letter of 26 January 1656. It is conceivable that he had passed Dutton, Marvell and their servants on their way down to Saumur from the capital. It is also possible that the Protectorate civil service was already lining up Marvell for a position, and was certainly using him as a correspondent for intelligence. René Augier in Paris wrote to John Thurloe on 19 or 29 January to report that 'I have according unto your Honour's Direction sent the Inclosed unto Mr Marvin [*sic*] att Saumur, and have also written unto him the place of my Abode here, that he maye make use of me for his Letters and Otherwise.'[55] Augier wrote again on 13 or 23 February to Thurloe, enclosing a packet from Marvell, and further mail for Dutton, which would otherwise have been lost, was forwarded from Paris on 7/17 March.[56] As ever, Marvell listened to and looked at what was around him. He drank it in. It would become a potent resource for both his poetry and his prose, and it would have formed valuable intelligence for Thurloe.

Marvell must have sustained a lively correspondence in this period, although all of it is lost, or as yet undiscovered. As we know, one correspondent at this time was Milton, with whom Marvell had already established a strong literary friendship and who was of course still useful to Marvell as a way to better employment. It would seem that just as Marvell had helped distribute copies of Milton's *Defensio Secunda* in England, so he had also given away copies of Milton's *Pro se defensio* in the summer of 1656, it having been published in August 1655. Milton refers not to Marvell by name, but to 'a friend of mine', which must almost certainly mean Marvell, in a letter of 1 August 1657 to Henry Oldenburg, later the first secretary of the Royal Society, but then another tutor in Saumur. Milton had sent one copy, but Marvell needed more, since this one copy had to go the rounds of the locality. Oldenburg was given more books: Marvell had reported that the book was in demand in the area (perhaps because in it Milton attacked the Scoto-French minister Alexander More).

As it was so tolerant a place, many Englishmen, Scotsmen and Irishmen of different kinds of loyalty and character gathered in Saumur. On 15 August,

James Scudamore, an Anglo-Irish Royalist, and the fourth son of John, first Viscount Scudamore of Sligo, wrote to Sir Richard Browne, Charles II's resident at Paris. (His sister Mary would eventually marry William Dutton.) He reported that among the many English living at Saumur, few were of note, but those who were included Lord Paget's son, Mr Dutton, 'calld by the french Le Genre du Protecteur' and 'whose Governour is one Mervill a notable English Italo-Machavillian'. Scudamore was scouting on behalf of Browne to find men loyal to the Stuarts who would be serviceable. Thus, it is no surprise that he found Marvell so closed and politique. This famous description is usually taken as corroborative of Marvell's interest in and knowledge of Machiavellian thought, itself reflected so prominently in the vocabulary of 'An Horatian Ode' and 'The First Anniversary'. However, and however true it may be in this literal sense, it was also a Royalist's pejorative description of a prudent man in the service of the enemy to all Royalists, Oliver Cromwell. And Marvell may very well have been gathering information on, among other matters, Royalist exiles, for Thurloe. It may also reflect Marvell's ability to talk to men of all opinions, and to appear to be open to all possibilities. He may have appeared to Scudamore to be no diehard Royalist, but certainly someone who was politically subtle and open to more than one possibility. Scudamore was also rash, being imprisoned for debts in Paris the following year. In all of this, Marvell was also in Scudamore's judgement 'notable'. Was he thus already famous?

He was certainly noted, for early in the previous October, just after the departure to Saumur, Samuel Hartlib received a letter from Dr John Worthington: 'There is one Marvel of 40. years of age who hath spent all his time in travelling abroad with Noblemens Sonnes and is skilled in several languages, who is now again to goe with one's Sone of 8. thousand a year, who is fitter to bee a Secretary of State etc.' The document went on: 'Hee is advised to make the like contract as Page hath done being thus far in years.'[57] Page was a 'fellow of Kings Colledge in Cambridge and once Orator there [who] hath from beginning of these troubles travelled into forraigne Parts and learned' and who had been newly employed 'by the Earl of Devonshire as Governour to his Son and hath an Annuity of an hundred lb. settled upon him'.[58] This would have been handsome indeed.

William Dutton and his tutor returned from France to England in September 1656. John Dutton's illness (a dropsy) had worsened and he felt that his end was near. He had raised with Cromwell the question of recalling William in June, and Marvell had received a letter warning him that return was imminent. Dutton renewed his request in August.[59] He wanted to pass on his estate to William with the greatest possible facility and ease, and that meant showing William how it worked. A description and inventory of the entire estate were made to help William remember its extent and contents. The Sherborne Estate, situated in the Cotswolds, was remarkable. Dutton had created Lodge Park in 1634 (see plate 17). Inspired by his passion for gambling and banqueting, he equipped it with what would later be called a grandstand, with its deer course and park. In a way, Marvell was becoming an estate steward. He lived with the Duttons at Sherborne, Gloucestershire, from September until January 1657, when John died, in the second week of the month. Dutton senior did not merely wish to familiarize his nephew with Sherborne: he also wanted to make sure that no one else either occupied the property or embezzled the goods, and he specifically suspected George Colt, husband of his only surviving daughter Elizabeth, or Lord Downe, the widower of his other daughter, in this respect. He sent Marvell to London probably in October to invite Henry Poulton, lawyer and husband of William's older sister Elizabeth, to visit Sherborne to discuss the settlement. Poulton was made a trustee of the estate at this point. Could it be that Dutton also feared a forced occupation? He thought the malcontents would make an 'incident molestacon', and asked Marvell to bring 'downe some good Companey off friends who might stich to his Nephew'.

Already in residence for some three months at Sherborne was the dramatist and Royalist Sir William Killigrew. He enjoyed Dutton's confidence and had knowledge of plans for the development of the estate, plans that he passed on to Marvell.[60]

Three days before he died Dutton sent Marvell off to London again to urge on Cromwell the match between his daughter Frances and William, and then called him back to tell him that he was leaving William an income of £4,000 a year, with a further £2,000 in reversion. Marvell was being put in a position of considerable trust. Nor was it merely a family dispute. Dutton was a Royalist but he had effectively compounded with Cromwell to keep his estate, and William was at the heart of that settlement. In 1652, Poulton had argued with John Dutton over the administration of Elizabeth's estate, and he would later claim that Dutton used Cromwell's influence then to avoid Poulton's pursuit of him in law. At this time, the projected match between William and Frances Cromwell was very much under discussion. But in 1656 that dispute was over. Marvell had been sent to London to talk to the Protector, and to take up the matter of the proposed marriage of William and Frances. Dutton had asked Killigrew to perform this task, but he had refused, so the duty fell to Marvell. The £4,000 a year was to be paid when William married. But in fact, Cromwell's attention in this respect was now again turned to Robert Rich, an even more eligible match for Frances, and the man whom she would soon marry.

Marvell's time as tutor to William Dutton came to an unlikely climax nearly a year later. John Dutton senior, William's uncle, finally died during the night of 13–14 January 1657. He had settled most of his estate on William, with a portion for William's younger brother Ralph.[61] In November 1657, the claim of the two brothers was challenged in Chancery by John Dutton's only surviving daughter Elizabeth and her husband George Colt. They claimed that a later will made by Dutton favoured Elizabeth, and they sought to have William evicted from Sherborne. In fact, Colt had had a forged will made, but it took an extensive investigation in the Upper Bench in November 1657 for this to be revealed. Marvell became involved as a witness on behalf of his former pupil. It was at the time a very public affair, not least because of Colt's fashionable reputation in town (even in the Protectorate 'gallants' populated the capital).

Documentation for the case was assembled several months earlier. Marvell's deposition is dated 22 June 1657, and he clearly testifies that John Dutton did not cease to show his great love and affection for William up to his death. It was indeed his concern for his nephew that had led him to write, with Cromwell's blessing, in September 1656 to recall him from France.

In the *Miscellaneous Poems* of 1681 is a poem entitled 'On the Victory obtained by Blake over the Spaniards, in the Bay of Santa Cruz, in the Island of Tenerife, 1657.' The news of the sinking of the Spanish silver fleet at Santa Cruz on 20 April 1657 reached London on 28 May. The Spanish fleet, consisting of five or six galleons and another ten or eleven smaller ships, had been anchored at Santa Cruz since early February. Having found no enemy ships off Cadiz in late March, Blake's fleet made for the Canary Islands and very shortly after its arrival engaged the Spanish fleet, which was arranged defensively in the harbour. This meant that the English ships had to come in close to land, and took fire from the shore defences. Nonetheless, after four hours the smaller Spanish boats were beaten back, and later the Vice-Admiral's ship caught fire, and the Admiral's exploded. The English losses were comparatively slight: no ships were lost; most of the slain (no more than fifty) or wounded (120) had succumbed to musket fire from the shore. That the wind had blown directly into the bay during the action, and then changed to enable the English fleet to sail away with ease, was regarded as an act of Providence. The victory concluded Blake's highly successful naval career. He was recalled to England, handsomely rewarded and loudly praised by Cromwell. But being by this time of frail health, he died of scurvy just off Plymouth on 7 August.

But this jingoistic verse is not like a Marvell poem and is decidedly inferior. It is now thought that Marvell was not the author.[62] It was probably by 'R.F.', whose signature remains on one surviving copy. Marvell had one too, perhaps on account of his proximity to Cromwell; possibly he received it from the author, who hoped that he would present it to the Lord Protector. Perhaps too it was a poem that Marvell hoped to rewrite, to turn into something more obviously his own, as he had done with other poems.[63]

CHAPTER 6

✳

CIVIL SERVICE

MARVELL'S GREAT CAREER HOPE was realized when, on Wednesday, 2 September 1657, he took up his appointment as assistant to Milton in his role as Secretary of Foreign or Latin Tongues. He was employed in the office of John Thurloe, secretary to the Council of State, and since December 1652 the Master of Oliver Cromwell's intelligence services, as the voluminous and fascinating records he left behind reveal. He was preferred to a 'Mr Sterry': presumably not Peter Sterry, Cromwell's chaplain, but perhaps his brother Nathaniel.[1] In May 1655, Thurloe had taken control of both domestic and foreign intelligence. Marvell was now at the heart of power and its exercise, and he has been seen as typical of a new class of civil officials who rose in the Protectorate and continued as a class after the Restoration. Samuel Pepys was another example. While Thurloe was technically Marvell's superior, and Marvell accepted instructions from him, in effect the new appointee worked for Milton. Most of Marvell's duties involved the translation of letters and other official documents from English into Latin, or vice versa. Milton's blindness meant that Marvell was kept busier than might otherwise have been the case. Apart from the translation of documents, he also attended foreign dignitaries in London. A salary of £200 was paid, in quarterly instalments, twice the amount that was considered a worthwhile salary as a private tutor. In Thurloe's office, Marvell would gain for the first time behind-the-scenes knowledge of how government worked. He worked for a government that has been judged in hindsight efficient, dedicated and relatively uncorrupt, even if hampered by lack of manpower and resources, outweighed by large and expensive armed forces, and challenged by the extraordinary potential for ideologically based subversion among its enemies. Thurloe bore a great responsibility for its successes.[2]

The first documented example of Marvell's work is a translation of a Latin dispatch to Thurloe from Hamburg concerning Baltic affairs dated on the day he entered the service. Marvell may have worked on this some three days after the document was dated.[3] A further dispatch from the same source, dated 8 September, was also translated.[4] The next known job, in late October, was the translation of a letter from Marshal Turenne to Bordeaux, the French ambassador, from the camp at Rumingen, and in part concerning the commitment of English forces in the war with Spain.[5] Those autograph translations that have been found are concerned either with French matters or with Sweden, the latter being somewhat more numerous: seven out of nineteen items. There are also several items concerning relations with the United Provinces. It is hard to discover any more specific details of the circumstances and conditions in which these documents were produced, but it is certain that on 18 February 1658 Marvell substituted for Milton in the rendering of a letter from Cromwell to the Elector of Brandenburg, Friedrich Wilhelm, into Latin. Milton's beloved second wife had died on 8 February, and we suppose that Milton was thus indisposed. Marvell appears to have taken down the letter in English by dictation from Cromwell before translating it into Latin.

At around this time, and in response to a petition by the Scottish Guinea Company seeking to recover the *St Andrew* of Edinburgh, captured as long ago as 1636 or 1637, when its men had been murdered on the order of the Portuguese Governor of São Tomé, John Thurloe also noted 'Mr Marvill. I desire you to write a Letter upon this petition to the K. of Portugall.'[6]

In Marvell's work as an interpreter he was called upon to receive foreign visitors. He assisted Nieupoort, the Dutch ambassador, on 27 November 1657, and he was probably present when the Dutch ambassador and the agent of the Elector of Brandenburg visited in August and September 1658.[7] His trips abroad and his broad literary knowledge and tastes would have equipped him extremely well for these duties.

When Marvell entered government employment, the major foreign concern was the war with Spain, and (to the English) the uncertain alliance with France that bolstered them against the Spanish. The King of Spain held positions in northern Europe (Flanders in particular, Dunkirk most of all) that would facilitate an invasion by Charles Stuart, backed by Spanish forces. Throughout the first nine months of 1657, the former Leveller Edward Sexby was active in Spain, in league with the Royalists, directly soliciting the financial help of Philip IV and hoping that an acceptance of the Crown by Cromwell would precipitate a revolt among the army officers, so that the Royalists and Spanish would be greatly aided by internal dissent and the decline into anarchy that might result from an army revolt. The English, who had troops in Flanders, wanted French help to take the territory around the Channel ports, and Dunkirk itself, which would eliminate both the Royalist and the Spanish threat, and the safe haven that the port offered to various pirates who harried English shipping. The French, especially their field commander, Marshal Turenne, were far less committed to this path, seeing little strategic advantage for themselves in what would be a costly and difficult military operation.

Mardyke was eventually besieged; it surrendered on 24 September, but the garrison was then open to counter-attack from the Spanish and the Royalists. When the English ambassador to Paris, Sir William Lockhart, arrived with French reinforcements, Turenne's advice was to abandon the fortress, and, Cromwell's views aside, even the Council of State was concerned about the cost of the operation. The Council in fact decided only on 6 November to keep Mardyke, and it was on this day that Turenne wrote from the camp at Rumingen to Bordeaux, the French ambassador to England, saying that he had taken such defensive precautions in Mardyke as would please the Protector. Whatever else the French intended, they must act as if Mardyke really mattered to them, and Turenne says he intuits that Cromwell wants to preserve Mardyke, but that if it should be lost, he wants neither the shame for its loss nor the expense. In this respect, he worries that English promises of arms and engineers have not yet been honoured. This is the letter that Marvell translated into English, presumably after it had been intercepted and opened. The same was the case with a letter written three days later by another French commander, d'Ormesson, writing from Calais, and probably also to Bordeaux, giving further evidence of French preparations in Bourbourg, and lamenting the delayed arrival of English arms. Bordeaux, if he is the addressee, is asked to make ready to dispatch a large quantity of English arms to Flanders.[8]

A week after he translated d'Ormesson's letter, Marvell's attention was directed to copying, perhaps taking down by dictation, a letter from the commissioners appointed by Cromwell to negotiate a treaty with the United Provinces to William Nieupoort, the ambassador from the Dutch States General. It is a stoutly worded document, indicating how far apart the Dutch and the English remained in 1657, and how maritime and mercantile affairs in particular divided them. Thurloe considered it sufficiently important to read it over, correcting, adding punctuation and endorsing. The content is concerned with the form in which agreements are expressed, and with the English insistence that treaties vary in their form and content. However unspecific the contents of this letter, the tone points up the ongoing 'uncomfortable embrace' of the English and the Dutch.[9] The treaty that followed the First Dutch War (1652–54), during which time Marvell wrote his accomplished satire, 'The Character of Holland', was supposed to have been followed by a further maritime agreement, but this had not occurred and Dutch complaints of English naval harassment grew. By 1657 the Dutch were in alliance with the Spanish, with whom the English were at war. But outright war with Holland was, in the mind of Cromwell, to be avoided at all costs. Despite the unceasing points of aggravation between the two nations, it still seemed far worse for Protestant states to fall into war with each other.

One month later came the first of a substantial body of translations by Marvell concerned with Anglo-Swedish relations. These are in stylish English, and are a record of Swedish views (given in spoken discourse by the Swedish commissioners on 7 December) on the necessity of the ships of both nations being free to navigate unhindered in their waters; there is specific reference to the unusual conditions that prevailed during the Anglo-Dutch wars, and to determining the specific dates of the conflict.[10] At stake was an alleged £100,000. It seems that Marvell was translating from Latin, and this is reflected in the notably subtle sentences: 'wherefore this or that ship, or the goods of either party, were taken, detained and afterwards dismissed, supposing all those things examined, agitated, disputed before-hand, and laid asleep after the sentences given'. In Marvell's hand are the English commissioners' reply of 14–16 December, and a translation from the Swedes of 19 December urging no further delay in reaching a settlement while still insisting on their understanding of the dates of the Anglo-Dutch conflict.[11] Then on 7 January in the new year Marvell translated a letter from George Fleetwood and Johan Friderich von Friessendorff, the Swedish envoy to England, to the Council of State requesting restitution for shipping losses owing to English depredations (and where the English commissioners are seen as not having lived up to treaty commitments). The letter recalled the services in yesteryear of the Swedes against the Dutch. Sweden's pursuit of Dutch war reparations continued: their requests and arguments remained unanswered. Marvell copied another document (this time an account of one of its authors; he did not translate it) from the Swedish commissioners on the same day. It resorted to natural law, and cited Justinian and Ulpian as authorities in order to justify the repayment of the value of lost shipping. George Fleetwood, brother of the influential Commonwealth soldier and politician, Charles, signed the document as one of the Swedish commissioners, along with Friessendorff: he had long been employed by Charles X.[12]

Thurloe was ill and was unable to stay at his desk throughout the rest of January: this stalled business with the ambassadors in France and Wismar, the Hanseatic port on the north German coast and Swedish territory since 1648; Marvell underestimated the significance of this illness even though it meant he wrote to ambassadors in his own right rather than as an amanuensis.

Then in this series came something quite other, in a wholly different key. The most substantial document that survives from this period is a forty-page translation of a political tract by von Friessendorff, written in Marvell's hand, and made in the second half of January.[13] The purpose of the tract was to persuade the Protector to send the English navy with the Swedes, under English command, against Holland and Spain. Strictly speaking therefore, and aside from letters, the translation may be considered Marvell's first known surviving prose work. The translation is extremely clumsy, in the sense that it appears to be a phrase-by-phrase rendering of the Latin text. There was probably no other intention than that it should serve as a policy discussion document, and so should be close to the literal meaning of the original. Annabel Patterson avers that it nonetheless chimes in places with Marvell's known views on liberty of conscience so much that it begins to sound like him rather than von Friessendorff, and therefore raises new questions about the sources of Marvell's views on religious liberty. Marvell's involvement in the Swedish embassy of 1654, albeit remote, had given him a knowledge of Scandinavian history sufficient to cope with the historical and political context of the document, and it must have helped sustain his interest in the north and the Baltic, references to which recur throughout his later writing.

Von Friessendorff presents Sweden as a parallel case to England. In his view, it became a virtuous state with the Vasa dynasty who were able to throw off centuries of Danish tyranny. Then it also became a Protestant state. The wars with Poland were not merely dynastic but confessional, and the worthy Protestant Swedes have to maintain a wary eye on the persistently perfidious Danes and Russians, to say nothing of the Polish affinity with the Austrian Habsburgs, which had caused Charles IX and his successor Gustavus Adolphus to take war to northern and central Europe. But the Swedes, having settled Europe so that Protestantism was protected, now have to deal with the unreliable Dutch, who have made an alliance with the arch-Catholic power, Spain. The Stuarts prevaricated when they should have been engaged in the Thirty Years War, and this failure is connected, it is argued, with their domestic difficulties, just as Kristina may have suffered God's vengeance for alienating her religion and for being too flexible with the Spaniards when negotiating the Peace of Westphalia. Cromwell and Charles X, like the biblical David and Jonathan, are the opposites to this: they are the Protestant hope pitted against Holland, which, like the 'Commonwealth of Venice', is driven by a commercial greed that will outweigh any other principle, and is therefore perfectly willing to play off one power against another to her own advantage, whatsoever the issues at stake. Von Friessendorff points to the poor treatment of George Downing, the English ambassador at the Hague, in these terms.

Striking too are the rhetorical devices that chime with Marvell's state poetry of the 1660s. The Dutch are revealed by the visual appearance of their culture: 'Let him that pleases looke upon the frontispiece of the new built town-house [i.e. the City Hall] of Amsterdam And he will see that the very stones speake concerning their disposition their mind their counsels.' 'He who painted Mercury with wings seems to have expressed their nature who follow him.' Then comes allusion to Aesop: the United Provinces are the wren that hides under the eagle in order to avoid the vulture, 'as if she were cutting diamonds of those that are more potent, she grinds the one with the other'.

The rhetoric hid, in hindsight not very effectively, the aggressive aims of Charles X's foreign policy. He favoured Swedish expansion by conquest and was determined to use the English as allies to this end. In this Cromwell and his advisers misjudged the Swedish king, since they did not see this aim, and were surprised when Charles turned out to be as dangerous to his Protestant neighbours as he was to the Catholic powers. Nonetheless, it had been possible to exercise restraint on Swedish ambition for two years. A war between the Dutch and the Swedes would have been disastrous for England, especially since her navy was preoccupied by the demands of the war with Spain. The Protector had to play a subtle waiting game: he was good at this, and while waiting Marvell took on lesser diplomatic tasks, like the writing of a demand from Cromwell that a Brandenburg sea captain be punished for the harsh treatment of an English counterpart.

During these first few weeks in his new position, with its very serious and time-consuming duties, Marvell would surely have noticed the marriage, at last, of Mary Fairfax on 24 September to George Villiers, second Duke of Buckingham, the man in whose company Marvell very probably was in 1646. It was not to be a happy marriage, and perhaps Marvell already knew that Buckingham's time in exile had sown the habits of loose living that would lead in the next twenty years to neglect, adultery and failure to produce an heir. Cromwell certainly did not like the match, and objected on the grounds that it let one of the chief Royalist families back into the ranks of the propertied aristocracy at a time when Buckingham's loyalties were not certain. Buckingham undoubtedly wanted his lands restored and the match with Mary Fairfax was one way towards this. Yet in 1657 the marriage seemed a fulfilment of the dynastic hopes expressed at the end of 'Upon Appleton House'.

One important piece of evidence concerning the wedding is the testimony of Fairfax's nephew, Brian Fairfax, who claimed in a brief life of Buckingham, not published until 1758, that Abraham Cowley and not Marvell, as might be expected, wrote an epithalamium for the wedding (it does not, so far as we know, survive).[14] Marvell was of course by this time tied down to Whitehall and its demands, but more importantly, he was now too close to Cromwell on this sensitive issue. Indeed, as Fairfax or Buckingham would have noticed, he had been of the Cromwell household since shortly after leaving Nun Appleton.

In his role as assistant secretary Marvell was at last a dignitary, and it would have been fitting for one in his position to have a portrait made. The 'Nettleton' portrait of Marvell, which the poet's great-nephew Robert Nettleton gave to the British Museum in 1764, may well date from this time (plate 18).[15] Nicholas von Maltzahn suggests that the picture may have remained in Marvell's possession during his lifetime and so he may have taken it with him when he left his lodgings in Whitehall, since the engraved frontispiece to the *Miscellaneous Poems* (1681) seems to derive from it.[16] It would also have been appropriate at this time for Marvell to be painted by the fashionable Sir Peter Lely. There is evidence that such a picture was made, although it remains lost.[17]

Marvell's skills as a poet were by now apparently known to the Cromwell family, because he was asked to prepare an entertainment for the marriage of Oliver's third daughter, Mary (1637–1712), to Thomas Belasyse, second Viscount Fauconberg (or Falconbridge; 1627–1700), on Thursday, 19 November 1657, at

Hampton Court. Indeed, Cromwell must have seen the Latin epitaphs on himself and Kristina, possibly a copy of the 'Letter to Doctor Ingelo', possibly 'The Character of Holland' and almost certainly 'The First Anniversary'. (He might have seen 'An Horatian Ode', but would he have understood its ironies?) Marvell wrote his 'Two Songs at the Marriage of the Lord Fauconberg' for this wedding. The internal evidence of both songs suggests that they would have been performed shortly after the wedding ceremony, but there is no absolute certainty since the celebrations are reported to have continued throughout the following week.

Sir William D'Avenant, whose works, as we have seen, Marvell carefully scrutinized, wrote an epithalamium for the marriage, which was entered in the Stationers' Register on 7 December, but the poem is not known to survive in printed or manuscript form. Fauconberg was related matrilineally to Fairfax, and was a Yorkshireman: it is therefore possible that he was well known to Marvell. Despite the closure of the theatres, and the public hostility of the Parliamentarian and Commonwealth regimes to plays, entertainments continued to be performed in private houses throughout the 1640s and 1650s, and pastoral themes and characters were popular.[18] Many Commonwealth grandees were in favour of drama, and various kinds of officially tolerated theatre began to be performed again in the 1650s. Cromwell himself was fond of music and maintained a considerable musical establishment, using it to entertain guests. Marvell's use of Platonic elements is a sign of the revival of Caroline masque themes inside Protectoral circles (although with the Restoration, this kind of masque was to disappear when the monarch failed to live up to the image of virtue anticipated and celebrated therein).

In comparison with the wedding of another Cromwell daughter, Frances (to the wealthy and eligible Robert Rich, and not Marvell's former pupil, William Dutton (see above, 110–13; 128–35), at Whitehall the previous week, this wedding was a modest and a private affair. Fauconberg in fact requested that the cost of the wedding be allocated to the dowry. But such modesty is not attributable to Puritanism. The women in Cromwell's family had Anglican preferences, and the Belasyses were known Royalist sympathizers (the groom had also, at one point, been suspected of Catholicism by the government). Perhaps for this reason the wedding was regarded with 'universal amazement', and the intimacy and indeed secrecy of the celebration was suited to the fact that many of Fauconberg's relatives would have been unable to attend on account of their Royalism, or in Fairfax's case, their difficult relations with Cromwell.[19] The marriage ceremony was conducted by Dr John Hewitt, a highly effective, yet tolerated, Anglican preacher, reputedly using the Book of Common Prayer.[20] However Puritan Marvell's songs appear to us today, they were written for and performed within a courtly and Anglican context. To this extent, they contributed to an atmosphere that must have felt somewhat like a reversion to the 1630s. The marriage itself represented a consolidation of the

Cromwell family's rise to the ranks of the nobility. The marriage settlement was worth £15,000, while Fauconberg's estate was worth £35,000 per annum.

The songs are pastoral in nature, and hence thoroughly in keeping with the tradition of the epithalamium – a poem written to celebrate a marriage – that Marvell would have known well. Spenser, for instance, had written a famous epithalamium. In the first eclogue, Endymion represents the bridegroom, Cynthia the bride, and Jove Cromwell himself. In the second, the bride and groom are alluded to under the names of Damon and Marina; Menalca is Cromwell.

It has been suggested that Henry Lawes, the composer of the music for Milton's masque *Comus*, may also have written the music for Marvell's songs, although other candidates are John Hingston, master of music to the Lord Protector, or perhaps one of the other seven Protectorate musicians, all of whom had former careers in the royal court. These men, together with 'two lads brought up to music', would presumably have performed the music at the wedding. Lawes played a prominent role in musical innovation, furthering the humanist goal of balancing text and melodic line. By the mid-seventeenth century English song had abandoned polyphony and conventional formulas for a monody that subjected musical line to the poetic text: this Italian fashion found its greatest English expression in the compositions of William and Henry Lawes.[21] The dramatized persona of the singing voice and the argumentative structure were emphasized, preferences that would have suited the fanciful, ironic and self-conscious nature of Marvell's poems.

These features make Marvell's marriage songs very different from most comparable entertainment verse, which is regular in nature. Marvell produced a verse that was expressive rather than formulaic, 'highlighting and emphasizing rhymes, line-ends, and particular points of argument rather than strophic, repeated, or ornamental elements'.[22] Although no music for the songs survives, it may well have been that the tension between regularity of poetic metre and discontinuity that falls during the cadences (in the style of the music outlined above) would also enhance the playfulness of Marvell's sophisticated prosody.

We can tell from the songs how some of the family members were represented in the entertainment. This may suggest that they even performed in the songs, but we cannot be certain. Cynthia is mentioned at line 7, the classical moon goddess, but she is plainly identified with Mary Cromwell at line 33. In Elizabethan iconography, Cynthia was Queen Elizabeth herself: Mary Cromwell thus takes her place as heroic Protestant female. Endymion is Lord Fauconberg, and, more interestingly, Anchises represents here Robert Rich, grandson and heir to the Earl of Warwick, who of course had recently married Frances Cromwell. Anchises consorted with Venus on Mount Ida on Crete, so Frances Cromwell is compared to the goddess of love. Since Anchises was the father of Aeneas, the implication is that the union between the Rich and Cromwell families will produce a new hero for the English nation. Marvell

followed a well-known Platonic allegory in representing the union of Mary and
Fauconberg: Cynthia lives in the realm of pure reason, and expects Endymion to
exercise his reason to reach her. At the end of the first song there is an allusion
to the marriage of Mary Fairfax and Buckingham. Cromwell would never have
allowed such an untoward marriage for his daughters: 'For he did never love to
pair/His progeny above the air.' Still another suggestion is that the lines refer to
an earlier rumour of marriage between Mary Fairfax and the future Charles II.
Menalca played by Oliver Cromwell, in fact iconographically apt, is also rather
absurd. Whilst reference to both Charles I and Charles II was often made in
pastoral terms, the reverse side of Cromwell's death medal depicted a shepherd
minding sheep, together with an olive tree. 'Joy to that happy pair,/Whose hopes
united banish our despair' picks up the theme of good in every sense that will
come from this marriage, just as it will from the union of Frances and Rich. The
political implications of the marriage were not merely a favourable alliance for
both the Cromwells and the Belasyses, but also a further healing of national division by the union of a former Royalist family with the Protectorate.

Marvell's Cynthia, Mary Cromwell, is presented as a coy mistress, but this
version of the Endymion story is extremely unusual. Characteristically, Cynthia
is portrayed as the more prominent force for desire.[23] Although the figure of
Cromwell remains apparently disinterested and aloof, the memory of the traditional Endymion story might well have suggested to an informed witness that
Marvell's intention was to point up the role of Cromwell in the making of the
match. The informed audience would have seen that the political reality was
different from that suggested by the masque, and in this dissonance signals
Cromwell's interestedness. Even in an epithalamic entertainment, Marvell
expressed with acute intelligence the exigencies of interest, just as he would
increasingly focus on its political dimensions in the future.

In light of the manner in which the wedding was conducted the sentiments
of the poem were, to say the least, hopeful. As with the earlier marriage
of Frances Cromwell, the marriage of Mary was greeted with dissatisfaction
by the army officers and seen as a sign of Cromwell's growing aristocratic
ambitions. Just seven months later the officiating divine, John Hewitt, would
be tried and executed for his alleged part in a Royalist conspiracy. But the
marriage itself, which had been arranged between Cromwell and Fauconberg
before Mary had any knowledge of it, turned out to be extremely prudent:
it was long and apparently happy. Fauconberg was much favoured after 1660
which meant that Mary was able to offer support to her sister Frances
whose marriage to the man of her choosing, Rich, ended in widowhood in
February 1658.

Finally, and after all, there was another poet behind these two wedding songs.
Marvell's poems came after Edmund Waller's poem on the marriage of Frances
Cromwell and Rich. While Marvell certainly takes some poetic guidance from
Waller in his revival of Caroline courtly entertainment modes, he certainly offers a

different conclusion to Waller. If the latter depicts Cromwell as a military dictator who has made possible the stable future of moderate aristocracy, Marvell presents a more nuanced scene: one in which the still unsettled resonances of the times, between Puritan gentleman-farmer-soldiers and their artisan-labourer-infantry followers on the one hand and powerful aristocrats on the other, between Roundheads and Royalists, between Cromwellians and republicans, is made subtly apparent. Only Oliver Cromwell himself makes everything come together. It was a chance for Marvell to answer Waller for his disapproval of 'The First Anniversary', but it would not be the last exchange.[24]

Marvell wrote to Sir William Lockhart, the English ambassador at Paris, on behalf of Thurloe on 11/21 January 1658, apologizing for Thurloe's ill health, promising that Lockhart's letters were read and announcing that a reply would be forthcoming.[25] This letter was intercepted, opened and copied by the French Post Office, and through that route it made its way into the hands of Henry Slingsby (one of Fauconberg's kinsmen), secretary to the Earl of Bristol and one of Charles II's agents.

The Swedish documents end in Cromwell's lifetime with a letter of around 9 April 1658 taken in English in Marvell's hand, but with revisions in another hand, to Sir Philip Meadows, envoy extraordinary to the King of Sweden.[26] Meadows was appointed instead of Marvell in 1653, and we must suppose that Marvell might have had hopes of being sent on such a mission in the future. Like Meadows he too by 1658 was a Baltic expert. It is a set of instructions: Meadows is asked to replace Major-General William Jephson as English ambassador in Sweden and to acquaint himself with the terms of the Swedish–Polish treaty currently being made. Meadows was to understand that he should be a mediator in the negotiations, and that, in so far as was possible, he should persuade Charles X to be willing to cede Prussia to the Poles. An equivalent approach to the King of Poland should be made, but if that approach did not meet with success, Meadows was to stand by Charles. Indeed, while Meadows was further instructed to reconcile the Swedes and the Brandenburgers, he was to follow Swedish directions, said Cromwell, in any relations with the Russians. The Protestant nature of this policy initiative is clear, since Meadows was to be sure to insist that the 'House of Austria', the Habsburgs, be kept out of the treaty. Not foreseen in this document is the rise of Prussia as a separate kingdom, which in the late 1650s was just around the corner.

After the Cromwells, the Oxenbridges again called on Marvell's attention, for on 23 April 1658 John Oxenbridge's wife Jane died. Jane Oxenbridge (b. 1620–1) was the daughter of Thomas Butler of Newcastle, merchant, and Elizabeth Clavering of Callaley. She married John Oxenbridge in 1634, shortly after he was expelled from Magdalen Hall, Oxford.[27] The epitaph by Marvell was written and then engraved on a black marble surface placed beneath Jane Oxenbridge's monument, erected on the south wall of Eton College Chapel, near the entrance to Lupton's Chantry. Over the monument was set the arms of

Oxenbridge impaling those of Butler. Under the epitaph was later set a shorter memorial inscription to Oxenbridge's second wife, Frances, daughter of the Puritan divine Hezekiah Woodward. Marvell's lines were obscured by white-wash at the Restoration: 'this larg epitaph giving offence to the Royalists at the Kings Restauration, an. 1660, it was daubed out with paint', and the monument itself was removed during alterations made in 1699. However, a copy of the epitaph, taken from Marvell's original copy in continuous prose form, was printed in the *Miscellaneous Poems*, and seven manuscript copies survive.

Anthony Wood later called the poem a 'large canting inscription' in which Oxenbridge made 'a grievous puling' after his wife, but he also confirmed the implication in Marvell's lines that Jane Oxenbridge was more than merely a pious wife, since he reports that she used to 'preach among ye women'. In *Athenae Oxonienses*, this statement was preceded by the observation that she preached 'amongst her gossips', a phrase among many objected to by Ambrose Barnes, brother-in-law of Jane Oxenbridge, in his *Memoirs*. Here he attested to Jane Oxenbridge's prowess as a scriptural commentator: 'a scholar beyond what is usual in her sex, and of a masculine judgement in the profound points of theologie, [her husband] loved commonly to have her opinion upon a text before he preacht from it'.[28]

By common reputation, Puritans and funerary monuments did not go hand in hand. Cavalier verse made much of godly contempt for monuments, and derided Puritan habits of commemoration. Extravagant expense was discour-aged by Puritans, and they objected to the use of images of the departed: this was seen as a kind of idolatry. There are recorded instances of the desecration of monuments by soldiers, and, allegedly, by Puritan separatists. Parliament, however, understood the importance of monuments as a means of sustaining social hierarchies through a visible and material sign of status and family iden-tity. Jane Oxenbridge's epitaph was very much in keeping with refined Puritan epitaphs, emphasizing her piety and her domestic virtues. A Royalist satire of her husband's patron, Oliver Cromwell, bitingly mocked Puritan scruples about monuments: 'no Stone/Shall stand this Epitaph; *That he has None*.' Ironically then, Marvell's Puritan epitaph of Jane Oxenbridge was itself a victim of Royalist iconoclasm. Part of the fashion of all epitaphs at this time, but particularly those of the godly, was a morbid obsession with the cause of death, which becomes in turn a source of poetic wit. Thus there is a conceit in which Jane Oxenbridge's death from dropsy is compared to the biblical deluge (Gen. 6–8), an image that would recur when Marvell came to commemorate the Protector himself. The flight of her soul from her body is likened to Noah releasing the dove from the ark to search for dry land (Gen. 8: 8–12). The conceit appears extravagant, of the kind that pushes comparison to breakdown or parody. However, the image is apt as an attempt to describe a grossly swollen body, even though the impres-sion of the soul being swept away by the deluge of retained body fluids defies the idea of the separation of body and soul that is the conceit's subject.

Official duties persisted during this time. They apparently included helping to raise money for the relief of foreign Protestants, perhaps individuals and families who had sought refuge in England. Thus, just a week after Jane Oxenbridge's death, Samuel Hartlib referred to Marvell when he wrote to Robert Boyle about a collection for Polish Protestants: 'But Mr Marvel did send again another express unto him [Roger Boyle, Lord Broghill], that his business was laid seriously to heart.' The ecumenicist John Dury, says Hartlib, had similarly pursued the London merchant Sir Thomas Viner.[29] Then, on 12 May, the Council of State delivered an order to Marvell that 'the Treasurers for the monies ariseing by the Collecion for the Poore Protestants Exiled out of Poland doe advance five hundred pounds for the releife of the xx[tie] Bohemian familyes; upon the Creditt of that Collection to be paid to such person and distributed in such manner as the Committee for that affaire shall direct.'[30] He was also ordered by the Council of State to attend to the business of 'the Committee on the Piedmontese Protestants to consider who shall receive the 500*l*. and how it shall be disposed of'.[31] The last letter in Marvell's hand in Oliver Cromwell's lifetime is a brief instruction of 9 July to George Downing, the English Resident at the Hague, from Thurloe, that he urge the Dutch to make as soon as possible a treaty of alliance with the King of Portugal. More minor but also repeated duties included requests to the Council of State for passes, usually for foreigners to leave the country, usually to France, sometimes elsewhere. At the same time, Marvell was expected to put up quite large sums for the transport of diplomats, which money was typically reimbursed annually from the government's chest. They were seventeenth-century travel receipts.

Willem Nieupoort, ambassador of the Dutch Republic, arrived at Gravesend in late July and Marvell was sent to greet him on the 24th. In addition to the normal reception, Marvell was instructed to promise barges, coaches and an entertainment – one perhaps, now lost, that Marvell himself might have penned. But, out of respect for the mourning for the death of Elizabeth Cromwell, Nieupoort refused these and said he intended to meet the Lord Protector on the 26th at Whitehall. Cromwell in fact stayed at Hampton Court which is where Thurloe finally conducted the Dutch ambassador. Nieupoort was delighted and impressed by Marvell's attention, as he wrote back to the States General.[32] There had been a considerable effort by Marvell in the first year of his appointment: he submitted on 1 September expenses for some fifty coach journeys to see Fleetwood, Friessendorff, Barkman (secretary to Friessendorff), Whitelocke, Petcombe the Danish Resident, Daniel Walker, Cromwell at Hampton Court, the Portuguese ambassador and Nieupoort himself, and he had been rewarded in August with a bonus payment of £15 by the Council of State for his 'publick Service'.

By the summer of 1658, Marvell had participated for nine months in a regime that itself had lasted some four and a half years. Cromwell could look back on his achievements both with pride and with some misgivings (see plate 19). However paranoid he may have felt about it, in part because of several assassination attempts, there was no mass support for the return of the Stuarts, even despite unpopular measures such as the closure of alehouses. Neither was the Protectorate a conservative regime: the measures that Cromwell took in many ways responded to the weakness of Stuart rule, and were to a large extent welcomed by the elites who ruled counties and boroughs. On top of this, and unlike the Barebones regime that preceded the Protectorate, Cromwell had fostered the return of ousted gentry JPs to their former positions; in general he tried to knit together the social fabric that had been stressed not merely by civil war and a revolution but also by one of the worst socio-economic crises of the early modern period during the late 1640s. With minimal central interference, local government seems to have proceeded well, and even progressively, in most respects in many places.

Marvell clearly had sympathy with the policy of relatively broad religious toleration pursued by Cromwell. The government had the power to appoint or eject ministers from livings, and sometimes – but rarely – did so. Tithes were maintained (much to the disgust of firm Puritans, like Milton), and supplemented by a scheme to enhance the income of poor clergy with funds from former ecclesiastical estates. But parishes were left alone and often carried on as they had under the bishops before 1640. The Prayer Book was replaced by the Directory for Public Worship, a Presbyterian document, but one that was relatively non-proscriptive. Cromwell was much less intolerant than the Presbyterians, many Independents and many of the MPs in his two Protectoral parliaments. The two famous heresy cases of John Biddle the Socinian in 1654–55 and James Nayler the Quaker in 1657, both of whom were on trial for their lives, reveal the split between Cromwell and his representatives. In the case of the former, the Protector's personal intervention saved Biddle's life.

Marvell's appointment was part of the two outstanding successes of the Protectorate: on the one hand, the relatively uncorrupt administration, and on the other a foreign policy that left England with a high diplomatic standing in the world. This was all the more remarkable given how inexperienced in foreign affairs most of Cromwell's officials were. Nonetheless, the regime made itself secure in Scotland and Ireland, and made an advantageous peace with the Dutch that forced Charles Stuart out of Dutch territory. There were further advantageous commercial treaties, and the navy successfully kept pirates and Royalists at bay. And yet far from being conservative, Oliver maintained his godly zeal in the cause of Reformation, causing serious disagreements with his parliaments, and seriously reducing his basis of support. When he fell ill for the last time in August 1658, this legacy did not bode well for those who came after him.

DEATH OF A HERO

Oliver Cromwell died at 3 p.m. on 3 September 1658, exactly one year after Marvell had joined the administration. The event would have profound effects for the Commonwealth and everyone in it. Cromwell's health had begun to fail earlier in the year, but he worsened greatly after the death from cancer of his favourite daughter Elizabeth on 6 August. Just one month later he passed away. It was an ominous moment in every respect, and the storm of 2 September, the day before Cromwell's death, was widely interpreted as a divinely induced sign – for some a manifestation of the wrath that came to take the tyrant away, and for others, like Marvell, a tremendous salute from heaven.

As one of the Latin secretaries to the Council of State, Marvell walked in Cromwell's funeral procession on 23 November, and had his mourning clothes paid for by the state. Famously, he walked alongside Milton, and with Dryden. The three poets worked together though Marvell and Milton would in many ways become poetic and literary enemies of the latter after the Restoration. With them were the other secretaries, Sir Philip Meadows and Nathaniel Sterry, and also Samuel Hartlib, the influential educational and scientific reformer, who sometimes undertook government tasks.

It was crucial for the Protectorate government to use a state funeral to demonstrate their sure grasp of power. Cromwell's body had to be embalmed and encased in lead soon after he died: the especially rapid putrefaction of the corpse surprised everyone. A private burial took place on 26 September in the chapel of Henry VII in Westminster Abbey. An effigy, dressed regally in purple and ermine, crowned and with a golden sceptre lay in state in Somerset House. Little expense was spared on the magnificent funeral, which cost £60,000 (to a state that was in severe financial difficulties). The funeral procession was long, and new mourning costumes or uniforms were procured for officials and soldiers walking in the procession or lining the route. The republicans and religious radicals who had fallen out with Oliver were outraged. The Royalists looked on in dismay or sullen anger and waited. Their day would soon come.

During this period, Marvell wrote his funeral elegy on Cromwell: 'A Poem upon the Death of his Late Highness the Lord Protector'; it was registered on 20 January 1659 to be published in a volume entitled *Three poems to the happy memory of the most renowned Oliver, late Lord Protector of this Commonwealth, by Mr Marvell, Mr Driden, Mr Sprat.* Marvell's poem is packed with allusion to newsbook and pamphlet publications from the autumn months of 1658 as the impact of Oliver's death sank in. It is a masterpiece of its kind and has been unjustly overlooked through the centuries, but for understandable reasons. Much of what was published in verse and prose to commemorate Cromwell was stiff, formal and awkward, not least because it had to be composed quickly. Cromwell's heroism, military prowess, nobility (even regality) and religious rectitude or apocalyptic role were stressed, often with a careful avoidance of ideological sensitivity, and hence with a tendency towards blandness and the conventional.[33] Marvell's poem is different.

Several commentators have felt that the poem reveals an unusual intimacy with the Cromwell family. Marvell's moving description of Cromwell's corpse at

lines 247–53 suggests that he was one of the few people to see it, as opposed to
the vast majority who saw only a wax effigy. Certainly, public information
surrounding the Protector's death was tightly controlled by the government:
both official newsbooks published identical accounts of Oliver's death and the
proclamation in the first week of September of Richard Cromwell as Lord
Protector.[34] Most of the information contained in the poem was publicly
available. Cromwell's love for his family was, for instance, acknowledged in
published literature: 'all these his Children, married and honourably disposed
of in his lifetime; so that we may truly say, that he lived, to be an Eye-witness of
God's great Mercy & Blessings, powred on himself and whole Family . . . a most
Tender and Indulgent Father'.[35] Cromwell's affection for his second daughter,
Elizabeth Claypole, his distress at her death on 6 August 1658, and its connection with his own deterioration, were also public knowledge.[36] But the focus on
the private side of Cromwell is both distinctive and apt. After Elizabeth's death,
Cromwell effectively ceased public activity, and Marvell's poem reflects nothing
of the Protector's elaborate and extravagant funeral ceremony. Yet neither is
there any trace of Elizabeth's funeral, which took place at midnight on Tuesday,
10 August in Henry VII's Chapel, and which Cromwell did not attend on
account of his gout.

Marvell idealizes Cromwell's relationship with Elizabeth, supposed, as we have
seen, to be his favourite daughter, but whose haughtiness as an adult (she is
frequently noted for assuming the status of a princess) gave Cromwell concern.
She interceded with her father on behalf of several political offenders, including
Harrington: she was able to assure the return of the confiscated manuscript of
Oceana to its author. On her deathbed she was also supposed to have reproached
her father for his bloodshed. Naturally, none of these details enters the poem.
Whatever the extent of Marvell's closeness to the Cromwell family, the presentation of the Lord Protector is in line with that of the private man who outdoes in
public life all monarchs and princes. The care for his daughter is consistent with
the elaborate state funeral accorded to his mother, Elizabeth, who died in
November 1654, aged ninety-three, an event celebrated in *The First Anniversary*
of 1655 (ll. 161–2).

Marvell's poem focuses upon Cromwell as an exemplary father and private,
godly man, as well as a martial hero, prince and agent of Providence. Thus,
although it is a well-defined example of the classical *epicedion*, or funerary poem,
describing deeds and lineage, its range of subjects is much broader than any
other example. Neither does the elegy easily fit with the general pattern of elegies
in the period. The execution of Charles I, and the spate of elegies that followed,
made Royalist elegy in the late 1640s and 1650s highly fashionable, and a distinct
branch of the genre. Parliamentarian, republican and Commonwealth elegy
tended to be as much panegyric as lament, and yet Marvell's poem manages to
create its own genuine and original terms of loss.[37] Moreover, Marvell's poem
defies the genre of funerary elegy in that it is called a 'poem' rather than an 'elegy'.

The other singular Cromwell elegy is George Wither's *Salt upon Salt: Made out of certain Ingenious Verses upon the Late Storm And the Death of His Highness Ensuing* (1659), which, unlike Marvell's poem, is critical as well as affirmative of the Protector, and meditates extensively on the sins of the nation and God's punishment of them, as well as (characteristically) Wither's own state of mind.[38]

One common feature of the elegies for Cromwell was an exaggeration of the topos concerned with the excellence of the subject. Cromwell defies the powers of all poets to commemorate him adequately, because he is such an outstanding leader and hero.[39] But Marvell's poem more closely resembles, and in some cases depends upon, the prose publications lamenting Cromwell's death and celebrating his achievements, where some space at least is given to Cromwell's private virtues and his domestic life.[40] Yet Marvell's poem still exceeds these in its concern with Cromwell's private life.

The further echoes of Milton's 'Lycidas' suggest that Marvell may have been attempting to generate a distinct kind of Puritan elegy in addition to revealing the growing influence of Milton on his own verse, despite Milton's own disillusionment with the Protectorate. Milton and Marvell had worked together in the government for one year when Cromwell died. There is evidence in 'A Poem' of textual connections with *Paradise Lost* as well as Milton's earlier poetry: Milton had begun to work on his great epic in this period.[41]

The apocalyptic and millenarian elements in the earlier two Cromwell poems, 'An Horatian Ode' and *The First Anniversary*, are almost wholly absent here (the one exception is line 272). In *The First Anniversary* (l. 139), 'Foreshortened Time' describes an imagined apocalypse brought on by Cromwell's excellent rule. In 'A Poem', there is a reversal in the very unapocalyptic image of Cromwell as a 'foreshortened' tree to human sight, whose immense height can only be appreciated when it is fallen and dead (ll. 269–70). There are several further references to *The First Anniversary*.[42] Hunting was a royal sport, but Charles I had been portrayed as a stag in Sir John Denham's *Cooper's Hill* (1641–2, 1655), Sir William D'Avenant had presented hunting as tyranny in *Gondibert* (1651, 1.2.24–41), and Edmund Waller's commendatory poem to Christopher Wase's translation of the hunting poem by Gratius, *Cynegeticon* (1654), had called for a poem on the modern hunting of 'beasts'. *The First Anniversary* answers that call, while 'A Poem' carefully avoids an image of hunting that presents Cromwell in his persecuting role, without sacrificing the association of Cromwell with hunting.

The major theme of mutuality and reflexivity that we have seen elsewhere in Marvell is his way of praising Cromwell's personal qualities. Thus, Providence, described as a mirror, looks into *itself* to discover Cromwell's fate. Nature and Cromwell are identical: Nature appears to fight Nature for Cromwell's death (l. 133). The infant Eliza replaced the milk in her mother's breasts with love (l. 36). Cromwell and his daughter are likewise mutual reflections of each other's love, to the extent that they become the same entity: as the disease 'melts' his daughter, so Cromwell also inwardly wastes away (here they are not mirrors – Eliza is a wax model of her father within him). This is compounded by vocabulary of 'doubling' (ll. 57, 66), and by paradoxes that enhance the sense of a closeness that is poignantly harmful to both father and daughter. Eliza's dying breath tarnishes the 'polished mirror' of her father's breastplate, and this is enough to start his decline (and later Richard Cromwell, the glittering image of his father, has his 'beams' 'obscured' by grief for his father's death). The image of life on the mirror of Cromwell's dead face (ll. 257–60) suggests that he will return to life.

By contrast there are a number of deliberately obscure passages.[43] Among the purported weaknesses detected by critics in the poem are the nebulous and difficult sentences, usually an effect of syntactical inversion, or hysteron proteron (e.g. ll. 13–18, 223–6, 273–6), and less commonly, ellipsis (e.g. ll. 189–90, 128, 216, 276). Ambiguity is not cleverly poised, as in the previous two Cromwell poems (and especially 'An Horatian Ode'), but is an effect of blurred and indistinct syntax. Would Marvell have let such a poem be entered for a collection that would eventually be published, or are the apparent blemishes genuine examples of poetic failure, perhaps induced by haste in the circumstances of the Protector's death? One answer is that the poem is marked by deliberate failures of poetic sentence: Cromwell's death brings about the end of good poetry. Ellipsis is a kind of 'choking' in the voice of grief – an effect by no means unknown in mannered seventeenth-century elegies. Moreover, what begins as characteristic inversion (ll. 15–18) ends as a deliberate distortion. The effect is the opposite of the distorted impression of height we had of Cromwell when he was alive (see ll. 269–70), and is an obscuring opposite to the bright mirrors and images of Providence, Cromwell and his two offspring who feature in this poem. Syntactic obscurity is also an effect of our dim, sublunary perceptions, in which 'we ourselves betray' (l. 298), while, more often than not, obscure lines are unravelled by the bright day of concluding couplets. To confirm this, lines concerned with the will of heaven are also syntactically difficult (e.g. ll. 107–8). Some sentences 'fool' the reader, appearing to point to one meaning for the first half, and then achieving a reversal and clarification in the second half: 'Pity it seemed to hurt him . . . more that felt/Each wound himself which he to others dealt' (ll. 197–8). Cromwell, these features tell us, though dead, is always ready to bounce back.

Marvell's elegy on Cromwell has attracted almost no sustained comment, despite Thompson's generous annotation: 'The English language does not boast a more elegant elegiack poem, than this to the memory of the magnanimous and noble Cromwell.'[44] Legouis confessed that the poem was Marvell's finest 'official' verse, but that despite its public function, it was 'so touching, so heart-felt, and so free from the political preoccupation' that it was as if it were 'a friend mourning for a friend'. Friedman regards the poem as a 'mixture of [Marvell's] best metaphysical techniques, confused sequences of images and subjects, and hackneyed terms of elegiac praise', and therefore considers it inferior to the elegies of Dryden and Waller. He is impressed by Marvell's 'undiminished ability to . . . express correspondences between individual events and their abstract meanings', and by the 'sincerity and depth of [Marvell's] sense of catastrophe', but regards lines 255–6 as particularly bad, and guilty of 'Shelleyan inanities'. Despite her defence of the poem's formal design, Patterson finds that it 'competes effectively neither with the strenuous mental activity of the earlier Cromwell poems nor with the voluptuous emotional activity of an elegy'. Donnelly argues that the poem's failure is a consequence of the resources in elegiac tradition being unable to match the man who excelled all men.[45] If in the light of these comments, Thompson's sentiments might be judged an exaggeration, the poem is nonetheless, and by a considerable distance, the best of all surviving elegies on Cromwell, and has been unjustly neglected. It is a small, highly intelligent, engagingly personal masterpiece.

Yet it belonged in a field of similar poems written by men many of whom belonged to one or other part of the establishment, and who therefore had distinct interests. Some of these poets were close to Marvell, and some close and still his enemies. The future dynamo of Augustan verse and confirmed Royalist, John Dryden, had joined the Office for Foreign Tongues as a clerk, perhaps as soon as a month after Marvell's employment. And Marvell's earlier poetic contestant Edmund Waller had already issued *Upon the late storme, and of the death of His Highnesse ensuing the same* as a broadside. This poem, much parodied by Royalists and some republicans, argues that the ominous storm was necessary to carry off so great a hero as Cromwell, whose virtue was in enhancing England's global reach and in ending civil war. Such a position has been seen to reflect Waller's own trading interests, even as he ignores the problem of the cost to the nation of these foreign exploits. Waller's poem is for the most part finely wrought, but its insouciance is obvious; was Marvell offering something far more thoughtful for discerning readers, attempting to draw them into loyalty to the Ricardian Protectorate? It must have been galling, then, if Marvell did not suppress his own poem, to find himself suppressed in the name of a much less substantial poem by his sometime enemy Waller, when the elegiac volume finally appeared in April 1659.

Not surprisingly Marvell was at the business of state just two days after Cromwell's death, delivering letters to Schlezer, the agent of the Elector of Brandenburg, concerning the Baltic conflict. On the 10th, he noted two petitions from a total of ten Turks escaped from Spanish imprisonment. On 1 October, he wrote two letters from Thurloe to Downing, and was still interceding for the ill Thurloe with the Dutch ambassador in respect of Baltic relationships.[46] A further letter and a large document written by Wolseley, Jones, Strickland and Thurloe was given by Marvell to Nieupoort on 17/26 November. In idiomatic French Marvell invited the Genovese republic on 20 November to send a representative to Cromwell's funeral.[47] On 16 December, he delivered an order from the Council of State that the Court of Admiralty review a complaint brought by Patrick Hayes against Hamburg for a shipping loss. It was reported that the Dutch had seized an English ship, and Marvell notified Nieupoort again on 23 December. Finally on the same day, under Marvell's hand, permission was granted to the Duke of Holstein to transport to Holstein one hundred barrels of gunpowder.[48]

RICHARD AND THE RUMP

The commonplace idea that Marvell decided to change career by becoming an MP in January 1659 is based on a mistaken apprehension.[49] Rather, the move from civil servant to MP makes sense as part of the career development of a man who had no choice but to be someone's servant, if a very well-educated and sophisticated one. Having been of service to Fairfax, Cromwell and the Protectorate government, he formed a rational plan to serve his own kin and native townsmen: this might in time lead to a more secure future. On 28 December 1658, Edmond Popple, then Sheriff of Hull, told the Board of the Corporation that his brother-in-law Andrew Marvell wished to be made a 'free Burgesse' of the Corporation.[50] Whether this was Marvell's wish alone, or part of a strategy designed with others, including Popple, to prepare the way for him to represent the town, is another matter. Such an entitlement made Marvell eligible to be elected as an MP, which duly came about when Richard Cromwell summoned his first Parliament on 10 January 1659 (see plate 20). Popple also refers to the services Marvell had already performed for the town. So, presumably as Assistant Secretary for Foreign Tongues, Marvell had done Hull good turns, and he had certainly worked at the Council of State's command in June 1658 on a committee made up of army officers and Hull worthies who were determining whether the town needed a magazine in the manor house. At any rate, the Bench records show that Marvell received his freedom while he himself was absent from Hull.

Marvell stood for election before an electorate of about five hundred freemen, and he was returned with John Ramsden, the most important merchant in Hull, although once again Marvell was absent from Hull during the election itself. His kinsman Matthew Alured was returned for the neighbouring constituency of Hedon. The other candidates were Thomas Strickland, Henry Smyth and the redoubtable republican, Sir Henry Vane the Younger, who had sat for Hull in the Long Parliament. It was thought to be a close-run affair: on 9 January, the day before the election, one observer, Captain Adam Baynes, thought that 'the town is soe much divided; but [I] beleive that one Mr Marveile who is the Lattin Secretary at White-Hall, and one Mr Ramsden a merchant may carry it, except Sir Henry Vane who has a considerable party, carry it by the divisions of the rest. . . . Hull chuses on Monday next.'[51] A fragment of letter by Marvell, almost certainly to Popple, survives, written on 15 January. It expresses affection for his 'cousin', and enquires of the views of eighty-six men of 'the businesse and of me', presumably a reference to the election and to a body of men who were pressured to support Marvell.[52] As we shall see, Marvell appears to have been seen by his electors as a Protectorate man, which is not surprising. The Protectorate court had certainly used its influence on his behalf against Vane, who was said to have had the majority in the Hull vote.[53]

Parliament met on 27 January. It was not long before the new MP was embroiled in its business. He was appointed on 5 February to the committee examining the petition of Elizabeth Lilburne, wife of the now-dead Leveller leader John. On the same day, he was also appointed appropriately to a committee considering whether the five northern counties were supplied with a 'learned, pious, sufficient and able' ministry.[54]

The new MP continued in his role as assistant secretary in Thurloe's office. No conflict of interest was either defined or seen in this period, as would undoubtedly be the case today, but it is clear that Marvell was not merely one of the Members for Hull. He was also MP for the Protectoral government – he could put its views in debate, and he could inform Thurloe of every speech and discussion he witnessed. His kinsman Matthew Alured put exactly the opposite view in this Parliament, speaking strongly against a Cromwellian tyranny as well as the Royalists.[55] The newsletter that Marvell wrote to Downing, Resident at the Hague, on 11 February combined secretarial and MP perspectives.[56] This means that Marvell writes as a Protectorate supporter, but he is officially standing in for Thurloe, who was too preoccupied to write. In domestic politics, Downing was a firm Cromwellian, and had been accused in republican pamphlets of bribery and of trying to orchestrate the creation of a monarchical dynasty.[57] Marvell all but denounces the republicans Heslerig, Vane, Weaver, Scott, St Nicholas, Reynolds, Cooper, Packer, Neville and Lambert (in their full numbers they amounted to about one-third of the House), who argued that the role of protector could not pass by inheritance since all power lay with the people and hence, on the death of Oliver, with their representative or, in person, the Speaker. To Marvell, however, this was a thinly disguised army plot, backed by orchestrated petitions. The republicans pushed their case hard and unceasingly, resorting to questions of procedure, since they were in a minority. As Marvell said, 'They haue much the odds in speaking but it is to be hoped that our justice our affection and our number which is at least two thirds will weare them out at the long runne.'[58] It is odd to find someone we think of as superbly eloquent on paper admitting insufficiency in public speaking, at least for his party. But it is the not the last time we shall hear it. Nonetheless, the bill on which this debate focused, to recognize officially Richard Cromwell as Lord Protector, passed on 14 February.

Marvell wrote a further letter of Thurloe's to Downing on 18 February, accompanying petitions for redress for damages to English shipping. Two weeks later the Hull Corporation met to consider the instructions they wished to send to Marvell and Ramsden.[59] Let us think back at this point to the election itself, and those eighty-six men. It is credibly reported that Richard's government wanted at all costs to keep Vane out of Parliament, and that it succeeded in denying him at Bristol and Hull, forcing him to be returned for Whitchurch in Hampshire. He complained of 'unjust practices'.[60] Was Marvell, with his obvious Protectoral connections, the engine by which Vane was not returned for Hull? Were the eighty-six men drummed in to produce a majority for Andrew? Unlike later polls, the voting numbers for this election do not survive, and that itself has been seen as a sign of potential dirty work, or at least of using undue local influence.[61] Did Edmond Popple and associates manufacture a result that would otherwise have returned Vane? It certainly seems so.

A second letter to Downing, of 25 March, underlines Marvell's role as a Protectoral MP with strong Cromwellian convictions.[62] While the ostensible reason for writing is to acknowledge receipt of two letters and to apologize for the lack of a reply from Thurloe, the third sentence begins to record Parliamentary debates, and the battle between the Protectoral MPs and their republican opponents. The republicans had tried and failed to have the pro-Cromwellian Irish and Scottish Members excluded. William Packer, a disaffected former Cromwellian deputy major-general, had been dismissed for being illegally elected at Hertford. Then William Petty was recalled from Ireland to answer charges of breach of trust in paying soldiers; and a petition alleged that Thurloe had improperly had someone imprisoned and sent to Barbados. There were similar charges against other Protectorate officials, and hostile MPs failed to have them thrown out.

Northern affairs continued to occupy Marvell: on 31 March he was named to a committee to examine whether the County Palatine of Durham should have parliamentary representation.[63] On 13 April he was named to a committee to examine the petition of the supernumerary disbanded forces in Lancashire.[64] But another committee was dealing with the more constitutionally pressing question of the preservation of records, hitherto a concern of the republicans, who feared that a tyrant might burn state papers:

> That it be referred to Mr Attorney-general, Serjeant Maynard, Mr Marvell, Mr Dixwell, Mr Scot, Mr Annesley, Lord Marquis of Argyle, etc. to consider how to remove, and where to place, the conveyances, records, and other writings, now remaining at Worcester House, so as they may be disposed of, for their safety, and the service of the Commonwealth.[65]

Marvell had written his elegy on Oliver Cromwell soon after his death, and inevitably with the necessity of paying respect to Oliver's son and successor as Protector, Richard. It has been argued that Marvell's poem is in fact a praise of Richard, appropriate to his powers of political reconciliation and sympathetic to the infant deaths among Richard's own children, despite the evident stress on Oliver's superiority to the unproven Richard. Many of the poems in the academic volume *Musarum Cantabrigiensium Luctus & Gratulatio: Ille In Funere Oliveri . . . Haec de Ricardi Successione Felicissima* (1658) praise Richard more confidently as well as lamenting Oliver, and some are concerned wholly with Richard. But by the time the poem was ready to appear in print, Richard had manifestly failed, and the poem had lost a large part of its moment. Thus it was that Marvell's poem was withdrawn from *Three Poems*, having been first registered with the Stationers' Company on 20 January; it was eventually replaced with Edmund Waller's 'Upon the Late Storme and Death of his Highnesse ensuing the same'. When *Three Poems* actually appeared, printed by William Wilson, Richard Cromwell's hold on power was uncertain, if not over. In these circumstances, Marvell's praise of Richard as a conciliatory ruler was singularly inappropriate. It was more fitting to reprint the well-known and conventionally martial praise of Oliver Cromwell contained in Waller's poem.

Richard Cromwell's Protectorate failed on 22 April 1659 when the army caused the dissolution of his Parliament; all of Marvell and his fellow Protectoral MPs' endeavours were in vain. The Rump Parliament was recalled just over a fortnight later, with the republicans now in the ascendant (see plate 21). The most immediate consequence for Marvell was that he was out of Parliament, having this time lost his seat to Vane, who rejoiced that 'the practices of some and the Influence of [the] Court party' were thwarted.[66] In June, the Corporation of Hull wrote to congratulate the restored Rump, and Marvell the MP was for the time being a lost cause, even though on 16 June the Mayor and Burgesses of Hull gave 'our well beloved friend Andrew Marvell of the Citty of Westminster Esquire' power of attorney 'to receive rent for the Hull Manor house' used as a magazine.[67] Marvell also retained his post as Latin secretary while Thurloe was dismissed, to be replaced by the regicide Thomas Scott. It is hard to believe that Marvell can have seen eye to eye with Scott, who was decidedly critical of the Cromwells. Still, the new government had its uses for Marvell and must have trusted him, for on 14 July the new Council of State voted a grant of lodgings to him in Whitehall, despite some shuffling around of rooms among different civil servants.[68] Here he seems to have drawn the short straw twice: first being told he could keep his rooms (14 July), then being displaced by Robert Goodwin (16 July) and again by Brampton Gurdon (18 July). No final mention is made of where he ended up. At the end of June Marvell drafted in English and Latin a ratification document for the Treaty of the Hague, after the dissolution of Parliament. Through the summer months he continued to work as Latin Secretary, mostly translating from English to Latin and vice versa, and on documents negotiating the Anglo-Dutch treaty, and communications with Martin Bökell, the agent for the Baltic port of Lübeck.[69] Meanwhile, in October, the Council of State appointed a committee of seven, with Marvell as secretary, to treat with the Portuguese ambassador, Francisco de Mello e Torres.[70]

Now it was at this point that the volume of elegiac poems of Cromwell was circulating, but without Marvell's contribution. Marvell had had to put up with Waller's poem replacing his own, a poem to which he may have been responding. The other two poems in the volume represent different challenges to Marvell's outlook and his particular configuration as an intellectual. At the front of the volume was Dryden's 'Heroic Stanzas' on Cromwell and if Marvell's poem represents a personal testimony, these lines embody a cool appraisal of Cromwell's achievement. Dryden's poem has an eye for caution and for the appropriate that goes beyond Marvell in finally reserving the position of the author. Perhaps Dryden was already seeing ahead to the end of the Protectorate, and this was aided by connections with Protectorate critics as well as by having relatives who were Protectorate servants. His poem has early sections that seem to respond to Marvell's figure of the coy mistress and his invocation of Machiavelli in 'An Horatian Ode':

> Fortune (that easy mistress of the young,
> But to her ancient servants coy and hard)
> Him at that age her favourites ranked among
> When she her best-loved Pompey did discard.
>
> (ll. 29–32)

But he goes on to suggest that Cromwell died borne down by the weight of his own fame, and that it is 'strange' how Cromwell's feats have been blessed on account of his dual qualities of piety and valour. 'Strangely' (l. 147) means wonderful but there is an undertow of 'surprising' there too. For all the praise that has been given to this poem, Marvell's still beats it, but Marvell must have seen Dryden's talent growing, and he would in time be forced to meet its challenge.[71]

The recalled Rump did not enjoy the confidence of the army any more than had Richard Cromwell, and in October it was expelled. Lambert played a key role in the coup. A Committee of Safety was established and chaired by Charles Fleetwood, whose wife was Cromwell's daughter Bridget. The Rump appears to have tidied up its business, voting on 25 October, the last day of its deliberations, that Milton and Marvell each receive £86 12s. in arrears pay, effectively salary since the Rump had been recalled in May.

This brief period during which the republic was re-established is marked by a frenzied return of the kind of public debate that not been seen since the 1640s. The printing presses were busy producing hordes of tracts, and this time the subject of debate was more political theory, and the correct constitution for England rather than religion. The older republicans, many of whom believed that the younger generation had been pacified by strong-arm, censorious Protectoral policies into political compliance with the Cromwells, sustained long speeches in Parliament, in part as a way of reintroducing virtuous speech and difference of opinion into the public sphere.

In the midst of all this speculation, and in many ways one of its intellectual centres, was the 'Rota' club founded by James Harrington, an association of gentlemen dedicated to the discussion of constitutions and constitutional reform. The hostile testimony of Samuel Butler is that Marvell was a member of this club, or at least he addressed it during the period when it met between November 1659 and February 1660.[72] Marvell was Harrington's friend and knew him until he died (as we shall see, the two would live very near each other in Westminster), and Marvell would write a (now lost) Latin epitaph for him. Whatever the truth of his supposed earlier affection for Charles I, Harrington had composed during the earlier and mid-1650s one of the most remarkable works of republican political theory ever penned. This was the *Oceana* of 1656, dedicated to Oliver Cromwell, but in fact a thinly veiled conceit with a warning: make the polity correspond to the description contained in the treatise or risk a slide into anarchy, which is what by 1659 the English republicans thought had already happened. In clearly stated opposition to Hobbes, Harrington argued that the balance of power in England lay with the propertied classes, and that these landowners had to be represented in a bicameral system of assemblies. A system of voting enabled decision-making to take place. However important a single prince might be in starting a polity, the business of government lay thereafter with these assemblies. Harrington justified his vision by recourse to earlier and ancient political writing, notably Plato, Aristotle and Machiavelli, and in succeeding defences of his views against controverters he showed the relevance of his views to contemporary predicaments, and especially the relationship between political representation and the army. Harrington was also a poet and a translator of poetry (Virgil's *Eclogues* and some books of the *Aeneid*). His poetry was another forum for his political theory: in his translations can be seen his interpretation of Roman history. This must have chimed with Marvell's interests in poetic history and the writing of bucolic and epic verse.[73] Passages of Harringtonian analysis crop up abruptly in Marvell's Restoration prose: Harrington's distinctive vision had a great impact on Marvell and its beginning must date from this time.[74]

Four months at most does not seem like a long collaboration, but when we realize that it appears to have met every evening, we become aware of the extraordinary intellectual energy in the Rota, and not least in Harrington himself. The period coincides exactly with the existence of the Committee of Safety. Cromwell is thought to have seen the danger implicit in *Oceana* when it first appeared (this was not difficult to see: its first publishers were the well-known Fifth Monarchist, Livewell Chapman and the populist republican John Streater, who had already called for Cromwell's assassination).[75] The Rota itself was in effect a new kind of political association. It met at the Turk's Head in New Palace Yard, Westminster. This was not an inn but a coffee house, and the company sat around an oval table with coffee being delivered from the centre

of the table (the server entered the centre space through a gap in the oval).
Aubrey described the Rotarians as both disciples of Harrington and 'Virtuosi',
and he remembered that the conversation took place with great eagerness, the
contents of the discussions being both ingenious and 'smart'. This sense of
almost overheated energy – to the point of mental distraction – is also a characteristic account of Harrington's own mental state. After the Restoration he
suffered from periodic bouts of insanity. The known members of the Rota
included Milton's friend Cyriack Skinner, the republican politician and satirist
Henry Neville, and John Aubrey himself.[76] The evidence for Marvell's membership of the Rota comes from the hostile testimony of the satirist Samuel Butler,
made in the 1670s, and whilst we have seen how Marvell is firmly associated
with Protectoral rather than republican circles and sentiments, the association
with Harrington and Neville and their writings is discernible in Marvell's later
works.[77] In any case, Marvell would have been thinking more broadly after the
fall of Richard Cromwell's Protectorate. His membership of the Rota, if indeed
he was a member, is highly significant.

   The Committee of Safety split the army itself: the Scottish army, commanded
by Monck, did not approve, declared for the Rump and marched south. On
25 February, Monck reached London, and permitted the MPs excluded as
long ago as 1648 to return to Parliament. Not the Rump, but now the Long
Parliament was recalled. Time was fast running out for the Commonwealth: the
Long Parliament, or what was left of it, declared itself dissolved, and called new
elections. On 25 April 1660, the Convention Parliament met and resolved to
invite back the King. The English had run out of ideas for an alternative form
of government to monarchy, even though there seems to have been no great
enthusiasm for its return. Harrington probably understood this after listening
to the discussion in the Rota: Aubrey reports that he often said at the end of
meetings that the King would 'come in' again. On 4 April, just two days after the
elections, Marvell undertook his last act for the Commonwealth, a letter in
Latin from himself to Francisco de Mello e Torres, the Portuguese ambassador,
concerning a treaty now under discussion, and the advantage to the ambassador at home and in England should he sign it; in signing off, Marvell seemed
to distance himself from the diplomatic pressure being exerted on the
Portuguese, and Mello signed the treaty with the Council of State on 18 April.[78]

RESTORATION

The restoration of the monarchy put Marvell in a difficult situation. This is not
surprising for a former servant of the Lord Protector and supporter of
'Protectoralism'. Some of the republicans, especially the more eminent ones,
were able to make their peace with the King, and like Anthony Ashley Cooper,
the future Earl of Shaftesbury, were invited to take a place in the Privy Council.
Charles knew that the regicides must be punished, but he also knew that the

future depended upon reconciliation between the parties, and hence the Declaration of Breda and the Act of Indemnity and Oblivion. Some have noted how comparatively few supporters of the Commonwealth were punished. Yet the signs of dire punishment were inescapable. The rotting corpses of Cromwell, Bradshaw, Ireton and Pride were dug up, dismembered and hung on the gallows at Tyburn, and some of the regicides were tried and executed, the most important of all being Sir Henry Vane (beheaded on 14 June 1662 after being convicted of treason earlier in the year). The senior secretariat of the Protectorate was treated with suspicion: Thurloe was imprisoned on a charge of high treason; Milton was jailed for some time and his books burned by the public hangman.

But Marvell was an elected member of the Convention Parliament, having been returned in place of Vane. He was clearly benefiting from the privilege of being an MP, and in this corporate sense, he had voted to invite the Stuarts back to the throne. His history and associations would be remembered more clearly in the Cavalier Parliament, which would not meet until May 1661. The Convention Parliament sat from 15 April until 29 December 1660, but it was able to resolve little beyond the restoration of the monarchy. There was a long adjournment from 13 September until 6 November. The Act of Indemnity was passed, as was a Navigation Act, and an Act for the Confirmation of Judicial Proceedings, but a wholly inadequate financial settlement was made, no religious settlement was reached, and the excise tax remained: these would be the dominant and difficult factors in politics for the next thirty years. On 29 May, the day that Charles II was officially restored, Marvell also wrote with his fellow Hull MP John Ramsden to the Commissioners of the Militia for Hull urging restraint in respect of present business because the Council of State had been abolished before they had been able to hear a communication from Hull.[79] Marvell and Ramsden were delicately signalling that new management had arrived.

In all of this Marvell's experience as a secretary was not forgotten. Thus, on 23 July he was asked by Parliament to confer with the MPs for the universities to prepare a letter of acknowledgement to Karl Ludwig, the Elector of the Palatinate, who had written to congratulate Parliament on the restoration of the monarchy. He also sat on several Parliamentary committees: to examine a petition of 25 June from the University of Oxford; to examine papers printed in the name of the King and bishops defaming Parliament on 30 June; to consider reparation of the Earl of Bristol on 29 August; to consider spending funds to buy ransoms for captives in Algiers and Tunis on 3 September; to report on fen drainage on 4 September, to settle the militia on 6 November, to examine a petition of Michael Crake, the Commons' Serjeant at Arms, on 9 November; to examine a bill preventing the voluntary separation of married persons, 14 November; to settle a chapel of ease in Waltham Forest, 15 November; and to consider the debts of the Earl of Cleveland on 26 November.[80]

He had, in other words, succeeded in accommodating himself to the new regime. And being an MP was by no means to be associated closely with the King or the court, or indeed – and, as it would turn out, more importantly – the administration of the King's chief minister, the Earl of Clarendon. Nonetheless, his public association with the restoration of the monarchy was evident in a printed work reporting that Marvell and Ramsden presented a statement of welcome from the City of Hull to the King at his return.[81]

Marvell's long correspondence with the Corporation of Hull, which provided his pension, began at this time; the first surviving letter is dated 17 November, and we know there was at least one before this.[82] He wrote directly to the Mayor; Christopher Richardson was in office at this time. The first issue was the matter of disbanding eight militia regiments. The cost of maintaining a standing army, and its potential threat to civil liberties, would have been apparent to any corporation, and Marvell thought the King was sufficiently moderate not to need such an army for the people to call on for protection. (In fact there were already Cavalier interests working to take control of the militia.) He predicted the disbanding of the entire army and looked back sentimentally to his childhood when the city's militia of young part-timers matched in their show of arms any soldiers he claimed to have seen since. Marvell's chronologer, Nicholas von Maltzahn, considers this an unusually colourful and candid letter, with much offering of personal opinion, quite unlike the guarded writing that would follow, much of it apparently only committing facts to paper.[83] Marvell wrote on 29 November that such letter composition was a pleasure after these demanding sessions. While records of Marvell's payment by the Corporation for his attendance begin in 1659, now also began the custom of providing from time to time each of the Hull MPs with a barrel of ale.

Other decisions taken in the House and mentioned by Marvell bespeak a 'country' as opposed to 'court' sentiment and outlook, although they are consistent with much of Parliament's dealing with all of the Stuarts from James I onwards. He is listed by the former Parliamentarian and Puritan Lord Wharton as a 'friendly' MP in 1660 and 1661.[84] Thus, Marvell voted not to approve a bill requiring Parliament to underwrite all of the cost of Charles's coronation. It was prudent, he claimed, to leave something for Parliament still to give, and also imprudent to risk the people's good will in giving away too much of the money supplied by taxation. The additional comment that the Stuarts had been subject to a terrible affliction of divine making, that lay upon the nation as well as them, looks like an attempt to accommodate himself, at least in so far as he was presenting his thinking to Mayor Richardson, to the Stuarts. The silent contrast would be to the Cromwells, whom, while Oliver was alive, God had favoured greatly.

The King had promised in the Declaration of Breda toleration for the Nonconformists. In December, Marvell acted as teller for the 'Ayes' in a bill enacting such an indulgence, but it was defeated. In the Convention Parliament could already be seen the Anglican intolerance that would characterize its successor, the Cavalier Parliament. Marvell wrote that now all hopes for toleration rested on the King alone. In respect of Parliament, 'his Majestyes goodnesse . . . hath hitherto been more ready to give then we to receive'.[85]

Marvell's friendship with Milton continued to develop, despite the younger poet's participation in a monarchical regime, and the older poet's precarious position in these new circumstances. The sketchy biographical sources suggest that Marvell visited Milton regularly in these times. Milton himself was in fact imprisoned for about two months between some point in October and 15 December because he had been excluded from the Act of Indemnity. A record of Parliamentary proceedings not published until 1808 by William Cobbett claimed that Marvell had complained in the Commons of the excessive jail fees charged to Milton (£150), who was now unemployed and unlikely to find any substantial income in the foreseeable future. Others in the House replied that as Cromwell's Latin Secretary (and by association, the author of works justifying the regicide as well as defending the Commonwealth), Milton was getting off lightly and deserved to be hanged. Although the *Commons Journal* attests that the matter was referred to the House's Committee of Privileges, Edward Phillips, Milton's nephew, wrote that Marvell acted on Milton's behalf in Parliament by organizing considerable support for him among other MPs.[86]

Before the December dissolution, Marvell was appointed to eleven committees, dealing with a variety of issues from examining the petition of the University of Oxford to examining questionable publications in the King's and bishops' names. In a further committee of the whole House, he tried, in league with some other MPs, to achieve a more 'mixed' restored church settlement: an episcopal church without deans and chapters. This committee worked towards the endowment of vicarages using funds formerly devoted to archbishops, deans and chapters. The view of the church that he had gained in the 1650s, and in Protectorate circles, and which would be so important later on, was already in some shape here. Marvell was a teller for the 'Yeas' in the vote on the Worcester House Declaration, a proposed church settlement intended to reconcile Episcopalians and Presbyterians, but which was unsuccessful. The declaration failed again on 28 November, and on 4 December Marvell wrote that he saw division in the church because key Puritans such as Calamy would refuse bishoprics.[87] In the same letter, he noted the order for the disinterring and dismembering of Cromwell, Bradshaw, Ireton and Pride, even though he also thought that Charles II was capable of moderation in other respects.

Marvell seems to have remained in London for at least some of the time when Parliament was out of session. He therefore promised extra-Parliamentary service to the Corporation of Hull on 3 January. Indeed on 12 January he undertook to write newsletters in place of Gilbert Mabbott, who went to a new post in Ireland. He promised to do it at no extra cost, and then launched into a page or

so of news, which included a rumour he had heard at the Exchange of a plot
against Hull, presumably by Fifth Monarchists, and a report that Belasyse, the
Governor of the garrison, had removed all those inhabitants formerly in the
Parliament's service. As Marvell said, one rumour cancels the other, and each is
as true (i.e. untrue) as the other; he both offers news and then instances its point-
lessness or at least its limitations. Then follows a characteristic piece of tenderness, and a recalling of the importance of Hull in his life, even after he has asked
for God's mercy on the measles-stricken royal children: 'It is hard for me to write
short to you. It seems to me when I haue once begun that I am making a step to
Hull & can not easily part from so good company.'[88] On 17 January, Marvell sent
a short newsbook instead of writing one at length, although he did mention the
recovery of Princess Henrietta and the expectation that the Fifth Monarchist
prisoners would be executed.[89]

The other main business to achieve was the making of a new legal commission that defined the authority of the lieutenancy of Hull as extending to the
town as well as the county. Marvell had covered the fees required for this to
happen, and he was reimbursed in March by the Corporation. A no less significant duty for the Corporation was the request, made during the next
Parliament in April 1661, for four wine licences for Hull.[90]

Outside London, he might have strayed as far as Lord Wharton's residences,
at Winchendon and Wooburn, where he would later venture. Within London
and by his own later admission, he visited Milton at his Jewin Street residence
(see plate 23). It was here, he claimed, that he first met his greatest enemy of
later years, Samuel Parker.[91] Milton's name and circumstances remind us of very
real matters of information control and intelligence at this time. On 19 and 21
March, all mail was simply stopped; perhaps this was tied up with the insurrections: 'You might be sure all was not right when you heard not from me.'[92]
Equally it mattered that he was able to pick up the mail from Hull the instant it
arrived, rather than wait for it to be carried around the city by the 'porters'. To
this end, he simply asked that mail for him be left at the house of William
Popple. In May 1662, he still felt apprehensive about the possibility that mail
would be indiscriminately opened and read and perhaps by people he did not
want to read it. On 8 May 1662, he warned Trinity House of discussing too
much business in letters.[93] During the Protectorate employment, he had been
very much a Westminster civil servant and, in his diplomatic role, a latter-day
courtier. Now as an MP with increasingly 'opposition' tendencies he was at last
becoming a Londoner.

And what of Marvell the poet at the time of the Restoration? Certain
evidence that Marvell's verse had circulated through the 1650s in scribal form,
and especially among the poets themselves, comes in Abraham Cowley's
anonymously published *Visions and Prophecies concerning England, Scotland,
and Ireland, of Ezekiel Grebner* (1660), which appeared in the following year in
a more forthright manner as *A vision, concerning his late pretended highnesse,*

Cromwell, the Wicked containing a discourse in vindication of him by a pretended angel, and the confutation thereof, by the Author. Grebner is a Parliamentarian and in some sense an enthusiast, but is horrified by the regicide; after witnessing Cromwell's funeral, he sees in a dream a giant who presents himself as Britain's guardian angel. On his skin are tattooed images of Parliamentary victories during the Civil Wars. However, the giant is in fact the devil, and Grebner debates Cromwell's reputation with him, maintaining strongly that Cromwell has caused irreparable damage to the nation. Grebner's redeemer in the dream against Cromwellian/demonic persecution is an image of Charles II as St George, but described in the same language as Marvell used to praise Cromwell at the beginning of 'An Horatian Ode':

> When, Lo, ere the last words were fully spoke,
> From a fair clowd, which rather ope'd, than broke,
> A flash of Light, rather than Lightning came,
> So swift, and yet so gentle was the Flame.
> Upon it rode, and in his full Career,
> Seem'd to my Eyes no sooner There than Here,
> The comelyest Youth of all th' Angelique race.
>
> (ll. 79–85)

This comes from Marvell's 'And like the three-forked lightning, first/ Breaking the clouds where it was nursed' (ll. 13–14), while the description of the 'Cromwellian devil' as a 'great Bird of prey' recalls Marvell's comparison of Cromwell to a falcon.[94] Cowley was thus attempting to erase Commonwealth poetry and its subjects of praise from literary memory, as well as to purge any trace of his own accommodation with the Protectoral regime. But anyone within the tight world of mid-seventeenth-century poetry would have recognized the strong association of Marvell with Cromwellian panegyric. Marvell was *the* Commonwealth and Cromwellian poet for these highly accomplished circles, and that was bound to carry some notoriety in the new order of things.

※

CHAPTER 7

CAVALIER REVENGE

. . . even I, who am none of the best Disputers of this world.[1]

The next Parliament, to which Marvell was elected, met first on 1 April 1661. Its adoption of the Clarendon Code (the laws that re-established the supremacy of the Church of England), and its hostility to any departures from a mixed-monarchical and Anglican norm, would earn it the title 'Cavalier Parliament'.[2] Since it remained one entire Parliament for eighteen years, long after the fall of Clarendon, it is also known as the 'Long Parliament'.[3] Appropriately, Marvell's fellow MP for Hull this time was not Ramsden, who was defeated, but Colonel Anthony Gylby, a Royalist spy during the 1650s, imprisoned in this period, and someone with whom Marvell, it is usually supposed, would never enjoy cordial relations. Yet Marvell had promised to the Corporation cooperation with Gylby if they were both elected: in a statement of 26 March, he had refused to see any 'inconsistence' between their interests.[4] Gylby had in fact been declared the candidate with the most votes. At first Gylby expected much from the partnership. He was cheered to find new lodgings, possibly at Mr Brim's house in St Peter's Street, only four or five doors from Marvell, and was impressed by his fellow MP's character and conversation. He was so confident in the relationship that he wrote to the Mayor and Aldermen of Hull on 9 May in these terms: 'I very well like of Mr Maruels conuersation, and I doubt not but wee shall both of us indeauour to be serviceable to those that sent us hither, and also very friendly to one the other, noe place beinge able to afford (for any thinge I can perceive) any two Members more of a Judgmt than we shall bee.'[5] Marvell, the former Secretary to the Protectorate regime, had clearly convinced a hard Cavalier that he was of the right party, and he must have needed much of his Machiavellian side to do this.

Two months later this amity had drastically deteriorated into open animosity, 'the bonds of civility' between them being, so Marvell thought, irreparably 'snappd in pieces'.[6] We might also note Gylby's comment that although he was living very close to Marvell, nothing was to be seen of him until the first day of Parliament: he was not a man to be found easily.[7] Marvell felt that the cause of the difference lay in some issues of understanding that had remained unresolved since the election, which could mean who had the most votes, but also might refer back to more fundamental disagreements. Gylby himself was prepared to put on at least a public front or an appearance of ultimate common purpose, writing to Hull on 27 June that Marvell had countermanded an instruction from Gylby to Charles Vaux, the Town Clerk of Hull. He presented this as a positive move, both men in the end striving to please the Mayor and Aldermen.[8] When Marvell said on 16 May that the Corporation must not presume from separate letters that he and Gylby were divided, and said that 'there is all civility betwixt us', he was in fact only signalling what would shortly become a huge difference.[9]

And indeed Marvell himself, writing to Hull on 1 June, used similar terms with a sense of embarrassment that the unhappy differences might compromise the effectiveness of the two MPs. The argument might, after all, result in a three-way breakdown in communication and understanding, a 'misintelligence', that would be a 'disadvantage' to the Corporation.[10] But the fact is that religious differences, specifically on matters of church government, were considerable between the two men. The issue at hand was a petition for legislation to make Holy Trinity Church separate from its original mother church at Hessle, to the west and on the banks of the Humber. The Corporation wanted the right of patronage in any new arrangements, although the patronage was originally the Crown's. Marvell did not want to press ahead with a direct approach to the King before the Mayor had resolved the issue of maintenance for the ministers. He did not want the Corporation to risk looking unready in the eyes of the King. He also worried that if patronage was not granted, the Corporation would be compromised, should the separation go ahead. A fortnight later he wrote again, saying that an Act had been framed according to the Corporation's wishes, but that the issue of maintenance for the clergy had to be resolved before there could be progress.[11] The means for maintenance in the proposed Act were opposed by some proposals that Marvell and Gylby had received. All this was happening against the background of national legislation for the reinstallation of the bishops of the Church of England and potential revisions to the Act of Indemnity (Marvell was named to the committee for confirming this Act). Locally and nationally, it was for the Hull community, as for everyone else, a tense time. As Marvell said at the time, if the King did not push all of this business on with expediency, 'we shall be broken against that rock'.[12]

Instructions did not arrive from Hull by 17 June, so Marvell wrote that he would oppose the Bill at its second reading unless the issue of maintenance was linked to that of the town's patronage.[13] He thought that Lord Belasyse would be with him in this respect. It would seem that Marvell did effect a delay, as Gylby's letter of the 27th seems to imply.[14] Marvell was named to a committee for considering the bill for dividing Trinity Church from Hessle on 29 June.[15] By then he knew of the further consequences of the split with Gylby, for on 20 June he had warned the Corporation that 'you also listen to no litle storyes concerning my selfe. For I believe you know by this time that you have lately heard some very false concerning me'. Rumours were afoot and the suspicion must be that they came from Gylby's camp.[16]

The Cavalier Parliament was the instrument of Clarendon's reign as chief minister of the Crown. He used its Anglican and hard Royalist majority to introduce the 'Clarendon Code'. On 18 December 1661, any Corporation office holder was required to conform to the Anglican church. The same applied to the Catholics, although the outcome in that context would not be known until after Marvell was dead, when the strongest proponent of Catholicism, James Duke of York, came to the throne. The implications of Charles's stated support for toleration would in this decade come to nothing. Marvell must have felt that he was in hostile territory most of the time, and this must have coloured his sense of the argument with Gylby, the former Royalist. Already in the Convention Parliament he had strongly supported several proposals in favour of Nonconformity that were voted down. On 8 May Sir Edward Turnor, later the subject of one of Marvell's most colourful satirical portraits, was chosen as Speaker.[17] Marvell was chosen to sit on a variety of committees again, including that dealing with the Acts of Pardon, Indemnity and Oblivion.[18] He was also named as one of the commissioners for tax assessment in Hull on 25 December, a role he held to the end of his life.[19] He noted in his constituency letter of 16 May the reversals suffered by former Commonwealth supporters or those thought to be so, like Sir John Morly, MP for Newcastle, who was prosecuted for correspondence with Cromwell and for having received pay from Sir George Downing, then the Commonwealth's Resident in Holland.[20]

The work of the Cavalier Parliament proceeded apace. The republican presence was erased. The body of Thomas May was exhumed from Westminster Abbey on 9 September, and on 7 November Milton's *Eikonoklastes* was burned, along with other works; the order was executed at Hull in the Common Hall.[21] Back in late June Marvell had warned that the Act of Conformity, which would settle the church, was imminent. On 19 May 1662, the Act of Uniformity, as it was finally called, received royal approval, and on Sunday 24 August, St Bartholomew's Day, it would come into force, a day thenceforth known as 'Black Bartholomew', coinciding with the anniversary of a notorious pogrom of Protestants in sixteenth-century Paris. Hundreds of Presbyterian ministers chose to resign their livings rather than conform.[22]

Indeed, it may have been, as attitudes hardened at the centre of power in court and in Parliament, that Marvell's past was catching up with him. Back in 1661, on 20 June, he had written to the Mayor of Hull, asking that no attention be paid to any malign rumours the Corporation might hear concerning him. This suggests more than differences with his fellow MP, and is indeed indicative of the surreptitious, near-conspiratorial activity that we know Marvell would engage in later in the decade, although by itself this speculation is not sufficient to explain the absence of correspondence between June 1661 and February 1662. Perhaps it was destroyed, and perhaps this was connected with the difficult political context of the day. This period undoubtedly proved very trying for Marvell, and perhaps too he was depressed. It was not an uncommon response among former Commonwealth supporters, the Quaker George Fox being a famous exemplar.[23] At least on 18 December, the Commons agreed to the revisions inserted by the Lords into the Act for separating Trinity Church from Hessle.[24]

Shortly before this, however, on 3 December, Trinity House in Hull wrote to Gylby requesting that he and Marvell help them secure the grant of the Spurn Head Lighthouse, the establishment of which would not only aid navigation but would put much revenue into the hands of Hull merchants. The negotiating, cajoling and letter-writing that would follow was to exercise both MPs for many, many hours. By 25 February Marvell and Gylby had prepared a draft petition, which they sent to Hull for review, together with the copy of a bill on the subject that had been read in the Lords on the previous 8 July. On 23 March Hull Trinity House recorded that it had given Marvell and Gylby the sum of £100 to spend on bribing potential supporters for the lighthouse scheme, and during the next month the two MPs would approach the Duke of Albemarle, the most important soldier in the kingdom. The Privy Council ruled on 12 May that only the King had the right to erect a lighthouse on Spurn Head, but Marvell delegated the solicitor John Cressett to act so that no further grant for the lighthouse be made without the case of Hull Trinity House first being heard. On the previous 2 August, the Corporation of Hull had instructed Marvell to act with its lawyer in London, Charles Vaux, in order to renew the town's charter.

It was then that Marvell acted as a teller for an amendment to the Poor Bill on behalf of garrison towns, which was defeated. Since the reconvening of Parliament on 7 January, he had been named to a further eight committees before a most revealing incident in March.[25] It involved both controversy and humiliation. It would seem that on 18 February Marvell argued publicly in the House with Thomas Clifford, the Member for Totnes, a closet Roman Catholic, soon to be a member of the court party, and a henchman for Arlington, Secretary of State during the Second Dutch War. Clifford's notoriously vile temper would not sit well with Marvell's, which was at least quick, and the quarrel heightened from the heated exchange of words to a scuffle.[26] The witness, John Scott, a Cavalier member for York, would not be sympathetic to Marvell. The Speaker, Sir Edward Turnor, conducted an investigation, and it was determined that Marvell, having given the first provocation, should make the first apology, and that Clifford should then apologize for the consequent exchanges. Sensationally, under the eyes of the House and the authority of the Speaker, Marvell refused to apologize. This led to an official reprimand ('gravely reprehended') from the Speaker 'for breach of the peace and privilege of the House', with all the protocol of the two MPs being called to their places in the House to receive it. Marvell then made his apology on his knees and Clifford followed. It was a grim moment, in which one of Marvell's limitations, his susceptibility to an extreme temper, was evident.[27]

It was at about this time that the so-called 'Hollis' portrait (after the eighteenth-century republican who had it engraved in 1760 and 1776) was probably made.[28] Quite unlike the Nettleton portrait of 1657, this showed Marvell, aged forty-two, as a sober if not also Puritanical gentleman, weighed down by deep concerns. His eyes are exaggeratedly watchful, and indeed a little fearful. From all we know of Marvell in this period, we cannot be surprised. He had been converted by the change of the times, and we might think again about depression, of travelling through adversity, of having to accept a much more limited lot in life.

TWO MISSIONS OVERSEAS

Shortly after the quarrel with Clifford had been formally resolved a sharp turn of events took Marvell away from Parliament for more than two years – much to the displeasure, it would seem, of some of his constituents back in Hull. He was asked by the Earl of Carlisle, Charles Howard, a member of the Privy Council (see plate 24), to undertake a secret mission to Holland. He could not tell the Hull Trinity House (no letter to the Corporation of Hull survives from this time, but he did apparently write to the Corporation) what he was doing, only that he was bound for the United Provinces and that, being aware of the consequences of his absence in Parliament, Carlisle would oversee the interests of Hull while Marvell was away.[29] Marvell repeatedly said that Gylby would be well able to look after Hull's interests in his absence, which is perhaps not the point.[30] And one wonders how he could have been right since he was appointed to four further Parliamentary committees in April, three of them with business related to northern interests, to say nothing of the preoccupying matter of the proposed lighthouse at Spurn Head.[31]

Marvell sailed by 13 May 1662; letters to London reporting his safe arrival were noted by the 24th. Upon landing in Holland, he made for the Hague, where he stayed in the residence of Sir George Downing, who happened to be the brother-in-law of Carlisle. Although almost nothing is known of this mission, the connection with Downing is a big hint. Downing had been the Protectorate's emissary in the Hague in the 1650s, and Marvell had corresponded with him, both on his own behalf and on that of Thurloe. As we saw earlier, Downing was no republican; rather, he wished to create a monarchy out of the Protectorate. Changing forms of government and allegiance were thus relatively easy for him, and he reappeared after the Restoration at the Hague as Charles II's Resident.[32] His main task in these early days of the new regime was to round up a number of Commonwealth exiles and have them sent back to England (several to be tried and executed). This he succeeded in doing. Carlisle himself did not stay for long, if indeed he left Westminster at all, since he appeared in Privy Council meetings soon afterwards.

Various reasons have been suggested for Marvell's usefulness to Charles II's government in Holland. He knew Dutch, and had been in the republic before. His mercantile connections, and his former diplomatic ones, it has been argued, may have been useful as a way of gathering intelligence on Dutch mercantile and military rivalry. When Marvell left England in the early summer of 1662, the outbreak of the Second Dutch War was only two years away. It is doubtful that Marvell was of any use to Downing in any military or mercantile context. Downing had served in the Dutch republic for a long time: he would have his own means of gathering intelligence on Dutch activity when he needed it; he boasted a remarkable facility in the running of spy rings. His contacts and knowledge of the scene would already have been far superior to anything that Marvell could have gathered for him.

Marvell's secretarial and linguistic skills counted for a lot, but his reference to specific pressure from a very powerful figure in the realm calls for more thought. Unlike Carlisle, Downing at least had some skill in languages and could encode correspondence. It is in fact to intelligence on Englishmen in Holland that Marvell's call to serve Carlisle and Downing relates. Carlisle had been brought up as a Catholic aristocrat. Despite early Royalist inclinations, he fought valiantly for the Commonwealth and Cromwell had rewarded him with political appointments in return for the delivery of that which the Howards and other northern aristocrats had provided for centuries in the far north of England: security in the border country. Carlisle naturally took an interest in the plight of Roman Catholics, but also in that of Protestant Nonconformists, and while an officer in Oliver Cromwell's bodyguard in the early 1650s had been a member of George Cokayne's Independent congregation. Like Marvell he was a supporter of Richard Cromwell, advised action against the army leaders and was imprisoned during the recall of the Rump on suspicion of collaboration with Royalists. No doubt this made his reconciliation with the restored monarchy easier, and before 1660 was out he was made a privy councillor in addition to being given a number of largely northern administrative and military appointments. As the Cavalier Parliament voted the Clarendon Code into law, with its harsh penalties against Dissenters as well as Catholics, Carlisle became the protector of all whose beliefs made them fall foul of the law. He wanted a broader religious toleration.[33]

Charles's Privy Council wanted to haul in regicides still at large, and to wipe out the diversity of religious practice that, in their view, had led to the Civil War and all the turmoil that had followed. That is to say, some of the Privy Council, like the Lord Chancellor, Clarendon, wanted this. Others, like Shaftesbury and

Buckingham, took a different view, and would for most of the decade find themselves out of the Council. It seems likely that Downing needed help in the form of an informed but relatively unrecognizable Dutch speaker, who could move around in the coffee houses, inns and other meeting places of the key cities – Amsterdam, Rotterdam, Middelburg, Leiden, Scheveningen, and so on – and locate those who were being sought. We know that although Marvell stayed at the Hague, he also moved around, and wrote one letter from Vianen. That Carlisle and Downing were seemingly in charge of this initiative is inter-esting. It means that they could control precisely who might be apprehended and who was left alone: one can imagine that they might go after out-and-out regicides but leave former Protectorate officials, religious radicals and former Levellers alone. Vianen was a self-proclaimed sovereign seigniory from the Middle Ages until 1795, and as a 'free city' was a haven for felons, escaped serfs and political fugitives. It was an obvious place for Downing to go hunting, and he caught four regicides.[34]

Whatever Marvell's skills as a secretary, he would soon be noticed in England as a creature who frequented coffee houses and bookshops, and his writings in prose and verse reveal how attuned he was to what was 'on the street', the literary public sphere of Restoration London. He would also soon be involved with what was left of the Commonwealth radical press, now decid-edly underground, and indeed seeking the protection of the Earl of Carlisle. In the 1670s, he was suspected of visiting the United Provinces in order to raise interest among English exiles in a republican conspiracy. As yet, we have no firm evidence to prove this hypothesis, but I think it highly likely that Marvell was a double agent for the government, just as Carlisle and Downing were, respectively, a double-sided aristocrat and a double-sided official.

Back in England, back in Hull, not all were pleased by the MP for Hull's absence. He had, after all, missed a great deal of Parliamentary debate and decision-taking (including the passing into law of the Clarendon Code). Near the beginning of February 1663, with the next session of Parliament looming, the Mayor and Aldermen of Hull wrote to Marvell asking him to return to his seat.[35] In February the Governor of Hull, Lord Belasyse, wrote to the Hull Corporation protesting about Marvell's absence, and urging that they should consider replacing him. The Corporation replied that they might well have to pursue this course of action. An interesting intervention: Belasyse (who was related to Lord Fauconberg, the husband of Oliver Cromwell's youngest daughter; Marvell had written the pastoral entertainment for their wedding at Hampton Court in 1657) had been a Royalist and, perhaps more to the point, a Catholic. Was he on the inside with regard to Marvell's mission, and was he at odds with Carlisle, and hence trying to diminish his influence? At any rate, he thought the Corporation should demand Marvell's return, and if he did not comply, they would then be justified in finding a replacement. The Corporation concurred in a letter of 27 February: they were considering electing a new burgess to replace Marvell. This was a serious matter. Belasyse saw an opportunity to enhance his influence by recommending one of his clients as a replacement.

The Mayor warned Marvell by letter that he should look to his back: dismay and resentment at his absence was building up. This prompted a quick return to Westminster. On 12 March, Marvell wrote from Vianen to say that he was placing his duty to the Corporation above his 'private concernments' and returning to the Parliament House.[36] What he described as a 'prudent and courteous letter' from the Mayor should be taken as a euphemism: the situation had been grave. He arrived back in time for the new session, and wrote on 2 April to Hull to confirm his presence and his eager application to his work. He also added that his place in the House he found empty, but wryly or even spikily added that he was aware that 'some persons would have been so courteous as to haue filled it for me.'[37] The repetition of neglecting his own 'private concernments' for the sake of the Corporation is there to assure Hull of his loyalty, but there is also a tone of resentment, of being pulled reluctantly into harness again. Between the lines of this courteous correspondence we can see the MP expressing frustration and the need for higher employment.

Marvell continued to correspond with the Corporation and Trinity House throughout the session, and at this time was resident again in St John Street, Clerkenwell, where he had stayed in 1642.[38] It was here that Carlisle had a house: was Marvell resident with him? While he reported to Hull Corporation that measures were being prepared to prevent the growth of popery and against Nonconformist conventicles, the major news in June was the unsuccessful plot in May by former members of the New Model Army, including the soon to be notorious Thomas Blood, to seize Dublin and the Lord Lieutenant.[39] The new regime did encounter resistance, and there was good reason for it to feel insecure.

By June, however, Marvell was once again being pressed by 'some private occasions' which this time related to public affairs, and which would once more require his absence from the House.[40] He had in fact been invited by Carlisle to be his secretary on a diplomatic mission to Moscow in order to re-establish English trade there; the Czar had cancelled English trade privileges that stretched back to 1555 after the regicide in 1649 but there seemed little sense for him to restrict trade partners in the future; Marvell had known about the mission since mid-May.[41] There would be stopovers in Sweden and Denmark on the way back. He was well aware that this was likely to cause further offence, so he offered as excuse the fact that there were precedents for MPs being absent from the House, and said that he would not go without the express permission of the Commons.[42] He wrote to Trinity House on 20 July that he had in the mission 'his Majestyes good liking, by leaue from the House and with the assent of our Bench [of the Corporation of Hull]'.[43]

At any rate, this was a different affair, public, with royal blessing, and obviously to the national advantage. No discussion took place at this time with regard to unseating Marvell even though the mission lasted nearly nineteen months, seven months longer than his maximum prediction of a year. The embassy itself was lavishly equipped with ceremonial dress, and with manpower (nearly eighty personnel in all), all packed into two ships, a man-of-war and a merchant vessel: the Muscovites were to be impressed. It was also the subject of a book-length report, written by Guy Miège, the under-secretary, Swiss and just nineteen years old when the mission began, which remains the major source for the embassy, along with Carlisle's letters, which were written in Marvell's hand, many of them sent back to the English Secretaries of State.[44] Marvell was on the man-of-war, the frigate *Kent* at Gravesend on 20 July; it sailed on the 22nd and reached Archangel a month later by sailing north around the coast of Norway and into the White Sea.

Here, Marvell was put to immediate use as an interpreter and negotiator. He was disembarked by Carlisle to present the embassy's credentials to the governor of the castle, and to have means provided for the Earl to be transported ashore. On shore he was met by six Russian gentlemen and 600 soldiers. We have no evidence that Marvell knew Russian, so we must presume that he communicated in Latin or French, most probably the former, and it may be inferred that the Russians wilfully misunderstood Marvell's Latin when they looked for disagreement; they would continue to do so during the entire course of the mission. However successful Marvell was in this initial encounter, the experience of the English became increasingly frustrating. Indeed, the gap of cultures told against Carlisle from the start, when even in Archangel the Muscovites were offended by some English and Dutch merchantmen firing their cannon in Carlisle's honour.

Still, sixteen boats collected the Earl and his party, and on 23 August 1663 Carlisle made his entry into Archangel and met the Governor, Osep Evanovich Ocolnitz. The English then waited until the merchant ship carrying the rest of their party and goods arrived on 5–6 September. Carlisle wrote to Clarendon on 27 August with news of the arrival at Archangel, some details of different nations' relations with the Russians, and some local details, such as the effect of a withdrawal of copper coinage.[45] An arduous journey followed, initially by river, the entire party travelling for some one thousand miles in six barges pulled by serfs (widely used for internal navigation in medieval and early modern Russia), and, following the northern Duina and Sucagna rivers but against their direction of flow, they reached Vologda on 17 October.

Ice had to be broken from time to time along the way as they went. At this point the Russian winter, which had already begun to set in, became unbearable. Despite equipping themselves with furs and sheepskins and, like the Russians, drinking vodka or another spirit, the English froze in the barges and decided to wait in Vologda until further freezing of the river that was late in coming meant that Carlisle's party could proceed more rapidly by sleigh. They celebrated Guy Fawkes Night with a feast, dancing and fireworks. Looking forward to expected and splendid meetings in Moscow, Carlisle had written to Patrick Gordon, the Scottish soldier serving in the Czar's army, and to Clarendon, asking for the supply of two silver trumpets, with banners, halberds and fringes in Carlisle's livery. On 21 November, Carlisle reported back in Marvell's hand on the experiences of the embassy so far, and the evident signs of mobilization against the Polish invasion. But Carlisle was well and court-eously treated in Vologda despite the persistent demands of servants for tips from the English. The embassy cannot have failed to be impressed by the cathe-dral of St Sophia, rebuilt by Ivan the Terrible in the sixteenth century, and Spaso-Prilutsky Monastery founded in 1371.

The arrival in December of agents from the Czar led, it was felt, to a deteri-oration of standards of diet and accommodation, although the English kept themselves going with hunting, music, dancing and some traffic in tobacco. The lesser servants were more officious and Carlisle felt they treated him idol-atrously, as an image of Charles II.[46] These circumstances meant a three-month wait, and a further fortnight's travel until, on 3 February, Carlisle's party reached a village, Yauza, close to Moscow. Then each Englishman apparently had a sleigh to himself, where he lay, wrapped in fur, fortified by spirits and mostly asleep. All along the way, the English had been reminded of the Russians' obsession with protocol and of their capriciousness. Carlisle's first encounter with an official in Archangel had involved a snub, and at Vologda the Czar's official, Offonasy Evanovich Nestrof, refused to supply the English with sleighs. Marvell was sent to remonstrate and was told by this man that the English should consider themselves lucky to have been sent such an important person from Moscow:

> To which the Secretary replied, that my Lord Ambassador acknowledged his quality, but he never thought it so great, that he and his associate ought to prefer themselves before him as they had done at their first visit.[47]

This was cheeky and sly, snide even, probably deserved, and clearly amused the English party. It is also decidedly reminiscent of the challenge of wit and honour that takes place between the speaker and companions in Marvell's satire 'Flecknoe, an English Priest at Rome'. Carlisle had Marvell compose a Latin letter making a complaint to the Czar about what he regarded as breaches of protocol, which had resulted in cumulative hardship for the English, and which, so it seemed to them, were insulting to the dignity of their mission and the monarch whom they represented. Redress was demanded. It was not an auspicious way to start.

The embassy prepared to enter Moscow formally on 5 February 1664 and the Czar and his family was ready to meet it, but there was a further delay so that ceremonies could be performed the following day. An uncomfortable night was spent in the village of Prutki. Marvell would surely have found what

happened next, to say the very least, full of irony. Muscovy's culture was deeply
embedded in ceremony, in a manner that was continuous with the practices of
the Eastern Orthodox church. No doubt as a way of flattering the Czar with the
significance of their status, Carlisle adopted a strategy of maximum display. He
entered the city in a procession of 200 sleighs on 6 February, with mounted
troops and loud music. Waves of cavalry peeled off to join the back of the
procession so that the impression of a greater host was created. This, plus gift
exchange, a further dispute about precedence, a formal Muscovite greeting and
English response, took three hours. The embassy did not enter the city itself
until after nightfall, although there were only candles and fires, torches not
being customary or known, and proceeded to its residence, a large stone house
belonging to David Rytz near the Kremlin. By then it had been given Offanasy
Evanovich Pronchissof as an attendant and one of the commissioners
dedicated to Carlisle's embassy. Four days were then spent attempting to
learn Muscovite protocol, and further sumptuous gifts were sent on. On
11 February, a first formal audience with Czar Alexei Mikhailovich took place,
Marvell riding with Carlisle, but standing up in the sled, without a hat, and
carrying on a yard of red damask all of the ambassador's credentials (letters
guaranteeing his authority), written on parchment, 'whose Superscription
contained all the Titles of the Czar in letters of Gold'. Even by seventeenth-
century standards, this was extravagant.

Yet it was designed to meet an imperial display that was more staggering to
the Englishmen. The Czar was covered in jewels, and Miège suggests that
Carlisle's party were literally dazzled by the appearance of Czar Alexei
Mikhailovich, who seemed to glow like the sun, as was no doubt the intended
effect. He was surrounded by 200 boyars, dazzlingly dressed, and had many
more troops and guards. Carlisle's Russian interpreter gave his speech in
Russian, which was then repeated in English by Carlisle, followed by Marvell's
Latin translation for submission as a written text. Marvell had composed a
series of Latin speeches, which he delivered, and gifts were presented,
including a gun used by Charles I and a pair of pistols worn by Charles II when
he entered London in triumph in April 1660.

At this first audience, the Czar's first comment had been an enquiry after
Henrietta Maria, the widow of that 'glorious Martyr *Charles* the First'. Could it
be that a monarchical ruler, heavily invested in the iconic status of the crown in
his own realm and enjoying something like godlike reverence from his subjects,
would be particularly affronted by the removal of a fellow monarch, to the
extent that he might feel it to be an attack upon himself? This must have been
the case, unless Alexei and his advisers were by nature insolent, since the
second audience, two days later, proved disastrous. At the first audience,
Carlisle's address was 'well approved of', gifts from the English to the Czar were
presented, and Carlisle and his gentlemen, including Marvell, were allowed to
kiss the right hand of the Czar, upheld by a boyar lest his master be tired. But

all was suddenly changed in the next meeting. The English were reproved by the Czar for their letter of complaint of 6 February, causing Carlisle to 'speak somewhat hard'. The Czar expressed his discontent at being called '*Illustrissime*' as opposed to '*Serenissime*' (the adjective given to Charles II), words chosen, of course, by Marvell himself. Choice of words had caused an international incident. No doubt some of this was due to the incompatibility of the two political cultures: the Russians regarded the Czar as greater than a European king, and indeed saw him as an emperor (Peter the Great would eventually use the term *imperator* in 1721). The word 'czar' came close to being untranslatable for west Europeans. It is not difficult to see how the disastrous confusion of terms of address in which Marvell was involved could arise. Moreover, Alexei (a man generally known for his piety, if also for fits of bad temper) said he was not granting the English their request since the Archangel Company (the Merchant Adventurers) had supported the revolution: an envoy had been sent by Charles I himself to inform the Czar. In any case, he thought the English were interested only in their own profit at the expense of the Russians.

This was a very considerable setback: nothing had been gained, despite a huge diplomatic effort, and a lot of bad blood had been generated. From the point of view of a secretary on a diplomatic mission, it was an embassy in crisis. Some attempt at reparation was made at dinner, on 19 February, and at a sitting lasting from 2 p.m. until 11, during which time Marvell was rewarded with an entire sturgeon's head. On 29 February, Carlisle made yet another attempt at an audience. But he did it without tact. He did not humour the Czar, but instead pressed again the complaint of bad treatment by the Czar's officials, and said that the Czar's letter to Charles II of 28 July 1661 had been an invitation to the Muscovy Company to renew its privileges. There followed a point-by-point attempt to refute the Czar's arguments. All of the English, Carlisle said, were in some sense involved in the Civil War and its aftermath, but the 'better part' remained free from guilt (presumably including the English Company of Archangel). Charles I's envoy to the Czar had been an impostor, a failed merchant desperately in search of succour. If the English had misnamed the Czar, why then so too had the Russians neglected to call Charles by his proper title, 'Defender of the Faith'. He added (and surely this must have come from Marvell himself) that the 'word Serenus signifieth nothing but still & calme': thus both Cicero and Lucretius called the night serene and gave further examples tending to the superiority in meaning of '*Serenissimus*' over '*Illustrissimus*'. It has been rightly shown that some of this language bears a close resemblance to Marvell's own poetry, so that the terms were, to say the least, not Carlisle's alone.[48] Indeed, since it is presumed that Marvell would have written Carlisle's letter, and therefore had been on hand to give advice, one cannot help but think that the entire approach was full of Marvellian testiness, as if his later satirical contestations with Parker and Turner were in style present here in an act of risky diplomacy.[49]

The English had entertained themselves all through their mission. They went duck and pigeon shooting while on the barges, or engaged in drinking contests with local governors. At Vologda they hunted white hare, skated, danced to the music of their six accompanying musicians, and celebrated 5 November with fireworks made along the way and a 'pleasant farce of Mascarads'. In Moscow, the embassy occupied a well furnished and well supplied stone house, raced horses, took saunas, and played football in front of the Czar, while the music master wrote a 'handsome Comedie in prose', which was acted in the residence. Marvell's duties, it would seem, kept him away from entertainments, in which he had by then some skill and experience. In Moscow they were entertained with feasts, one of which consisted of nearly 500 dishes served continuously. On the Czar's birthday (17 March) a huge dinner was sent to the English embassy by the Czar himself. The English watched the huge Palm Sunday procession on 3 April, and witnessed the Easter celebration in the form of the giving of coloured eggs for fifteen days.

In a series of further speeches, Marvell found himself on Carlisle's orders denouncing former pro-Commonwealth friends and colleagues. But Alexei would not be moved. He played a waiting game, and on 10 and 19 March, raised the issue of English military help against the Poles and the Tartars. The Polish threat was clearly a major preoccupation.[50] Carlisle thought that emergency war taxes would be borne by the population with great difficulty, and that the impressments of men would benefit the Czar little since they were cowed by slavery and in poor physical condition.[51] The Czar's commissioners were nettled by the tone of Carlisle's comments about the Russian posts and titles, and continued to insist on English military help before trading privileges would be restored. Carlisle wrote to the King in Marvell's hand, bitterly complaining of the way the winter slowed down all activity, and hence all the Muscovites. At a final private audience on 22 April 1664, just after the Orthodox Easter, nothing was gained, and nothing was agreed, even though Carlisle spoke in the first person to suggest that Charles II was present to negotiate with the Czar. He offered English mediation with Poland and Sweden. Interestingly, these letters were signed only by Marvell, Carlisle refusing to sign them. Was Marvell, as Downing had suggested, actually making up policy? Carlisle would eventually sign only on the condition that his English sense was observed. Was there a difference of view with Marvell, or was Carlisle very insecure indeed about his poor languages? He was at the very least concerned to avoid being susceptible to any Russian attempt to find fault or take offence. A month later, on 24 and 27 May, the Czar's commissioners again refused all of Carlisle's demands, and apparently misinterpreted the Latin to his disadvantage. Charles II assented to the idea of English mediation between Muscovy and Poland, and put this to a new set of commissioners, but he saw the repeated offer of privileges after the cessation of war with Poland as a ruse. Carlisle left after a final public audience on 24 June. Ten days earlier he had written to Charles II reporting his failure, and dictated other letters to Marvell

1 St German's Church, Winestead.

2 Holy Trinity Church, Hull.

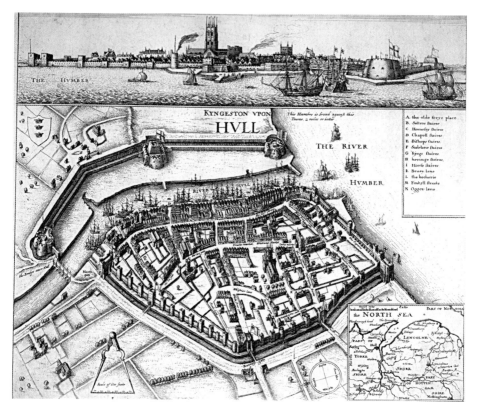

3 Wenceslaus Hollar, Plan of Hull (*c.*1640). The Charterhouse where Marvell lived as a boy was situated to the west of the River Hull (not the Humber) and north of the town walls, at the lower left-hand side of this map.

4 Henry Hawkins *Partheneia Sacra* ([Rouen], 1633), sig. [Avi[v]].

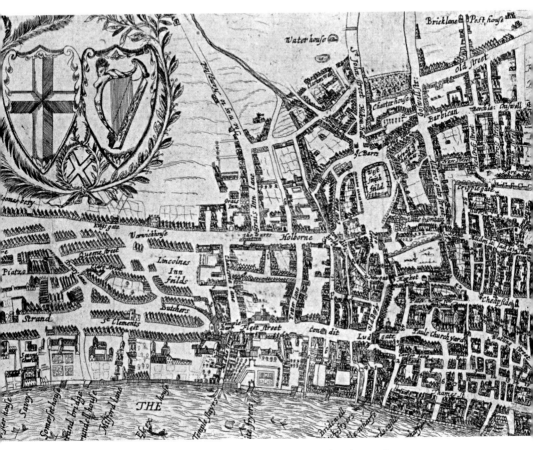

5 Detail of a map (1654) of Clerkenwell, Smithfield and environs by Thomas Porter.

6 Gian Lorenzo Bernini, *Apollo and Daphne* (1622–5).

7 Sixteenth-century representation of the statue of Pasquino in Rome, from Antoine Lafréry, *Speculum Romanae Magnificentiae* (1575).

8 Attributed to Jusepe Leonardo, *Palace of the Buen Retiro* in 1636–7 (detail).

9 *Oliver Cromwell* (1649) by Samuel Cooper.

10 Robert Overton, painter unknown.

11 *Thomas Fairfax, 3rd Baron Fairfax of Cameron* by William Faithorne, after Robert Walker.

12 Daniel King, Appleton House.

13 *Oliver St John* (1651) by Pieter Nason.

14 *Walter Strickland* (1651) by Pieter Nason.

15 Oliver Cromwell (1653) by Robert Walker.   16 *John Dutton,* after Franz Cleyn.

17 Lodge Park, Gloucestershire.

18 Andrew Marvell: 'Nettleton' portrait (*c.* 1657).

19 *Oliver Cromwell (*1655)
by Samuel Cooper.

20 *Richard Cromwell*
(*c.* 1650–5).

21 Copy of the Seal of the Parliament of the Commonwealth of 1659, imitating the Great Seal of 1651. Although Marvell was not elected to this particular, short-lived Parliament, he was a member of its immediate predecessor and two successors.

22 Engraved frontispiece and title page of *Miscellaneous Poems* (1681).

MISCELLANEOUS
POEMS.

BY
ANDREW MARVELL, Esq;
Late Member of the Honourable House of Commons.

LONDON,
Printed for *Robert Boulter,* at the *Turks-Head*
in *Cornhill.* M. DC. LXXXI.

23 *John Milton* (1670) by
William Faithorne.

24 *Charles Howard,
1st Earl of Carlisle* by
William Faithorne.

for Clarendon and for Henry Bennet, Charles's Secretary of State, in which he confessed his frustration at Russian capriciousness, in a country where diplomats were considered to have no privileges. The Czar gave Carlisle a parting gift of sables, to be distributed to the ambassador's train according to rank. But having gained nothing, Carlisle did not see that he could honourably accept gifts. To the dismay of his party, who nonetheless saw his point of honour, the sables were sent back. Carlisle had Marvell write a Latin letter on 30 June near Tver, from which they were shut out, asking that an Englishman called Caspar Calthov, who had been in the Czar's service, now be permitted to return to England rather than be arrested and jailed, as was intended.

By 3 August 1664 the party reached Riga via Novgorod and Pskov by horseback, three coaches and 200 wagons. They were impressed by the majestic rivers flowing across vast plains, and amused by the fear they incited in the local peasantry, but they suffered from hard saddles, an unrelenting diet of beef and mutton, and a summer affliction, the 'persecution of the flies'. Perhaps the high point was on 22 July when they left the territory of Muscovy and Nihuysen and entered Livonia, which then belonged to Sweden. But a further Latin letter sent from Pskov, the last Muscovite outpost, regarding Calthov, and a returning of borrowed tents and coaches at this border and not at Riga, was taken by the Czar as extremely insolent, and resulted in an emissary being sent to England to complain about Carlisle. In Livonia the entire party now travelled on rather poor horses, but they were well provisioned and were greeted by frequent artillery salutes.

In Riga, the second-largest city in Swedish territory, they were well received by the Swedes; there were three days' entertainment, appreciative audiences with Count Oxenstierna, and the distractions of featherbeds. The weather was stormy but all were said to be glad to be out of Muscovy. After resting at Riga for fifteen days, they sailed for Stockholm on 18 August, but poor weather delayed them, stretching provisions. The waters off Stockholm were not reached until the 31st, and the embassy did not enter the city until 8 September. Here, they were received in the court of Charles XI, who was just nine years old. Ten years earlier, Marvell had written a Latin poem in praise of, and that was read to, his father's cousin, Queen Kristina. Marvell delivered a Latin address after Carlisle had given it in English, and then gave it in French the next day to the Queen Mother, Hedwig Eleonora of Holstein-Gottorp. The English delighted in the civility of the Swedes, their Lutheran piety, and their dinners and deer hunting. There was a review of the Swedish fleet in which an early submarine was demonstrated. Although nothing was directly gained here either, perhaps because of Swedish fears of commitment to England at a time when the likelihood of war between England and Holland was rising, Carlisle tried to build the grounds for an Anglo-Swedish-Danish alliance that would discountenance the United Provinces and Muscovy. He had to dissuade the Swedes from the view that the English were allying against them.

On 13 October, the embassy left Stockholm for Copenhagen, which they reached on the 27th, although not without a storm delaying departure and further postponing embarkation. Two days before there had been ceremonial leave-taking, with Miège noting Marvell's oratorical skill, including a pause in both English and French to convey that he was lost for words in praise of the Queen Mother's excellence.[52] During the voyage the company was entertained by the two tame bears that had been presented at the huge feast in Moscow on 19 February. They wrestled and one sucked the fingers of anyone who was brave enough to let him. On the 21st, while they were at sea, Marvell's step-mother Lucy Alured had been buried in Beverley. Upon arrival in Copenhagen, Marvell was again dispatched to present Carlisle's credentials at the court. Compliments were exchanged, hospitality was extended (at first three days of entertainments), negotiations took place, and for six weeks Carlisle attempted to pull the Danes into alliance with the Swedes and the English. Perhaps this is not surprising: the Danes were the formal allies of the Dutch, and Charles II's paternal grandmother had been a Danish princess. A cordial audience took place with Frederick III, King of Denmark under the new Danish absolutist monarchical constitution, with Marvell translating Carlisle's English into Latin, or French for the Queen and possibly Crown Prince Christian. The English embassy left in mid-December, but an initial attempt to go by sea from Helsingør failed since the water was frozen and the weather stormy. Carlisle was in fact running out of money: in Marvell's hand he wrote to Bennet noting the debts incurred in running the embassy, and saying that his wife's pregnancy meant a further fortnight's stay (Carlisle's second son Frederick Christian was christened on 17 November). The bad weather meant a further six days anchored off Helsingør, and another attempt to sail was prevented by further inclement weather. It was then determined that they should travel overland, but as swiftly as possible this time: the embassy was low in resources and war would shortly be declared between England and Holland.

The mission made its final way home overland to Hamburg. On the road out of Hamburg, on the next stage towards Bremen, comes one of the most colourful events in Miège's account and Marvell's life, and one that is indicative of impatience, a hot temper and desperate action growing from frustration. One supposes in the circumstances of such arduous travel and after such trials that tempers would be frayed. At the village of Buxtehude, a wagoner said he would not drive Marvell unless his comrade, whom the English did not wish to use, came along with another wagon. Reason not working, Marvell pulled a pistol on the wagoner, which was immediately wrested from him by other villagers. A scuffle ensued, and Marvell had to be rescued by his countrymen from 'a barbarous rout of peasants and Mechanicks'. Then while he was in Buxtehude itself complaining of his treatment (which seems risky; he had after all pulled a gun), a mob gathered and the English were jostled; a page was tossed up and down, and only the return of Carlisle restored order. The party rode on through Bremen (6–8 January), Münster (11 January), Cologne, Malines (Mechelen), Brussels and Calais, from where they sailed for Gravesend, arriving on 30 January 1665.

Carlisle was debriefed by Charles. Already, the King had received reports from the Russian ambassador Dashkov in London protesting on behalf of Czar Alexei at the insolence of the English embassy, specifically complaining about the letters sent from Tver and Pskov, and mentioning Marvell as well as Carlisle, who would be asked by Charles to write an account of the embassy that could be used to challenge the Russian account. It is likely that Marvell wrote Carlisle's 'The Lord Ambassadors Apology'. Charles was satisfied, and Miège published it in full in his book, itself an indication of growing public interest in foreign affairs. We might also add that Miège's account reflects the substantial presence of Marvell's particular temper and wit with words. He appears to have been as much an architect of the English embassy as his immediate superior, the Earl of Carlisle himself. But the mission had been a disaster, and while Carlisle, the Czar and his officials must bear much of the blame, some negative reflection must surely have remained in the King's eyes about Carlisle's secretary too.

THE POLITICS OF PLAGUE

When Carlisle's party was journeying across Russia towards the Baltic coast, John Trott died. He was the son of Sir John Trott of Laverstoke Manor in Hampshire, a 'country' MP who had been a Commonwealth official and who was evidently known to Marvell. Marvell might have picked up such news when he arrived with Carlisle's party in Stockholm, although it seems more likely that even if he did learn it there he waited until his return to England before he wrote his Latin epitaph for John. Or perhaps he heard the news later still in August 1667 when Sir John's second son, Edmund, also died from smallpox, although this seems far less likely given the very different nature of the two Latin epitaphs Marvell wrote.[53]

Whatever did happen, Marvell evidently returned to his duties as a Hull man in London. This was no doubt prudent in view of Hull Corporation's desire to have their pennyworth of their MP. Thus, presenting merely symbolic unity, we find Marvell on 4 February witnessing a Trinity House document alongside Gylby, Ramsden and Cressett.[54] The signatories were headed by Robert Bloome, soon to become mayor himself. On 16 March Marvell was paid £10. 6s. 8d. for thirty-one days' attendance in Parliament. Four weeks after his return, on 4 March, war was declared on the United Provinces.

In Marvell's absence – a total of eighteenth months – a great deal had changed in English politics, very little of it to Marvell's liking. The year 1664 was a crucial one, during which the hold of the Cavalier Parliament and Clarendon had intensified. The Triennial Act, guaranteeing the calling of Parliament every three years, had been repealed and the Conventicle Act, which imposed severe penalties on Dissenters, was introduced. Anglican reaction against Dutch support for Nonconformity was one factor behind the trade restrictions imposed on the Dutch in the same year. Carlisle and Marvell might both have resisted these developments in their respective spheres, and it was certainly convenient for the Cavaliers to have Carlisle out of the way.

Marvell arrived in time to deal with a crisis that had been brewing at Trinity House, the mercantile and marine institution in Hull that he also represented in London, and to attend the last thirty-one days of Parliament in the current session, which was prorogued on 2 March 1665 until 21 June.[55] The Yorkshire MPs were enlisted as members of a committee for the Bill to repair Bridlington pier on 8 February, and on the 25th for the draining of Deeping Fen, Lincolnshire. But the major business of the session, and one that would have profound consequences, was the official declaration of war on the United Provinces on 4 March 1665, although military preparations had been taking place since the autumn and Dutch colonies had been attacked in December 1664.[56] There is no correspondence addressed to the Corporation of Hull for this period, but that may be a consequence of the fact that a probable close relative of the then Mayor, William Skinner, gave the letters written at this time to 'the pastry-maid, to put under pie-bottoms'.[57]

Initial victory against the Dutch was undermined by an inability to exploit naval advantages, and by a failure of the war administration. The navy was hampered by a dual authority structure in which one half was often at odds with the other. Money became increasingly scarce. Supply to the fleet and preparation for coastal defence were inadequate. English trade was paralysed, even to the extent that English colliers were kept out of London in the winter of 1666–67. Coal could not be had for heating (this seems to be mentioned in one version of Marvell's 'The Second Advice to a Painter', l. 60). A psychological victory had been won by the Dutch who, by contrast, had men, munitions and money.

On 3 June 1665 was fought the first major naval action, the Battle of Lowestoft, where the English navy failed to press its advantage to complete victory; this action was succeeded by its embarrassing failure to punish the Dutch fleet at Bergen in Norway. This indecisiveness was very decisive for Marvell's future poetry, as we shall shortly see. In the meantime, Marvell's First Dutch War satire 'The Character of Holland' had been published for the first time by the very proper hands of Roger L'Estrange, Surveyor of the Press, and Octavian Pulleyn of the Stationers' Company. It may well be that the poem, with its new eight-line conclusion applying it to the context of 1665 and praising the Duke of York, was prepared entirely without Marvell's knowledge; on the other hand, in releasing and revising it, he may have been looking for further promotion:

Vainly did this *Slap-Dragon* fury hope,
With sober *English* valour ere to cope:
Not though they Primed their barb'rous mornings-draught
With Powder, and with Pipes of Brandy fraught:
Yet *Rupert, Sandwich*, and of all, the *Duke*.
The *Duke* has made their Sea-sick courage puke.
Like the three Comets, sent from heaven down
With Fiery Flailes to swinge the'ingratefull Clown.[58]

A further edition was published in York probably at the beginning of August, and this seems to have coincided with the Duke of York's visit as a precaution against any possible new northern uprising or possible defections of Englishmen to the Dutch navy.[59] This edition was published by Stephen Bulkley as a two-column broadsheet intended to be pasted on walls, such as those of inns; the text was taken from a corrected copy of Robert Horn's London edition.

Then came a calamity. The Great Plague of London (1664–66), an outbreak of bubonic plague, struck London and was particularly violent during the hot months of August and September of 1665. In one week, 7,165 people died. The total number of deaths was about 70,000. People called it the Black Death, black for the colour of the telltale lumps that foretold its presence in a victim's body, and death for the inevitable result. The explanation that has usually been accepted is that the disease was carried by fleas that lived on black rats, although this is now challenged by epidemiologists, who point to waterborne disease as more likely to cause such a rapid spread of infection.[60] It was generally incurable, and its effects were terrible – fever and chills, swelling of the lymph glands, eventual madness and death. It had first appeared in Britain in 1348, and the islands had never been totally free of plague since then; it had been accepted as an unpleasant possibility that people just learned to live with, as was the case in Hull in the later 1630s. In 1665, however, matters were different.

In 1663 plague had ravaged Holland. Charles II forbade trade with the Dutch, partly out of wise concern, and partly because of the build-up to war. Despite the precautions, the early spring of 1665 brought a sudden rise in the death rate in the poorer sections of London. The authorities ignored it. As spring turned into one of the hottest summers in memory, the number of deaths escalated and panic set in.

People had no idea what caused the disease or how to control its rapid course. Victims of the plague were buried in large pits. Many people fled from London. The nobility left the city for their estates in the country; they were followed by the merchants and the lawyers. The Inns of Court were deserted. Most of the clergy suddenly decided they could best minister to their flocks from far, far away. The College of Surgeons left for the country, which did not stop several of its members from writing learned papers about the disease they had been at such pains to avoid. The court moved to Hampton Court Palace. By June the roads were clogged with people desperate to escape London. The Lord Mayor responded by closing the gates to anyone who did not have a certificate of health. These certificates became a currency more valuable than gold, and a thriving market in forged certificates grew up.

By mid-July over 1,000 deaths per week were reported in the city. The death toll mounted and graveyards soon became full. Vacant land was used for 'plague pits' and quicklime was used in them. In spite of gravediggers literally working night and day, they could not keep up with deaths and so corpses were piled up awaiting burial. The epidemic was at its worst in the third week of September 1665 when the death toll was estimated at well over 10,000. A cold autumn reduced the toll to 900 deaths in the final week of November and the crisis had ended by the time the King returned to London on 1 February 1666.

It seems sensible to assume that Marvell, like most people of at least some means, fled to the country, as the summer and the deaths came on. Perhaps he went back to Hull, or retreated to one of the houses of the great whom he served: Lord Wharton and his grand houses at Winchendon and Wooburn, Buckinghamshire. With the Second Anglo-Dutch War came an intensification of the King's policy of proroguement. Parliament did not meet between 2 March and 9 October 1665 – seven months – and when it did the presence of the plague in London compelled a meeting in Oxford.

In the late summer of 1665 anyone anywhere near London was mainly concerned about the plague epidemic that was fast reaching its height. This fact certainly made an impact on the Oxford historian Anthony à Wood.[61] But whatever leisure Marvell had in October, it may have been hard to find, since Robert Stockdale reported that he was too busy to write to the Corporation of Hull on the 12th.[62] Marvell was becoming a little tired of the Hull Corporation's failure to supply the responses he had requested to the legislation that was soon to be enacted: principally the King's proposed war supply and the Five Mile Act, which compounded the legislation that already existed against Nonconformists. He had not been present to give his views when the Conventicles Act was debated and passed in 1664. But the abuses of the war and problems with its administration were beginning to surface: specifically at this juncture, the embezzlement of prizes.[63]

Marvell was in Oxford by late September and the King had arrived earlier in the month. Marvell signed his letters simply from Oxford; it seems unlikely that during Michaelmas Term he would have found, along with the others, lodgings in a college.[64] He is recorded on the 30th as being a visitor to the Bodleian Library, almost alone among the visiting MPs, but we have no evidence of his reading, and there is nothing from these years that relates to the specific content of books Marvell might have found in the Bodleian.[65] At any rate, this would have merited a more positive approbation from local residents than that accorded the King and his courtiers, whose fine appearance was belied by their unhygienic manners, for they left, claimed Anthony à Wood, 'their excrements in every corner, in chimneys, studies, colehouses, cellars'. They were, he went on, 'Rude, rough, whoremongers; vaine, empty, carelesse'.[66] Marvell wrote to the Mayor of Hull, Robert Bloome, concerning a vote in the Commons for a supply of £1.2 million a month for the Dutch war, even though Parliament was not in session. Several other bills were discussed, including bills for restraints on swearing and drinking by penalty, and for prohibiting ejected ministers from living near towns.[67] This was on 15 October; one week later there were further bills to limit the import of Irish cattle and to deal with the improper embezzlement of prize goods. More surprising are the imprisonment of the Dutch ambassador's secretary, and the snubbing of the French ambassadors. Marvell was certainly interested in the fact that the Bishop of Münster had succeeded in forcing the Dutch to open their dykes. But, as he predicted, the session ended soon, on 2 November, with the result that much of the discussed legislation passed, together with the issuing of attainders for the arrest of three English republican defectors in Holland: Thomas Dolman, Thomas Scott and Francis Bamfield, all of whom were believed to be helping the Dutch against the English. Legislation designed to assist the passing of the plague met with resistance from the Lords, who did not want to board up their houses. Just over a week before the closure, Marvell and his fellow poet Edmund Waller were appointed to a Parliamentary committee investigating the embezzlement of prizes in the war.[68] This is highly significant, not only as a clear sign of a growing concern with corruption but also because it may well yield us a vital clue in explaining Marvell's next remarkable move as a poet. Marvell might have felt uneasy at the reintroduction of book licensing, in addition to penalization of Nonconformists. On 13 December, it was ordered that Marvell be paid £7 6s. 8d. for his twenty-two days' attendance at Parliament. Gylby, it would seem, did not go to Oxford: he was busy managing the garrison at Hull during the plague visitation.

It is worth dwelling on the uses Marvell might have made of the Bodleian. He had no such library to call upon in Westminster and, as is now known, he probably wrote The Rehearsal Transpros'd in the Earl of Anglesey's private library.[69] So he may also have been taking the opportunity to read in a more preliminary way in the fields that would power his polemics of the 1670s. One obvious candidate for an earlier composition, researched in Oxford, that was later published, suffixed to Mr Smirke, was the History of General Councils, a likely project because of the context of the recently introduced conventicle legislation, and its notable exposure of episcopal turbulence in church history.[70]

As we have seen, the King did not return to Westminster until the beginning of February 1666. It looks as though Marvell may well have returned by early December, since he signed a letter jointly with Gylby to Trinity House on the 9th.[71]

There is then a gap of about ten months for which no correspondence survives. This is not necessarily unusual: it may mean that the constituency correspondence for this period was simply lost. But events that would intimately concern Marvell were beginning to develop. Parliament met on 20 February and eleven days later the second, longer and more elegant version of Edmund Waller's state praise poem *Instructions to a Painter* appeared (the first had appeared as a broadsheet in 1665), no doubt intended as a book that would appeal to MPs and noble peers in the light of what the government proclaimed as a successful prosecution of the war. But that claim could not be sustained.

CHAPTER 8

✳

THE PAINTER AND THE POET DARE

THE RETURN OF PARLIAMENT to Westminster provided the context for a number of grievances to be aired. The King prorogued it from 20 February to 23 April, and finally to 18 September. It is to April 1666 that the dating for the emergence of the outspoken and sensational verse satire 'The Second Advice to a Painter' is ascribed. Marvell is now thought with some assurance to be at least part author of this poem.[1] In one rescension of the manuscript, the poem (like its followers) is addressed to 'the Company of Drunken Poets', which implies joint publication by a group of the disaffected, be they MPs or others.[2]

As events unravelled, it became clear that the naval administration and the government behind it were inadequate to fight and win this war. Logistics carried successive shortfalls; corruption was rife. It used to be thought that the cause of the war was trade – the mercantile competition between the two countries – but now economic enmity is seen to have been precipitated by the ideological differences that had emerged between the dominant power blocs in each respective country in the 1660s (and which stemmed back to mid-century divisions) – the Anglican Royalists in England and the republicans in the United Provinces, each fearing that the other appealed to and supported its enemies at home. Thus, the English feared the republican exiles in Holland (who were understood to have helped the rebellion of disaffected Nonconformists and republicans in the north during the autumn of 1663), and the Dutch republicans feared English support for the Prince of Orange, who was at that time substantially excluded from power.[3] For the Anglican Royalists, Dutch trade was part and parcel of a new attempt at universal monarchy. Much in Marvell's writings and in the deliberations of his superiors, like George Downing, supports this view.

On 20 February 1666, Parliament was prorogued until 23 April, and then until 18 September. Marvell had a lot of free time on his hands. Some of his time at least was usually dedicated to his family. On 9 April in the company of his nephews William Popple and Thomas Alured, he witnessed certificates of the Cambridge bookseller Anthony Nicholson and Dorothy Pocock that they had been cured respectively of the King's Evil and a breast tumour by Valentine Greatreakes, who performed miracle cures by 'stroking'.[4] At this time Greatreakes was under the patronage of the Boyle family. The next month we know Marvell was back in Hull, since Trinity House accounts record payments for food and wine when they entertained Marvell and Gylby on the 17th.[5] In other words Marvell was free of the constraints on his time imposed by Parliamentary sessions; he was able to observe Restoration England closely, and to watch how it had taken shape while he had been away – and how very different it was from Commonwealth England.

These weeks in 1666 were taken up with other matters that return us to the meeting place of art, high politics and war. The fashion for portraiture in the Restoration is well known, and drew attention to itself at the time: it stood out as a special interest of the English elite, and was noted as such by continental visitors. Other kinds of painting did not fare so well in this period when the wealthy did not stint in spending money on other kinds of luxury goods, from the building of houses to the upgrading of coaches for transport.[6] While some painters, notably Lely, had been prolifically painting portraits of eminent people during the Commonwealth, no one failed to notice a distinct change of style. Away went heroism and the Cromwellian era version of Van Dyck and along came an almost incandescent fleshliness that could only be redolent of the libertine ethos of the King and his closest courtiers. Kevin Sharpe has drawn attention to the fact that Charles had a remarkable number of pictures painted of the royal bastards, so that he may be seen to be celebrating his own profligacy.[7] Painting was the final accoutrement of the libertine courtier, the mirror in which ego and style were reflected back, and in which both truth and disguise were evident.[8]

So it was totally appropriate, when criticism of the government reared its head, that painting should be the arena of engagement. Edmund Waller had celebrated the English naval victory over the Dutch at Lowestoft in June 1665 with *Instructions to a Painter*, published first in short form as a broadsheet in 1665, then in 1666 as a printed book, entered in the Stationers' Register on 1 March. In response, the Advice-to-a-Painter poems appeared, most probably first in manuscript, then shortly afterwards in print. The poems were part of a series of verse satires on the Second Dutch War, which developed from a concern with naval maladministration and court corruption into an attack on the bishops of the Church of England. They constituted a major means by which discontent with Clarendon's government was registered, and opposition focused, before the divisions of the Exclusion Crisis led to the clear identification of Whig and Tory factions. Marvell was following the dictate of Horace, *De arte poetica*, lines 9–10, that the painter and the poet are alike in 'daring all', although Waller had maintained that only poets can describe battles.[9] While 'The Second Advice' amply shows this, Marvell deftly reworked images from his earlier verse, some of which must have been self-reflexive, to depict the characters in the battle. Hence James Ley, third Earl of Marlborough, emerges in his heroic death as an unfortunate lover, in the Marvell poem of the same name, perhaps revealing a relationship of mutuality between poet and hero as seen by Marvell.

Looking back in 1667 on defeat, plague and possibly also the Great Fire, the Quaker George Bishop reminded the King of a prophetic warning that had come to him from God just after the battle, in which Bishop was told that plague would come on England because of the persecution of Dissenters.[10] In the court and in Parliament several emerged who championed calls for a more efficient government, and more religious toleration: foremost among them were Buckingham, Arthur Annesley, Earl of Anglesey, and Philip, Lord Wharton. Buckingham would be invited to be the King's chief minister, and would quickly fail; Anglesey was a gifted administrator and trained lawyer; and Wharton was already well known as a leading pro-Parliamentary aristocrat during the 1640s, and was a dedicated patron of Nonconformists. Marvell was already associated with Wharton by 1660, and with all three he would have much to do in the late 1660s and 1670s. When Parliament was not sitting it would become a matter of course for Marvell to attend these men, provide advice and do their bidding, much as he had done for John Dutton in 1656–57. He was what was called their 'client' but the political context of the mid-1660s made the client relationship decidedly more intense.

'The Second Advice' was probably written and intended to be circulated to coincide with the calling of Parliament on 23 April 1666; this follows the entry in the Stationers' Register of the complete version of Waller's *Instructions to a Painter* by one month: it is the patriotic spirit of this poem that Marvell's retort satirically unwinds. His poem may well have been withdrawn from circulation with the proroguement until 18 September. It was only then that Christopher Wase responded to it with his poem *Divination* and Pepys did not see a copy until 14 December.

The criticism of the government and the courtiers begins during the Battle of Lowestoft. What should have been a crushing victory was marred when a courtier (Henry Brouncker) pretending to have the authority of the Lord High Admiral, the Duke of York, called off the pursuit of the Dutch fleet. Marvell's poem presents this debacle as but one example of a series of manifestations of courtly behaviour that were doing great damage to the nation. Towards the end of the poem, two further naval failures are described. In July de Ruyter, returning with a weakened East India convoy, managed to evade Sandwich's fleet off the Dogger Bank (ll. 245–52, 259–70). At the same time, a foolish attempt to subvert the alliance between the Danish and the Dutch resulted in an English squadron under Sir Thomas Teddeman suffering severe loss and damage from combined Dutch and Danish fire as he tried to attack a Dutch fleet in Bergen harbour (ll. 253–8, 271–86). Finally, although Sandwich did capture part of the Dutch East Indies fleet, he allowed the cargo to be looted, even taking some of the goods himself. This led to further criticism at home, while at sea, once again, the naval advantage was not pressed home. Charles saved Sandwich by appointing him ambassador to Spain (ll. 287–316). The naval scenario ends in the poem with the division of command between Rupert and Monck in early 1666.

Marvell's Commonwealth and Protectorate sympathies are not far from the surface of the poem. The heroes are, by and large, men who had prospered in the Commonwealth navy: of these, Sandwich was the most eminent. The villains are former Royalists, many of whom were in exile during the 1650s, who returned to reap honours and profits under the restored monarchy. Marvell's estimations of men thus often differ from those of other commentators. Pepys greatly valued Sir William Coventry as mentor and colleague, but Marvell presents him as the minister of death. He was effectively constructing the 'patriot' tradition, so valued by those supporters of the Glorious Revolution who encountered 'The Second Advice' as part of the 'Poems on Affairs of State' in the editions of 1689, 1694, 1697 and thereafter.[11] Marvell's poem is notable for its degree of equivocation: the Dutch are reviled less than the representatives of English corruption. This is in contradistinction to Jasper Mayne's *To His Royall Highnesse The Duke of Yorke* (Oxford, 1665), a verse panegyric on the Battle of Lowestoft that points up Dutch greed, murderousness, religious toleration and republicanism.

The poem is one of the earliest English Painter poems and the first in the long series inspired by Waller's panegyric.[12] As such, it is closely related to Waller's poem (which it exceeds in length by only thirty-two lines), often closely if not patiently inverting Waller's original, and re-using much of Waller's vocabulary. Later poems in the series are less governed by Waller. The poem is less carefully constructed than the prosodically and imagistically intricate (and sometimes majestic) 'Last Instructions'. This, and the assumption that the latter did not in all probability circulate widely, while the 'The Second Advice' did, points to probable hasty composition in order to meet the needs of a defamation campaign. It may also mean joint composition. In one of the manuscript recensions, authorship is attributed to the 'Company of Drunken Poets'. This may have been the circle of poets in Parliament and its fringes, although not Waller himself. Perhaps it also relates to circles surrounding the opposition peers: again Buckingham's group comes to mind.

The major political objections to Waller's poem are twofold: first, that the patriotic, self-sacrificial courage celebrated in *Instructions to a Painter* should more properly be angry rebuke at an irresponsible home government; second, the war may not have been just, but was rather a design to aggrandize the Duchess of York and the other courtiers. Not everyone was impressed by Marvell's poem, but it is a clever travesty, and was influential on contemporary Dutch war verse. The painter is now on the verge of 'shaking' (l. 3), presumably with rage, or pitiful laughter. The painter, as much as his painting, is now a spectacle. The poem introduces mock-heroic spectacles (e.g. ll. 8, 87–8, 93–4), but the action described is plainly unheroic: a poetics of cowardice is the result. Where Waller's poem expounds its propaganda function openly in the instructions to paint, 'The Second Advice' inserts the domestic and courtly causes of neglect as a framing device before the description of the naval engagements. The other remarkable feature is the inclusion of a disaffected speaker (ll. 135–54), akin to similar voices in ancient satire.

By the time Parliament did meet on 18 September, the nation's capital had been devastated by the fire of a fortnight before. The long days and nights of that terrible event cast a lasting shadow over the deliberations that would last until 8 February 1667. Marvell would in fact play a central role in the interrogation of informers and suspected arsonists. But before then it seems he, possibly with the help of others, took up the pen again, composed and put into circulation 'The Third Advice to a Painter': a response to Christopher Wase's *Divination* (1666), an attack on the political critique of 'The Second Advice', although admiring of its poetic achievement.

Although the press had been subject to severe censorship since the Restoration, it is now accepted that public opinion played an important role in the politics of the war and of toleration.[13] Although the crisis of the late 1660s was not a party dispute, contemporaries were conscious of a survival of issues from the 1640s and 1650s. The government, through its information officer and censor, Sir Roger L'Estrange, certainly identified a republican fifth column: the *Intelligencer* reported that a republican faction had encouraged the Dutch to war on the grounds that the English government would misuse the supply it had been voted. Wase suspected the author of 'The Second Advice' of Commonwealth sympathies (*Divination*, l. 160). Opinion invented spectral identities that would feed the fears of various participants, and which, though unfounded, were very real in that they could determine the decisions of key actors. In this context, the Painter poems played a key role.

Throughout the cycle of Painter poems, Marvell's knowledge of events and personalities is not tied to any particular source (e.g. specific newsbooks); rather, it appears to be based upon a conglomeration of opinions and information on events. Although he often differs in his estimation of people from as well-informed an observer as Pepys, his intelligence is as apparently discerning and accurate. Indeed, the account of the Battle of Lowestoft in 'The Second Advice' bears a very close resemblance to a letter of intelligence from William Coventry to Albemarle, that Pepys read.[14] That all three Painter poems presented here were written some months after the events they describe suggests the use of accumulated information, unlike the partially informed nature of publications closer to the events. None of this is surprising, given that on 26 October 1665 Marvell had been appointed to the Parliamentary committee investigating the misappropriation of prizes.[15] In this context, the Painter poems may be seen as a more intimate kind of poetic as well as political exchange: another member of the same committee was Waller himself. The questioning of the justness of the war in 'The Second Advice' (ll. 313–30) is particularly apt in this context, and reads almost as a list of a committee's findings, and in one of the early printed editions and several manuscripts these lines are placed at the end of the poem.[16]

The anonymous authorship of controversial material by an MP was advantageous: 'Inside knowledge could, in effect, create an outspoken but anonymous lobby for positions which could only be held discreetly in the House.'[17] Perhaps in order to divert attention from his true intentions, Marvell spoke against Clarendon's impeachment several times. For whatever reason, after Clarendon had fled, in December 1667, he joined the committee that arranged Clarendon's banishment. Earlier in 1667, he was involved in illegal Nonconformist pamphlet activity. The three Painter poem pamphlets published in 1667 were printed and distributed by surviving members of the radical press of the Commonwealth years.[18]

The second and third 'Advices' were ascribed to Denham, but there is no imitation of any of the poetic modes in which Denham wrote. Rather, Denham's name functions as a disguise (or a decoy) and a joke, although his activities in Parliament at this time were significant. The answering of Waller's panegyric in its own terms is the starting point of the cycle, but in 'The Third Advice' and 'Last Instructions' it is only the starting point. The three poems attributed to Marvell are united by their concern with the poetic interpretation of paintings. They therefore relate to the central Renaissance topos of *ut pictura poesis est*, even to the extent of literalizing in the 'Third Advice' (through the figure of the Duchess of Albemarle) the idea of the speaking picture. The tradition had its origins in classical sources in the continental Renaissance and spread to seventeenth-century English culture.[19] Marvell's grotesque portrayals of courtiers employ a licence that is faithful to Horace's original dicta in his *Ars poetica*, as opposed to the strictures on unacceptability of the Italian theorists. Marvell's satires may be seen as a brave disturbance and reversal of the entire tradition of Stuart art and letters. The Painter device permits the poet a critical stance in opposition to the heroic narrative beloved of Waller, Dryden and other apologists for the government.[20] The fusion of heroic narrative and painting was a feature of influential Italian art theory, and in addition to the imitation of Waller, and like him, the poems adopt in some respects the manner of contemporary painting manuals. Marvell's new guise then was that of the painter.

Marvell (and whoever else may have helped write the second and third 'Advice' poems) revealed himself to be a serious and reflective comic satirist. The thematic elevation of paintings may also be seen as a reflection of the difficulty of publishing printed attacks on the government in these years. It was particularly appropriate in light of the widespread fashion for heroic portrait and naval painting. Such works are frequently noted in contemporary descriptions of public and private rooms. In this context, the Painter poems may be seen as a central part of a critical counter-culture of official portrayals of national life. In the official culture, the King was presented as sensitive to the importance of the advancement of trade through naval prowess and colonial endeavour.

'The Third Advice' is concerned with the Four Days' Battle (1–4 June 1666), where Monck suffered considerable losses against de Ruyter's fleet. The English fleet was weakened since Prince Rupert had commanded a squadron of twenty ships that had left late in May to encounter a French fleet under the duc de Beaufort in the Bay of Biscay. Only Prince Rupert's last-minute arrival saved the English from total defeat. Through the voice of Monck's wife, Anne, Duchess of Albemarle, the poem blames the reversal on corruption and bad administration. Although Monck and Rupert would later allege that Arlington's intelligence had falsely reported Beaufort at Belle-Ile (in an attempt to lay the blame on Arlington and Coventry, rather than Clarendon), they were fully responsible for their action. Arlington claimed he had acted on what he thought was genuine intelligence. As the poem acknowledges (ll. 32–4), Monck engaged de Ruyter's superior fleet thinking he could win. Later on, it became clear that Albemarle's letter, requesting Rupert's immediate support, was delayed by Coventry and Arlington.

Unlike the Battle of Lowestoft, the Four Days' Battle took a very heavy toll. The English lost twenty ships, either destroyed or taken, two admirals (one captured) and 8,000 killed and wounded, or taken prisoner, as against Dutch losses of two admirals, four to seven ships and 2,000 killed and wounded. Lack of men willing to serve in the navy was now alarming. Impressment was common: many of the dead men floating in the water after the battle were still wearing their dark Sunday suits, having been impressed directly from church.

Marvell's poem also responds to two poems that defended the regime and the war policy. The first was Wase's *Divination*, an attack on the political critique of 'The Second Advice'; 'The Third Advice' appears to pick up on Wase's accusations. The second was Dryden's *Annus Mirabilis* (composed in the summer and autumn of 1666, published January 1667), which offered a heroic, indeed Virgilian, account of three failures (the division of the fleet, the Four Days' Battle and the Great Fire of London), and, in its preface, a juxtaposition of the heroic with the grotesque burlesque. Marvell's poem replies with a grotesque (and in his view, justified) response to Dryden's (in Marvell's view, naïve) heroism, and along the way supplies several alternative renderings of events described in *Annus Mirabilis*. But this means that Marvell must have seen a manuscript copy of Dryden's poem and its preface before it appeared in print; however, this seems extremely unlikely.

The poem also offers other kinds of travesty. Official accounts of the Four Days' Battle stressed English prowess and suggested that victory was with them. One such work was *A True Narrative of the Engagement between his Majesties Fleet, and that of Holland* (1666) in which a first person plural voice is associated with Monck, as if the Admiral himself were speaking. In 'The

Third Advice', the 'truth' is provided by the female voice of his wife, speaking in the genre of *parrhesia*, free speech by someone not in power urgently addressing a crisis. The Duchess is likened to a series of classical prophets – the Cumaean Sibyl, the Pythia of Delphi, Cassandra, Philomela – and she is characterized as an 'engastrimyth' or ventroloquist rather than a true divinely inspired prophetess. Comparison to various animals gives her a further truth-telling perspective since in this sense she is neither human nor subject to human folly.[21]

After the Four Days' Battle, printed verse was certainly more willing to confess the horror of a naval battle than was Waller, as the lurid vision of Richard Head's *The Red-Sea* (12 June 1666) made clear. But criticism of the government was still absent from these poems. Like its predecessor, 'The Third Advice' is written within the framework of a painter painting a picture, this time by Richard Gibson, the dwarf miniaturist, as if (in a manner akin to Book II of Swift's *Gulliver's Travels*) little people show the folly of the great in magnified clarity, while expressing it in appropriately trivial tiny form. Gibson is preferred to Sir Peter Lely as the dominant artist whom the poet will imitate. Lely was Dutch, so Marvell wittily supposes that his brush will in fact help the Dutch more than the English (which is indeed what Marvell's pen appears to do in sections of the Painter poems). The realism of Lely's Dutch training might also be considered too embarrassingly revealing for these English follies. Indeed, the first movement of the poem closes with commands that the painter should not paint the Four Days' Battle because it is so shameful to the English. If there is anything worth painting, it is compressed into tight allusion. 'Yet, if thou wilt, paint Myngs turned all to soul;/And the great Harman charked almost to coal' (ll. 115–16) refers to two exceptional heroes of the battle. Sir Christopher Myngs (1625–66) led the van in the *Victory*. He was fatally wounded on the fourth day of the battle and died later, on 10 June. Sir John Harman (d. 1673) was Rear Admiral of the white squadron, whose ship, the *Henry*, was fired. Many of the crew fled, and Harman himself was lamed by a falling mast, but he managed to extinguish the fire and save the ship. Lely's portrait of Harman is very dark, as if charcoal had been used: this is reflected in Marvell's 'charked' which plays upon, and is the opposite of, 'to chalk', to mark with chalk, and hence, to make white. But the best solution, says the narrator, is for the painter to mask the shame in a series of mythological representations. Thus, Prince Rupert appears as Perseus rescuing Andromeda from the sea monster (Albemarle). And having vigorously attacked the Dutch (although Rupert had as a child been protected with his family by the Dutch Stadholder), he was only too grateful, having had his ships also disabled by chain-shot to be protected by descending clouds:

> a propitious cloud betwixt us stepped
> And in our aid did Ruyter intercept.

Old Homer yet did never introduce,
To save his heroes, mist of better use.
Worship the sun, who dwell where he does rise:
This mist does more deserve our sacrifice.

('The Third Advice', ll. 157–62)

The poem divides abruptly at line 169 where the Duchess of Albemarle is introduced. The Duchess's speech contains many locutions appropriate to her original lowly status, in addition to being the 'Presbyterian sibyl'. To this extent her speech should be compared with that of the nymph complaining, although her complaint also adopts the 'popular' diction of the Presbyterian poet Robert Wild, whose celebration of Monck's role in bringing about the Restoration, *Iter Boreale*, is echoed in her voice. The Duchess is a grotesque, who is given a repulsive, indecorous physical enormity that contrasts with the dwarf painter. The painting context is appropriate: Pepys records dining on disgusting food at Albemarle's Whitehall lodgings in the presence of a considerable collection of paintings. Gibson, not unlike Marvell himself, was a great survivor, having been a page in the court of Charles I, then Cromwell's portraitist, before becoming official miniaturist to the court of Charles II. Anne, Duchess of Albemarle, was a Presbyterian, and aligns herself with the Nonconformists who, though expelled from the national church in 1662, remained loyal to the Crown. She stands for those religious Nonconformists whom Marvell would defend in his prose works of the 1670s.

The Fire changed everything, and the political fallout became a major preoccupation, to say nothing of recovery and reconstruction after the devastation. Parliament had gathered just two weeks before 'The Third Advice' was written, and perhaps first circulated, just ten days after the Fire, but apart from being added to the Committee on Elections and Privileges, Marvell was involved in nothing, and appears not to have spoken, until 2 October. It was then that he was added to the committee of inquiry into the causes of the Fire. This committee would hear evidence every day until the end of the month, and formed the opinion that the Fire had been started by a member or members of a Roman Catholic conspiracy. Marvell was convinced by the findings of this committee; his own scepticism had this time been overridden. On 13 November, the committee was ready to report to Parliament, just after the King had published a proclamation 'against Papists', but two weeks passed and at the end of the month the committee went to work again, sitting into December. This was partly because of the weight of business of different kinds, as the letter of 23 October to Hull implied, and because there was much deliberation upon the justice or not of laying such a heavy burden on taxpayers, and 'a desire therefore to do it in the most prudent eligible and easy manner'.[22] On 27 October the Commons resolved to ask the King to banish all non-native or court Catholic priests and Jesuits within thirty days. As the committee gathered

further evidence, the Commons wanted a tightening up of the anti-Catholic
laws, especially the matter of taking oaths of loyalty, and thought that all
who refused such an oath should be disarmed.[23] Still the matter of supply
snared Parliament, while the Corporation of Hull wrote to Marvell and Gylby
on 6 November requesting that the King and his Council be asked to negotiate
a prisoner exchange with the Dutch so that Hull seamen could return home.[24]
Marvell and Gylby in fact approached Downing, who looked at the list and
thought that several men named on it had already been released. Sad news too
reached Westminster: Francis, Lord Willoughby, a veteran of the Civil War who
had been appointed to a governorship in the Caribbean, had perished with
many of his men in a hurricane while on a mission against the French in
August. Also worthy of mention was the embarrassing matter of Lord Mordant
and a threatened Scottish incursion.[25] While Parliamentary business of less
urgency passed, the broader context of opposition to the administration
defined events, tying together poetic defences of the regime, such as Dryden's
Annus Mirabilis, which appeared in print on 22 November, and the discoveries
of the Fire committee. Matters seemed to be heading to a huge crisis in church
and state, as the Painter poems, now freely in circulation, did their work.

ANNUS HORRIBILIS

January 1667 came round in a businesslike way, Marvell being appointed on
the 5th to a committee for setting the price of wine, on the 7th to a committee
for assuring a share of the manor of Iron Acton to Sir John Poynz, and on the
10th to a committee for settling the estate of the late Henry Hilton's charities.
Such was the humdrum life of an MP, a participant in good housekeeping on
a national scale. As Marvell would later say, kings moved in a rather different
sphere. But few can have felt much optimism at this point, with the dreadful
consequences of the Fire so close in time, and its causes still under investigation by a Parliamentary committee. The 'Third Advice' was circulating within
official circles: Pepys was sent a copy by his Admiralty colleague John Brisbane
and noted how 'bitter' was its attack on Albemarle, an interesting response that
says a lot about Albemarle's very high reputation.[26] We might laugh at the way
he is made to suffer a humorous loss of dignity, but that hubris in its context,
together with Albemarle's splendid guarantee of the Restoration, could only be
taken as a crushing fall.

Marvell's constituency letters at this time are packed with business, and
there are lots of them: six for January alone.[27] The poet must have spent many
long hours in the House and in committees. Indeed it must have been wholly
distracting, with very many boring, exhausting hours. Just as well then that
Parliament would be prorogued from 8 February until 25 July.

In his signing-off letter to the Mayor and Aldermen of Hull at the end of the
session in February, Marvell expressed concerns about the proliferation of fires

but whilst he describes fire as a kind of disease, and England as in a season of disease, it must have been in his mind still that the report of the committee on the cause of the Fire had blamed it on a malign, probably popish, or at least French, design.[28] No action was taken on the report in Parliament or by the government; it is no surprise that more publications, like *London's Flames* (1667), containing accounts of the report would begin to circulate, quite unofficially of course. A fire of discontent was beginning to kindle, fuelled by the underground press.

Marvell himself was free to rest and refresh his resources. He wrote a long and warm letter to his friend and patron Philip, Baron Wharton. This was also a newsletter, so that in addition to reporting London news, Dutch war preparations and political developments, Marvell enclosed a sermon by Stillingfleet and Simon Ford's Latin poem on the Fire. The letter tells us that Marvell was in a by now long relationship with Wharton and that he had nothing 'mature enough in the businesse we used to discourse of, which might be worthy of your notice'.[29] This must mean more than merely writing Wharton a newsletter when he was not at Westminster. It probably refers to some political strategizing in which Marvell acted in the Commons for Wharton. It might refer further to the writing of the Painter poems themselves.

Wharton was on his estate at Winchendon (or perhaps Wooburn) in Buckinghamshire, estates that Marvell knew and that may have provided further inspiration for his garden and estate poetry. Having been painted, in handsome splendour, by Van Dyck, in 1632 at the age of nineteen, Wharton had gone on to amass one of the most impressive collections of portrait paintings in the country: precisely the kind of materials from which the Painter poems could emerge. Equally significant, however, is the fact that Marvell had disappeared from Westminster and instead listed his address as 'London'. Why would one move into the city when most of it had just been destroyed by fire? Marvell might have travelled up to Wharton's houses during the recess, but he had not done so by April. Indeed, everything in the letter to Wharton suggests a careful imbibing of the streets of London, of coffee house and newsbook culture, of the rumour and gossip passing about on the streets.

It is important to dwell on these matters because one of the most crucial claimed events in Marvell's life, an event that remains to be either confirmed or denied, was about to happen. Marvell married. Allegedly. In evidence given much later, in 1682, Mary Palmer/Marvell claimed after Marvell's death that the couple were married on or about 13 May 1667 in Holy Trinity Minories, one of the two churches in the capital where secret marriages took place, since the church did not need to publish banns or issue a licence.[30] Mary said that her husband imposed an agreement of strict silence upon her. She must never, ever talk about this matter. She claimed that the church marriage register recorded the union, but it does not survive. Perhaps in 1682 it was known not to have survived. Then again, who did Mary think she was kidding? She could not stand up in court and tell a lie. I believe that if the evidence shows only inconclusively that Marvell was married, it is equally inconclusive in respect of whether he was *not* married.[31]

If, as Mary claims by her description, he wanted his wife to be a landlady or housekeeper, why did he not just employ one? It surely would have been much cheaper. One thing for sure is that this marriage was not a conventional partnership for the purposes of procreation. We always encounter Marvell as a single visitor, either to friends or acquaintances. Mary was accused of being the widow of a tennis court keeper, but was she rather connected with the bookseller Thomas Palmer who was later in trouble for distributing Painter poems? And did this Thomas Palmer have anything to do with another Thomas Palmer who lived in St John's, Clerkenwell?[32] Did Marvell marry someone who was related to key players in the radical press? Was this perhaps to ensure her silence if he were ever prosecuted in court, since wives were unable to give testimony against their husbands?

Also during the Parliamentary recess, Marvell must have begun to assemble in his head a very different kind of Painter poem, and his most ambitious poem yet. It would in part amount to an artistic redemption, at long last, of all those tedious hours spent in Parliament. Now they would be recast as part of the vital life of one of the most original and outstanding poetic satires written in seventeenth-century England. 'The Last Instructions to a Painter' is remarkable in its detailed and chronologically accurate description of the events of the first three-quarters of 1667. By the mid-1660s, the confidence that accompanied the early days of the Restoration, and in particular the government of Charles II's Chancellor, Clarendon, had dissipated. There were accusations that Clarendon had designs on the throne himself, and had married his daughter to the Duke of York, the King's brother and heir, in order to achieve this. A further series of incompetent acts and decisions led to naval embarrassment at the hands of the Dutch – quite contrary to the successes of the Commonwealth navy in the previous decade.

However disunited and inferior in naval terms the Dutch appeared to be, they had able commanders and a system of public credit far superior to England's. Holland had the lead in a war of attrition, and the English government underestimated the country. The Dutch were determined to secure a treaty that enhanced not merely their honour but also their national profit. For this reason, they were disinclined to compromise in the negotiation at Breda, which began on 4 May 1667. Instead, they decided on a daring military policy that would force major trading concessions from the English. Sixty-four warships – some with Englishmen serving on them – left Holland on 27 May. Admiral de Ruyter arrived off Kent on 5 June and on the 10th bombarded Sheerness Fort. On the 12th, his fleet broke the chain across the Medway, burned three of the biggest English ships moored near Chatham, and captured the *Royal Charles*, the pride of the Royal Navy. After an attack on the dockyard at Chatham was foiled, the

Dutch retreated to the mouth of the Thames, where they set up an indefinite blockade. So many senior English commanders were present during the Thames and Medway attack that confusion was rife. Marvell's poem follows the energetic response of the government, and the initial investigations into the embarrassments of June 1667, but gives no account of the further recriminations consequent upon the recall of Parliament in October 1667.

Literary attacks on court corruption had intensified. In April, the King watched and then suppressed *The Change of Crowns*, a play by Edward Howard (brother of the opposition MP Sir Robert) in which preferment by bribery was exposed. In the aftermath of the Dutch raid, popular discontent, and disquiet within the government and the court was rife, and registered for contemporaries by the circulation of satirical verse:

> Libels are daily sent . . . and brought to ye King by my Ld Anglesey who sayd he found it in ye outward Co^rt at Whitehall another in Harry ye 8th's Chayre in ye Gallery a 3rd at ye K: bedchamber door, strangely insolent. All wch I suppose will bee printed since ye Inclosed written long since, & passing from hand to hand in Manuscript now appears publique, wch I therefore send y^t y^r Grace may see to w^t height of extravagance ye humours of ye people rise: Of this Sr Fr: [escheville] Hollys ye young angry sea-Captayne is supposed ye Author: I did on Saturday forbear ye folly of ye D. of Buckingham, and am angry I have nothing July, 1667.[33]

In addition to the poems that would eventually be published in the 'poems on affairs of state' collections, several other works critical of Clarendon and the court circulated in manuscript.[34] Of these, 'The Century book printed at Oxford', a satirical list of fictitious publications, is particularly close in some respects to 'The Last Instructions'.[35] And it was in early July, as we have seen, that Pepys saw the first printed edition of the second and third 'Advice to a Painter' poems. Francis Smith, the great opposition publisher, was connected with the printing of this, and *London's Flames* was found (perhaps available only for the first time) on another underground press.[36]

Marvell's part in this focused poetic attack upon Clarendon began in July, not with 'The Last Instructions', but with 'Clarendon's Housewarming'. The last line of the poem refers to the calling of Parliament on 25 July (St James' Fair) as a forthcoming event: it had been officially summoned on 25 June. Although the metrical awkwardness of some parts of the poem make it hard to believe that Marvell was the author (indeed, computer stylistics evidence denies Marvell the authorship), and although the use of Marvellian topoi could be seen as another poet's reworking of Marvell, a series of phrases and individual words (see ll. 7–8, 17–20, 43–4, 56, 87–8, 94–6) suggest finally that Marvell was the author at least in part, although I am not inclined to view the two epigrams that followed the poem as Marvell's.[37] Sir William Empson argued that the poem was the joint production of several people, all of them probably MPs.[38] He imagined Marvell as a ringleader, and proposed that the verses that do scan (ll. 41–52, 93–100) are Marvell's. The first two stanzas are also given by Empson to Marvell, who is imagined beginning a round of composition for four or five other participants. The first line of the poem is highly prosaic, and was perhaps given to the poet as a starting point. Given the politics of the court at this time, one wonders if Buckingham himself was the author, as he and his supporters jockeyed for favour with the King:

> When Clarendon had discerned beforehand,
>   (As the cause can eas'ly foretell the effect)
> At once three deluges threatening our land;
>   'Twas the season he thought to turn architect.
>
> (ll. 1–4)

At any rate, it is not hard to imagine the poem as a product of some opposition wits meeting in an inn in July 1667.

Why attack Clarendon's residence? When he returned from exile in 1660 to become Charles II's chief minister, Edward Hyde, Earl of Clarendon, lived in rented accommodation. After much debate, and with the encouragement of the King, who made a grant of open land, a residence was planned and building was begun in 1664. Clarendon House was completed in late 1666 or early 1667, designed by Roger Pratt.

Many reported its grandeur and its architectural success: it was the first great classical house in England, and was to be much imitated in the following decades. The interior was notable for its large and distinguished picture collection and its library. It stood on the north side of present-day Piccadilly, between Tyburn Ditch and Sackville Street, straddling Albemarle Street. A significant symbol of Clarendon's power, it looked down upon and dwarfed St James's Palace. Building costs outran expenditure by one-third, to Clarendon's great embarrassment and financial ruin. In the context of war, plague and the Great Fire, Clarendon found himself deeply unpopular, his house the object of violent popular demonstrations: 'at my Lord Chancellor's, they have cut down the trees before his house, and broke his windows; and a gibbet either set up before or painted upon his gate, and these three words write: "Three sights to be seen: Dunkirke, Tangier, and a barren Queene." '[39]

The poem is a parody of a country-house poem, and the genre of poems celebrating civic buildings. It is also metrically various: 'To describe the metre of *Clarendon's Housewarming* as anapaestic may create a false impression of regularity.'[40] In fact, only twelve lines are properly anapaestic, but anapaestic feet recur throughout the poem, and create its dominant rhythm, although there are extravagant, indeed, completely unmetrical, departures from it. In a true 'drollery', Marvell and the other collaborator poets use accentual verse, a form associated with popular or archaic poetry, one that went against the preference for heroic couplets. It may be that a 'popular' verse form was used in order to evoke the popular discontent that Clarendon was suffering. At the same time, the form would have facilitated easy and rapid composition. There are for instance frequent feminine rhymes. While noting Marvell's powers of analysis, isolation and judgement in his satirical couplets, Legouis defends the prosody of this poem for its robust heartiness, and its fluid capacity to carry insults and obscenities. Within these paradigms, the sense of 'Upon Appleton House' and 'The First Anniversary' in reverse is unmistakable:

> He had read of Rhodopis, a lady of Thrace,
> > Who was digged up so often ere she did marry;
> And wished that his daughter had had as much grace
> > To erect him a pyramid out of her quarry.
>
> But then recollecting how harper Amphion
> > Made Thebes dance aloft while he fiddled and sung,
> He thought (as an instrument he was most free on)
> > To build with the Jew's-trump of his own tongue.
>
> > > > > > > > > > > > > > > (ll. 13–20)

It is a delightful and amusing poem, and one that certainly delivers a punch.

The effort, however, was wasted. Parliament duly met on the 25th, and deferred most of its business to the 29th. On that day it learned from the King that peace had been made with the United Provinces, and that it would not be meeting again until 10 October. It was a peace by no means honourable to the English; criticism was forestalled by dispersing the assembly. Yet the free time gave Marvell the space to work on his larger, greater project.

Indeed, Marvell was thinking of sober patriots as opposed to corrupt and decadent courtiers. In mid-August he wrote to the country MP Sir John Trott, expressing condolences for the death from smallpox of his two sons.[41] There is veiled reference to Clarendon, and the clear sense that it would be better for Clarendon to leave public office sooner rather than later. But in purely personal terms, Marvell in his letter shows surpassing empathy, imagining how hard it will be for Trott to suffer the second acknowledgement of a son's death among his community when he returns to Hampshire: 'I know that the very sight of those who have been witnesses of our better Fortune, doth but serve to reinforce a Calamity.' He must have been thinking of his parents' deaths, or perhaps a very early memory of his brother's death when he was three, or his cousin Andrew's when he was eight: 'I know the contagion of grief, and infection of Tears, and especially when it runs in a blood.' These are uncommonly acute words. No surprise to learn then that some of the images, especially that of the rainbow, are shared with the poet's earlier poetic elegy on

Lord Francis Villiers. It is not without humour either: Marvell warns against an over-indulgence in grief but nonetheless thinks the example of Eli permissible, 'the readiest and highest complement of mourning, who fell back from his seat and broke his neck'. There is a hint of Donne's 'Hymn to God, my God, in my Sickness' in the suggestion that to learn about grief and yet to be the exemplar of dealing with it is 'as if a man should dissect his own body and read the Anatomy Lecture'. Before referring to the elegy, Marvell recommends the Bible, the society of good men, the books of the ancients and 'diversion, business, and activity' as the accoutrements of assurance in adversity. And then the personal crunch: 'But I my self, who live to so little purpose'. Does this refer to Marvell's unmarried state, even at the age of forty-six, his want of children, his sense that he could perform neither as father nor son? It is the voice of a man who, however preoccupied with service to the town of his birth and his patrons, was acutely aware of the corner of life into which he was seemingly painted.

The relationship between intimate private life and public responsibility is a major feature of Marvell's unquestionable triumph with the Painter poem 'Last Instructions to a Painter'. It has been argued that the criticisms of the court offered in the Advice-to-a-Painter and other satirical poems were answered in poetic apologies for the court, such as Dryden's *Annus Mirabilis* (1667).[42] Dryden himself was aligned with some of Marvell's targets, notably the Duchess of York, and opposed to the Duke of Buckingham.[43] Dryden sought 'to recall the more hopeful days when royal paternity might tangle together sexual vigor and national abundance', an association played on by Marvell in his opening salacious picture of Henry Jermyn, Earl of St Albans, a survivor from Charles I's court (ll. 29–48), and more generally in his linking of 'enormity, appetite and luxury' with 'sterility and death'. If the association of whoring and misgovernment was a common perception in anti-court satire, Marvell's poem took the mode to new extremes of pointed refinement, exploiting the symbolic association of distended courtly bodies and a deformed body politic. It should be no surprise that other anti-court satires, including the outrageously frank verse of Rochester, accompanied Marvell's poem in the printed texts and the manuscripts. When the poem was published in 1689 it stood alongside 'Rochester's Farewell', a verse satire now thought to be the work of Henry Savile.

Marvell's attack on the court also involves a construction of patriotism in terms of elements dissociated from publicly known Stuart preferences. The heroes and virtuous of the poem are those furthest from the court and its ways: Douglas the Scot and probable Catholic and de Ruyter the Dutch Admiral. Treasonous republicans like Thomas Dolman, the English pilot who led the Dutch ships into the Medway, is merely chastised (l. 431), treated with mock-horror, and given a just motive for being poorly treated by his masters (ll. 583–4). The Dutch themselves were not without civility in the act of war:

Sheerness was invaded and held for three days, but the Dutch paid for the meals provided by the townsfolk.

In the autumn Parliament began to investigate the conduct of the war, and the role of Clarendon. It is notable how poets played a major role in the transactions of the House of Commons, in this instance in a manner not dissimilar to the echoing of other poets within Marvell's poetry:

> After the article of the charge had been debated Mr Marvell pressed that the words that were said to be spoken against the King should not be passed over in silence but be declared; the words as it [is] said are these:
>
> 'The Chancellor should say that the King was an unactive person and indisposed for government.' Sir Robert Howard pointed at Mr Seymour, who indeed gave the first hint of them. Mr Seymour produced Sir John Denham and Sir John Denham he affirmed that he had it from another who would justify that the Chancellor said so, and made a most excellent and rational speech.[44]

'Last Instructions to a Painter' is far more thematically and aesthetically unified and ambitious than either the second or third 'Advice', but (in part because it is so long) it falls into several discrete sections, each with differing sources. The most discrete is the elegiac section on Douglas (ll. 649–96), which was redeployed with minor alterations in 'The Loyal Scot.' It may well be that these lines were composed as an entirely separate poem. In general, the purpose of reference to painting in poetry was to enhance the epic scope of the latter. Marvell's frustration with the painter–poet analogy in his poem points up the unsuitability of his subject matter for dignified treatment.

The sections of the poem concerned with courtly women are parodies of the Advice-to-a-Painter poems that were part of the lyric tradition. At the same time, Marvell's poem has affinities with some of the verse published on the Great Fire of London.[45] Poetic descriptions of the Fire helped Marvell describe urban and naval conflagration, and his poem shares the pictorial motif and aesthetic assumptions of some of the Fire poetry, for instance 'The Author to the Graver upon occasion of a Draught expressing London in Flames' published in Simon Ford's *The Conflagration of London* (1667), ll. 349–494.

Marvell's reversals of Waller's confidence function on the level of representation as well as theme. Where Waller's painter works with a 'bold pencil', Marvell's painter has a 'desperate' and 'lab'ring' pencil, that risks his curse and is outpaced by the poet's pen. The concern with pictorial art extends beyond the Advice-to-a-Painter poems. Explicit and implicit references to court painting that point up the failings of the English court have been detected.[46] Rubens is named in the poem but his own painting of Lady State is not mentioned: Lady State, and the other genres of state painting, are of course travestied. Marvell understood that painting, like poetry, relied upon decorum: the mode of representation should fit the moral state of the subject. The poem accordingly invents a fitting series of written images for the court, while calling on the lower forms of painting and drawing in ll. 9–12 for help, culminating in the inverse parody of a Lady State picture, where Charles is shown attempting to seduce 'England or the peace'. The topos of sea triumph (specifically not a picture of a naval victory, since the Dutch did not have to fight) is reserved for de Ruyter's journey up the Thames, that of the noble death detected in the death of Douglas. But in addition, as the portrayals of the failing or frustrated painter suggest, painting is outdone by a series of verbal devices.

Another important frame of reference is provided by the optical discoveries of the natural philosophers, then very recently made. The poem makes use of the invention of the microscope and the minuscule world that it revealed. There are specific references to Robert Hooke's work, published in his seminal *Micrographia* (1665). This should not surprise us: as we saw, Marvell knew Robert Boyle and was evidently keenly familiar with the new science and the inventions that were making possible its discoveries. The microscope's extraordinary powers of perception, so the poem argues, reveal truths about courtiers and politicians that are hidden from normal view. Further aspects of natural philosophy in the poem are discussed by various authorities. Painting is presented as an inferior art to empirical investigation. It may be efficient as a means of delivering appropriate praise or blame, but it cannot objectively and dispassionately describe, as the microscope and the telescope do. There is always the danger that truth will be lost in the painter's attempt to flatter. The painter must therefore aspire to the perceptive powers of the empiricists. By contrast, St Albans and the Duchess of York appear as false empiricists, lost in corrupt pursuits for sensual pleasure and personal advancement, which are perversions of disinterested enquiry.

Sexual satire had been used as a way of criticizing the behaviour of courts, monarchs, parliaments, republic, Puritans and Protector throughout the seventeenth century, though with particular vigour from the mid-1640s onwards.[47] The treatment of sexual corruption in this poem is, along with other poems by Marvell, an acknowledgement of the 'force of sexuality in imaginative exploit, in the argument of heroic venture, in the calculation of human potential, and in the luxuries of retreat'.[48] The reign of Charles II was publicly celebrated at the Restoration as a renewal of fertility; Marvell responds by attacking the body politic on the level of sexual morality. The language of sexual innuendo is present in the poem to the extent that it has the capacity to render entirely different readings of passages from the ostensible ones. The forms of sexual representation in the poem belong to the context of both learned and elite, or scurrilous pornography, especially in pictures, in the tradition stemming from Aretino's *Postures*. The sexual satire is an example of 'low burlesque'. The initial portraits are grotesques, 'gargoyles stuck in the face of the edifice', but the passage dealing with the excise debates is mock heroic. Thus, even those in Parliament who share Marvell's views are implicated in the 'mindless chaos that England faces'. Appropriately, the description of de Ruyter ('Clarendon', ll. 523–34) begins heroically and in a pastoral idyll, but degenerates until the Dutch Admiral succumbs to a sexual appetite not far removed from that of the English courtiers: another opportunity for a contrast with Douglas. Still, what does this say of a poet who could so readily evoke an underworld of shady inns graffitied with lewd charcoal sketches?

The one exception to the satirical and parodic modes of the poem is the passage dealing with the heroic death of Archibald Douglas, a Scottish soldier of famous lineage and, ironically, almost certainly a Roman Catholic.[49] The passage may have pictorial sources in paintings of Ovidian scenes and contains a fusion of Christian and pagan allusions, characteristic of Rubens, and a baroque, fantastic mode in the style of Bernini. Indeed, the readiest comparison would be, as we have seen, Bernini's ecstasy of St Teresa (1647–52), in the Cornaro Chapel, Church of S. Maria della Vittoria, Rome.[50] The aesthetics of Roman Catholic Europe are suggested. Others argue that the visual point of Douglas's death is the distinction between his 'shape' and the fire enfolding him: 'the identification between what is without and within is complete, because the act of immolation simultaneously registers and enacts his heroism'.[51] In this way, the poem offers a poetic version of martyrological iconography – the truth in painting, in contrast to the allegorical victory painting of Cornelis de Witt, Deputy Admiral to the Fleet, presiding over the raid. The English could now plainly not deploy such images. The similarity to Bernini's depiction of St Teresa's ecstasy where the holy flames look like sheets, and which Marvell would have seen in Rome, is evident.[52]

The Douglas passage contains clear, extensive and complicatedly intelligent allusions to Virgil's Aeneid. It is one of the more obvious examples of the way in which Marvell was writing his own version of epic language as a form of critique of the epic language that was publicly praising the regime.[53] Dryden's dense allusions to and echoes of Virgil in Annus Mirabilis, his reflections on heroic verse in his letter to Howard prefacing the poem, and the portrayal in the Fire poetry of London as a burning Troy, were among the immediate triggers. After the Medway raid, the Troy of London is threatened by the Greece of Holland and France. The use of epic in the politics of allegiance or opposition was a major feature of literary life during the Civil War, Interregnum and Restoration periods. Translations of ancient epics were used to describe public events, while various kinds of mock epic were produced by Royalists, originally as a part of Cavalier drinking culture, later as a more engaged form of criticism. The 1660s saw the publication of Samuel Butler's Hudibras (1663–4) and Charles Cotton's translation of Scarron's travesty of the Aeneid, Scarronides (1664). Marvell takes none of these mock epics as his models (although he sometimes uses the false accents, bad rhymes, absurd analogies and clumsy allusion to the technique of *Hudibras*) but instead develops his own distinctive epic poetry. The poem thus 'resolves itself not into a consistent caricature of unheroic heroes, but into what is in effect an epic in reverse – an epic of defeat and demoralization, not of triumph and victory . . . the epic value of the joys of conquest is presented, with a tragic irony, through the eyes of the enemy'.[54] The appearance of the first edition of Milton's *Paradise Lost* in the autumn of 1667, with its strong public resonances, which Marvell was especially well qualified to notice, provides another important context. Sections of it appear to be echoed in Marvell's satire.[55]

The Medway raid was celebrated in Holland by a large and various body of publications, including printed maps and charts, detailed scenic engravings, letters from naval commanders in ships anchored in the Thames and Medway, verse and even celebratory goblets presented to the victorious naval commanders. Marvell's later confession that Dutch satirical iconography rendered a more truthful picture of the English than any native assessment presupposes a knowledge of Dutch anti-English literature. It is highly likely that Marvell saw some of this material, and used it, or at least was helped by its perceptions, to fashion his critique of the government's mismanagement of the war.[56]

'Last Instructions' consists of three central narrative sections: the sitting of Parliament in 1666 (ll. 105–396); the attempt of the court to secure peace (ll. 397–522); and the Dutch invasion of the Thames and the Medway (ll. 523–884). These are preceded by pictures of courtly corruption and debauchery, and succeeded by the depiction of Charles II attempting to force erotic favours from his vision, the naked 'England or the peace', which is followed by the forty-one-line address to the King, where the Advice-to-a-Painter motif is not used. These sections are informed by three elements: first, often fragmentary narration and description of the actual world; second, the 'instructions' through which artistic coherence is given, but which, in the debate between poetry and painter (and momentarily between poetry and music), is shown to be impossible; third, a new 'tectonic' structure which abandons the known artistic forms in order to restore faith in an ideal order.[57] Throughout the poem, media and different parts of experience are confused, in order to suggest the difficulty of describing the subject.

The longer passages not explicitly concerned with the painting analogy sustain the motif by imitating the painting genre of large-scale events, such as sea battles, and satirical engravings.[58] In some cases, these are executed with considerable accuracy. In fact, the entire poem is a series of modulating, intricately composed poetic pictures imitating a variety of contemporary pictorial modes: effectively a history of vision. Each example participates in an aesthetic of inversion, just as the English fleet is unbuilt and hence unprepared for battle, and the only battle is to describe the debate over the Excise in Parliament.[59] This leads to a series of crises of representation, where either pictures or words, or both, fail to capture the subject matter. In this context, the appeal to the King (ll. 943–8) is an appeal for the restoration of the *ut pictura poesis* tradition.

Marvell's cursory treatment of aesthetic debate in the poem is a further part of the intended design because 'any conventional method will be inappropriate to this chaotic, unconventional situation.'[60] The poem displays considerable flexibility in its use of the rhymed decasyllabic couplet, ranging from the measuring of chaotic subject matter with highly controlled and dignified verse (i.e. the mock heroic), to grotesque couplets that reflect grotesque subject matter:

> Two letters next unto Breda are sent:
> In cipher one to Harry excellent.
> The first instructs our (verse the name abhors)
> Plenipotentiary ambassadors
> To prove by Scripture treaty does imply
> Cessation, as the look adultery,
> And that, by law of arms, in martial strife,
> Who yields his sword has title to his life.
>
> (ll. 449–56)

The poem was a triumph in the art of satire but far fewer people saw it in the period immediately after its composition, when it was most intended to have an impact, than read the earlier two long verse satires.

The Parliamentary session called on 10 October 1667 lasted until 9 May 1668 and was interrupted only twice, with an adjournment from 19 December to 6 February. It was an intense session not least because it was dominated by the urge to blame someone for the naval and diplomatic failures of the previous months. In his correspondence with Hull, Marvell saw it at first as a great opportunity, a Machiavellian *occasione*: 'there neuer appeared a fairer season for men to obtain what their own hearts could wish either as to redresse of any former grievances or the constituting of good order and justice for the future.'[61] It was also a sign at last that the King was listening to good counsel and had himself seen the light. Charles played up this theme when he explained to Parliament that the long prorogation of the previous months had indeed been a chance for him to do 'some things' beneficial to the country. It is clear that Marvell completed 'The Last Instructions' by the end of November: Clarendon fled the country on the 29th, of which there is no mention in the poem. Peter Pett, the Navy Commissioner at Chatham until 1667, was generally held to blame for the Medway catastrophe, and on 31 October he had been brought before the Commons on a charge of negligence in defence of the fleet. The House considered detailed evidence, including narratives by Albemarle and Prince Rupert. Marvell was one of three MPs (the other two being John Swinfen and Edward Boscawen) who defended him and argued against his imprisonment in the Tower. They are described as 'sectaries' in accounts of the proceedings.[62] Marvell refers in 'The Last Instructions' to the scapegoating of Pett (ll. 765–90), but this is a reference to much earlier investigation in the summer by the Privy Council. Pepys witnessed the interrogation of Pett by a Privy Council committee and felt sure that he was being framed by Arlington and Coventry, who were seeking to protect themselves.[63]

Yet the main business of this parliament was to investigate Clarendon's conduct and to see if there were grounds to impeach him. Much to our surprise, we find that Marvell did not want to impeach the King's disgraced adviser. It may be that given the dangerous nature of his poetic statement – which may be said to have carried a seditious if not openly treasonous character – it was crucial for him to maintain an absolutely orthodox and loyal front as an MP. On 3 October, he wrote to the Mayor of Hull praising the 'prudency and constancy' of the King and his governance. The House of Commons was busy voting thanks to the King for his various acts (such as disbanding the army on 25 July at the end of the war). Marvell distinguished himself, speaking in a debate on 14 October against voting thanks to the King for 'laying [Clarendon] aside', on the grounds that it was a condemnation of the Earl before an investigation of his conduct had been made. The House, he said to Hull, was intemperate in its eagerness to punish.[64] This is what Marvell is reported to have said in Henry Capel's account. On the one hand, Marvell says that it is no business of the House to discuss the King's choice of advisers, and on the other that the House must not be seen merely to be reflecting popular happiness or discontent. But as always with Marvell, silent implications mean much. Clarendon would be investigated, and if found wanting, what then the implications for the King's conduct of government? It was just three days later that Marvell was named to the committee of inquiry into misconduct in the war, and a further committee investigating the reasons for the sale of Dunkirk. Marvell's effectiveness as a speaker has been questioned: he was usually too subtle, confused or angry. But it seems in this instance that he was highly effective within a strict, legalistic understanding of the terms of the representative and its function. It was a stand on principle. It is significant that Waller, the panegyrist of official policy, now wanted to see Clarendon impugned by the Commons: in his view, the crimes were manifest and needed investigation. The findings of an official investigation of course would carry more weight than allegations bandied about in Parliament.

Clarendon's impeachment began on the morning of 26 October, as the committee investigating miscarriages began to ask questions, summoning statements from Albemarle and Prince Rupert. Marvell again stood for principle:

> The raising and destroying of favoritts and creatures is Kings sport not to be medled with us by Kings in their choise of their Ministers[. Kings] move in a sphaere distinct from us. Its sayd because the people rejoysed at his fall wee

must thanks the King. The people allsoe rejoyse at the restoration of the Duke of Buckingham the other day obnoxtious. Shall we not thank the King for that too? Its sayed we hat[e] him not, Should any man in this house be willing to have such a vote passe upon him?/Wee are to thank the King for this matter of his Speech[.] This is not in particular any part of it and comes regularly before us.[65]

He stood against calling witnesses (if they could be called) who might testify merely on grounds of objections to great personalities without considering details that would take time to discover and clarify. All of this was setting up the terms in which the impeachment would be conducted. On 29 October, Marvell again stood up and desired that he: 'Would have the faults hunt the persons – Would not have a sudden impeachment by reason of the greatness of the person or danger of escape, Lord Clarendon not being likely to ride away post – Witnesses of that quality not to be had.'[66] It may also be inferred that Marvell's position is that of someone close to a powerful member of the House of Lords (such as Wharton or Buckingham): Clarendon, he said, was to be tried by his peers. Buckingham was at this stage assuming that Clarendon would survive, and had hopes of him as an ally against Arlington: Marvell's questions are strategically consistent with Buckingham's position. It's also possible that Marvell saw Clarendon as favouring incorporation of some of the Nonconformists at this point and so as being worth protecting. The impeachment proper began on 6 November, and he must have been glad of the barrel of ale presented to him by the Hull Corporation the next day, although he would not see it for another month. He was noted for his acute insight in the debates. Most significantly, he wanted to know the source for the statement that Clarendon had said the 'King was an unactive person and indisposed for government' ('whoever brought in the article of . . . [sh]ould publish the person that gave him that information').[67] The circulation of the rumour was traced back from Sir Robert Howard to Edward Seymour to Sir John Denham, who said he had it from someone else, but who it was was not divulged. Neither was that charge carried, although the impeachment resolution followed directly in the Commons, and was carried up to the House of Lords on the 12th.

Two days later and the sense of pressure from work was mounting. In addition to debates in the House and membership of the committees listed above, in November alone Marvell was placed on eight more committees, and in December another five. Late in the day on the 14th, he said 'I lose my dinner to make sure of this letter.'[68] There were cases of tested honour and rectitude everywhere and not just in the matter of Clarendon. Sir John Ashburnham was deprived of his seat because he accepted a bribe from some French wine merchants after a ban on the importation of French produce. Marvell was asked to sit on a committee investigating this matter on 25 November.[69] And to add to his duties, the Hull Corporation asked Gylby and Marvell to exert themselves so that the town would be reimbursed for garrison expenses during the Dutch war.[70]

The House of Lords was not persuaded that Clarendon should be committed to custody without a specific cause, and this led to a debate between the two Houses that became notably hot in the last week of November. But then on the 30th, leaving a five-page petition of protest, Clarendon fled (Marvell had said he would not do this), considerably altering the course of proceedings. The next day that Marvell wrote to Hull, 3 December, Clarendon actually arrived in France, and on the same day the House of Lords received a long petition of some five sheets of paper from the Earl explaining what he had done. The Earl had cast the die himself for his future, as well as avoiding the severe disagreement between the Lords and the Commons that was threatening, since he had left Parliament little option but to banish him, and on the 16th Marvell was named to the committee for his banishment, which Act was rapidly expedited and voted into law by the 19th.[71]

It is significant that the third volume in the Advice-to-a-Painter poems series, 'Directions to a Painter', appeared in December just after Clarendon fled. It was an altogether more ambitious and complicated piece of work than its predecessors. Not only did it print all four advice poems (now styled 'directions to a painter'), but it added 'Clarendon's Housewarming' and two further anti-Clarendon squibs: 'Upon his House' and 'Upon his Grand-Children'. Whoever was responsible for the volume bypassed the texts previously printed and went straight to a different copy text. Closer scrutiny suggests that either Marvell had lost control of his poems, or he was prepared to be involved in high-risk publication ventures. But the second edition of 'Directions to a Painter' had been altered so that 'all lines specifically criticizing the king are absent' from the fourth 'Advice'.[72] This edition was therefore a bowdlerized edition of the 'Directions', which in turn has led to the suspicion that it was a pirated text (if one can properly speak, that is, of an unlicensed work being pirated). As Martin Dzelzainis suggests, 'someone, possibly a radical like Francis Smith but more likely one of the grandees of the Stationers' Company, was evidently cashing in on the notoriety of "*Directions to a Painter*" while at the same time attempting to minimize the risk by removing the most offensive and provocative passages'.[73] This is especially so given that the fourth and fifth 'Advices' seem to have been in the eyes of contemporaries more bitingly critical of the court than were the first two satires.

It was at this point that more serious attacks on monarchy, much to the alarm of L'Estrange, began to appear, such as *The Saints Freedom* (1667): an assertion of the popular origins of divinely sanctioned earthly power, in the name of scriptural revelation and 'Natural Reason'. It was resurgent radical Puritan, in places Leveller, political theory convincingly couched in the language of the late 1640s sects: 'Acts of Royalty put out, proves not the Authority to be from God; but is ground of strong suspicion (if not of demonstration) That the *Power* and

Authority which is acted and influenced from the Devil, is not of Gods appointing or ordaining; but only by Gods permission and suffering in his just Judgements.'[74] On 15 March 1671 the bookseller Thomas Palmer was fined and pilloried for selling two subversive books, *Nehushtan* (1668), attributed to Joseph Wilson, another classic of the surviving Puritan resistance to the entire edifice of Anglican worship, and 'Directions to a Painter', part or all of which he also circulated in manuscript. L'Estrange refused to grant Palmer's petition that he be spared these punishments.[75]

The government censors were taken by surprise by the printed Painter-poem phenomenon. From the evidence of surviving copies and manuscript copies made from the printed book, it would seem that the volume circulated widely and was not at first intercepted by the authorities. It was only in 1670–71 that they really began to understand what had happened, and this part of the story will be resumed later. For now it is sufficient to recognize that Marvell had managed to function as a satirical poet with enormous political influence and exceptional artistic force, and that he had emerged as a most serious voice for justice in Parliament. He began the decade as a civil servant with considerable influence on the working of diplomacy. He ended as an agent of opposition politics, where that opposition was compelled to use surreptitious and subversive tactics.

CHAPTER 9

✻

CABAL DAYS

WHAT WAS THE DISAPPEARANCE of Clarendon supposed to achieve? The unity of interests and personalities that had contributed so decisively to his downfall disappeared almost as soon as the ex-Chancellor had boarded the packet for France. The Cavaliers, who had felt betrayed by Clarendon (many of whom indeed thought he had been too friendly to the Dissenters), were outraged by the clientage of Buckingham, who was now in his ascendancy. It was Buckingham who consistently pressed for religious toleration, although it is hard to discern consistentcy in his views in any other sphere, and his sense of the limits of royal authority see-sawed wildly, which was alarming because he enjoyed great personal authority over the King. Arlington, on the other hand, wanted a more extensive system of ministerial control in the court and in Parliament. Both were now preferred advisers to Charles, but quickly quarrelled with each other, and thus aggravated instability. The Cavaliers were displeased by Buckingham's preferred policies, and the 'country' MPs – be they disaffected old Cavaliers or 'Presbyterians' (that is, old Puritans) – were upset by the Arlington-inspired attempts to manage the Commons.[1] Anyone might have been appalled by the growing group of advisers who accompanied the King everywhere, slowing down business, as Pepys thought, and unable among themselves to reach conclusions.[2]

Where did Marvell stand in all of this? The short answer would be as a kind of 'opposition' MP, a kind of 'Presbyterian', but rather independent minded and increasingly so. As we have seen, he publicly attacked some of the terms on which Clarendon was impeached, which was far less expected than his resistance to the attempts to bribe the Commons into compliance. Not all of the 'opposition' figures who replaced the Clarendonians in office would have found favour with Marvell: Anglesey yes, perhaps Howard (but surely not always), and certainly not Osborne, the future Earl of Danby and master operator in Parliament.

All in all, the fall of Clarendon had seriously weakened the Cavaliers, so that those who opposed the deposed and banished Chancellor had more power than at any time since 1660. And yet confusion reigned. If any single figure exploited the political situation in the late 1660s and early in the next decade, it was Charles himself. Even as the Commons pressed on with the investigation of the mismanagement of the war, even as the presence of Clarendon was erased, Charles made a sensational and outrageous move in foreign policy which was at first secret. In early 1668 he had publicly signed the Triple Alliance with the United Provinces and Sweden, which was designed to limit French ambitions. But soon afterwards he began talks with Louis XIV, negotiations which were concluded in the secret Treaty of Dover of 22 May 1670, which was anti-Dutch, and where French assistance to the English Crown was linked to an assurance (in the most secret clause of all) that Charles would announce his conversion to Catholicism (French troops would be present in abundance if Charles's announcement provoked a revolt by the English).[3] The most secret clause was not known until Charles's death, but several ministers were involved in the negotiations, including Marvell's two most significant enemies at this stage: Arlington and Clifford. But then, for different reasons, people with whom Marvell was or would be associated, and who were also in the know, including Buckingham and Lord Ashley, the future Earl of Shaftesbury, were equally in favour, and wanted to see a French-strengthened English monarch as a way of overcoming the Commons' majority resistance to toleration for Dissenters. This group, with the Duke of Lauderdale, the King's chief minister in Scotland, formed an inner circle of advisers known as the 'Cabal', the acronym being formed from the initial letters of their names. Although there was enough scope in personal relations for details of the secret negotiations to leak out, the Commons appeared to know nothing of what was going on. But as time went by, Parliamentarians of all kinds, Cavalier and anti-Cavalier, began to feel excluded from the decision-making processes of government, or simply that their institution's compliance had been bought. It was not the kind of mixed monarchy they had believed England was. As events unravelled in these years, Marvell would find himself torn between two extremes that both belonged to the government: he sympathized with much of the toleration agenda, but would become increasingly appalled by the King's growing willingness to use his prerogative.

As Parliament reassembled in early February 1668 after its recess, Marvell noticed the purge of Clarendon's family from all official posts and from the royal household. This included Clarendon's eldest son, Lord Cornbury, Chamberlain to the Queen, who had been satirized in 'The Last Instructions', and who was dismissed from the court in early February.[4] The week that followed was one of the most remarkable in Marvell's life. When he next wrote to the Corporation of Hull, he was concerned to report how the debates on the miscarriages of the war had gone, and that after heavy debate, it was voted that the division of the fleet in the Four Days' Battle had been a mistake; and furthermore that not revoking the order for the division of the fleet after intelligence of the presence of a Dutch fleet was also an error.[5] 'I haue been so busy this weeke that I could not write before,'[6] he says, and all this debate was certainly consuming of time and energy, but what he had done on this day, 15 February, or the day before, was to stand up and attack in a 'moste sharpe speech' the King's Secretary of State, Arlington, among other members of the Privy Council, charging him with personal corruption and with rendering poor service to His Majesty; fiddling, so to speak, while Rome burned:

> Mr Marvell, reflecting on Lord Arlington, somewhat transportedly said[:] We have had Bristols and Cecils Secretaries, and by them knew the King of Spain's Junto, and letters of the Pope's cabinet; and now such a strange account of things! The money allowed for intelligence so small, the intelligence was accordingly – A libidinous desire in men, for places, makes them think themselves fit for them – The place of Secretary ill gotten, when bought with 10,000l. and a Barony – He was called to explain himself; but said, The thing was so plain, it needed it not.[7]

The first half of the sentence sees absolutism, tyranny and possibly religious persecution as a consequence of the high-handedness of would-be administrator courtiers, especially George Digby, second Earl of Bristol, notorious in the early 1660s. However, the latter comment was the most outspoken and outrageous Marvell would make in the chamber, and his self-defence when challenged was decidedly assured. Seldom is Marvell's anger, which was abundant enough, so forthrightly seen. That powerful adverb 'transportedly' is very significant. Marvell's comments come in the context of various attempts by courtiers and councillors to blame each other for events: two such libellous letters were received by the Speaker earlier on the 14th. Nonetheless, a slight majority in the House clearly wanted blood in these issues and was prepared to concede nothing in respect of the Privy Council's actions under pressure of war. The Commons' collective opinion was indeed completely harmonious with the viewpoint of the second and third 'Advices'. Now those poems looked like the secret unconscious of the nation finally brought to official acknowledgement after the sad events they recount. The discoveries were debated and voting continued through the session, making the surreptitious poems a prophetic history of a desperate episode, and this may help to explain why they were so frequently copied all the way through to the early eighteenth century.[8]

The tone of Marvell's first intervention (we may infer that it was driven by anger) confused some members. He was asked to explain himself, and he fizzed: 'The thing was so plain, it needed it not.' Another MP, the Welshman John Vaughan, well known for his opposition views, averred that it mattered neither who attacked nor who defended Arlington, but the Secretary himself clearly felt that he was being attacked. 'Mr Marvel hath struck hard at me, upon the Point of Intelligence,' wrote Arlington on the 17th, but felt that his adversary had shot himself in the foot by invoking the King's speech, which delayed further consideration of the charge against Arlington.[9] Four days later Marvell joined the protest concerning the paying of seamen in tickets, when there was ready money available: a matter that had been a serious cause of failure of morale in the navy. The protest was first levelled at Lord Brouncker, one of the chief butts of 'The Second Advice', but further exchange caused confusion and Marvell spoke to insist that someone from among the officers must come forward to explain the bad decision

Much of the business in which Marvell participated during the first session of 1668 was effectively to do with accountability: with investigating the mismanagement of the Dutch war, but also ensuring that future voted supplies would be well spent. Most time was spent debating where taxes would be levied in order to provide the funds for the supply. There was concern that strict measures of enforcement were required to make people pay these levies. This is the stuff of his letters to Mayor Lambert of Hull.[11] But at the same time the Cavaliers were clearly worried by what they claimed were disturbances of Anglican worship initiated by Dissenters, and a toughening of the Conventicle Act was promised. The House was also concerned that intimations of royal or Parliamentary intent were creeping out to circulate in the provinces. Here and there Marvell writes something terse that gives away an ocean of anxieties: 'Other things are of a privater nature,' he wrote on 29 February.[12] A fortnight before, a bag of libels had been left at the door of the Commons indicating that the realm was by no means pacified. Would Marvell have been in favour of the Triennial Bill, compelling regular elections of new parliaments every three years, proposed by Sir Richard Temple and debated on 18 February?[13] Surely so, but others felt that this would have been a severe and negative limitation on the King's prerogative power.

Some very sensible ideas preoccupied MPs – principally the need to foster national resources that were sometimes scarce, and to encourage the country to become richer. But as a whole they did not want the Nonconformists to step beyond their (Parliament's) authority, and with the encouragement of a majority in the Commons, the King made his proclamation against meetings of Dissenters and Catholics on 11 March 1668. So whilst some have seen Marvell's growing fears of royal power as the major concern in this period, it cannot have been his absolutely predominant concern, since he was equally interested in the fate of the Nonconformists, who were likely to suffer a harsher fate at least at this point in time at the hands of Parliament than they would at the hands of the King. Marvell spoke twice in the Commons in favour of the Nonconformists: once on 13 March in the company of several MPs (but to no avail) and then again on 30 March.[14] Perhaps this context explains why, along with other factors, such as Marvell's sometime acquaintance with Buckingham and his participation in an embassy, he was thought of as a court supporter, and appeared in a list of those inclined to the Duke of York assembled by Sir Thomas Osborne (the future Lord Danby) in April 1669.[15]

In all of this, being an MP required regular correspondence with his constituents, and in particular their elected leader, the Mayor of Hull. In and around the reports of Parliamentary business in these letters comes other information, which is of a parochial nature, even if its origin was in London. Thus, Marvell learned from Gylby, he wrote on 7 March, that Lord Belasyse, who was governor of the garrison at Hull, and who had tried to have Marvell replaced as MP in 1663, was very ill, and this explains the delay in the Corporation hearing from him concerning some insolences among the soldiers.[16]

At the end of this session (the King adjourned Parliament on 9 May until the following 10 November; it would not in fact meet in session until 19 October 1669), a dispute between the Lords and the Commons broke out, the former having taken the side of a petitioner against the East India Company, Thomas Skinner, and the latter defending the Company. Each claimed the action of the other was illegal, and Marvell's account in his letter to Lambert on 9 May suggests a constitutional crisis of considerable proportions.[17] Several figures in the Lords were involved with whom Marvell was or would be closely connected: Buckingham, Anglesey and Holles. Charles hoped he could resolve the dispute while Parliament was not sitting, but four East India Company officials remained at the judicial mercy of the Upper House. As we shall see, Marvell was involved at the heart of this dispute and in a way not quite proper.

To read Marvell's constituency correspondence is to miss almost entirely the sense of what it was generally like to be in the capital and near the court at this time. We know from a letter addressed to him on 5 March 1669 that he was living at an inn called the Crown, near Charing Cross.[18] If anything, the extraordinarily libertine morals of the court intensified in the days of the Cabal. Just before Parliament was recalled in early 1668, Buckingham fought a duel with the Earl of Shrewsbury, with whose wife he was conducting an affair, and emerged the winner. Shrewsbury was wounded and died two months later, very possibly as a result of his injuries.[19] Public knowledge of court behaviour was widespread and indeed extended into the city: where else were many of the King's and courtiers' mistresses to be found? I am not the first and cannot be the last person to observe that Pepys's diary records the naval administrator's emulation of courtly practice: the prevalence of libertine practices and the books that reported or facilitated them is evident on every page. It would have been very difficult indeed for an educated middle-class man in London to avoid being influenced. Marvell was affected no less than Pepys, as we shall see.[20]

Popular resentment of this culture boiled over in the 'Bawdy-House Riots' of Easter 1668: violent demonstrations by apprentices against brothels in the capital. On 9 May Marvell wrote to Anthony Lambert that four people were hanged, drawn and quartered for the 'late insurrection of Apprentices'.[21] This is what happened. During the Easter holiday, which in 1668 fell in late March, apprentices gathered to pull down brothels, establishments that had existed under terms of great secrecy during the Interregnum but which had now become highly visible in the new era. The violence lasted for three days, from 24 to 26 March, and began in Poplar but spread to Moorfields. The riots were a large display of popular justice – a very violent charivari of a shaming ritual, coupled with more than a tinge of Puritan disapproval, and increasingly so as the riot progressed, with reported cries of 'Reformation and Reducement' and 'Liberty of Conscience'. There was evidence of popular approval; some rioters imprisoned in Clerkenwell were freed by another mob. The court panicked and feared insurrection: they heard that the rioters would not stop short of demolishing the 'grand bawdy-house of Whitehall', and that the rioting was orchestrated by 'men of understanding' from Cromwell's army. Mock petitions in verse and prose from the whores, and from the citizens and apprentices, flew, backwards and forwards. The most telling was in the voice of the Countess of Castlemaine, thereby linking the charges of courtly and city corruption, although its source might easily be within the court.[22] Heavily armed guards rather than the trained bands were required to pacify the crowd, but even they were forced back with stones, while the rioters easily evaded capture in the urban environment by being swift of foot. Lord Craven was encountered by Pepys hysterically ordering soldiers about 'like a madman'.[23] It became difficult to move around the city as watches frequently halted coaches. Throughout the court, fears of Puritan or republican insurrection spread, and the Crown responded to this element through the judiciary with charges of high treason. Whilst the single genuine apprentice indicted after the riots was not convicted, four of the eight indicted at the time were dismembered.[24] Was Marvell in sympathy with them?

At five in the morning, presumably earlier on the same day, 9 May, an exhausted Marvell wrote a brief letter to his friend Philip, fourth Baron Wharton (1613–96).[25] His eyes were 'scarse open' at the end of what had been a day-and-night's sitting in the House of Commons. But the MP was eager to inform Lord Wharton of the votes that night. Wharton needed an up-to-the-minute account of the Commons' proceedings in part because they were pointedly not communicating their votes in any formal way to the Lords. This was owing to the contest over privilege between the Houses. The adjournment expected that very day was to put an end to the impasse that had developed late in the session. The problem lay with Skinner's case. The claim against the East India Company had been granted by the Lords, only for the Company then to take the matter to the Commons, who voted both Skinner's complaint and the Lords' ruling illegal. That vote the Lords then ruled illegal in turn. In Marvell's brief letter to Wharton, which he signed with his monogram, he now reports the four further votes in which the Commons reacted sharply to this renewed breach of their privileges.

This was not a matter on which we might expect to find Marvell leaking the proceedings of the Commons to, in this context, its constitutional enemy, the Lords. But Marvell was pulled to Wharton by the latter's support for Nonconformity. And so, just before Parliament was adjourned, Marvell decided to work around the Commons with its Anglican majority. No doubt through some consultation with Puritan peers, and Wharton in particular, he drafted an appeal on 7–9 May from the Lords to the King to use the royal prerogative to help the Nonconformists. It was the beginning of the policy of indulgence that would eventuate in 1672.

Marvell and Wharton prepared 'An Addresse from the House of Peeres to the King to make use of his prerogative in Ecclesiasticall affayres for the better composure and union of the minds of his protestant subjects in the intervall of the present adjournment'. It complains of the Commons' breaches of privileges. The recess brought on by the Skinner contest prevented the House of Lords from discussing the better union of Protestants that Charles had asked for in his speech to both Houses at the beginning of the session on 10 February 1668.[26] The joint Marvell–Wharton address therefore asks Charles to take matters into his own hands: 'that You will be graciously pleasd in the intervall of this instant adjournment to take such course therein as to Your Majesty shall seem fit according to the Power inherent in You in Ecclesiasticall affairs by the Prerogatiue annext to Your Imperiall Crown'. The draft was not read in the House of Lords, but Wharton certainly remembered it in later years. For someone with such a reputation for defending the rights of the Commons, Marvell's willingness to appeal to royal prerogative is remarkable, especially when the two Houses had been so recently and deeply divided. With such long prorogations, it might be seen as pragmatic to work by direct appeal through a powerful aristocrat to the monarch. In any case, the climate within Parliament was not looking good, despite the removal of Clarendon. An Anglican–Royalist clampdown filled Marvell with revulsion. The tone in his letters is deadpan and neutral, but we can read between the lines: state violence is tyranny, but that violence came from the body of which he was an elected member. It was a concern that would grow in the following years. As the session came to its tense end, the supply was finally voted, but there was insufficient time to allow the Conventicle Bill to pass.

In the summer recess, Marvell had time to reflect upon matters that were not so closely connected with Parliament and the political scene, and the extended repercussions of the crises of 1667. He had, perhaps, been married for a year, not that we can tell anything about that from his letters. The time he spent with Wharton in the country also suggests other and earlier contexts to do with the country house and with poetry. Wharton's first house was at Winchendon, Buckinghamshire, but although he had much improved it, and continued to invest in its modernization, he had in the 1660s come to prefer another Buckinghamshire property acquired through his second marriage.

This was at Wooburn near Beaconsfield, some eight miles north-north-east of Eton, and on this house and garden he lavished huge sums. Wharton had passions for architecture, painting, gardens and poetry. He built a long gallery at Wooburn, in which hung his unmatched collection of Van Dycks and Lelys.[27] He commissioned portraits as well as purchasing them. His houses and gardens were regarded as a source of wonder.

Marvell had stayed at these estates, and it may be that a sojourn here, as the spring grew into the summer of 1668 and as the leisure of the recess afforded him the chance to read, enabled him to compose one of his greatest poems, 'The Garden'.[28] This poem was once regularly associated with the Nun Appleton years of the early 1650s, but on account of echoes in the verse from the collected works of Katherine Philips (1667) and Abraham Cowley (1668), the later date now seems much more likely.[29] Being removed from the city and from Westminster after such a demanding year of hard work might well have made solitude on a country estate seem particularly attractive. One of the echoed poems is Katherine Philips's 'Upon the Graving of her Name upon a Tree in Barnelmes Walks', and Barn Elms, across the Thames from Hammersmith, is where Cowley lived in retirement and Pepys liked to walk.

Marvell sees in his poem the potential for the garden to present to man at least a hint of the paradisal garden from which Adam and Eve were expelled after their Fall. Abraham Cowley's poem 'The Garden', addressed to John Evelyn, praises married life, with the wife's beauty compared to a garden, whereas Marvell's paradise is one of a solitary male, before the creation of Eve, even for some the androgynous Adam Kadmon of kabbalistic tradition.[30] The speaker's invigorating interaction with the fruit and flowers (ll. 34–40) does bear a broad comparison with kabbalistic writing, but the genuine kabbalistic and Hermetic poetry of Samuel Pordage in *Mundorum Explicatio* (1661) is far removed from Marvell's verse.

We should also read the poem as has very rarely been done before, against the backdrop of the momentous collapse of Clarendon's administration and humiliation by the Dutch. The poem may be seen as a turning away from the courtliness that has failed the nation, and in this respect it is related to the views of loyal Stuart supporters who nonetheless were deeply troubled by the morals of the court. Such figures would include poets like Cowley and natural philosophers like John Evelyn, both of whom wrote in favour of gardens and garden reform. Marvell's solitary figure, a latter-day Adam, progressively dissociates himself from all contact with the world until he is simply conscious of himself, nature in the garden and the state of his solitary reflections. Perhaps he should be seen as a counterpart to Captain Douglas, having found his state of virtue. The same could be said for the Mower speaker in 'The Mower against Gardens', now also dated to 1668, who rails against horticultural experiment ('forbidden mixtures there to see') that he represents as unnatural coition to produce a 'green seraglio'. Sterility is one result of this departure from the order of nature, in the stoneless cherries, another hint at the emasculation that is taking place at the nerve centre of power. In '*Hortus*', the Latin companion poem to 'The Garden', there is a covert reference to Charles II as Jupiter reunited with the Royal Oak, but which might also be taken as a further jibe at the Countess of Castlemaine ('*Jupiter annosam, neglecta conjuge, Quercum/Deperit*'; 'Jupiter, neglecting his wife, is dying about an aged oak').[31]

Marvell continued as a faithful and sensible broker for Hull. In October a difficult matter challenged the Corporation and its relationship with the government. Lieutenant Wise, an officer in the garrison at Hull, had insulted the Mayor, Anthony Lambert.[32] It appears to have been over a matter of debt between the Lieutenant and a townsman. Wise had run for cover to Sir Jeremy Smith and Lord Belasyse, the Governor of Hull, who oversaw the garrison. It was a serious matter since good relations between the town and the garrison were crucial, especially when wars and the threat of invasion by foreign powers were never far away. Marvell was key to effecting a reconciliation by way of an apology from Wise to the Mayor. In this he acted with William Lister the Recorder, although the two were resident at a distance from each other in London. Marvell effectively signed some of the letters for Lister as well as for himself even though Lister and he had not discussed all of the contents. In another letter Lister was complicit in this.[33]

The issue was sensitive not merely in a local sense. The Lord General of the King's forces was the Duke of Albemarle, who was of course important enough, but the commander-in-chief was the Duke of York, the heir to the throne, and Wise was in a very proper military sense his officer. Intervention was certainly necessary and it was successful. It would seem that both, as well as Belasyse, were persuaded to pressure Wise into an apology.[34]

But if with retirement came the chance to elaborate it as a theme, so also it would seem that Marvell's presence in the city, and his involvement in politics, meant that his poetry had a chance to circulate in the urban world, a world now indelibly corrupted by popular politics and journalism in the way that is so berated in 'To his Noble Friend Mr Richard Lovelace, upon his Poems'. And thus we find the shorter version of 'To his Coy Mistress' in the Haward Manuscript, a collection of mid- to late 1660s verse that catches the raunchiness of the era. This version of the poem has been plausibly connected with an emergent homosexual culture in Restoration London.[35] While it was reported that George Larkin was employed by Captain John Seymour to print the 'Directions to a Painter' volume, he is also known to have liked poetry himself, to have venerated the muse.[36] Perhaps Seymour had a taste for poetry too, like Colonel John Scott, another radical, who possessed in 1678 a copy of 'A Dialogue, between the Resolved Soul, and Created Pleasure'. Retirement and contemplation could enter the city too.

Loyal Scots

Nothing is heard of Marvell in the records for the following January and for most of February 1669 until the last week when an issue was raised by Hull Trinity House that had run in the background of Marvell's affairs and would continue to do so for most of the rest of his life. Trinity House wanted to build a lighthouse on Spurn Head and to make a profit from it. They faced competition from other like-minded interests and a legal battle took place in the lawcourts of London over several decades. On 23 February, after the issue had lain dormant for some time, Trinity House wrote to Marvell to warn him that hostile interests were again at work. Marvell's solution, out of sorts with his later image as an incorruptible patriot, was to suggest that Sir Philip Frowd, secretary to the Duchess of York (Anne Hyde, the butt of Marvell's satire in 'Last Instructions'), be bribed. He also requested documents concerning the matter on 5 March.[37]

Parliament met on 1 March, having adjourned on the previous 10 November, but was immediately prorogued by the King until 19 October. In a letter to the Corporation of Hull on 2 March, Marvell mentioned that while there was talk of electing a new parliament, the King had been said to be strongly in favour of keeping the present one together.[38] Soon, the poet-politician would come to feel with anger the constraint on the nation of this policy. At this point he was living or at least receiving mail at 'the Crowne over against the Greyhound Taverne neere Charing Crosse London'. In the absence of Parliament, a daily routine of letter-writing followed by walks across town and visits to friends is discernible here and there in the correspondence. On 16 March, Marvell told Mayor Duncalfe he was off for a walk to fashionable Hatton Garden, 'where I intend to see one Sam', while also reporting concern for the health of Albemarle.[39]

By mid-March a contention between Sir Robert Cary (or Carr) and a Mr South on the one hand and the Corporation on the other had come to a head. It would seem that Cary and South had improperly used Corporation money or had impugned members of the Corporation, which, as Marvell saw it, left the Corporation with the option of prosecuting Cary and South in the King's Bench court if a settlement could not be reached. But it was negotiated, in a meeting on 17 April, witnessed by Robert Stockdale the Recorder and Richard Aston for Marvell, and two of Cary's friends. Cary and South agreed to pay £10 each to the three injured parties and to make a donation to Hull's poor (£10 more) as well as pay the Corporation's costs (£10 more still). This was duly accepted by the Corporation and the matter happily settled. Cary's letter to the Corporation of 17 April was part of an official language of reconciliation (although his manner in the meeting was none too civil), and evidently Marvell was the linchpin in the entire business, which itself is signified by his four detailed constituency letters on the matter.[40] Stockdale attests as much in his own account to the Mayor and Aldermen, and in another letter two days before the meeting he made it clear that he would regard Marvell's presence as important in carrying the business successfully.[41]

Such business went on over a long period – some seven months – when Parliament did not sit. Thus, Stockdale reported in a further letter of 15 June that he was off to find Marvell to show him a batch of papers sent from the Mayor and Aldermen. But Stockdale, like Marvell, had his eyes on national matters too: in the same letter he noted that Richard Baxter had been arrested under the terms of the Five Mile Act against Dissenters, the assumption being that the government was trying to suppress the mass of Dissenters by hitting hard at the leaders and figureheads: 'if they nipp but ye heads, ye roots will wither.'[42]

Marvell would be named for duty in ten committees during the three-month session from November 1669, as well as being a teller in one vote. As soon as business began the King pressed for commissioners to be appointed in order to establish a union between the two kingdoms of England and Scotland. This was a theme that Marvell apparently picked up in his last long verse satire, 'The Loyal Scot'. It may have taken a long time to write, in the sense that the whole poem was developed in response to the events of the 1670s, but the original poem began with the lines on Captain Douglas in 'The Last Instructions'. The idea of a union with Scotland goes back to James VI and I's arrival in England in 1603 but such visions had not been realized and the 1650s had seen Scotland quelled by an occupying English army, during which time the absorption of southern Scotland into England had been discussed.

The poem is remarkable for its claim that national boundaries are human inventions, and should at least in some circumstances be removed:

> Prick down the point (whoever has the art),
> Where Nature Scotland does from England part.
> Anatomists may sooner fix the cells
> Where life resides, or understanding dwells:
> But this we know, though that exceed their skill,
> That whosoever sep'rates them doth kill.
> Will you the Tweed the certain bounder call
> Of soil, of wit, of manners, and of all?
> Why draw we not as well the thrifty line
> From Thames, Trent, Humber, or at least the Tyne?
>
> (ll. 75–84)

While acknowledging the difficulties of perception that would have to be overcome, the finale is even more positive in its evocation of union:

> Nation is all but name as shibboleth,
> Where a mistaken accent causes death.

In paradise names only Nature showed,
At Babel names from pride and discord flowed;
And ever since men with a female spite
First call each other names, and then they fight.
Scotland and England! Cause of just uproar,
Does 'man' and 'wife' signify 'rogue' and 'whore'? . . .

. . . For shame, extirpate from each loyal breast,
That senseless rancour against interest.
One king, one faith, one language, and one isle:
English and Scotch, 'tis all but cross and pile.

                                           (ll. 262–9; 274–7)

It has been noted that the poem embodies a complete reversal of sentiments from the anti-Dutch satire 'The Character of Holland' (1653).[43] It is also true that Marvell's explanation of national division is humanistic, showing the source of nation-naming to be the linguistic confusion caused by the Fall. Yet this is but the beginning of the poem's teaching.

Marvell's treatment of nationhood may indeed be seen as a response to, and a reflection upon, the tensions between the two nations, despite the monarch they shared. These relationships were further complicated by the different powers of the monarch in each country. However Charles II used his ministers in the 1660s, he had to contend with a parliament, whereas in Scotland he was more absolute in church and state, operating through a very few aristocrats. Where in England, a restored episcopal church gradually if grudgingly accepted toleration of Dissent, in a context of considerable denominational diversity, in Scotland a reimposed episcopacy attempted to impose conformity on a laity that was, in large parts of the country, highly Presbyterian. If English Dissenters were imprisoned and subjected to abuse, and some violence, the Scottish Presbyterians (or Covenanters) claimed massive violent persecution in a vivid literature that was republished down to the nineteenth century, and that still carries substantial echoes today. Under John Maitland, Earl, then Duke, of Lauderdale, obstructive bishops like Alexander Burnet (see below, 296–300) were replaced by others prepared to sanction extreme measures against the Covenanters.[44] In 1670, preaching in conventicles was made a capital offence. Matters were exacerbated by periods of relative toleration, when the King hoped to win over more Presbyterian clergy to the episcopal church. The beginning and end periods for the composition of this poem (1669 and 1674) correspond to two periods of intense persecution. Such was the nature of obstacles to political union that Charles II and Lauderdale had abandoned all hopes of a negotiated settlement. They allowed the talks to continue in order to provide a ruse for the government to negotiate with Louis XIV in pursuit of an anti-Dutch alliance, a highly contentious matter since

French money and military support were offered in exchange for the advancement of the Catholic cause in England.

To Marvell, the Covenanters looked like English Puritans, even though they
had not supported the regicide, and although he had written in support of the
republic's invasion of Scotland in 1650. The Solemn League and Covenant of
1643, the document that bound the Parliamentarians together, was essentially a
result of Scottish pre-eminence at that early stage of the Civil War: it was
publicly burned during the early days of the Restoration. Marvell had sympathy
with the Covenanters (but ultimately not with Lauderdale, whom he regarded
as a violent persecutor and a danger to Parliamentary freedoms),[45] who would
have appeared as fellow-travelling Puritans, under even fiercer persecution
than their English brethren. The poem is aimed at combating the widespread
view that, in the light of the events of the 1640s, the Scots were unreliable.
Marvell's attitude may also have been coloured by his northern associations: the
Fairfaxes were Presbyterians, and collaborative, pro-Scottish attitudes existed
more commonly in the north and far north, literally through the experience of
proximate coexistence.[46]

The poem is spoken by the persona of the ghost of the poet and satirist, John
Cleveland (1613–58), author of the satirical poem 'The Rebel Scot' (1644).[47]
Like all of Marvell's poems about other poets, 'The Loyal Scot' is a means for
Marvell to measure himself against the achievements, reputation and opinions
of an influential poet. Cleveland's presence in Marvell's earlier verse is strong.
Both poets were in Cambridge at the same time: Cleveland was admitted to
Christ's College in 1627, and moved to St John's in 1631, becoming a fellow in
1634. He would have known Marvell's associate John Hall: some of Hall's poems
were ascribed to Cleveland. Unlike Hall's tutor, John Pawson, Cleveland, a
fervent Royalist, was ejected from his fellowship by the Parliamentarians in
1645. He then served Charles I as a journalist and judge, and survived during
the Interregnum as a private tutor, but not without interference and imprisonment at the hands of Protectorate officials. Where Marvell eventually benefited
from employment by the Protectorate, Cleveland was forced to petition
Cromwell for his release from prison. He managed nonetheless to publish his
poetry and prose works (in which his Royalism was easily discernible), and
allegedly ran a poetic club with Samuel Butler in London.

As would become the case with Marvell after his death, and Denham in
the 1660s, 'Cleveland' was the name under which a variety of poems were
published, but in his case all of them were Royalist, and most of them approxi-
mated to the highly extravagant, conceited verse for which Cleveland was famous.
By the time he wrote 'The Loyal Scot', Marvell was beginning to acquire a similar
reputation as the voice of opposition poetry through his involvement in the
Advice-to-a-Painter poems, and their accompanying materials. Although his use
of Cleveland as speaker of the poem cannot be regarded as an attempt to frustrate
the establishment of an authentic canon for Cleveland (which occurred after

'The Loyal Scot' was written), the imitation and then reclamation of Cleveland's voice for a kind of early Whiggery was an exploitation of the instability of Cleveland's canon.[48] Dryden had drawn attention to Cleveland's poetic manner in *Of Dramatick Poesy: An Essay* (1668), creating the label 'Clevelandism' to name the poet's habit of catachresis, 'wresting and torturing a word into another meaning', and making unfavourable comparisons between Donne and Cleveland, yet reserving for the younger poet the distinction of being the only English poet quoted in the essay (and 'The Rebel Scot' is one of the two poems quoted).[49] Cleveland's achievement and reputation were very prominent in literary affairs when Marvell came to write his satire. To put the elegy on Douglas (lines that are markedly Marvellian) into the mouth of Cleveland's ghost is to replace Cleveland's voice with Marvell's.

'The Loyal Scot' is a revision of 'The Rebel Scot' (1644), which was written on the occasion of the Scottish army's entry into England (in support of Parliament). Cleveland's ghost atones for the views he expressed while alive; anti-Scottish sentiment is converted to praise of heroic Scots and a demonstration of the unity of the two nations. Marvell had used echoes from Cleveland to construct his satire of the Dutch in 'The Character of Holland', a work that uses national stereotypes for xenophobic purposes. Now he puts Cleveland to work in a contrary way, although his later satire is still hostile to the Dutch. Although the ghost speaks a poetry purged of the extravagant conceitedness for which Cleveland was famous, there are several echoes of his verse, especially 'The Rebel Scot', in addition to imitations of Cleveland's manner.[50] The informed reader still recognizes the poem as Cleveland's, allowing the poet to conceal his imitative method of composition under the disguise of a Menippean satire. The description of Douglas's fiery death, borrowed from 'The Last Instructions', becomes a heroic reversal of the satiric description of Scots in 'The Rebel Scot' as red-haired people, inflamed with disease, and the rage of the satirist, described as a fire. The homoerotic description of Douglas now appears in contrast to Cleveland's own quizzical treatment of hermaphrodites (see, for example, Cleveland, 'The Authour to his Hermophrodite'): this as we will see is highly significant.

The bishops are treated as deceitful actors: this view is rooted in a long tradition of Protestant anti-clerical suspicion, as opposed to the heroic acting of Douglas, although both are, in this life, shown to be subject to forces of fragmentation and instability.[51] Moreover, the lines that follow the Douglas passage in 'The Loyal Scot' continue the pattern of metamorphosis, making Douglas's melting the source of the political fusion of the two nations. On the generic level, this Ovidian addition to the version in 'The Last Instructions' is seen explicitly to replace the ballad of Chevy Chase, the divisive tale concerned with Anglo-Scottish border hostilities. In fact, the poem may be said to develop two forms of metamorphosis: heroic and desirable in the case of Douglas, and revelations of sin and punishment in the case of the bishops. The poem's brilliance lies in the fact that its couplet form is put to the service of imparting an experience of division versus unity: syntax offset against rhyme, and especially as the poem shifts from the elegance of the Douglas passage to the plainer manner concerned with Scotland. The divisive bishops are appropriately assigned triple rhymes, and they are seen to divide the island into 'sees', thereby making Britain itself into an archipelago.[52]

The poem has been noted for its 'piecemeal composition and its digressiveness', making it the most 'miscellaneous and formless' of Marvell's verse satires.[53] And yet the insights into the double nature of identity surface again and survive the poem's relative lack of integrity. They are Marvell's insight not only into the nature of the poet's identity, but into human nature itself; identity is never rooted in a central self (most certainly as a Puritan would have seen it) but is contained in a split self where two versions are always in a relationship of mutual reflexivity. It is in this poem that we can see a concept of human identity with related senses of sympathy and respect emerging. There is an obvious relationship with notions of religious toleration, but most significantly these insights are reached through poetic process: the representation of people and predicaments in poetic language. In the adverse circumstances of the Restoration, Marvell was making his former modes of praise and lyric expression do serious ethical work. It is an aspect often overlooked by literary critics, and by intellectual historians unfamiliar with Marvell's writings. But this is an extremely important milestone in Marvell's work, as John Kerrigan argues: 'Captain Douglas, by virtue of his name and lineage, and his death on behalf of Anglo-Britain, shows how an historical Scottish (and Franco-Scottish) threat to England can become a source of strength if the riven borders which the Douglases almost incarnate are allowed to knit into scar tissue and unify the island.'[54] More than this, however, if old, much-disputed and mutable borders can be made to seem so ephemeral, and people of different cultures and a partially shared language happy under one king's wise rule (ll. 276–89), does Marvell imply a potentially universal human sympathy?

At any rate, this vision looks something like a Presbyterian Britain (in a way that many Englishmen, not least Milton, would have found particularly hard to accept), since the villains of the poem are the divisive Scottish bishops, and by implication (and in a few places explicitly) they are associated with their English counterparts. Parts of 'The Loyal Scot' were probably written later in the 1670s when Marvell was preoccupied with the public presence of High Anglican divines and their arguments for episcopal supremacy. We will return to the poem and its concerns.

As we have seen, even before the autumn session of 1669 was over, the issue of religious liberty had reared its head. While careful work to circumvent the obstructions of Sir Philip Frowd was taking place in respect of Trinity House business and the proposed lighthouse at Spurn Head, a libel attacking the

King's evil counsellors was circulated. Called 'The Alarme', and aimed at a 'patriot' audience, it was once attributed to Marvell by the historian Narcissus Luttrell, but this seems unlikely given Marvell's interest in exploiting the Cabal, or his loyalty to some of its members.[55] Luttrell was writing at the end of the century and no doubt took good note of Marvell's attack on Arlington. Nonetheless, he missed the broader context, and none of Marvell's contemporaries attributed the piece to him. The Commons were edgy: the bookseller Richard Chiswell had been summoned, so Marvell wrote on 19 October, for publishing a work addressing the House of Lords' punishment of Sir Samuel Barnardiston, who as Deputy Governor of the East India Company appeared for them in their dispute with Skinner. It was 'seeming of most dangerous consequence to the Libertyes of the Commons of England'.[56] This was one of the areas of dispute between the Lords and the Commons, the Lords claiming that they had the right to try persons in this way. Chiswell claimed he was acting on the instruction of Lord Holles, to whom the tract is attributed. An act concerning Parliamentary procedure was duly drafted.

A new Conventicles Act was expected: Marvell mentioned this on 4 and 9 November, and then reported on the 13th how the debate about a possible second reading of the Conventicles Bill had taken up all the time allotted to discuss Carteret's case, a matter of alleged gross mismanagement of naval accounts during the Dutch war.[57] Indeed, the business of the King's supply was held up not only because the Lords and Commons were at odds over the issue but because they had decided not to proceed until the irregularity of Carteret's conduct was resolved. But the House was apparently scared by a report of a sudden rise in conventicles. There was a report that the old Commonwealth general Edmund Ludlow had returned from exile and was gathering support around him: 'Commonwealths men flock about the town & there were meetings said to be where they talkt of new Modells of Government'.[58] These reports increased through the next week, with the further suspicion that the arch-republican Henry Neville was back in town. When Buckingham was implicated too, Marvell picked up a wry sense (perhaps also his own) that the threat was less dangerous than at first might have seemed: Neville which 'some thought of much others of lesse moment', and Buckingham 'without making that impression wch some apprehended'.[59] But Albemarle's report that a confederacy of old army, commonswealthmen, council of state members, outlaws and foreigners was afoot was seriously and gratefully received. On 22 November was published a Church of England reaction to the current absence of a Conventicles Act: Samuel Parker's Discourse of Ecclesiasticall Politie, one of the works that would aggravate Marvell in three years' time. It was on 5 December that Elizabeth Calvert, widow of the great publisher of radical books, Giles, was indicted for publishing the 'Directions to a Painter' volume, the significance of which I discuss elsewhere.[60]

On 7 December, Marvell acted with Henry Henley as teller for the unsuccessful 'Noes' on the question of whether the churchman Peregrine Palmer had been elected for Bridgwater over Sir Francis Rolle who was sympathetic to Dissenters.[61] Many of Rolle's supporting voters were disqualified under the Conventicles Act. Business was coming to a head in respect of many pieces of legislation but attendance was becoming thin. Adjournment until February was considered but then it was heard that proroguement was imminent, so the Commons, having suspended Sir George Carteret from the House, having voted him guilty on ten counts of maladministration during the Dutch war, asked also that he be banned from the court and deprived of all offices.[62] Something had snapped in Marvell on the matter of prorogation, which meant that all of the legislation of that session would be lost, including the Conventicles Act. He referred sarcastically to Charles's 'princely wisdom' in suspending the Parliament, and while leaving much silent, expressed a great deal of contempt at this wasteful managing of the political process: 'It is enough to tell you that prorogation makes all bills votes and proceedings of this session null & void as if nothing had bin done or said. God direct his M[ty] further in so weighty resolutions.'

PERSECUTION AND DECEPTION

Marvell spent some or much of his time with his nephew the young merchant William Popple who had been based in London for the latter half of the 1660s.[63] Early in the new year, Popple moved to Bordeaux to develop his role in the wine trade. This was the pretext for a long and important series of letters from Marvell to Popple, in one of which he spoke freely and without the constraints noticeable in the constituency letters.[64]

Marvell returned to Parliamentary business with the opening session of 1670. There was much to be discussed and recorded in respect of duties on wine and the supply that would have to be decided later in the session. The dispute between the Lords and the Commons that had dragged out for two years was finally forgotten during the first month of the session, with each House agreeing to erase records of the dispute from their respective journals. Indeed, Marvell recorded how on 22 February the Commons en masse attended the King in the Banqueting House, first to be asked to erase the records (in respect of Barnardiston and Skinner's cases) and second to tell the King that this had been done. Such oblivion, wrote Marvell, was full of royal 'prudence justice & kindnesse'.[65] But was this an ironic reference? It was oblivion aided by alcohol, since the meeting was followed by binge drinking in the royal cellars for all MPs, orchestrated by Marvell's enemy Sir Thomas Clifford.[66] Might we detect irony in Marvell's letter here? The Commons agreed to erase the records on 21 February, the Lords shortly afterwards and before the 26th.

Marvell's overriding concern was the Conventicles Bill, which, he wrote to Mayor Tripp on 26 February, he expected to pass soon into law. In addition to receiving news from its MPs, the Mayor and Aldermen of Hull also received accounts from their hired intelligencer, Robert Stockdale, who served diligently throughout the Restoration. That Marvell had given Stockdale some notes in early March (he did the same a month later) deterred him from writing at length to Mayor Tripp, but five days later he was prolix with detail.[67] Supply and taxation quickly gave way to the details of the Conventicles Bill. Reports of insurrections and seditious attitudes to the monarchy once again pushed the Commons towards restrictive, punitive measures, against Roman Catholics as well as against Nonconformists. The Bill was given its first reading in the first week of March. Under its proposed terms, no one could meet for a religious purpose in groups of five or more outside an established church service on pain of a 5s. fine for a first conviction, and 10s. thereafter. Huge £100 fines were to be levied on those caught preaching if they were not local figures, £50 on anyone who allowed a meeting on his property. Law officers were entitled under warrant to break into any property where they thought such a meeting might be taking place, and to arrest anyone discovered in a conventicle meeting. The Bill was passed by 138 votes to 78 and sent up to the Lords. Exhausted and with the post about to leave, Marvell finished his longest letter to Hull, containing these details, on 10 March.[68]

Against the will of Parliament, the King could deliver toleration, or at least prevent the Conventicle Act taking hold. But to do this he would need to exercise power that threatened the constitution of mixed monarchy, of King in Parliament. Thus, Marvell wrote warily and fearfully to Popple on 21 March of the achievements of Lauderdale in Scotland.[69] He was able to exploit Presbyterian and episcopal weakness in order to render the King absolute in matters of religion, to have an army that could march anywhere in the three kingdoms, and to allow the King to name commissioners in Scotland for the proposed union with England. Lauderdale had raised the prospect of arbitrary royal power in Scotland, and Marvell reported murmurs that impeachment proceedings would be brought against him. While the King's prerogative in context might help the Dissenters in England, it was an aid to arbitrary power in Scotland. The Commons held on to their role as guardians of public accountability: slowing down the rate of supply so that Charles felt the pinch and accordingly addressed Parliament in 'Stylo minaci & imperatorio' in order to impress upon Parliament the need for more money.[70]

Indeed, the Conventicles Bill, the 'terrible Bill', 'the Quintessence of arbitrary Malice', as Marvell put it, would probably pass, since the necessary majority of MPs had been bought.[71] One wonders, however, how constant or clear-sighted Marvell's mind was at this stage, or indeed that of any political observer. He did not like the King's power to determine church ordinances in Scotland, but Charles was one source of hope for the Nonconformists. Yet the King himself said, according to Marvell, that he was bound to pass the Conventicles Bill because he needed the supply money. Marvell's point here is that it is the King who has been bought: 'the Price of Money'.[72] Three weeks later, he was concerned by Charles's insistence on an ancient practice that the monarch should sit in the House of Lords during debates – a stratagem employed in this instance for curbing the Duke of York's influence there (especially in respect of Lord Roos's bill for divorce). And Charles seems to have had his way with voting in the Lords: the Commons had to persuade the Lords to take back a bill that would have restored all the King's privileges since the conquest of 1066: a 'Piece of absolute universal Tyranny'.[73] Throughout the system everyone could be 'bought' by everyone else, and this boded ill when at the imminent meeting with French courtiers at Dover there were rumours of Charles taking a French princess, presumably after a divorce ('The King disavows it; yet he has sayed in Publick that he knew not why a Woman might not be divorced for Barrenness').[74] Perhaps echoes of the reign of Henry VIII were evident. The theme of arbitrary power had indeed emerged from the tangle over religious liberty and was threatening to become dominant. And yet in late March, the Lords had so revised the Conventicles Bill, adding 'a reserving clause for his Majestyes ancient prerogative', that he might be able to suspend the execution of its terms entirely. Good for religious liberty, but bad for the constitution.[75]

Not for the first time Marvell felt the passing away of an older, better world, not respected in the present. George Monck, the Duke of Albemarle, military and naval hero of the Commonwealth, the architect of the Restoration, and still the best senior soldier in England, had died on 3 January. He lay in state for three months at Somerset House and was ignored ('he yet lys in the Dark unburyed, and no Talk of him').[76] Marvell suggests that this was because Albemarle's son, Christopher, was unwilling to pay for a great funeral and felt that the King should do so (he was, however, perfectly willing to support a funeral for his mother, the chief speaker in 'The Third Advice to a Painter' who died twenty days after her husband). When the service for the Duke finally took place, it was a diminished affair, with few walking in the train. So much for the man who was to many, including Marvell, the most impressive Englishman of the 1660s.

Marvell and Gylby had had to deal on behalf of the Hull Corporation with another figure who behaved like Sir Robert Cary. This was Sir Charles Wheeler, who owed the Mayor and Aldermen some money. Writing on 14 March, Stockdale reported that after being addressed by the two MPs, Wheeler had promised to pay the money at another meeting with Stockdale and Marvell, which appointment he failed to meet. Stockdale's scorn must have been shared by Marvell, who would have heard Wheeler speak 'like a Senator' in the House of Commons.[77] Stockdale at least promised to keep an eye out for Wheeler: he would not be allowed to get off the hook.

On 22 March Marvell was added to the committee investigating a disputed election at Tamworth between John Ferrers and Charles Boyle, Lord Clifford; the latter was another son of Richard Boyle, second Earl of Cork, and had benefited from Boyle's substantial Yorkshire interests. We may assume that Marvell would have been prone to side with Lord Clifford; although an arrogant courtier, he eventually became a patriot.

The King achieved much in the elongated session (Marvell had once again entrusted Stockdale to write up his notes as a newsletter when the work pressure came towards the end on 2 April; he also noted the thinness of attendance in the House).[78] On 11 April, at five in the evening, Charles summoned both Houses to the Lords, where thirty-eight acts were passed, many of them private, but among the most important the legislation for rebuilding London, the Act for Roos's remarriage, and finally the Conventicles Act. Parliament adjourned until the following 24 October, and the King left for Newmarket and the races. Marvell sent printed copies of the acts to Hull and as if to monumentalize the work of this Parliament, they were bound into a volume by Alderman Foxley and presented to the Corporation Board on 16 June.[79] The King said in his speech that he was delighted with so much progress, with the degree of unity between the two Houses, and with the steps made towards the union of the two kingdoms.

The demands on MPs at this time were intense: they were required to debate morning and afternoon, and into the evening. Writing to Mayor Tripp on 19 March, Marvell again confessed that Parliament drained him, depriving him of the energy to write letters.[80] He said the same to Edward Thompson on 17 December of the same year, referring to days on end of continual sitting, if not in the House then in committee.[81] Stockdale was given Marvell's notes to write to Hull in the meantime. Once free from the demands of Commons business, Marvell was able to write at length and more reflectively of events to William Popple on 14 April, two days after the adjournment.

While the Corporation of Hull and Trinity House were rewarding Marvell for his services on 16 April, verse satire began to circulate, critical of the King. In particular, 'The Kinges Vowes', also known as 'Royal Resolutions', made fun of royal habits and pretensions. We know copies were about in May:

> When the plate was at pawn, and the fob at low ebb,
> And the spider might weave in our stomach its web;
> > Our pockets as empty as brain;
> > > Then Charles without acre
> > > Made these vows to his maker –
> > If ere I see England again,

> 1
> I will have a religion then all of my own,
> Where Papist from Protestant shall not be known;
> But if it grow troublesome, I will have none.

> 2
> I will have a fine Parliament always to friend,
> That shall furnish me treasure as fast as I spend;
> But when they will not, they shall be at an end.

3

I will have as fine bishops as were e'er made with hands,
With consciences flexible to my commands;
But if they displease me, I will have all their lands.

(ll. 1–15)

In 1703 these verses would be attributed to Marvell, and would be included in the most important Marvell poetry manuscript, but not all editors have agreed that they were his. If the verses resemble a drinking song, that certainly fits Marvell's known address (at least his correspondence address) at this time 'att Mr Richard Hill's howse the Rhenish wine howse in Westminster'.[82]

One month later, Marvell was writing uncharacteristically out of session to warn the Mayor and Aldermen of Hull that they should expect an audit from Westminster in respect of the state of the town's defences, which, it was felt in the capital, should be maintained at the town's expense. Marvell advised that it would be prudent for the Corporation to appoint a high steward from the Privy Council who could represent Hull directly to the executive power. Marvell's choice was the Earl of Sandwich, not least because he was Vice-Admiral of the nation, but he urged that there should not be a visible competition for the post, since 'Competition is not honourable'.[83] The Corporation was suitably grateful in its reply.[84]

It was in June that the King decided to reform himself in some ways, perhaps partly in the light of the satires mentioned above. He banished his mistress, the Countess of Castlemaine, to the provinces, first conferring on her the title of Duchess of Cleveland. She continued to exert considerable influence, but she was no longer a visible presence. Whitehall Palace, which had remained unoccupied, was renovated, its mourning removed. But London remained a tense place, while criminal violence was reported throughout the country. Court corruption was assumed to be widespread. In now lost letters, probably to Thomas Rolt, Marvell was held to have said that 'no one could expect promotions, spiritual or temporal, unless he made his court to the king's mistresses'.[85] In Hull, the climate was reflected in a dispute within the congregation of Holy Trinity. This reached the ears of the Archbishop of York, Richard Sterne, who wrote from his palace at Bishopthorpe to the Corporation on 8 June to instruct politely yet firmly that he wanted differences within the congregation quelled. He may not have been able to impose his own Conventicles Act on the congregation of the church but within any one congregation there might yet be conventicles (as there literally had been in the 1650s): 'I . . . desire you for the time to come to take care to prevent such irregular meetings, & the tumults which may arise thereupon.'[86] The effect on the surrounding country concerned him as much, and he feared that this might result, one way or another, in complaints to the government: in other words, more openly expressed political dissent.

On 24 October Parliament gathered again, and the King was after money. Despite, or perhaps precisely because of, the secret Treaty of Dover, he referred to the growth of armed forces in France and Holland as a reason for substantial military expenditure in England. The Triple Alliance required him to have forces that he could contribute to those supplied by Holland and Sweden, even though secretly he had other intentions. In addition, he presented himself as a successful diplomatic and commercially minded monarch: treaties with Spain had left England with Jamaica and other possessions in the Caribbean, and advantageous treaties had been made with Denmark, Portugal and Savoy, as well as France and Holland. Such was his success, so he claimed, that he needed Parliament both to provide funding for naval refurbishment, and also to pay off debts which were now incurring very large sums of interest. As ever, Charles was keen to resolve the matter of supply as quickly as possible, and then have everyone leave Westminster and return to their estates. Marvell said he would send on to Hull the document from which these statements are drawn (the King's speech, if it was printed) but we learn in the next letter, written a week later, that the printing was forbidden by Arlington.[87] In the intervening week, the House had considered thanking the King for all his efforts in commerce and against conventicles, but had instead fallen to examining the state of the kingdom's finances, which had become more and more engrossing. A week later still, Marvell reported that rather than endure a general tax of 20 per cent on all property, many would rather have a land tax and home excise, which, he reports, would have given the King exactly what he wanted in the first place. However much he accepted that the supply was necessary, it is clear that too much taxation threatened to subject people to duress, or possibly a kind of tyranny: a proposed tax of 50 per cent on foreign (i.e. French) clothes would be effectively a 'prohibition', he wrote on 29 November 1670.[88]

During this intense period of letter-writing, Marvell voiced his concern that as few people as possible be allowed to read the letters: only the bench of the Hull Corporation. Was he concerned that the privileges of the House would be broken by the spread of restricted knowledge? And why is he so alarmed when he is offering not interpretations and opinions but a 'plain account'? Precisely because it contained such 'openesse of my writing & simplicity of my expression'.[89] It might perhaps be needless, as he said, to worry on this account, but on the other hand, it is too easy for us to forget that this was classified information and was meant to be read by the Mayor and Aldermen alone. All in all, it is extremely detailed material on the practicalities of taxation alternatives. Although significant names are suppressed, it might indeed look to some as if privileged information was being leaked, ultimately with seditious intent. Marvell was sensitive to the sometimes conflicting senses of trust in which he was placed: by Parliament and by the Corporation of Hull. At this time Marvell and Gylby were also functioning as tax advisers to the Corporation itself, on the matter of whether two bakers' ovens served by one chimney are liable for one or two charges of tax, and whether blacksmiths' forges should be taxed at all.[90]

The Corporation was also trying to have its own Act of Parliament passed, giving it permission to levy duties upon goods passing through the port. Marvell and Gylby both advised caution here, pointing to problems experienced by other ports such as Boston in Lincolnshire which had gone down this road and noting that duties were not popular with the customers: the merchants who used the port. Marvell in particular said representatives would need to be sent from Hull to explain to MPs in detail the needs of the port. Then finally there was the issue of time, which would have to be found from a very busy schedule in order to secure the passage of a private bill through Parliament.

If proposed taxes on commodities were not to be publicly discussed, the MP's continuing correspondence with his nephew would certainly have given the King's censors much to ponder. A surviving letter of 28 November 1670 records Marvell's distress at the consequences of the Conventicles Act.[91] London's local governors, including the Lord Mayor, Sir Samuel Starling, and Sir John Robinson, the Lieutenant of the Tower, went after the Nonconformists with vigour. The London officials, like many elsewhere in the country, had been 'purged' for fear that they would be too sympathetic to the Dissenters. The trained bands or local militia marched to the beat of drums through the streets of London, there was a permanent guard on the Exchange, and patrols searched for Nonconformist ministers. The bands alarmed the King, who, fearing an insurrection akin to Venner's rising of 1661, gave them more troops, with the Duke of York appearing as commander on Sundays. The Nonconformists defied the law and met; the soldiers went in to clear assemblies, wounding many and killing some more (Marvell mentions Quakers in this respect). It was also alleged that the soldiers had been hindered from approaching the pulpits, been verbally abused and had brickbats thrown at them. James Hayes and John Jekyll were indicted, the former on the grounds of trying to bribe the last Lord Mayor with publicly collected money into leaving the Dissenters alone.[92] They were offered either astronomically large (and in Marvell's view illegal) bonds of £5,000 per person or custody. Marvell spoke in Hayes's defence in the Commons on 21 November, attempting to have the case heard by a committee of the House rather than generally at its Bar and under the terms of the Act.[93] Three days later, with the King declaring an Act of Grace, the Commons discharged them.

But a trial had begun the previous September at the Old Bailey of the Quakers William Penn and William Mead. They were found not guilty by the jury, in response to which the Lord Mayor and the Recorder kept the jury shut up with neither food nor water for three days. The result was the establishment of the precedent that judges could not punish juries for their verdict, while the entire event allowed the Friends to publish an account of what almost amounted to Quaker martyrdom, which immediately became a key document in the new wave of persecutions.[94] In it, the Recorder is alleged to have commended the Spanish Inquisition, claiming that England, in Marvell's words, 'would never be well till we had something like it'.[95] Significantly, it was on 5 December that Elizabeth Calvert, widow of the great radical publisher Giles, was indicted, for publication of the 'Directions to a Painter'. Although the indictment referred back to an offence committed on 20 May 1668, the full details of this event would not become clear for some time.[96] On 8 December, Marvell reported to the Corporation of Hull further amendments to the proposed Conventicles Bill, including the provision that anyone who refused to give his name or to pay 5s. would be liable to have his house entered without a warrant.[97] By late November the House of Commons was again so sparsely attended and obsequious that it just did what the King wanted, and a 'terrible Act of Conventicles' would be the result.[98] On 3 December, Marvell wrote of the measures discussed in the House to make MPs attend sessions. In the same week, the Conventicles Bill had been read twice and committed. He was quietly outraged that conventicles were now defined in law as 'riots'.[99]

At this point Marvell provides a fuller picture of the supply issue of late October and early November. It was proving hard to raise the supply requested by the King: the money could only be found by a combination of feverish city bargaining and the special efforts of the 'Fanatics', who managed to raise £40,000, twice as much as the city could deliver. In other words, wealthy Nonconformist merchants thought that if they helped the King with his financial needs, he would exercise a restraining influence on the application of the Conventicles Act. The House, thinned by poor attendance, became 'obsequious', and the vote was given not positively but 'Nemine contradicente', with few affirmatives and 'rather a Silence as of Men ashamed and unwilling'.[100] Worse than this, however, must have been the defection to the King at this point of several prominent opposition figures: Sir Robert Howard, Sir Robert Carr, the Speaker Sir Edward Seymour, Sir Richard Temple and Denzil, Lord Holles. Writing to Thomas Rolt nine months later, Marvell thought this buying off had been so extensive, 'it is a Mercy they gave not away the whole Land, and Liberty, of *England*'.[101]

Marvell's job was also to protect the interests of his constituents, or associates, in the north. In this respect, he reported to Edward Thompson in mid-December the mentioning of Thompson's brother, Sir Henry, by name, for not paying duties, and stressed that he had rebuked his fellow committee members for mentioning any names at all.[102] Marvell felt that Sir Henry had been unjustly and dishonourably treated, and that it behoved a burgess to defend the honour of a gentleman. Edward Thompson was a close friend, and so Marvell claimed was Sir Henry, but he would become much more than that. The Thompsons were a prosperous York merchant family who had made a fortune in the wine trade and through small lending; Sir Henry was seriously wealthy and was busily transforming himself into one of the great landowners of Yorkshire. In 1668 he acquired from the Howard family the estate at Escrick, six miles south of York. He and his successors would add to the land and improve the buildings so that it became one of the most impressive large estates in northern England. At about this time, Sir Henry was building a toll road between Escrick and York, the path of which would later become the A19 trunk road. He was an important patron for Marvell and, as we shall see, Marvell did not much disappoint him.

A telling episode in December 1670 that pointed to an insolent, disrespectful court, and one that delayed the business of taxation, concerned Sir John Coventry. As recorded by Marvell it was an assault on Sir John Coventry, MP for Weymouth, by a company of the Duke of Monmouth's guard.[103] Coventry had joked in the Commons against Sir John Berkenhead's defence of the playhouses because they were of a great service to the King, by asking whether Berkenhead meant the male or the female actors. The reference to the King's proclivities was obvious. This was on the last day before the Christmas recess, 19 December, and that evening soldiers lay in wait for Coventry and attacked him at two in the morning as he returned from dining at the Cock on Suffolk Street. They threw him to the ground and inflicted a lasting disfigurement by nearly slicing off the end of his nose. Further damage to Coventry was avoided by the arrival of others. Sir Thomas Sandys, the commander of the troops, and Charles O'Brien, son of the Earl of Inchequin, were named ringleaders in what was seen as an assault on Parliamentary privilege, as well as on the liberty of the subject. It could have been construed as part of an alarmingly violent trend: earlier in the month, the King's viceroy in Ireland, the Duke of Ormond, was nearly abducted on St James Street by a mounted gang led by Thomas Blood.[104] The King was rumoured to be considering whether to interrogate Coventry for his words, and in an inflammatory way, ordered the release of Wroth and Lake, two lower-ranking soldiers who had been arrested. When the Commons resumed business, the matter was initially not discussed. The House resolved to do nothing until it had dealt with the soldiers: on 10–12 January they were summoned on pain of severe punishment, and banished on 16 February. Arguments about the details of the Act making this law and how it should be recorded went backwards and forwards between the Lords and the Commons in late January and early February 1671. Sandys and O'Brien did not appear: they remained attainted and outlawed, with no possibility of pardon, but the statute book carried a law (later known as the Coventry Act), as Marvell humorously put it, 'against cutting Noses'.[105]

In addition to the Coventry matter, there was serious concern about the extent of taxation consequent upon the King's supply. Writing to Hull, Marvell suggested on 10 January that Hull merchants persuaded their wine customers to delay returning any account until the whole sum required by the King, £800,000, had been collected.[106] In a letter to Edward Thompson on 5 January, he reflected more poetically on the predicament: 'My word we need no frost nor snow this winter. The Bills will pinch us enough. There will be noe sort of men in the nation but we shall make them tingle to the very fingers ends.' And more directly: 'The mony will goe hard but the ways of collecting are so severe that it will spend all mens patience.'[107] He hoped that a retrospective operation of the foreign excise would be dropped. It is also clear from Marvell's letter to Sir Henry of 5 January 1671 that he was deeply indebted to the Thompsons, not least for the help they had given to William Popple's career.[108] It is evident from another letter of January that Marvell was promoting Popple's business elsewhere: he knew that his friend the admiral Sir Jeremy Smith, then in Tangier, was ordering supplies from Popple.[109] Every move of political affairs had a consequence for the network of relationships of which Marvell was a part, and he knew this intimately.

In early February came further evidence of the tough administration of the Conventicles Act, with reports of people arrested violently during sermons or even while receiving communion.[110] At the same time, the Commons became fearful of the growth of popery, there being reports of more priests and followers in Monmouthshire and Herefordshire, and the rise to prominence of influential Catholics at court. In parts of the English/Welsh border it was said there had been a tenfold increase in practising Catholics. A committee of inquiry was established to investigate these reports, and added, remarkably, Jews to the remit. At the beginning of March, Marvell would be named to this committee. On 21 February he reported that the Commons asked the King to put the laws in action against the dangerous growth of popery. A bill was sent to the Lords for their concurrence. A week later, the Commons had prepared a bill 'for the better convicting & proceeding against them'.[111] By 11 March, this Bill had been sent up to the Lords, and a further bill against profanation of the Sabbath was also under commitment.[112] On 14 March the King promised to issue a proclamation against Catholic priests, and apply the law to those who had lately converted, but said he had to respect those who had been brought up Catholic and had been loyal to his father and himself.[113] On 22 March Marvell seems to have helped win a tactical victory for the Nonconformists by being a teller for the successful 'Noes' in a vote that upheld a reduction of liabilities against offenders in the Conventicles Bill. He was delighted conventicles were no longer to be defined as riots; the only threat that remained in his view was continuing indemnity for those who were proven to have exceeded the law in prosecuting Dissenters.[114] A further attempt to indemnify those who had been prosecuted under the old Conventicles Act failed, the Bill was read on 5 April for the third time and sent to the Lords, where it was narrowly maintained.[115]

Much of Marvell's time in the early part of the year was consumed by rekindled interest in the Spurn Head lighthouse matter. Another party, Charles Whittington, had gained the right to erect lighthouses at Humbermouth. This had upset Frowd by mid-February, and Marvell wrote that he hoped for the sake of Hull Trinity House to stir up the two against each other. This took up much time in February, but in its last week they were back to square one: Whittington's hopes had been dashed by lack of royal and ducal patronage and Frowd was as full of delay as ever.[116]

In the meantime, the Coventry affair resolved itself unpleasantly. James, Duke of Monmouth, Charles's eldest and illegitimate child by Lucy Waters, was a thug and something of a rascal. He had protected O'Brien by hiding him in his lodgings after the attack on Coventry. Writing to nephew William at the end of the following April, Marvell reported – but assumed that news had already reached Bordeaux, such was its notoriety – on another fracas, in which Monmouth, abetted by several other gentlemen, had fought with the watch and killed a beadle. To the scandal of everyone, it would seem, they had all received the royal pardon. Attempts to break Charles's peculiar interpretation of the constitution met with no success either, reported Marvell. Lord Lucas had spoken against the readiness of the Commons to give supply, in addition to the 'Looseness' of the administration, and Lord Clare had argued against the presence of the King in the Lords. Lucas's speech was deemed a libel by the Lords, and was burned by the hangman. The King continued to attend the Lords, but Marvell laughed at the hangman's mistake: he burned the House of Lords' order with the copy of the speech.[117]

Is it any surprise then that Marvell should write in late January to his nephew that 'The Court is at the highest Pitch of Want and Luxury, and the People full of Discontent'?[118] He was in fact looking for a way out, and he wrote to Popple in late April that 'I think it will be my Lot to go to an honest fair Employment into *Ireland*'.[119] Would this have been as a secretary, or perhaps even as a superior officer? This might have been through the influence of the Boyle and Jones families, respectively the Earls of Cork and of Ranelagh, powerful elements of the Anglo-Irish aristocracy. Marvell had met Katherine, Lady Ranelagh, who had recently moved to a house in Pall Mall, London, with her daughter Frances, and had witnessed the work of their protégé, the miraculous curer Valentine Greatreakes in 1666. Marvell had known Lady Ranelagh's brother Roger Boyle, Lord Broghill, now Earl of Orrery, since 1660, when he had tried to persuade the Earl to contribute funds for the relief of Polish Protestants. There was also the connection with Marvell's friend Sir William Petty, who had been involved in Irish economic affairs since the 1650s, and with the Earl of Anglesey, another of the great Irish landowners, a Puritan of complicated political opinions, with whom Marvell would shortly have to do in an important way. Whatever the case, even if, as Marvell recorded, you might smell the influence of the Papal court in Ireland, at least one would be out of the stench of the English one. Some have read the mention of an 'honest fair Employment' as an ironic reference to espionage, but there is no clear evidence that points this way.[120]

What was happening was a kind of moral malaise as the King continued to exploit divisions in Parliament, forcing the two Houses together when it suited his purposes, and doing nothing to render the court accountable for its excesses. He prorogued Parliament on 22 April for an entire year. In the event, it would not meet for eighteen months. A hoped-for short prorogation that would have allowed differences between Lords and Commons over the Foreign

Commodities Bill to disappear vanished along with most of the more significant legislation, including the Conventicles Bill and the Bill against Catholics. All were lost.[121] And all the time, Charles was drawing inexorably towards concerted action with Louis against the Dutch. Marvell described this as a 'bewitching', and also as a national disease. Louis XIV would do nothing against the English, because they would 'dy a natural Death'. 'For indeed never had poor Nation so many complicated, mortal, incurable, Diseases', he said, associating this in the next sentence with the recent death on 31 March (from cancer) of the Duchess of York.[122] The House of Commons had been bought off by the Crown and was in consequence 'odious to the People'. Many aristocrats and former patriot MPs were now farming the customs and taxes, and the Duchess of Cleveland, so severely rebuked in 'The Last Instructions', was making most of all in this way, in addition to her considerable control of court patronage.

As the year drew towards its last quarter, Marvell, like many of his countrymen, could begin to see where royal policy had led. England was a client to France: 'we truckle to *France* in all Things, to the Prejudice of our Alliance [with Holland and Sweden] and Honour'.[123] Equally worrying was the situation with Parliament. Quarrelling between the two Houses had surfaced again. With the Commons controlled by Arlington and Clifford, the country gentlemen there formed a somewhat unlikely alliance with Buckingham, who was by now exercising resistance to Arlington in the Lords.

It was possibly during the summer recess of 1671 that Marvell sought and found refuge from London and Westminster by obtaining the use of a cottage in Highgate, a short ride from the capital, but then still pleasantly bucolic. Commentators have associated the chance of retreat to Highgate with Marvell's spare, unadorned and faithful rendering of Seneca's *Thyestes*, lines 391–43:

> Climb at court for me that will
> Tottening favour's pinnacle
> All I seek is to lie still.
> Settled in some secret nest
> In calm leisure let me rest;
> And far off the public stage
> Pass away my silent age.
> Thus when without noise, unknown,
> I have lived out all my span,
> I shall die, without a groan,
> An old honest countryman.
> Who exposed to others' eyes,
> Into his own heart ne'er pries,
> Death to him's a strange surprise.

The echoes that others have found in the poem of Milton's *Paradise Regained*, published earlier in the same year, and Cowley's version of the same lines from

Seneca, sustain the idea of stoical retreat from a corrupt world of courtly politics, but without the amplification of retreat found in Cowley.[124]

In 1671 another smaller-scale event took place that would eventually have a profound impact on Marvell's life. A partnership of several merchants formed: Richard Thompson, Edward Nelthorpe, John Farrington and Edmund Page came together to make a bank and to trade.[125] The former two were Hull men and were related to Marvell. Thompson's son was clerk to William Popple in Bordeaux; Nelthorpe was or would become extremely intimate with Marvell: this will have to interest us. Thompson was a coffee house and news addict, to the neglect of his business responsibilities, while Nelthorpe was prone to highly speculative commercial projects. Suffice it to say for now that mercantile matters and kinship were intimately bound up and that they would affect the shape of the Marvell household and the action that the players in it took.

Whatever calm was afforded by the prorogation was quickly dispelled by a sensational event in early May 1671. Summarizing the year's news in August, Marvell looked back to May, when:

> One *Blud*, outlawed for a Plot to take *Dublin* Castle, and who seized on the *Duke of Ormond* here last Year, and might have killed him, a most bold, and yet sober, Fellow, some Months ago seized the Crown and Sceptre in the Tower, tooke them away, and, if he had killed the Keeper, might have carried them clear off. He, being taken, astonished the King and Court, with the Generosity, and Wisdom, of his Answers. He, and all his Accomplices, for his Sake, are discharged by the King, to the Wonder of all.[126]

Thomas Blood was a former Commonwealth JP who had been rewarded with property in Ireland, which he then lost at the Restoration.[127] He had sought redress for his loss of property in the plot at Dublin in 1663 that was designed to seize Ormond, had been involved in the armed risings of the Covenanters in Scotland in the Pentland Hills in November 1666, and the ambush of Ormond (on 6 December 1670; allegedly at the instigation of the Duke of Buckingham), who spiritedly resisted his attackers despite his advanced age. Informants helped the authorities quickly establish the identity of the attackers, but the gang remained at large until the attempt on the Crown Jewels. Charles and his councillors were as much impressed by what Blood knew as by the grace of his speech, and he was soon, like Larkin the printer, functioning as a double agent: informing on republican and Nonconformist activity, but also helping to reconcile former Cromwellians with the regime.[128] It was important for the government to have the best inside knowledge of Nonconformity in the light of the forthcoming war with Holland; knowing who might collaborate with the enemy and the prevention of this was a serious intelligence goal. Marvell's Latin lines on Blood, and the English version that was also deployed within the text of 'The Loyal Scot' and appears to respect the act of mercy that betrayed the Crown Jewels plot, focuses more acutely on Blood's mastery of disguise:

Epigram: Upon Blood's attempt to steal the Crown

When daring Blood his rent to have regained
Upon the English diadem distrained,
He chose the cassock, surcingle and gown,
The fittest mask for one that robs a crown.
But his lay pity underneath prevailed,
And while he spared the keeper's life he failed.
With priest's vestments had he but put on
A bishop's cruelty, the crown had gone.[129]

This relates of course to one of Marvell's own great concerns: the cruelty of bishops. Marvell seems to enjoy the aptness of Blood's use of clerical disguise – the epitome of greed and violence – so that his respect for the subject is enhanced by the aptness of Blood's choice. Clerical abuse was already much exercising Marvell. Whatever Blood's crime, says Marvell, that of the bishops was worse, a theme that he would play up for the rest of his life; Blood's action was an emblem of the deceitful ill at the heart of the state. A poem replying to Marvell's in one of the manuscript copies of the poem took the opposite view: the act was 'a rebus [a pictorial representation of words or ideas] of ye good-old-Cause'.[130] As we shall see, Marvell and Blood were to be linked together by others in the future. But Blood's skills with disguise had a completely different goal to those of Marvell. Indeed, one judgement, admittedly a Victorian one, finds in him a complexity of motivation not out of keeping with either the novel or with that Calvinist paradox, the 'justified sinner': he kept a long list of examples of how Providence had permitted him many lucky escapes.[131] 'He assumed various disguises and continually changed his places of refuge, sometimes assuming to be a Quaker, sometimes an Anabaptist, an independent, and even a Roman Catholic priest. Rapidly flitting about among all sorts of people, entering sympathetically into their grievances and family affairs, instead of shrouding himself in mystery and thus exciting suspicion, he succeeded in baffling pursuers, and became acquainted with many desperate characters'.[132] This degree of stated sympathy in 'Blood and the Crown' points to the fact that Marvell and Blood were already associated, probably through a common connection with Buckingham, perhaps even with Wharton. The King's spymaster, Sir Joseph Williamson, was informed on 21 September that Marvell had travelled with Blood either from Buckinghamshire (where both Wharton and Buckingham had houses) or from Buckingham himself, wherever he was.[133]

It seems that also at this time Marvell was trying to revive, such as it was, his reputation as a poet. In July or soon afterwards he decided to compete in a competition instituted by Louis XIV's administrator Colbert for the best inscription to be set up on the pediment of the great colonnade of the Louvre, which had been completed in 1670. The prize was 1,000 pistols, a very considerable sum of money (was this an attempt by Marvell to better his financial health?). The pediment stones were hoisted into position in 1672. No record of any winning distich being inscribed on the stone actually survives, but George Gordon, fourth Marquis of Huntly and later Duke of Gordon, was judged the winner.[134] Marvell's distichs were written for the competition, notwithstanding his suspicion of most things French at the time. Louis had announced his competition throughout Europe, and it was reported that many poets in France and Italy busied themselves with the prospect. Whether Marvell's lines were presented in the French court is unknown.[135] Did he hear about the competition from William Popple? Were they to have been sent with a member of an English embassy, as was the case with the poetry heard by Queen Kristina in 1654? Access even to Louis XIV was not as difficult as might at first be imagined: Wharton's sons were taken by the English ambassador for a royal audience.[136]

The lines are exquisite achievements, written in the wake of Emanuele Tesauro's popular *Il cannocchiale aristotelico* (1655) which elevated epigraphy to a distinct and demanding rhetorical art. Tesauro also redefined epigraphy to include all 'eulogies, epitaphs, dedications, epigrams, mottoes, and every kind of inscription', whether written or carved in stone.[137] He made the genre fashionable again. Marvell was in some sense out of step, yet very adventurous: there were complaints that elegies were the wrong genre for this subject: on metrical grounds alone, heroic verse was more effective for the purpose.

Inscribenda Luparae

Consurgit Lupurae dum non imitabile culmen,
    Escuriale ingens uritur invidiâ.

Aliter
Regibus haec posuit Ludovicus templa futuris;
    Gratior ast ipsi castra fuere domus.

Aliter
Hanc sibi syderam Ludovicus condidit aulam;
    Nec se propterea credidit esse deum.

Aliter
Atria miraris, summotumque aethera tecto;
    Nec tamen in totò est arctior orbe casa.

Aliter
Instituente domum Ludovico, prodiit orbis;
    Sic tamen angustos incolit ille lares.

Aliter
Sunt geminae Jani portae, sunt tecta Tonantis;
Nec deerit numen dum Ludovicus adest.

To be written on the Louvre

While the inimitable roof of the Louvre rises
The huge Escorial burns with envy.

Another
Louis built this temple for future kings,
But the camp was a more pleasing home to him.

Another
Louis built this starry palace for himself,
Nor did he believe on that account that he was a god.

Another
You marvel at the halls, and the sky pushed up by the roof;
Yet there is not in the whole world a less roomy house.

Another
Louis founding this house, the world came forth;
Yet thus he inhabits a cramped household.

Another
These are the double gates of Janus, these are roofs of the Thunderer;
Nor is divinity lacking while Louis is present.

The poems are typically inscrutable, apparently panegyrical, but there is also something else. Are they not drily double-edged, as are the other contributions we know about? Is Marvell frowning as he is smiling in order to expose the pretence of absolutist posture?

Perhaps it was at Highgate that Marvell wrote one of his longest, most intimate and most affecting letters on 9 August. The letter, the original of which is now lost, and which was first published by Cooke in 1726, was written to Thomas Rolt, who had travelled to Persia in 1668 and had been appointed as chief of the East India Company there. His mission was to increase Company trade there, in the face of stiff and at the time superior Dutch competition, and to make better use of English relations with the Persian rulers, which was difficult in a situation of political and dynastic fragility. Gombroon had been established after the fall and destruction of Hormuz in the early sixteenth century. It was originally a Portuguese possession but was recaptured by the Persians under Shah Abbas around 1615, from which it takes its modern name Bandar' Abbasi or Abbasi. The East India Company regarded the port as full of opportunity. Rolt had made his way in a Company ship to Gombroon, but 'hath bin very sick these 3 months & now very weake here', with the implied fear that there would be no recovery.[138] But Rolt recovered, providentially, it seemed to Marvell, and went on to succeed within the East India Company in a very remarkable way. Marvell explained his hopes in a metaphysical conceit that owed something to Donne's famous compasses image: 'your own good Genius, in Conjunction with your Brother here, will, I hope, tho at the Distance of *England* and *Persia*, in good Time, operate extraordinary Effects; for the Magnetism of two Souls, rightly touched, works beyond all natural limits'.[139] Rolt was sent by the Company to replace another agent, who it believed had overspent the Company's money. Rolt struggled, no doubt literally and physically, in the extreme heat for which Gombroon was famous among English seamen. But he too fell foul of the Company's strict rules of business management, and was for a while in dispute with it. He also deeply disliked the elevation of his erstwhile junior Gerald Aungier over his head to be appointed Governor of Bombay. But by 1677, the year before Marvell died, Rolt had prevailed, prospered and was himself Governor in Bombay. The profits made by the Rolts in Persia and India were very considerable, exciting in London 'Malice, Envy, and Detraction'.[140] Rolt returned to England an extremely wealthy man, and purchased in 1688 the estate at Sacombe, Hertfordshire, which would become one of the great land-scaped projects of the following century.

All that was a long way ahead in August 1671. The Rolts had profited under the Protectorate and had suffered something of a fall in 1660. They were Bedfordshire people related to the Cromwells. Thomas's brother Edward had risen to be one of Oliver Cromwell's two gentlemen of the bedchamber, and had ridden directly next to the bier in Cromwell's funeral procession. He had been the Protector's ambassador to Sweden in 1656, where he had been sent with sumptuous trappings, and where he was treated by Charles XI with equal grandeur. But he had necessarily fallen on hard times at the Restoration. He had not been imprisoned, and indeed was allowed by Parliament to wander freely and armed in Westminster. In Pepys's diary, he appears as an intimate, Captain Rolt, one of a small band of the diarist's friends, who shared in his delight of musical performance. Pepys himself was well aware of Rolt's some-what straitened circumstances.[141] Marvell's letter presupposes an ongoing correspondence with Edward Rolt: a previous letter from Marvell had gone missing in transit, and Marvell is replying to a letter of October 1670 – a clear indication of the delay caused by the slow nature of long-distance travel in this era. The lost letter had been carried by an Armenian, 'Cojan Karickoes', who had been in England in 1670, and who was considered by the English crucial in providing help in negotiations with the Shah. Marvell seems to know about Rolt's dispute with the Governors of the East India Company, for he reports that Rolt's reputation and activities have given an advantage to his friends, and have begun to turn around the hearts of his enemies. This did not stop Marvell

from offering two pieces of exquisitely stated advice stemming from the observation that 'a good Cause signifys little, unless it be well defended'.[142] First, a
good cause will not stand alone without action to support it: 'A Man may starve
at the Feast of good Conscience'. Second, when taking action, be sure of the
absolute rule of combat in any sphere – strike first: 'My Fencing-master in
Spain, after he had instructed me all he could, told me, I remember, there was
yet one Secret, against which there was no Defence, and that was, to give the
first Blow'.[143]

One further observation must be made of this letter. Marvell says he will
commit nothing too personal to a letter that might pass to a third party: 'the
Thoughts of Friends are too valuable to fall into the Hands of a Stranger'.[144]
And yet the letter contains two notable statements. The first is the concern for
Rolt's current affliction which has meant that he could not use his writing
hand. The second is Marvell's sense of the friendship, or dare we even say, the
love, that existed between the two men, as somewhat harmful to Rolt, when he
might otherwise be protecting his standing with the East India Company: 'If I
could say any Thing to you towards the Advancement of your Affairs, I could,
with a better Conscience, admit you should spend so much of your precious
Time, as you do, upon Me'. This is telling, and he clearly liked the attention.

The continued leisure afforded by the absence of a sitting Parliament meant
that Marvell was free to serve his noble friends and their personal concerns. On
23 December, and on behalf of Wharton, he wrote to Benjamin Worsley, the
prominent Hartlibian, enquiring of a Mr Cabell's daughter in Devon, who was
being considered confidentially as a wife for Wharton's eldest surviving son,
Thomas.[145] Four days later, Worsley replied to Marvell, who was evidently
staying at Winchendon, and Marvell wrote back on the 29th.[146] It seemed like a
match that would work well.

CHAPTER 10

✳

INDULGENCE AND REHEARSAL

MARVELL HAD MANY PREOCCUPATIONS during this long period without Parliament. During the normal recess, in very early January 1672, he continued to help Lord Wharton arrange a marriage for his son, Thomas, who had been down to Honiton on a visit but found himself rejected. What is most significant in these letters is the intimacy of Marvell and Wharton, with Marvell passing on Benjamin Worsley's letters, revealed with his own seal and with a note. Worsley and Marvell learned together how advantageous the Cabell match might be to the Wharton family. But Worsley himself was not always convinced of Marvell's judgement, as he questioned his attempt to dissuade Wharton from helping to release a victim of religious persecution because he anticipated a general release of all people held in this way.[1] During the early days of January (the 5th to the 7th), Marvell also spent time with the country MP and later actor in the Popish Plot, Sir Thomas Lee. Lee lived at Hartwell House, near Aylesbury, Buckinghamshire. Hartwell had originally been home to the Hampdens, famous in the opposition to Charles I at the outbreak of the Civil War. The Lees had married into the Hampden family in the 1650s. Lee had long been a hero of Marvell's, as his praise in 'The Last Instructions', line 299, makes clear: 'equal to obey or to command'.[2] He was also a famous entertainer, and we can imagine the dinner meeting of like-minded country interest politicians.

While Marvell was hoping to help settle Puritan dynasties in Buckinghamshire, the King, never short on surprises, rocked the city by ceasing to repay government debts. He needed cash, could raise no further loans, and adopted a plan of Clifford's against the advice of everyone else in his Privy Council. The system of circulation was halted: bankers were ruined, and those dependent on the bankers suffered in consequence. But Charles was now by his secret alliance committed to war, so he needed all the funds he could raise. The notoriously anti-Dutch Sir George Downing was sent off to the Hague as ambassador with harsh demands from Charles, including the provocative call for the salute to English ships whenever they were encountered in English waters. The Dutch correctly intuited an Anglo-French alliance against them, and Charles began to talk freely about his intentions – even with those who were not in his immediate circle of courtiers. War was just weeks away.

It was indeed the Committee for Foreign Affairs that launched the second major initiative of this year – a complete reversal of the Conventicles Act. Clifford proposed that the King exercise his own authority to suspend punitive legislation. Negotiation within the committee took place, with the King concerned to maintain some control over Nonconformist meetings while Clifford was looking for toleration for Catholics. With political opportunism on the brink of war to be exploited (Charles wanted pliant Nonconformists in the context of a Dutch war in order to minimize defection and to enhance espionage), agreement was reached, and with no Parliament to be obstructive, the Declaration of Indulgence (in line with the thinking propounded by Marvell and Wharton four years previously) was published on 15 March. It suspended all penal laws on ecclesiastical issues, and allowed Nonconformists freedom of worship under a licensing system, while Catholics were allowed to worship in private houses.

Two days before, Admiral Sir Robert Holmes had picked a fight with the Dutch Smyrna fleet sailing off the Isle of Wight, but already English troops had been sent to France in advance of what would be Louis XIV's devastating invasion of the Low Countries. On 17 March, two days after the Declaration of Indulgence, war was declared on Holland, thereby violating the Triple Alliance. Two months went by, however, before the first significant naval engagement of this, the Third Dutch War. The Battle of Sole Bay began on 28 May. Marginally a Dutch victory, it was notable for the heavy casualties inflicted on both sides, including that of the Earl of Sandwich, whose flagship, the *Royal James*, caught fire. Sandwich, who seems to have grown in Marvell's estimation since his portrayal in 'The Second Advice', was the last man seen alive on her; his body was washed ashore nearly two weeks after the fighting began.[3]

The 28 March saw the death of Frances Jones, Lady Ranelagh's daughter, born in 1633 and unmarried. Marvell wrote her epitaph, which is engraved on a monument in the crypt of St Martin-in-the-Fields. For some time, Marvell had been welcome at Lady Ranelagh's house in Pall Mall. She had moved there in 1669 after her husband's death. No disappointment to her pedigree, she maintained an impressive intellectual salon, and visited Milton in the 1650s when he lived in Petty France. Much of this information points to a Puritan household, and so it was.

The poem, Marvell's only verse epitaph in English, both exploits and criticizes the contemporary mood of nostalgia in epitaphs: he 'simultaneously attacks those who idealize the dead out of partisan self-interest and, while purporting not to, idealizes the deceased for his own polemical purposes as a virginal, virtuous Protestant whose exceptional virtues reveal all that is wrong with the Restoration settlement and society'.[4] Unlike other early seventeenth-century epitaphs, Marvell's does not suggest that the poem and its subject can influence society: Frances Jones's ideals have no currency in her age. Yet the age itself is judged by her. The very deliberate echoes of Donne and Jonson (ll. 9, 19–20) have been seen as an instance of Marvell's attempt to show poetry's loss of power in a decadent age.[5]

Where epitaphs were supposed to sum up the virtues of the deceased, Marvell claims that the full extent of Frances Jones's virtue was the evident every day of her entire life. By protesting poetic disempowerment, Marvell's speaker imitates the self-denying lifestyle of the godly Puritan. The poem ends in a sharp turn that emphasizes the absence inherent in epitaph representation, so making the 'reader feel the loss of one whose perfection he or she can only know from a distance, through a distorting representation, once it is gone':[6]

An Epitaph upon Frances Jones

Enough: and leave the rest to Fame.
'Tis to commend her but to name.
Courtship, which living she declined,
When dead to offer were unkind.
Where never any could speak ill,
Who would officious praises spill?
Nor can the truest wit or friend,
Without detracting, her commend.
To say she lived a virgin chaste,
In this age loose and all unlaced;
Nor was, when vice is so allowed,
Of virtue or ashamed, or proud;
That her soul was on heav'n so bent
No minute but it came and went;
That ready her last debt to pay
She summed her life up ev'ry day;
Modest as morn; as midday bright;
Gentle as ev'ning; cool as night;
'Tis true: but all so weakly said;
'Twere more significant, 'She's dead.'

Did Marvell think in a similar way about Lord Fairfax, his old employer and patron, who had died on 12 November?[7]

As if on cue, the lighthouse issue emerged two weeks later as a distraction. Justinian Angell who owned the land at Spurn had raised his interest in erecting a lighthouse. Once again, Marvell could see success for this third party only if he joined forces with Frowd, and Hull Trinity House requested

Marvell to bring the different parties together; this he did on 11 June. But Angell took this as a design against Frowd and proposed terms to enhance this strategy. Marvell insisted in talking further and in reconciling him to Frowd: he managed to have them meet for negotiation on 24 June, and Trinity House hoped that their good name would be kept out of proceedings.

Just over a fortnight later Parliament reassembled only to be prorogued (as a prior proclamation had announced) until 30 October. Yet while the King and his Council pondered their next move in the war, events developed on foreign and domestic fronts which showed that public opinion now played a significant role in politics. The government knew that a war in alliance with the French would require the massaging of public concern: long-standing fears of France and Catholic monarchy, and anxieties about making war on another Protestant state. It tried to justify the war in print, and to control anti-war sentiment, but these measures failed, and they were soon dealing with a well-orchestrated pro-Dutch propaganda campaign.[8] The Declaration of Indulgence had also failed to impress most Protestants. While the Independents and Baptists applied for licences, other Nonconformists, hoping for an eventual union with the national church, felt further forced into a schismatic position. Others still felt that the licensing system enabled the authorities to have too much knowledge of the conventicles, which could be put to persecutory ends at will. The Quakers argued that the state had no power to control worship at all: they refused to buy licences. Most thought that the Catholics had been put in far too advantageous a situation, since they were not scrutinized. Above all, there was widespread disapproval of a monarchical action that had put aside the laws of Parliament. Yet now that he had moved on his strategy, or moved as a part of Louis XIV's strategy, the King was not having it all his own way. As a Parliamentarian Marvell's position was apparently compromised, for he was in support of a measure made by the exercise of royal prerogative alone, little less than an absolutist decree.

And so when Marvell wrote to William Popple in June, and said that 'Affairs begin to alter', he was catching a sense of the swinging mood. There would soon be peace with Holland, he said, but would not disclose in the letter why he thought so: 'it is my Opinion it will be before *Michaelmas*, for some Reasons not fit to write'.[9] Louis's armies had swept across Holland: five of the republic's seven provinces were seized; only the opening of the dykes halted the French. Internal strife wreaked its worst in Holland, described by Marvell as enduring at once 'an Earthquake, an Hurricane and the Deluge'. Charles's nephew, William, Prince of Orange, had originally been excluded from a commanding military position. Now a frightened and angry public turned against the republican faction. Its leader Johan de Witt was stabbed in June and Marvell thought him dead. In fact, he and his brother, Cornelis, were both murdered in August. William was suddenly very popular, and was made stadholder. In this context, both Louis and Charles negotiated to carve up the United

Provinces, reducing it to powerlessness, an endgame that William was determined not to allow. This impasse is probably the context in which Marvell
wrote to Popple, although it is clear that his sympathy is with the Dutch, as
opposed to 'potent and subtle' France. He had written of the smaller fires
that broke out in London and Hull in the year after the Great Fire almost as
omens, and again now he described to Popple five distinct major fires, and
some more. What did they portend? Were they a sign of yet more censorship
('the old Talk . . . a severe Proclamation issued out against all who shall vent
false News, or discourse concerning Affairs of State'), or was the censorship the
harbinger of a final deliverance?[10] Whatever the reason, Marvell pointed out to
Popple that this very letter was a breach of the attempt at information control.

In the same month Marvell began work on a project that would finally
render him famous, and for some infamous. It would also place him in a most
complicated relationship with Charles II, one that clearly worked in the opposite direction from the dismay he had registered at royal policy throughout
1670–71. It was an attempt to tackle the question of toleration, but in a way
that went to the time before the Declaration of Indulgence, to the toleration
and anti-toleration debates of the later 1660s and to Charles's promise in the
Declaration of Breda in April 1660 to deliver 'liberty to tender consciences'.

The fall of Clarendon had resulted in a renewal of the public debate in
print on the pros and cons of toleration for Dissenters. Against an array of
Puritan divines and statesmen, the Anglican divines, led by Gilbert Sheldon,
Archbishop of Canterbury, voiced resolute opposition. Persecution was good
and necessary because it worked. Two of Sheldon's chaplains, Thomas Tomkins
and Samuel Parker, the latter the most prolific and significant, wrote in harsh
terms against Dissent. Nonconformist divines, like John Owen, and opposition
intellectuals, like John Locke, resisted and replied. Marvell's sensational *The
Rehearsal Transpros'd* was a late arrival on the polemical stage in this debate,
although it was given extra fuel by the Conventicles Act, and unusual currency
by the Declaration of Indulgence. Many close to Marvell were among those
who accepted the Declaration and purchased licences, including Marvell's
bookseller, Nathaniel Ponder. The Declaration itself looked back to the jointly
framed proposal of Wharton and Marvell in May 1668.

To some extent, then, *The Rehearsal Transpros'd* must be considered a work
that looked at least in part to the views of some members of the Cabal. Marvell
took as his starting point Parker's preface to his edition of Archbishop John
Bramhall's *Vindication of himself and the episcopal clergy, from the Presbyterian
charge of popery, as it is managed by Mr Baxter in his treatise of the Grotian religion: together with a preface shewing what grounds there are of fears and jeal-
ousies of popery*, which was advertised in the Term Catalogue on 24 June and
entered in the Stationers' Register on 7 September.[11] Bramhall (*c.* 1594–1663),
a Yorkshireman with a brilliant skill in defending the Church of England and
another gift for determined church administration (notably in Ireland in the

1630s), had risen, despite having attached himself to the Yorkshire Royalists and suffering a long period of exile in Europe, to be Archbishop of Armagh at the Restoration.[12] Parker admired Bramhall's defence of the English episcopal order and his firm anti-Puritanism: 'the Method he prescribed to all dissenting Parties, in order to a Catholick Agreement, and a sober Reformation to forego all their upstart and unwarrantable Innovations, and return to the ancient and Apostolical simplicity; a thing very easie and very practicable, were not Interest and Ignorance engaged against it.'[13] To Puritans like Owen and Baxter, Bramhall looked like a Papist, and it was a charge Parker wished to dispel. In his view, Owen and company were merely disguising their own version of 'Popery'. Parker proceeded to indulge in a detailed demolition of words and phrases from Owen's Puritan lexis that he viewed as arrant 'enthusiasm'. He would also begin to develop the view that the Nonconformists were to be associated with republicanism and atheism, versions of disobedience that dissolved the social glue that God had placed, via monarchy and episcopacy, in society. It is one reason why Parker himself is ambivalent towards Hobbes: taken by his approval of strong state authority, but alarmed by his materialism.[14] This view in particular would be developed in the longer response to Marvell in 1673.[15]

Marvell claimed at the end of *The Rehearsal* that it was the sheer arrogance of Parker's presumption that had prompted him to write; secondly, his repetition or tautology, and in consequence his disrespect for merchants, princes, the Bible, prayer, the Holy Spirit and Jesus alike.[16] True in large part as this was, there were deeper reasons that may be discerned in the context. Parker was one of a number of Anglican divines, and certainly not the most talented, who had refuted their Puritan backgrounds and hitched their coat-tails to the new orthodoxy in church and state. Moreover they had proclaimed their modernity at the same time by associating the established episcopal church with the new philosophy or new science that had gained assent during the middle years of the century.[17] In their view, the Royal Society and the Church of England went hand in hand, and the more vocal apologists for this institutional conjunction were quick to condemn former Commonwealth supporters whose thinking and beliefs did not fit: Milton and the prolific chaplain to Sir Henry Vane, Henry Stubbe, were both treated in this way despite their own interests in natural philosophy. Parker had played his part in two earlier publications, literally linking physics and episcopacy as a defence against atheism, and attacking the Platonists: *Tentamina physico-theologica de Deo* (1665) and *A free and impartial censure of the Platonick philosophie* (1666). These were substantial statements, although Joseph Glanvill occupied a more visible position in this field, and he was in principle just as intolerant of Dissent as Parker.[18] In the light of Marvell's association with the Boyles, and with Benjamin Worsley, an important natural philosophy figure before 1660, with his evident interest in the new discoveries – Hooke's *Micrographia* (1665) being an important source for 'The Last Instructions to a Painter' – this must have been a hard and very uncomfortable new reality. In the eyes of men like Glanvill and Parker, you could not be a Dissenter and a natural philosopher at the same time.

On the same day that Bramhall's work was recorded in the Stationers' Register, Buckingham's play *The Rehearsal*, his satirical attack on D'Avenant, Dryden and their heroic drama, was also listed (it had first been performed on 7 December of the previous year). The appeal of Marvell's pamphlet was rooted in its hilarious fusion of satirical drama and ecclesiastical controversy – an irreverent subversion of religious propriety that was guaranteed to produce titters, or outrage. Marvell's editors see the source of his chosen technique in John Owen's objection to Simon Patrick's use of Aristophanes to ridicule Nonconformists, and Parker's contrary suggestion that Ben Jonson's anti-Puritan drama would have been a more appropriate model.[19] Behind this still lay the Marprelate tradition: 'Martin Marprelate' was the anonymous Elizabethan Puritan who had used the humanist jestbook mode to abuse the bishops in the name of Presbyterianism in the late 1580s and early 1590s.[20] But Marvell's choice of Buckingham's play as a satirical sounding board, which is densely and playfully alluded to and echoed throughout the text, can also be seen as a form of appropriate praise or signalling of affiliation, just as Marvell's Cromwellian poetry uses ideologically appropriate poetic models. Marvell was exploiting the love of wit that prevailed in Buckingham's circle, which included the King, who certainly thought that some of the bishops deserved to be mocked. In doing so he was broadening the appeal of the tolerationist position he defended, and took discursively and hence ethically a very different line from the gentler style adopted in most of the pro-toleration tracts: John Humfrey's *A proposition for the safety and happiness of the King and kingdom, both in church and state* (1667), John Corbet's *A Discourse of the Religion of England* (1667) and Sir Charles Wolseley's *Liberty of conscience upon its true and proper grounds* and *Liberty of conscience the magistrates interest* (both 1668), in addition to Owen's *A peace-offering in an apology and humble plea for indulgence and liberty of conscience* and *Indulgence and toleration considered* (both 1667). Owen explicitly disapproved of the use of satire, and in that respect proved himself to be in line with Puritan objection to ad hominem calumny.[21]

Parker's attack was vigorous, acute and should not be underestimated. In several works before his preface to Bramhall he cumulatively established a powerful and coherent dismissal of Puritanism, republicanism and libertinism. But this time he was in effect attacking the King as well as leading courtiers, and the aristocratic defenders of Nonconformity. In this respect, Marvell had to respond to a controversialist who had exposed himself to a serious charge of disloyalty. There must also have been a personal motif: it was spectacularly galling to see an ex-Puritan one knew changing sides, and in such biliously offensive public rhetoric, a topic that would particularly vex Marvell.

The Rehearsal Transpros'd is extremely learned. It is now understood that the huge range of works cited in the text was due to Marvell's access to the Earl of

Anglesey's library, which he used extensively at this time. As we saw earlier, Anglesey had moved back into the King's confidence in the early months of 1672. So there was much more than mere association with some of the leading peers in favour of Nonconformity, such as Wharton and Carlisle, with whom he had already worked. The hurry to finish the piece in time for Parliament was eased by the postponement on 17 September from 17 October 1672 to 4 February 1673, and it would seem that in the following month Marvell assembled his satirical response. If he was using Anglesey's library, part of it was not where we usually locate it, in his house at Drury Lane in Covent Garden. Marvell had returned from the country on 29 October, and he must surely have been working on it before his return, so the library, or at least part of it, is more likely to have been in the house of his country estate at Bletchingdon in Oxfordshire, which he had owned since 1666. Production began in early November, and rapidly, with possibly as many as three presses at work on the book, which would have meant that it was ready to be bound in a fortnight or so, and could therefore have appeared before the end of the month.[22]

In Buckingham's *The Rehearsal*, Dryden (and D'Avenant) appears as the buffoon Mr Bayes, and Marvell's intention is to show that Parker and Bayes 'do very much Symbolize' each other. The dramatic framework allows Marvell to make the vagaries of ecclesiological animadversion acceptable to those who would normally prefer the stage, the coffee houses or the court. While claiming to be led anarchically astray by the 'rambling' and 'perpetual maze' of Parker's discourse, Marvell organizes his attack into three sections: the first a discussion of Bramhall's anti-Puritan idea of a single church, the second an analysis of Parker's *Discourse* and his *Defence*, and the third a huge exploration of church–state relations in the reign of Charles I. The middle section makes a mockery of Parker by reducing his thought to six main points, and then by showing how his two different works are at odds with each other, while also allowing John Owen, in the shape of Owen's text, to answer Parker back. Owen was involved in the material production of the book too, despite his objections to satire: perhaps in order to safeguard Marvell's identity, he was present at the printing shop to make proof corrections.

Parker's preface, unlike his later riposte to Marvell, is at least initially compellingly vitriolic. Later on, Marvell would be able to expose the failure of Parker's wit. Here Parker distils the essence of unpleasantness and Marvell knew it for what it was. He also knew he had to answer back. Parker chose to mock Owen's language as a form of debased heroic chivalry. This is perhaps not surprising, given the love of the romance genre by Bramhall's generation of Royalists, and the rise of mock-heroic anti-Puritan satire, most influentially Samuel Butler's long poem *Hudibras* (1663). Indeed, we have already seen the extent to which this register was embedded in Marvell's own verse of the 1640s and 1650s.[23] But now Marvell had a ready hook on which to hang an attack on Parker.

The Rehearsal was written in 1664 but its first performances were severely delayed by the great plague that closed the theatres.[24] Its first performance was on 7 December 1671. The original anti-hero, Bilboa, a parody of Robert Howard, was refashioned after 1667 to make Bayes, still principally a reflection of Dryden, also a composite of Arlington, all four of the Howard brothers, Thomas Killigrew, Robert Stapylton and Marvell's old literary target D'Avenant. After reading the play, the modern reader might be surprised to learn of its popularity (it was constantly in repertory for over a hundred years), and that it became the most influential of the sub-genre of rehearsal plays. Emptiness was of course one of Buckingham's themes (Mr Bayes has written a plotless and hence in a sense a contentless play that has meaning only in terms of a series of discontinuous heroic and romance conventions), and Marvell rescues Buckingham's farce by giving it vital content in the context of the toleration controversy. That sense of discontinuity might have been imparted by the fact that the play was a collaborative effort. Buckingham employed several writers to help him: Martin Clifford, Thomas Sprat and Samuel Butler. As evidence of rehearsal, the play is misleading, since it relies upon Buckingham's knowledge of French theatrical practice: Mr Bayes is an amateur and lower class, both elements that were inconsistent with English Restoration stage practice. The play's erroneous characterization of rehearsal was actually taken for fact (unlike their French counterparts, English actors did not engage in endless repeated rehearsal).[25] Dancing masters were usually hired to instruct actors in dancing, but in The Rehearsal Mr Bayes exasperatedly teaches his actors, and this is because the part of Bayes was played by the greatest of Restoration actors John Lacy, also a dancing master. Lacy had been a soldier during the Civil War, so that his very presence was doubly ironic in the heroic drama of the period. He had recently acted the part of Almanzor in Dryden's Conquest of Granada (1670), a self-made soldier who becomes a national leader. The echoes of these roles must have come down in the play, just as Bayes himself represents mock-heroic deflation, and just as rebellion and deposition are also represented as farce, including a 'snuff' scene where all on stage kill each other.

Marvell's The Rehearsal Transpros'd takes from this cosmopolitan dimension, using the play to facilitate rich and humane prose satire. Buckingham took considerable pains to teach the actors the precise manners and gestures he wanted mocked. The force of the play lay in how good the acted mimicry was. Buckingham himself was known to be a good mimic, and so in his verse was Marvell. Indeed, Buckingham never attacked the idea of rehearsal itself, and it was this that led many to see aspects of the Duke in Bayes himself. Marvell builds on this structure, pointing to the fact that both bishops and actors were in the habit of 'exposing' and 'personating' the Nonconformists, in line with the fashion for imitating the sermon styles of different confessions.[26] Where Parker lists as great wits several bishops as well as Raleigh and Bacon, Marvell subverts in appropriately theatrical terms by adding Richard Tarlton, the clown of Shakespeare's theatre, who becomes another figure for Parker himself (a fool for princes or, more appositely and snidely, prince-bishops).[27] Marvell imagines Parker's statue standing next to that of King James in the Exchange, in a niche left vacant by the removal of Charles I's statue in 1649. Not only is Parker in Marvell's view a fool, he is also presumptuous, and, like Charles I, he could also be removed.[28]

Marvell's greatest misgiving about Samuel Parker was his view that the magistrate should have complete control over the beliefs of subjects. Liberty of conscience in Parker's opinion should not or did not exist; anyone claiming it did was the victim of a dangerous illusion. In contrast Marvell offers 'authorities' as his witnesses and sources of guidance: in addition to published books, the very channels of public communication that constituted the 'public sphere' of Restoration England: the gossip and hearsay, some of it reliable, some of it not, that coursed through the coffee houses.[29] Conscience and public opinion existed for Marvell. Parker's view, as relayed by Marvell, is made to seem at one point consonant with Hobbes: that order is preserved by an earthly sovereign power determining exactly how meaning and significance in language are to be understood.[30] Marvell's reply is that the history of variant spellings and interpretations proves such authority impossible to sustain.

With such an explosive powder keg on his hands, Marvell had to be very careful. Some of the figures he attacked were left anonymous in order to protect himself, so that the reader had to use hints to work out who they were – which was of course part of the fun of reading the text. However, the recently or not so recently deceased were treated to open mockery, and sometimes, as in the case of Laud, this was delivered in a back-handed way, since ostensibly in Marvell's text, Laud was praised. The brunt of Marvell's satire was determined exposure of the power-hungry pretensions of the bishops, a tendency he saw as beginning in the third and fourth decades of the century. In other words, Marvell's text contains a version of what has become known as the 'rise of Arminianism' thesis: that under the patronage of Archbishop Laud, the English Arminians prospered, and in return for their success were loyal to strong royal and episcopal authority. (They rejected Calvinist predestination theology, preferring to believe in the exercise of human free will in matters of salvation; at the same time, their idea of ecclesiastical power was extremely authoritarian.) Marvell notes the schism threatened by Richard Montague's *Appello Caesarem* (1625), which was ordered burned by the House of Commons after its denunciation by Archbishop Abbot. In Marvell's view, Parker elevated loyalty to King and church over salvation.[31] Marvell had known two of the chief exponents on both sides of the Arminian controversy at Eton, Francis Rous, the great Calvinist politician, and John Hales, who had been at the Synod of Dort. As we saw earlier, Hales represented to Marvell the acceptable face of Arminian theology, without the ecclesiastical bigotry and authoritarianism that came with it in the English church (Parker would later challenge Marvell's account of Hales). Indeed, in a history of English established religion that belongs to the 'anti-priestcraft' tradition, Marvell argued that the English Arminians had appropriated a theology that had originally been put to far different purposes in Holland, the country of its origin, and used it as the official ideology of an English 'papacy'.[32] Marvell's line may well connect to his father's own views of the matter.[33]

It is not long before Marvell builds this into an attack upon authoritarian bishops by using highly relevant forms of comparison. Parker, he claims, wants to elevate the liturgy and the published explanation of it into such widely accepted terms that they will be a universal language of the kind debated by the intellectuals of the Royal Society.[34] Far better to have the sort of divine who explains in his sermons the kinds of disputes over definitions that have led to a history of difference, and indifferentism, in the church. Marvell's cited example was Nathaniel Hardy (d. 1670), the Archdeacon of Lewes and Dean of Rochester.[35] The considered reflection that Marvell imagines is the preserve of the universities, and, he says, is ignored by the bishops, who take their pattern from the 'Pedantry of Whipping' of the schoolmasters, or, before them, the cannibals.[36]

It is not abstract political theory that exercises Marvell in *The Rehearsal Transpros'd* so much as practical observations that are directly connected with the disasters of 1667. In this context, he lambasts Parker for preferring in Latitudinarian style moral theology over the theology of grace, and then further exposes hypocrisy when Parker maintains that debauchery is a better and even more tolerable evil than religious difference or heresy.[37] In a passage that looks back to the anti-Clarendon satires, and reflects Miltonic thinking on civic or republican vigour, moral decay and luxury are offered as the causes of national defeat. It is easy in this context for Marvell to represent Parker as a tyrannical Roman emperor, with deft historical parallels to instances of tyranny in the Roman historians, like Suetonius, or even later imitators of classical tyrant portrayals, like Shakespeare in *Richard III*.[38] Perhaps, Marvell thought, Parker would like to put Nonconformists into galleys as rowing slaves: after all, the King had acquired two galleys in 1671 to patrol the Straits of Gibraltar against Islamic pirates. It is important that Marvell praised merchant communities and activity in this respect (he was after all representing one in Parliament, and merchants were his kinsmen) against Parker's charges that trading leads to sedition and heresy. This should be coupled with Marvell's observations on the advantageousness of popular restraints on various monarchs in Europe, all of which point to the fact that princely power should not be unlimited.[39]

To this extent, Marvell is advocating a transformation of the Restoration polity. He may not have been ostensibly advocating a radical transformation, and certainly his critique never extended to the millennial and apocalyptic language of the sectarians.[40] Nonetheless, he clearly thought that the magistrate's power to interfere in matters of belief was limited, and that the extent of religious (or other) speculation allowed to the individual was extensive. In this he lines up not only with Owen, but also with Humfrey and Wolseley. One would also expect to find the economic liberalism of republicans like Slingsby Bethel, given his Yorkshire mercantile connections, but one does not.[41] Similar extensiveness might be claimed for the other more profound or original aspects of the pro-toleration argument: that it made the kingdom more secure and was hence in its interest, and would establish the proper 'balance' therein; that there should be a separation of church and state (a persecuting magistrate being contrary to nature). However, it is hard to see here something like William Penn's idea of freedom of conscience as a fundamental birthright, or that liberty of conscience was necessary for the progressive recovery of religious truth.

In fact, Marvell's initial focus was on writing – the enormities as he saw them of Parker's style; and he played upon the fact that Parker had promised, after his two earlier defences of episcopacy, to be quiet. Not being quiet, he deserves the most appropriately witty mockery. Thus, picking up on Parker's charge of Owen's 'whining', Marvell shows Parker himself to be guilty of what in Guarini's 'whining' Italian is 'translated' ('transpros'd', even) from the irresistibility of sinning to the irresistibility of writing. He cares about style to the detriment of theology.[42] Parker is likened to a howling wild animal, an exponent of the 'Rhetorick of Barking' and fits of spitting. Later on, his style is seen as the symptom of a mental illness, like swellings on the skin or even buboes. Or he is the alchemist of railing. Marvell's tactic of portrayal has been traced to Milton's likening of Salmasius to a werewolf in his *Defence of the English People*, and here Marvell is signalling his affiliation with the elder poet. Such a 'parallel allows Marvell to suggest that Parker is digging up the dead bodies of those hanged for regicide in order to serve them up to the King. The rhetorical ploys of Milton and Marvell are at one: to combat superstition by including and exposing to derision an object of superstition.'[43] It is to Owen's credit, argues Marvell, that he has answered Parker only once, and then soberly ('with his *Hat*, or with *Mum*'), and without raising his eyebrows while speaking.[44] Then Marvell moves hilari-ously into accusing Parker in his Preface of setting up Bramhall as fit for the fashion of the times: he means not only the caps of the bishops but also the extravagant wigs of Restoration women. Tucked into this is a charge of Parker's effeminacy. He is likened by Marvell to the Duchess of Newcastle, the prolific author known for her extravagant appearance.[45] Yet in his discourse Marvell returns immediately to dwell on Parker's further objection to the printing press in what has often been seen as a crucial analysis of the relationship between the invention of printing and Reformation habits of mind. Parker is a dull wit compared with the poetic mocker of the Puritans, Samuel Butler, who, claims Marvell, would have been even more effective in satirizing the bishops.[46]

It is worth pointing out that Marvell reworks his own poetic imagery in his polemic. Parker is accused of representing Bramhall as in a distorting mirror, just as Damon the Mower, after the Cyclops Polyphemus, saw his own distorted image in a scythe blade. Like the Dutch sailors who in drunkenness try to carve each other as if they were the ancient sculptor Deinocrates (see

'The Character of Holland', l. 94), sculpting Mount Athos into the figure of a man, the bishops praised by Parker have inordinate and unworkable aims. These unrealistic ecumenical goals are as unrealizable as the attempts to drive canals through the Isthmus of Corinth or to connect the Red Sea and the Mediterranean (so it was thought at that time), and this figure of division looks like the opposite of the figure of unity that Marvell sees between England and Scotland in 'The Loyal Scot'. Parker's elevation as Archbishop Sheldon's chaplain is described in terms of the soul's sense of vertigo at being trapped in the upright body in 'A Dialogue between the Soul and the Body', one of several instances of a reworking of the poetry in the prose already noted by Marvell's editors.[47] In other words, the works of prose controversy share their vision with the poetry, and this is highly significant.

When *The Rehearsal Transpros'd* appeared, it was immediately praised for its wit, and it changed the way in which controversy was conducted; it is a watershed text. Even Catholics admired its arguments, the Earl of Castlemaine using it as a means of attacking the Anglicans.[48] *The Rehearsal Transpros'd* may have been timed to appear at the start of the Parliament of October 1672 but this was prorogued. The pamphlet was nonetheless printed and appeared towards the end of November. The second edition was, however, seized in the press at John Darby's works on 2 December and censored by L'Estrange's agents.[49] Darby had printed the first edition; now he printed the second for the publisher Nathaniel Ponder. Ponder complained to Anglesey, who then met with both Ponder and L'Estrange at the same time. Anglesey protected Ponder by allowing the book to appear, although some alterations were made by L'Estrange, some of them softening the attack on Laud and Parker. Anglesey alleged the personal involvement of the King, who is supposed to have said 'he will not have it supprest, for Parker has done him wrong, and this man has done him Right'.[50] L'Estrange also conceded that Ponder's propriety had to be protected, which made publication inevitable. Nonetheless, in Anglesey's presence L'Estrange tried to gain the absent Marvell's consent to the changes, including giving an accurate place of publication, and indeed revealing the author. The Stationers' Company clerk, George Tokefield, refused to enter it, even after L'Estrange's and Anglesey's personal intervention, which meant that Ponder had to print a different title page in order to make the already distributed first edition saleable, and to appear to be censored. But it was not: this was noticed and the second edition lost its licence. Further negotiation later in December resulted in a second licence being granted, even for an edition with the imprint so disliked by L'Estrange. But some uncensored sheets for this edition found their way into the bindings, which meant that there were some partially uncensored editions available.

Contemporaries noted this confusion, which added to *The Rehearsal Transpros'd's* notoriety. Benjamin Woodruffe wrote to the Earl of Huntingdon that he could not recommend *The Rehearsal Transpros'd* but everyone was reading it: "'tis called the *Rehearsall* transprosed. it hath beene stopt from spreading, but is againe allowed to be brought.'[51] Yet Ponder the publisher was happy to appeal to L'Estrange in order to have John Winter's pirated edition of the first uncensored edition suppressed. Ponder, L'Estrange's assistant Richard Jefferys and John Darby raided Winter's house in Cock Lane and seized sheets of the duodecimo edition (so Darby's wife would later testify on 24 January).[52] Despite the support of Anglesey and Shaftesbury, who had been made Lord Chancellor on 17 November, the government (notably Arlington) pressured the printer and publisher, while Marvell himself was targeted: the government was desperate for someone publicly to avow Marvell's authorship; they knew very well he was the author. Marvell would claim that *The Rehearsal Transpros'd* was deemed a theological book so that it could be more readily prosecuted, and that Parker 'procured that I should be asked by good Authority whether the *Rehearsal Transpros'd* were of my doing, which I under my hand avowed'.[53]

There's a long tradition of disparaging Marvell's prose satire, in the face of its evident contemporary popularity. 'Marvell's prose satire is learned, witty, occasionally enlivened by flashes of vigorous language and vivid metaphor, but it lacks the immediacy, pace, rapid clarity and narrative invention of Swift.'[54] But it was none other than Jonathan Swift who admired its wit, and who said that long after Parker was dead, *The Rehearsal Transpros'd* would be read and admired.[55] Moreover Marvell and Swift share the technique of having the narrator or speaker voice the opinions under attack, a quintessentially Swiftian characteristic that has its origins in earlier heresiography such as that of Thomas Edwards.[56] *The Rehearsal Transpros'd* commends itself by its explosive, daring, flagrantly disrespectful yet funny humour, and that for its contemporary audience endorsed the spirit of toleration by broadening the range of human experience usually available in theological writing. The conversation within the coffee house is present in the text as an authority, with enough apparent verisimilitude to imply that such conversations really took place.[57] The implications in the innuendo bubble infectiously in the reader's mind as an endless source of pleasure. All the jibes (such as the use of Italian) originate in Parker's text, so that he can be said to be responsible for them.

If Bramhall is made to be effeminate, Parker is a sexual travesty. His energetic verbal superabundance is complicit with a sexual intemperance, so Marvell suggests: he is the slave of a mistress as well as a bookseller, the child of his invention inseparable from the work of his loins. Later on, his overblown rhetoric makes him a lover of Bishop Bramhall ('he should make a dead Bishop his Mistress'). His love of uncontrolled discourse makes him an enthusiast, the very kind of Puritan he wishes to attack, and the climax of his pleasure is not to be hidden from public view. Indeed, in a parody of Aretino, Marvell has Parker running naked and erect down the street, a phallic travesty of Archimedes, perhaps with more water to displace: 'But there was no holding him. Thus it must be and no better, when a man's Phancy is up, and his Breeches are down; when the Mind and the Body make contrary Assignations, and he hath both a Bookseller at once and a Mistris to satisfie; Like Archimedes, into the Street he runs out naked with his Invention.'[58] Picking up on a common Restoration theme, heroic boasts are indicative of unbounded priapic energy. Elsewhere, we glimpse Parker as a sexual deviant, a sadist deriving sexual pleasure from the punishment he wreaks on Nonconformists: 'down with their breeches as oft as wants the prospect of a more pleasing *Nudity*'. Taking this pathology further, Marvell sees that this attitude may have an educational root. Parker had formerly been under John Owen's sway when the latter was Vice-Chancellor of Oxford. Now in the driving seat in the Restoration, Parker can transfer his abuse to Owen, to say nothing of the spy networks that Marvell associates with this persecutory attitude.[59]

In all of this, the concentrated attack on Parker must have required many hours poring over lengthy, complicated ecclesiological pamphlets. One is tempted to relate Aubrey's comment that Marvell was fond of a bottle of wine to this intense animadversion.[60] There is a hint in *Mr Smirke* (1676) of long writing sessions, the wit induced, Jonson-like, by more than a single glass of wine: 'for the good news, Mr Exposer, I will give you four Bottles (which is all I had by me, not for mine own use, but for a friend upon occasion)'.[61]

Whatever the circumstances, *The Rehearsal Transpros'd* is an impressive document precisely because in his derogation of Parker Marvell articulated himself: he poured his own identity into the pages of his satire in an uninhibited way. During the course of ecclesiological and political discussion we are given many fragments of autobiography and many components of poetic identity. And by focusing on the ethical standing of a man as a mere citizen in a community, as opposed to a cleric, Marvell had relocated the place of the clergy in society. Part of this had already happened but Marvell was no longer a member of the church even though he could write in a dazzlingly well-informed way about it. *The Rehearsal Transpros'd* was one of a very few texts that used scurrilous wit to change for ever the way in which sacred matters and sacred history would be used.

It would have been a distraction while *The Rehearsal Transpros'd* was being assembled and printed for Marvell to persevere with Frowd and hence to try to finalize the agreement between him and Hull on the lighthouses. On 8 November Trinity House indicated to Marvell that Angell was apparently stealing a lead on Frowd. Despite the fact that he found Frowd's slowness insupportable Marvell managed to frustrate Angell's bid for support at Deptford Trinity House by dining there and engaging in a debate in late November. While the merchants of Trinity House were more interested in gaining convoy protection for their ships from Dutch attack, and had Marvell consulting Sir Jeremy Smith about how this might be obtained, the MP was amused to report on 2 January that Frowd was so frustrated that it seemed Hull and Deptford Trinity Houses could combine to set up a series of lighthouses. Hull Trinity House was happy to learn that Angell was not being supported by their brothers in Deptford, and once again they were happy to wait while the war took its course.[62]

Wit in Crisis

Now *The Rehearsal Transpros'd* may have been permitted to circulate by force of powerful people, including the King, but there were many interests against it. Ponder was the enemy of the Stationers' Company which spared no effort.[63] On 15 January 1673 Darby the printer was forced by the Stationers' Company to dismantle one of his three presses. With the new session of Parliament looming Arlington pressured the Company to control the presses. In response, five days later, the Stationers consulted three times at Whitehall about *The Rehearsal Transpros'd*. Ponder was threatened with prosecution for debt and moneys owed from published English stock to which the Company had the copyright. The Secretary of State Henry Coventry even interrogated L'Estrange, and it was here that the government learned about the unlikely collusion of L'Estrange, Ponder and Darby. This was confirmed in a further testimony of Darby's wife Joan given on the 24th. Ponder himself was examined the next day, and testified that John Owen was to the best of his knowledge the only person to have seen the proofs of *The Rehearsal Transpros'd*, while acknowledging Shaftesbury as well as Anglesey as among the book's supporters.

With no declaration from Marvell that he was the author of *The Rehearsal Transpros'd*, Parliament met on 4 February. It was business as usual. The MP for Hull was indeed named on the 7th as usual to the Committee of Elections and Privileges, but on the same day *A Common Place-Book out of the Rehearsal Transpros'd* was advertised, pointing out that the author of *The Rehearsal Transpros'd* would now be preoccupied by weighty matters of state, and asking angrily what the son of a vicar was doing insulting Archbishop Laud.[64] The anonymous author saw Marvell as a secular invader of ecclesiastical privileges, and the most talented politician and orator of the remnants of the 'Good Old Cause', citing further his links to Owen and to Milton. The tradition of reference to Marvell as a jesting 'merry Andrew' begins here. Private correspondence confirms that rumours of Marvell's identity as author were spreading widely. On 19 February, the Hartlibian and Royal Society fellow John Beale, although he had certainly prevailed within the church during the Protectorate and harboured millenarian and prophetic beliefs, denounced Marvell in a letter to the hard Royalist man of letters Christopher Wase who in April 1669 had been appointed historiographer in the office of Sir Joseph Williamson, the Secretary of State. Beale, writing in Yeovil to Wase in Oxford, treats Marvell as a despoiler of learning, 'who deservs to be brought on his Knees in that house where he sits; and from thence to be sent to O Cs quarters, since apparently he justifies that foule cause. And, if the Universityes would now bestirre themselves, as they ought to do, I doubt not, but they might make Mervell an example, for a terror to others. But common fame doth promise nothing of Spirite, Resolution, or Activity, or yet of Conduct, from such men.'[65] Beale thought that the English lacked the vigour, self-discipline and inventiveness that was serving their enemies the Dutch so well, while Wase, in addition to translating Greek and Latin texts, and writing the recent history of France, was gathering information to disprove that Hobbesian view that grammar schools were sources of social dissent. At this juncture Marvell looked like a counter-example, displaying nationally destructive disobedience.[66] Yet looking back on this period from a few years in the future Gilbert Burnet was sure that *The Rehearsal Transpros'd* and *The Rehearsall Transpros'd: The Second Part* were the wittiest books on the market, and that when the King read them, though not a great reader, he could not put them down.[67]

Under pressure from the Anglican consensus that threatened in Parliament to deny him the supply he wanted, Charles withdrew the Declaration of Indulgence on 8 March. For 'the Price of Money' (i.e. in order to secure the supply) he began to realign himself with the Anglican interest. At the end of March a Test Act was passed, which enabled Roman Catholics to be removed from public office.[68] While the Supply Bill became law on 26 March, Anglesey's attempt to introduce a bill that would exempt Protestant Dissenters from the reinforced penalties failed: an adjournment cast the Bill into limbo, just when the Commons had expressed anxiety about a clause introduced in the Lords enabling the King to suspend statutes when the Parliament was in recess (it looked too much to them like the old Declaration of Indulgence). In fact, although the Declaration was revoked, the licences that had been purchased were not, and although some JPs tried to discount them, they were regarded in law as still standing.

Meanwhile, the economic duress that Marvell had feared would be caused by the supply measures began to bite. While he was preoccupied with committees concerned with parliamentary representation for Durham, the prevention of moor-burning in Yorkshire and the north, and the improvement of London's streets and sewers, the Corporation of Hull had received a petition from Hull and York merchants with regard to the effects of the farming of wine duties: they were losing money in extra duties to a monopoly.[69] Members of the Corporation in turn wrote to their MPs. In this context Hull Trinity House expressed its concern to Marvell and Gylby that the proposed Spurn lighthouse be understood as the most significant upcoming expenditure.[70] On 5 April, however, Marvell counselled prudent delay in a further letter to his kinsman Edmond Popple.[71] There were communication worries too, since Marvell was also asked to represent the Corporation and the merchants to the Postmaster General: in fact he talked to Colonel Roger Whitley the Deputy Postmaster on 29 March, and further discussion was expected.[72]

The supply was of course needed especially to fight the war with the United Provinces. Here a new feature entered Marvell's life. The King's secret treaty with France, once known, would create much opposition where formerly there had been support. Sympathy would grow for Holland. In this respect, one of Marvell's earlier biographers, Thomas Cooke, reported in 1726 on the basis of documents he had obtained from the Marvell family that Marvell was very friendly with one Abraham Vanden Bemde, a naturalized Dutchman with Yorkshire associations living in Westminster. In March 1673, Vanden Bemde was seen lobbying MPs on behalf of the Dutch as he walked through Westminster Hall and the Court of Requests.[73] This kind of connection would become increasingly important in the following year.

But the main preoccupation of this year remained *The Rehearsal Transpros'd*, the response to which had been more extensive and sensational than could possibly have been imagined. Marvell was transformed by it in reputation and, perhaps more interestingly, in how he understood himself as an author. By the end of 1673, just before *The Rehearsall Transpros'd: The Second Part* appeared, he was held responsible for having started a new literary fashion, the 'Vitious sort of Buffoonry'.[74] He read and carefully considered the many attacks upon *The Rehearsal Transpros'd* and considered his response. To Sir Edward Harley he wrote on 3 May 1673 that he would wait for the advice of his friends (presumably he meant the influential ones) before replying to Parker, who had published his response, *A Reproof to the Rehearsal Transprosed* in May and was rumoured to be at press with it during the previous month, but the sense in this letter is that he was going to answer back anyway.[75] *The Rehearsall Transpros'd: The Second Part* would be a more coherently sustained attack on Parker, and Marvell responded to his critics by tightening up the standard of reference, especially to his opponent's work, which would appear in copious marginal notes. It would be a work in which Marvell began to entertain serious questions about the origins of government, with further implications too for fundamental religious questions.

The printed responses to *The Rehearsal Transpros'd* were written largely in kind, in a sense celebrating the wit that his had developed by writing in this mode, but suggesting that his use of it was directed to an improper end. Wit of course was a major way of guaranteeing a readership. Edmund Hickeringill's *Gregory, Father-Greybeard, with his Vizard Off* (advertised on 16 June) imitated *The Rehearsal Transpros'd's* humour across 331 octavo pages, but then claimed that Marvell's attack on Anglicanism and clerical supremacy was profoundly misguided.[76] There are frequent allusions to Samuel Butler's popular anti-Puritan and anti-Commonwealth satire *Hudibras*, as well as lines of verse that appear to be Hickeringill's own. Hickeringill would have known well many aspects of the positions that Marvell defended since, like Marvell, he had been a Commonwealth official. Indeed, he had even been a Baptist, as well as a JP and fortress commander in Cromwellian Scotland, and had had numerous difficulties in deciding a confession for himself before conforming in 1662 and occupying in 1664 a living in Colchester, where he epitomized the simple tenets of ceremonial worship and duty that typified the Restoration church.[77] The very first objection to *The Rehearsal Transpros'd*, Henry Stubbe's *Rosemary and Bayes* (?December 1672), was an attack on both Parker and Marvell. Stubbe was a prodigious scholar who had come up under Sir Henry Vane's patronage, and his

independent-mindedness was reflected in the charge that he was an atheist.[78]
The Transproser Rehears'd (6 May 1673)[79] lays out Marvell's crimes as a heinous
reintroduction of Commonwealth principles, while it is itself an epitome of
both the old and new Cavalier ethos. The tract was once thought
to be the work of the actor Richard Leigh, but is now attributed with more
certainty to Samuel Butler himself.[80] The transproser's false modesty is
regarded as a front for an aggressive Machiavellian republicanism not afraid of
distorting historical sources, with the help of John Rushworth's impeccable
Commonwealth documentation, in order to blame the High Church bishops
for harmful acts of statecraft. The discussion of John Hales is erroneous, Butler
claims, failing to disclose his denunciation of his treatise on schism, and his
return to the loyal Anglican fold, shepherded by Laud. In so doing, Marvell is
Milton in little:

> This Doctrine of killing Kings in their own Defence, you may safely vindicate
> as your own, it was never broacht before. And from such unquestionable
> Principles may we reduce your Account of the late War, p. 303. Whether it
> were a War of Religion, or of Liberty, is not worth the labour to enquire.
> Which-soever was at the top, the other was at the bottome; but upon consid-
> ering all, I think the cause was too good to have been fought for. Which, if I
> understand not amiss, is nothing but Iconoclastes drawn in Little, and
> Defensio Populi Anglicania in Miniature.[81]

Another jibe notes Marvell's paraphrase of Milton's *Areopagitica*.[82] The tract is
indeed among the most insightful and perceptive analyses of Marvell, as we shall
see in later pages. *S'too him Bayes* (May 1673) and *A Common Place-Book out of
the Rehearsal Transpros'd* (7 February 1673) were two further anonymous and as
yet unassigned traductions. The former, attributed by Wood to one William
Burton of Oxford, notes the poverty of the author of *The Rehearsal Transpros'd*,
while also drawing attention to his *politique* insights, and his view that Parker
deserved scorn for not anticipating the Declaration of Indulgence. It did not
command the respect of readers. But Marvell would save the greater portion of
his response to the longest and most substantial of the ripostes, Samuel Parker's
A Reproof to the Rehearsal Transprosed, which weighed in at a hefty 539 pages.
Commonwealth principles and insufficient scholarship were the charges against
Marvell found in the other attacks on *The Rehearsal Transpros'd*, but Parker,
affronted by his own treatment in *The Rehearsal Transpros'd*, did not stint in ad
hominem attack, incorporating a malign biography in part based on the information in *The Rehearsal Transpros'd* itself. He registered his tract on 15 March, and
Thomas Blount the antiquarian and lexicographer noted on 22 April in correspondence with Anthony à Wood that Parker was preparing his tract for the press
with the help of John Eachard, which was possibly a reference to Eachard's own
sneer at Marvell in *A Free and Impartial Inquiry into the Causes of that very great*

Esteem and Honour that the Non-conforming Preachers are generally in with their Followers (7 April 1673).[83] Despite Eachard's widespread use of wit, for which he was famous (his *Grounds and Occasions of the Contempt of the Clergy and Religion Enquired into* of 1670 was ranked by Anthony à Wood alongside *The Rehearsal Transpros'd* and Butler's *Hudibras* as among the most droll and buffooning books of the age), he objected to the recourse to jest in place of disputation, 'downright raillery' in place of 'sober words' and, a further instance of the decay of the times, saw its author as the victim of 'an impotent and enraged passion'.[84] Still, Blount thought that *The Rehearsal Transpros'd's* wit placed its author on safe ground.[85]

Before he had seen all of Parker's *Reproof*, for somehow he had seen (?proof) sheets of some 330 pages, Marvell wrote an important and candid letter to Sir Edward Harley, one of the great country MPs of this period, former Parliamentarian soldier and the father of Sir Robert Harley, later Earl of Oxford, leader of the Tory party during Queen Anne's reign.

The Harleys are mainly associated with their country seat of Brampton Bryan Castle, Herefordshire, which was subject to two sieges during the Civil War, and the defence of which was organized by Lady Brilliana Harley, Sir Edward's mother.[86] Marvell had been meant to meet Harley in London or Westminster, presumably at the end of the Parliamentary session and before he had retreated westwards. He had missed Harley in town and then had a further engagement at Stanton Harcourt in Oxfordshire, the home of another country MP, Sir Philip Harcourt. His interest in Harley was such that two years later he asked to be remembered to Harley, probably by the Presbyterian Thomas Jacombe.[87] Note that these residences were old: manors or castles, and not the vastly expensive renovations and new building associated with Wharton and Buckingham. Indeed, the Harleys and the Harcourts were and would be interconnected in domestic and political life for several generations. Harley certainly knew who wrote *The Rehearsal Transpros'd*, and its author confidently spoke to him on 3 May 1673 of the triviality of most of the replies published so far to *The Rehearsal Transpros'd*. Using terms that threw back at Parker the descriptions he had used of Marvell, he wrote that the *Reproof* was 'the rudest book, one or other, that ever was publisht (I may say), since the first invention of printing'.[88] Interestingly again, Marvell believed he was dealing with a 'noble and high argument', presumably a reference to ecclesiology and toleration (or is he being ironic again?). He did not see what he was doing as at all trivial, and indeed hoped that contemporary taste could cope with it: 'I will for mine own private satisfaction forthwith draw up an answer that shall haue as much of spirit and solidity in it as my ability will afford & the age we liue in will indure.' Yet he wanted his friends to say that Parker needed no reply (on the pretence that the *Reproof* was worthless, scurrilous and self-evidently ineffectual). In closing Marvell asked that letters to him be addressed to Richard Thompson (Marvell's merchant friend) in Woolchurch Market, London, a sure sign that he was still concealing his identity; this must have mattered now more than ever. It is surprising that a letter of this candid kind was even written in the circumstances. Perhaps it involved a calculated risk.

So what did Parker say? Within the first two pages of the *Reproof*, Parker had called Marvell a 'Gamester' (alluding to his confession of gambling in *The Rehearsal Transpros'd*, a biographical issue of which Parker makes much), ignorant (there was no 'fifth epistle' from Augustine to Marcellinus; Marvell was citing the first one), ridiculous, perverse and indecorous. He was not to be taken seriously, and was a 'yelper'. Why spend more than 500 pages on him then? Why claim that he is virtually treasonous for suggesting that it is possible the King might be assassinated, reflecting the old minimalist definition of treason – to imagine the death of the King?[89] Being essentially a fanatic, says Parker, Marvell can only assert, and he asserts merely the supremacy of the civil magistrate in all religious matters. Clearly, this latter allegation was the spur to Marvell's more serious consideration of the matter in his second reply to Parker. First of all, however, he had to put up with the weight of Parker's abuse, which becomes tedious in extensive repetition, and unconvincing as nouns and adjectives, fused under the imperative of invention, sit uneasily together: 'you trifling wretch'.[90] Nothing could be more true than Parker's own admission: 'I have been much more tedious than at first I design'd, and indeed than was necessary to correct such a Yelper.' In the broader and long-term reception of the controversy, Parker would find himself condemned by his own words: 'I must confess I have lost not only my labour but my Understanding.'[91] Nonetheless, he felt justified because he had been so abused, he said, by John Owen as well as by Marvell in *The Rehearsal Transpros'd*, which was an unprovoked attack, and he had to reply point by point. Parker is more pertinent when he wonders why Marvell asserts the magistrate's authority when he is so obviously on the side of history's rebels against such authority; the Münster Anabaptists are one of the best-known examples he cites. Parker's ground is that supreme magistracy in the English Reformation sense is incompatible with the respect of tender consciences: all must conform to one confession under a sovereign authority. Otherwise, the reformed state, English style, cannot work. He denies again that conscience exists – certainly in the sense that Marvell means it; it is a fiction, 'some little Spirit or Puppet Intelligence within you distinct from your selves', 'of no more certain signification than the clinking of a Bell, and that is as every man fancies'. At the very least, any Act that does not bind the conscience to obey it is no law. And since conscience is nothing but what a person chooses to think, it cannot be appealed to alone: there must be a principle behind its being invoked. To appeal to it thus means both everything and nothing, and conscience itself may as well be named by any of the passions. Marvell's invocation of John Hales gives Parker the opportunity to point up Hales's early associations with the Socinians and Socinus's own intentions of becoming a Nonconformist demigod like Calvin (bearing in mind that Owen himself accused Parker of Socinianism as well as popery).[92] For Parker, strong state authority is the great benefit of the English

Reformation vision against the harmfully divisive claims of popery and presbytery: 'when I asserted the Soveraign Power to be Absolute and Uncontroulable,
'tis apparent nothing else could be intended than that it is not to be controuled
by any distinct Power, whether of the Pope or the Presbytery (for they are the
only Rivals of the Princes of Christendome)'.[93] The experience of grace, claimed
Parker, must be visible in this world and coupled explicitly to morality: otherwise exclusively claimed grace, such as that of the Puritans, justifies anything,
and is an excuse for economic reliance on others, or even rapaciousness.

Behind this is Parker's sense, which many must have shared, that Marvell was
modelling *The Rehearsal Transpros'd* on the Martin Marprelate tracts of 1589–91
(see above, p. 239). It was a natural historical departure point for an articulation
of the insult that he felt he had suffered from Marvell: 'according to *Decorum*,
i.e. like a Buffoon; the very same Request word for word that *Martyn-Mar-
Prelate* has often put up to his Readers to be allowed the same freedom with his
Nuncka John the Arch-Bishop of *Canterbury*'.[94] Dryden would later call Marvell
the Marprelate of his time in the preface to *Religio Laici* (1681), and he probably
also saw John Eachard's *Free and Impartial Inquiry* (1673), from where he took
the charge against Marvell that since Parker could not be beaten in argument,
he had to be 'laughed and jested' out of his assertion.[95] The catch there of course
was that Parker and Marvell had known each other since at least the 1650s, both
being associated with the Commonwealth: 'Sir, you might have used this familiarity with me without all this ado, for I perceive we are so intimately
acquainted, that we have no doubt sometime heretofore either rob'd Orchards or
lampoon'd the Court together.' To this end, Parker had said that he would not
have minded at all had Marvell confronted him privately with his misgivings.[96]

In theological terms Marvell is guilty of indecorum, casting theology as
fable. Any tendency Parker had exhibited in this way in his earlier commentary on Bramhall was nothing when compared with Marvell's poetic imagination set loose on the Church of England.[97] This set of observations allows
Parker to dissociate Marvell from proximity to the King, whom, after all,
claims Parker, Marvell had presented as 'a *mad horse kicking and flinging most
terribly*'.[98]

Yet Parker was no wit, or at least few thought so at the time, and his writing
is extremely hard to read. He tried to imitate Marvell's humour, but his real
stylistic inflection is that of *gravitas*, and the latter does not sustain the former.
Sometimes he manages something rhythmically more energized:

> Thou Prevaricatour of all the Laws of Buffoonry, thou dastard Craven, thou
> Swad, thou Mushroom, thou Coward in heart, word, and deed, thou *Judas*,
> thou Crocodile, thus (though it were in thy greatest necessity) after having
> profess'd wit and rithm these fifty years, to snivle out such a whining submis-
> sion in publick is past all precedent of Cowardize from the Trojan war to this
> very day; but that thou shouldest do it of thy own accord and without any

provocation is more sneaking than the flattery of a Setting-dog. Thou shalt wear a Collar, and thy name shall be *Trey*.[99]

But Parker writes largely in a dead tone and makes it easy for Marvell to riposte. The defence of Bramhall is notably unsuccessful, degenerating to mere rebuttal without argument: Marvell uses 'Fanatique Malice and Impudence to bespatter the most worthy persons with such foul reproaches under profession of so much love and sweetness'.[100] And it seems so very lacking in wit simply to quote Marvell's ribald comments about senior clergymen and assume that the reader will be suitably outraged by the quotation alone: 'You see how little Execution is to be done upon the Church of *England* with the *But-end of an Arch-Bishop*, as you express it with equall Wit and Manners'.[101] Here he seems only able to capture some of Marvell's humour, without establishing his own authority either as controversialist or wit.

Nonetheless, the apology for Latitudinarianism, as Parker understood it, is appealing, compelling Marvell to answer the accusation of Parliamentarian and Commonwealth tendencies. For instance, on the savagery of Charles I: 'accuse him for turning his three Kingdoms into *one great Prison*, in so much that *many thousands of his Subjects* that had no mind to rot in Jails, *were constrain'd to seek another Habitation*'.[102] For Parker, Charles is a martyr, and his Royalist followers committed acts of martyrdom in his cause. For Parliament to assault royal sovereignty was the greatest act of absolutist government; Marvell's tract is part of an 'old War against Faction and Non-conformity'.[103] Parker's theology is also markedly different to the scriptural fundamentalism that Marvell adopts from the Puritan tradition: 'Now I doubt it will be found upon enquiry, that the design of the Church of *England* in her Reformation was to casheir all these Scholastick Innovations, and to retrieve the Old and Apostolical Christianity; and that the plat-form she propounded for her direction were not the decisions of the Schools, but the Holy Scriptures, and the four first general Councils'.[104] Parker also has to be credited for a very accurate understanding of Marvell's strategy: 'all your profest fooling either by way of Similitude or Rithm or Story; your playing upon single words, your confuting introductions and transitions, your smutty imaginations, your general and insolent censures, with abundance more of such bold and immodest stuff, that though it signifies nothing by it self, yet is almost enough to beat any modest man out of countenance by pure force of brow and confidence'.[105] To this should be added Parker's attack on Marvell's lack of breeding: growing up in Hull among cabin boys, and being once the master of a watch. At the heart of the dispute was a definition of reason. Marvell's use of humour was associated with an indirect approach and enabled Parker to accuse him of making no sense, of confusing the reader with twelve separate beginnings:

Away you trifling Wretch, talk you no more of Ecclesiastical Policy, and hereafter never pretend to any knowledge that pretends either to Reason or

Modesty! for had you any sense of the former, you would never have been so silly as to be so seriously scared at such an innocent and undeniable proposition; or any of the latter, you could never have been so impudent as to bray forth such a confident and heinous censure against it, as if it were notoriously evident without proof that it directly subverts all the Principles of Religion and Government. And therefore I would fain know in good earnest what your meaning was, in making your first onset upon this Grand Thesis? If you intended its Confutation, why have you not discharged so much as one semi-vowel of exception against it?[106]

Parker's scolding is tired enough in this example to include indecorous repetition.

Despite this, freedom of thought for Parker is a perversion of understanding, one that enables both religious radicals and philosophical libertines to unite in a dangerous alliance of irrationality: 'the Gnostick Fanaticks of old, and the *German* Anabaptists of late, that whenever *occasion* was pleased to be *debonair*, had this pretence always in ready pay to warrant any Rebellion and disobedience'.[107] There is also an innate violence that Parker sees in Marvell: a man who needs thuggery to survive: 'were your Fangs as good as your Throat the whole Order would in a very little time be torn and woried in pieces'.[108] It is, says Parker, and not without insight, all to do with parentage:

> For take but an Hunger-starved Whelp of a Countrey Vicar, and enter him in a Committee-Pack for plunder'd Ministers, and let him but once draw blood of the Church, and tast the sweetness of Ecclesiastical Sequestrations, and if ever after he get view of any regular Clergy-man, though an Arch-Bishop, he opens and pursues with all the rage of a Phanatick Blood-Hound.[109]

The threat of corporal correction in return is raised by Parker, who jokes that Marvell deserves the gentler correction of the stocks, even if Marvell considers himself too 'gentle' (i.e. in social rank) for them. Puritans like John Owen also take refuge, claims Parker, in the invocation of apocalyptic justice upon their enemies – a kind of irrational cowardice in his view, as well as a huge mistake.[110]

Parker was quick to see the print potential of *The Rehearsal Transpros'd* and how Marvell had so cleverly exploited it, picking up again on the metaphor from Milton of print as dragon's teeth: 'What think you now of a publick Tooth-drawer to wrench out its old ugly rotten teeth? there is no outfacing this printed black and white, and nothing could be more rashly and indiscreetly done than for you to attempt it.'[111] Marvell's neologisms were in Parker's view unacceptable from someone with a secretary's training.[112] Is the invocation of Julius Caesar meant to bring Oliver Cromwell to mind, to whom Marvell was indeed a secretary? The concern with print and with toleration must have triggered in Parker's head something he knew at first hand: that Marvell and Milton had been intimately associated in the Commonwealth. This means, alleges Parker, that Marvell can mean only one thing: 'if we take away some simpering phrases, and timorous introductions, your Collection will afford as good Precedents for Rebellion and King-killing, as any we meet with in the writings of *J. M.* in defence of the Rebellion and the Murther of the King'.[113] This makes Marvell as well as Milton part of the grand master plot of the revolution:

> Both these [the Parliamentarians] and the Zealots were excellent Tools of Sedition, but they were no more than Tools, the Master-workmen were the cunning and reserved Members of the Republican Faction. For it is plain enough, that all things were govern'd in both Houses by a Cabal of such as had from the beginning (as appeared afterwards) a design upon the alteration of the Government.[114]

In his defence, Marvell rebuts the allegation that Milton has helped him write *The Rehearsal Transpros'd*. Although Marvell suggests disingenuously that Milton has kept an expiatory 'retired silence' since the restoration of the monarchy, his analysis of Milton's gifts ('of great Learning and Sharpness of wit as any man'; Milton, he says, has lived 'ingenuously and Liberally') is a testimony to what will follow in relation to literary values.[115] There is an apparent reference by Parker to lines at the end of 'Upon Appleton House', which would betoken real familiarity with that body of Marvell's poetry that was as yet unknown to the reading public, and a plain allusion to that embarrassing incident of the correct way to address the Czar of Russia.[116] Marvell's wit, claims Parker, is a result of his foreign travels, which have corrupted his appetite and his mental faculties: he is far too sophisticated and confused for the plain-speaking Anglican Englishman. Marvell's poor ability to calculate (perhaps reflected in his gaming fortunes) is coupled with his inability to reason: to argue that debauchery permitted is a less serious crime than toleration. After all this, Marvell might rightly have felt skewered.

A less pugilistic but nonetheless critical view was supplied by the anonymous *Character of a Coffee-House*, published on 11 April 1673. Marvell's powers as a town wit are celebrated under the name of 'Merry Andrew', and with some acuteness. He has set the coffee houses ablaze with curiosity, so that they have become a bizarre zoo of wit, and he has done this anonymously so that he can enjoy the scene vicariously: 'The wax candles burning, and low devout whispers sometimes strike a kind of Religious Awe, whilst the modish Gallant swears so oft by Iesu, an Ignorant Catholick would take it for a Chappel'.[117] It is notable that this author knows that Marvell is a poet, and possibly also that he was part of the republican discussion group, the Rota:

> The Ingeniosi use it for an after Rehearsal, where they bring Plays to Repetition, sift each Scene examine every uncorrected Line, and damn beyond the fury of the Rota, whilst the incognito Poet out of an overweening affection to his Infant Wit, steals in muffled up in his Cloake, and sliely

Evesdrops like a mendicant Mother to praise the Prettyness of the Babe she
has newly pawm'd on the Parish.[118]

Likewise, Samuel Butler appears to know that Marvell was the author of 'An
Horatian Ode', 'The First Anniversary', and the Advice-to-a-Painter poems.
Butler only alludes obliquely to the Painter poems because of his association
with Buckingham: he cannot afford to reveal publicly the identity of those
involved in the campaign against Clarendon.[119]

Marvell's most potent suit was indeed his support of the King's policy of
indulgence, which presented Parker in particular with problems. How can he
argue against Marvell and avoid insulting the King's indulgent position, with
which, of course, he certainly did not agree? The answer was a series of statements that indirectly place the bishops as the true guides to the King. Hence the
praise of Calvin's policy of restraint on kings: 'the greatest thing that can be said
in Mr *Calvins* praise, is, that he was the first founder of that *Modern Orthodox*
Doctrine. That it is the duty of Subjects to moderate the licentiousness of Kings,
and to punish or depose them when they play the Tyrants, or wantonly insult
on the Common People.'[120] The King's thinking that leads to the Declaration of
Indulgence is made to seem well intentioned but not part of serious policy,
and is juxtaposed with the monstrous image of the King unwittingly playing
into the hands of the Presbyterians:

> They care not what becomes of King and Parliament and Kingdom too, so
> they may gratifie their own Pride and peevishness. Not that I believe they
> have all formed designs against the State, (they are most of them too simple
> to entertain thoughts so great) but yet they are easily acted by those that have;
> they are conceited and froward, and apt to pick quarrels and take offence at
> the present management of affairs, be it what it will.[121]

Moreover, in the political embarrassment that followed the Chatham raid of
June 1667, the Nonconformists seized the moment by reasserting the claims of
conscience against episcopal authority, and coupled this with the promulga-
tion of republican political ideology: a treacherous attempt to undermine the
church–state settlement.

While Parker worked away, important, long-term matters of state were being
determined. The Duke of York resigned all his offices in June, thereby
declaring his Catholicism, and on 20 September married by proxy in Modena
the devoutly Catholic Mary, Duchess of Modena, niece of Cardinal Mazarin.
He had declined to take the sacrament the previous Easter, which was the
occasion of a widespread scandal, not least because it came immediately after
the passing of the Test Act. The marriage was unpopular and reviled in
Parliament.[122] Mary arrived in England on 12 November.

Clifford's Catholicism had become public in May, when his coach overturned on leaving Somerset House, revealing him in the company of a Catholic priest. Serious discontent on the matter of the war and the prospect of Catholic succession unsettled the Privy Council. When Parliament gathered in October, this turbulence increased as solutions to the disquiet and impasse were expected. Marvell's old adversary, Clifford, died on 17 October, possibly by suicide.

Shaftesbury learned of the secret clauses of the Treaty of Dover on 3 November (also the date of a letter sent to Marvell threatening violence against him if he published against Parker).[123] Six days later he was dismissed from the chancellorship and the Privy Council. The days of the Cabal were over; another direction in government would be taken. Shaftesbury moved immediately into opposition, and the die was cast for the rise of the Whigs, with as backdrop the widespread mood of fierce anti-Catholicism, and growing hostility to France and to the war with the Dutch.

The Rehearsall Transpros'd: The Second Part appeared in December; Ponder attempted to pre-empt piracy by issuing both an octavo edition and a duodecimo one, the latter featuring some authorial correction and nearly all surviving copies bearing the date 1674. By the end of the month it was circulating with ease and drawing much interest. It had been much anticipated: Thomas Blount knew that it was being searched for and heard a rumour in July that it was to be called 'a Whip for a Lambeth Ape'.[124]

The context of the political revelations makes *The Rehearsall Transpros'd: The Second Part* particularly apposite since the heart of the tract was a powerful if short passage on the origins of government. To what extent was it retrogressive and formed by the debates of the previous century? Or did it look forward to the theories of contract and consent that, in the pen of Locke, and under the aegis of the events of 1688–89, would dominate the following century? The Scottish Nonconformist Robert Ferguson was one controversialist who would use the arguments of *The Rehearsal Transpros'd* and *The Rehearsall Transpros'd: The Second Part* in his writing in the 1680s.[125] What is clear is that while Marvell might have been thinking these complicated matters through for some time, there can be no mistake that he finally provoked into expressing this synthesis by the Royalist and Anglican view of power that Parker set down in the *Reproof,* and especially in the final hundred pages where he gave an analytical account of the origins of the Civil War and the subsequent revolution.

Marvell began his statement by saying that the magistrate's power was there by divine right. Note that Marvell said 'magistrate' and not 'monarch', and within an admittedly long paragraph was undermining the authoritarian implications of this statement. The issue should never be debated, he said, because princes should exercise their power with a generosity inherited through the generations. This was clearly aimed at Charles and his own attempts to appear benign: by the 'third Life', Marvell means the reign of the third Stuart monarch. The service and revenue rendered by subjects to the King naturally produce 'tenderness' in the monarch towards them. Those who have governed by a 'sanguinary' course and have not adopted moderation have usually reached unfortunate conclusions for themselves as much as for their people. Then follows a series of natural and pastoral analogies that look similar to some of the Advice-to-a-Painter poems. 'The wealth of a Shepheard depends upon the multitude of his flock', and shepherds cannot hope to gain if they 'hare their People, driving them into Woods, and running them upon Precipices', all images potentially culled from the poetry. Later on, there is a similar analogy of magistrates as parents to their loving children the people. If early Christians were set apart by being persecuted by pagan magistrates, modern magistrates should follow suit. Christians are obedient, and so Christian magistrates undermine themselves when they persecute. These good relations are certainly put at risk when the church is corrupted by worldliness, as it was under Constantine.[126] Marvell's immersion in church history shows, and the resonances with current churchmen are clear. Earlier obsession with rites and ceremonies resulted in the simplicity of church services becoming a 'Mosaical rubbish', while they placed their dependants, such as their concubines, outside the secular law. And here magistrates have to clean up society or risk rebellion, which is unlawful, but may in these circumstances be unavoidable. In this respect, he alludes to the English Revolution, calling it a 'dismal effect'. Again, Marvell presents this as a natural process – rather like the idea of his friend the republican theorist James Harrington that society is subject to the same natural forces as the world of nature itself.[127]

The Rehearsall Transpros'd: The Second Part was carefully organized in other ways too, not least because Marvell understood that Parker had chosen not to engage him first in respect of the salient themes of toleration, conscience and the power of the magistrate. It began with a precise 'anatomizing' of Parker, explaining his outraged response to *The Rehearsal Transpros'd* as a medical condition caused by Marvell's tract, and in a manner that owed a lot to Rabelais's satirical method. It is as if Marvell picks up on the French comic genius, having previously used Cervantean mock romance to represent the bishops in the closing pages of *The Rehearsal Transpros'd*.[128] Parker has to be 'purged' of his unnatural 'heat' with the evangelical medicine of *The Rehearsal Transpros'd*, as Gargantua was purged by his author. Marvell confesses that he has made Parker sweat until he has vomited up the unpleasantness of the *Reproof*. Even at the end of his anatomizing, Marvell bewails, 'it hath been thus far the odiousest task that ever I undertook, and has look'd to me all the while like the cruelty of a Living Dissection, which, however it may tend to publick instruction, and though I have pick'd out the most noxious Creature to be anatomiz'd, yet doth scarce excuse or recompence the offensiveness of the scent and fouling of my fingers'.[129] The offensiveness of befouling and stench is very notable. The first section was followed by a long passage discussing the ethical position Marvell had decided to take in *The Rehearsall Transpros'd: The Second Part*, and how it was caused by Parker's own poor ethics of authorship, before an even longer disquisition on Parker's origins. Seriousness is treated deservedly (as we saw above), but where Parker prevaricates or is scurrilous, 'I shall treat him betwixt Jest and Earnest.'[130] Hence the image of Parker as a whale tossing the barrel that Marvell has thrown to him, and noting that he so mires himself in it that he renders himself caught. Although this image was used by Sebastian Münster in his *Cosmographia Universalis* (1559), it was Marvell's deployment that would eventually trigger Swift's eponymous image in *A Tale of a Tub* (1704).

Within all of this come a series of remarkable revelations of selfhood, more so than in *The Rehearsal Transpros'd*, and in particular personal states of mind and inclinations perhaps as revelatory as any statement elsewhere by Marvell about himself. He felt compelled to defend himself against Parker's questionings of his attack on the clergy when he himself was the son of a clergyman. It was, he said, precisely because he held the 'Sanctity of their function' in such regard that he persisted in the attack on their corruption. Yes, he was caustic to some extent in character: it was a necessary defence in a wicked world; it was, said Marvell, always necessary to carry some 'ill Nature' in one's pocket. In 1672, the *Philosophical Transactions* of the Royal Society reported that a viper's head could be swallowed as a preservative against a venomous snake-bite.[131] Perhaps it is the chemical hint in the reference to medicine that led Marvell to refer to his clerical family background as his 'extraction'. More significantly, in respect of the clergy's wives, he says (following Richard Hooker) that while he certainly did not worship them, neither did he utterly disrespect them, or consider them the worst clergymen's wives in the world. Does this imply a view that could be generalized to all women? It is after all the most equivocal and yet pointedly revealing statement about the clergyman's wife that immediately precedes these observations: '*if they come short* of other Women *in point of Efficacy, yet they have the advantage* of other Women *in point of Security*'.[132] There is also a level of disingenuousness in all of this since Marvell's self-confessions involve untruths. He says he did not know Parker personally until at least after 1668, perhaps even later, an assertion that is almost certainly untrue.[133] Later in *The Rehearsall Transpros'd: The Second Part*, there comes the better-known statement by Marvell that he knew nothing of Commonwealth politics until he became a disinterested politician in 1657, which in the light of the Cromwell poems is really not true at all.[134]

Marvell seems to have discovered more about Parker's background, if he was not aware of it already. In particular, he associates the future bishop with the unsavoury parts of London where he had himself once lived: Saffron-Hill in Holborn, Clerkenwell and Farringdon.[135] And Parker's father's career as a pro-Parliamentary judge is discussed, not least the offence he caused the House of Lords. Marvell suggests that Parker senior's pro-Engagement tract of 1650 was written in order to buy back favour. Parker himself was a greedy undergraduate, Marvell discovered, and splendidly Puritan in worshipping in the house conventicle of the laundress Elizabeth Hampton (at the command of a Presbyterian tutor he also lived on a diet of oatmeal and water and was known as a 'greweller'), even though this necessitated his moving from Wadham to Trinity College after the Restoration. These details are confirmed in Anthony à Wood's *Athenae Oxonienses*: one wonders if Marvell corresponded with Wood at this time; certainly access to Wood's knowledge may have been through John Aubrey, a friend of both men. Tellingly, one of Parker's greatest crimes was his betrayal of Milton, especially since he was a visitor to Milton's house near Moorfields in the early 1660s. It was actually in Milton's house in Jewin Street that Marvell and Parker first met.[136]

At any rate, Marvell's 'sharpness of Stile' was permitted by the circumstances (an ancient doctrine most famously expounded by Horace – *decorum personae*: the punishment suited the crime). Parker, Marvell writes, has a 'Ruffian-like stile', and Marvell is Robin Hood, or, in his own perception, Falstaff, robbing only those who have already stolen. Elsewhere, Parker is described scatologically as like the Dutch in Java, who on one occasion fired excrement to the great vexation of the Javanese.[137] The best kind of writing is naturally mature: 'the generousest wine drops from the grape naturally, without pressing, and though piquant hath its sweetness'.[138] This points to Marvell's *goût* for wine, but also connects convincingly to the sense of fullness in his greatest lyric poetry, although there has been a slippage in the reasoning: pleasant writing is not necessarily the preserve of all mature people. Marvell offers a serious attack on the ethical status of Parker's writing. An author who engages in such an attack on another's reputation must be very sure of his own reputation; otherwise he risks sacrificing his credit with his readers. Humility, says Marvell, is what is required but this is precisely what Parker does not offer: his writing is finally an offence to 'the bonds of Society', and without good cause Parker suffers an unfortunate metamorphosis himself, appearing as a satyr, with 'prick-ears, wrinkled horns, [and] cloven feet', one who will need to be hunted out of the neighbourhood 'thorow the woods with hounds and horn home to his harbour'.[139]

Reference to Killigrew and D'Avenant's plans for a trainee theatre or 'nursery' for actors gives yet one further indication of Marvell's understanding of highly relevant contemporary issues. And from here, Marvell drew in his tract on his colourful knowledge of city life. It was one thing for Marvell to admit gambling, quite another to have Parker as another gambler, increasing the stakes at every throw of the dice ('buttering' is the slang term used by Marvell), which is to say that he increases the level of insult, and needs to be answered with each successive publication. Exploiting the licensing system for his own ends, Parker is presented as a card trickster who rigs the game in his favour.[140] Suddenly, the urban and the theatrical are amplified to become the high seas – Hobbes's state of nature on water – where Parker is a pirate of a special order: like Sir John Falstaff in Shakespeare's *I Henry IV*, he robs people of the goods they have already stolen. This is the image for what he had done in speaking so persistently ill of so many people: he was an 'open Pirate of other mens Credit', and Marvell does not even need an official licence to attack him. The six responses to *The Rehearsal Transpros'd* are likened to *Scaramuccios* – the stock figures of Italian farce, being given actual resonance in the spring and summer of 1673 with the visit of Tiberio Fiorilli's acting company.[141] In all of this, Marvell has located the church and its politics not in sacred space but in the feckless, highly insecure early modern urban melee. This is no longer merely ecclesiastical controversy.

It is clear that once *The Rehearsal Transpros'd* was out, Parker and Marvell also engaged in personal if indirect communication. Marvell claimed that he had warned Parker that further calumny against himself would reflect poorly on the chaplain, and Parker assured Marvell, perhaps in a letter, that he would not injure Marvell's reputation, only to establish what Marvell describes as machinery, first for searching out any hints concerning Marvell's activities, and then for establishing a 'Calumny Office by which he might hear and propound' as much anti-Marvell material as possible.[142] This set of perceptions readily feeds into Marvell's general view of ecclesiastical corruption.

Marvell was himself acutely aware of the relevance of his exchange with Parker to the operation of licensing and censorship. Parker, he claimed, exercised his influence in order to stop further publications that might defend *The Rehearsal Transpros'd*. He also abused his permission to publish by behaving like a licenser in such a way as to make libelling authorized. Parker's happy relationship with L'Estrange's own publishing strategies while Surveyor of the Press is evident here, and Marvell's image of Parker as an arsonist is telling: 'it looks too like a man that shall lay a train of Gun-powder, and then retire to some obscure place from whence after he has applyed his match'.[143]

While Marvell makes much of the importance of printed literature, and is decidedly against interference in book publishing, he also made use at crucial points of non-printed materials. Important in this was his friendship with John Rushworth, the former parliamentarian, journalist, historian and lawyer whom Marvell had known well since at least 1659 when they were both elected to the last Protectoral Parliament. Rushworth, like Marvell a north country man with connections to the Fairfaxes, was steadily releasing unpublished state papers, and Marvell clearly had the run of the unpublished materials at this time.[144] He quoted from a petition of the City of London against the right of the King to impropriate any subject's property.[145] At the same time, the cost of Parker's *Reproof* is presented by Marvell as a kind of financial burden on the established clergy, who were strongly encouraged to buy it, and the Nonconformists, by force of Parker's advertising, are virtually compelled to buy it.

We have noticed drama and controversial literature in *The Rehearsal Transpros'd* and *The Rehearsall Transpros'd: The Second Part*. It is also important to recognize that poetry was working virulently through Marvell's imagination

as he wrote the tracts. The *pièce de résistance* here is the extensive series of allusions to and quotations from Donne's 'Progress of the Soul', as metempsychosis
is used to show the changing shape of persecution from pamphlet to
pamphlet.[146] This is followed by the genealogy of the name Parker, an 'Upon
Appleton House' in reverse, although like it a combination of romance and
history. In a similar category would come the extensive allusions to Suetonius'
History of the Twelve Caesars, and the likening of Parker to Nero and Caligula,
and later on Julian. It has been conjectured that Marvell was using his own translation of Suetonius here.[147] Moreover, Marvell reveals the modernity of his scholarship, arguing for the importance of Grotius's novel annotations of the New
Testament, and later on the critical scholarship of Lipsius, the Scaligers, Vossius
and Selden.[148] It comes as wonderfully witty that Marvell should end this section
with an apparent revision of a nursery rhyme: '*Thou should'st have had a Silver
Stye,/And she her self have pigg'd thee by*.'[149] The method becomes highly auto-
biographical in a double sense. Following a hint in Parker, Marvell compares a
fantasy image of Parker presenting a medal commemorating the founding of the
English republic with a very royalist medal that D'Avenant was imagined, in a
poem by Sir John Denham, to have presented to some of those who rescued him
from his imprisonment.[150] The true nature of Parker is revealed: a turncoat of no
principles. At least D'Avenant was true to his cause. Denham was of course the
fictitious author of the second and third 'Advices', and Marvell probably arranged
at least in part to adopt such a disguise. Denham's later career permits the chance
of further vilification of Parker, since he was allegedly cuckolded by the Duke of
York and was also for some time temporarily insane.

Finally, after all the digression and different modes of argument and satire,
Marvell amusingly and scarily reaches a Rabelaisian conclusion. He tells the
story of a conjuror at the medieval Bohemian court who amused his monarch
by ingesting the king of Bavaria's trickster and spitting him up in a tub of water.
He refrained from swallowing the conjuror's shoes because they were muddy.
Just so, says Marvell, the stomach of his wit was stretched beyond conception
and was polluted by Parker's challenge: 'I have spit out your dirty Shoon.'[151]

But that is still not all, because one phrase in an early attack on *The
Rehearsal Transpros'd* makes an astonishing claim about Marvell's sexuality.
The Character of a Coffee-House (1673) vilifies Marvell for his coffee house wit,
and in doing so talks of the company he kept:

> By these Arts dexterously manag'd he engrosses a vaste Repute, The grave
> Citizen calls him shrewd man, and notable Headpiece, The Ladies (we mean
> the things so called of his acquaintance) vote him a most accomplisht
> Gentleman, and the Blades swear he is a Walking Comedy, the only Merry
> Andrew of the Age, that scatters Wit wherever he comes, as Beggars do Lice,
> or Muskcats perfumes, and that nothing in Nature and all that can compare
> with him.[152]

'The Ladies (we mean the things so called of his acquaintance)': the ladies look suspiciously like men, or does this mean women of no rank, or prostitutes? Samuel Butler likewise identified masculine deviance, which he put down to genital damage in an unfortunate but obscure circumstance:

> Nature, or Sinister Accident has rendred some of the Alteration-strokes useless and unnecessary. This expression of mine may be somewhat uncouth, and the fitter therefore (instead of Figleaves, or White Linnen) to obscure what ought to be conceal'd in Shadow. Neither would I trumpet the Truth too loudly in your ears, because ('tis said) you are of a delicate Hearing, and a great enemy to noise; insomuch that you are disturb'd with the tooting of a Sow-gelders Horn.[153]

Butler then trails off to imagine in rhyme a sexual liaison between Milton and Marvell in the Protectorate Office of Foreign Tongues. This matter we will have to judge in a later chapter.

Through all this, Hull business had continued. Marvell had been delighted in June to inform Trinity House that Angell's scheme had failed, which left the Hull cause hopeful. Yet on 6 August, he also noted that Angell had even begun to build a lighthouse but that it was not supported by Deptford Trinity House: he promised to pursue the matter further.[154] Hull and Deptford proceeded to negotiate through Marvell in order to circumvent Angell, whose actions they took as a slight.

✳

CHAPTER 11

BRUTE DIVINES

1674

MARVELL'S ENTRY INTO CONTROVERSIAL satire continued to make him famous. Probably in 1674 Lady Sarah Cowper listed extracts from *The Rehearsal Transpros'd* in her manuscript sequence 'The Medley' and one other miscellany, and included a further passage and two poems attributed to 'AM', one of which might be Marvell's. The sentence goes 'He who can write well and yet is of a dul conversation, it's a sign he is not rich himself, but has a good credit and knows where too take up.' The poem, possibly Marvell's (but it is very poor verse), called 'Affliction', echoes the closing lines of the Cromwell elegy: 'Small ills to men kind heaven in mercy send/And shews us that no greater it intends/So watry Rain-bows that Produce a sho[w]re/Secure us from a deluge any more.'[1] Lady Sarah was helped by Martin Clifford, who was part of Buckingham's circle. To these people Marvell was a wit, a controversialist and a poet. More works were appearing that gave Marvell the victory in the fight with Parker, and here Marvell was a regarded as a 'protestant of so much wit and note'. He was enjoying literary influence. John Wilmot, Earl of Rochester, the notorious libertine, incorporated phrases from *The Rehearsal Transpros'd* in one of his most important verse satires, 'Tunbridge Wells', building on Marvell's portrait of the chaplain as lazy and dull to depict Parker as an obese, inappropriately jolly drunkard:

> Listning I found the Cob of all this Rabble,
> Pert Bays, with his Importance Comfortable:
> He being rais'd to an Archdeaconry
> By trampling on Religion's liberty,
> Was grown too great, and lookt too fatt and Jolly
> To be disturb'd with care, and Melancholly,
> Thô *Marvell* has enough Expos'd his folly.

> He drank to carry off some old remains
> His lazy dull distemper left in's veins.

(ll. 68–76)

That collocation 'Importance Comfortable' would find itself widely repeated to describe any presumptuous and pretentious figure in the future.[2] As a defender of clergymen would write, while Marvell had undoubtedly beaten Parker in the contest of wit, he was simply obeying fashion in stirring up hatred of the clergy.[3] Marvell's writing then had occasioned a decline in public morals, but it was part of a larger cultural movement. The mode of *The Rehearsal Transpros'd* also seemed to take opponents over, even as they supposedly wrote against him. Thus 'Theophilus Thorowthistle' reprimands Marvell in a *faux* conjuration that only ends in praise:

> Marvel of Marvels, for that is the Character given you by a certain sort of Impertinent People who love mischief; Mischief your Minion Medium, which like a rich vein runs through the heart of all your Syllogismes, to the utter impoverishing of their Consequences; for, from a vicious medium (as unfledg'd a Logician as you are) you may Cock-sure, inferr, there must necessarily follow a vile consequence.
>
> But, how defective soever you are in your Syllogismes, you make ample satisfaction.[4]

Lamely, the author claims that his tract will offend no authority since it is devoid of offensive political or religious reference. A closer imitation than 'Thorowthistle' was Vincent Alsop's attack on William Sherlock, *Anti-Sozzo*, which appeared on 8 March 1675. Not so lame either was a manuscript poem in the commonplace book of Sir George Ent entitled 'A Love-Letter to the Author of The Rehearsall Transpros'd'.[5] Just as in *Sober Reflections*, this poem hinted at Marvell's sexual amphibiousness ('neither Flesh nor Fish, nor good Red-herring') and alleged, repeating Butler, that Marvell had been surgically castrated. In an episode that seems to echo uncannily some matchmaking that would shortly take place, the anonymous author presents a Nonconformist church trying to decide how to reward Marvell for his help. They know he is poor and in straitened circumstances, but are reluctant to bestow the proceeds of a collection on 'one, who could not propagate'. Hanging then is the best thing for him, or transfer to the Turks, who might best use him for sodomy or as a eunuch attendant in a harem.

Nonetheless, *The Rehearsal Transpros'd* and *The Rehearsall Transpros'd: The Second Part* produced a more measured response in some places. The anonymous author of *An Apology and advice for some of the clergy* (1674), sometimes thought to be Joseph Glanvill himself, was sure that Marvell had the better of Parker in respect of pure reproach, but thought that the clergy were in a difficult position: to be truly unblemished they could not answer back; when they did they were hated even more; indeed people liked to hate them. Marvell had, in the view of this author, played into the lamentable passion of the times: clergy-baiting. This is what Marvell had said he had not done, but as we will see, his anti-clericalism was in fact not merely the fashionable one of the court rakes – it would become, if he did not already understand it as such – more intellectually coherent and profound. The author of *An Apology* recommended that clergymen must therefore (and here the finger points at Parker) refrain from engaging on these terms, and must simply practise an even more virtuous and pious life.

When Parliament gathered after Christmas, the effect of the new align-ments of power, and the disarray in government, told immediately. In the Lords, Carlisle, Shaftesbury, Holles, Salisbury and others spoke strongly against popery and exerted their influence in the Commons for a move against the King's 'evil councillors'.[6] Lauderdale was condemned; Buckingham too was crit-icized on counts of treachery in respect of the war and the immorality of his not so private life (he continued to live with the Countess of Shrewsbury). He tried to incriminate Arlington, and sensationally appeared before the Commons, but before an address for his removal was made, the King had stripped Arlington of office. Arlington was interrogated in impeachment proceedings that began on 15 January 1674 but he survived. What did not survive from this tempes-tuous week in early January was Marvell's constituency letter, which is a shame, given the dominant subject at that point.

To all intents and purposes, Marvell was an MP, a representative in a constit-uted government that was at war with another state, Holland. Indeed, Marvell reported to Mayor Rogers of Hull on 24 January the terms of the proposed peace with the United Provinces, which had been delivered in a speech by the King in the Lords to both Houses on the same day.[7] On 3 February, Marvell was also named in the Commons to a committee to draw up reasons for a conference with the Lords concerning the address for peace.[8] In February alone he was named to six committees before the proroguing on 24 February until the following 10 November. Yet there were other dealings taking place outside the assemblies.

The Dutch had of course successfully distributed propaganda in England, winning sympathy for their cause. As in the Second Dutch War, a body of discontented republicans, Fifth Monarchists and other strong anti-Catholics had aided the Dutch with advice and arms. While Dutch propaganda entered England, orchestrated by Pierre du Moulin, a stream of intelligence reached the Hague from English soil.[9] Du Moulin was a member of a distinguished Huguenot family, and had been a protégé of Arlington as a civil servant; pro-French foreign policy forced him out of favour and eventually into William's service in 1672.[10] William of Orange was effectively running a spy network, featuring the former Fifth Monarchist, William Medley, and William Carr. Undercover names were endemic (Medley was known as 'Mr Freeman'), and there were double agents, such as Carr. Carr reported to Sir Joseph Williamson, the Secretary of State and chief of intelligence for the government, that someone who looked like Marvell travelled in January and February, during the Parliamentary session, to the Hague under the name of 'Mr George' and spoke with the Prince of Orange before returning after one night.[11] Remember that Williamson and Marvell went back a long way, having coincided when younger as tutors to gentlemen in Saumur in the 1650s. If Marvell did indeed visit the Hague clandestinely, was he plotting with the man who would eventually become England's next Protestant king just as the political lines at Westminster hardened? If so, it was reported that du Moulin did not give the kind of message of support for which these would-be agents of insurrection looked. Did Marvell nonetheless gain knowledge of the Dutch position that would have helped him and the Commons, or the nascent opposition, as they established themselves as a kind of political party? Carr reported this information to Williamson in May, and it would seem that Marvell was again in Holland in June, perhaps for some weeks, since he twice appears in a list and the letter of du Moulin's under the pseudonym 'Mr Thomas'.[12] It is in this part of the evidence that Marvell appears to be blamed for a rift between English agents and the Dutch.[13] Marvell's activities constitute a part of the politics that is now understood as a tri-state interaction involving France, the United Provinces and England, so that in this sphere there were three closely interconnected political societies as opposed to separate nation states.[14]

The increase of leisure time meant further work for Wharton in March, this time concerning the courtship of his second son Goodwin, while he chased Hull Trinity House with regard to retainer fees for the lawyer Sir William Jones who was providing in Marvell's view valuable advice in relation to the light-house business.[15]

After mid-April Marvell began to compose his considered response to Milton's *Paradise Lost* in the form of a prefatory poem, written for and published in the second edition of the epic, which would finally be advertised on 6 July, four months before Milton died. Marvell's friendship with Milton was now more than twenty years old. Quite apart from the opportunity provided by Milton's earlier works, notably the 1645 poems and the anti-episcopal tracts, for deep reflection on several personal and poetic themes, Marvell had read both *Paradise Lost* and the 1673 poems very carefully. His poem is a subtle and often amazing commentary on Milton's achievement. It was also a contribution to the debate concerning the use of rhyme in heroic verse, a dispute between Dryden and Sir Robert Howard that began in the 1660s and that was given new perti-nence for Marvell through Dryden's creation of a stage version of *Paradise Lost* (*The State of Innocence*, licensed on 17 April 1674). Dryden's use of couplets provoked Marvell's dismissal of him as a hack poet, the 'Town-Bayes', even though he himself uses rhyme and confesses the 'shortcoming' at the end of the poem. That Marvell had already attacked Samuel Parker as a rhymer in prose leaves a loose association of the two as part of the same party, guilty of the same shortcoming. The poem is certainly part of a continuing defence of Milton, which began in *The Rehearsall Transpros'd* and was extended to meet the charges in Samuel Butler's *The Transproser Rehears'd* (1673), where Milton is accused of hypocritical internal rhyming. Marvell himself was accused by Butler of 'rhyming' in prose, which is to say jesting, and this was little different from writing unrhymed blank verse, which by Milton and Butler's equation is also tantamount to republicanism. Marvell went back to his old letter to Milton of 1654, presumably from memory, and sought to vindicate Milton while preserving his own still secret identity as the 'transproser'. Marvell imitates Ben Jonson's prefatory poem to Thomas May's translation of Lucan and in doing so implies that Milton's poem is a Lucanic enterprise, a covert critique of empire in the name of republicanism, and a piece of resilient Stoicism, understood as resistance in retirement rather than a sacrifice of its cause. To this extent Marvell is being true to Jonson's poetic ethos as much as to Milton's.

There are many detailed imitations of the notable style of *Paradise Lost* in the poem, even as Marvell contributes a major piece of early 'Augustan' verse, with imagery subordinated to the speaker's finely discriminating tone.[16] The most significant feature here is Marvell's taking of the convention of praise by initial doubt to an extreme, 'straining praise through the sieve of doubt'. It almost seems as if Marvell's narrator is a Miltonic one, submitting himself to error, seeing events through 'Satanic' spectacles, then correcting that vision, and finally affirming the truth. This sense that Milton is to be regarded critically is unmistakably present through Marvell's adoption of Milton's own character of Samson to represent the poet (ll. 9–10). Despite Marvell's qualification of the critique, it stays in the reader's mind (most famously in the image of Milton as Samson 'groping' in his blindness for the pillars in the Theatre of Dagon), alongside the repeated references to the vastness of Milton's design. 'Vast' (l. 2) in any case is a word usually associated with Satan: Marvell's tactic is a fitting response to the double-sidedness of Milton's epic. The joke in the poem at lines 49–50 comparing rhyme words to the tags and points that held clothes together refers back to the phrase Milton used when he gave Dryden permission to adapt *Paradise Lost* in rhyme ('Mr Milton received him civilly, and told him he would give him leave to tagge his verses') but the fact (as D'Avenant had noticed) that tags and points had already been superseded by hooks and eyes makes the reference also one that evidently refers to a former age.[17] Marvell knew that Milton was old, but he also knew even at this stage that the poem would be extremely influential; and that it contained a veiled attack on monarchy. For all that, Marvell's touch on the issue of sublimity in poetry and the theory of the sublime did not satisfy all readers. In 1793 Capel Lofft noticed that Marvell had acknowledged in his poem Milton's attempt to follow the great ancient creation poet (and atheist) Lucretius, but thought that Marvell should then have written a more appropriately Lucretian poem in praise of Milton's epic. But Marvell's poem reflects Milton's continued embattlement, the fact that *Paradise Lost* and the other two major poems spoke for a defeated cause and were rearguard actions on its behalf. A more open statement Milton himself could not make: in this same year of 1674 L'Estrange refused a licence to an edition of Milton's letters of state.

As he wrote, Marvell waited for William Popple to arrive from Paris: they were to travel to Yorkshire together.[18] Near the end of May Marvell finally made the trip to the north and Hull, where he was welcomed handsomely by Trinity House in a reception at the Hull postmaster George Mawson's house.[19] Marvell apparently stayed until mid-September, when there was another reception at Mawson's to see him off. These months would have been spent with members of his family, giving him time to nurture some of the fond sentiments expressed in later letters.[20] But they were also months in which clandestine visits to Holland may well have been paid.

The Hull connections developed further when Marvell returned to London, which he did by riding via York on 17 September.[21] The Hull Corporation wrote on the 28th concerned that lead mined in Derbyshire was passing through Hull without the payment of duty, and the MP was asked to speak about this issue with Sir William Lowther, Sir William Thompson and Captain Garroway. On 20 October, Marvell met the Duke of Monmouth, the High Steward, and gained his assurance that he would look after Hull (the order telling Marvell to do so had arrived on 28 September). Monmouth was embarrassed by the gift of six gold jacobus coins (worth 22s. each) and Marvell had to insist that Monmouth not give them back in order to avoid embarrassment for the town (he had been asked by the Corporation to acquire them).[22]

In another kind of loyal act, Marvell wrote on 24 September to Sir Henry Thompson at Escrick, expressing that sentiment through an apology for being a tardy correspondent.[23] Marvell's wit here extended to the confession that his memory was the only faculty that was not exceeded by Thompson's courtesy, but even that must be defective since his 'Imagination' and 'Understanding' cannot sufficiently comprehend his obligation to Sir Henry. He has a lot of will, he says, by which he means an intention to be good, but however much his soul belongs to Thompson, it is but a little one. Thompson had won a by-election the previous year in York, effectively replacing Sir Thomas Osborne, who had been raised to the peerage, and defeating Danby's candidate Sir John Hewley.

The body of the letter was foreign news: this seems to have been its purpose. It concerned the campaign fought between the French and the Dutch on the borders of eastern France, and the fates and reputations of various aristocratic figures. English troops supporting the French were incensed that their bravery had not been reported in newsbooks. The joke here was that the losses among the English were so great that soon there would be no complaints at all: they would all be dead. Marvell did not think armies were worth great expense, and he quibbled over whether it was worth helping the French gain a victory or trying to guess whether there would soon be a rebellion in Scotland to face.

Most of the last part of the letter is concerned with an assassination attempt on Louis XIV, whom Marvell had already disapprovingly mentioned as *the* supreme ego because of his order that the words 'Pour moi gloire' be cast on French ordnance. There is a careful filleting of rumour and hearsay from reality, in respect of whether the assassination attempt was part of a planned rebellion. The crucial opinion seems to be that there were no Protestant plotters involved, while some very famous Catholics had been fingered. It was, says Marvell, too early to tell what it all meant.

Just over a week later, Marvell wrote on 5 November to Sir Henry's brother Edward, who was a merchant in York.[24] The letter is addressed playfully or affectionately to 'Monsieur Eduaoart Thompson', and so he was named at the end of the letter to Sir Henry, possibly reflecting a career in France. The letter contains thanks for taking care of George, the eldest son of the Admiral, Sir Jeremy Smith. Among general political gossip and international news were the King's intentions in summoning a meeting of some of the bishops in Ossory, and Arlington heading for Holland in an atmosphere of distrust between the two nations, although Prince William was rumoured to be coming to England in order to marry the Duke of York's daughter. Significantly, Marvell noted an attempt on the Holy Roman Emperor's life, and connected it with that on Louis XIV reported in the previous letter. He was in fact 'glad' that the clergy had returned to their old king-killing role for it showed them in their true light.

No later than the end of October, Marvell may have written a satirical poem, 'The Statue in Stocks-Market', on the corruption of the Lord Mayor of London, a situation which paralleled that within the government. Sir Robert Viner (1631–88), alderman of Langborn in the City of London (later Lord Mayor) and Charles II's principal banker, had unveiled an equestrian statue of the King on 29 October 1672.[25] The horse was acquired in Italy and had a figure of Charles added to it.[26] The alterations made to the statue (Sobieski to Charles II, the Turk to Oliver Cromwell) left the Turk's turban in place: it was embarrassing evidence of the conversion. Viner may have had the statue for some time: a similar gift from him had been declined by the Royal Exchange in 1669.

The poem uses the occasion of the statue's unveiling to highlight a number of court and government failings: financial chaos, and the associated charge of decadent overspending; the motives of the government in starting the Third Dutch War. But the treatment of Viner is at least as critical: his court connections and his authoritarian attitude to the governance of the City of London made him the enemy of many within the city Corporation with whom Marvell had connections.[27] The crushing irony is that the gift of the statue was an apparent reward for the ruin that the King's closure of the Exchequer had caused in the city in 1672. But the satire then suggests that the statue is an insult because so poorly executed, and was Viner trying to portray himself instead of the King? The imagery of calm and storm at line 8 suggests that

Marvell is the author, but the outright accusation of royal corruption is not characteristic, certainly not in this period:

> But a market, they say, does suit the king well,
> Who the Parliament buys and revenues does sell,
> And others to make the similitude hold
> Say his Majesty himself is bought too and sold.
>
> (ll. 21–4)

If Marvell was not the author, perhaps this poem was the inspiration for another likely Marvell composition 'The Statue at Charing Cross', probably meant to be a companion poem to this one.[28] The clever sense of doubleness in these lines – both the King in his person and his image in the statue – and the call to have the statue improved introduce a sense of repetitive seasonal change. This itself is Marvell's way of expressing Charles's capriciousness and his endless deferral of the enactment of Parliamentary legislation by proroguing Parliament rather than calling for new elections. The last stanza is appropriately weary; and ominous, with the threat of the Catholic Duke of York:

> But Sir Robert affirms we do him much wrong;
> For the graver's at work to reform him thus long.
> But alas! he will never arrive at his end,
> For 'tis such a king as no chisel can mend.
>
> But with all his faults restore us our King,
> As ever you hope in December for Spring,
> For though the whole world cannot show such another,
> Yet we'd better by far have him than his brother.
>
> (ll. 53–60)

Marvell too must have been aware of Milton's purpose in his published translation of Sobieski's election document: to point to the decidedly republican possibility of election as a way of resolving the succession crisis in England.[29]

Parliament was once again prorogued on 10 November until the following 13 April. With nothing else to report, Marvell wrote to the Corporation of Hull on much the same subjects as in the letter he had sent to Edward Thompson on the 5th, and indeed to Sir Henry again on the 10th.[30] He wrote to Sir Henry again on 1 December after more work for the Board of Deptford Trinity House, upon which he now sat.[31] Thompson wanted news of business as well as politics, and he was given it: how Lord St John had missed a financial killing in lead by spending too much time at Boulogne. The forgery that he had perpetrated was exposed, many involved had fled, although Marvell thought that St John's reputation was not entirely lost. Then he mentioned the monopolies settled on the two chief royal mistresses and other courtiers. Marvell also thought it worth mentioning the society marriages that had been arranged, such as that of (the King's mistress) Louise de Kerouaille's sister, Henriette, to the Earl of Pembroke.[32] Into the final section comes mention of the other York MP, Sir John Hewley, with whom Thompson had disagreed in respect of the election. Marvell was clearly finding it extremely hard to negotiate with him, and this is uncharacteristic: 'The thing might make a Play tis so foolish an humor and in good faith methinks I never saw so meere a Cully.'[33] As he said to Edward Thompson ten days later, both Hewley and Marvell himself were too modest to start an argument.[34] But there is no mention anywhere in Marvell's surviving correspondence of the death of Milton between 8 and 10 November and his burial on the 12th. Marvell must have been affected; it is hard to believe that he was not involved in some way in the funeral, although he would have been preoccupied enough with the brief meeting of Parliament and Trinity House issues. Now 'On Mr Milton's Paradise Lost' might be read as an elegy.

But at least on 15 December, there was a sense of expectation: Arlington was coming to London, and the bishops had been in a secret negotiation the details of which were expected. The fate of a priest condemned to be hanged, drawn and quartered remained in the balance, and Burnet had preached to a very fashionable congregation in Covent Garden, in complaint against Lauderdale and for being banned from preaching within twenty miles of London. The expectation had turned to embarrassment for Marvell when he had to confess in his next newsletter to Sir Henry that he had 'done just nothing' about the Hewley business. It is very unusual to find Marvell confessing his inefficiency with embarrassment as if he was expecting to be berated. He even found it easier to defer to John Rushworth, Hewley's solicitor but one of Marvell's friends: 'I can do it more freely then with Sr John, discourse the thing very plainly with Mr Rushworth ouer a pint of wine and I will doe so and that ere long.'[35] Which might be a small age. Thompson is again given foreign news – nearly all of it showing Louis XIV's absolute power to make or break aristocratic marriages – and repeated English news, with nice gossipy details here and there filling out older stories: 'Her sister [Henriette de Kerouaille] was on Thursday married to the Earle of Pembroke he being prity well recoverd of his Clap.'[36] All money made from the supply or other taxes was to be redistributed to the royals, including illegitimate children. While the King was receiving the freedom of the City of London in the form of a golden box, Clarendon died, on the same day as Justice Sir John Vaughan, both to be reconciled finally in heaven as they were not on earth, Marvell thought.

The year 1674 also saw increased activity at Trinity House in Hull concerning its long pursuit of erecting a lighthouse at Spurn Head at the mouth of the Humber. As its agent in London, Marvell was busy. In January he had warned the Corporation and Trinity House of the possible dangerous consequences of a continuing duty for ships (including those from Hull) to pay on coal delivered to London.[37] The land where the lighthouse might best be built was owned by Justinian Angell, and although Trinity House wanted the lighthouse in a

different place (so they wrote on 21 April), they nonetheless wanted to throw in
their lot with Angell.[38] Marvell's job was to push things along in this direction,
not least with the assistance of Sir Jeremy Smith. He was himself pessimistic
about moving the lighthouse location since many thought it well placed.
Nonetheless he promised to seek Smith's help when he returned from his naval
duties at Chatham.[39] On 8 May, Marvell was elected as Elder Brother of Hull
Trinity House's sister organization at Deptford, also known as Trinity House,
and where Smith was a master. He was thereafter present at regular monthly
meetings, where one of the major functions was the distribution of funds to the
dependants of the House. The election required a payment of £30 on Marvell's
part.[40] The trip north to Hull in early June was largely connected with Trinity
House business, and after his return in mid-September, he was able to report on
22 October that the Commons were taking the Humber lighthouse issue seriously; Angell had presented his papers and patent, and the issue of the position
of a new sandbank had to be resolved.[41] One week later, Marvell was among the
signatories of a letter from Deptford Trinity House asking their brethren in Hull
for the best location for a new lighthouse that would take account of the new
sandbank.[42] In November Deptford Trinity House told Hull through Marvell
that it entirely opposed Angell's scheme, and Hull Trinity House agreed with
this, even though they saw new sand as a good reason for a lighthouse at Spurn.
And so it went on at the two Trinity Houses into the next year, with Marvell and
Smith both signing a letter from Deptford asking Hull for advice on Sir John
Clayton's proposals for north coast lighthouses.[43] On 4 March 1675, Marvell
was chosen and sworn as deputy assistant to Sir Thomas Allen.[44] The lighthouse issue was enlivened by the apparent circulation of a counterfeit letter
in March suggesting that Angell had already set up a lighthouse and that it
was operative.[45] Hull Corporation were in fact unimpressed by Marvell's
membership of Deptford Trinity House since they thought it meant he could
not represent them in certain respects with regard to the lighthouse: Hull and
Deptford had finally come to have different views.

1675

There were two meetings of the Board of Deptford Trinity House, upon which
Marvell sat, in January 1675: on the 21st and the 28th. On the latter day,
Marvell wrote this: 'I . . . who haue no imployment but idlenesse and who am
so oblivious that I should forget mine own name did I not see it sometimes in
a friends superscription.'[46] The middle fifties might well be a time when one
seriously begins to experience memory loss, and in April Marvell would
complain that his now shorter memory was preventing him from producing
full reports of Parliamentary business.[47] It might also be a time when fits of
anger (called 'choler' in the seventeenth century, under the terms of humour
theory) came easily, as when Marvell exploded on 4 February to hear that his

name was being used without his knowledge in business dealings with Bordeaux and involving the Thompsons.[48] It may have been that Sir Henry Thompson had inadvertently allowed this use, but Marvell was not certain since he had not seen the correspondence in detail. His own honour and his friendship with the Thompsons seemed to be at stake, in the latter case because the letter appears to suggest that Marvell and Thompson were negotiating with each other: 'I should be supposed to barter thus with you and deale with so meanly upon conditions with one to whom I am so farre engaged.' Marvell was mystified because he could not see the correspondence in which his position had been alleged, according to Robert Steward, an associate of William Popple's whom he had run into in London. Revealingly it was important that Marvell should want to tell Thompson that he showed no emotion to Steward.

The previous week, Marvell had addressed how Sir Henry remained in a position of dispute with Sir John Hewley concerning the election in York. Marvell remained obliged, it would seem, to speak with Sir John on the matter. He reported that one of Hewley's lawyers, Hartlib, son of the natural philosopher and educational reformer, had put himself in debt through extravagant expenditure and had fled to Holland.[49] Marvell reports that he had spoken with Rushworth (son of the New Model Army clerk, historian and his great friend) who had advised Hewley to rest his claims against Thompson, and that his chance of support therein from Danby the Lord Treasurer was very slight, and if it came, he (Hewley) would risk becoming Danby's pawn. In any case Hewley had not arrived to attend Parliament, so it might be inferred that he was losing interest in the dispute with Thompson. Marvell hoped that, come Easter Term, he and Rushworth might jointly persuade Hewley. A week later, it appeared that Hewley's intention to come to Westminster for Easter Term was a sign that he remained in contention. Marvell further reported, effectively elaborating on the issue of the power of Danby, that Danby had continued to pressure the Lord Mayor of London, Sir Robert Viner, to marry his stepdaughter to Danby's son, Lord Dunblane, which meant in turn pressuring a clergyman to deny that he had married Viner's daughter, Bridget Hyde, to her cousin John Emerton.[50] The Act of Habeas Corpus was invoked in order to bring Mrs Hyde out of confinement. Meanwhile, Marvell was suspicious of the continuing secret meeting of the bishops with Heneage Finch, the Lord Keeper, and Lauderdale. In a further letter to Mayor Daniel Hoare of 6 February, Marvell said that he felt there would be a substantial Parliament when the prorogation expired, and in the meantime the weekly meetings of Deptford Trinity House proceeded.[51]

On 17 February, Marvell performed a function that showed how vital he was to the Corporation of Hull. Two aldermen, William Foxley and William Skinner, the former of whom would be, the latter of whom had been, Mayor of Hull, had travelled to London to seek legal advice. The Corporation found itself in a property dispute, and needed help. Marvell met Foxley and Skinner at James Shaw's chambers in Gray's Inn. Shaw would be the solicitor, while it was agreed that Marvell and Sir Jeremy Smith would approach an eminent lawyer, Sir John King.[52] Without their assistance, the aldermen would have been helpless. Foxley and Skinner had hoped that the Attorney General would represent their plea, but they found out that he was representing their opponent. The question then revolved around whether the Corporation should appeal directly to the King and his Privy Council or to common law. It was here that Marvell's skill in drafting documents was invaluable: he compressed two letters into one elegant and effective statement and, with the help of his friend Sir Jeremy Smith, was able to pass the letter to Sir John King, one of the King's counsel, and soon to be the top practitioner in Chancery, who advised that a direct and successful appeal to the King might not work: the opponents might still hold their course on the grounds that a royal command did not contravene the common law.[53] The Corporation should instead place a bill in Exchequer, where it would still require royal assent, but this could not be resisted by the other party. It was resolved that the aldermen should meet with Marvell and King in the latter's chambers a week later in order to design such a bill. A letter expressing gratitude to Marvell and Smith was ordered to be sent by the Mayor and Corporation.[54]

This exchange took place on 4 February. Two days later, Marvell wrote to Mayor Hoare in the expectation that, after a long prorogation, Parliament would be recalled. It gathered on 13 April. Buckingham had returned to London shortly beforehand and had begun to negotiate with the country MPs. It was expected to be and would turn out to be a memorable few months. Whether Marvell had been asked to supply Hull with more frequent and detailed letters, or whether he felt this to be his duty, the fact is that Marvell's correspondence markedly increases in frequency at this time, there being a total of thirty-nine constituency letters for this year, with twenty-five being written for the first session of Parliament alone.

Parliament met on 13 April, and Marvell dutifully wrote to Mayor Hoare reporting the contents of the King's speech – his desire for unity of purpose between himself and his subjects, and his awareness that some worked against this (possibly Catholics, republicans or Fifth Monarchists; we are not told), that he would always uphold the Church of England, and that the navy needed much money for repairs. Marvell said he would send this gracious speech in printed form, when available, to the Mayor, and reports that both Houses voted thanks to His Majesty.[55] Two days later he wrote again, this time referring to a debate on the 14th concerning explorations into Parliamentary history: concerning procedures for passing bills into law, against impressments, and the terms by which men could be imprisoned on the King's warrant.[56] There was a debate on the Duke of Lauderdale (who had been made Earl of Guilford and Baron Petersham in the English Peerage on the previous

25 June) occasioning a renewal of the resolution to ask the King to remove him from office. In the afternoon, the MPs attended His Majesty at Whitehall with their vote of thanks, and the next morning the actual records considered the previous day were presented to the Commons, but it was decided to have them translated from Law French before proceeding further. Marvell heard and reported that some in the Lords had protested about their vote of thanks since, unlike that of the Commons, it was not limited to the matter of defending religion and property, and to the very calling of a parliament.

That is what Marvell said, but what he might have been doing was quite another thing. For when the MPs gathered, they found in their places *His Majesty's Most Gracious Speech to Both Houses of Parliament*, a mock speech that is now regarded by some as Marvell's.[57] It is a parody of the King's speech of 8 March 1673, and is a satirical exposure of administrative rapaciousness, with the King asking for ever greater sums and the Lord Treasurer Danby presented as guiding him behind the scenes. Charles's real politic instincts – his sense that the Commons were already unpopular, so they will have to give the King what he wants in order to have a friend – are on display, as are his allegedly risible attempts to control household spending. The speech had been seen early in March by the Venetian ambassador, Girolamo Alberti, who reported that it was being sold by hawkers in Westminster and London. It was precisely the product of an idle period, while men waited for Parliament to be reassembled, and was clearly part of a renewed opposition campaign. Whoever wrote it, Marvell or someone else, it may be seen as writing that demanded the accountability of the King, and as such has been seen as literature that adapts republican argument from the Interregnum period to Restoration circumstances without explicitly attacking the institution of monarchy.[58]

The Commons proceeded to assert itself. Between 15 and 17 April, a bill was debated for a new religious test, this time being softer on Dissenters and much harder on Roman Catholics. The King cannot have been pleased. Then an address to the King was planned, asking him to recall subjects fighting for Louis XIV in France and requesting that further recruitment be forbidden. In accordance with this sentiment, on 22 April Marvell was one of the tellers for the successful 'Yeas' in the second reading of a bill preventing MPs from taking public office. In a letter of the same day, he set out the wording of the Test Bill, which remained unconfirmed by the Lords, and pointed up the Commons' interest in controlling expenditure and accountability in respect of the navy, the militia and the hospitals.[59]

No cause for an impeachment of Danby could be found, and the only way forward with Viner was to bring him in together with the minister, John Brandley, who had been pressured to deny marrying Bridget Hyde. No doubt Marvell's contemptuous comments against Viner ('detestable', 'ignominious') were fuelled by the fact that Viner had already been in dispute with Marvell's business acquaintances in London, Richard Thompson and Edward

Nelthorpe.[60] Both had spoken in the Common Council of London against Viner's influence in the appointment of a judge to the Sheriff's court.[61]

On 30 April Viner was interrogated in the Commons, but it was decided that there was too little evidence in the instance of the marriage fiasco for impeachment of Danby. And on 4 May, Danby was acquitted on the rest of the articles. Marvell was writing by every post at this point to send news back to Hull. This meant writing every other day rather than once a week, although it is hard to see why he should have changed practice. It certainly creates the impression of a very busy world, with some letters being written immediately after sessions ended, such as at ten at night, and with the MP distinctly trying to show the relevance of legislation to his constituency: for example a bill for suppressing pedlars.[62] On 10 May the Commons had unsettled itself when the tellers could not agree on the numbers in a vote, making the committee work wasted and requiring each member to stand up and promise not to feel any resentment or dislike of what had happened. 'Both Parties grew so hot, that all Order was lost; Men came running confusedly up to the Table, grievously affronted one by another; every Man's Hand on his Hilt.'[63]

So busy was Marvell that he fell down on one significant literary duty. John Aubrey had gained a promise from Marvell to supply notes on Milton for his growing collection of biographies. They never arrived and Aubrey turned instead to Cyriack Skinner.[64] Marvell continued to witness the war between the Lords and Commons, which he much regretted, and hoped on 20 May that reason would prevail in a conference, so that differences would be resolved. He evidently further hoped that more absent MPs would be persuaded to come to Westminster and sit: the subject of a long debate on 26 May.

While the Lords continued to debate the Test Bill, on 3 June Marvell along with the other Yorkshire MPs were added to the Committee for Abolishing the Writ for Burning Heretics, *de haeretico comburendo*.[65] The issue of the authority of the two Houses vis-à-vis each other was once again at stake, and the stakes were rising, to the extent that Marvell worried that a list of legislation he was sending to Hull might miscarry and be lost: it would be worse than too bad. Arrest and counter-arrest continued until 5 June, when the King instructed both Houses to adjourn and then to attend him in the Banqueting House at Whitehall, where he attempted to reconcile them in a speech. But deadlock followed, with Sir John Robinson, Keeper of the Tower, either defended by the Commons or having habeas corpuses slapped on him by the Lords. Finally, on 9 June, Parliament was prorogued until 13 October, and Marvell let the King's speech explain why to the Corporation of Hull. For Marvell it meant more attendance at Deptford Trinity House, and another salmon preserved in salt and vinegar from Hull Trinity House.[66]

There was also some correspondence to catch up on: to Sir Henry Thompson he sent a newsletter on 6 July expressing gratitude for the King's safe arrival after a week on a stormy sea travelling from Gravesend to the Isle of Wight.[67]

Then followed for Marvell a retreat to the cottage in Highgate and a chance to write an extremely long letter to William Popple.[68] Will had written on 17 July, and Marvell's reply on the 24th offered a kind of fantasy of the extraordinary events that had recently taken place. Will was to imagine himself, not unlike Thomas Rolt, in the East Indies, to account for the delay in receiving the letter. Then Marvell laid into court corruption, or at least political imbalance: Danby, Lauderdale and York carried chief influence, the former two being so unpopular they had to reinvigorate alliances with the bishops and the old Cavaliers in order to enhance their security and make sure there would be a supply. Particular and ironic contempt is reserved for Danby who is insultingly called by the name of his son-in-law, Coke. The Duke of York was being exempted from the Test legislation, and there were rumours of Machiavellian ruses so that the legislation would be followed by a Parliament that might reverse all or some of it. All of this was riding over the huge divisions that existed between the various parts of the 'royal' interest.

Perhaps it was for this reason that Marvell probably responded to the announced erection of Charles I's statue at Charing Cross with a satirical poem on the subject. There was even talk of reinterring the remains of the King, 'to make a perfect Resurrection of Loyalty'. Overtones of *Eikon Basilike*, of Charles I as Christic martyr-king, are obvious in this phrase. What really irritated Marvell was a tightening of the laws against 'Fanatics and Papists'.[69] Danby had escaped impeachment, Marvell claimed, by bribery. Somehow it was appropriate that *Scaramuccio* was playing at Whitehall, 'and all Sorts of People flocking thither, and paying their Mony as at a common Playhouse; nay even a twelve-penny Gallery is builded for the convenience of his Majesty's poorer Subjects'.[70] While he urged Will to look after himself, to gain what wealth he needed as soon as possible before returning to England, and to find other people to be his drudge, he celebrated the death of the staunch Anglican Sir Giles Strangways, satirized in 'The Last Instructions', who had recently been made a privy councillor. Strangways had used informers, an episode that would be raised again somewhat later by Marvell. And in this way he was, says Marvell, leading the church to wrack; at least Buckingham had given the bishops a hard time, 'never the like, nor so infinitely pleasant: and no Men were ever grown so odiously ridiculous'.[71] Lauderdale's words were so treacherous that Marvell had to repeat them:

Dr *Burnet*, one of *Lauderdale's* former Confidents, witnessed, at the Commons' Bar, that, discoursing to *Lauderdale* of the Danger of using such Severitys against the Nonconformists in *Scotland*, while the King was engaged in War abroad, *Lauderdale* said, *He wished they would rebel*. How so? *Why, He would bring over the irish Papists to cut their Throats*. Farther, concerning the Parliament, *if they be refractory, I will bring the scotch Army upon them*: But it will be difficult to persuade them. *No, the Prey of England will draw in a great many*. Nevertheless, *Lauderdale* is in as much Favour as ever.[72]

The poem itself took as its subject the bronze equestrian statue of Charles I, cast by Le Sueur in 1633, but it remained to be erected when the Civil War broke out. Parliament sold the statue to Rivet the brazier, who sold bronze-handled cutlery to Royalists after the regicide because they believed the cutlery to have been cast from the bronze in the statue. Rivet had in fact kept the statue. Danby acquired it after the Restoration and erected it at his own expense in order to appeal to popular sentiment in 1675. Thus it was indicative of Danby's tactics, corrupt of course in Marvell's view, of directing funds frivolously when there were more pressing causes. It is in fact a very sophisticated analysis of Danby's tactics throughout his career, and repeats the accusation that his wife was behind his actions:

> Does the Treasurer think men so loyally tame
> When their pensions are stopped to be fooled with a sight?
> And 'tis forty to one if he play the old game
> He'll shortly reduce us to forty and eight. . . .

> Let's have a King then, be he new be he old;
> Not Viner delayed us so, though he was broken
> Though the King be of copper and Danby of gold,
> Shall a treasurer of guineas a prince grudge of token?
>
> (ll. 21–4; 37–40)

When Parliament reassembled on 13 October, Marvell sent to Hull the King's and Lord Keeper's speeches, and then, on the 19th, set about explaining the continuing determination of the Commons to prevent breaches of privilege (as in the case of the infirm Colonel Thomas Howard who published a letter on 30 August impugning two Parliamentarians, Lord Cavendish and Sir Thomas Meeres, for allegedly insulting his brother John, who had died commanding English troops in the service of France) and to limit the supply to the King (a committee of the whole House voted very narrowly not to allow supply on account of anticipated debts – thought to be in the order of £1 million).[73] He also felt his job was made difficult by some indiscretion on the part of the Mayor and Aldermen so that the contents of one of his letters had become known to John Cressett the lawyer. As he said on 21 October, 'seeing it is possible that in writing to assured friends a man may giue his pen some liberty and the times are something criticall beside that I am naturally and now more by my Age inclined to keep my thoughts private, I desire that what I write down to you may not easily or unnecessarily returne to a third hand at London.'[74] On the 25th the Corporation wrote to Marvell claiming that no such letter had been written to Cressett.[75]

Three days before this, he had written to Sir William Petty, the foundational mind in the field of political economy, whom he acknowledged as a friend of some years' standing, wishing him success in his new Irish venture (Petty was beginning to run his Irish 'farm') and recommending one Joseph Watson and his brother for employment in the mission.[76] As suggested before, perhaps it was Petty as well as the Boyles who tied Marvell to Ireland with an offer of potential employment.[77]

Distressingly, a run on Richard Thompson and Edward Nelthorpe's bank began as November 1675 came around.[78] More concern still of a personal kind followed. On 3 November, Marvell witnessed the death of Sir Jeremy Smith at 11 p.m., 'dying very peaceably and with perfect understanding memory and speech to the last gaspe'. It was the circumstance of Smith's death, with Marvell being able to convey to the Corporation his last good wishes, and the Corporation's letter of the 25th that reconciled Smith and the Corporation. But Marvell persisted in his belief that his letters were being read: 'there is some sentinell set both upon you and me,' he wrote on 4 November to Mayor Shires.[79]

Indeed, he felt he had to apologize to the Mayor and Aldermen for his preoccupation with the arrangements for Sir Jeremy's funeral, since all his time was taken up. In the second week of November, he seems to have been functioning as an executor for Smith's estate; and, having been party to making the arrangements for the funeral, he accompanied the corpse as it was borne out of London on its way for burial at Hemingborough, now North Yorkshire, Smith's home village on the Ouse, downstream from Cawood where it is joined by the Wharfe, the river that Marvell knew so well from Appleton House.[80] Back in the House of Commons, the concern with atheism, impiety and debauchery again surfaced in debate, and anxieties were voiced about the machinery for tax collection. A bill against the printing of scandalous libels was read. On 22 November, Parliament was prorogued for more than a year and would not meet until 15 February 1677.

Marvell spent the rest of the year looking after the interests of the Thompsons, providing both brothers with newsletters, and at one point noting that Shaftesbury's influence on the appointment of Customs Commissioners might have proved advantageous to the Thompsons, but that a published speech in Shaftesbury's name had made him many enemies in the House of Lords.[81] He speaks of a pair of 'ugly distichs' that had been posted over the door of the King's bedchamber, which complained of Charles's disloyalty to those who had helped him. One might have thought this was Marvell obliquely talking about his own writing, as was customary, but they are very bad lines and the sense of them does not fit his interests: 'in vaine for help to your old friends you call, when you like pittied them they must fall.'[82] Some of the news touched closer relations: in late December Marvell reported that a run on the banks in Lombard Street by their creditors, for no good reason in his view, had severely strained the system, but it had not damaged the bank of the two Yorkshiremen and friends of Marvell, Richard Thompson and Edward Nelthorpe. In return Sir Henry Thompson reaffirmed his friendship and patronage of Marvell in a letter probably written around 7 December, claiming to drink his health every night in

thanks for the help Marvell gave him (this despite his coach dangerously overturning near Doncaster). Like many of Marvell's friends in Yorkshire, Thompson
looked forward to the summoning of a new Parliament and had further
hopes that he might sit in it. How disappointed he would be. He reminded
Marvell of his other Yorkshire friends – Sir John Hotham and Robert Witty –
but more significantly mentioned a recently widowed rich Nonconformist,
Priscilla Brookes, in York: a potential and perhaps highly appropriate wife for
Marvell.[83] She was in fact Marvell's senior by ten years, and was a patroness of
Nonconformist ministers who preached in the chapel she had built near
Ellenthorpe, near Boroughbridge, in 1658. Thompson clearly thought that the
Nonconformity connection was a ground for compatibility between the two;
and, being rich, she would have eased Marvell's condition of dependency. Like
Thompson's election to Parliament, the marriage would never happen.

Mr Mitchell

In January 1676 a matter that had been in the making for several years came
to a head. For Marvell's inquisitiveness would result in the composition, very
probably at this time, of one of his most overlooked but starkly successful and
intelligent poems, and it would take his attention back to Scotland.

James Mitchell, a 'conventicle preacher', graduated from Edinburgh
University in July 1656, having at the same time signed the National Covenant
and Solemn League and Covenant. Described as 'a youth of much zeal and
piety', he became a preacher, a schoolteacher in Galloway, and a household
chaplain.[84] By November 1666 he was an active rebel, and had joined the
rising of the Covenanters in the west at Ayr and the Pentland Rising. He was
pronounced guilty of treason on 4 December 1666 and was excluded from
the pardon given to those in the rising on 1 October 1667. Mitchell fled to
Holland, but returned in 1668 and opened a tobacco and spirits shop, which
some would later argue was a front for further seditious activity.

On 11 July 1668 Mitchell attempted to assassinate the Archbishop of
St Andrews, James Sharp, by shooting him with a pistol in Edinburgh. He had
apparently been plotting for some time. Mitchell's shots missed Sharp and
went into the arm of the Bishop of Orkney. Mitchell escaped by taking refuge
in a friendly house and then emerging in disguise. Sharp survived, although
Andrew Honeyman, Bishop of Orkney, died nearly eight years later from
consequences of the wound to his wrist. On the following Monday, 13 July, the
Scottish Privy Council met, wrote to the King to tell him of the matter, set a
price of 5,000 marks for the villain's discovery, and ordered further searches of
the town and the rounding up of all persons involved in the late rebellion.
Mitchell was again forced to flee and spent five years as a fugitive in 'Holland,
England, and Ireland', until the end of 1673 when he returned to Scotland. He
was arrested the following February and placed in custody.

At first Mitchell denied any involvement in the assassination attempt, but when offered a promise that his life would be spared, he confessed. Two days later a trial by the Justiciary Court was ordered, but in it Mitchell withdrew his confession; it was the only evidence that could be brought against him. On 24 January 1676 the Privy Council ordered that he be tortured in order to extract a further confession of his part in the 1666 rebellion. In certain extreme conditions, this was legal under Scottish law. Mitchell would endure the most common instrument of torture, a device imported from Russia and used sufficiently by Lauderdale to become known as 'Lauderdale's Boot': an iron box that encased the leg; staves were driven into it to compress and eventually shatter the leg. Unsurprisingly, a person tortured with the boot was often unable to walk for some time; they would be permanently maimed:

> the executioner . . . began his Strokes; at every one of them enquired, if he had no more to say, or would say more? Mr *Mitchel* answered, No more, my lords. And thus he continued till he gave Nine strokes upon the Head of the Wedge: At the Ninth Mr *Mitchel* fainted through the Extremity of Pain; upon which the Executioner cried, Alas! my Lords, he is gone.[85]

No further confession had been made and he was carried by friends back to the Tolbooth. A year later, on 1 February 1677, Mitchell was taken to the Bass Rock and in January 1678 a new trial began, restricted to the assassination attempt. In it a number of important figures – Rothes, Halton, Lauderdale himself and Sharp – perjured themselves by denying that any promise of life was ever given to the accused. Mitchell was convicted and executed on 18 January 1678 at the Grassmarket in Edinburgh. For his part, Sharp was assassinated by Covenanters in May 1679 on Magus Muir.

Word would have reached London in late January 1676, and a new and brilliant poem by Marvell was one response, although it is largely overlooked because it is in Latin. In the words of one of its best scholars, Marvell's 'Scaevola Scoto-Brittannus is . . . something of a first, since in it Marvell turns his attention to a living example of a torture victim – a religious dissenter suspected of involvement in seditious activity in Scotland in the 1660s and 1670s. Marvell takes the opportunity to renew a familiar practice – attacking bishops who persecuted nonconformity . . . he also makes his fullest exploration of the attitude of martyrdom and the precise sensibility that inspires Mitchell's remarkable display of resistance.'[86] Mitchell was to become the subject of several poems and controversial pamphlets, most of them hostile (where the fact of his torture was played down or omitted), but some sympathetic (where Mitchell emerges as a martyr figure). What makes Marvell's contribution especially significant, however, is that it pre-dates all of these accounts and that it focuses on Mitchell's torture. The absence of any details from Mitchell's trial or execution strongly suggests that Marvell's poem was written before January 1678. Marvell would have been keenly aware of Archbishop Sharp, who had been in London in 1674 and 1675 as Lauderdale's assistant. Mitchell's treatment was a part of a crackdown on Covenanters, after calls for further indulgence to them in late 1675. In turning to Mitchell, and creating a martyr to extol the Nonconformist cause, Marvell's poem would have been very timely indeed in the early part of 1676.

If it seems strange that English poet-politicians should take such a strong interest in the Scots, it should also be noted that the Scots were certainly interested in the English, and in particular the ecclesiastical controversies gripping the reading public. The Scottish Presbyterian Robert McWard wrote a preface to his friend John Brown's *Christ the Way and the Truth and the Life* (Rotterdam, 1677) in which he referred to Marvell the author of *The Rehearsal Transpros'd*, 'who did so cudgel and quell that boasting *Bravo* [Parker], as I know not if he be dead of his wound, but for any thing I know, he hath laid [i.e. killed] his speech'.[87] Both men were protégés of the great Puritan divine Samuel Rutherford, himself so influential in Civil War England as well as Scotland, who had chosen exile in the Netherlands rather than accept the re-establishment of episcopacy in Scotland. In the United Provinces McWard and Brown cultivated positive relations with a number of Dutch theologians, including the leading and very firm Calvinist Gisbertus Voetius. Short of assassination, they were just as uncompromising as Mitchell; like Mitchell, McWard had been imprisoned in the Edinburgh Tolbooth. They both appear to have acted in the interest of the Dutch government against that of the Stuart monarchy and the episcopal church. McWard had even preached against the English during the Second Dutch War. Like Marvell they were by the 1670s engaged in an international political and religious scene in which the Dutch States General and the Stadholder stood as a greater guarantor of liberty for their religion than the reigning king of Scotland and England.[88] Before it became a party term in England, 'Whig' was used to describe the uncompromising Scottish Puritans typified by Mitchell, Brown and McWard: the radical Covenanters. At the point at which Marvell was mentioned by McWard, both he and Brown had been officially banished from the United Provinces at Charles II's request, although the edict was not enforced.[89]

Marvell's poem is rightly described as operating through a pair of juxtapositions. The significant one is the comparison of Mitchell and Sharp (ll. 1–8, 29–36). Marvell does not condone assassination, but he does suggest that Mitchell is the victim of unjust ecclesiastical tyranny. This discriminating treatment connects with his view of Parker, and several parallels, conceptual and verbal, have been seen between Marvell's English chaplain and the Scottish archbishop. Marvell's poem shows caution as well as probable acknowledgement of the debate taking place over Mitchell's claims to divine inspiration. But Mitchell wins the high moral ground precisely because he was subjected to such violence and because in the event he did not confess even under duress. In this sense, for Marvell, he defeats his torturer.

The occasion of the poem gave Marvell yet another opportunity to explore the matter of mirroring and self-reflexivity that pervades his work. In Paul Mathole's words, 'When the torture begins Mitchell is described as "*ut proprii sedet ad spectacula cruris*", "like a spectator at his own torture" (19); he is imagined among the crowd watching his own suffering.'[90] Obviously in enacting this treatment Marvell radically extends the apprehension of sympathy in his reader, attaching it to his call for toleration.

Finally Marvell compares Mitchell and Sharp by developing the allusion in the poem's title to the celebrated Roman hero, Gaius Mucius Scaevola: '*Scaevola si Thuscum potuit terrere Tyrannum,/Fortius hoc specimen Scotia nostra dedit*' (ll. 29–30: If Scaevola was able to terrify the Etruscan tyrant, our Scotland has given in this man a braver example). The parallel is inviting: in an attempt to kill the occupying king Porsenna, Mucius by mistake slew his secretary standing next to him. Arrested, and threatened with being thrown into a fire, Mucius thrust his own hand into the flames and held it there as one who felt no pain. The King, amazed by this display, set Mucius free; thereafter Mucius was known as 'Scaevola' or 'left-handed'. In return, Scaevola told Porsenna that there were 300 other men ready to take his life.[91] The point quickly becomes clear: through his conduct under duress, Mitchell has proved himself. Like Scaevola, Mitchell volunteers his own torture to show that he disregards his body in the cause for which he fights.

Marvell's representation of Mitchell is a highly significant development of the understanding of the scope of human subjection to violence. Put in terms with another of Marvell's writings, his posture mirrors inversely that of the Roman Emperor Caligula whom Marvell invoked to castigate Samuel Parker in *The Rehearsall Transpros'd: The Second Part* (1673).[92] In using the example of a tyrant, he specifically recalled Caligula because he 'had a singular quality for which he admired himself, and gave it a peculiar name of *Adiatrepsia*, which was his unmoved constancy in assisting at, and looking upon the most horrid executions.'[93] This achieved indifference (ironically invoking the Greek term which Marvell so liked about moderate English churchmanship – indifference (*adiaphora*) – which requires no compulsion of belief or practice) whilst looking upon suffering was used by Marvell to depict Parker as one who had an equal insensitivity in the face of human anguish. Now in Mitchell Marvell explores an alternative: indifference while undergoing physical torture.

Sharp was for Marvell a Scottish version of Parker, but with a greater record of actual persecution. Once a Presbyterian, Sharp accepted a position within the episcopacy at the Restoration and from then on was regarded as a turncoat by his former brethren. A harshly critical life of Sharp probably written in 1675 may have circulated in manuscript at this time, and many felt Sharp's treatment of Mitchell in particular and the Scottish Covenanters in general deserved punishment, which is precisely the implication at the end of Marvell's poem.[94] Marvell's poem was part of a series of poems, all of them playing ironically on the precise national identity of the subject. Thus Sharp was bitterly mocked as 'Misanthropos, Judas, Scoto-Brittanus his Lyfe, Lamentatione and Legacie'.[95] And of course, the poem was also an attack on Lauderdale, an absolutist bugbear for Marvell for five years, who by early 1676 was the chief opponent of Shaftesbury. It was alleged at the time that Shaftesbury sought to undermine Lauderdale in the Scottish Parliament, and was in communication with those in Scotland suffering under Lauderdale's policies.[96] The poem then was intended as an intervention in the religious politics of Scotland, possibly for circulation in Scotland, and certainly for circulation in Westminster, where Lauderdale's policies were assessed in court and Parliament. The poem is a prophecy of Lauderdale's end (his fall from power would begin in June 1678), and of Sharp's murder in May 1679, when Charles could no longer ignore the voices of Scottish aristocrats appalled at the Duke's repeated harsh repression.

MR SMIRKE

The second group of printed controversial exchanges in which Marvell was involved took up much of 1676, although the controversy itself had begun the previous spring during the battles in Parliament over supply, the attempts to impeach Lauderdale and Danby, and the struggles over privilege between the Lords and the Commons. A small group of moderate bishops in dialogue with leading Nonconformists had begun to push for a form of broad compre-hension for Dissenters within the national church towards the end of the first Parliamentary session of 1675. Marvell's defence of their most prominent spokesman, Herbert Croft, resulted in two tracts, published together in the summer of 1676 although they had probably been finished by the end of April: *Mr Smirke; or, The Divine in Mode* and *A Short Historical Essay, Concerning Councils, Creeds, and Impositions, in Matters of Religion*.

Herbert Croft was Bishop of Hereford.[97] He had been a Roman Catholic (originally converted by his father), but had re-converted in the 1630s at the urging of Laud and Thomas Morton, the Calvinist Bishop of Durham, and by the later 1660s was an advocate of the comprehension of as many Protestants as possible within a broadly defined national church, while being unrelentingly anti-Catholic.[98] He helped to introduce a Comprehension Bill in 1667, and had opposed the Conventicles Act of 1670, significantly in conjunction with Marvell's friend Sir Edward Harley. At a meeting of five bishops (including the pro-comprehension Edward Reynolds, but also the anti-Nonconformist Thomas Barlow) with two Nonconformist ministers (William Bates and Thomas Manton) present in May 1675, Croft was nominated to propose the position for comprehension by writing a pamphlet, designed originally to circulate at the end of the Parliamentary session. Croft wrote *The Naked Truth: or, the True State of the Primitive Church* and arranged for 400 copies to be printed, with the express purpose of circulation within the two Houses of Parliament. But Charles prorogued Parliament on 9 June, and Croft ordered the printer to stop his presses and withhold the book until the next session. However, the tract was pirated by another, unknown printer, who circulated this unofficial edition in the late summer or autumn of 1675. The delayed authorized edition, with a new and apologetic preface, appeared in late October or, more probably, November.

Croft's authorship was readily guessed, even though his name did not appear in either edition, and both editions caused a sensation, provoking rapid and often deeply hostile responses from a number of Anglican divines, including Peter Gunning, the Bishop of Ely (who had in fact edited posthumous works by Marvell's friend John Hales), and Francis Turner, chaplain to the Duke of York. Had *The Naked Truth* been published in 1673 its reception might have been different. But by 1676 both Parliament and Sheldon himself had hardened against comprehension.[99] Gunning's attack in the form of a sermon, originally preached before the King on 20 February, had appeared in print before 18 February, and Turner's tract seems to have appeared even before this, having been advertised in the government newsbook, the *Gazette*, of 6–7 February, although both of its editions carried the imprimatur of Henry Compton, Bishop of London, who was not appointed until 23 February, and it did not appear in the Term Catalogue until 5 May. This suggests that Turner's *Animadversions upon a Late Pamphlet* was backed in very high places indeed. On 3 March Stationers' Company officials went on the offensive and L'Estrange authorized searches for Croft's tract on the 29th.[100] We can make the circle of political associations larger too, for on 10 March the head of the government's intelligence, Sir Joseph Williamson, was told that since Richard Thompson's bank had collapsed, he would presumably no longer be a voice of such prominence and, for the government, difficulty, on the London Common Council.

Marvell mentioned Gunning in his reply on behalf of Croft but the real focus of his attack was Turner, who had chosen to vilify Croft with a number of ad hominem gibes. Marvell must have begun planning, perhaps even writing, *Mr Smirke* in the second week of February, but his creativity was spurred by the first performance of Etherege's *The Man of Mode; or, Sir Fopling Flutter* on 11 March at Dorset Garden, and by Turner's irritated observation that *The Naked Truth* was the talk of the town.[101] At the end of the *Essay*, Marvell also made a reference to a third attack on Croft, *Lex Talionis* (attributed to Philip Fell, but sometimes also thought, among others by Marvell, to be by Gunning), which was advertised in the *Gazette* of 4–8 May, so the complete two-piece pamphlet must have been in the press at this time, and coming to a conclusion. By 8 May, in fact, the Wardens of the Stationers' Company were searching for it. Although the two works are indubitably tied together, it is likely that Marvell was working on the *Essay* before he began his satire of Turner, in the long term as part of his anti-episcopal thoughts during the *The Rehearsal Transpros'd* controversy of 1672–73 (or perhaps even earlier), and in the more immediately preceding period of the prorogation of Parliament of nearly three months, between 22 November 1675 and 15 February 1676.[102] Nonetheless, Marvell's views on the harmfulness of creeds responds directly to their defence by Turner.[103]

Mr Smirke is more thoroughly anti-clerical than either part of *The Rehearsal Transpros'd*. Marvell takes strength from the character of wit as it was being offered in burgeoning London society and in particular the theatre. He then uses it to enforce the identity of his speaking persona, and at the same time to objectify the clergy. In *Mr Smirke* they begin to emerge as an idiot caste, despite the careful qualifications in defence of virtuous clergy. The result is a dry humour offered in a tightly bound sentence:

> It hath been the Good Nature (and Politicians will have it the Wisdom) of most Governours to entertain the people with Publick Recreations, and therefore to incourage such as could best contribute to their Divertisement. And hence doubtless it is, that our Ecclesiastical Governours also (who as they yield to none for Prudence, so in good Humor they exceed all others,) have not disdained of late years to afford the Laity no inconsiderable Pastime. Yea so great hath been their condescension that, rather than fail, they have carried on the Merriment by men of their own Faculty, who might otherwise by the gravity of their Calling, have claimed an exemption from such Offices. They have Ordained from time to time several of the most Ingenious and Pregnant of their Clergy to supply the Press continually with new Books of ridiculous and facetious argument.[104]

Marvell writes to correct the want of wit among the clergy, and with a refinement he had not yet deployed in prose spans the amusing analogy between apostolic succession and the conferring of wit. It is in fact an elaboration of the same concern with the witty writer that occurred in *The Rehearsall Transpros'd: The Second Part*:

> It is not every man that is qualified to sustain the Dignity of the Churches Jester: and, should they take as exact a scrutiny of them as of the Non-conformists thorow their Diocesses, the number would appear inconsiderable upon this Easter Visitation. Before men be admitted to so important an employment, it were fit they underwent a severe Examination; and that it might appear, first, whether they have any Sense: for without that how can any man pretend, and yet they do, to be ingenious? Then, whether they have any Modesty: for without that they can only be scurrilous and impudent. Next, whether any Truth: for true Jests are those that do the greatest execution.[105]

Francis Turner 'took up an unfortunate resolution that he would be Witty' but such was his shortfall, it was as if he had sinned against nature, an assertion that has been seen to carry associations of simony and sodomy.[106] The consequence of the unnecessary terms of Turner's attack upon Croft is a polluting of the public, a folio's worth of falsehood inside one side of quarto, and 'that Calumny is like London-dirt, with which though a man may be spatter'd in an instant, yet it requires much time, pains, and Fullers-earth to scoure it out again'.[107] It is only fitting for Marvell to conclude a section with a quotation from Rochester's 'Satire against Reason and Mankind', which had an added section attacking 'prelatic pride'.[108]

Yet Turner is no fool. His style may have been inelegant but he offered a skilful defence of the Church of England together with some stringent criticism of Croft's arguments. His appeal to creeds and some tradition in external matters such as vestments, logic, as well as authors of unsurpassable authority (Augustine, George Herbert) makes sense as a description of a reformed church embattled for survival. Turner can only see a disastrous confusion in Croft that will lead to the end of the church. This is why Turner regards Croft as a would-be heretic, fanatic and Socinian: a destroyer of God's order. Turner can command impressive imagery from ancient and patristic literature: events concerning St Augustine's mother, the line in the sand drawn around Antiochus by Popilius, Livy's account of how the behaviour of a Roman imperial guard dissuaded the Senate from moving the imperial throne out of Rome. Marvell sees that Turner is unable to find the model of modest, simple Christianity in Croft's writing: in his view it is a recipe for the end of Christianity in England. Marvell's sympathies are quite the opposite. Croft's treatise represents a springboard into another kind of piety: one without compulsion, and one answering to the collaborative vision of laymen and clergy in *The Rehearsal Transpros'd*. Turner's world, claims Marvell, is one of spiritual tyranny and 'temporal slavery' with a clergy intent on imposing print censorship.[109]

The Stationers' Company's quest for *Mr Smirke* took place in May, and involved searches at the houses of four printers: John Darby, Nathaniel Ponder, Thomas Ratcliffe and Nathaniel Thompson. Both Henry Coventry, Secretary of State, and Henry Compton, the Bishop of London, were interested in tracking down and suppressing the tract. On 10 May, Ponder was indicted for printing Marvell's book without a licence on the evidence of being found with papers from Marvell, including directions specifically from Marvell for the printing of the books.[110] Anglesey, as Lord Privy Seal, tried to prevent the imprisonment of Ponder, but he was overruled by Heneage Finch, the Lord Chancellor. Williamson noted that Ponder was to be imprisoned in the Gatehouse for 'carryng to the Prese to be printed an unlicensed Pamphlett tending to Sedition and Defamation of the Christian Religion'.[111] Darby was interviewed on 18 May by Coventry and confessed that he had been asked by Ponder to print the book: the intention had been to use two printers to produce 1,500 copies in order to circumvent action taken by L'Estrange or the Stationers' Company. The strategy of having parts of the tract produced in different printing houses resulted in a process that has been called 'inconsistent,

interrupted and highly pressurized'. The number of different states of the tract
is very great indeed, even to the extent of resisting the conventions of bibliographic description, in some cases making definitive description impossible.[112]
Darby confessed that Marvell was the author. For all this information, it was
decided not to punish Darby, who in any case, and perhaps disingenuously, had
said that he was himself unwilling to print the book, and had only composed
one sheet and printed none.[113] It took a petition, a promise of future good
behaviour and a £500 bond for Ponder to be released, on 26 May.

Marvell's authorship then was known widely and to the government from the
beginning, but no attempt was made to indict him. Not so much as an approach
was made, despite the feeling of some that he should be punished and humili-
ated 'for his insolence in Calling Dr Turner, Chaplain to His Royal Highness,
Chaplaine to Sir Fopling Busy'.[114] At the same time, the tract was selling, despite
the attempts to suppress it. It is reported that *Mr Smirke* sold for as much as half
a crown (Turner's tract was listed for only 6d.) and that it was widely distributed
by Nonconformists, who were delighted by the attack on a High Churchman.[115]
This latter information makes sense of a wry joke in a letter from Marvell to
Harley that summer that a rich Presbyterian had offered to buy the entire
impression in order to suppress it.[116] Marvell was implying by negative irony that
the tract was being purchased by Nonconformists for distribution through their
networks. Indeed, it was soon to be the case that three separate editions of the
tract were being distributed, the second probably by the Nonconformists.

In the meantime, the King had decided to stifle discussion of the *Naked Truth*
controversy by closing the coffee houses; perhaps the failure of Gunning's
sermon to appear in print was connected with this order. Strong protest at this
measure resulted in a delay of its implementation from 8 January until 24 June,
with the proviso that coffee house keepers allowed no seditious papers in their
premises.[117] But of course it is precisely the coffee house and its role in the operation of the public sphere and the formation of public opinion that Marvell's
pamphlet assumed, exploited and celebrated. Coffee houses were part of the
innovations in print distribution that made the later Stuart period so distinctive,
along with the clubs that met there and improvements in the postal system.[118]

Etherege's *The Man of Mode* was performed for the first time in early March
1676 at Dorset Garden, although it was not licensed for publication until
3 June. Whereas in *The Rehearsal Transpros'd* Marvell had identified his chief
target of attack, Samuel Parker, with Buckingham's chief character, Mr Bayes, in
Mr Smirke, Marvell picked a minor character, Mr Smirke, a divine who is kept in
a cupboard until he is required to perform a marriage, as his analogue for Francis
Turner. It was a decidedly acute piece of reductive humour: Turner was represented by an idiotic, well-dressed, shallow, biddable divine. He is chaplain to
'Lady Biggot', which itself is of course a gibe at the Duke of York. Etherege was
against Nonconformists so he may well have felt slighted himself by Marvell's
appropriation of his character: he dedicated the printed text of his play to Mary

of Modena, the new Duchess of York, whose marriage had excited so much protest in the Commons in 1673.[119]

Mr Smirke follows *The Rehearsal Transpros'd* in portraying the Anglican clergy of Turner's ilk as harmfully intolerant. Their hard definition of heresy becomes for Marvell a logical impossibility. His presence on a Parliamentary committee charged with abolishing the statute of *de haeretico comburendo* in March 1677 testifies to a personal interest in the matter.[120] Marvell also finds Turner's insistence on formal creeds, as opposed to Croft's emphasis on authentic faith, repellent. On the matter of the Godhead, he is quick to point out Turner's ignorance of theology (for instance in supposing that Judaism regarded the Holy Ghost as a second person in the Godhead), a matter that points back to Socinian knowledge in Marvell's background. Marvell pours scorn on Turner's apparently shallow suggestion that Christian creeds are essentially the same (and Trinitarian) and differ only in the 'Inadequation' of language.[121] He cannot translate, Marvell alleges, and he uses the witness of ancient Greek pagans to judge the Christian Greeks.

There is more to say about Turner's tract. Marvell's offence is triggered by the fact that its haughtiness of manner makes it difficult to read, especially when compared with *Lex Talionis*. It may have contained powerful arguments but it was also vulnerable as well as offensive in its manner, and that is partly why Marvell attacked it. He knew he had a target, and one that would work well if he developed the techniques he had used in *The Rehearsal Transpros'd*. Such premeditation suggests that Marvell was thinking and writing in conjunction with known associates, especially Sir Edward Harley with whom he had been corresponding since the publication of *The Rehearsall Transpros'd: The Second Part*. Harley was a friend of Croft's, and like his Episcopal colleagues, Croft had been working for comprehension with the colourful Colonel John Birch, in fact no friend of Croft's, Harley's or Marvell's (and allegedly deeply self-serving; he was an excise official, the 'Black Birch' of 'The Last Instructions', ll. 143–4), but a long-standing Herefordshire landowner, former Parliamentarian officer and strong believer in religious toleration and Parliamentary liberty; also with Sir Robert Atkyns, an Exchequer judge, fiercely anti-court, future designer of the Bill of Rights and someone who had prospered during the Interregnum.[122] That the opponents of Croft could see in *The Naked Truth* the same position as John Hales's, letting in broad toleration and even denigrating episcopacy through an appeal to reason, and hence destroying the church by a disastrous own goal, is another point of connection with Marvell.

But back to Turner, who is worth quoting here in order for us to see what Marvell saw in him:

> I Confess when first I saw this Jewel of a Pamphlet, and had run over two or three pages of this Chapter, I suspected our Author for some Youngster that had been dabling among the *Socinian* Writers, and was ambitious of shewing us his

Half-Talent in Their way. I was quickly delivered from this Jealousie by his Orthodox Contradictory Expressions in other places: But I find he is one of the *Men of the Second Rate* (as I take leave to style them) that hardly ever see to the Second Consequence. Therefore once for all I protest, that I do not charge him with many of his most obvious Consequences as his opinions: for 'tis plain, he does not discern them. But the Church may justly complain of him, for thrusting out such crude, indigested matter, without communicating these Conceptions as his opinions, to some that have shew'd him the weak and blind sides of them.[123]

Lex Talionis is clear that Croft is dangerously misguided but Turner is arrogant and condescending, and to this Marvell could reply in a manner that was a distinct and confident riposte to Turner's hauteur. It had to be so because Turner lifts from Marvell in *The Rehearsal Transpros'd* the invocation of John Owen as J.O. The humour of Marvell's opening passage is that he argues that no one should be offended by his lay person's discourse concerning the clergy even though that is exactly what he has sought to do: to offend Turner and his party to the point of inducing apoplectic rage. After all, 'albeit Wit be not inconsistent and incompatible with a Clergy-man, yet neither is it inseparable from them'.[124] The tract then becomes implicitly a mockery of ordination, claiming that wit is a harder thing to transmit than the ceremonies of the Church of England.[125]

Marvell's *Essay* has not been given the attention it deserves as an original, discrete work, largely because it was placed at the end of *Mr Smirke*. Its questions are certainly powerful enough: 'How came it about that Christianity, which approved it self under all Persecutions to the Heathen Emperours, and merited their favour so far, till at last it regularly succeeded to the Monarchy, should, under those of their own Profession be more distressed? ... Were there some Christians then too, that feared still lest Men should be Christians, and for whom *it was necessary*, not for the Gospel reason *that there should be Heresies*.'[126] Perhaps for this reason all of *Mr Smirke* is 'signed' by Andreas Rivetus, Jr., a title that more readily relates to the *Essay*, and in *Mr Smirke*, Turner is charged with arguing that a church is really a general council. André Rivet (1572–1651) was a towering figure in west European Protestantism, tutor to the young Prince of Orange in the earlier seventeenth century and author of a series of critiques of Catholic hermeneutics, as well as Protestant 'heresies', including Socinianism and the universalism of the later Saumur theologians.[127] Marvell's treatise imitates Rivet's recourse to the church fathers in a work of 1620 that stressed the role of secular rulers as nursing fathers to religion, but he turned Rivet's materials to different uses.

Marvell used exactly the same sources as Rivet and added only one, and that in a very occasional way. But by referring back to a Latin and (as it happened) Counter-Reformation Latin translation of the Greek of the three patristic church historians (Eusebius, Socrates Scholasticus and Sozomen) he was able to make his own strategic translations from the Latin, always in ways that treated bishops reductively, and presented them as unable to govern their own charges within the church. Some of the translation work even functions to reverse the sense that his authors originally intended. As a whole the *Essay* has a compelling rhythm in its exposition of episcopal cruelty. The *Essay* also involved a complicated *politique* history of the debates leading up to and taking place at the Council of Nicaea, where the doctrine of the consubstantiality of the Father and the Son were affirmed – the beginnings of the doctrine of the Holy Trinity. The corrupting quest for strict creeds, be they Nicene or Arian (the opponents of the Trinity), or later ones, is apparent. Constantine the Great, who stands for Charles II, is praised for his good intentions and moderation, although he had to suppress the Novatians for their intolerance (Marvell compares the Novatians to the Puritans) and chided them for letting the bishops get above themselves. As with *Mr Smirke*, comparisons with seventeenth-century England are often made: Hilary of Poitiers's fourth-century complaint against disunity in the church is seen as a direct precursor of Croft's *Naked Truth*.[128] Marvell compares the earthquakes that had ruined Nicaea in Valens's reign with earthquakes reported in England in early 1676.[129] The final three pages, added as an aftermath and perhaps an entirely separate composition, focus exclusively on the comparison with the Church of England.[130] Such disputes are the infection that wrecks Christianity from within: 'these Symptoms broke out at last like a Plague-Sore in open Persecution'.[131] Heresy in this period, Marvell reminds us, merely meant opinion, rather than anathema: a decidedly Miltonic view. Although Milton was far less charitable to Constantine, his late views in *Of True Religion* (1673) on the importance of a simple unifying scriptural faith, with lots of room for difference on many other matters, are echoed in the *Essay*, together with some of his favourite scriptural passages.[132] And from Marvell's history, Arius, the great anti-Trinitarian, emerges as wholly wronged and wilfully misunderstood by his episcopal opponents, while Athanasius is depicted as falling into jealous corruption after his virtuous boyhood (although Marvell will show how there had been persecuting Arian bishops and emperors, and he displays a republican preference by criticizing emperors like Valens who used mercenary armies instead of citizen militias).[133] Ultimately, bishops will convince secular rulers that their subjects are their enemies. It is a further inducement to think in the Machiavellian tradition and that of interest theory and reason of state: 'Hence it is that having awakened this jealousie once in the Magistrate against Religion, they [that is, the bishops] made both the Secular and the Ecclesiastical Government so uneasie to him, that most Princes began to look upon their Subjects as their Enemies, and to imagine a reason of State different from the Interest of their People: and therefore to weaken themselves by seeking unnecessary & grievous supports to their Authority'.[134] Constantine's exasperated delivery by himself of a singular understanding of Christ's nature at the end of the Council of Nicaea puns wittily in order to echo Horace's phrase concerning the mountain that was pregnant with a mouse: 'And thus this first, great, General Council of Nice, with which the world had gone big

so long, and which look'd so big upon all Christendom, at last was brought in
bed, and after a very hard labor deliver'd of *Homoousios*.'[135] As the editors of
Marvell's prose have noticed, in the *Essay*, biblical citation replaces literary allusions, achieving a remarkable and effective religious *gravitas* hitherto unseen in
Marvell's writing. This is wholly appropriate for a work that reaches out to
Dissenters in its opening pages: Christianity is defined as a suffering religion, and
the parallel between the bishops and the Pharisees is readily made. The taming of
conscience by an external authority is a kind of slavery: 'a good Christian will not,
cannot atturn and indenture his conscience over, to be represented by others'.[136]
To anyone whose understanding was grounded in the Thirty-Nine Articles of
the Church of England, Croft's sense of the limitation of human understanding
of the Trinity looked shockingly unorthodox, but Marvell defended him.[137] In a
game of name-shifting, again with modern resonances, it is in Marvell's view as if
the bishops were trying to claim that the episcopacy *was* the church. In Marvell's
view, the clergy themselves are nothing more than dressed-up laity, which was at
the time a very advanced view of churchmanship.[138]

Above all, Marvell's writing reveals the work of a poet as a critic of the clergy.
The opening sections of both *The Rehearsal Transpros'd* and *Mr Smirke* make a
similar point by having lines of verse punctuate successive paragraphs. This
containment by rhyme functions as a critical device: a rhyming sentence in
Francis Turner is used to criticize purported laziness of faith in the use of creeds
or a simple confession of faith without internal conviction. Harping on a string
and scanning on one's fingers are instances of poetic club-footedness being used
to demonstrate incompetence in the realm of controversy. Being vulnerable to
unguarded passions is a trait of the characters such as Flecknoe whom we see
mocked, gently or less so, earlier on in the poetry, and Marvell's intimate knowledge of raunchy Restoration London (however much elsewhere he appears to
have disapproved of it) further startles the reader.[139] But what makes us sit up here
is the picture of ecclesiastical hectoring as the thuggish tactics of a desperate and
unsubtle playwright. The vestry has become a tiring room, the mode of discourse
the new one of dramatic criticism, fused with coffee-house-cum-newsbook
observation. By virtue of theatrical analogy, wit is dressing up. The tone is startling, the dramatic tension and irony exquisite:

> The Vestry and the Tiring-room were both exhausted, and 'tis hard to say
> whether there went more attendants towards the Composing of Himself, or of
> his Pamphlet. Being thus drest up, at last forth he comes in Print. No Poet, either
> the First or the Third day, could be more concern'd; and his little Party, like men
> hired for the purpose, had posted themselves at every corner, to feign a more
> numerous applause: but clap'd out of time, and disturb'd the whole Company.[140]

It is Marvell's gift as an animadverter that he gives the impression of being
able to voice his opponent's hidden intentions. This is very well done,

involving the use of quotations from Turner, who in turn is shown to be conducting an indecent textual anatomy on Croft. The effect in Marvell's text is indeed proto-Swiftian, since Turner is revealed to be a cruel and violent persecutor, and mad: 'Such like also is his talking, that *this is stripping the Church to skin, nay skin and all*, and *skin for skin*: so wretchedly does he hunt over hedg and ditch for an University Quibble . . . I have heard a Mad-man having got a word by the end ramble after the same manner.'[141] The key words are developed beyond Croft's and Turner's texts so that the references to skin come from the tempting Satan in Job 2: 4, but Turner's mocking obsession with the skin references in Croft reveals him to be concerned only with his own skin (*curare Cuticulum*). Where Marvell had looked with discomfort at a poet-priest like Flecknoe in earlier years, because Flecknoe represented a destiny that could have been his, in these later years the distance from the clergy is complete. Parker and Turner have become other creatures, utterly distanced from the humane and *politique* MP.

In the prose itself the energetic deployment of surprisingly unusual, out of context, out of decorum, words marks the presence of a poet. In *Mr Smirke*, printed dispute is represented as a fist fight with words that embody the physical: the game of 'Hot-cockles'; while to 'expose' is to execute (in that it suggests a flaying), and the same is made to seem true of 'extended'.[142] Animadversion is likened to throwing eggs at those in the pillory or stocks, underwritten by a further list of kinetic vocabulary: 'galls', 'hank', 'Dint', 'Culls', 'Tiring' (a hawking word), 'snush' (meaning the enforced taking of snuff); in addition to vivid portrayals of compelled communion and baptism in the Church of England as force-feeding and drowning. Likewise, Turner's dull humour results in a cruel torture for Croft, like execution done with blunt instruments: 'To be raked and harrowed thorow with so rusty a Saw!'[143]

In the *Essay*, this intricate and wholly literary exposure of cruelty results in what has been claimed to be a modern sense of martyrdom, not for faith or bravery but for reason: 'For one that is a Christian in good earnest, when a Creed is imposed, will sooner eat fire then take it against his judgement. There have been Martyrs for Reason, & it was manly in them: but how much more would men be so for reason Religionated and Christianized!'[144] In this respect, Marvell's text begins to articulate something that looks exceedingly like Enlightenment religion, and it is notable that in the final sentence he offers his book and himself up to a fiery martyrdom to be burned, if necessary, by Turner in a spirit of reconciliation. Marvell's sense of martyrdom has been seen as political in the modern sense in which the term began to be used in the later seventeenth century, but there is still a sense of martyrdom for faith, although it is certainly a politicized community of faith.[145] Thus he spurns the claims by the bishops that the Holy Spirit was always present at council meetings: 'Nor needs there any strong argument of his absence, then their pretense to be actuated by him, and in doing such work. The Holy Spirit! If so many of them when they got together, acted like rational Men, 'tis enough in all reason and as much as could be expected.'[146] Without reason, anathematizing men turn into beasts, *'bite at one another, we are now all of us torn in pieces.'*[147] In all of this history, the heroes were saintly men like St Gregory Nazianzus, the Croft of his time, reluctantly a bishop, and Ammonius Parotes, who mutilated himself in order to avoid being a bishop, and this Marvell treats as a kind of martyrdom.[148]

Croft's *Naked Truth* offered a unified version of the Church of England, reunited with most of the Dissenters, especially the Presbyterians. To the orthodox, like the author of *Lex Talionis*, it seemed as if Croft was identifying bishops with presbyters. Between them is a very considerable gap with regard to how a Christian community is to be defined. Croft argues plaintively for unity and comprehension, the minimizing of differences based on a simple but strong affirmation of Protestant faith (all of the time he fears that division within Protestantism is a golden opportunity for Roman Catholics). The author of *Lex Talionis* believes in an exclusive Christianity that denies heretics according to a tradition as old as the patristic period. Arius was the first of many deceiving and self-deceiving heretics; these people and their beliefs must be cast out of the church in order to keep it pure. Faith involves denunciation and castigation. Marvell stood against this, articulated its unpleasant human dimensions as perpetrated by the clergy, and, with all of his affinity for martyrdom, looked towards a revival of suffering as a form of tolerant sympathy. It was quite a vision.

What we know about Marvell for the rest of 1676 is mostly concerned with the reception of *Mr Smirke*, apart from the regular meetings of Deptford Trinity House. He sent copies of Croft, Turner and his own *Mr Smirke* to Popple in May, even though the publication date was 4 June. In early June he went away for three weeks 'in the Country', almost certainly beyond Highgate.[149] It was reported by Sir Christopher Hatton that Marvell's new tract was much harsher on Turner than *The Rehearsal Transpros'd* had been on Parker. It may have been droll, but some thought it too satirical, even those on whose behalf it was written. Perhaps Marvell was happy that its author was understood to be a Presbyterian MP. The government made sure that the responses to it in tracts were well advertised. Anthony à Wood rumoured that Marvell had been clapped up in the Tower of London, and others begged to see copies of *Mr Smirke*.[150] Marvell wrote to Harley, anticipating that the letter might be opened, and so reported indirectly that *Mr Smirke* was considered by divines inferior to *The Rehearsal Transpros'd* and that the *Essay* was superior as a piece of writing but written to a poor end. He noted that some Nonconformists, like William Bates, were against his views on church councils. He was clearly enjoying his relative anonymity and immunity: 'the book said to be Marvels makes what shift it can in the world but the Author walks negligently up & down as unconcerned'.[151] Croft wrote to thank Marvell for his defence in early July; Marvell wrote back even daring to suggest surreptitiously that Croft had been too harsh on his own enemies, and implying the irony of the almost violent tone of Croft's letter when compared with his argument for gentle terms of comprehension.[152] Croft he called a 'fool', but that was because Croft called himself one, in the sense of the holy fool who speaks against the wisdom of the world (Prov. 26: 5); in fact he thought that Croft had looked after himself well and had protected himself against further answers in print. On 15 or 17 July, he slyly told Popple that *Mr Smirke* was 'slight and superficial' but not without use; its very nature meant that it would be hard to answer. Marvell also told Popple he thought that Stillingfleet might have had *Mr Smirke* and the *Essay* in mind when he attacked early church councils.[153] The High Churchers were furious for Marvell had abused the Bishop of London, and in October Simon Patrick attacked Anglesey's *Truth Unveil'd* (1676) for being kind to Marvell, and specifically attacked the *Essay*.[154] Patrick objects to Anglesey's characterization of Marvell as 'candid and facetious'; while much of his genuine ire is reserved for the attack on creeds, the satire of Parker in *The Rehearsal Transpros'd* is reviled for its 'smuttiness'. Patrick sees an arrant anti-Trinitarian in Marvell, and irresponsible gullibility in Anglesey, who should have acknowledged that Marvell had '*out-done all others in scurrility, calumny and prophaneness*' but instead he 'sobb'd and sigh'd, and sate down full of Marvel'.

In keeping with this newly exposed scepticism, Marvell mentioned to Popple in mid-July that he was unimpressed by the book he had been sent on astrology on the recommendation of the graphologist Maniban and Popple's wife.[155] Instead he recommended Cornelius Agrippa and Pico della Mirandola against the astrologers. And with a now familiar sense of his mortality, he enquired, again in Latin, about the state of William's finances, hoping that he would soon be able to return from Bordeaux to England, so that the two might more readily enjoy each other's company – before it was too late.

It was probably around this time that Marvell wrote his Latin poem on Maniban, who had apparently been shown a letter of Marvell's by the Popples. This would surely have been at least a surprise to the secretive Marvell; the poem itself rounds on those who would seek knowledge from something so apparently detached from the mind, and from someone not known to the interpreter: 'the flexings of the pen' making the shapes of the words rather than their significance. The unease at being read in this way is registered anatomically, as if the poet were being dissected, or sacrificed in ancient Tuscany in order to have predictions made from his extracted organs. Since Maniban fused graphology with astrology in his readings, the second half of the poem refers to the influence of the stars, yet while he does not deny that such maps in the book of nature represent something, how that truly relates to mankind in the present is not clear. What can an astrologer really foresee? '*Grammatomanti*' means both diviner and schoolmaster, while the echo of Ovid in line 4 points back to the secrecy that Marvell so valued. In this most refined and wry of poems, the irony is that the entire poem should not really exist: normally, a probing of his secrecy should be met with silence.[156]

Through the autumn, Marvell kept up his newsletters to the Thompsons in Escrick and York. He kept a close eye on matters of publication censorship, and instances where the Nonconformists prevailed. Already in July, he noted that Sir Robert Payton had been imprisoned in the Gatehouse for moving in the Common Council of London that there be a petition for a new Parliament.[157] Sir Robert Carr, although an 'old Cavalier', had been accused of fomenting similar sentiments; as had Ratford and Cornwallis. All were acquitted in court, but it was evidence for Marvell of a growing tyrannous administration.[158] He noted significantly the return of Shaftesbury to London at the beginning of December, but warned that pamphlets claiming that Parliament had been dissolved so that there would be a fresh election were utterly false.[159] A curious reference to the Virginia rebellion of Nathaniel Bacon (which liberated servants and African slaves but projected the removal or extermination of all native Americans in the colony) presented the disturbance very much as in the balance, as if it were an analogue of English politics, but finally expected that the Governor, Sir William Barclay, would prevail.[160]

At the end of the year too, local matters became more strained as Hull Trinity House tried to pursue in law Edmund Clipsham, who had been attempting to avoid duties owed to Trinity House on some fir (cut up into sections: 'deals') he had imported. Until the matter was resolved, the deals were impounded at the haven in Hull.[161] This meant for Marvell liaison with lawyers in London, including Sir Francis Pemberton and Sir Thomas Allen. He learned, having gone with Thomas Coates, another member of Hull Trinity House, to visit the Attorney General that the more expensive route of pursuing the case in the Exchequer meant that Clipsham would pay costs if he lost.[162] A good lawyer would have to be found to represent the Corporation. At the very end of the year he expressed regret to Hull Trinity House that it had decided to pursue Clipsham in common law, which would make much work for him in London. He feared that the Trinity House men would dawdle: he understood it as imperative that swift action be taken in preparing the necessary bill to be presented to Parliament, as he said to Edmond Popple, chiding him also that Trinity House had waited too long before it had turned to law. Their own charter was not 'Magna Carta', and 'Country Counsell like ill Tinkers make work for those at London'.[163] Some feverish work procured the solicitor John Fisher to represent Trinity House in the Exchequer, alongside Sir Robert Sawyer, who was a member of the Bar and an MP, and Marvell had the bill drafted in the last days of December.[164] All was set expediently, so that Clipsham was served with a subpoena in January 1677.[165]

Politics would become much hotter the following year. Before then it is important to note that Marvell saw himself as having evolved a different stance from the Puritans or at least the Presbyterians in his *Essay*. He could afford to tell Harley this, and he does so in a way that suggests finally his own surprise: 'Marvell, if it be he, has much staggerd me in the busnesse of the

Nicene & all Councills, but had better haue taken a rich Presbyterians mony that before the book came out would haue bought the whole Impression to burne it. Who would write? What saith the poor man.'[166] Indeed it was a matter of encountering censure amongst one's own natural supporters. But in writing and publishing the *Essay* Marvell was no longer a Puritan; he had become indelibly a freethinker: 'He may be a *Socinian*, or at least an *Arian*, or perhaps believe Nothing.'[167]

CHAPTER 12

✳

ARBITRARY POWER

THE YEAR 1676 WAS A momentous one: it was the year that saw Marvell's engagement with church politics (*Mr Smirke*) and the political consequences of church politics (the Mitchell affair) in the fullest and most ethically developed sense. These engagements also showed how far Marvell had moved towards the heart of Restoration culture. Whatever might have been seen of the remnant of Commonwealth outlook in his 1660s poems and satires, there is no doubt that 1676 sealed his reputation as one of the fiercest critics as well as recorders of the new age.

Marvell's strategies of anonymity had resulted in a reorganization of lifestyle. Probably late in the year he acquired the use of a room or an apartment in Maiden Lane, Covent Garden, where, as we will see, his wealth was allegedly kept. It was, in his own terms, his 'study', clearly somewhere he could go to write undisturbed. It was probably also the case that his lodging in the Little Almnery, Westminster, just over a mile distant from Maiden Lane, was now well known.

Through January 1677, and indeed for the rest of the year, the business of Hull and Trinity House continued, with attention given to the Clipsham affair. More lawyers had to be retained and the subpoena itself had to be prepared and sent to Hull so that it could be served on Clipsham. This was done in the early days of January, in which time Marvell learned that Popple was wavering, fearing that Clipsham would find a way of resisting, and hence the money would be spent in vain. Popple wanted to give Clipsham one last chance, and Marvell, with all his Cromwellian experience, knew about steadfastness: 'I can not but wonder that . . . you should so soon begin to wamble which is enough to discourage or turne giddy of one of so weak a braine and experience. Surely, Brother, it is better to steere steddy and hauing once set saile to follow ones course.'[1] At the same time, other matters become clear concerning Marvell's circumstances. In or about February, Marvell was due to pay a debt of £14 for some books to his publisher Nathaniel Ponder: his circumstances were thus not secure.[2]

His notoriety was now extensive. Without even naming him, the Anglican divine and apologist Thomas Long noted that those (like Marvell) who praised the tolerationist attitudes of converted Roman emperors ignored the strict discipline exerted by many of them. Two months later, other Anglicans would fall back on the old claim that ecclesiastical debate should not involve 'spleen'.[3] Such comments in printed books accompanied the intensified embattlement of the political nation that would come when Parliament was reconvened on 16 February 1677 after a very long prorogation. It would stay in session for another fourteen months. On the second day, Buckingham, Shaftesbury, Wharton and the Earl of Salisbury were imprisoned in the Tower of London by order of the House of Lords.[4] The charge against them was that they had insisted that the prorogation meant that the Cavalier (or for some 'Long') Parliament was dissolved and perhaps also that they had written and circulated pamphlets that encouraged sedition and rebellion.[5] Marvell's 'party' of opposition was increasingly identified; party politics, as opposed to faction, was about to rear its head in the nation for the first time during the extended period known as the Exclusion Crisis, from late 1678 until 1681, even if, in respect of local matters, Marvell insisted that he was disinterested. A Libels Committee of the House of Lords met for the first time on the 19th and was to remain in being until 9 April: the tenseness of the atmosphere was apparent. Marvell was a teller for the unsuccessful negative vote on 21 February in an attempt to have the very pro-court Sir Richard Temple removed from chairing the committee of the whole House concerning the supply, and on the 26th in an unsuccessful attempt to bar Henry Savile, perceived to be a client of the Duke of York, from taking up his seat.[6] On 27 February, Marvell reported that the Lords Libels Committee was close to discovering the author of a libel against Parliament; two days later Nicholas Cary was fined £1,000 for having a book 'concerning Parliament' printed without revealing its author.[7] From where were these statements and allegations in print coming? In the Lords, Holles was compelled to rebut the rumour that he was the author of *The Grand Question*.[8] Later in March, *Mr Smirke* was listed as one of the libels printed improperly by members of the Stationers' Company.[9]

On 3 March Marvell wrote to Trinity House in Hull to apologize for some adversity in the Clipsham case. They appear to have lost a commissioner to act for Trinity House, and Marvell had spent time trying to align more dignitaries with Hull connections, such as the Hothams, to exert pressure for Trinity House. In any case, the lawyers were not worried by the mischance. On 6 March came the debate that would be so definitive for the nation: one in which was so evident the fear of the influence of French power, in and of itself, and also in respect of its tainting the King and his government with absolutist tendencies. For the next month and ten days the debates in Parliament would provide the backbone for Marvell's finest and purest work of political analysis, *An Account of the Growth of Popery and Arbitrary Government*. In many ways, the pamphlet reflects majority views in the Commons, which warned the King of encroaching French power in an address, a copy of which Marvell sent to Hull on 10 March. Many MPs thought that war with France was inevitable and necessary; they were only surprised that it was taking the King so long to make a declaration.[10] There were many sensitive aspects of the French issue: such as alarm felt in the Commons that English soldiers had been impressed into French service.[11] Marvell certainly made sure that whatever he personally thought, and whatever the views of the interest he guarded, the tract would appear to be the obviously 'common sense' view of Parliament.

On the 24th, a Bill of Habeas Corpus passed through the House, which Marvell gratefully acknowledged was 'so necessary for the subject'.[12] Whilst he was named on the 26th for a committee charged with designing legislation to abolish the law for burning heretics (the last case had been in 1612), he was more troubled by the so-called 'Bishops' Bill' that had come down from the Lords on 15 March.[13] This was an attempt to ensure that bishops remain Anglican and that royal children be educated as Protestant Anglicans even if the reigning monarch had refused to take the Test Act (and in the event of the Duke of York succeeding his brother to the throne, was a Catholic). Marvell strongly expressed his view in the Commons on 27 March in a rare speech, saying that the Act was cumbersome, a potentially tyrannous machinery itself, that would not achieve its aim: ''tis an ill thing, and let us be rid of it as soon as we can'.[14] As usual, he did not report this intervention back to Hull. He said that the Bill amounted to Anglican absolutism, so to speak, a version of arbitrary power that might seriously hamper the proper functioning of the monarch. Marvell's speech lined up with the views of the country party, Shaftesbury at their head (but like Buckingham at this point, Shaftesbury was imprisoned in the Tower of London): they did not want the possibility of a Catholic succession in the monarchy to be prevented by strengthened episcopal power.[15] Marvell's argument in the Commons was strategic but it did reveal some patterns typical of his way of thinking and writing. The language of the Bill too readily presented the demise of Charles II, but Marvell also saw acutely through to the mutability of phrases: we should not be discussing treason as meaning 'to imagine the death of the King', but as its opposite: 'not to imagine the King's death'. Evidently Marvell felt that the King did not need to be so compelled at this time and that royal prerogative was being compromised. Although Marvell acknowledged that the bishops may not have been the authors of the Bill, he insulted them and their office by suggesting that the King's test oath might be administered by any group, such as the College of Physicians: he even proposed that this be tried out, like a scientific experiment or 'tryal'. And to voice even a hint of the King's death was to make that demise and all of its associations present in the House of Commons. The Bill was committed for further discussion in committee, against Marvell's desires (and in this he was supported by Sir Robert Howard and John Maynard), but he joined that committee and there it died.[16]

Marvell's speech, as Grey reports it, is awkward, and as has been often noted, his perceptions and wit, as he himself admitted, were not suited to this kind of discourse. But no one doubted his intent: the Speaker, Sir Edward Seymour, strongly criticized him on 28 March, when he was absent from the chamber, for endangering national interest by slandering the bishops.[17] All of his views on ecclesiastical power were behind his stratagem in Parliament. Then on 29 March Seymour tried to slander Marvell by seizing on the fact that he had appeared to hit Sir Philip Harcourt on the side of the head, after stumbling in the House. Seymour would not listen to Marvell's explanation that Harcourt was a friend, and tried to use the occasion to embarrass Marvell. It was of course an attack on Marvell's politics too. Presumably Seymour had not seen the poet's picture of him in 'The Last Instructions to a Painter', or if he had, he did not know that it was by Marvell. But he might have done. Another butt in Marvell's great verse satire, Sir Job Charlton, insisted that Marvell be sent to the Tower (like the opposition peers dispatched there the previous month).[18] Despite Harcourt's further explanation that the collision was accidental, Marvell was forced to make an official apology in the House. In it, the business of the collision bleeds into Marvell's riposte to Seymour's first objection. Marvell said that since the Speaker had traduced him in his absence the previous day, he hoped that he would look to keep himself in order as well as the rest of the House. Now that was disrespectfully intransigent, more so then than it would be today, and we can see that Marvell played into the hands of his enemies by letting the wit of the satirist come out inappropriately in the arena of Parliamentary debate. Either he was, not for the first time, politically clumsy, or he just could not stop himself. Perhaps he was playing in jest with Harcourt; perhaps too fatigue and irritation were showing in the two MPs. Marvell's frustration, brewed over a long time and much pent up, had in this context betrayed him, and it took the concerted efforts of his political allies at this point – Sir Robert Howard, William Garroway (or Garway) and Sir Thomas Meeres (or Meres) – to stifle the matter.[19] Marvell's apology blamed his lack of oratorical skill in the House, and affirmed his respect for the Speaker ('He is not used to speak here, and therefore speaks with abruptness'), but the fact is that he did not respect Seymour, and he had to be rescued by his fellow 'country' MPs.[20]

But Seymour would have known too that Marvell was close to being exposed or even punished in Parliament for being the author of *Mr Smirke*. Furthermore, while the Commons were busy rebutting the Lords' Bill against recusants which a majority of them (including Marvell) felt actually to be working in favour of the Catholics, the Lords Libel Committee had finally uncovered the uncomfortable fact that Mearne the stationer had testified that the King had ordered the publication of *The Rehearsal Transpros'd*.[21] L'Estrange had licensed it the day after Mearne had seized it: the committee saw L'Estrange's letter of instruction.[22] Embarrassment of Marvell would have been a major political victory for the Cavalier–Anglican axis and no doubt a very distressing matter for Marvell himself: he simply did not like this kind of public exposure. But, on 16 April, Parliament was adjourned until 21 May, and it must have been some comfort to Marvell to know that the King was angry that the Commons had not been able to vote the supply before the adjournment, even though relations with France, after Louis's taking of St-Omer, had deteriorated further in the direction of war.

It was a significant moment, and as in the crisis of the later 1660s, Marvell noted in a letter of 25 April to Sir Henry Thompson the sighting of a comet and an approaching eclipse of the sun. In May, presumably before the demands of the session took his attention, Marvell began to compose *An Account of the Growth of Popery and Arbitrary Government*, looking back at the debates of the preceding session while also summarizing the session that would begin on the 21st. This suggests that the tract was largely composed in this interval. The March debate, his role in it and his humiliation in the House by his enemies, had precipitated the need for revenge, and he resorted to writing to find it. At the same time, Shaftesbury listed Marvell as 'thrice worthy' in a tally of MPs, a significant demonstration of alignment. When Parliament did gather again – for just a week from 21 May – the pressing issue was whether to go to war with France. Parliament insisted that Charles form alliances with other powers, especially the United Provinces, before any moneys were voted. It was altogether preoccupying and Marvell could not be reached by any of the Trinity House agents in London.[23]

After the adjournment on 28 May, a famous domestic event in Marvell's life occurred. He asked Mary Palmer to end the lease of the house in the Little Almnery and to rent a house in Great Russell Street, Bloomsbury, from a Mr and Mrs John Morris. She was to use her name and not his, even though others still would be paying the rent. The purpose of this was to hide Marvell's family and Hull associate, Edward Nelthorpe, who was bankrupt and trying to protect his assets. These took the form of deposits of the very considerable sum of £500 left with the goldsmith Charles Wallis, but with Marvell himself named as the payee, thereby making Nelthorpe's money invisible. At or around this time, Marvell seems to have borrowed from Nelthorpe £150, even though he was bankrupt. In the middle of the month Nelthorpe and Richard Thompson went into hiding with the remaining cash and instruments of the bank they had founded with Farrington and Page. Farrington was soon in jail, the creditors having been persuaded by Thompson and his wife that he possessed the records of the bank.

Money, its relationship to international affairs and the stability of states, was much in the air in the Marvell family. In the next decade, resistance to James II would in part depend upon the viability of certain banks, as well as the recourse to arms.[24] Mary Popple, wife of Marvell's nephew William, wrote from Bordeaux to Edward and Mary Nelthorpe that she was consulting the 'Abbé' (presumably Maniban) on money matters, and an astrological figure for Sir William Cowper, but that the abbé needed more information to make a discerning calculation.[25] Mary Popple also referred to the publication of the Zohar, one of the kabbalistic texts. This must have been the first volume of *Kabbala denudata*, prepared by Christian Knorr von Rosenroth and published in 1677 at Sulzbach. She mentions that Francis Mercurius van Helmont, who had become famous in England when appointed Lady Conway's physician in 1670, was trying to dissociate himself from this publication, even though he had helped Knorr with copies of several important texts, and contributed a dialogue defending the kabbala's description of the origins of matter. What Marvell might have made of the Zohar is an interesting question. The Fairfax poems and 'The Garden' contain hermetic and Neoplatonic elements consistent with some kabbalistic ideas (e.g., the androgynous Adam Kadmon extant before the creation of Eve, and the Adamic and perfect language of nature spoken by mankind before the Fall), but this does not sit so readily with his castigation of another kind of mystical prognostication in Maniban's graphology.[26]

Meanwhile, back in Westminster, the plight of the Parliamentarians was a preoccupation for the poet-politician. While the French armies advanced across the southern Netherlands, the trial of Joseph Brown for publishing the prorogation tracts continued (effectively calling for new Parliamentary elections), and the four lords remained in the Tower, with Shaftesbury pleading at the King's Bench for the law of Habeas Corpus.[27] All of this Marvell noted at the end of June; on 16 July Parliament met only to be adjourned until 3 December. This had been an expected manoeuvre by the King, with court MPs upsetting the procedure by demanding an adjournment before the order by which the Commons had last been adjourned could be read. To the opposition MPs, that last adjournment had been irregular, but as Marvell noted, too few MPs cared. They probably cared even less than they did about the sexual crimes that had been prosecuted at the previous sessions.[28]

But the imprisoned lords were fighting back. Salisbury, Wharton and Buckingham had been released upon petitions in late July while Shaftesbury remained in the Tower, his plea to be released on health grounds refused by the King.[29] Marvell also noted in a moving letter to Sir Edward Harley that conventicles in Scotland had been violently suppressed: the point of writing '*Scaevola Scoto-Brittannus*' was entirely justified and had, it would seem, come to nothing.[30] On 9 August, the hand of the opposition lords became apparent to the government as L'Estrange had detected the clandestine printing of prorogation tracts, pamphlets defending the imprisoned lords, and a tract expressing fear that the Duke of York and Danby would bring in popery. The latter, it has been thought, might be *An Account*.[31] Whether it was or not, L'Estrange was fairly sure that Francis Smith was at the heart of this: the underground press was once again doing its work.[32]

Marvell continued in the business of both Hull and Deptford Trinity Houses in early September but on the 7th came the startling news of the death of his friend and sometime neighbour the political philosopher, James Harrington.[33] Aubrey claimed that Marvell wrote a splendid Latin epitaph for Harrington that would have given 'offence' (although this was based on hearsay: he had not seen it). An innocuous epitaph was placed in St Margaret's, Westminster, but this was not by Marvell, whom Aubrey had listed as second only to Neville among Harrington's friends.[34]

Harrington's real contribution could only be remembered secretly by 1678, and with great preoccupation in the country for the marriage of William of Orange to Princess Mary, a Stuart, daughter of the Duke of York, it was as if there was another kind of conspiracy to that of the proto-Whigs and republicans, with the Dutch subjected to William and the English to Charles; both to Catholicism. But the Clipsham business required further attention in September. The Commission had finally been executed, and for his part Clipsham had threatened not merely to resist but to challenge the right of Trinity House to charge primage. Reporting a conference between himself, Coates and Fisher, Marvell offered the view that Clipsham's claims were most unlikely to be sustained.[35] The only issue would be whether he would be made to pay Trinity House's costs. Marvell said Clipsham was irrational and dishonest; he wanted to put his brethren's mind at ease, but there must have been some sense of apprehension while the case played out.

A further royal proclamation postponed Parliament for a further five months, until 4 April 1678.[36] This at least gave Marvell a break in the pressure to produce *An Account*, the printed text of which was at the time being prepared by the Baptist printer John Darby.[37] It also gave him time to see through to the end Trinity House's case. On 3 November, the hearing was anticipated, after much preparation, involving liaison with Fisher the solicitor, and the two Hull men in London, Thomas Coates and the lawyer George Trueman. He still had not exhausted the money entrusted to him by Trinity House for the case.[38] The hearing came on 15 November, and Trinity House was granted all it wanted, except for its fees, which Marvell considered unimportant compared with the victory over Clipsham.[39] A decree was prepared for dispatch to Hull, so that proof of the judgment was manifest. All had behaved well, except for Sir Robert Sawyer, who though paid had not appeared to represent his clients.[40]

While the Clipsham affair finally came to its successful end for Trinity House (the following February Marvell would be rewarded with ten guineas, presented personally by Coates), he did further duty for Hull by procuring at their wish six Jacobus pieces of gold in a silk purse for presentation to the Duke of Monmouth, the Lord Lieutenant, as his 'annual honorary'. The order was made on 20 December; Marvell presented the gold on 1 January.[41] He also wrote to Harley apologizing for being unable to enclose the next instalment of what we presume was *An Account*. At a lunch meeting with Denzil, Lord Holles, however, further alarm was expressed concerning French power, against a background of popular demonstrations against popery.[42] It was perhaps just as well that at the 3 December meeting of Parliament, which was only to acknowledge a further adjournment, the next session was brought from April back to 15 January: Charles had lost his secretly negotiated subsidy from Louis XIV, and there was in the court a strong move to pull in the supply from Parliament and mount a war against France if only to distract hostile popular attention from the court itself.[43] Marvell had little choice now but to bring his *Account* to a rapid conclusion and publish it. As he did so, he now openly referred in his text to the oncoming January meeting.

An Account of the Growth of Popery and Arbitrary Government

Early in January, or perhaps even in the closing days of December, *An Account* finally appeared. Darby's edition was followed by a second edition also in quarto, but with an uncertain date and printer, and this was the starting point for several further editions. It was a classic underground press production but perhaps Marvell's method of anonymous publication was no longer an effective disguise: several surviving copies contain early manuscript attributions to him.[44] Such were the conditions of haste and secrecy governing the production of the first edition that the text bears little resemblance to Marvell's own habits of spelling, capitalization and punctuation: it was probably copied by the ex-Cromwellian officer Henry Danvers and then taken by Ann Brewster to Darby's press.[45]

'Popery' is not, for Marvell, merely Roman Catholic worship and church government. After all, we have already seen in Marvell a degree of sympathy for individual Catholic figures, such as the Earl of Castlemaine and Archibald Douglas. 'Popery' as Marvell conceives it is a form of corrupt political behaviour that alienates Englishness and English political and religious identity by ignoring or bypassing the traditional relationship between the monarch and Parliament. The first part of Marvell's tract is a history of events from 1667 onwards, charted to show the rise of a conspiracy of pro-French court-associated MPs. The second half of the tract is a more detailed account of the sessions of 1677, and in particular the Bishops' Bill for the Protestant education of royal children, to which Marvell had made such objection in the House of Commons, and of the debates about war with France from March to May. Marvell was clearly working very hard at certain points, and without much leisure, to solder together disparate materials. He just about succeeds in making the whole governed by his irony, and he further succeeds in demonstrating how the King was attempting to draw supply without first declaring war on France; by establishing a pro-Catholic conspiracy between Danby, the Duke of York and the bishops. Despite this, Marvell's claim that the politics of the early 1670s was the same as that of the late 1670s has been judged at best rhetorical and at worst 'specious'. After all, first Buckingham and then Shaftesbury were ministers for Charles II in the early 1670s, and Marvell silently implicates Buckingham in the making of the secret treaty with France, and Buckingham and George Savile, Viscount Halifax, in pressing impossible terms on the Dutch in June and July 1672 (while also over-looking Shaftesbury's support for the Third Dutch War itself).[46] In Marvell's view, Buckingham's reputation is rescued because when the conspirators were pressured, Buckingham was made a scapegoat. Deprived of office, he was restored to his natural respect for English liberty. The proroguing of Parliament on 22 April 1671 is seen in hindsight as a blunt consequence of the supply having been voted, rather than the dispute between the two Houses.[47] The Declaration of Indulgence, which Marvell had once supported, is seen as a stratagem to distract attention from the outbreak of the Third Dutch War in 1672, as well as an introduction of popery by royal dictate.[48] Perhaps *An Account* demonstrates Marvell's tactic of silent implication at its most accomplished and most daring: the King is not mentioned as a responsible actor throughout the tract, but 'Charles was the common link between all the steps towards absolutism and popery'.[49] It is impossible to read the King's speech in the Banqueting House on 28 May 1677 as anything less than extreme constitutional arrogance. The blunt accusation that the Commons had invaded his prerogative in foreign affairs may have been made in 'his *Majesties* name' but it was spoken by him too, and to that extent he was an agent, even if the speech he read 'out of his Paper' was not entirely his own composition. And in response, the House of Commons is 'appalled', and the reader is meant to be so too, by the attempts of the Speaker and others to stop an immediate response to the speech, since the King had also adjourned Parliament at the end of his speech.[50]

The Bishops' Bill is cited in full in *An Account*, reflecting Marvell's own interest in seeing it fail, and by focusing on it he makes the tract as much anti-episcopal as against French power. The extensive reporting of the Bill makes the bishops look demented (again, Marvell used the technique of speaking in the voice of his enemies), and they are mocked by the irreverent typesetting ('Bishop-prick'; 'Arch-bishop-prick') that does not seem entirely accidental.[51] It also greatly disrupts the flow of the tract's political narrative. Marvell takes the attack to the Court party in the Commons too, notably Seymour (once praised by Marvell when he was a supporter of Buckingham), Williamson the spymaster and Sir Robert Holmes, once an aggressive naval commander against the Dutch.[52] These were some of the MPs trying to embarrass Marvell during the 'box on the ear' affair in March 1677. Williamson was in Marvell's view an arch-conspirator, but it is Holmes who emerges as more intrinsically evil, rapacious and someone who today would be termed an 'utter bastard'. By contrast, the heroes of *An Account* are Buckingham, Shaftesbury and James Harrington, although Marvell never quite speaks from a position absolutely identical to Shaftesbury's.

Other aspects of Episcopal policy, such as a bill that the Commons thought was too lenient towards recusants, are passed over by Marvell: finally *An Account* is not a comprehensive history of the business of Parliament.

The brilliance of Marvell's argument is to name the court politicians as 'conspirators' (perhaps taken from Sallust's *coniuratories*)[53] who were damaging what ought to be a unitary national political culture: the interest of England, as opposed to the interest of France. The country MPs were thus not a faction but guardians of the central national interest. More brilliant still is Marvell's portrayal of the 'conspirators' with ironic sympathy. With great insight, Nicholas von Maltzahn writes: 'The *Account* presents the conspirators almost as they might see them themselves – as if high-minded, and not just high-handed – only then to expose such deceit as scarcely veiling the most naked private interest.'[54] Marvell's lack of personal authority, so limiting in his speeches, served his capacity for irony in his writing. In some passages it is hard in the grammar to detect agency on the part of the conspirators, Marvell's intent being to show how insidious was their power, how hard to detect, and how omnipresent. Thus the Bishops' Bill 'dyed away' in committee, even though 'some indeed having, as is said, once attempted it in private . . . but were discovered.'[55] More local effects are less than ironic: the conspirators looked to Louis XIV for support in enhancing royal power in England, finding there a 'Back for their Edge', which is to say the weight and support on the back of a knife blade, so that its edge works with maximum cutting or piercing effect. Likewise the Triple Alliance is winningly described as 'a hook in the French nostrils'.[56] In reality, Marvell is at pains to suggest, the French are winning at the expense of the English at every point: Louis is shown to be particularly skilful in promoting French trading interests at the expense of English merchants.[57] The sarcasm here is sometimes deafening. The conspirators called Louis XIV 'the King of France' in the autumn of 1675, but in fact his armies were trudging over several parts of Europe (reinforced by the presence of English troops in their ranks), and they might have called him 'King of England'.[58]

Another aspect of this tract that follows from its indebtedness to Parliamentary debate and political life is its composite make-up. Marvell appears to have written his narrative of events in 1676–77 in May 1677 (pp. 70–85), and to have begun later the longer-term explanation of the previous decade (pp. 27–69). Then other documents were assimilated to the text without transcription by Marvell or anyone else, such as the copy of Bridgeman's speech (pp. 20–26) and the list of ships captured by the French navy added at the very end of the first quarto edition, which the printer set off distinctly. It may be that the material concerned with the debates on war with France in March–May 1677 also came from a separate narrative source or sources, which were summaries of debates in the House of Commons (pp. 101–7, 122–48). This means that it has been possible to break the text down into seven different components, each of which has various subsections, making a total of twenty discrete units.[59] Marvell saw the problem, and did what he could to give his reader a 'thread to guide himself by thorow so intreaguing a Labyrinth'.[60]

The presence of political theory in the tract is not to be overlooked. The second paragraph refers to the 'proportion' retained by mere subjects in the English legislature, and this arithmetical sense suggests a debt to James Harrington's analytical terms. The same can be said of the sentence that follows: 'the Ballance of publick Justice being so delicate, that not only the hand only but the breath of the Prince would turn the scale'. The image is of the blind figure of Justice, and the subject is royal power, but the concept of the balance is Harringtonian.[61] The picture of the English monarchy is so perfect that it is clearly ironic, but also echoes the utopian dimensions of state formation in Harrington's *Oceana*, in the figure of Olphaus Megalator, an idealized Oliver Cromwell.[62] It is an exquisitely clear piece of political journalism in which the witty satire of 'Flecknoe, an English Priest at Rome' is retooled as a piece of incontestable observation. Marvell praises by way of ironic comparison the strict law-keeping of the Spartans in the ancient world, another favourite republican example.[63] Of Catholic worship Marvell writes: 'by a new and antiscriptural Belief, compiled of Terrours to the Phancy, Contradictions to the Sense, and Impositions on the Understanding their Laity have turned Tenants for their Souls, and in consequence Tributary for their Estates to a more then omnipotent Priesthood.'[64] The allegation of priestcraft is part of Harringtonian republican theory, but Marvell was also relying upon his Miltonic connection, the 'character' of popery reaching back through Milton to Sarpi's *History of the Council of Trent*. The allegation that priestly celibacy is a violation of nature and a cause of adultery is more recognizable Protestant apology, but the charge that princes use Catholicism as a means of enslaving their subjects, and that this is like a Hindu priest sleeping with a bride on her wedding night in order to better ensure her future devotion, is altogether more exotic. One source was Neville's republican and libertine parody of the Book of Genesis, *The Isle of Pines* (1668).[65]

Marvell draws an analogy between the constitutional protection of property and the protection of religion, which involves the propriety of conscience. The Declaration of Indulgence was therefore a robbery of what Englishmen had gained through Parliament in respect of religion: 'men ought to enjoy the same Propriety and Protection in their Consciences, which they have in their Lives, Liberties, and Estates: But that to take away these in Penalty for the other, is merely a more Legal and Gentile way of Padding [robbing on the highway] upon the Road of Heaven, and that it is only for want of Money and for want of Religion that men take those desperate Courses.'[66] And at the very beginning of the tract, Marvell is utterly sure that everyone in the kingdom is represented, and that this relationship turns precisely on the matter of the supply: 'here the Subjects retain their proportion in the Legislature; the very meanest Commoner of England is represented in *Parliament*, and is a party to those Laws by which the Prince is sworn to Govern himself and his people. No Money is to be levied but by the common consent.'[67]

Finally, the role of poetry and art in politics is of great interest to Marvell. He notes wryly the stretched way in which the English claimed a cause of war in Dutch pillars, medals and paintings celebrating victories in the Second Dutch War, and especially the Chatham Raid, even though the mould for the medals had been broken in 1670. By comparison, he noted a Polish poem provoking a declaration of war by Russia in the 1650s and ironically stated that the English cause of war was so weak it needed Dutch satirical art to make its case. Hidden in here is a plea for the power of political art since it stimulates the imagination of the powerful: 'the Pillars to add Strength, the Meddals Weight, and the Pictures Colour to their Reasons.'[68] His controverter Marchamont Nedham would see a comparison in Marvell between Shaftesbury and Cicero, and he presents this in a negative light, even while detecting the probable source for both himself and Marvell in Ben Jonson's *Catiline*.[69]

Marvell wrote from Covent Garden on 15 January 1678 that Parliament had gathered only to be adjourned until the 28th of the month. The government announced that a further week would enable the King to make a significant and positive announcement with regard to the position in Europe. However, of more concern was the fact that the Speaker adjourned the House without putting the question and thereby violated its ancient privilege, with MPs lining up to speak. It was a matter to which the contents of *An Account* related, and it did not take at all long for the recently published tract to raise the ire of the government and its agents, even as the House of Commons was debating a reinterring of Charles I's body, 'his late martyred Majesty'.[70] Even former acquaintances, like Nedham, were troubled by the disturbing power of *An Account*. On 19 February 1678, Samuel Mearne, the King's Stationer, was licensed to enter any suspicious house or other premises in order to find who was printing *An Account*.[71] Two days later, another stationer, William Whitwood, seized copies of the pamphlet from Samuel Packer of Cornhill. Packer himself was imprisoned in the King's Bench where he is reported to have died. In fact, either the dating is wrong or he managed to remain in hiding in mid- and later March, corresponding in secret with his wife, but every minute fearing violent seizure and imprisonment.[72] It was on 21 March that Goodman Atwood, the Deputy Marshal of the King's Bench prison, wrote to Danby reporting that he had taken Packer for distributing *An Account*, and asked that he be reimbursed for the cost of the imprisonment and rewarded for making the arrest. He had also searched the house of Francis Jenks, a linen draper and key distributor of opposition publications, where behind a mirror and in a closet several copies of tracts, including those concerned with James Harrington and Joseph Brown, were found.[73] The Wardens of the Stationers' Company paid for a porter to carry twelve seized copies of *An Account* to Whitehall. On 22 February the bookbinder Thomas Bedwell was committed to Newgate for dispersing treasonable and seditious libels, including *An Account*. He would have to wait until his mother successfully petitioned for his release on 3 May.[74] On the following day the Wardens of the Stationers' Company were summoned by the King and Privy Council, as they sought to hear the results of the many searches that had taken place. On the 25th, Danby pushed further in the Lords to aid L'Estrange by asking that the Surveyor be allowed to investigate the manuscripts of the libels condemned by the Lords during the previous March: he thought he would be able to establish a link between them and *An Account*.[75]

This predicament is anticipated in the tract itself, in so far as Marvell notes that attempts to have Commons addresses and other apologies printed in May 1677 were denied, handwritten copies suppressed, and the King's speech printed in the *Gazette* so that the House of Commons was defamed as 'Run-away Servants, Lost Doggs, Strayed Horses, and High-way Robbers'. It was a public humiliation, and from a country viewpoint an unconstitutional manoeuvre, noted in political correspondence at the time.[76]

It was a distraction more personally relevant than Clipsham's that Marvell was named to a committee on 12 February for the better discovery of the estates of his bankrupt friends Nelthorpe and Thompson and others, brought by their former associate Farrington. But Marvell had of course given them shelter in the rented house on Great Russell Street.

That Shaftesbury's release from a year's detention on 26 February was mentioned by Marvell is significant.[77] Shaftesbury had finally apologized to Charles and Parliament; it is thought that he wanted some influence in the issue of raising an army, especially if, beyond the context of war with France, it was to become a standing army.[78] Nedham's *Honesty's Best Policy, or, Penitence the sum of Prudence*, an attack on Shaftesbury, presented *An Account* as a mouthpiece for him, a purported friend of its author, and as the creation of his patronage. 'It looks ugly,' thought Nedham, and he further labelled the *Account* a tragicomedy and its author a 'virulent Scribe'.[79] On 18 May, as distinguished a writer as the Tory pamphleteer Edmund Bohun noted Nedham's perspicuity in analysing Marvell's 'most infamous libell' in this work.[80] Williamson was told by the stationer William Leach on 1 March of Samuel Packer, who had asked Leach to bind a copy of the pamphlet. As we heard above, Packer was soon in hiding, deeply anxious and trying to avoid harm being done to his family: 'they prosecute att present so violently that I dare nott stir out of doores unlesse by stealth. If I should I should be inevitably taken and miserably used which I hope thou desirest nott I dare nott come to any Friend not they to me butt by Notes and Letters there is A thousande Pounde bidd for me as soone as their Rage is A little over I will send for thee God willing to meet me.'[81] He hoped to arrange to meet his wife secretly, but these meetings would never happen: Packer was taken around the 21st of the month. Searches of various premises began to bring results: in addition to the raid on Francis Jenks's property near the Royal Exchange, from the stationer Joseph Lee came frustratingly unverifiable hints of a secret press at one 'Cartwrights' and that John Harrington had had a hand in the production of *An Account*.[82] As if in confidence, the administration published in the *London Gazette* an offer of a substantial reward for further informers on printers, publishers and distributors of seditious and libellous pamphlets. They knew they should attempt to break up the allegiances of the printers, offering to set up any informer from the printing industry with the freedom to establish a printing house. Rewards were claimed months after the advertisement first appeared. As Nicholas von Maltzahn suggests, the advertisement in the *Gazette* for 21–25 March then prints a notice for Dryden's *All for Love* as if it were a direct riposte to and correction of *An Account*: the advertisement commended Danby and the government for achieving a monarchy with liberty beyond a commonwealth and yet no tyranny.[83]

In April, L'Estrange himself entered the printed debate by publishing *An Account of the Growth of Knavery, Under the Pretended Fears of Arbitrary Government and Knavery*, the most direct and searching attack on Marvell so far. Although there are ways in which the pot was calling the kettle black, L'Estrange chose to attack Marvell's ethos – the grounds of authorship and, as he saw it, the way the speaking voice in the tract allied itself with sedition and also concealed its identity. He associated Marvell's *Account* with the list of court MPs in *A Seasonable Argument* (which was named in a search and seizure warrant of 6 April) and referred to the author as a 'Merry-Andrew', a skilled writer but not skilled in business or in delivering a clear opinion; he tied the tract to both *The Rehearsal Transpros'd* and the Painter poems in this sentence: 'By his vein of improving the Invective Humour, it looks in some places as if he were *Transprosing* the *First Painter*.' But L'Estrange also had to show how *An Account* was dangerous, and so on a national political level he likened its opening to the Grand Remonstrance of December 1641, sent by Parliament to Charles I.[84]

A further and important satirical attack came in the form of a pamphlet masquerading as a secret letter from within the ranks of seditious opposition: *A Letter from Amsterdam to a friend in England*, which called for new *Accounts*, and praised Marvell as the key anti-papal writer, while also accusing him of confused religious opinions and of being an unsuccessful poet.[85] It appeared on 18 April.[86] Marvell's identity and achievements, as his enemies saw them, were becoming clearer and clearer in the public eye.

INGENIOUS TO THE END

Marvell himself was happy at least that William Sancroft had been made Archbishop of Canterbury in January.[87] But for now there was the business of the bankrupt kinsmen to deal with. Marvell was paying, or was having paid, or someone was having paid in his name, £15 half-year interest on the £500 loan. Richard Thompson was in hiding in Chichester. Was Nelthorpe in the house in Great Russell Street? Somebody wanted to know because at the end of the month, on 31 January, the *London Gazette* advertised for their discovery.[88] Parliament met on 15 January only to be adjourned until the 28th. But the Speaker had not raised the question about adjournment, which, maintained Marvell, would itself be a cause of debate when the 28th came. The irregularities were raised on that day, in a string now stretching back some time over several adjournments. Surely the government had brought about the situation in which a new Parliament must be called.[89] Other pamphlets had appeared, like *A Seasonable Argument*, which listed all the Parliamentarians who were allegedly in the pay of the court and hence bound to vote for it.[90]

For some while Marvell had been drafting another prose work, *Remarks upon a late disingenuous discourse: writ by one T.D. under the pretence De causa Dei, and of answering Mr John Howe's letter and postscript of God's prescience, &c., affirming, as the Protestant doctrine, that God doth by efficacious influence universally move and determine men to all their actions, even to those that are most wicked by a Protestant*, a defence of the moderate Nonconformist John Howe and in the context of an attack on Howe by Thomas Danson. It had been licensed on 17 April and entered in the Stationers' Register for James Astwood, although it appeared, unsigned, in May with Christopher Hussey named as its printer. Howe (1630–1705) had asserted the 'middle way' of Richard Baxter against those who maintained the traditional Calvinist belief in predestination. He was a typical ejected minister: removed from the living of Great Torrington, Devon, in 1662 but appointed chaplain to Sir John Skeffington, second Viscount Massarene in 1670, and from 1676 minister to a Presbyterian congregation at Haberdashers' Hall, Staining Lane, London. Howe had been at Christ's College, Cambridge, where he had come under the influence of Henry More in the later 1640s, whose objections to high Calvinism were by then well developed. In 1656, as personal chaplain to Oliver Cromwell, Howe had met Baxter and the influence of the latter on the former was great. Both pursued the goal of accommodation between all Protestants in the 1660s.[91] It was in the court of Oliver that Marvell would have first met Howe as well as Baxter. Howe was closely associated with Richard Cromwell too, and the second Lord Protector visited the elderly Howe shortly before he died.

Howe's original tract, a 154-page octavo entitled *The Reconcileableness of God's Prescience of the Sins of Men, with the Wisdom and Sincerity of his Counsels, Exhortations, and Whatsoever Other Means he Uses to Prevent Them*, appeared in the early summer of 1677. It took the form of a letter addressed to Robert Boyle the natural scientist, who, along with the rest of his illustrious family, was a patron of Nonconformist ministers and an advocate of toleration. Howe's approach is epitomized in this quotation:

For they really signifie the obedience, and blessednes of those his Creatures that are capable thereof, to be more pleasing and agreeable to his Nature, and Will; than that they should disobey and perish. (which is the utmost that can be understood meant, by those words, *God will have all men to be saved and come to the knowledg of the truth*) But withal, that he so apprehends the indignity done to his Government, by their disobedience, that if they obey not (as the indulgent constitution and temper of his Law, and Government now are, in and by the Redeemer) they must perish.[92]

Howe was answered first by Theophilus Gale and later by Thomas Danson.[93] All three had been fellows of Magdalen College, Oxford, in the early 1650s, and Gale and Danson were, like the then President, Thomas Goodwin, Congregationalists. Danson's was the more significant attack, taking exception to Howe's dissociation of reason and predestination.[94] For Danson, developing an argument close to John Owen's attack in the 1650s on the Socinian John Biddle, Howe had replaced God with man:

God is justled out of his proper place; I mean, of being the first cause of all the Creatures actions, and the Creature put in his stead, as being represented able to use its powers, as it pleases. That one great Perfection of the Divine Nature, *viz.* Foreknowledge of future Contingencies, is separated from it, by denying the only true ground of such Foreknowledg, the Divine Decrees.[95]

As has been indicated by its editor, Marvell's *Remarks* is in and of itself an innovation in several ways. To call a work on theology 'remarks' is wholly unusual and almost certainly an innovation in 1678. The word 'remarks', coming into English from French usage, was never used as a title before the Restoration; after 1660 it gained currency for essays on current affairs, biographies and topographical works and its heyday came in the 1680s and 1690s. This lexical acuity is of a piece with Marvell's more famous 1670s works, and it is matched here by a remarkable refusal to engage in the conventional structures of theological controversy. Danson is not controverted point by point. Instead his actual argument is ignored: the tract is a discussion of the ethics of good writing, and in another way this anticipates Swift's satire in *A Tale of a Tub* while continuing the central concerns of *The Rehearsal Transpros'd* and *Mr Smirke*. Danson himself is mockingly obliterated as an authorial presence, since Marvell argues that he will enhance the author's desire for anonymity by assuming that his initials, T.D., mean 'The Discourse'. He says he wants to divorce author from discourse in order to avoid calumny; he and we know in practice that this is impossible. Marvell mocks theological controversy by taking issue with the smallest incidental detail in Howe's conclusion (his apology that he wrote the tract while on a journey), and raises many silly questions concerning the difficulty of writing while travelling, only to conclude that Howe would have been better off remaining at home. Reflecting back on his own method, Marvell notes that Howe's discourse is so impartial it is free of laughter.[96] By contrast, Danson is not merely ethically repellent, he is also in his misuse of logic nonsensical.[97] And if his application of logic to Howe's text is splitting hairs, it is also deeply tedious: 'so unimaginably dull an argument, that really it requires a proportionable dullness in the Reader, or an extraordinary acuteness to comprehend it'.[98]

Even this does not quite prepare us for the text of *Remarks*, which begins with a likening of ministry to Adam in Paradise, and then, on the contrary, the postlapsarian gathering of grapes from thorns and figs from thistles (Matt. 7: 16). This most unusually modulates, via an initial attack on school logic, to an account of the vexed relationship between travel by horse and thinking (the two are not compatible, especially not in Marvell's experience). For all of his travels around England and between England and Ireland, Howe could still argue against predestination, just as some can play chess while travelling, and chess, Marvell maintains, is an emblem of predestination. Marvell reveals the extreme arduousness of travel in his day, but there are also lightly humorous hints here of the mock-heroic journey. The attack carries on in this way, constructing images of journey from Marvell's sources. Danson's image of two ferrymen as representing God and Adam turns into another precarious image of the ferry passenger (mankind in history) who is exposed by the two ferrymen: 'This is the same in T.D. as if *Its concurrent Wherry-men*, p. 27. after they had taken in their Fare, should be long pulling off their Doublets, and then carry a man to another Stairs than they were directed: The one shows that they had but little heart to their labour; the other, that they know not the River, unless perhaps they have a design, if they can find a place convenient to rifle the Passenger.'[99] Buried here is a biographical reference to Marvell senior's death allegedly at the hands of an incompetent ferryman.

Marvell attacks intemperance, whether from the pen of the chaplains Samuel Parker and Francis Turner or of the Puritan Danson. One consequence of intemperance is a misuse of logic. Marvell subtly shows how Danson misreads Howe, incidentally supporting his case with details of inaccuracies in Danson's page references to Howe's tract. Danson also introduces superfluous logical terms in order to attack Howe, the result being a virtual verbal jumble: Danson's introduction of logic turns 'concourse' into 'conconcourse'.[100] The image of the journey returns, as Danson himself is imagined as a seasick passenger on a stormy sea, seeing wildly disturbed scenes on the land. If the boat is Danson's *Discourse*, no one knows where it is bound. To wholly unethical ends, for if Danson is so full of hatred, and God is in the Calvinist view the author of all things, not only does Danson allegedly manifest hatred towards God, he also makes God hate the world.[101] Howe's sensible terms and well-chosen or well-developed distinctions are a salve for travellers: in Marvell's analogy they prevent galling, or rubbing until sore from horse riding. It is a profound insight on Marvell's part into the relationship between theology and lived experience.

The other strain of imagery is that of animals. Marvell alleges that Danson tries to catch Howe's discourse rather like the keeper who trains a camel to dance to music by playing while the animal walks on a hot surface. When the keeper then plays his fiddle the animal responds by moving his feet, although this has nothing to do with the music the keeper is making. But then Danson's use of syllogism is so awkward, he is like a camel dancing with five feet, changing his terms often but having no impact upon Howe's argument.[102] Yet Danson is a tyrant, his discourse full of spiteful tyrannous laughter and in places predicated upon false friendship. He is also so short-sighted he is like Antipheron, who saw himself, and everything else, distortedly reflected in the 'mirror' of the air around him. Whatever Danson sees he makes in his own image and it is a hallucination.[103]

Whatever position we might take on Danson, howsoever modern liberal views chime with Marvell's critique, Danson was not speaking for such an outdated theological view. Indeed, we may say that he took a figurative beating at Marvell's expense.[104] It looks like the recapitulation of an old battle. Marvell was settling a score in favour of a view that had won out at the Cromwellian court against the unmitigated application of predestination theology, and in this light Danson was a relative 'out', left behind by Howe in an Oxford college in the earlier 1650s.

One further important matter remains to be discussed here. Did Marvell really believe the position he was defending? Is the authorial identity of 'a Protestant' genuine, in the sense of Marvell being in the same position as Baxter or Howe, or very close to them? Given Marvell's position as it had evolved to the *Essay on Councils*,[105] it is very hard to believe. Marvell may have approved of the calmness of Howe's discursive manner, but there would surely have been areas of consideration in church history where they disagreed. The opening sounds almost sarcastic: 'Of all the Vocations to which men addict themselves, or are dedicated, I have always esteemed that of the Ministry to be the most noble and happy Imployment; as being more peculiarly directed to those two great Ends, the advancement of God's Glory, and the promoting of Man's Salvation.'[106] One can hear the libertine jesting of Henry Neville behind some of the sentences: 'if men by this fansied *opening of their Eyes,* have attained to see more clearly, and acknowledge the wickedness of their own Actions, it resembles the modesty of our First Parents, discerning their *Nakedness*.'[107]

The personnel in Parliament were beginning to change. When the Commons had gathered on 11 April, Marvell wrote to Hull, saying that Coventry reported that the Speaker, Sir Edward Seymour, was grievously ill; Sir Robert Sawyer was installed in his place, and the business of making the supply proceeded.[108] But in the House of Commons the temper of the times was strongly against the threat of popery and there was little stopping the Commons themselves wanting a war with France. On 30 April, reports had been read in the Commons of open meetings of Catholics, the public celebration of the mass and the spurning of legal controls on recusants in Monmouth, Hereford and even Middlesex. This was as the Dutch and the Spanish alliance was being settled; in the Commons intense consideration was given to the former in early May, for fear that the Dutch would instead make an alliance with France. It was a frantic time that caused Marvell to use poor quills ('ill tooles').[109] Ordinary business did nothing to forestall in Marvell a sense that something was exercising MPs: 'the House . . . is much fuller then ordinary . . . there seems a more then usuall concernment among all men as if some great and I hope good thing were to be expected'.[110] The Commons wanted Charles to declare war on France.

But the moment of war drifted away as Holland and Spain came to terms with France. Moves to disband the armed forces now hastily took place, although fears of a Catholic rebellion from within remained high. The House remained watchful of a recusant called Sir Salomon Swale who was refusing to appear before the Commons on the grounds of ill health, while it concerned itself with economically protective measures, such as ensuring the law required that everyone dressed and was buried in woollen cloth, or promulgating still further duties ('the Additional Impost upon Wines').

Marvell wrote to William Popple in Bordeaux on 10 June, first expressing his admiration for the Covenanters in Scotland (having noted a fortnight before that the King had not received visiting Scottish lords personally nor had he granted their desires).[111] But then he referred to the continuing inability of the government to establish the author of *An Account*, even as the Bill against the growth of popery was read for the first time. Why then, asked Marvell, had he not been questioned in Parliament? Perhaps the answer was that the net was not quite sufficiently tightly drawn. Williamson was still interrogating people: on 6 July he summoned the pamphlet's distributor Packer from custody, and had his dwelling searched by warrant on the 8th.[112] Packer, it would seem, was to be prosecuted, while the bookseller Francis Smith, also suspected of involvement, had part of his stock of books destroyed: perhaps almost the entire print run of the second quarto edition, which was an unusually high figure for the time.[113] Smith appealed to a noble protector who might be able to stop this: the episode would form part of his monumental account of the persecution of printers, and the ruin to which many of their families were brought.[114] There was a search for Axtell, son of Daniel, the regicide, thought to be harbouring a stock of seditious books in a warehouse. Axtell's house was in Newington, south of the Thames, although in fact he stayed in Drake's at Tokenhouse Yard. Packer was examined by Williamson probably on 19 July and, in an attempt to protect himself, claimed that the book was only left 'in his seat upon the Table'.[115] He was released towards the end of the month.

Soon afterwards Marvell himself was in Yorkshire, meeting Hull Corporation on 29 July to discuss the state of town affairs and, with Gylby, being an honoured guest at a dinner hosted by Trinity House. On 1 August, Parliament was prorogued and would remain so until 21 October. Nonetheless, Marvell returned to London on approximately 9 August in order to conduct more business in Chancery on behalf of Trinity House. On the 10th a great deal of correspondence was dispatched to Marvell and others from Trinity House concerning their dispute with Angell, which was now drawing to a close, and for the Hull merchants it would be a successful conclusion. Trinity House also acknowledged the good testimony that Marvell had given of Witty for his part in reconciling Angell to the brethren; on this account they were going to reward Witty in the near future.[116] It had, however, all been too much for the MP, and shortly after reaching London Marvell contracted a tertian ague, a shaking fit and in effect a late manifestation of malaria. He summoned a doctor, who bled him but then induced a coma with 'a draught of Venice treacle' and many layers of blankets; on 16 August, Marvell died comatose of an 'apoplexy', which could mean from a stroke or from internal bleeding.[117]

The medical authority Richard Morton noted angrily that an ounce of quinine (Morton produced a manuscript on the preparation of quinine or 'Peruvian bark' in 1680) instead of the treacle would have produced a cure for Marvell in a day or so. Since Morton was also an ejected minister, we may suppose that he might have wished Marvell alive for other reasons.[118] Also writing in 1680, the Yorkshire physician and Helmontian William Simpson, coincidentally a rival of Marvell's friend Robert Witty, claimed that he had cured a relative of Marvell's, possibly one of the Popples or Alureds, using 'ninsing root' or 'nean', so that the family called him 'Lazarus the Second'.[119] The relative was severely emaciated after a long fever and an 'ulcer of the lung'. 'Ninsing', which name is not recorded in the *Oxford English Dictionary*, was from the Far East, and Simpson claimed it would cure consumptions, asthma, 'psitticks' and rheumatic conditions. Simpson had his patient restored again after a daily dose of ninsing in red cow's milk, so that his skin was like that of a child, his appetite restored together with his ruddy complexion. So a rare cure from Asia was used to cure one man from Hull, and another rare cure from South America was sadly not administered to cure another.

CHAPTER 13

✳

AFTERLIFE AND REVELATION

THERE WAS A LOT of grief at Marvell's death. Robert Witty professed himself a 'syncere mourner', the brothers of Trinity House in Hull 'very sorry and . . . unhappy'.[1] Witty, then in London, was for the time being entrusted with the correspondence intended for Marvell. The Corporation of Hull and Trinity House, Deptford, began to think about replacements. Monmouth proposed John Shales to be Marvell's replacement in the House of Commons, and this was supported by the Duke of York, although in fact it was William Ramsden who was elected.[2] Hull Corporation put forward the not inconsiderable sum of £50 for Marvell's funeral and the erection of a gravestone. Very much later monuments would be erected in St Giles-in-the-Fields church, London, where he had been buried on 18 August, and in Hull.

BIRTH OF A HERO

The unfolding of political events in the months after Marvell's death reads like the prophecy of *An Account* come true. The evidence of a widespread conspiracy of Roman Catholics, indigenous and foreign, designed to ensure a Catholic succession of the monarchy and future for England was widely believed and caused a massive crisis in church and state.

In these circumstances Marvell's political verse began to have a greater impact: John Oldham's 'Satyr II' bore particular traces of 'The Loyal Scot' and the Blood epigram; other works showed that he had read Marvell's prose.[3] More echoes still of his poetry and prose appeared in other poems. The attributions of opposition poetry to Marvell grew although many of these were incorrect: Marvell's reputation and association with a certain kind of poem (for instance, the Painter poem) was the cause. Even a Whig Nonconformist poet might occasionally resist the 'desire to be deified after Marvel's manner'.[4]

After Marvell's death, it was possible for him to be named on the title page of *An Account*, and this is what happened with the third edition, an imposing folio with corrections that helped establish Marvell as a significant author in the Whig canon, and someone with the same status as Shaftesbury and Buckingham.

An Account was translated into French with other oppositional materials in 1680, and became highly influential: other tracts repeated its prophecy of encroaching tyranny unless something was done. The number of titles using some variant of 'popery and arbitrary government' in the few years after 1678 was very great. Attacks on country and Whig pamphlets accused their authors of a misrepresentation of Anglicanism, and a masking of Presbyterian and Commonwealth principles. Marvell after all was 'Oliver's Latin Secretary', and guilty of 'dullness and insufficiency'. For the other side, in 1681 the Nonconformist and future supporter of Monmouth's rebellion William Disney incorporated long passages from *The Rehearsall Transpros'd: The Second Part* and *A Short Historical Essay* in *Nil dicum quod non dictum prius or, A transcript of government considered as it is in the state of nature or religion*, a defence of Parliamentary sovereignty over and above all royal prerogative.[5] Thomas Brown did the same with *The Rehearsal Transpros'd* in a text attacking Dryden in 1687. In 1682 appeared *The Second Part of the Growth of Popery and Arbitrary Government*, probably written by the Scottish Whig and conspirator Robert Ferguson. More generally Marvellian perceptions entered the language of controversy (such as the idea from *Mr Smirke* that censorship made the publishing of a good book a sin). The republican and deist John Toland in particular was indebted to Marvell.

As the Exclusion Crisis built up, the persecution of printers and publishers connected with Marvell's *Account* and other tracts continued. The 1680 reissue of 'Directions to a Painter' was ordered by the Privy Council to be burned on 23 February.[6] The publishing of the *Miscellaneous Poems* in 1681 (plate 22) was no less of a political act, although it remains the major witness for all of Marvell's lyric verse. The fact that the Cromwell poems were omitted from most copies has usually been taken to signify last-minute concern on the part of the publishers, as opposed to the intention to produce a special version with the Cromwell poems designed for limited circulation.

Another dimension was established when Thomas Shadwell created a dramatic character for Mr Smirke, called 'Smerk' in *The Lancashire Witches* (1681), which was allowed to play in September before it was censored by the Master of the Revels. The character of Sir Edward Hartfort obviously represented Marvell's friend, the country leader Sir Edward Harley, although Hartfort has also been seen as a reflection of Marvell himself. With the revolution of 1688–89, the further anthologizing of Marvell's *Account* along with his 1660s verse satires in a series of publications consolidated his reputation as a patriot hero, the defender of proper constitutionalism and Protestantism. In the *State Tracts* of 1689, in which *An Account* appeared as sixth in a series decrying Stuart rule, that reputation was a tool in the establishment of the radical Whig cause.

It was also known as we have already seen that Marvell, like other poets, specifically Jonson and Cowley, died poor, even though they were all 'incomparable' poets. The important point to remember is that Marvell was not unrecognized as a poet until the later nineteenth century, as has often been claimed. His poetry was very much admired, and by the experts, the makers of literary taste. Addison quoted him at length, and if sometimes Marvell was thought to have written some mediocre verse, he was regarded as exceedingly accomplished while being surpassed only by George Herbert (this from a judgement in 1753).[7] Perhaps the most astonishingly imaginative use of Marvell was by Laurence Sterne who took his fellow Yorkshire writer's landscapes and love of wit and made them a vital part of the framework of his polyphonic novel of sentiment and sociability, *Tristram Shandy*.[8] The Hull poet William Mason also saw cause to celebrate Marvell's literary and political accomplishments in 'To Independency' (1756). It was a broadly accepted judgement that Marvell was the 'Poet Laureat of the Dissenters'. An earlier dimension of this praise was that Marvell was the poet of the Painter poems, which suggests veneration of a particular aesthetic as well as political dimension, however broadly the canon of these poems was defined.

MARRIAGE

On 31 March 1679, seven months and thirteen days after Marvell died, Mary Marvell and John Greene, a lawyer, took out an administration on Andrew Marvell's estate.[9] Greene was in fact a front for John Farrington, who claimed to be Marvell's creditor in his role as administrator of Edward Nelthorpe's estate. Beforehand, and soon after Marvell's death, Farrington had issued a legal instruction to the Prerogative Court of Canterbury that no one be granted an administration of Marvell's estate without him knowing. This instruction stood for six months, and explains why Mary Marvell/Palmer waited for seven months before acting. Nelthorpe, who had died on 18 September 1678, had lent money to Marvell; that money, claimed Farrington, was now owed to him. The goldsmith Charles Wallis had £500 in a bond from Marvell and Nelthorpe (as we have seen, Nelthorpe had asked Marvell to entrust the money to Wallis in order to avoid the discovery of his own name): only by proving Mary Marvell's marriage to Marvell could it be released to her. One month later, Farrington was made administrator of Marvell's estate. Then, in a counter-move, on 30 September the Prerogative Court of Canterbury made Mary Marvell and Greene the joint administrators (Greene seems also to have been a front for Mrs Nelthorpe since it was important still to keep Nelthorpe's name secret). This was confirmed one year later on 31 March 1680.

In the meantime Richard Thompson had gone to live in the Great Russell Street house, and began to pay 'Mrs Palmer' to keep it. On 1 June 1681 Farrington filed a bill of complaint in the Court of Chancery against Greene, Wallis and Mary Marvell, alleging that the money in Wallis's possession was payable to Nelthorpe's estate, not Marvell's; Marvell himself not being capable of lending such money. Mary Marvell answered that her husband Andrew did have money, and that Nelthorpe acquired the contents of the Maiden Lane lodgings after Marvell's death, even though he had been in France at the time. She claimed that Farrington had tried to deceive her, concealing his knowledge of the existence of the Wallis bond but trying to persuade her to give power of attorney.

On 7 November Wallis issued a bill of complaint against everyone hitherto named and Edmund Page, alleging that he had repaid Nelthorpe in guineas a few days after the loan had been made. He accused Farrington of a conspiracy to obtain money from him, and for pressuring Greene and Mary Marvell to help him. Farrington doubted even that Marvell knew about the bond Nelthorpe had raised in his name. Few others knew about it, or they knew about it only at a late date, including Greene, Farrington himself and Mary Marvell. Farrington was at this time in jail for debt and wanted the money to rectify his situation.

When Mary Marvell challenged Farrington, Greene and Wallis, and complained that they were trying to defraud her of the property, once her husband's, that was now hers, the marriage itself was thrown into doubt. Farrington alleged that Mary *Palmer* was merely Marvell's servant. But Mary defended herself, described when and where the marriage took place, and explained the unusual nature of the household relations. The next phase established that Marvell was poor, and indebted for £150 to Nelthorpe. On 15 November 1682 a trial in Chancery was ordered to settle the matter between Mary Marvell, Greene and Farrington. But nothing happened, and on 28 January 1684 the Court of Chancery intervened so that a settlement could be reached. Sir John Cole was entrusted with the business and he reported on 13 March that he had drafted a settlement. A trial was held at some point between then and 2 June, when the contestants were summoned for a judgment, which was that Farrington should be allowed to pursue the money in Mary Marvell's name, so long as he reimbursed her for any costs she incurred. At this point both Farrington, who was still in jail, and Mary Nelthorpe complained that the Thompsons had defrauded them and lived a life of comfort within the rules of the King's Bench prison.

This was in the first part of 1684. The judgment gave Farrington the administration after all. He then pursued Mary Marvell and Thompson, alleging that they held much of the bankrupts' money. What was happening was that after Nelthorpe's death, the former partners in the ex-bank were trying to secure the funds that Marvell had entrusted to Wallis. He had done this originally in order to try to protect the bankrupts. But on 24 November 1687, Mary Palmer died and was buried under this name. It was all over.

What had been going on? Mary certainly had Marvell's 'papers' by October 1680 when she signed the certificate printed at the front of the *Miscellaneous Poems*. It was only late in the series of issued complaints outlined above that Mary's status as Marvell's wife was challenged: in response to her complaints having proven that Greene was acting 'in trust' (that is, as a front) for Farrington. This is significant. The volume of the marriage register of Holy Trinity, Minories, where Mary claimed that she and Andrew were married in 1667, is missing. Do we believe her? Most of those trusting their common sense and the balance of probability have said no, and assumed that she was lying in order to try, perhaps desperately, to get her hands on Marvell's assets (which turned out in the end to be purely fictional), or that she was persuaded to conspire with Farrington and Greene in an intricate conspiracy to make sure that all the funds associated with the Nelthorpe–Thompson–Farrington bank came to Farrington, and freed him from his creditors. But we cannot be certain that this was not an unusual marriage. By Mary's own admission it certainly was, and it has been regarded as some evidence of the way in which the household was arranged at this time.[10] Was it a 'political' marriage: that of a man who had no interest in marriage for propagation, romance or companionship, but who knew that a wife could not give evidence in court against her spouse, and who thus had found a way to make sure that his housekeeper could never be made to talk? There's no evidence of a libertine marriage, although scurrility is celebrated in places by Marvell. While her evidence points to a marriage based on affection, however unorthodox, other figures associated with free-thinking and republicanism, such as Henry Marten, did have what would today be called cohabiting partners, and their reputations suffered for it.[11]

HUSKS AND KERNELS

The evidence that stands out as among the most solid is that Marvell liked being alone – in Highgate, or in Maiden Lane. He had few friends and generally did not trust people. He liked drinking but would not drink in company. In his last years he conducted his business in a purely private place. Privacy and in some sense invisibility were requirements for most of his professional duties. Being an MP and a secretary required discretion, and sometimes operating behind the scenes in such a way as not to be detected. This was necessary because of the surveillance systems operating at the time, and in particular the ability of government agents to open letters. Being a spy always required secrecy, and we suppose that Marvell was employed in secretarial work that was to do with intelligence: another arena where discretion was utterly necessary. Most of these spheres required the development of a professional, public or civic persona that entirely denied oneself as a person, indeed as a late Renaissance 'self-fashioned' man of letters, or a humanist adviser to a prince. One's identity was part of someone else's or one did not have an identity: one was a blank. Marvell's poetry is full of the confession of this erasure or impossibility of expressed identity. The poet is always a shadow of the object of praise, be it the hero Oliver Cromwell or Mary Fairfax. The poet is the invisible opposite of these centres of charisma, and often Marvell confesses that it is the hero who is the real poet, the real source of energy. In this sense, the poetry expresses accurately and sensitively the patronage relationships upon which Marvell was dependent, from Lord Fairfax and Lord Wharton to the Corporation of Hull and Trinity House.[12] From here follows a long series of insights in Marvell's writing with regard to how this poet's art is a kind of negation: it is an imitation of someone else's art even to the extent of gathering so many fragments of others together that they return as the final integrated fulfilment of a great number of clichés. Marvell found his poetic identity in this negative way, a shadow presence in the pastoral, helping to make it, but barely perceptible in its landscape. Indeed, in some senses, sacrificed by it: witness the witty martyring by drowning of the speaker in 'Upon Appleton House' (ll. 623–4). The drowning is in one of its senses a matter of being overwhelmed by so much other poetry and painting, to the extent that the poet 'chokes' on it: witness too the mockery of so much aesthetic pretension, again in 'Upon Appleton House'. It was also a figure of the patron's presence and 'interest', and is precisely not 'disinterested': 'His decorum, or courtesy, which [T.S.] Eliot struggled to define as wit, rises to the challenge of interestedness. But this is exactly not disinterest or that much-vaunted impersonality celebrated by Eliot and by much subsequent criticism indebted to him.'[13]

All this evidence suggests that Marvell suffered a good deal of personal denial. There are serious signs of a frequently frustrated and disappointed person. The outbursts of anger, especially when not being understood or when unable to communicate optimally (for instance when speaking publicly), are striking. The description of Marvell as a sneering wit suggests someone permanently jealous of others; a sense of an outsider slightly outcast; a person who was let down repeatedly by causes and sources of protection (Andrew Marvell senior, the Royalists, the Protectorate, Charles II, the Church of England), and who was compelled to respond; someone whose intelligence was ahead of his ability to communicate it; but someone who could write fluently, translate from and manipulate other languages with excellence.

It also suggests someone suppressing pain, someone who could readily sympathize with those who suffered (one thinks, for instance, of his worry about the plight of the Scottish Covenanters in 1677).[14] We have already encountered the significance of Marvell's father's death. It is no surprise that the sea, and Milton's elegy for a drowned acquaintance, Lycidas, figure significantly in Marvell's imagination. His father had not finished providing a framework,

discipline and means for his son when he drowned in the Humber. The lasting
sense of trauma in Marvell is well explored in the reading of 'The Unfortunate
Lover' provided by Professors Zwicker and Hirst.[15] We should also mention the
pain at loss expressed by the Nymph. Was there something more to hide? Was
Marvell not merely without means but also damaged or defective, not merely
psychologically but also physically, as Butler and the anonymous poet of the Ent
commonplace book suggest?[16] Certainly while Marvell did not experience
fatherhood, he greatly treasured the role of uncle and mentor to William Popple.
The letter to Sir John Trott of August 1667 is particularly sensitive to the issue of
the failure of patrilineal descent.[17] Marvell was told of a likely wife by Sir Henry
Thompson, who clearly understood his need for a propertied partner. Nothing
came of it. Popple aside, the 'love' that he could express in his writing was a
further manifestation of the variety of desires driven by his dependencies – the
attachments of patronage he needed to make his life liveable. The opposite
perception in Marvell's writing, but intimately attached to this understanding of
'love', is the passion-driven portraits of the courtiers in the verse satires and the
clerics in the prose satires.

In so far as we can construct a picture of Marvell's life, poetry was a welcome
refuge as well as a means of political intervention. It was a place where one
could escape and where strife would disappear. So much of the poetry avoids
the passionate clash of opposites, of lovers harmonious or disharmonious, in
order to seek solitary enlightenment and fulfilment. Take for instance 'The
Garden'. The lover loves himself, or himself through his environment. The
mower appears to be a miserable frustrated poet in some places, but in others
a figure who is fulfilled by his true connection with nature. The world of
women to the mower is figured as unnatural ('The Mower against Gardens')
and some of Marvell's women are unattractive witchlike crones ('Upon
Appleton House'). The speaker poet is more interested in the mower than
in Julia; the sweat of the mowers in 'Upon Appleton House' is sweet (although
the mowers' women are also 'fragrant': ll. 428–9). If Marvell's women
are goddesses, and so unapproachable, they are also unknowable. The great
moment of sexual passion in Marvell, in 'To his Coy Mistress', is not so much
personal as a brilliant feat of poetic appropriation, imitation and reorganization. It is exciting because of this, and the limits of the speaker's epicurean
persona, through partially hidden dramatic ironies, are evident. Neither is it at
all personal, in the way we see real people flit through the poetry of, for
instance, Dante, Petrarch, Surrey and Donne. Intimacy in Marvell's lyric verse
is absent. There is certainly sexual intercourse: in 'To his Coy Mistress' and
'The Match', stylized, glorious, and a goal for literary inventiveness. All the
same, it is a performance rather than a means to intimacy.

Marvell's poetry is one of fulfilment in a kind of self-love. The object of
desire is finally a reflection of a subject identified as oneself. It is therefore no
surprise that the straitened world of Puritan behaviour, of the 'reformation of

the household', with its rules of denial and its concealing of body parts, could be attractive for Marvell. Hence the delicately observed assessment in the epitaph on Frances Jones, which nonetheless is also a poem of distance. 'Clorinda and Damon' is a surprising rejection of pastoral dalliance for the sake of rigorous piety. Other poems are accounts of the mutual binding of disparate aspects of a person to each other: 'A Dialogue between the Soul and Body' is a document of closure. Hence also the remarkable poems on the life of the soul, in Latin as well as English, which manage to set the balance between earth and heaven, soul and body, with perfect poise. And the soul for Marvell is admirable on account of its enclosure from the temptations of the world, as in 'Ros', lines 29–32. It's hard to imagine so lay a writer, such a Machiavellian, writing like a divine: think of them all – Donne, Herbert, Crashaw, Henry More, Isaac Watts – all clerics. Perhaps Milton is the one notable exception who comes near Marvell. But Marvell, like Milton, was never totally a Puritan: the academics, the bishops and the Catholics saw to that.

'Young Love' suggested a world of sanitized older man/young woman relations, but one devoid of identities if not feelings. We never quite see who the young love is, although there is a hint in the third stanza that it is female; this sense then disappears, and the poem remains a highly abstract expression of mutuality. The conclusion of 'Mourning' suggests that women are as difficult to understand as the poet himself: access to the full array of feminine deliberation is not granted. Neither do we see the male lover's intentions except by sly inference in 'Daphnis and Chloe'. What is clear is that Marvell's collection of lyric poems contains markedly alternative and even deviant versions of heterosexual love. First there is the *senex* and the younger lover in 'Young Love', and the related scenario of a voyeuristic older man and a young girl in 'The Picture of Little T.C.' This is not exactly paedophilic poetry, and certainly not in terms of the ancient tradition from which it comes, but it does nonetheless challenge a norm, though less so in terms of the classical tradition. There's also the presence of homosocial and perhaps also homoerotic verse: in the Villiers elegy, in 'Last Instructions to a Painter', and the manipulation of source poems, in 'To his Coy Mistress' and 'Damon the Mower'.[18] In other words, and to say the very least, the lyric poems offer collectively a dispersal or dissolution of the sexual energies we are meant to find in a lyric verse collection of this period. A good deal of the energy of the verse goes in these sexually heterodox directions. Marvell may not have been as frank as Rochester in his libertine verse (and Rochester's verse was beginning to circulate in Marvell's lifetime and was read by him) but it is arresting and disturbing in this sense.

The level of control or restraint in these portrayals also suggests more denial or repression, deliberate or not. Parker and Butler's portrayal of Marvell as a pervert, a man who chose to go in disguise to public places, and to gratify himself with male or female prostitutes, might be part of ecclesiastical satire, but it is also not to be entirely dismissed. It certainly has to be put alongside the stereotype of Marvell as incorruptible, right-headed patriot hero, and a poet who could live above the passions he described. And in this light the accomplishment of the poetry looks like a brilliant sublimation of a set of social and sexual confusions and frustrations. The hours of musing and the love of solitariness is where that sublimation occurred, allegedly often through the power of wine. Yet it is precisely because that musing occurred that Marvell was able to make a leap from his personal perceptions to his political assertion of liberty. For it is in the satires, especially the verse satires, that we see a full and alarming human portrait. Through the veil of satire's need to ridicule, the portrait of the courtly and other actors is not without sympathy or pity, repellent though the frank portrayals of courtly sexual appetites can be. It is here that tyranny and sexuality are seen to connect, however partial Marvell's picture of events. There doesn't seem a great deal of distance here between the Countess of Castlemaine and the hero-martyrs of virtuous behaviour: Archibald Douglas and James Mitchell. He may not have been aware of it, but the sum of his writing in poetry and prose was 'a program that deconstructs the very bases of heterosexuality and patriarchalism alike'.[19] Marvell's notions of liberty in the escape from political and spiritual tyranny were inherently linked to this acknowledgement of alterity. The eighteenth, nineteenth and twentieth centuries might have had little use for the full dimensions of his revelations, the teachings of his life. That is something for us and our future, an appreciation that might seek to requite those many disappointments and denials that produced his vision.

Such a vision did not ground liberty merely in a series of satirical portraits. It reached conclusions about ethical behaviour based on a critique of the nature of a traditional kind of privilege and power domination: that of the clergy. It saw the source of this domination – bullying, in short – in the entire educational practice of the nation, in how we grow up. He saw this in Parker, in Turner and to a lesser extent in Danson. He saw related ramifications in courtly politicians and administrators, and in power-hungry members of the church who let their desires pervert their understanding of Scripture. The meandering wit of *The Rehearsal Transpros'd* is a refusal of the logic of orthodox power, so-called legitimate power in the name of an alterity – the power of intelligent laughter. I see this in aesthetic terms as a mirrored 'truth', an existential 'rhyme' that accompanies the scheme of legitimacy. This is taken in the 1670s tracts even to the point of unwinding the confessional viewpoint common to most Protestants: Marvell's critique was not merely mildly and sometimes slyly libertine; it was freethinking, proto-deist and looked forward into the years after 1689. The persistence of this witty undoing of clerical pomposity and political tyranny is directly related to Marvell's lyrical troubling of stable identities, and for that matter his brilliantly perceptive portrayals of heroes (Lord Fairfax, Lord General Cromwell, the Lord Protector Oliver Cromwell) who grapple with the forces of history and prevail. To have seen all these things, and to have seen them in so arrested a fashion, as if the camera of history has stopped, as if one was looking at events encased in amber, was viewed by Marvell's hostile contemporaries as a revolt against the dominant sexual order, as if Marvell was outside that order. No doubt his friends would not have put it like this, or even owned up to this, but they respected his solitary disposition and his ability to see into the nature of the world from his unusual stance. We cannot say for sure whether or not he had been damaged or mutilated so that his vision of alternatives arose from a position of exclusion, shyness and the need to hide. But if there is anything that comes clearly home in those hostile portraits it is of Marvell as eunuch, an identity confirmed in one of his Latin poems, and where sexual sterility is converted into poetic power, because it is a condition of that power:

> Do not believe that you are sterile, albeit, as an exile from women, you are unable to thrust a sickle at the virgin harvest or to sin in our manner. By you will Fame be forever pregnant, and you will lay hold of the nine sisters from the mountain, while Echo, repeatedly struck, will give birth to music as your offspring.[20]

The person who finally resisted all corruption in an age of corruption needed such a privation, as well as the sustained experience of privation, to see how the social whole could be pervasively persecutory. Marvell stands for liberty – liberty of the subject, liberty in the state, liberty of the self, liberty from political and personal tyrannies: the domination of the public self and the interior private consciousness. The story that his experiences told him gave him the power to analyse these liberties, and he could so analyse because he found himself standing outside the lines of authority that would have had him exercising power. It seems never too much of a good thing to have such insights, and an inestimable benefit to have them so well expressed, to be made a keystone of beauty.

ABBREVIATIONS

AMC	Nicholas von Maltzahn, *An Andrew Marvell Chronology* (Houndmills and New York, 2005).
AMP	Andrew Marvell, *The Poems of Andrew Marvell*, ed. Nigel Smith (Harlow, 2007, rev. edn).
ATH	Hull, Trinity House, administration files.
BJHS	*British Journal for the History of Science.*
BL	British Library.
BLJ	*British Library Journal.*
BN	Bibliotheque National, Paris.
Bod.	Bodleian Library, Oxford.
CJ	*Journal of the House of Commons.*
Cooke	Andrew Marvell, *The Works of Andrew Marvell*, ed. Thomas Cooke, 2 vols (1726).
CPW	John Milton, *Complete Prose Works*, ed. Don M. Wolfe et al., 8 vols (New Haven, CT, 1953–82).
CSPD	*Calendar of State Papers Domestic.*
CUL	Cambridge University Library.
DNB	*Dictionary of National Biography.*
DTH	Deptford, Trinity House.
E in C	*Essays in Criticism.*
EHR	*English Historical Review.*
ELH	*Journal of English Literary History.*
ELR	*English Literary Renaissance.*
EMS	*English Manuscript Studies.*
ES	*English Studies.*
FTH	Hull, Trinity House, finance files.
HCA	Hull City Archives.
HCL	Hull City Library.

HJ	*Historical Journal.*
HMC	Historical Manuscripts Commission.
HTH	Hull, Trinity House.
HUA	Hull University Archives.
IELM	*Index of English Literary Manuscripts*, compiled by Peter Beal and Margaret M. Smith, 4 vols in 12 (London and New York, 1980–97).
JDJ	*John Donne Journal.*
JHI	*Journal of the History of Ideas.*
JMH	*Journal of Modern History.*
LJ	*Journal of the House of Lords.*
MAH	Mayor and Aldermen of Hull.
MLR	*Modern Language Review.*
MP	*Modern Philology.*
MPW	*Prose Works*, ed. Annabel Patterson, Martin Dzelzainis, Nicholas von Maltzahn and N.H. Keeble, 2 vols (New Haven, CT and London, 2003).
N & Q	*Notes and Queries.*
NH	*Northern History.*
NS	new series
NTH	Hull, Trinity House, navigation files.
ODNB	*Oxford Dictionary of Nation Biography.*
PBA	*Proceedings of the British Academy.*
PBSA	*Publications of the Bibliographical Society of America.*
Pepys	Samuel Pepys, *The Diary of Samuel Pepys*, ed. Robert Latham and William Matthews, 11 vols (1970).
PL	*Poems and Letters*, ed. H.M. Margoliouth, rev. edn, Pierre Legouis with E.E. Duncan-Jones, 2 vols (Oxford, 1971).
PMLA	*Publications of the Modern Language Association of America.*
POAS	George de F. Lord et al., eds, *Poems on Affairs of State*, 7 vols (New Haven, CT, 1963–75).
PRO	Public Record Office.
RES	*Review of English Studies.*
RO	Record Office
SC	*The Seventeenth Century.*
SEL	*Studies in English Literature.*
SP	*Studies in Philology.*
SR	Stationers' Register. *A Transcript of the Registers of the Worshipful Company of Stationers. 1640–1708.* ed. G.E. Briscoe Eyre. 3 vols (London, 1913–14).
TC	*Term Catalogues.*
Thurloe	*A Collection of the State Papers of John Thurloe*, ed. Thomas Birch, 7 vols (1742).
TLS	*Times Literary Supplement.*
YES	*Years Work in English Studies.*

*

NOTES

(The place of publication is London, unless otherwise noted.)

CHAPTER 1: INTRODUCTION: THE PROBLEM OF ANDREW MARVELL

1. With old dating, '1677' appeared on the title page.
2. The best description of *An Account* is Nicholas von Maltzahn's introduction in *MPW*, II.179–221.
3. Thomas Osborne, Earl of Danby and eventually first Duke of Leeds (1632–1712): see *ODNB*.
4. For this Parliament see Annabel Patterson, *The Long Parliament of Charles II* (New Haven, CT, and London, 2008).
5. *HMC* Ormonde, NS 4:423.
6. See J.P. Kenyon, *The Popish Plot* (1972).
7. See Mark Knights, *Politics and Opinion in Crisis, 1678–81* (Cambridge, 1994).
8. See life in *ODNB* by Warren Chernaik.
9. These texts are discussed by Nicholas von Maltzahn in 'Marvell's Ghost', in W. Chernaik and M. Dzelzainis, eds, *Marvell and Liberty* (Basingstoke and New York, 1999), 50–74.
10. Roger L'Estrange, *The Parallel or, An Account of the Growth of Knavery* (1679), sig. A2^{r-v}.
11. Thomas Cooke, 'The Life of Andrew Marvell Esq', in *Works*, ed. Thomas Cooke (1726), II; Edward Thompson, 'The Life of that Most Excellent Citizen, and Uncorrupted Member of Parliament, Andrew Marvell', in Andrew Marvell, *Works*, ed. Edward Thompson, 3 vols (1776), III.433–93. Thomas 'Hesiod' Cooke (1703–56) and Edward 'Poet' (but also naval officer) Thompson (?1738–86): for both, see *ODNB*.
12. Cooke, 'The Life of Andrew Marvell Esq', II.2.
13. See James Barry's *The Phoenix or the Resurrection of Freedom* (1776), reproduced on the dust jacket of Chernaik and Dzelzainis, eds, *Marvell and Liberty*. In later years, Marvell would be seen as a standard of virtue that American politicians could not reach: J.R. Lowell to C.F. Briggs, 8 August 1845, in E.S. Donno, ed., *Andrew Marvell: The Critical Heritage* (1978), 128. See also the less critical comments of J.G.Whittier in Donno, ed., *Andrew Marvell*, 199–200.
14. [?Henry Rogers], 'Notice of the Author', in Andrew Marvell, *Poetical Works* (Boston, 1857), xliii; Thompson, 'The Life . . .', 442–3.
15. [?Henry Rogers], 'Notice of the Author', xxii.
16. Thompson, 'The Life . . .', 443; *AMC*, 171.

17. See Donno, ed., *Andrew Marvell: The Critical Heritage*, 141, 169; see also 188–96.
18. Thompson, 'The Life of that Most Excellent Citizen, and Uncorrupted Member of Parliament, Andrew Marvell', III.435–6.
19. In Donno, ed., *Andrew Marvell: The Critical Heritage*, 143.
20. Hartley Coleridge, *The Worthies of Yorkshire and Lancashire* (1832), 61–4, reprinted in Donno, ed., *Andrew Marvell: The Critical Heritage*, 158–9; John Ormsby, in *Cornhill Magazine*, 20 (July 1869), in Donno, ed., 221.
21. Pierre Legouis, *André Marvell, poète, puritain, patriote, 1621-1678* (Paris and London, 1928); see David Masson, *The Life of John Milton*, 7 vols (1859–94).
22. T.S. Eliot, 'Andrew Marvell', *TLS*, 31 March 1921; republished in T.S. Eliot, *Selected Essays* (London and New York, 1932).
23. Nicholas Murray, *World Enough and Time: The Life of Andrew Marvell* (1999), 4.
24. Ibid., 38.
25. Nicholas von Maltzahn will produce the next edition of Marvell's letters.
26. Hilton Kelliher, *Andrew Marvell, Poet & Politician, 1621-78: An Exhibition to Commemorate the Tercentenary of his Death* (1978).
27. Hilton Kelliher, 'Marvell's *Last Instructions to a Painter*: From Manuscript to Print', *EMS*, 13 (2007), 296–343; *ODNB*.
28. See above, vii–viii, 'Acknowledgements'.
29. John M. Wallace, *Destiny His Choice: The Loyalism of Andrew Marvell* (Cambridge, 1968); Annabel M. Patterson, *Marvell and the Civic Crown* (Princeton, 1978), rev. as *Marvell: The Writer in Public Life* (Harlow and New York, 2000); Warren Chernaik, *The Poet's Time: Politics and Religion in the Work of Andrew Marvell* (Cambridge, 1983); Derek Hirst, ' "That Sober Cromwell": Marvell's Cromwell in 1654', in John M. Wallace, ed., *The Golden and the Brazen World: Papers in Literature and History, 1650-1800* (Berkeley, CA, 1985), 17–53; Derek Hirst and Steven N. Zwicker, 'High Summer at Nun Appleton, 1651: Andrew Marvell and the Lord Fairfax's Occasions', *HJ*, 36 (1993), 247–69; David Norbrook, *Writing the English Republic: Poetry, Rhetoric, and Politics, 1627-1660* (Cambridge, 1999), 158–82, ch. 6, 337–57; Blair Worden, *Literature and Politics in Cromwellian England: John Milton, Andrew Marvell, Marchamont Nedham* (Oxford, 2007), chs 3–6. See also Edward Holberton, *Poetry and the Cromwellian Protectorate: Culture, Politics and Institutions* (Oxford, 2008), and Nicholas McDowell, *Poetry and Allegiance in the English Civil Wars: Marvell and the Cause of Wit* (Oxford, 2008).
30. John Dixon Hunt, *Andrew Marvell: His Life and Writings* (1978), e.g. 26–56, 80–81, 101.
31. For Williamson, see below, 132, 241, 261, 281–2, 301, 303, 322, 326, 332; and for Sir Philip Meadows in particular, see below, 109, 145.
32. J[ohn] A[dams], 'To Mr Creech on his Translation of Lucretius', in *T. Lucretius Carus, the Epicurean Philosopher: his six books, De natura rerum, done into English Verse with Notes* (2nd edn, 1683), sig. C2^v.
33. *PL*, II.321.
34. Thompson, 'The Life . . ', 435; Paul Hammond, *Dryden and the Traces of Classical Rome* (Oxford, 1999); *PL*, II.316.
35. [Samuel Butler], *The Transproser Rehears'd* (1673), 134–5.

CHAPTER 2: ROOTS

1. George Fox, *The Journal*, ed. Nigel Smith (1998), 70–1. The reference is to the third book of Joseph Hall, *The Discovery of a New World* (1st edn, 1609).
2. *ODNB*; *AMC*, 15–16.
3. Yorks., East Riding RO, PE85/1, 7^v.
4. Yorks., East Riding RO, PE125/1/4^r.
5. HCA, BRB 3:127; *AMC*, 17–18.
6. *AMC*, 18–20.

7. R.A. Marchant, *The Puritans and the Church Courts in the Diocese of York, 1560–1642* (1960).
8. Claire Cross, *Urban Magistrates and Ministers: Religion in Hull and Leeds from the Reformation to the Civil War*. University of York, Borthwick Papers 67 (1985).
9. See Richard Perrot, *Iacobs vovve, or The true historie of tithes* (Cambridge, 1627).
10. 'Things to be considered about the Hospitall called God's house', HCL, MS 'Sermons &c. of the Rev. Andrew Marvell'. See also John Cook, *The History of God's House of Hull, Commonly called the Charterhouse* (Hull, 1882).
11. *MPW*, I.288–9.
12. Audrey Howes and Martin Foreman, *Town and Gun: The 17th-Century Defences of Hull* (Hull, 1999).
13. *AMC*, 18.
14. *PL*, II.2.
15. HCL, MSB, fol. 9^r.
16. Thomas Fuller, *The History of the Worthies of England* (1662), 159.
17. See, e.g., BL, MS Lansdowne 891, fol. 118.
18. London, Inner Temple Library, MS 531.C.
19. BL, Harley MS 6356, fols 153–62.
20. 'Israel and England parallel'd', London, Inner Temple, MS 531 C.
21. See Timotheus of Miletus, *The Fragments of Timotheus of Miletus*, ed. J.H. Hordern (Oxford, 2002).
22. See below, 112 and *AMP*, 227.
23. The quotation from Horace is 'Olim francus eram ficulnus, inutile lignum:/ Quam faber incertus scamnum faceretne Priapum,/ Malum esse deum' (*Satires*, I. viii. 1–3).
24. See above, n. 15.
25. HCL, MSB, 'For in Christ Jesus, neither circumcision availeth any thing; nor ancircumcision: but a new creature', fol. 137^r.
26. HCL, MSB, fol. 137^v. 'Fooliana' is a reference to the third book of Joseph Hall's *The Discovery of a New World* (1st edn, 1609). Hall had been a fellow of Emmanuel College, Cambridge, but left in 1601, the year in which Marvell senior matriculated.
27. HCL, MSB, fol. 121^r.
28. HCA, BRL 247, 247a, 247b.
29. HCL, MSB, n.p., three pages on two leaves, bound after Racovian Catechism and Latin theological notes, and scriptural index.
30. CUL, MS Notes 4.12.
31. Fuller, *Worthies*, 159.
32. HCL, MSB: the translation of the Racovian Catechism is also unpaginated and takes up the first fifty-one leaves, after two preliminary leaves. The volume is unusually bound, dividing the text of the Catechism, binding the pages front and back, and also reversing their order.
33. See Sarah Mortimer, *Reason and Religion in the English Revolution: The Challenge of Socinianism* (Cambridge, 2010).
34. *AMC*, 27. For Best, see also *ODNB*.
35. See John Marshall, *John Locke: Resistance, Religion, and Responsibility* (Cambridge, 1994); Rob Iliffe, *Newton: A Very Short Introduction* (Oxford, 2007).
36. See Paul Chang-Ha Lim, *In Pursuit of Purity, Unity, and Liberty: Richard Baxter's Puritan Ecclesiology in its Seventeenth-Century Context* (Leiden, 2004), 166.
37. HCL, MSB, fol. 121.
38. BL, MS Lansdowne, 891, fol. 118.
39. HCL, MSB, fol. 202^r.
40. HCA, BRM 166. For Neile, see *ODNB*.
41. Marchant, *Puritans and the Church Courts*, 262; *AMC*, 25–6.
42. HCL, MSB.
43. 'Complaint against the perverse behaviour of some of the Inhabitants of Kingston upon Hull', HCL, MSB, fols 207–11.

44. John Lawson, *A Town Grammar School through Six Centuries; A History of Hull Grammar School against its Local Background* (London and New York, 1963).

45. Alan Stewart, *Close Readers: Humanism and Sodomy in Early Modern England* (Princeton, NJ, 1997), 88–104.

46. *MPW*, I.85.

47. *MPW*, I.162.

48. *MPW*, II.45–6.

49. *MPW*, II.55.

50. *AMC*, 22.

51. *AMP*, 5–9.

52. For Overton, see Nicholas McDowell, *The English Radical Imagination: Culture, Religion, and Revolution, 1630–1660* (Oxford, 2003), 52.

53. *AMC*, 25.

54. Hilton Kelliher, *Andrew Marvell: Poet and Politician 1621–1678*, 22–3; *AMC*, 26.

55. See G.A.J. Rodgers et al., eds, *The Cambridge Platonists in Philosophical Context: Politics, Metaphysics, and Religion* (Dordrecht and Boston, 1997).

56. John Sherman, *A Greek in the Temple* (1641), 2–3.

57. *ODNB*.

58. Christine Rees, *The Judgment of Andrew Marvell* (1989), 128; see further *AMP*, 107–11.

59. Henry More, *The Immortality of the Soul* (1659), 3.2.1.

60. Basil Smallman 'Endor Revisited: English Biblical Dialogues of the Seventeenth Century', in *Music and Letters* (1965), 137, 140–1. Timothy Raylor, 'Marvell's Musical Dialogues', *Explorations in Renaissance Culture*, forthcoming.

61. E.E. Duncan-Jones, 'Marvell: A Great Master of Words', *PBA*, 61 (1975), 267.

62. See below, 254, 279 and Nigel Smith, 'Freethinking Marvell', forthcoming. For Clifford, see Giovanni Tarantino, life in *ODNB* and *Martin Clifford, 1624–1677: deismo e tolleranza nell'Inghilterra della Restaurazione* (Florence, 2000).

63. I am most grateful to Ian Parker for drawing my attention to this volume, neglected since Legouis's editorial work on Marvell.

64. See *ODNB* and George Saintsbury, *Minor Poets of the Caroline Period*, 3 vols (Oxford, 1921, 1968), III.424.

65. See Nicholas von Maltzahn, 'Death by Drowning: Marvell's "Lycidas" ', *Milton Studies*, 48 (2008), 38–52.

66. *HCA*, BRL 247.

67. Ibid.

68. See Alison Shell, *Catholicism, Controversy, and the English Literary Imagination, 1558–1660* (Cambridge, 1999).

69. See Anthony Milton, *Catholic and Reformed: The Roman and Protestant Churches in English Protestant Thought, 1600–1640* (Cambridge, 1995).

70. See Nicholas McDowell, 'The Beauty of Holiness and the Poetics of Antinomianism: Richard Crashaw, John Saltmarsh, and the Language of Radical Religion in the 1640s', in Ariel Hessayon, ed., *Rediscovering Radicalism in the British Isles and Ireland, 1600–1700* (Aldershot, 2009), forthcoming.

CHAPTER 3: A DECADE OF CRISES

1. *HCA*, L. 243, dated 10 August 1635; *HCA*, L. 272, 29 May 1640.

2. John Tickell, *The History of the Town and County of Kingston upon Hull, from its Foundation in the Reign of Edward the First to the Present Time* (Hull, 1796), 308.

3. Donald Woodward, *Men at Work: Labourers and Building Craftsmen in the Towns of Northern England, 1450–1750* (Cambridge, 2002), 8. By the mid-eighteenth century the population had doubled to *c.* 12,000.

4. Tickell, *The History*, 309–11. In fact, no printed version appears to survive, but there is an MS copy at BL, MS Harl. 6356, fols 153–62.

5. Thomas Fuller, *History of the Worthies of England* (1662), 159; *AMC*, 28.

6. London Metropolitan Archives, H1/ST/E79/24, m. 37; *ODNB*, *AMC*, 28–9.

7. Steven N. Zwicker and Derek Hirst, 'Eros and Abuse: Imagining Andrew Marvell', *ELH*, 74 (2007), 371–95.

8. Trinity College, Cambridge, Conclusions and Admissions Book, 1607–73; *AMC*, 29.

9. As happened to Thomas Gage, who recorded it in *The English-American his travail by sea and land, or, A new survey of the West-India's* (1648).

10. *AMC*, 28.

11. W. Clavert Watson, *The Charterhouse Bill. The Story of the Charterhouse* (1886), 22.

12. Richard Tames, *London: A Cultural History* (Oxford, 2006), 26.

13. See *ODNB*.

14. Robert Wilcher, *Andrew Marvell* (1985), 72.

15. [Abraham Cowley], 'Francis Cole', *The Prologve and Epilogve to a Comedie Presented at the Entertainment of the Prince, His Highnesse, by the Schollars of Trinity Colledge in Cambridge in March last, 1641* (1642), 3.

16. On exile, see Geoffrey Smith, *The Cavaliers in Exile, 1640–1660* (Houndmills and New York, 2003).

17. See Hilton Kelliher, *Andrew Marvell, Poet & Politician, 1621–78: An Exhibition to Commemorate the Tercentenary of his Death, British Library Reference Division, 14 July–1 October 1978* (1978), 125–6.

18. PRO SP 18/33/152; Milton, *CPW*, IV.ii.859; *AMC*, 38.

19. T.S. Eliot, 'Andrew Marvell', *TLS*, 1002 (31 March 1921), 201. The best introduction to Marvell's exploration of European verse remains J.B. Leishman, *The Art of Marvell's Poetry* (1966, 2nd edn, 1968).

20. Sheffield University, Hartlib Papers, 29/5/50A.

21. See, e.g., Simon Schama, *The Embarrassment of Riches: An Interpretation of Dutch Culture in the Golden Age* (1987); Jonathan Israel, *The Dutch Republic: Its Rise, Greatness and Fall, 1477–1806* (Oxford, 1995).

22. See Lisa Jardine, *Going Dutch: How England Plundered Holland's Glory* (2008).

23. See below, 106–9.

24. See *AMC*, 91.

25. See Anston Bosman, 'Renaissance Intertheater and the Staging of Nobody', *ELH*, 71 (2004), 559–85.

26. See N.F. Streekstra, *Afbeeldingsrelaties: een taal- en letterkundig essay over Huygens' Donne-vertalingen* (Groningen, 1994); Peter Davidson and Adriaan van der Weel, eds, *A Selection of the Poems of Sir Constantijn Huygens (1596–1687)* (Amsterdam, 1996).

27. For the relevant Marvell passages, see *AMP*, 218, 231–2. (Trans. Peter Davidson.)

28. The relationship between politics and literature is treated very subtly by Christian Jouhaud in *Les Pouvoirs de la littérature* (Paris, 2000).

29. Trans. Cynthia Nazarian.

30. See e.g. BN, MS Fr. 19145.

31. See e.g. BN, MS Fr. 15220.

32. See Anon., *Satyre sur la barbe de monsieur le Président Molé* (1649), ll. 99–101, a mazarinade (www.textesrares.com/poesie/b6_315.htm). See also Hubert Carrier, *La Fronde: contestation démocratique et misère paysanne: 52 Mazarinades* 2 vols (Paris, 1982); Orest A. Ranum, *The Fronde: A French Revolution, 1648–1652* (New York, 1993). For mixtures of amorous, satirical and political lyric and song, see, e.g., BN, MS Fr. 12801.

33. Thomas Hobbes, *The Correspondence*, ed. Noel Malcolm, 2 vols (Oxford, 1994), I. letters 29, 30, 32–4, 36, 57, 59, 60.

34. *MPW*, I.70–73.

35. See below, 88 and *AMP*, 96–7.

36. The Villiers brothers were travelling and present in Rome at this time. Marvell says he knew Lord Francis Villiers: see below, 69–73. See *AMP*, 11–55, 166; Edward Chaney, *The Grand Tour and the Great Rebellion: Richard Lassels and 'The Voyage of Italy' in the Seventeenth Century* (Geneva, 1985), 348–50.

37. See Richard Flecknoe, *Prose Characters*, ed. Fred Mayers (New York, 1987).
38. Flecknoe, *Ariadne Deserted by Theseus* (1654), sigs A4^v–A5^r.
39. Ibid., sig. A7^r.
40. Edward J. Reilly, 'Marvell's "Fleckno", Anti-Catholicism, and the Pun as Metaphor', *JDJ*, 2 (1983), 51–62.
41. *MPW*, I.241.
42. See above, 40–1.
43. See the satires against poets and painters, and the engraved print *Alexander the Great in the studio of Apelles*, etching (*c.* 1662).
44. I owe this insight, as in many other matters, to Leonard Barkan; it was discussed in Nigel Smith and Leonard Barkan, 'Marvell's Roman Holiday', BBC Radio Three, *Twenty Minutes* broadcast 7 November 2005, produced by Julia Adamson.
45. See Jeremy Robbins, *Love Poetry of the Literary Academies in the Reigns of Philip IV and Charles II* (1997).
46. 'Romance' (1582); translation adapted from John Dent-Young, ed., *Selected Poems of Luis de Góngora* (Chicago, 2007), 26–7.
47. See below, 219–20.
48. *PL*, II.324.

CHAPTER 4: POETRY AND REVOLUTION

1. For the circulation in manuscript and print of Royalist verse, see Robert Wilcher, *The Writing of Royalism, 1628–1660* (Cambridge, 2001).
2. HCL, Andrew Marvell Meldreth deed; Hilton Kelliher, 'Some Notes on Andrew Marvell', *BLJ*, 4 (1978), 125–9; *AMC*, 2.
3. See Nicholas McDowell, *Poetry and Allegiance in the English Civil Wars. Marvell and the Cause of Wit* (Oxford, 2008).
4. *ODNB*.
5. See the headnotes and footnotes in *MP* for details. Much work in scholarship has been expended on this topic; the most impressive and early collection of discoveries, showing Marvell's indebtedness to continental as well as English verse, remains J.B. Leishman, *The Art of Marvell's Poetry* (1966, 2nd edn, 1968).
6. See McDowell, *Poetry and Allegiance*, Ch.1.
7. Robert Wilcher, *Andrew Marvell* (1985), 64.
8. See *AMP*, 43–5, and Estelle Haan, *Andrew Marvell's Latin Poetry: From Text to Context* (Brussels, 2003), 87–94.
9. Gary Kuchar, *The Poetry of Religious Sorrow in Early Modern England* (Cambridge, 2008), Ch.3.
10. Wilcher, *Andrew Marvell*, 13–20 (see below n55).
11. Robert Ashton, *Counter-Revolution: The Second Civil War and its Origins, 1646–8* (New Haven, CT, and London, 1994), 408.
12. Edmund Ludlow, *The Memoirs of Edmund Ludlow, Lieutenant-General of the Horse in the Army of the Commonwealth of England, 1625–1672*, edited with appendices of letters and illustrative documents by C.H. Firth (Oxford, 1894), I.198.
13. *The Parliament-Kite*, 8 (29 June–13 July 1648), 44–5.
14. John Hall in *Mercurius Britannicus* (11 July 1648), 70; for Hall, see *ODNB*. The associations of his writings with Marvell's are many: see, e.g., *AMP*, 21–2, 26, 84, 274–5.
15. See McDowell, *Poetry and Allegiance*, 167.
16. James Loxley, 'Prepar'd at Last to Strike in with the Tyde? Andrew Marvell and Royalist Verse', *SC*, 10 (1995), 47–8.
17. Jerry Brotton, *The Sale of the Late King's Goods: Charles I and his Art Collection* (2006), 208, 244, 327, 335.
18. Paul Hammond, 'Marvell's Ambiguities', ch. 4, in *Figuring Sex between Men from Shakespeare to Rochester* (Oxford, 2002), 213.

19. Samuel Parker, *A Reproof to the Rehearsal Transpos'd* (1673), 274.
20. *AMP*, 13; John McWilliams, ' "A Storm of Lamentations Writ": *Lachrymae Musarum* and Royalist Culture after the Civil War', *YES*, 33 (2003), 273–89.
21. See Peter Beal, *In Praise of Scribes: Manuscripts and their Makers in Seventeenth-Century England* (Oxford, 1998), 148.
22. None of the three elegies mentions the King's execution, which in itself suggests an early date, given that the regicide was an irresistible topic for Royalist elegists after January 1649. It is therefore impossible to say with certainty whether the three elegies under discussion pre- or post-date Marvell's elegy. Fur further discussion of this manuscript volume, see forthcoming publication by John McWilliams, for whose help I am especially grateful.
23. This aspect is explored more extensively by Blair Worden, *Literature and Politics in Cromwellian England: John Milton, Andrew Marvell, Marchamont Nedham* (Oxford, 2007), 58–60, 62, 71, 102.
24. Michael Craze, *The Life and Lyrics of Andrew Marvell* (1979), 8.
25. See further, McDowell, *Poetry and Allegiance*, 170–73.
26. See, e.g., 'The Unfortunate Lover', sts V–VIII; 'The Nymph Complaining', ll. 1–24; 'Daphnis and Chloe', sts VII, XVII, XXV.
27. McDowell, *Poetry and Allegiance*, 186–7; for Hall, see *ODNB*; David Norbrook, *Writing the English Republic: Poetry, Rhetoric, and Politics, 1627-1660* (Cambridge, 1999), 169–80, 212–21.
28. See Esther Cope, *Handmaid of the Holy Spirit: Dame Eleanor Davies, Never Soe Mad a Ladie* (Ann Arbor, 1992), and *ODNB*.
29. See Hugh Trevor-Roper, *Europe's Physician: The Life of Theodore De Mayerne* (New Haven, CT, and London, 2006).
30. Lyndy Abraham, *Marvell and Alchemy* (1990), 303–4.
31. Jeremy Maule, 'Marvell's Hastings Elegy: A Supplementary Note', *RES*, n.s., 37 (1986), 399.
32. Apollodorus, *The Library*, II.x.3. For Rubens's portrait of Mayerne as Aesculapius, see *AMP*, 28.
33. See Ovid, *Metamorphoses*, I, ll. 521–4; Milton, *Comus*, ll. 628–40; Lady Eleanor Davies, *Sions Lamentation* (1649), 2.
34. M[archamont] N[edham], 'On the Untimely Death of the Lord Hastings', in *Lachrymae Musarum* (1649), 81–5 (II. 1–2).
35. See Blair Worden, ' "Wit in a Roundhead" ', in Susan D. Amussen and Mark A. Kishlansky, eds, *Political Culture and Cultural Politics in Early Modern England: Essays presented to David Underdown* (Manchester, 1995), 321–2; Blair Worden, *Literature and Politics in Cromwellian England: John Milton, Andrew Marvell, Marchamont Nedham* (Oxford, 2007), 24–5, 92–3, 96, 110, 129, 220, 223, 296, 317; Nigel Smith, *Literature and Revolution in England, 1640-1660* (New Haven, CT, and London, 1994), 182–7; McDowell, *Poetry and Allegiance*, ch. 5.
36. See Aristotle, *Politics*, III.xiii.1–2.
37. See untitled poem [by John Ravenshaw] at Folger Shakespeare Library, Washington, DC, MS v.a.148, fol. 35^v.
38. See above, 36.
39. Houghton Library, Harvard University, fMS Eng. 645.
40. On Lucretius and his reception in early modern culture: see Stuart Gillespie, 'Lucretius in the English Renaissance', in Stuart Gillespie and Philip Hardie, eds, *The Cambridge Companion to Lucretius* (Cambridge, 2007), 242–53; Gerard Passannante, 'The Art of Reading Earthquakes: On Harvey's Wit, Ramus's Method, and the Renaissance of Lucretius', *RQ*, 61 (2008), 792–832.
41. Norbrook, *Writing the English Republic*, 269–70.
42. Abraham Cowley, 'To the Reader', *The Mistresse* (1647), 115.
43. Worden, *Literature and Politics*, 85.
44. Alastair Fowler, *Triumphal Forms: Structural Patterns in Elizabethan Poetry* (Cambridge, 1970), 76–84.
45. Archivo General del Reino, Simancas, Valladolid, Spain.

46. J.A. Mazzeo, 'Cromwell as Machiavellian Prince in Marvell's *An Horatian Ode*', *JHI*, 21 (1960), 1–17. See also Hans Baron, 'Marvell's "An Horatian Ode" and Machiavelli', *JHI*, 21 (1960), 1–17.

47. See Barbara Everett, 'The Shooting of the Bears: Poetry and Politics in Andrew Marvell', in R.L. Brett, ed., *Andrew Marvell: Essays on the Tercentenary of his Death* (Oxford, 1978), 74.

48. Bod., MS Wood F39, fol. 414.

49. See Allan G. Chester, *Thomas May: Man of Letters, 1595–1650* (Philadelphia, PA, 1932), 11–30.

50. BL, MS Add. 28002, fol. 59.

51. See Blair Worden, 'The Politics of Marvell's Horatian Ode', *HJ* 27 (1984) 525–47; Richard Tuck, *Philosophy and Government, 1572–1651* (Cambridge, 1993), 221–53, and Smith, *Literature and Revolution*, 177–200.

52. Warren L. Chernaik, *The Poet's Time: Politics and Religion in the Work of Andrew Marvell* (1983), 177.

53. Matteo Palmieri, *Vita Civile* (1429), ed. Gino Belloni (Florence, 1982), 198–208.

54. See further, *AMP*, 119.

55. E.E. Duncan-Jones, 'A Great Master of Words: Some Aspects of Marvell's Poems of Praise and Blame', *PBA*, 61 (1975), 77.

56. Anon., *The Earle of Pembroke's Last Speech* (1650), 3.

57. John Wilson, *Fairfax: a Life of Thomas, Lord Fairfax, Captain-General of all the Parliament's Forces in the English Civil War, Creator & Commander of the New Model Army* (1985), 162–3; see also Andrew Hopper, *Black Tom Sir Thomas Fairfax and the English Revolution* (Manchester, 2007).

58. See above, 27 and *ODNB*.

59. See BL, MS Egerton 2146, fol. 6ff.

60. Timothy Raylor, 'Dr Witty and a Nun Appleton Poisoning', *N&Q*, n.s. 249 (2004), 27.

61. Robert Witty, 'The Translator to the Reader', in James Primerose, *Popular Errours* (1651), sig. A6^r.

62. See *ODNB*.

63. Sir John Denham, *Poetical Works*, ed. T.H. Banks (2nd edn, 1969), 159.

64. Ibid., 160.

65. Norbrook, *Writing the English Republic*, 283.

66. Ibid., 287

67. BL, MSS Stowe 185, fol. 1811; Stowe 189, ff. 72, 73.

68. This is the argument of Blair Worden, *Literature and Politics*, Appendix I.

69. Derek Hirst and Steven N. Zwicker, 'High Summer at Nun Appleton, 1651: Andrew Marvell and Lord Fairfax's Occasions', *HJ*, 36 (1993), 247–69.

70. Sketched by Daniel King *c.* 1656; Bod. Gough Maps 1, fol. 1, see fig. **00**; Lee Erickson, 'Marvell's "Upon Appleton House" and the Fairfax Family', *ELR*, 9 (1979), 158–68 (163–5).

71. See Jane Partner, ' "The Swelling Hall": Andrew Marvell and the Politics of Architecture at Nun Appleton House', *SC*, 23 (2008), 225–43.

72. See, e.g., Samuel Colvile, 'Ad Illustrissimum Heroem Dominum Thomam Fairfaxium Baronem de Cameron (1650), Anon., Ad Fairfaxum Imperio post attritas regis copias usum' (1651).

73. Hirst and Zwicker, 'High Summer'; Michael Wilding, *Dragon's Teeth: Literature in the English Revolution* (Oxford, 1987), 143.

74. Patsy Griffin, ' "Twas no Religious House till now": Marvell's "Upon Appleton House" ', *SEL*, 28 (1988), 61–76 (62–7); Gary D. Hamilton, 'Marvell, Sacrilege, and Protestant Historiography: Contextualising "Upon Appleton House" ', in Donna B. Hamilton and Richard Strier, eds, *Religion, Literature, and Politics in Post-Reformation England, 1540–1688* (Cambridge, 1996), 161–86.

75. See *ODNB*.

76. Hirst and Zwicker, 'High Summer', 260–2.

77. Anne Cotterill, 'Marvell's Watery Maze: Digression and Discovery at Nun Appleton', *ELH*, 69 (2002), 103–32.

78. As shown by Alastair Fowler, ed., *The Country House Poem: A Cabinet of Seventeenth-Century Estate Poems and Related Items* (1994).
79. Leeds University, Brotherton Library, Fairfax MS Acc. No. 24719, fols 295–6.
80. John M. Wallace, *Destiny His Choice: The Loyalism of Andrew Marvell* (Cambridge, 1968), 240ff.
81. BL, MS Egerton 2146, fol. 2ᵛ.
82. See *AMP*, 128–30, 135–45.

CHAPTER 5: THE TUTOR

1. PRO C24/814/26; Art Kavanagh, 'Andrew Marvell and the Duttons of Sherborne in 1657', *N&Q*, 248 (2003), 183–8; *AMC*, 37.
2. See Joad Raymond, *Pamphlets and Pamphleteering in Early Modern Britain* (Cambridge, 2003), 151–5; Nicholas McDowell, 'Urquhart's Rabelais: Translation, Patronage, and Cultural Politics', *ELR*, 35 (2005), 273–303.
3. For dating, see *AMP*, 74.
4. Christine Rees, *The Judgment of Marvell* (1989), 93.
5. Jules Brody, 'The Resurrection of the Body: A New Reading of Marvell's To His Coy Mistress', *ELH*, 56 (1989), 53–79 (74).
6. Rosalie L. Colie, *'My Ecchoing Song': Andrew Marvell's Poetry of Criticism* (Princeton, NJ, 1970), 59.
7. Joshua Scodel, 'The Pleasures of Restraint: The Mean of Coyness in Cavalier Poetry', *Criticism*, 28 (1996), 239–79.
8. Charles Kay Smith, 'French Philosophy and English Politics in Interregnum Poetry', in Malcolm Smuts, ed., *The Stuart Court and Europe: Essays in Politics and Political Culture* (Cambridge, 1996), 177–209 (183).
9. See Smith, 'French Philosophy', 205.
10. Zachary Crofton, *Bethshemesh Clouded* (1653), 3–4.
11. Robert H. Ray, 'Marvell's "To His Coy Mistress" and Sandys's Translation of Ovid's *Metamorphoses*', *RES*, 44 (1993), 386–8.
12. Paul Hammond, 'Andrew Marvell's Sexuality', *SC*, 11 (1996), 112–13.
13. J.B. Leishman, *The Art of Marvell's Poetry* (1966), 70.
14. B.J. Sokol, 'Logic and Illogic in Marvell's "To His Coy Mistress"', *ES*, 3 (1990), 244–52.
15. Ibid.
16. Brody, 'Resurrection of the Body', 71–2.
17. Smith, 'French Philosophy', 207.
18. Trinity College, Cambridge, MS R.5.5, undated; see also Arnold Hunt, 'The Books, Manuscripts and Literary Patronage of Mrs Anne Sadleir', in Victoria Burke and Jonathan Gibson, eds, *Early Modern Women's Manuscript Writing* (Aldershot, 2004), 205–36.
19. David Crane, 'Marvell and Milton on Cromwell', *N&Q*, n.s. 33 (1986), 464; *AMP*, 274.
20. PRO SP 18/33/152; Milton, *CPW*, IV.ii.859–60; *AMC*, 38.
21. See Hugh Dunthorne, 'Resisting Monarchy: The Netherlands as Britain's School of Revolution in the Late Sixteenth and Seventeenth Centuries', in R. Oresko et al., eds, *Royal and Republic Sovereignty in Early Modern Europe: Essays in Memory of Ragnhild Hatton* (Cambridge, 1997), 125–48, and Steven C.A. Pincus, *Protestantism and Patriotism: Ideologies and the Making of English Foreign Policy, 1650–1668* (Cambridge, 1996), 15–79.
22. *AMP*, 247–8.
23. See below, 224–5.
24. See *ODNB*.
25. Milton, *CPW*, IV.ii.860.
26. See *ODNB*; see also David Trotter, ' "Practic Resurrection": The Sermons of John Hales', *YES*, 9 (1979), 236–45.
27. See *ODNB*; see also above, 92–4.
28. C.B. Hardman, 'Row Well Ye Mariners', *RES*, 51 (2000), 80–82.
29. See McDowell, *Poetry and Allegiance*, 218.

30. See *ODNB*, entry for John Oxenbridge; *AMP*, 192–5.
31. Lucius Cary, Viscount Falkland (1610–43).
32. *MPW* I.134.
33. John Aubrey, *Brief Lives*, ed. Andrew Clark, 2 vols (Oxford, 1898), I.279–80.
34. See *ODNB*.
35. Edward Holberton, 'Bellipotens virgo', *TLS*, 21 November 2008, 14–15.
36. Susanna Åkerman, *Queen Christina of Sweden and her Circle: The Transformation of a Seventeenth-Century Philosophical Libertine* (Leiden, 1991); *The Diary of Bulstrode Whitelocke 1605–1675*, ed. Ruth Spalding (Oxford, 1990), 316.
37. Essentially it is a complete text of the copy made by Jean Scheffer and published in Johann Arckenholtz, *Mémoires concernant Christine reine de Suède* (1751–60), with the extra two lines, but in place of a number of Arckenholtz variants it reads as *1681*.
38. See below, 253.
39. Iiro Kajanto, *Christina Heroina: Mythological and Historical Exemplification in the Latin Panegyrics on Christina Queen of Sweden* (Helsinki, 1993).
40. For fuller analysis of the poem and the other poetry used in the embassy, see Edward Holberton, *Poetry and the Cromwellian Protectorate: Culture, Politics, and Institutions* (Oxford, 2008), ch. 1.
41. *PL*, II.306.
42. See above, 53–62.
43. See above, 34.
44. David Norbrook, ' "This Blushing Tribute of a Borrowed Muse": Robert Overton and his Overturning of the Poetic Canon', *EMS*, 4 (1993), 220–66; Sidney Gottlieb, 'George Herbert and Robert Overton', *George Herbert Journal*, 18 (1994–95), 185–200; Barbara Taft, "'They That Pursue Perfection on Earth": The Political Progress of Robert Overton', in I. Gentles et al., eds, *Soldiers, Writers and Statesmen of the English Revolution* (Cambridge, 1998), 286–303.
45. Noel Blakiston, 'Andrew Marvell at Eton', *TLS*, 2610 (8 February 1952), 109.
46. James Harrington, *Oceana*, ed. J.G.A. Pocock (Cambridge, 1977), 37.
47. [Marchamont Nedham], *A True Case of the State of the Commonwealth* (1654), 51
48. See John M. Wallace, *Destiny his Choice: The Loyalism of Andrew Marvell* (Cambridge, 1968), 106–44; Derek Hirst, ' "That Sober Cromwell": Marvell's Cromwell in 1654', in John M. Wallace, ed., *The Golden and the Brazen World: Papers in Literature and History, 1650–1800* (Berkeley, CA, 1985), 17–53.
49. Timothy Raylor, 'Reading Machiavelli, Writing Cromwell: Edmund Waller's Copy of *The Prince* and his Draft Verses towards *A Panegryick on my Lord Protector*', Turnbull Library Review, 35 (2002), 9–32; idem, 'Waller's Machiavellian Cromwell: The Imperial Argument of *A Panegyrick to My Lord Protector*', *RES*, n.s. 56 (2005), 386–411.
50. Alexandra Walsham, *Charitable Hatred: Tolerance and Intolerance in England, 1500–1700* (Manchester, 2006), 302–5.
51. See below, 328–31.
52. *MPW*, I.233.
53. Pierre Legouis, 'Marvell and the two learned brothers of St. Marthe', *PQ*, 38 (1959), 450–8.
54. *MPW*, I.362.
55. Bod. MS Rawlinson A34, 599; *Thurloe*, 4:437; *AMC*, 43.
56. Bod. MS Rawlinson A35, 132; *Thurloe*, 4:533; PRO, SP 18/125/50[r]; *AMC*, 43–4.
57. Sheffield University, Hartlib Papers, 29/5/50A, yielding a departure date a little later than implied by Henry Poulton.
58. Hartlib Papers, 29/5/8A–B, 29/5/43A.
59. Benjamin Billingsley deposition, PRO, C24/814/26; *AMC*, 44.
60. *AMC*, 44.
61. See Art Kavanagh, 'Andrew Marvell and the Duttons of Sherborne in 1657', *N&Q*, n.s. 50 (2003), 183–8.
62. E.E. Duncan-Jones, 'Marvell, R.F. and the Authorship of "Blake's Victory" ', *EMS*, 5 (1995), 107–26.
63. See above, *AMP*, 242–5.

CHAPTER 6: CIVIL SERVICE

1. *PL*, II.380.

2. See Philip Aubrey, *Mr Secretary Thurloe: Cromwell's Secretary of State, 1652–1660* (London and Rutherford, NJ, 1990).

3. Bod. MS Rawlinson A53, 242–3; Hilton Kelliher, 'Some Notes on Andrew Marvell', *BLJ*, 4 (1978), 130.

4. Bod. MS Rawlinson A53, 302; Kelliher, 'Some Notes', 130.

5. Bod. MS Rawlinson A55, 221–2; *Thurloe*, 6:578–9; Kelliher, 'Some Notes', 130.

6. PRO, CO1/13/84; *PL*, 2:380; *AMC*, 47.

7. Thomas Birch, ed., *A Collection of the State Papers of John Thurloe*, 7 vols (1742), 7:513.

8. Bod. MS Rawlinson A55, 255; Birch, ed., *A Collection*, 6:584–5; Kelliher, 'Some Notes', 130.

9. Bod. MS Rawlinson A55, 249–50ᵛ; *Thurloe*, 6:601–2; Kelliher, 'Some Notes', 130.

10. Bod. MS Rawlinson A56, fols 65–6, 153, and *Thurloe*, 6:677–9; Kelliher, 'Some Notes', 130.

11. Bod. MS Rawlinson A56, 178–9 [with Latin 174–6], and *Thurloe*, 6:684–6; Kelliher, 'Some Notes', 130; Bod. MS Rawlinson A56, 246 [with Latin 244–5], and *Thurloe*, 6:696–7; Kelliher, 'Some Notes', 130.

12. Bod. MS Rawlinson A63, 27–9 [Latin is MS Rawlinson A57, 82–4]; and *Thurloe*, 6:735–8 [also 7:813–16]; Kelliher, 'Some Notes', 131.

13. BL, MS Add. 4459, 175–96ᵛ; Kelliher, 'Some Notes', 130, 131, 133; *MPW*, I.441–9.

14. Brian Fairfax, *A catalogue of the curious collection of pictures of George Villiers, Duke of Buckingham . . . With the life of George Villiers, Duke of Buckingham, the celebrated poet* (1758), 31.

15. Now at the National Portrait Gallery (discussed and reproduced in Kelliher, 'Some Notes', cover and frontispiece, 80), and elsewhere: *AMC*, 47.

16. *AMC*, 47.

17. C.H. Collins-Baker, *Lely and the Stuart Portrait Painters*, 2 vols (1912), I.217.

18. See Dale J.B. Randall, *Winter Fruit: English Drama, 1642–1660* (Lexington, KY, 1995).

19. Edward Holberton, *Poetry and the Cromwellian Protectorate: Culture, Politics, and Institutions* (Oxford, 2008), 143.

20. See Anon., *The true and exact speech and prayer of Doctor John Hewytt* (1658); *ODNB*.

21. See Ian Spink, *Henry Lawes: Cavalier Songwriter* (Oxford, 2000). Among several recordings of the Lawes brothers' music, *Lawes: Songs* (Hyperion, 2007) is particularly literary.

22. Donald M. Friedman, 'Marvell's Musicks', in Claude J. Summers and Ted-Larry Pebworth, eds, *On the Celebrated and Neglected Poems of Andrew Marvell* (Columbia, MO, 1992), 27–8.

23. Holberton, *Poetry and the Cromwellian Protectorate*, 155.

24. See above, 128.

25. PRO SP78/114/17, printed from original in *Thurloe*, 6:743; the manuscript copy is Bod. MS Clarendon 57, 42; *PL* II:306.

26. Bod. MS Rawlinson A58, 380–7, and *Thurloe*, 7:63–4; Kelliher, 'Some Notes', 130.

27. See above, 110, 113–15.

28. Ambrose Barnes, *Memoirs of Mr Ambrose Barnes*, Publications of the Surtees Society, 50 (Durham, 1867), 63.

29. Robert Boyle, *Works*, ed. Thomas Birch, 5 vols (1744), 5:274; *AMC*, 51.

30. PRO SP 25/78/615; *AMC*, 51.

31. PRO SP 25/78/615.

32. Bod. MS Rawlinson A60, 262–6; *Thurloe*, 7:298–9.

33. These tributes are now admirably summarized in Holberton, *Poetry and the Cromwellian Protectorate*, 162–7.

34. *The Publick Intelligencer*, 141 (30 August–6 September 1658), 794–[800]; *Mercurius Politicus*, 432 (2–9 September 1658), 802–8.

35. Thomas L'Wright, *A More Exact Character of . . . Oliver Cromwell* (1659), 5–6.

36. Henry Walker, *A Collection of Severall Passages Concerning His Highnesse* (1659), 1, 10.

37. See Nigel Smith, *Literature and Revolution in England 1640–1660* (1994), 287–94.

38. For Wither's poetry, see David Norbrook, *Writing the English Republic: Rhetoric, Politics and Poetry 1630–1660* (Cambridge, 1999), 140–58, 238–42, 351–7, 384–6.

39. E.g. 'G.G.', in *Musarum Cantabrigiensium* (1658), sig. G4^r, 'Mars envi'd thee, nor can we blame him for't; . . . Saturn *in brazen walls thou didst confine,/ Joves thunder was not so much feard as thine.*'

40. See, for instance, Anon., *The Portraiture of his Royal Highness, Oliver Late Lord Protector* (1659), 7–8, 57–8; Holberton, *Poetry and the Cromwellian Protectorate*, 180–1, sees particular resonances between Marvell's elegy and ?Charles Harvey or ?Henry Walker, *A Collection of Several Passages Concerning His Late Highnesse Oliver Cromwell* (1659).

41. See *AMP*, 290.

42. See further, *AMP*, 302–3.

43. *AMP*, 303–4.

44. Edward Thompson, ed., *The Works of Andrew Marvell, esq.*, 3 vols (1776), III.513.

45. Pierre Legouis, *Andrew Marvell, Poet, Puritan, Patriot* (Oxford, 1965), 111; Donald M. Friedman, *Marvell's Pastoral Art* (Berkeley, 1970), 284; Annabel Patterson, *Marvell and the Civic Crown* (Princeton, NJ, 1978), 94; M.L. Donnelly, ' "And still new stopps to various time apply'd": Marvell, Cromwell and the Problem of Representation at Midcentury', in Summers and Pebworth, eds, *On the Celebrated and Neglected Poems of Andrew Marvell* (Columbia, MO, 1992), 167–8.

46. Bod. MS Rawlinson A61, 33; *Thurloe*, 7:373; PRO SP 18/182/159, 194; BL MS Add. 22919, 51–3; Kelliher, 'Some Notes', 131; *AMC*, 53–4.

47. Archivio di Stato di Genova/Archivio Segreto, Inserto 1; *AMC*, 54.

48. Bod. MS Rawlinson A61/2, 275–6, 279–80; *Thurloe*, 7:434, 513; PRO SP 31/17/33, 307, 326–7, 349–50, 357–8; *AMC*, 54–5.

49. A common assumption in scholarship: see, e.g., Lawrence W. Hyman, *Andrew Marvell* (New York, 1964), ch. 6; Harold E. Toliver, *Marvell's Ironic Vision* (New Haven, CT, 1965), 116; Pierre Legouis, *Andrew Marvell: Poet, Puritan, Patriot* (Oxford, 1965), 105–6.

50. HCA, BRB 4:274; *AMC*, 55.

51. BL, MS Add. 21427, 262^v; see also *AMC*, 56.

52. *PL*, II.307.

53. HCA, BRB 4:277; Edmund Ludlow, *Memoirs*, ed. C.H. Firth, 2 vols (1894), II.51.

54. *CJ*, 7:600; *AMC*, 56–7.

55. *ODNB*.

56. BL, MS Add. 22919, 78; *PL*, II.2:307–8.

57. Although to Royalists, Downing often appeared imbued with republican principles. It is hard to regard him as a strict republican, like a Vane or a Milton: see Jonathan Scott, *Commonwealth Principles: Republican Writings of the English Revolution* (Cambridge, 2004), 70, 316–17, 344; idem, ' "Good Night Amsterdam". Sir George Downing and Anglo-Dutch Statebuilding', *EHR*, 118 (2003), 334–56.

58. *PL*, II.308.

59. BL, MS Add. 22919, fols 81–2.

60. HCA, BRL 635.

61. Nicholas Murray, *World Enough and Time: The Life of Andrew Marvell* (1999), 96.

62. BL, MS Add. 22919, 14–15; *PL*, II.308.

63. *CJ*, 7:622.

64. *CJ*, 7:638.

65. Thomas Burton, *Diary*, ed. J.T. Rutt, 4 vols (1828), IV:425–6; *CJ* 7:639.

66. Sir Henry Vane to MAH, HCA, BRL 635.

67. HCA, BRD 867; *AMC*, 58.

68. Bod. MS Rawlinson C179, 178; compare *PL* II:382; Bod. MS Rawlinson C179, 187; Bod. MS Rawlinson C179, 196; *AMC*, 58.

69. PRO SP 82/9/219^r (217^r original); Kelliher, 'Some Notes', 132; Bod. MS Rawlinson A66, 15; Kelliher, 'Some Notes', 132; PRO SP 82/9/243 (245 original); Kelliher, 'Some Notes', 132; Bod. MS Rawlinson A65, 403–6, and *Thurloe* 7:705; *CJ*, 7:754; Kelliher, 'Some Notes', 132; PRO, SP 84/162/322^r–323^v [original 324]; Kelliher, 'Some Notes', 132.

70. Hilton Kelliher, 'Some Uncollected Letters of Andrew Marvell', *BLJ* 5 (1979), 148.
71. Holberton, *Poetry and the Cromwellian Protectorate*, 203–4.
72. John Aubrey, *Brief Lives*, ed. Andrew Clark, 2 vols (Oxford, 1898), I.289–91.
73. [Samuel Butler], *The Transprosed Rehears'd* (1673), 46; *AMC*, 59.
74. See below, 273, 320, 322–4.
75. James Harrington, *Political Works*, ed. J.G.A. Pocock (Cambridge, 1977), 'Introduction';
    Nigel Smith, 'Milton and Popular Republicanism in the 1650s: John Streater's "Heroick
    Mechanicks"', in D. Armitage, A. Himy and Q. Skinner, eds, *Milton and Republicanism*
    (Cambridge, 1995), 137–55.
76. Aubrey, *Brief Lives*, I.289–91.
77. [Samuel Butler], *The Transproser Rehears'd*, 146.
78. Sotheby's, 24 July 1978, lot 108; BL, RP 3791 (photocopy); Kelliher, 'Some Uncollected
    Letters 59.
79. *PL*, II.309.
80. *AMC*, 60–1.
81. *To His most Excellent Majesty Charles the Second, by the grace of God, of England,
    Scotland, and Ireland, King, Defender of the Faith: the humble address of the maior,
    aldermen, ministers and burgesses of the town of Kingston upon Hull* (1660).
82. *PL*, II.1–3.
83. *AMC*, 61.
84. Bod. MS Carte 81, fols 80[r], 82[r]; see also fol. 77[r]; *AMC*, 59, 63.
85. *PL*, II.6.
86. *CJ*, 8:208–9; *AMC*, 62–3.
87. *PL*, II.7–8.
88. *PL*, I.17.
89. *PL*, II.18.
90. HCA, BRB 4:356.
91. See below, 227, 250–77, 279–82, 289–9.
92. *PL*, II.21.
93. *PL*, II.250–1.
94. As noted by Nicholas McDowell, *Poetry and Allegiance in the English Civil Wars:
    Marvell and the Cause of Wit* (Oxford, 2008), 257–8.

Chapter 7: Cavalier Revenge

1. *MPW*, II.106; see also 1 Cor. 1: 20.
2. Paul Seaward, *The Cavalier Parliament and the Reconstruction of the Old Regime,
   1661–1667* (Oxford, 1989).
3. See Annabel Patterson, *The Long Parliament of Charles II* (New Haven, CT, and
   London, 2008).
4. *PL*, II.21.
5. HCA, BRL 651, Gylby to MAH, 9 May 1661; *AMC*, 65.
6. *PL*, II.21.
7. HCA, BRL 651, Gylby to MAH, 9 May 1661.
8. HCA, BRL 661.
9. *PL*, II.23–4.
10. *PL*, II.27.
11. *PL*, II.27.
12. *PL*, II.31.
13. *PL*, II.31–2.
14. HCA, BRL 661.
15. *CJ*, 8:224; *AMC*, 66.
16. *PL*, II.32–3.
17. *AMC*, 65.

18. *CJ*, 8:249; *AMC*, 65.
19. *AMC*, 67.
20. *PL*, II.23–4.
21. May's exhumation has been seen as a context for the harshest lines of 'Tom May's Death', and hence an argument for a later dating of the poem: see above, 84–8.
22. See N.H. Keeble, *The Literary Culture of Nonconformity in Later Seventeenth-Century England* (Leicester and Athens, GA, 1987), 24–33.
23. George Fox, *The Journal*, ed. Nigel Smith (1998), 308–9.
24. *CJ*, 8:335–6; *AMC*, 67.
25. *AMC*, 68–9.
26. *CJ*, 8:389; *AMC*, 69.
27. *CJ*, 8:391; *AMC*, 69–70.
28. For the career of Thomas Hollis, see Annabel Patterson, *Early Modern Liberalism* (Cambridge, 1997), ch. 1.
29. *PL*, II.250–51.
30. *PL*, II.250–54.
31. *CJ*, 8:394, 403, 415; *AMC*, 70–1.
32. See above, 170–2.
33. For Carlisle, see *ODNB*.
34. *ODNB*; see also Blair Worden, *Literature and Politics in Cromwellian England: John Milton, Andrew Marvell, Marchamont Nedham* (Oxford, 2007), 399–404.
35. HCA, BRB, 4:503; *AMC*, 72–3.
36. *PL*, II.34.
37. *PL*, II.34–5.
38. *PL*, II.34–9.
39. See further *The horrid conspiracie of such impenitent traytors as intended a new rebellion in the kingdom of Ireland* (1663), and Richard L. Greaves, *Deliver Us from Evil: The Radical Underground in Britain, 1660-1663* (New York and Oxford, 1986), 140–50. For Blood, see *ODNB* and below, 236, 240–4.
40. *PL*, II.37.
41. *PL*, II.37.
42. *PL*, II.37–8.
43. *PL*, II.254.
44. Guy Miège, *A Relation of Three Embassies from his Sacred Majestie Charles II to the Great Duke of Muscovie . . .* (1669) which is used throughout this chapter, unless otherwise noted. Carlisle also wrote a report for the King with copies at Bod. MS Clarendon 80, 165ff. and PRO SP 29/81/223ff.
45. Bod. MS Clarendon 80, 166^r.
46. Ibid., 277^r.
47. Ibid., 105.
48. See Stephen Bardle, 'Literature and Dissent in the 1660s: The Restoration Careers of Ralph Wallis, George Wither and Andrew Marvell', unpublished D.Phil. thesis, University of Oxford, 2008.
49. See below, Chs.10, 11.
50. Bod. MS Clarendon 81, 124^v.
51. Ibid., 277^r.
52. This performance when it occurred in Sweden is interpreted differently by John Dixon Hunt, *Andrew Marvell: His Life and Writings* (1978), 148, with Marvell failing to give a sense of spontaneity in his French version.
53. *AMP*, 195–8.
54. *PL*, II.373n.; *AMC*, 88.
55. *AMC*, 88–9.
56. *AMC*, 89.
57. *AMC*, 257.
58. *AMP*, 246.

59. John Barnard, 'The 1665 York and London Editions of Marvell's The Character of Holland', *PBSA*, 81 (1987), 459–64.

60. Justin Champion, *London's Dreaded Visitation: The Social Geography of the Great Plague in 1665 by Justin Champion* (Historical Geography Research/Series 35, 1995).

61. Anthony à Wood, *Fasti*, 4 vols, ed. Bliss (1813–20), II.228.

62. HCA, BRL 1194/17; *AMC*, 90.

63. *PL*, II.40.

64. *AMC*, 90.

65. *AMC*, 90.

66. Anthony à Wood, *The Life and Times of Anthony à Wood, abridged from Andrew Clark's Edition and with an Introduction by Llewellyn Powys*. ed. Andrew Clark (1932), 127.

67. *PL*, II.40.

68. *CJ*, 8:621; *AMC*, 99.

69. Martin Dzelzainis and Annabel Patterson, 'Marvell and the Earl of Anglesey: A Chapter in the History of Reading', *HJ*, 44 (2001), 703–26.

70. I am grateful to Nicholas von Maltzahn for this suggestion.

71. *PL*, II.256.

CHAPTER 8: THE PAINTER AND THE POET DARE

1. *AMP*, 323–4.

2. See *AMP*, 446.

3. Steven C.A. Pincus, *Protestantism and Patriotism: Ideologies and the Making of English Foreign Policy, 1650–1668* (Cambridge, 1996), 198. However, this view has been challenged by an explanation rooted in economic and political opportunism: see Gijs Rommelse, 'The Fishing Industry as a Cause of the Second Dutch War, 1660–1667', *Dutch Crossing*, 26 (2002), 115–22.

4. Henry Stubbe, *The Miraculous Conformist* (Oxford, 1666), 83–5; *AMC*, 92.

5. FTHS 1/5; *AMC*, 92.

6. Helen Jacobsen, 'Ambassadorial Plate of the Later Stuart Period and the Collection of the Earl of Strafford', *Journal of the History of Collections*, 19 (2006), 1–13.

7. See Catharine Macleod, Julia Marciari Alexander, Kevin Sharpe and Tim Harris, eds, *Politics, Transgression, and Representation at the Court of Charles II* (New Haven, CT, 2008).

8. As in the portrait of John Wilmot, Earl of Rochester, attributed to Jacob Huysmans, *c.* 1665–70.

9. 'The Second Advice', ll. 87–98.

10. George Bishop, *The Warnings of the Lord* (1667), 19.

11. See George de F. Lord, *Poems on Affairs of State*, 7 vols (1963–75), I.xxv–lvi, *PL*, II.225–34; Nicholas von Maltzahn, 'Marvell's Ghost', in W. Chernaik and M. Dzelzainis, eds, *Marvell and Liberty* (Basingstoke, 1999), 50–74.

12. See Mary Tom Osborne, *Advice-to-a-Painter Poems, 1633–1856: An Annotated Finding List* (Austin, TX, 1949).

13. Pincus, *Protestantism and Patriotism*, chs 18–19.

14. Pepys, 6.122–3.

15. *CJ*, 8:621; *AMC*, 90.

16. *Directions to a Painter, For Describing our Naval Business: In Imitation of Mr Waller* (1667).

17. Annabel Patterson, *Marvell and the Civic Crown* (Princeton, NJ, 1978), 33.

18. See below, 210–11, 227, 235.

19. Patterson, *Marvell and the Civic Crown*, 117–39, revised as *Marvell: The Writer in Public Life* (Harlow, 2000), 79–85.

20. See, e.g., Samuel Wiseman, *Londons Fatal Fire* (1667).

21. See Martin Dzelzainis, ' "Presbyterian Sibyl": Truth-telling and Gender in Andrew Marvell's *The Third Advice to a Painter*', in Jennifer Richards and Alison Thorne, eds, *Rhetoric, Women and Politics in Early Modern England* (2007), 111–28.

22. *PL*, II.42.
23. *PL*, II.42–3.
24. HCA, BRB 5:76.
25. *PL*, II.46–7.
26. Pepys, 8.21.
27. *AMC*, 94–5.
28. *PL*, II.55.
29. *PL*, II.309.
30. John Farrington, bill of complaint; Mary Marvell answer, PRO C6/242/13.
31. Fred S. Tupper, 'Mary Palmer, alias Mrs Andrew Marvell', *PMLA*, 53 (1938), 367–92; Art Kavanagh, 'Andrew Marvell's Widow', unpublished paper. I am most grateful to Mr Kavanagh for sharing his work with me.
32. As noted in the London Guildhall Poor Rate Books.
33. Bod. MS Carte 35, fol. 568ʳ.
34. See *POAS*, 34–158
35. Bod. MS Eng. Hist. C. 57.
36. See below, 319–20, 332.
37. See John Burrows, 'Andrew Marvell and the "Painter Satires": A Computational Approach to their Authorship', *MLR*, 100 (2005), 281–97.
38. See William Empson, 'Natural Magic and Populism in Marvell's Poetry', in R.L. Brett, ed., *Andrew Marvell: Essays on the Tercentenary of his Death* (Oxford, 1979), 53–5.
39. Pepys, 8.269 (14 June 1667).
40. Pierre Legouis, *Andrew Marvell, Poet, Puritan, Patriot* (Oxford, 1965), 187.
41. *PL*, II.311–13.
42. Steven N. Zwicker, *Lines of Authority: Politics and English Literary Culture, 1649–1689* (1993), 98–9.
43. John Dryden, 'To the Right Honourable, The Earl of Rochester' [? September 1673], in *Dryden, Marriage A-la-Mode*, ed. David Crane (1991), 3–6.
44. John Milward, *The Diary of John Milward, Esq., Member of Parliament for Derbyshire, September, 1666 to May, 1668*, ed. Caroline Robbins (1938), 116.
45. See below, 197, 203, and Robert Arnold Aubin, ed., *London in Flames, London in Glory: Poems on the Fire and Rebuilding of London, 1666–1709* (New Brunswick, NJ, 1943).
46. Michael Gearin-Tosh, 'The Structure of Marvell's "Last Instructions to a Painter"', *E in C*, 22 (1972), 48–57.
47. See Sue Wiseman, ' "Adam, the Father of All Flesh": Porno-political Rhetoric and Political Theory in and after the English Civil War', in James Holstun, ed., *Pamphlet Wars: Prose in the English Revolution* (1992), 134–57; James Grantham Turner, *Libertines and Radicals in Early Modern London: Sexuality, Politics, and Literary Culture, 1630–1685* (Cambridge, 2002).
48. Steven Zwicker, 'Virgins and Whores: The Politics of Sexual Misconduct in the 1660s', in Conal Condren and A.D. Cousins, eds, *The Political Identity of Andrew Marvell* (Aldershot and Brookfield, VT, 1990), 86.
49. For Douglas, see *ODNB* and Martin Dzelzainis, 'Marvell and the Earl of Castlemaine', in Chernaik and Dzelzainis, eds, *Marvell and Liberty*, 290–312.
50. Grateful thanks to Leonard Barkan for help with Bernini's St Teresa.
51. Donald F. Friedman, 'Rude Heaps and Decent Order', in Chernaik and Dzelzainis, eds, *Marvell and Liberty*, 139.
52. See further *AMP*, 387–9 and above, 351, n.44.
53. Nigel Smith, ' "Courtesie is fatal": The Civil and Visionary Poetics of Andrew Marvell', *PBA*, 101 (1999), 185–6.
54. Ruth Nevo, *The Dial of Virtue: A Study of Poems on Affairs of State in the Seventeenth Century* (Princeton, NJ, 1963), 173–8 (175).
55. See, e.g., l. 70.
56. *MPW*, II.260.
57. David Farley-Hills, *The Benevolence of Laughter: Comic Poetry of the Commonwealth and Restoration* (London and Totowa, NJ, 1974), 77–8.

58. Earl Miner, 'The "Poetic Picture, Painted Poetry" of The Last Instructions to a Painter', *MP*, 63 (1966), 288–94 (289–90).
59. Patterson, *Marvell and the Civic Crown*, 160.
60. David Farley-Hills, *The Benevolence of Laughter: Comic Poetry of the Commonwealth and Restoration* (London, 1974), 78.
61. *PL*, II.57.
62. BL, MS Add. 33413, fol. 37ᵛ, Milward, *Diary*, 108, 127.
63. BL, MS Add. 35865, fols 25ʳ⁻ᵛ.
64. *PL*, II.59.
65. BL, MS Add. 35865, fols 25ʳ⁻ᵛ, 10ʳ; Milward, *Diary*, 328.
66. From 'Debates in 1667: October', *Grey's Debates of the House of Commons*, I (1769), 1–14 (14); http://www.british-history.ac.uk/report.asp?compid=40334.
67. From 'Debates in 1667: 1st–15th November', *Grey's Debates of the House of Commons*, I (1769), 14–41 (36–7); http://www.british-history.ac.uk/report.asp?compid=40335.
68. *AMC*, 100–2; 101.
69. *CJ*, 101; *AMC*, 101.
70. HCA, BRL 770.
71. *CJ* 9:40–1; *AMC*, 102.
72. Martin Dzelzainis, 'Andrew Marvell and the Restoration Literary Underground: Printing the Painter Poems', *SC*, 22 (2007), 401.
73. Ibid.
74. [A.B.], *The Saints Freedom from Tyranny Vindicated* (1667). Signed 12 December 1667 (pp. 30, 40).
75. *PL*, I.376; PRO SP 29/142.2/68; *AMC*, 126.

Chapter 9: Cabal Days

1. N.H. Keeble, *The Restoration: England in the 1660s* (Oxford and Malden, MA, 2002), 168–71.
2. Pepys, 9.5.
3. Keeble, *The Restoration*, 170–1; John Spurr, *England in the 1670s: This Masquerading Age* (Oxford, 2000), 11–12, 15, 21.
4. *PL*, II.64–5.
5. *PL*, II.65.
6. *PL*, II.65.
7. 'Debates in 1668: 1st–19th February', *Grey's Debates of the House of Commons*, I (1769), 70–85; http://www.british-history.ac.uk/report.asp?compid=40338.
8. See Harold Love, *English Clandestine Satire 1660–1702* (Oxford, 2004), especially 107–14; *Index of English Literary Manuscripts*: Part 2, 1625–1700, 2 vols (1980–97), II; Hilton Kelliher, 'Marvell's *Last Instructions to a Painter*: From Manuscript to Print', *EMS*, 13 (2007), 296–343.
9. *The Right Honourable the Earl of Arlington's Letters to Sir W. Temple, Bar.*, ed. Thomas Bebington (1702), 226; *AMC*, 104.
10. BL, MS Add. 33413, fol. 62ʳ; *AMC*, 104.
11. *PL*, II.65–76.
12. *PL*, II.67.
13. Grey, *Debates*, 18 February 1668: http://www.british-history.ac.uk/report.asp?compid=40338.
14. BL, Add. MS 33413, fol. 71ʳ, 75ᵛ.
15. BL, MS Egerton, 3345, fol. 7ʳ.
16. *PL*, II.68.
17. *PL*, II.75–6. Skinner (*c*. 1616–95) had accrued considerable property in Sumatra in the later 1650s but was an unauthorized trader and had been dispossessed by the Company: see *ODNB* life by Ruth Paley.
18. NTH 52/1; *PL*, II.373; *AMC*, 108.

19. This was Francis, eleventh Earl of Shrewsbury (c. 1623–68): see *ODNB* for Charles Talbot, Duke of Shrewsbury (1660–1718).
20. See below, 269.
21. *PL*, II.76.
22. James Grantham Turner, *Libertines and Radicals in Early Modern London: Sexuality, Politics, and Literary Culture, 1630–1685* (Cambridge, 2001), 166, 178.
23. Pepys, 9.129. William, Earl of Craven (1608–97).
24. Turner, *Libertines and Radicals*, 181.
25. Bod., MS Carte fols 81, 37; *AMC*, 106. This moment was explored and brought to public attention by Nicholas von Maltzahn, 'Marvell's Constant Mind', *TLS*, 21 June 2002, 14–15; and idem, 'Marvell and the Lord Wharton', *SC*, 18 (2003), 252–65. For Wharton, see *ODNB* and G.F. Trevallyn Jones, *Saw-Pit Wharton: The Political Career from 1640 to 1691 of Philip, Fourth Lord Wharton* (Sydney, 1967).
26. Bod., MS Carte 77, 597–8.
27. Many of which are now in the collection of the State Hermitage Museum, Moscow.
28. As suggested by Nicholas von Maltzahn, 'Marvell and the Lord Wharton', *SC*, 18 (2003), 252–65. Once dated c. 1652, now c. 1668, although not without continuing controversy: see *AMP*, 152.
29. See Allan Pritchard, 'Marvell's "The Garden": A Restoration Poem?', *SEL*, 23 (1983), 371–88.
30. Maren-Sofie Rostvig, *The Happy Man: Studies in the Metamorphoses of a Classical Ideal, 1600*, 2 vols (Oslo, 1954–58), I.261.
31. *AMC*, 5
32. *PL*, II.77–82.
33. HCA, BRL 780, William Lister to MAH, 27 October 1668.
34. HCA, BRL 779, William Lister to MAH, The Strand, 29 September 1668.
35. Paul Hammond, 'Marvell's Sexuality', *SC*, 11 (1996), 87–123.
36. See above, 210, n.72.
37. *AMC*, 107; *PL*, II.373.
38. *PL*, II.82.
39. *PL*, II.83. 'Sam' remains unidentified.
40. HCA, L.498; Sir Robert Cary to MAH, 17 April 1669; PL, II.83–5; HCA, L. 497, Richard Aston to MAH, Furnivall Inn, Holborn, 17 April 1669. See also HCA, L. 49?6, Cyriack Skinner to MAH, The Strand, 23 March 1669.
41. HCA, L. 1194 (174), L.1195 (175) (Robert Stockdale to MAH, 15 and 17 April 1669).
42. HCA, L. 1194 (187); Stockdale to MAH, 15 June 1669.
43. Annabel Patterson, *Marvell and the Civic Crown* (Princeton, NJ, 1978), 167–70.
44. For Lauderdale's complicated life, see *ODNB*.
45. *PL*, II.341–3.
46. Sarah Barber, 'Attitudes towards the Scots in Northern England, 1639–1652: "the lamb and the dragon cannot be reconciled" ', *NH*, 35 (1999), 93–118.
47. See L.A. Jacobus, *John Cleveland* (1975), and *ODNB*.
48. See John Cleveland, *J. Cleaveland Revived: A Facsimile Edition with Introduction and Indexes*, ed. Hilton Kelliher (Aldershot and Brookfield, VT, 1990); *AMP*, 401–2.
49. John Dryden, *Works*, 20 vols (1956–96), ed. Edward Niles Hooker and H.T. Swedenberg, Jr., XVII (1971), 10, 29–30.
50. See *AMP*, 12–13, 63, 75–80, 120, 262, 301nn.
51. Diana Trevino Benet, ' "The Loyall Scot" and the Hidden Narcissus', in Claude J. Summers and Ted-Larry Pebworth, eds, *On the Celebrated and Neglected Poems of Andrew Marvell* (Columba, MO, 1992), 198–9.
52. Thereby being a central poetic example in John Kerrigan, *Archipelagic English: Literature, History, and Politics 1603–1707* (Oxford, 2008), 274–80. See also David J. Baker, *Between Nations: Shakespeare, Spenser, Marvell, and the Question of Britain* (Stanford, CA, 1997), 152–68.
53. Warren L. Chernaik, *The Poet's Time: Politics and Religion in the Work of Andrew Marvell* (Cambridge, 1983), 196.

54. Kerrigan, *Archipelagic English*, 277.
55. Oxford, All Souls College, MS 167, 10ʳ–16ʳ; *AMC*, 110.
56. *PL*, II.86–7.
57. *PL*, II.111.
58. *PL*, II.92.
59. *PL*, II.93.
60. See above, 222–3 and below, 247, 347. Corporation of London Record Office, Sessions File 205; *AMC*, 121.
61. *CJ*, 9:118–19; *AMC*, 112–13.
62. Only prorogation saved Carteret from impeachment: see *ODNB*.
63. For Popple (1638–1708), merchant, tolerationist, associate of Penn and Locke and eventual secretary to Locke in the Board of Trade, see below, 237, 284, and brief *ODNB* entry in the life of his grandson William Popple (1700/1–65); Caroline Robbins, 'Absolute Liberty: The Life and Thought of William Popple, 1638–1708', *William and Mary Quarterly*, 24 (1967), 190–223; a measure of Popple's influence and connections will be found in Sarah Hutton, ed., *Benjamin Furly 1646–1714: A Quaker Merchant in his Milieu* (Florence, 2007), 2–5, 52–3, 58–61, 65–6.
64. At least two letters have not survived from the early months of 1670, and one from Popple to Marvell, dated 1 March 1670: *PL*, II.313, 384.
65. *PL*, II.97.
66. *PL*, II.314.
67. *PL*, II.100–3.
68. *PL*, II.100–3.
69. *PL*, II.313–16.
70. *PL*, II.314.
71. *PL*, II.314.
72. *Pace* Nicholas Murray, *World Enough and Time: The Life of Andrew Marvell* (1999), 158–9.
73. *PL*, II.317.
74. *PL*, II.317.
75. *PL*, II.116–17.
76. *PL*, II.315.
77. HCA, BRL 1194 (291); Stockdale to MAH, 14 March 1670; for Cary, see above, p. 221.
78. *PL*, II.105–7.
79. HCA, BRB 5:215; *AMC*, 118.
80. *PL*, II.104.
81. *PL*, II.319.
82. NTH 52/1; *AMC*, 117.
83. Edward Montagu (or Mountagu), first Earl of Sandwich (1625–72).
84. *PL*, II.108–9; HCA, BRB, 5:216; *AMC*, 118.
85. See Reginald L. Hine, *Confessions of an Un-Common Attorney* (1945), 7; *IEHM*, 21; *PL*, II.325. For Rolt, see below, 243–5.
86. HCA, BRL 807, Richard Sterne to MAH, 8 June 1670.
87. *PL*, II.109–11.
88. *PL*, II.119.
89. *PL*, II.112–13.
90. HCA, BRB 5:231; *AMC*, 119–20.
91. *PL*, II.317–18.
92. See *ODNB*.
93. 'Debates in 1670: 21 February', Grey, *Debates*, 294. URL: http://www.british-history.ac.uk/report.aspx?compid=40351.
94. See *The peoples ancient and just liberties asserted in the tryal of William Penn, and William Mead* [London: s.n.], 1670; Craig W. Horle, *The Quakers and the English Legal System, 1660–1688* (Philadelphia, PA, 1988).
95. *PL*, II.318.
96. Corporation of London Record Office, Sessions File 205; Nigel Smith and Maureen Bell, 'Andrew Marvell and the "femina periculosa" ', *TLS*, 26 January 2001, 14–15.

97. *PL*, II.120.
98. *PL*, II.318.
99. *PL*, II.120.
100. *PL*, II.318.
101. *PL*, II.324–5.
102. *PL*, II.319.
103. Coventry was a Roman Catholic, but also a follower of Shaftesbury: see *ODNB*.
104. For Blood see above, 173 and below, 240–2.
105. *PL*, II.325. Marvell tells Coventry's story in detail in his letter to Popple of *c.* 24 January 1671: *PL*, II.321–2.
106. *PL*, II.124.
107. Colorado College, Tutt Library, Alice Bremer Taylor Collection, MS 0145; *IELM* 1993, facsimile II; *AMC*, 123.
108. *PL*, II.320–1.
109. *PL*, II, 322.
110. *PL*, II.130.
111. *PL*, II, 132–3.
112. *PL*, II, 135.
113. *PL*, II, 136.
114. *PL*, II.137.
115. *PL*, II.138.
116. NTH 52/1; ATH 47/1; *AMC*, 124–5.
117. *PL*, II.322–3.
118. *PL*, II.322.
119. *PL*, II.323.
120. Murray, *World Enough and Time*, 171.
121. *PL*, II.140–1.
122. *PL*, II.323.
123. *PL*, II.325.
124. Admittedly, no letter survives from Highgate before 24 June 1673 but Marvell's habit of echoing recently published poetry in his own is usually a reliable guide; *AMP*, 190. Von Maltzahn, *AMC*, 138 prefers 1673. The translation could be later still: it bears some comparison with one by Matthew Hale, published in *Contemplations moral and divine by a person of great learning and judgment* (1676), pp. 121–2, which did not circulate until that year.
125. *PL*, II.348, 394–5; *AMC*, 122, summarizes the legal documentation in PRO detailing the operation of this bank.
126. *PL*, II.326.
127. See *ODNB*.
128. See Alan Marshall, *Intelligence and Espionage in the Reign of Charles II, 1660–1685* (Cambridge, 1994), 186–223.
129. Editors have accepted that the English version of the epigram is Marvell's but it was attributed to Sir Fleetwood Sheppard in 1707: *AMC*, 127.
130. Arbury Hall, MS 185, attr. 'Dr Fuller'.
131. Bod. MS Rawlinson A185.
132. Entry on *DNB*; see also the much updated entry in *ODNB*.
133. PRO SP 29/293/31–2; *CSPD, 1671*, 496; *AMC*, 128.
134. With 'Non orbis gentem non urbem gens habet ulla/Urbsve domum Dominum vel domus ulla parem'. [The world has no comparable people, no people such a city, no city such a palace, nor any palace such a master.] BL, MS Add. 18220, fol. 74^r. See Harold Love, 'Sir William Petty, the London Coffee Houses, and the Restoration "Leonine" ', *SC*, 22 (2007), 382.
135. E.E. Duncan-Jones, 'Marvell's "Inscribenda Luparae" ', *TLS*, 2878 (26 April 1957), 257.
136. Entry on Thomas, Lord Wharton, in *ODNB*.
137. See Armando Petrucci, *Public Lettering: Script, Power, and Culture* (Chicago, 1993); William Stenhouse, *Reading Inscriptions and Writing Ancient History: Historical*

Scholarship in the Late Renaissance (2005). The translation that follows is from *The Latin Poetry of Andrew Marvell*, ed. W.A. McQueen and K.A. Rockwell (Chapel Hill, NC, 1964), 41.

138. William Whitehorne writing on the ship *The Return* to the East India Company, 11 November 1668: BL, East India Company Records, G/36/105, fol. 31ᵛ.
139. *PL*, II.324.
140. *PL*, II.324.
141. Pepys, 2.108, n.1; 6.320–1, 323; 8.29; 9.166, 175.
142. *PL*, II.324.
143. *PL*, II.324.
144. *PL*, II.324.
145. (1648–1713), later first Marquess of Wharton, first Marquess of Malmesbury, first Marquess of Catherlough, and future Whig politician (1648–1715). See *ODNB*.
146. Bod. MS Rawlinson Letters 50, 123–4, 129ʳ; Nicholas von Maltzahn, 'Marvell's Constant Mind', *TLS*, 21 June 2002; idem, 'Marvell and the Lord Wharton', *SC*, 18 (2003), 252–65; *AMC*, 129.

CHAPTER 10: INDULGENCE AND REHEARSAL

1. Bod. MS Rawlinson Letters 50, 126–7, 129–30, 132–3, 149–50; *AMC*, 129–30.
2. Bod. MS Rawlinson Letters 50, 149ᵛ; *PL*, II.327; *AMC*, 130. See also *ODNB*.
3. For Marvell on Sandwich, see *PL*, II.19, 72, 109.
4. Joshua Scodel, *The English Poetic Epitaph: Commemoration and Conflict from Jonson to Wordsworth* (Ithaca, NY, and London, 1991), 225–30.
5. Ibid., 232.
6. *AMC*, 128.
7. Ibid., 230.
8. John Spurr, *England in the 1670s: This Masquerading Age* (Oxford, 2000), 35.
9. *PL*, II.327.
10. *PL*, II.327–8.
11. *TC*, 1:109: serial publications in catalogue form that early modern booksellers issued in joint ventures in order to inform customers and other book traders about recent publications; first published in 1668 by John Starkey. 'Term' was a reference to the fairs held by the book trade four times a year. *AMC*, 133; *SR*: 2:446, *AMC*, 134.
12. See *ODNB* entry on Bramhall by John McCafferty.
13. Samuel Parker, Preface, in John Bramhall, *Bishop Bramhall's vindication of himself and the episcopal clergy, from the Presbyterian charge of popery* (1672), sig. A4ᵛ.
14. See Derek Hirst, 'Samuel Parker, Andrew Marvell and Political Culture, 1667–1673', in Derek Hirst and Richard Strier, eds, *Writing and Political Engagement in Seventeenth-Century England* (Cambridge, 1999) 153–4.
15. See below, 261–78.
16. *MPW*, I.199–202.
17. See further Margaret C. Jacob, *The Newtonians and the English Revolution, 1689–1720* (Ithaca, NY, 1976).
18. For Glanvill, see *ODNB*.
19. *MPW*, I.10.
20. See Raymond A. Anselment, *'Betwixt jest and earnest': Marprelate, Milton, Marvell, Swift and the Decorum of Religious Ridicule* (Toronto, 1979), chs 3, 5, and now Joseph L. Black, ed., *The Martin Marprelate Tracts: A Modernized and Annotated Edition* (Cambridge, 2008).
21. John Owen, *Indulgence and toleration considered* (1667), 11. See further, Gary S. de Krey, 'Rethinking the Restoration: Dissenting Cases of Conscience, 1667–72', *HJ*, 38 (1995), 53–83; Hirst, 'Samuel Parker, Andrew Marvell, and Political Culture, 1667–73', 145–64.

22. The details of production and publication are set out by Martin Dzelzainis and Annabel Patterson in *MPW*, I.22–33.

23. See above, 47, 52, 56–60, 84–7.

24. For modern editions of the play, see George Villiers, Duke of Buckingham, *The Rehearsal*, ed. D.E.L. Crane (Durham, 1976); Robert D. Hume and Harold Love, eds, *Plays, Poems, and Miscellaneous Writings associated with George Villiers, Second Duke of Buckingham*, 2 vols (Oxford, 2007), I.333–454.

25. Tiffany Stern, *Rehearsal from Shakespeare to Sheridan* (Oxford, 2000), 128–39.

26. See Abraham Wright, *Five Sermons, in Five Several Styles; or Waies of Preaching* (1656).

27. For Tarlton's life, and the many fictional aspects of it that circulated in the century after his death, see *ODNB* life by Peter Thomson.

28. *MPW*, I.142–3.

29. For the coffee houses, see Steven C.A. Pincus, ' "Coffee Politicians does Create": Coffee Houses and Restoration Political Culture', *JMH*, 67 (1995), 807–34.

30. *MPW*, I.156–7.

31. *MPW*, I.82.

32. For Dutch Arminianism, see Jonathan I. Israel, *The Dutch Republic: Its Rise, Greatness and Fall, 1477–1806* (Oxford, 1995), 450–77; Martin Mulsow and Jan Rohls, eds, *Socinianism and Arminianism: Antitrinitarians, Calvinists, and Cultural Exchange in Seventeenth-Century Europe* (Leiden, 2005).

33. See above, 23, and below, 264–5.

34. See now Rhodri Lewis, *Language, Mind and Nature: Artificial Languages in England from Bacon to Locke* (Oxford, 2007).

35. See *ODNB*.

36. *MPW*, I.162.

37. *MPW*, I.102–4.

38. *MPW*, I.105.

39. *MPW*, I.163–5.

40. The activities of the radicals have been documented by Richard L. Greaves, *Deliver Us from Evil: The Radical Underground in Britain, 1660–1663* (New York, 1986); idem, *Enemies under his Feet: Radicals and Nonconformists in Britain, 1664–1677* (Stanford, CA, 1990); literary aspects are documented by Thomas Charlton, 'Continuity and Change in English Radical Writing, 1659–1675', unpublished Ph.D. thesis, University of Cambridge, 2006.

41. See de Krey, 'Rethinking the Restoration', 53–83.

42. *MPW*, I.128–9.

43. See Karen Edwards, 'Milton and Marvell against Lycanthropy', paper delivered to Modern Language Association Convention, Chicago, December 2007.

44. *MPW*, I.126, 141.

45. *MPW*, I.44.

46. A claim repeated in *RT* 2: *MPW*, II.413.

47. See also Nigel Smith, 'The Boomerang Theology of Andrew Marvell', *Renaissance and Reformation/Renaissance et Réforme*, 25 (2003), 139–55.

48. *MPW*, I.21, n. 47.

49. For Darby, see *ODNB*.

50. Leicestershire Record Office, Finch MSS, DG7, Box 4985, Bundle IX, 9/2; *MPW*, I.23–5.

51. Huntington Library, MS HA13634; *AMC*, 136.

52. Longleat House, Coventry MSS, vol. 11, fol. 10; *MPW*, I.25; *AMC*, 139.

53. *MPW*, I.251.

54. Murray, *World Enough and Time*, 178.

55. Jonathan Swift, *A Tale of a Tub* (1704), ed. A.C. Gulkelch and D. Nichol Smith (2nd edn, Oxford, 1958), 165–87.

56. See Nicholas McDowell, 'Tales of Tub Preachers: Swift and Heresiography', *RES*, forthcoming.

57. *MPW*, I.69–70.
58. *MPW*, I.48.
59. *MPW*, I.89.
60. Aubrey, *Brief Lives*, ed. Andrew Clark, 2 vols (Oxford, 1898), II.54.
61. *MPW*, II.109–10.
62. NTH 52/1; *PL*, II.277–8; *AMC*, 138–9.
63. For Ponder, see *ODNB*.
64. *TC*, 1:128; *AMC*, 140.
65. Oxford, Corpus Christi College, CC MS 332, fols 22ᵛ–23ʳ. Thanks to William Poole for drawing my attention to this document.
66. See *ODNB* for life of Beale by Patrick Woodland and life of Wase by Richard E. Hodges.
67. BL, MS Harley 6584, fol. 221ʳ; *AMC*, 242.
68. *AMC*, 142.
69. HCA, BRB 5:319–21; *AMC*, 141.
70. NTH 52/1; *AMC*, 141.
71. *PL*, II.278–9; *AMC*, 142.
72. *AMC*, 141–2.
73. PRO SP 29/334/357; Cooke, 1:9; *AMC*, 141.
74. Anon., *Raillerie a la mode consider'd, or, The supercilious detractor a joco-serious discourse* (1673), 3.
75. *PL*, II.328–9.
76. *TC*, 1:142; *AMC*, 145.
77. See *ODNB*.
78. See James R. Jacob, *Henry Stubbe, Radical Protestantism and the Early Enlightenment* (Cambridge, 1983).
79. *TC*, 1.135; *AMC*, 144.
80. Nicholas von Maltzahn, 'Samuel Butler's Milton', *SP*, 92 (1995), 482–95.
81. [Samuel Butler], *The Transproser Rehears'd* (6 May 1673), 72, 147–8.
82. Ibid., 131–2.
83. *SR*, 2:547; *AMC*, 141; John Eachard. *A Free and Impartial Enquiry into the Causes of that very great Esteem and Honour that the Nonconforming Preachers are generally in with their Followers* (7 April 1673), 34–5.
84. For Eachard's life by Hugh de Quehen, see *ODNB*.
85. Bod. MS Wood F40, fol. 161ʳ; *AMC*, 142.
86. See Jacqueline Eales, *Puritans and Roundheads: The Harleys of Brampton Bryan and the Outbreak of the English Civil War* (Cambridge, 1990), and life of Sir Edward Harley by George Goodwin, rev. David Whitehead in *ODNB*.
87. *HMC, Portland, III*, 349; *AMC*, 160.
88. *PL*, II.328.
89. Samuel Parker, *A Reproof to the Rehearsal Transprosed, in a Discourse to its Authour by the Authour of the Ecclesiastical Politie* (1672), 196.
90. Ibid., 7.
91. Ibid., sig. A4ᵛ.
92. Ibid., 136–7.
93. Ibid., 16.
94. Ibid., 105.
95. Eachard, *Free and Impartial Enquiry*, 34.
96. Parker, *Reproof*, 106.
97. Ibid., 118.
98. Ibid., 106, referring to Marvell, *The Rehearsal Transpros'd*, *MPW*, I.98.
99. Parker, *Reproof*, 268.
100. Ibid., 150.
101. Ibid., 155.
102. Ibid., 76–7.
103. Ibid., sig. A3ᵛ.

104. Ibid., 201–2.
105. Ibid., 226–7.
106. Ibid., 4.
107. Ibid., 44.
108. Ibid., 77.
109. Ibid., 77–8.
110. Ibid., 125–6.
111. Ibid., 192.
112. Ibid., 208.
113. Ibid., 212.
114. Ibid., 406.
115. *MPW*, I.417–18.
116. Parker, *Reproof*, 105. See above, 176–7.
117. Anon., *The Character of a Coffee-House* (1673), 6.
118. Ibid. For the Rota, see above, 159–60.
119. [Samuel Butler], *The Transproser Rehears'd*, 72, 112, 132, 138.
120. Parker, *Reproof*, 253.
121. Ibid., 438.
122. The parodic Parliamentary speech in the voice of Shaftesbury was attributed to Marvell but as late as 1705: *IELM*, 24, 26–7.
123. Cooke, ed., *The Works of Andrew Marvell, Esq*, I.14; *AMC*, 147.
124. Bod. MS Wood F40, fol. 166^r; Theo Bongaerts, *The Correspondence of Thomas Blount (1618–1679). A Recusant Antiquary* (Amsterdam, 1978), 141.
125. *AMC*, 147, 232–5, 238–9.
126. *MPW*, I.329.
127. Gordon Schochet, 'Samuel Parker, Religious Diversity, and the Ideology of Persecution', in Roger D. Lund, ed., *The Margins of Orthodoxy: Heterodox Writing and Cultural Response 1660–1750* (Cambridge, 1995), 119–48.
128. *MPW*, I.171–2.
129. *MPW*, I.266.
130. *MPW*, I.268.
131. *Philosophical transactions . . . VII* (1672), 87.5063.
132. *MPW*, I.241.
133. *MPW*, I.247.
134. *MPW*, I.288.
135. *MPW*, I.258–9.
136. *MPW*, I.418.
137. *MPW*, I.437; see also, I.414–15.
138. *MPW*, I.245, 242.
139. *MPW*, I.237. Dzelzainis rightly notes the witty allusion to Hobbes's theory of civil society: in this instance, it is not a physical threat to the security of subjects but Parker's satire that has dissolved the bonds of civil society.
140. *MPW*, I.252.
141. *MPW*, I.252, n.152; *PL*, II.320.
142. *MPW*, I.249.
143. *MPW*, I.242.
144. For Rushworth, see *ODNB*.
145. *MPW*, I.315 and note.
146. *MPW*, I.253–6, 266.
147. But the case for Marvell as the translator of Suetonius is not accepted by all scholars: 'If it is AM's translation, it seems odd he should have had it to hand only for *RT2* and not *RT*': *AMC*, 131. *MPW*, I.302–12. For the comparisons with Julian, see *MPW*, I.375–81, 383, 393.
148. *MPW*, I.398–9. See Jason Rosenblatt, 'A Subtle Circumcision in Andrew Marvell's *The Rehearsall Transpos'd*: The Second Part', *N&Q*, n.s.57 (2010), 57–8.

149. *MPW*, I.309.
150. *MPW*, I.288, n.348.
151. *MPW*, I.438.
152. Anon., *The Character of a Coffee House*, 5.
153. [Samuel Butler], *The Transproser Rehears'd*, 135.
154. NTH, 52/1; *AMC*, 146.

CHAPTER 11: BRUTE DIVINES

1. Hertfordshire RO, MSS D/EP F.37, fols 13, 262; *AMC*, 149.
2. See, e.g., *AMC*, 165.
3. Anon., *An Apology and advice for some of the clergy* (1674).
4. 'Theophilus Thorowthistle', *Sober reflections, or, A solid confutation of Mr Andrew Marvel's work in a letter ab Ignoto ad Ignotum* (1674).
5. Royal Society, MS 32, 41–54; dated 30 January 1674, but possibly written earlier in 1673 with the final lines added when *RT2* appeared.
6. *LJ*, 12:606–8, 612.
7. *PL*, II.141–2.
8. *CJ*, 9:302; *AMC*, 151.
9. John Spurr, *England in the 1670s: This Masquerading Age* (Oxford, 2000), 49–54.
10. See *ODNB*.
11. PRO, SP 105/222/127^r; *AMC*, 153.
12. R.A. Fagel, Fagel Papers, Rijksarchief, The Hague, Folder 244, as reported in K.H.D. Haley, *William of Orange and the English Opposition, 1672–4* (Oxford, 1953), 58, 63.
13. Fagel, The Hague, 244.
14. See Charles-Edouard Levillain, 'William III's Military and Political Career in Neo-Roman Context, 1672–1702', *HJ*, 48 (2005), 321–50.
15. Bod. MS Rawlinson Letters, 51, 218; *AMC*, 152; *PL*, II.281–2.
16. For further details, see *AMP*, 182.
17. John Aubrey, *Brief Lives*, ed. Andrew Clark, 2 vols (Oxford, 1898), II.72.
18. *PL*, II.282.
19. FTH 1/5; *AMC*, 154.
20. FTH 1/5; *AMC*, 155.
21. NTH 52/1; *AMC*, 155.
22. HCA, BRB 5:383; *AMC*, 155.
23. *PL*, II.329–31; *AMC*, 155–6.
24. *PL*, II.331–2.
25. See *ODNB*.
26. One thought erroneously to be an entire statue acquired on the continent depicting the Polish King Jan III Sobieski (1629–96) in victory over the Turk. See Martin Dzelzainis, ' "What a do with the Kings and the statues is here": Milton, Marvell and John Sobieski', in *Through All the Compass of the Notes: Essays in Early Modern Collaboration and Interdisciplinarity in Honour of Richard G. Maber*, ed. Paul A. Scott (Manchester University Press, forthcoming).
27. See Gary de Krey, 'London Radicals and Revolutionary Politics, 1675–83', in Tim Harris et al., eds, *The Politics of Religion in Restoration England* (Oxford, 1990), 135–6.
28. See below, 293.
29. As opposed to playing up Sobieski's tolerance (he was not tolerant, despite provision in the Polish–Lithuanian constitution of 1573), or appealing to the claims of the Duke of Monmouth: Dzelzainis, ' "What a do" ', and Christopher Hill, *Milton and the English Revolution* (1977), 219–20.
30. *PL*, II.143–4, 332–3.
31. *PL*, II.333–4.

32. Philip Herbert, seventh Earl of Pembroke (1653–83), another (and particularly violent) rake; see *ODNB*.
33. *PL*, II.334.
34. *PL*, II.334.
35. *PL*, II.335.
36. *PL*, II.336.
37. HCA, BRB 5:359; BRL 674; *AMC*, 151.
38. HTH, NTH 52/1; *AMC*, 152–3.
39. HTH, NTH52/1; *PL*, II.282; *AMC*, 153.
40. *AMC*, 153.
41. HTH, NTH 52/1; *PL*, II.282–3; *AMC*, 155.
42. HTH, NTH 52/1; *PL*, II.374; *AMC*, 156.
43. HTH, NTH 52/1; *PL*, II.374; DTH, Select Entries, 1670–76, 149–51; *AMC*, 159.
44. DTH, Court Minutes, 1670–76, 163; *AMC*, 160.
45. *PL*, II.159; DTH, Court Minutes, 1670–76, 184; *AMC*, 163.
46. *PL*, II.337.
47. *PL*, II.145.
48. *PL*, II.339.
49. *PL*, II.339.
50. *PL*, I.150. Peregrine Osborne (1659–1729), Viscount Dublane, 1674–1709, later Earl of Danby, Marquess of Carmarthen and second Duke of Leeds.
51. *PL*, II.144.
52. HCA, BRL 842; *AMC*, 159.
53. See *ODNB*.
54. William Foxley and William Skinner to Mayor of Hull, 18 February 1675: HCA, BRL 842; *AMC*, 159.
55. *PL*, II.14–15; *AMC*, 161.
56. *PL*, II.145–6.
57. *MPW*, I.460–4. The editors of *MPW* (I. xxviii, xlviii) accept Marvell's authorship but exceptionally Nicholas von Maltzahn is far more cautious, noting that the earliest known attribution to Marvell by name came thirty years after the speech's appearance: *AMC*, 160.
58. J.G.A. Pocock, *The Machiavellian Moment: Florentine Political Thought and the Atlantic Republican Tradition* (Princeton, NJ, 1975), 406–9; Warren Chernaik, ' "Such a king as no chisel can mend": Marvell, Charles II and Republicanism', in G. Sambras, ed., *New Perspectives on Andrew Marvell* (Reims, 2007), 103–19.
59. *PL*, II.148–9; *AMC*, 161.
60. *PL*, II.149–50; *AMC*, 161.
61. See further L.N. Wall, 'Marvell's Friends in the City', *N&Q*, 204 (1959), 204–7.
62. *PL*, II. 153; *AMC*, 162.
63. *PL*, II.342.
64. Bod. MS Wood F39, fol. 296ʳ; *AMC*, 162.
65. *CJ*, 9:352; *AMC*, 163.
66. FTH 1/5; *AMC*, 163.
67. *PL*, II.340.
68. *PL*, II.341–3: *AMC*, 164.
69. *PL*, II.342.
70. *PL*, II.342.
71. *PL*, II.343.
72. *PL*, II.343.
73. *PL*, II.164–5; *AMC*, 165.
74. *PL*, II.166; *AMC*, 166.
75. HCA, BRB 5:446; *AMC*, 166.
76. BL, MS Add. 72850, 145; *AMC*, 165. For more details of this incident, see Spurr, *England in the 1670s*, 75, 170.

77. For Petty, see *ODNB*; Tony Aspromourgos, *On the Origins of Classical Economics: Distribution and Value from William Petty to Adam Smith* (1996); Alessandro Rocaglia, *Petty: The Origins of Political Economy* (New York, 1985).

78. *AMC*, 166.

79. *PL*, II.169; *AMC*, 169.

80. *PL*, II.173; *AMC*, 167.

81. BL, MS Add. 60391, 33–4; Hilton Kelliher, 'Some Uncollected Letters of Andrew Marvell', *BLJ*, 5 (1979), 145–7; *AMC*, 168. The tract associated with Shaftesbury was *Two Seasonable Discourses Concerning the Present Parliament* (1675), which claimed to repeat arguments used in the debates of 20 November. It agreed that a new Parliament would vote the King money, preserve the church, grant liberty of conscience to Dissenters, and end penal laws against Catholics if they were banned from court and prevented from holding office and bearing arms.

82. Sir Richard Bulstrode, *The Bulstrode Papers* (1897), I.324; *PL*, II.391.

83. HUA, MS DDFA 39/26; *PL*, II.392.

84. *ODNB*; Robert Wodrow, *The History of the Sufferings of the Church of Scotland from the Restoration to the Revolution*, 4 vols (Glasgow, 1828–30), II.115; George Hickes, *Ravillac Redivivus* (1678), 13.

85. Robert Wodrow, *The History of the Sufferings of the Church of Scotland, from the Restauration to the Revolution*, 2 vols (Edinburgh, 1721), I.513. See also Clare Jackson, 'Judicial Torture, the Liberties of the Subject, and Anglo-Scottish Relations, 1660–1690', in T.C. Smout, ed., 'Anglo-Scottish Relations from 1603–1900', *PBA*, 127 (2005), 75–101 (80–85).

86. Paul Mathole, 'Marvell and Violence', unpublished Ph.D. thesis, University of London, 2004.

87. Robert McWard, 'Preface to the Christian Reader', in John Brown, *Christ the Way and the Truth and the Life* (Rotterdam, 1677), sig, c5[r].

88. See above, 262–3, 282, 284.

89. See *ODNB*.

90. Mathole, 'Marvell and Violence'.

91. Livy, *Ab urbe condita*, II.xi–xiii.

92. See above, 277.

93. *MPW*, I.311.

94. Anon., *The Life of James Sharp, Archbishop of St Andrews* (1st printed edn, 1719); see also Julia Buckroyd, *The Life of James Sharp, Archbishop of St Andrews: A Political Biography* (Edinburgh, 1987); and *ODNB* entry by David George Mullan.

95. NLS, MS Wodrow, Octavo xxix, no. 11, fols 113[r]–128[v].

96. Mathole, 'Marvell and Violence', wonders whether the *Life of Sharp* was a Shaftesburian creation.

97. See *ODNB* life by William Marshall.

98. See *ODNB* entry on Croft by William Marshall.

99. See Walter G. Simon, *The Restoration Episcopate* (New York, 1965).

100. *AMC*, 169–70.

101. Francis Turner, *Animadversions upon a late pamphlet entituled The naked truth, or, The true state of the primitive church* (1676), sig. [A]2[r].

102. See above, 270–7.

103. Turner, *Animadversions*, 2–5.

104. *MPW*, II.37–8.

105. *MPW*, II.40.

106. *MPW*, II.42.

107. *MPW*, II.58.

108. *MPW*, II.61.

109. *MPW*, II.52.

110. PRO SP 29/366/80; *AMC*, 171–2.

111. PRO PC 2/65/217; *AMC*, 171–2.

112. Beth Lynch, '*Mr Smirke* and Mr "Filth": A Bibliographic Case Study in Nonconformist Printing', *The Library*, 1 (2000), 46–71.
113. Longleat House, Coventry MSS, vol. 11, fol. 128; *AMC*, 172.
114. *Hatton Correspondence*, 1:128; *AMC*, 172.
115. Bod. MS Wood F40, 214; Bongaerts, 166.
116. *PL*, II.344–6; *AMC*, 174.
117. *CSPD*, 1676, 510.
118. Mark Knights, *Representation and Misrepresentation in Later Stuart Britain: Partisanship and Political Culture* (Oxford, 2005), 17.
119. See above, 271.
120. *CJ*, 9:406; *AMC*, 183.
121. *MPW*, II.89; Turner, *Animadversions*, 7.
122. See *ODNB*.
123. Turner, *Animadversions*, 1.
124. *MPW*, II.38.
125. *MPW*, I.39.
126. *MPW*, II.168.
127. See above, 128–33; Huibert Jacob Honders, *Andreas Rivetus als invloedrijk gereformeerd theoloog in Holland's bloeitijd* (The Hague, 1930).
128. *MPW*, II.153.
129. *MPW*, II.164.
130. *MPW*, II.172–6.
131. *MPW*, I.126.
132. *MPW*, II.145.
133. *MPW*, II.157.
134. *MPW*, II.170.
135. *MPW*, II.139; also a punning reference to Horace, *Ars poetica*, l. 139, 'Parturient montes nascetur ridiculus mus' [The mountain groaned, and delivered a mouse]. See also *MPW*, I.223. *Homoousios*: term promulgated at the Council of Nicaea in AD 325, to express the doctrine that the Son is 'of one substance' with the Father, as opposed to the term *Homoiousios*, where the Son is of 'like substance' to the Father.
136. *MPW*, II.146. 'Atturn' = 'attorn', to turn over, assign or transfer to another.
137. *MPW*, II.84.
138. *MPW*, II.149.
139. As with 'An Epitaph on Frances Jones': see above, 247–9.
140. *MPW*, II.43.
141. *MPW*, II.45.
142. *MPW*, II.56.
143. *MPW*, II.65.
144. *MPW*, II.146.
145. Mathole, 'Marvell and Violence'.
146. *MPW*, II.148.
147. *MPW*, II.153.
148. *MPW*, II.158–9, 161.
149. *PL*, II.344, *AMC*, 174.
150. Oxford, Corpus Christi College, CC MS 310, fol. 17^r; Bod. MS Wood F41, fol. 300^r; *AMC*, 174.
151. *PL*, II.346; *AMC*, 175.
152. *PL*, II.347–8.
153. *PL*, II.346, 393.
154. E.M. Thompson, ed., *Correspondence of the Hatton Family*, 2 vols, Camden Society, n.s. 22–3 (1878), 1:128, *AMC*, 172; Simon Patrick, *Falsehood unmaskt: in answer to a book called Truth unveil'd* (1676), 22–5; *AMC*, 176. Simon Patrick (1626–1707), at this time Dean of Peterborough.
155. *PL*, II.346–8.
156. *AMP*, 163–4.

157. Another prominent member of the opposition, an associate of Buckingham and Shaftesbury, and leader of a republican group: 'Peyton's Gang': see *ODNB*.
158. *PL*, II.345; *AMC*,174.
159. *PL*, II.349-50; *AMC*, 177.
160. *PL*, II.348-9. For Bacon (1647-76), see *ODNB* and W. E. Washburn, *The Governor and the Rebel: A History of Bacon's Rebellion in Virginia* (Chapel Hill, NC, 1957).
161. *PL*, II.295.
162. *PL*, II.286.
163. *PL*, II.286-7.
164. *PL*, II.287-8. For Sawyer, see *ODNB*.
165. HTH, NTH 571/1; *PL*, II.285-90, 375; *AMC*, 177-81a.
166. *PL*, II.346; *AMC*, 174.
167. Louis Daillé, *A lively picture of Lewis du Moulin drawn by the incomparable hand of Monsieur Daille, late minister of Charenton* (1680), 10.

CHAPTER 12: ARBITRARY POWER

1. *PL*, II.289.
2. PRO C24/1069.2/36; Art Kavanagh, 'Andrew Marvell "in want of money": The Evidence of *John Farrington v. Mary Marvell*', *SC* (2002), 206-12; *AMC*, 180.
3. Thomas Long, *The History of the Donatists* (1677), sig. A5ᵛ; John Warly, *The Reasoning Apostate: Or Modern Latitude-Men Consider'd* (1677), sig. A4ᵛ; *AMC*, 181-2.
4. James Cecil, third Earl of Salisbury (d. 1683).
5. Bod. MS Wood, Diaries 1677, fol. 9ʳ; *PL*, II.178-9; *AMC*, 180.
6. *CJ*, 9:386, 388-9; *AMC*, 181. For Temple (1634-97) and Savile (1642-87), courtier, drinker, dueller, debauchee, associate of Rochester, see *ODNB*. Some poetry formerly attributed to Marvell is now thought to be by Savile: see *MP*, 462. Marvell's insulting wit and Savile's were compared by contemporaries: *AMC*, 172.
7. *PL*, II.182-3. This was *Some considerations upon the question, whether the Parliament is dissolved by it's prorogation for 15 months?* (1676).
8. Denzil, first Baron Holles (1598-1680); see *ODNB*.
9. *PL*, II.183-4; *HMC 9th Report*, App. 2, 76b; *AMC*, 183.
10. HCA, BRL 879; *AMC*, 183.
11. *CJ*, 9:400-1.
12. *PL*, II.190-1.
13. See Ian Atherton and David Como, 'The Burning of Edward Wightman: Puritanism, Prelacy and the Politics of Heresy in Early Modern England', *EHR*, 120 (2005), 1215-50; *CJ*, 9:399-400, 406.
14. Grey, *Debates*, IV 321-5; *AMC*, 183
15. See Mark Goldie, 'Danby, the Bishops and the Whigs', in T. Harris, P. Seaward and M.Goldie, eds, *The Politics of Religion in Restoration England* (Oxford, 1990), 75-105.
16. For Howard, see above, 199, 204-5, 212, 235, 254, 282, 317; for Sir John Maynard (1604-90), see *ODNB*.
17. Grey, *Debates*, IV:326-7, 329.
18. Sir Job Charlton (1614-97); see *ODNB*.
19. William Garway (Garraway, Garroway; 1617-91); Sir Thomas Meres (Meeres; 1634-1715).
20. Grey, *Debates*, IV.328-31; BL MS Egerton 3345, 41; John Reresby, *Memoirs*, ed. Andrew Browning; 2nd edn, Mary K. Geiter and W.A. Speck (1991), 115; *AMC*, 186.
21. *PL*, II.194-5.
22. *HMC, 9th Report*, App. 2, 78b; *AMC*, 187.
23. NTH 57/1; *AMC*, 189.
24. Steven C.A. Pincus, *England's Glorious Revolution, 1688-1689: A Brief History with Documents* (New York, 2006), 122-3.
25. For Maniban, see above, 311.

26. Hertfordshire RO, MSS D/EP F.81, penultimate item; *AMC*, 190. For Van Helmont, see Alison Coudert, *The Impact of the Kabbalah in the Seventeenth Century: The Life and Thought of Francis Mercury van Helmont (1614–1698)* (Leiden, 1999).
27. *PL*, II.353–4.
28. *PL*, II.205–6, 353–4.
29. John Spurr, *England in the 1670s: This Masquerading Age* (Oxford, 2000), 249.
30. *PL*, II.355–6.
31. *AMC*, 193.
32. PRO SP 29/401/321; *CSPD 1677–78*, 691–2; *AMC*, 191.
33. It comes as a surprise in all of this to hear something like the real Puritan in Marvell speak when he reported to the Mayor and Corporation of Hull on 31 March that deliberations on the Bill for suppressing hawkers and pedlars, on the committee for which Marvell had sat, was coming to a conclusion: *PL*, II.193–4.
34. John Aubrey, *Brief Lives*, ed. Andrew Clark, 2 vols (Oxford, 1898), I.293; *AMC*, 192.
35. *PL*, II.294.
36. *AMC*, 192.
37. *MPW*, II.187–9.
38. *PL*, II.294–5.
39. *PL*, II.295.
40. *PL*, II.295–6.
41. ATH 47/1; *PL*, II.296–7, 375–6; *AMC*, 197, 208–9.
42. *PL*, II.356–7.
43. Spurr, *England in the 1670s*, 250–1.
44. *AMC*, 195.
45. PRO SP 29/406/49; *MPW*, II.207. For Danvers (*c.* 1619–87/8), General Baptist and republican insurrectionist, see *ODNB*.
46. For the career of George Savile, first Marquess of Halifax (1633–97), see *ODNB* and *The Works of George Savile, Marquis of Halifax*, ed. M.N. Brown, 3 vols (Oxford, 1989).
47. Spurr, *England in the 1670s*, 252; *MPW*, II.243–4, 251, 275–6.
48. *MPW*, II.256–7.
49. Spurr, *England in the 1670s*, 253.
50. *MPW*, II.368.
51. *MPW*, I.232, 316.
52. *MPW*, II.255, 279, 289, 308–9, 339, 348, 368–9, 371, 373.
53. Sallust, *Bellum Catilinae*, LII.17; *MPW*, II.193–4.
54. *MPW*, II.194.
55. *MPW*, II.323.
56. *MPW*, II.240, 250.
57. *MPW*, II.265.
58. *MPW*, II.287.
59. *MPW*, II.209–14.
60. *MPW*, II.241.
61. *MPW*, II.225–6. For Harrington's idea of balance, see James Harrington, *Political Works*, ed. J.G.A. Pocock (Cambridge, 1977), 36, 188–9.
62. See above, 127, 151, 159–60.
63. *MPW*, II.258.
64. *MPW*, II.229.
65. *MPW*, II.234, n. 54.
66. *MPW*, II.257.
67. *MPW*, II.225.
68. *MPW*, II.260.
69. Marchamont Nedham, *Honesty's Best Policy, or, Penitence the sum of Prudence* (1678), sig. A4ᵛ.
70. *PL*, II.210.
71. PRO SP 44/334/457; *AMC*, 197.
72. PRO SP 29/405/189–94; *AMC*, 198–202.

73. For Jenks (or Jencks), a key figure in London opposition politics, and son-in-law of the Leveller William Walwyn, see *ODNB*. See also Gary de Krey, *London and the Restoration, 1659–1683* (Cambridge, 2005).

74. PRO PC2/66/248; 319; *AMC*, 198, 204, 207.

75. *LJ*, 13:161; PRO SP 29/40/232ʳ; *AMC*, 198.

76. *MPW*, II.369, n.671; Bod. MS Carte 72, fol. 361ᵛ.

77. *PL*, II.219.

78. See *ODNB*.

79. Nedham, *Honesty's Best Policy*, 9, 15.

80. Edmund Bohun, *Diary*, ed. S.W. Rex (Beccles, 1883), 40–1; *AMC*, 208. For Bohun (1644–99) see *ODNB*.

81. PRO SP 29/401/337; SP 29/405/192; *AMC*, 200.

82. PRO SP 29/402/192; *AMC*, 203.

83. *London Gazette*, 1288 (21–25 March 1678); Hilton Kelliher, *Andrew Marvell: poet & politician 1621–78: An Exhibition to Commemorate the Tercentenary of his Death* (1978) 113; *AMC*, 202–3.

84. L'Estrange, *Account*, 10–11, 44, 46.

85. Anon. *A Letter from Amsterdam to a Friend in England* (1678), 4–5.

86. *SPD*, Car. II, Case G; *CSPD 1678*, 121–3; *AMC*, 205.

87. *PL*, II.208–9.

88. PRO C6275/120; C7/589/82; *London Gazette*, 28–31 January 1678; *AMC*, 196.

89. *PL*, II.209–11.

90. Anon., *A Seasonable Argument* (1677).

91. See *ODNB*.

92. Howe, *The Reconcileableness of God's Prescience of the Sins of Men* (1677), 94.

93. For Gale and Danson, see *ODNB*.

94. For a further discussion of Howe's theological views, see Sharon Achinstein, *Literature and Dissent in Milton's England* (Cambridge, 2003), 172–3.

95. Thomas Danson, *De Causa Dei* (1678), 121–2.

96. *MPW*, II.418–20.

97. *MPW*, II.429.

98. *MPW*, II.443–4.

99. *MPW*, II.422.

100. *MPW*, II.423. For further examples see Marvell's discussion of Danson's description of definite articles and conjunctions in *MPW*, II.427.

101. *MPW*, II.434.

102. *MPW*, II.436.

103. *MPW*, II.435, 447.

104. See William Lamont's life of Danson in *ODNB*.

105. See above, 306–8.

106. *MPW*, II.415.

107. *MPW*, II. 417.

108. *PL*, II.228.

109. *PL*, II.231.

110. *PL*, II.234–5.

111. *PL*, II.357.

112. PRO SP 44/334/514, 518, SP 29/405/96, PC2/66/370; *AMC*, 210–11.

113. Francis Smith, *An Account of the Injurious Proceedings* (2nd edn, 1681), 19; *MPW*, II.201–3.

114. Smith, *An Account*, 19, lists a number of important publishers and printers, all associated with radical and opposition printing: Thomas Brewster, Giles Calvert and Livewell Chapman.

115. PRO SP 29/405/116, SP 44/334/522; *AMC*, 211–12.

116. NTH 52/1; *PL*, II.376; *AMC*, 213.

117. Richard Morton, *Pyretologia* (1691), 96–7; Hilton Kelliher, 'Some Notes on Andrew Marvell', *BLJ*, 4 (1978), 118–19; *AMC*, 214.

118. For Morton, see R.R. Trail, 'Richard Morton (1637–1698)', *Medical History*, 14 (1970), 166–74.

119. William Simpson, *Some Observations upon the Root called Nean* (1680), 3–4. I am grateful to William Poole for this reference. For Simpson's development of the chemistry of Johann Baptista Van Helmont, see Antonio Clericuzio, 'From van Helmont to Boyle. A Study of the Transmission of Helmontian Chemical and Medical Theories in Seventeenth-Century England', *BJHS*, 26 (1993), 303–34.

CHAPTER 13: AFTERLIFE AND REVELATION

1. HTH, NTH 52/1; *PL*, II.376; *AMC*, 215–16.
2. HCA, BRL 893; BRB 5:594; *AMC*, 215, 217.
3. See *ODNB* life and Paul Hammond, *John Oldham and the Renewal of Classical Culture* (Cambridge, 1983).
4. [Thomas Brown], *The reasons of the new convert's taking the oaths to the present government* (1691), sig. A2ʳ⁻ᵛ.
5. See *ODNB*.
6. PRO PC 2/68/401; *AMC*, 222.
7. Edmund Carter, *History of the University of Cambridge* (1753), 323; *AMC*, 273.
8. See Thomas Keymer, *Sterne, The Moderns and the Novel* (Oxford, 2002), 191–211.
9. The following discussion is based on a series of depositions in the Court of Chancery: PRO B6/53/88; B6/54/25; C6/242/13; C6/275/120; C6/276/48; C7/581/73; C7/587/95; C7/589/82, 87; C8/252/9; C10/216/74; C24/1069.2/36; C33/261/308, 560; C38/1683/A–G, and in PRO SP 29/417/234; 421.2/16. Thanks also to Art Kavanagh for help with understanding these documents and for allowing me to read his as yet unpublished paper on Marvell's marriage.
10. Phil Withington, *The Politics of Commonwealth: Citizens and Freemen in Early Modern England* (Cambridge, 2005), 224–7.
11. For Marten's relationship with Mary Ward, see Sarah Barber, *A Revolutionary Rogue: Henry Marten and the English Republic* (Stroud, Gloucestershire, 2000), ch. VII.
12. As discussed by Nicholas von Maltzahn, 'Andrew Marvell and the Prehistory of Whiggism', in David Womersley et al., eds, *Cultures of Whiggism. New Essays on English Literature and Culture in the Long Eighteenth Century* (Newark, DE, 2005), 47–53.
13. Von Maltzahn, 'Andrew Marvell and the Prehistory of Whiggism', 33. See also Nigel Smith, ' "Courtesie is Fatal": The Civil and Visionary Poetics of Andrew Marvell', Chatterton Lecture 1998, *PBA*, 101 (1999), 173–89.
14. *PL*, II.356–7.
15. Derek Hirst and Steven N. Zwicker, 'Eros and Abuse', *ELH*, 74 (2007), 371–95.
16. London, Royal Society MS 32 (the commonplace book of George Ent), 41–54, contains the poem 'A Love Letter to the Author of the Rehearsall Transpos'd These – To his ever drolling Friend, The mery Gentleman that penn'd The Non Pariello for a Treatise Call'd the Transpos'd Rehearsall at his Dwelling in Hull', dated 30 January, 1674. In it Marvell is described as having been subject to a surgical castration, possibly as a result of contracting a venereal disease, to his great embarrassment in the eyes of his erstwhile Puritan friends.
17. *PL*, II.311–13; See Derek Hirst and Steven N. Zwicker, 'Andrew Marvell and the Toils of Patriarchy: Fatherhood, Longing, and the Body Politic', *ELH*, 66 (1999), 629–54.
18. See Paul Hammond, 'Marvell's Sexuality', *SC*, 11 (1996), 87–123. It is far harder to see Empson's argument that marriage to Mary Palmer freed Marvell from guile to imagine or practice same-sex encounters. See John Haffenden, *William Empson: Vol.II Against the Christians* (Oxford, 2006), 382–3, 615–16.
19. Hirst and Zwicker, 'Andrew Marvell and the Toils of Patriarchy', 631.
20. *AMP*, 188.

INDEX

NOTE: Works by Andrew Marvell (AM) appear by title; works by others under author's name